Beginning
SharePoint® 2007

Beginning
SharePoint® 2007
Building Team Solutions with MOSS 2007

Amanda Murphy
Shane Perran

Wiley Publishing, Inc.

Beginning SharePoint® 2007:
Building Team Solutions with MOSS 2007

Published by
Wiley Publishing, Inc.
10475 Crosspoint Boulevard
Indianapolis, IN 46256
www.wiley.com

Copyright © 2007 by Wiley Publishing, Inc., Indianapolis, Indiana

Published simultaneously in Canada

ISBN: 978-0-470-12449-9

Manufactured in the United States of America

10 9 8 7 6 5 4 3 2

Library of Congress Cataloging-in-Publication Data

Murphy, Amanda, 1976-
  Beginning SharePoint 2007 : building team solutions with Moss 2007 / Amanda Murphy, Shane Perran.
    p. cm.
  Includes index.
  ISBN 978-0-470-12449-9 (paper/website)
  1. Intranets (Computer networks) 2. Web servers. 3. Web portals. I. Perran, Shane, 1973- II. Title.
  TK5105.875.I6M97 2007
  004.6'8--dc22
                          2007013840

No part of this publication may be reproduced, stored in a retrieval system or transmitted in any form
or by any means, electronic, mechanical, photocopying, recording, scanning or otherwise, except as permitted under
Sections 107 or 108 of the 1976 United States Copyright Act, without either the prior written
permission of the Publisher, or authorization through payment of the appropriate per-copy fee to the Copyright Clearance
Center, 222 Rosewood Drive, Danvers, MA 01923, (978) 750-8400, fax (978) 646-8600. Requests to the Publisher for permission should be addressed to the Legal Department, Wiley Publishing, Inc., 10475 Crosspoint Blvd., Indianapolis, IN 46256,
(317) 572-3447, fax (317) 572-4355, or online at http://www.wiley.com/go/permissions.

For general information on our other products and services please contact our Customer Care Department within the
United States at (800) 762-2974, outside the United States at (317) 572-3993 or fax (317) 572-4002.

Trademarks: Wiley, the Wiley logo, Wrox, the Wrox logo, Wrox Programmer to Programmer, and related trade dress are
trademarks or registered trademarks of John Wiley & Sons, Inc. and/or its affiliates, in the United States and other countries, and may not be used without written permission. SharePoint and Microsoft are registered trademarks of Microsoft
Corporation in the United States and/or other countries. All other trademarks are the property of their respective owners.
Wiley Publishing, Inc., is not associated with any product or vendor mentioned in this book.

Wiley also publishes its books in a variety of electronic formats. Some content that appears in print may not be available
in electronic books.

I dedicate this book to my mother, father, and two awesome brothers for their love, encouragement, and support over the years. This book is also dedicated to the memory of our recently lost loved ones, Tom Ryan, Helen Chaplin, and Eric Murphy.

—Amanda Murphy

I dedicate this book to my family and to the special friend I lost while writing it. To the one who rests in Witless Bay, may you never catch your tail.

—Shane Perran

About the Authors

Amanda Murphy is a Microsoft Most Valuable Professional for Microsoft Office SharePoint Server located in St. John's, Newfoundland and Labrador. She has been working as a consultant and trainer with SharePoint since the release of the first version of the product in 2001. Amanda is a regular speaker and presenter at user group meetings, webcasts, and Microsoft Events on topics such as Microsoft SharePoint, InfoPath, and Project Server. She has maintained a SharePoint focused weblog at blog.funknstyle.com since 2003. In her spare time, Amanda is a member of the Board of Directors for INETA NorAm and manages the St. John's .NET User Group.

Shane Perran is a Microsoft Most Valuable Professional for Windows SharePoint Services living in St. John's, Newfoundland and Labrador. He has been designing online user experiences for more than a decade. His strong passion for visual presentation, web standards, and usability has paved the way for a successful transition into the SharePoint Products and Technologies space where Shane has become well known in the SharePoint customization space over the past five years. Shane's SharePoint Customization Blog, graphicalwonder.com, is a popular stop for customization experts across the globe.

Credits

Senior Acquisitions Editor
Jim Minatel

Technical Editor
David Schmitt

Production Editor
Martine Dardignac

Copy Editor
Mildred Sanchez

Editorial Manager
Mary Beth Wakefield

Production Manager
Tim Tate

Vice President and Executive Group Publisher
Richard Swadley

Vice President and Executive Publisher
Joseph B. Wikert

Compositor
Maureen Forys, Happenstance Type-O-Rama

Proofreader
Nancy Hanger

Indexer
Jack Lewis

Anniversary Logo Design
Richard Pacifico

Contents

Introduction   **xvii**

Chapter 1: Getting Started with Microsoft Office SharePoint Server   1

Introducing Portal Technologies and SharePoint   **2**
What is Portal Technology?   2
Why Does an Organization Invest in Portal Technology?   2
What Is SharePoint?   3
Comparing WSS and SharePoint   **4**
WSS Primary Benefits   5
Why Choose Windows SharePoint Services?   6
SharePoint Primary Features   8
Why Choose SharePoint ?   8
SharePoint Components Overview   **10**
SharePoint Lists   10
SharePoint Libraries   10
Web Parts   11
Workflow   11
Content Types   11
Sites, Workspaces, and Site Collections   12
Enterprise Features   14
Summary   **15**
Exercises   **15**

Chapter 2: Working with SharePoint Lists   17

What Is a List?   **17**
Understanding List Elements   18
Discovering SharePoint List Types   18
Understanding the Standard List Templates   **20**
Understanding and Creating Contact List Columns   20
Creating Calendar Lists   22
Understanding Announcements Lists   26
Understanding Discussion Boards   27
Understanding Links Lists   28
Understanding Tasks Lists   29
Exploring Project Tasks Lists   31

Contents

Exploring Issue Lists — 31

Exploring Survey Lists — 32

Working with Lists — **33**

Working with List Content — 33

Tracking List Content Updates — 39

Exporting Data to Excel — 42

Summary — **43**

Exercises — **44**

Chapter 3: Working with SharePoint Libraries — **45**

Understanding Libraries and Documents — **45**

Creating and Managing Documents in a Library — 48

Updating and Sharing Documents — 54

Review Document Version History — 59

Understanding SharePoint Library Templates — **61**

Document Libraries — 62

Form Libraries — 65

Wiki Page Libraries — 68

Picture Libraries — 71

Translation Management Libraries — 77

Data Connection Libraries — 78

Slide Libraries — 79

Summary — **83**

Exercises — **83**

Chapter 4: Managing and Customizing Lists and Libraries — **85**

Creating an Environment that Reflects Your Business — **85**

Best Practices for Building a Dynamic System for Managing Content — **87**

Ensure that Your Changes Add Value — 87

Follow Similar Processes and Practices — 87

Provide Guides and Descriptions — 87

Working with Columns — **88**

What Is a Column? — 88

Exploring Column Types — 90

What Are Site Columns? — 98

When to Use a List-Centric Column versus a Site Column — 102

Creating and Customizing Views — **102**

Working with the Standard View — 103

Setting up a Gantt, Calendar, or Datasheet view — 106

Working with Access Views — 110

Working with Custom Lists and Libraries   **112**
 Custom List Basics   112
 Managing Version Control   119
 Managing Document Templates   121
Summary   **124**
Exercises   **124**

Chapter 5: Working with Workflow   **125**

Types of Workflow Solutions   **125**
 Understanding the Workflow Templates   126
 Understanding the Workflow Creation Process   127
Using Workflow Templates   **128**
 Collect Feedback Workflow   129
 Collect Signatures Workflow   137
 Approval Workflow   144
 Translation Management Workflow   148
Custom Workflows with SharePoint Designer   **154**
Summary   **158**
Exercises   **158**

Chapter 6: Working with Content Types   **159**

Content Types Overview   **159**
Base Content Types   **163**
 Business Intelligence Content Types   164
 Document Content Types   164
 Folder Content Types   165
 List Content Types   165
 Page Layout Content Types   168
 Publishing Content Types   169
 Special Content Types   169
The Anatomy of a Content Type   **169**
 Name and Description   170
 Parent Content Type   170
 Group   170
 Template   171
 Workflow   173
 Site Columns   176
 Document Information Panel Settings   176
 Policy Management   180

Contents

Managing Content Types   **183**

  Enabling Content Type Management on a Library   184

  Managing Multiple Content Types in a Library   185

  Customizing List or Library Views Based on Specific Content Types   187

Summary   **189**

Exercises   **190**

Chapter 7: Working with Web Parts   **191**

The Anatomy of a Web Part Page   **191**

Web Parts Basics   **194**

Using the Various SharePoint Web Parts   **203**

  List and Library Web Parts   204

  Business Data Web Parts   207

  Content Rollup Web Parts   208

  Dashboard Web Parts   210

  Filter Web Parts   213

  Miscellaneous Web Parts   217

  Outlook Web Access Web Parts   219

  Search Web Parts   220

  Site Directory Web Parts   221

  Default Web Parts   223

  The Data View Web Part   228

Summary   **231**

Exercises   **231**

Chapter 8: Working with Sites and Workspaces   **233**

Understanding Sites and Site Collections   **233**

  What Is a Site?   234

  What Is a Site Collection?   234

  What Is a Workspace?   238

Site Management Overview   **239**

  Creating Navigation   240

  Using Regional Settings   243

  Enabling Features   245

Understanding and Working with the SharePoint Site Templates   **247**

  Working with Collaboration Templates and Sites   249

  Meeting Templates   266

  Enterprise Templates   269

  Publishing Templates   279

  Creating Custom Templates   280

Modifying the Look and Feel of a Site   **282**
   Using Themes   283
   Understanding Master Pages   285
Summary   **286**
Exercises   **287**

Chapter 9: User Management, Audiences, and Profiles   289

Understanding User Access Management and Personalization   **290**
   What Is the Difference Between User Access Management and Personalization?   290
   How Do Users Log In to a SharePoint Site?   290
Managing Access in SharePoint   **293**
   Understanding the SharePoint Membership Groups   294
   Working with Site Groups and Permission Levels   295
   Understanding the Different Levels of Access in SharePoint   304
Understanding User Profiles   **310**
   Adding and Updating User Profiles   311
   Configuring Profile Updates   316
Working with Audiences   **316**
   Membership-Based Audiences   318
   Profile Property-Based Audiences   325
Summary   **326**
Exercises   **327**

Chapter 10: Working with Forms Services   329

What Is InfoPath?   **330**
Creating and Customizing an InfoPath Form   **331**
Using the Design Tasks Pane   **338**
   Layout   339
   Controls   340
   Data Source   346
   Views   348
   Design Checker   349
   Publishing a Form Template   349
Working with Form Templates   **350**
   Designing a New Form   350
   Publishing a Form Template to a Library   358
   Customizing a Form Template   362
   Advanced Form Publishing Options   371
Summary   **376**
Exercises   **376**

Contents

Chapter 11: Working with Excel Services   377

Excel Services Overview   **378**
The Report Center   378
Publishing a Workbook to SharePoint   388
Excel Web Access Web Part   392
Data Connections   **393**
Business Scorecards   **397**
Creating a KPI List   398
Using KPI Web Parts to Display Performance Data   403
Summary   **407**
Exercises   **408**

Chapter 12: Working with the Business Data Catalog   409

Business Data Catalog Overview   **410**
What Is the Business Data Catalog?   410
Primary Roles for the BDC   411
Configuring a BDC Application   **412**
Importing the Application Definition File   413
Viewing Entities   414
Understanding Actions   415
Application Permissions   415
Working with Web Parts and Lists in the BDC   **417**
Business Data List Web Part   418
Related Business Data List Web Part   424
Business Item Web Part   428
Business Data Actions Web Part   431
SharePoint List Integration   **431**
Summary   **435**
Exercises   **435**

Chapter 13: Getting Started with Web Content Management   437

Web Content Management   **437**
Publishing Features Overview   **439**
Creating a Publishing Portal   439
The Publishing Portal's Lists and Libraries   441
Working with Variations   **443**
How Do Variations Work?   444
Understanding Labels   446
Managing Translation Workflows   449

Customizing the Look and Feel of a WCM Site   **454**
   Master Pages   455
   Page Layouts and Content Types   459
   Understanding Document Conversion   465
Enabling Publishing on a Team Site   **472**
Summary   **475**
Exercises   **476**

Chapter 14: Working with Search   **477**

Understanding SharePoint Search   **477**
Working with the Search Feature   **479**
   Using the Basic Search   479
   Using the Advanced Search   482
Customizing and Managing Search   **490**
   Create Content Sources   490
   Schedule Content Source Updates   494
   Manage File Types   498
   Create Search Scopes   499
   Using the Search Center   505
   Create Custom Keywords   508
   Finding People in Your Organization   511
Summary   **515**
Exercises   **516**

Appendix A: Answers to Exercises   **517**

Index   **533**

Introduction

Microsoft Office SharePoint Server 2007 has improved and changed dramatically over previous versions of the product. The capabilities of the platform have expanded greatly with the inclusion of an automated workflow engine, web content management capabilities, and a vast number of document management enhancements. However, the value of this tool to an enterprise will depend primarily on the ability of individuals in the organization to understand the features and capabilities of the platform and effectively map those to specific business requirements. This book is designed to mentor and coach business and technical leaders in an organization on the use of SharePoint to address critical information management problems. It gives detailed descriptions and illustrations of the product's functionality and also includes realistic usage scenarios to provide contextual relevance and a personalized learning experience to the reader.

Whom Is This Book For?

The mission of this book is to provide extensive knowledge to information workers and site managers that will empower them to become SharePoint Application champions in the organization. This book should be the premiere handbook of any active or aspiring SharePoint expert.

To complete the exercises in this book, you should have a basic comfort level using Microsoft Office application to create content and a general understanding of how to interact with a website through the browser. This book is intended as a starting point for any SharePoint 2007 user whether that user has never used SharePoint before or has some familiarity with a previous version and just wants to understand the differences with the new release.

What Does This Book Cover?

Chapter 1: Getting Started with SharePoint Server

The first chapter of the book is targeted at users who have either never used SharePoint before or are already familiar with SharePoint Portal Server 2003 or Windows SharePoint Service v2 and are looking to gain an understanding of what has changed in SharePoint 2007. This chapter lays out the foundation for important terminology and concepts explored in the following chapters of the book.

Chapter 2: Working with SharePoint Lists

This chapter introduces one of the core mechanisms for sharing and organizing content in a SharePoint site. You will review what lists are, how they are used, and then explore the various templates that exist in SharePoint.

Chapter 3: Working with SharePoint Libraries

After reviewing some of the fundamental concepts relating to lists, the chapter introduces the other major storage mechanism in SharePoint known as libraries. This chapter discusses some of the various templates that exist for libraries as well as brand-new concepts in 2007, such as slide libraries and wiki page libraries.

Chapter 4: Managing and Customizing Lists and Libraries

SharePoint templates for lists and libraries provide a great starting point for collaboration and information sharing. This chapter introduces how you can extend these base templates to address an organization's specific requirements for a collaborative site or information management tool.

Chapter 5: Working with Workflow

Workflow is a new feature available in SharePoint Server 2007. This chapter discusses the templates that SharePoint provides for workflow, as well as demonstrates how to create a custom workflow solution using the SharePoint Designer.

Chapter 6: Working with Content Types

Most organizations have information and documents, which often utilize consistent templates, processes, and policies each time they are created. Therefore, SharePoint 2007 has introduced the concept of a Content Type to allow an organization to package templates and information to ensure that reusable components are rolled out in the organization to enforce consistency and ease of use. This chapter demonstrates what content types are and explores how they can be used through some hands-on examples.

Chapter 7: Working with Web Parts

Web Parts are an important element in SharePoint because they display information in sites to users. A variety of Web Parts exist in SharePoint 2007 to address the many ways that teams want to present information. This chapter explores the various groups of Web Parts in SharePoint, including examples on how specific types of Web Parts can be configured and used to present information in a desired manner.

Chapter 8: Working with Sites and Workspaces

The fundamental components of any SharePoint environment are the sites and workspaces that it contains. These collaborative work areas contain all the components discussed in previous sections and represent how each of those items come together to provide an effective environment for collaboration, communication, and document management. In this section of the book, topics such as site templates, features, and look and feel are covered.

Chapter 9: User Management, Audiences, and Profiles

Effective management of users is of ultimate importance to any information system. The two primary tiers of effective user management include securing content and personalizing information on the portal. This chapter explains in simple terms how to effectively secure a SharePoint environment at the site level, the list or library level, and down to the unique content items stored on a SharePoint site. In addition, an introduction to personalization is presented to ensure that readers understand how to effectively target information to users in a portal.

Chapter 10: Working with Forms Services

InfoPath is the ideal companion to SharePoint for many business solutions. This chapter introduces readers to creating simple business applications using InfoPath and SharePoint including new features in 2007, such as template parts and browser based forms.

Chapter 11: Working with Excel Services

SharePoint addresses the need that many organizations face for better visibility and accessibility to data that is often stored in Excel spreadsheets or external business applications. This chapter demonstrates how to improve the overall decision making of an organization by providing access to important information by utilizing browser-based worksheets, visual indicators of performance information, and building personalized interactive dashboards.

Chapter 12: Working with the Business Data Catalog

The Business Data Catalog is completely new to SharePoint in 2007 and offers a fantastic way to access information stored in other business applications through the SharePoint portal interface and elements. This chapter introduces the concept of the Business Data Catalog, explaining each of the key roles in detail and then focusing on usage scenarios from the perspective of the business analyst and end-user roles.

Chapter 13: Getting Started with Web Content Management

All the functionality previously available in Content Management Server 2002 has been incorporated into the SharePoint platform for 2007. This convergence of technology allows for the creation, review, and publishing of web content from a single environment. This chapter provides an overview of the web content management capabilities of the system including the use of publishing sites and features, the automatic provisioning of multilingual content through variations, and user-interface customization.

Chapter 14: Working with Search

An information system is useful to an organization only if stakeholders can easily access and locate the information it contains. This chapter discusses the search engine capabilities of the SharePoint platform including methods that improve the search experience through the use of custom search scopes, content sources, and best bets.

What You Need to Use This Book

To effectively complete the examples in this book, you should have access to a Microsoft Office SharePoint Server environment or site collection in an administrative role. If you do not have administrative rights to your server, you may have to gain the assistance of your server administrator for some exercises in this book.

For the chapter covering the Business Data Catalog, you will require access to a properly defined business application in the BDC. Although the definition and configuration of a business application in the BDC is not covered in this book, the exercises depend on the existence of an application. For the exercises in this book, the Adventure Works sample database is used based on the SDK sample available at the following location:

```
www.microsoft.com/downloads/details.aspx?FamilyId=6D94E307-67D9-41AC-B2D6-
0074D6286FA9&displaylang=en
```

You should also have a client computer running either Windows XP or Windows Vista along with Microsoft Office 2007 Professional or Enterprise. While many exercises can be completed with earlier versions of Office, certain exercises related to workflow, Forms Services and Excel Services are dependent on features only available in the Enterprise versions of Office 2007.

Conventions

To help you get the most from the text and keep track of what's happening, we've used a number of conventions throughout the book.

Try It Out

The Try It Out is an exercise you should work through, following the text in the book.

1. They usually consist of a set of steps.

2. Each step has a number.

3. Follow the steps through with your copy of the chapter resource, when one is available. Sometimes, exercise steps build on Try It Outs previously presented in the chapter, or you may need something off the Wrox website to perform the steps. You can download chapter resources by searching for the title of this book at www.wrox.com.

How It Works

After each Try It Out, the code you've typed will be explained in detail.

```
Occasionally, in Try It Outs, you see text in this format, which means that this is
code you need to enter.
```

> **In a Try It Out, boxes like this mean that there is text for you to enter during the course of the exercise. Boxes like this can also hold important, not-to-be forgotten information that is directly relevant to the surrounding text.**

Tips, hints, tricks, and asides to the current discussion are offset and placed in italics like this.

As for styles in the text:

❑ New terms and important words are *highlighted* when introduced.

❑ Keyboard strokes appear like this: Ctrl+A.

❑ File names, URLs, and code within the text appear like this: `persistence.properties`.

On the Website

As mentioned in the "Conventions" section, some of the Try It Outs in this book require that you download chapter resources from the Wrox website to perform the steps. These chapter resources are available at `www.wrox.com`. Once you are at the site, simply locate the book's title by using the Search box, and then choose what you want to download.

Because many books have similar titles, you may find it easiest to search by ISBN; for this book, the ISBN is 9780470124499.

Errata

We make every effort to ensure that there are no errors in the text. However, no one is perfect, and mistakes do occur. If you find an error in one of our books, such as a spelling mistake or faulty piece of code, we would be very grateful for your feedback. By sending in errata, you may save another reader hours of frustration; at the same time, you will be helping us provide even higher quality information.

To find the errata page for this book, go to `www.wrox.com` and locate the title using the Search box or one of the title lists. Then, on the book's detail page, click the Book Errata link. On this page, you can view all errata that has been submitted for this book and posted by Wrox editors. A complete book list including links to each book's errata is also available at `www.wrox.com/misc-pages/booklist.shtml`.

If you don't spot "your" error on the Book Errata page, go to `www.wrox.com/contact/techsupport.shtml` and complete the form there to send us the error you have found. We'll check the information and, if appropriate, post a message to the book's errata page and fix the problem in subsequent editions of the book.

p2p.wrox.com

For authors and peer discussion, join the P2P forums at `p2p.wrox.com`. The forums are a web-based system for you to post messages relating to Wrox books and related technologies, and to interact with other readers and technology users. The forums offer a subscription feature to email you topics of interest of your choice when new posts are made to the forums. Wrox authors, editors, other industry experts, and your fellow readers are present on these forums.

At `http//:p2p.wrox.com`, you will find a number of different forums that will help you not only as you read this book but also as you develop your own applications. To join forums, just follow these steps:

1. Go to `p2p.wrox.com` and click the Register link.

2. Read the terms of use and click Agree.

3. Complete the required information to join as well as any optional information you wish to provide and click Submit.

4. You will receive an email with information describing how to verify your account and complete the joining process.

> *You can read messages in the forums without joining P2P, but in order to post your own messages, you must join.*

Once you join, you can post new messages and respond to messages other users post. You can read messages at any time on the Web. If you would like to have new messages from a particular forum emailed to you, click the Subscribe to This Forum icon by the forum name in the forum listing.

For more information about how to use the Wrox P2P, be sure to read the P2P FAQs for answers to questions about how the forum software works as well as many common questions specific to P2P and Wrox books. To read the FAQs, click the FAQ link on any P2P page.

Getting Started with Microsoft Office SharePoint Server

The goal of this book is to provide you with the knowledge you need to become the master of your organization's SharePoint environment. Along those lines, this chapter introduces you to the new and exciting features and capabilities of Microsoft Office SharePoint Server 2007. With it, you learn how to put the platform to work for your organization to create scalable team solutions. In this chapter, you learn about the following topics and concepts:

❑ The differences between Windows SharePoint Services 3.0 and Microsoft Office SharePoint Server 2007

❑ Common usage scenarios for Windows SharePoint Services 3.0 and Microsoft Office SharePoint Server 2007

❑ Differences between SharePoint Portal Server 2003 and Microsoft Office SharePoint Server 2007

❑ An overview of important SharePoint concepts and features such as:

   ❑ Sites and workspaces

   ❑ Lists

   ❑ Document libraries

   ❑ Web Parts

   ❑ Content types

   ❑ Workflow

   ❑ Enterprise features such as search, business data reporting, and Forms Services

Introducing Portal Technologies and SharePoint

Before getting started on the technical tasks associated with managing and working with SharePoint content, it is important to understand the purpose and common usage scenarios for the technology.

Organizational stakeholders often suffer from what's been termed *information overload*. Because computers play such an integral part in any business, not surprisingly, more and more of the information that is created, consumed, and shared in an organization is digital. The more business that you have and the more successful your business, the more information you have to manage. Usually, you have some form of document for just about every process and transaction that plays out during the day-to-day operation in your company. From proposals to legal documents, from sales receipts to human resource policy documentation, the amount of information required to function is staggering.

To manage your information overload, SharePoint offers tools with which you can build business applications to better store, share, and manage digital information. With it, you can create lists, libraries, and websites for your various company teams to help run your business processes more efficiently.

What is Portal Technology?

A corporate *portal* is a gateway through which members can access business information and, if set up properly, should be the first place an employee goes to access anything of importance. Portals differ from regular websites in that they are customized specifically around a business process. In SharePoint, a portal may actually consist of numerous websites, with information stored either directly on those sites or in other systems, such as fileshares, business applications, or a regular Internet website. Because making informed business decisions is key to becoming and remaining successful, it's important that the information you place on a portal is secure, up-to-date, and easily accessible. Because a business's marketplace may span the globe, an organization also needs to have the information that reflects the needs of employees from multiple specific regions.

As an example, consider a new employee who has just joined an organization. In addition to learning her new job responsibilities, this employee must quickly get up-to-speed on the various company processes and policies. A good portal should provide all the company reference and policy information that the employee needs to review as well as links to all the information systems and websites that employee needs to do her job. Information should be stored in easy-to-browse locations, based on subject or topic. In situations where the location of a document or information is not obvious, the employee should be able to type words into a search box and receive suggestions. The employee should also be able to share information with others. In many ways, a good portal should act as a table of contents for all the information and websites related to an organization or topic.

Why Does an Organization Invest in Portal Technology?

The following list provides eight reasons why many enterprise organizations opt to invest in portal technologies:

1. The recent adoption of the web and web-related technologies makes portal technologies an obvious choice. Because portal technologies are web-based, decision makers can access important information via the Internet regardless of where they are located.

2. Portal technologies allow information workers to handle day-to-day tasks from a single starting point where previously things were spread out across multiple places and applications.

3. With important regulatory initiatives, such as Sarbanes Oxley, organizations are using portal technologies to ensure that an accurate audit trail is kept on important documents and that business processes remain compliant.

4. The fileshare based approach previously used to store most information was highly dependent on the habits and practices of the person creating it. Portal technologies store and share information based on the organizational structure, making them intuitive to everyone in the organization. This structure translates into productivity boosts because workers can more easily locate and retrieve information.

5. Portal technologies such as SharePoint scale with an organization, offering a model that will grow as your company grows.

6. While the typical business portal product incorporates many common business practices, your organizational needs may dictate a customized process. Because SharePoint offers an extensible infrastructure, you can build custom solutions.

7. Although a company may be tempted by the latest and greatest information management system, most organizations still have legacy systems and data sources. You can massage portal technologies to integrate with these systems, allowing easier data mining or migration.

8. Much of today's digital information is created and managed using the Microsoft Office system. It, therefore, makes sense to use SharePoint as the portal technology. SharePoint integrates seamlessly with these tools, allowing you to create, store, manage, and collaborate on this information from a single location.

What Is SharePoint?

SharePoint is an extensible and scalable web-based platform consisting of tools and technologies that collectively form what's known as *SharePoint Products and Technologies*. The total package is a platform on which you can build business applications to help you better store, share, and manage digital information within your organization. Because you can build with or without the need for code, the package empowers the average business user to create, deploy, and manage team websites, without depending on skilled resources, such as systems administrators or developers. Using lists, libraries, and Web Parts, you can transform team websites into business applications built specifically around making your organization's business processes more efficient.

SharePoint Products and Technologies has two major offerings:

❑ *Windows SharePoint Services 3.0* is a free offering available to Windows Server 2003 and Small Business Server 2003. It contains the core functionality needed for document management and collaboration, such as document libraries and lists.

❑ *Microsoft Office SharePoint Server 2007* is a newer version of SharePoint Portal Server 2003. It offers the same features of WSS in addition to the functionality required for Enterprise Content Management as well as Excel and Forms Services, Business Data Catalog, and Business Intelligence. SharePoint also features a more robust and customizable search engine as well as special features for displaying information stored in the SharePoint environment in a more customizable and aggregated format than is possible with WSS.

SharePoint 2007 and SharePoint Portal Server 2003

If you're familiar with SharePoint Server 2007's predecessor, SharePoint Portal Server 2003, you might appreciate a quick look at the changes in the new version.

While SharePoint Portal Server 2003 offered a great method of aggregating content from multiple sites to a single, easy-to-navigate location, the process was dependent on a user's manual actions to publish the links to the portal areas, a dependency that highlighted the platform's shortcomings. If the person who updated content forgot to publish a link to the portal, business decision makers could not access information.

Microsoft responded with SharePoint Server 2007, which offers tools and features that automate business processes and content aggregations. Built-in Web Parts, such as a site aggregator and Content Query Web Part meant that the site administrators can specify what content should automatically roll up to the main portal sites, eliminating manual updates and resulting in sites with up-to-date information.

With 2007, the technology in the top-level portal sites is exactly the same as that available on the team sites. This was not the case for SharePoint Portal Server, where there was a very distinct difference between working in a team site and working with portal content. Users had to learn each separate tool and there was confusion as to what activities were appropriate for each location.

The architectural changes and feature enhancements make it possible for you to use SharePoint for a wider range of organizations and scenarios. SharePoint Portal Server required that users authenticate using a Windows-based authentication system and Active Directory for user profile information. Because of its platform enhancements, SharePoint 2007 uses a variety of systems for authentication due and supports multiple authentication providers as well as LDAP sources for user profile information. In addition, SharePoint has much better support for extranet and Internet-facing scenarios.

SharePoint Portal Server 2003 has no mechanism for automated workflow or business processes. SharePoint 2007 includes several workflow templates that business users can further customize to suit their specific requirements.

Comparing WSS and SharePoint

Many organizations struggle with understanding which of the SharePoint products is most appropriate for their needs. The following sections identify some differences between the products and usage scenarios for each. While this book has been written to specifically review SharePoint from the perspective of

SharePoint, the following section discusses some comparisons between WSS and SharePoint. To start you off, you should remember the following:

❑ *Windows SharePoint Services 3.0*, often referred to as *WSS*, has the core document management and collaboration platform features. With WSS, the average information user can build web-based business applications without numerous technical resources. Because WSS is available free to the Windows Server 2003 system, deploying web-based applications has never been easier. This is largely because of templates and existing site modules that allow users to add documents, images, and information via a simple form rather than by using code. You can create a new site based on an existing template in just a few seconds. Windows SharePoint Services is also tightly integrated with Microsoft Office Word, Excel, and Outlook so users can create and share content using a familiar, comfortable environment.

❑ *Microsoft Office SharePoint Server 2007*, often referred to as *MOSS 2007*, is the nexus of the Microsoft Office system. It delivers the robust, enterprise-targeted features of SharePoint Products and Technologies, which accelerate business processes across the intranet, extranet, and Internet. SharePoint delivers the tools to create, publish, and manage web-based content from a cohesive environment. SharePoint also offers the tools to automatically aggregate content from the Windows SharePoint Services team sites, rolling up content from multiple sources to a central location, making information management even easier.

WSS Primary Benefits

The primary features of WSS revolve around document and information management and collaboration. The following sections outline the major features of the platform that have been responsible for its wide adoption across the enterprise.

❑ **More Effective Document and Task Collaboration:** Team websites offer access to information in a central location as well as the following capabilities:

   ❑ An extranet-extendable single workspace for teams to share documents and information, coordinate schedules and tasks, and participate in forum-like discussions.

   ❑ Libraries provide a better document creation and management environment. Libraries ensure that a document is checked out before editing, track a document's audit history, or allow users to roll back to past revisions.

   ❑ Document level security settings ensure that sensitive information is secure and available only to select individuals.

   ❑ Advanced task-tracking lists and alert systems keep users updated on current and upcoming tasks.

   ❑ Templates for creating wikis and blogs to share information across your organization quickly and easily.

❑ **Reduced Implementation and Deployment Resources:** Because WSS is available to Windows Server 2003 customers as a free download, implementation time and cost is greatly reduced, resulting in the following benefits:

   ❑ Deploying team collaboration sites is easy, so organizations can free up skilled resources and focus on more important tasks.

❑ Users can immediately apply professional looking site themes.

❑ Customized workspaces have prebuilt application templates for most common business processes, such as workflows.

❑ Because WSS offers seamless integration with the Microsoft Office system, employees can use common applications such as Outlook email to create and manage documents without the need for a custom implementation.

❑ **Better Control of Your Organization's Important Business Data:** Windows SharePoint Services offer the following enhancements for data and information management and security:

❑ Enhanced browser and command-line based administrative controls allow you to perform site provisioning, content management, support, and backup. Subsequently, a business can become more efficient and reduce costs.

❑ You have more control over your corporate infrastructure. IT has access to security and policy settings at the lowest item level using enhanced administration services. WSS's increased security and easy deployment mean your organization can reduce its dependency on skilled IT resources.

❑ Using advanced administrative features, IT can set the parameters under which business units can provision sites and allow access, ensuring that all units fall within an acceptable security policy.

❑ The Recycle Bin item retrieval and document versioning capabilities provide a safer storage environment.

❑ **Embrace the Web for Collaboration:** By extending and customizing WSS, you can:

❑ Create collaborative websites complete with document libraries that act as central repositories for creating, managing, and sharing documents with your team.

❑ Create, connect, and customize a set of business applications specific to scaling your organizational needs.

❑ Take advantage of Sharepoint Designer to customize and brand your team sites and applications.

Why Choose Windows SharePoint Services?

This section has a fictional but realistic scenario to illustrate how an organization uses Windows SharePoint Services to cope with the overwhelming amount of information generated by projects from their various teams. The fictional organization, Rossco Tech Consulting, offers professional services and technology mentoring to startup companies. The following scenario outlines the Rossco's experience with SharePoint Products and Technologies, beginning with WSS and later expanding to SharePoint. Because so much of Rossco's business revolves around process documentation, having a central repository to manage information surrounding projects is imperative. Because Rossco was using Windows Server 2003, Windows SharePoint Services became the obvious and most cost-efficient foundation on which to build solutions to manage their projects.

Planning

To identify what improvements they needed to make to enhance efficiency, the company asked team leads about the problems they were encountering when they shared information within their respective teams. From these results, the company identified the common issues each team shared and created a site hierarchy that best represented the organization's corporate culture and business processes. Because the organization consisted of only three divisions (Finance, Marketing, and Operations), they opted for a single collection of sites: a main site for the organization as a whole, and three subsites, one for each division.

Because each division followed similar processes for most projects, the company could use SharePoint's template system to create a single "project" site template that all teams could use to create a collaborative project location. The sites created from this template would then have the following features:

- ❏ A document library to create, store, and organize any documents related to the project
- ❏ A contact list to store and organize important contacts involved with the project
- ❏ A task list to coordinate important tasks for team members involved with the project
- ❏ An issue tracking list to highlight any potential project concerns

The template was created and then saved in a central site template gallery where each division could use it to generate a new site for each project.

Because Rossco had invested heavily in the creation of its corporate identity, it was imperative that this brand be carried over to the intranet and extranet sites. Using a combination of the built-in site themes, custom style sheets, master pages, and free downloadable application templates, Rossco transformed the default SharePoint environment into a more familiar, corporate-branded interface.

Moving from Plan to Practice

After defining the organization structure via team sites on the intranet, it was time to for Rossco Tech Consulting to put their hard work and planning into real-world practice. As teams began to understand the tools that they now had available, the following practices started to drive more efficient operations within the organization:

- ❏ Projects were quickly defined via sites created using the project site template. This allowed teams to set up a central environment to create, store, and share information about a particular project with the entire organization in just seconds.
- ❏ Appointments and important deadlines were created and tracked from a single shared calendar on the project site that everyone on a team could easily view.
- ❏ Contact information was added to a central location so that team members could easily contact one another and other key partners or stakeholders for the project.
- ❏ Important project documents were moved to the document repository of their respective project sites where changes became easier to track and security became more manageable.
- ❏ Users began to create email alerts on the task and issues lists, ensuring that tasks and issues were dealt with in a timely manner.

As each division began defining its role in important projects, executives realized that they now had a bird's eye view of operations within the organization — a discovery which was met with great enthusiasm.

SharePoint Primary Features

SharePoint provides enterprise tools that connect people, processes, and information in a central location. The following sections outline some of the more commonly used Enterprise features in SharePoint.

❑ **Web Content Management:** You use familiar applications, such as email or a web browser to create and publish web content. Built-in tools make it easy to:

❑ Control documents via rights management and extensible policy management.

❑ Centrally create, store, and manage documents using built-in document library settings to define workflow and retention settings or even add new content types.

❑ Manage web content using page layouts and master pages to create reusable templates and variations to control multilingual content.

❑ Reduce the need for manual data entry with electronic web-based or InfoPath client-based forms.

❑ Use workflow tools to automate content approval and publishing processes.

❑ **Monitor Key Business Activities:** Using enterprise tools, you can effectively manage and monitor business events across your organization to:

❑ Manage critical business data through business intelligence portals using Dashboard capabilities, key performance indicators, and a sophisticated Report Center.

❑ Quickly connect people with information using enterprise search. Use the Search Center to find people and information in your SharePoint environment and external systems.

❑ Access important business information in real-time right from the browser, using features such as the Business Data Catalog and Excel Services.

❑ Aggregate information from a wide variety of SharePoint sites onto a single page to provide a personalized rollup of relevant information based on customizable criteria.

❑ **Simplify Collaboration:** SharePoint's collaboration tools allow you to:

❑ Enhance customer and partner relationships by connecting them with important data through intranet, extranet, and Internet-facing portals.

❑ Work offline with SharePoint lists and libraries using Outlook, making it easier to work with information even when not connected to the corporate network.

❑ Use people networks to connect people inside and outside your organization, ensuring that your organization has easy access to subject matter experts.

❑ Personalize operations using My Sites. Display personal information about colleagues, managers, and groups.

Why Choose SharePoint ?

You commonly use SharePoint in enterprise-level organizations where you must track and maintain operations via multiple mini-portals and business applications within the same main infrastructure. You can then gather the important data from all units up to a central location. A common place you might see SharePoint is a software support company. This section again presents the fictional company, Rossco

Tech Consulting, to show how SharePoint operates. Rossco Tech Consulting has expanded operations to support a major software manufacturer. This means providing English-, French-, and German-speaking customers with an Internet support portal where they can access up-to-the-minute information on the manufacturer's various software offerings.

Planning

While doing needs analysis, the following factors were major contributors in Rossco's decision to use SharePoint as the platform on which to build its customer support portal:

❑ The portal must accommodate multiple products from a central Internet-facing location. Each product has its own unique support materials.

❑ The portal must serve up content in multiple languages, though the original content would be created in English and then translated.

❑ For legal reasons, support documentation must be published via a strict approval process involving several individuals in the organization.

❑ The portal must accommodate speedy publishing of up-to-date information on emerging products.

❑ Additional documentation exists beyond what is stored in the SharePoint sites. This content must be indexed and accessible via the SharePoint search interface.

❑ Specific reporting requirements exist for dashboard scorecards on progress related to specific requirements, as well as the aggregation of information from multiple sources on a single page.

Moving from Plan to Practice

With the planning needs in mind, Rossco set out to plan and implement a SharePoint solution. The following section outlines the company's experience.

❑ **Internet-Facing Sites in SharePoint:** Because users will access a major part of the portal via the Internet, they created the initial site collection with a special publishing feature available only in SharePoint 2007 (this feature was previously in Microsoft Content Management Server 2002, and is now known as *Web Content Management* or *WCM*). This makes it possible to publish content through an automated and scheduled process from an internal and secured location to an external anonymous Internet-facing site.

❑ **Multilingual Design:** Because the portal needed to service three languages, the company used *Variations*, a feature unique to SharePoint 2007, which helps you create a site hierarchy for each language. Variations simplify content management in multiple languages by creating a source site and a site for each language.

❑ **Content Creation:** After creating the main subsites, the product teams created intuitively named lists and libraries (introduced later in this chapter) and added important documents and information. Making use of built-in features such as content types, site columns, and views, they created and presented the data more efficiently. To ensure that the portal was in line with the corporate brand, the portal was customized. Using the master pages feature, they created custom style sheets, page layouts, and content types to remodel the look and feel of the portal. This transformed the original site with its generic SharePoint look into an easy-to-use support interface. Using page layouts, they were able to empower key business users with no programming knowledge to create and publish branded web content such as newsletters and product updates.

❑ **Automating Operations:** Taking advantage of SharePoint's workflow features, Rossco created a strict content approval process that routed documents from approver to approver before they were finally publishing them to the Internet-facing portal.

❑ **Content Aggregation:** Using built-in Web Parts, such as the Content Query Web Part, Rossco could gather the most sought-after and important information in its sub sites and funnel this information to the Internet-facing portal where users had quick and easy access to support information for multiple products at a glance.

SharePoint Components Overview

SharePoint includes several components and elements that are key to the effective use of the system and will be very important concepts to master as you progress through this book. Although each of these items is addressed in detail in later chapters, the following sections offer a brief overview.

SharePoint Lists

The *list* is a fundamental component of SharePoint Products and Technologies. They act as both the store for the information and the vehicle for creating, adding, and sharing information from the store. For a to-do list that you might create using a notepad and pen, each task is an individual item and has certain properties or characteristics that differentiate it from the others in the list. In SharePoint, you can create a digital to-do list with each new task requiring that you fill out a form to describe the task. This means you can view a list of all completed items and rank them in order based on when you must complete them, or when they will start, or even how long each will take.

Although advanced and dynamic, SharePoint lists are easy to create, requiring absolutely no code, special development skills or tools. In the past, such lists took time to create and required using an application and hiring a developer or user with technical skills. By using SharePoint, users most familiar with the information tracking and sharing needs of the organization can create the tools they need.

You can use lists to store virtually any type of information. The most commonly used list types are Contacts, Tasks, Issues, Announcements, and Calendar lists. You can create other lists for just about any usage scenario to track and share information related to a single item. Chapters 2 and 4 examine the common list templates and how you can extend them to meet your team's goals and objectives.

SharePoint Libraries

Libraries are much like lists with one major difference: their intended content. Whereas lists store information about items such as events, contacts, or announcements, libraries store documents. You can think of libraries as superfolders that help users find files faster and easier than ever through the use of special properties or keywords such as *status*, *owner*, or *due date*. Once you add a number of properties to documents, you can create special views or reports to filter, sort, and organize documents based on those properties.

Through SharePoint 2007-specific technologies such as content types, document libraries can now manage multiple types of files and templates from a single library, making it possible to quickly create and manage common document types such as Word or Excel right from the browser. Chapters 3 and 4 explain how you can use document libraries within your SharePoint sites to further customize them to meet your team's needs.

Web Parts

When you create a list or library, SharePoint automatically generates a corresponding Web Part that you can later add to a Web Part page. You can think of *Web Parts* as mini-applications or modules that display information on a page or perform a special function. Web parts can perform any number of functions, from allowing a user to add custom text and images to a web page without using HTML code, to displaying a financial report based on information stored in a completely separate application.

While many common business Web Parts come with SharePoint, the model is extensible, and you can customize Web Parts to integrate the specific needs of your organization. You store Web Parts in a *Web Part gallery* and you place them on a web page by dragging and dropping them into an appropriately marked *Web Part zone*. Users can reuse, move, and customize Web Parts on multiple pages. For example, you can place a small module on the page to display the weather and have each division in your organization decide whether and where to display it on their site. In Chapter 7, you will examine the various types of Web Parts that are available in SharePoint and discuss common usage scenarios of each primary category.

Workflow

A *workflow* automates a business process by breaking it into a set of steps that users must take to complete a specific business activity, such as approving content or routing a document from one location to another. Automation eliminates manual tasks and reduces the chance of data entry errors or documents getting lost in the system.

Workflow can be as simple or complex as your organization's needs. They can be very rigid and clearly defined or offer a greater level of flexibility and decision making. You can use several built-in templates as a starting point for creating rules more customized for your organization. Templates come with common processes complete with tasks, which users must complete. If a user fails to respond to a task, the workflow reminds him of the task and tracks when it is past due.

You can customize basic workflow templates so users can utilize the browser for activities, such as giving approval, responding to a request for feedback, or signing a document. You can also design more specialized workflows using Sharepoint Designer 2007 or Visual Studio 2005. You look at some of the templates and ways in which workflow can be used in Chapter 5.

Content Types

A *content type* represents a group of informational items in your organization that share common settings. They allow you to manage multiple types of content from a single location. You can associate content types with a document library — for example, to manage multiple file types, such as Word, PowerPoint, and Excel documents. Content types can also manage multiple templates of the same document type, a shortcoming of all previous versions of SharePoint Products and Technologies. As you associate a content type with a document library or list, it appears in the library's or list's New drop-down menu.

Content types make extensive use of global properties known as *site columns*, which means you can associate metadata with your items to more easily find it. *Columns* are properties that help define an item, similar to the way you can use a field in a form. For example, for a task list, the field value for describing when an item is due is a column, as is a field that identifies who is responsible for completing a task. In the previous version of SharePoint, you could only apply a field to a single list. For example, to associate a customer's name with a task list to help better define the tasks, you created a Customer column. If you later decided to add a Customer column to your document library so that you could also track documents by customer for which they were created, you had to create yet another customer column. Site columns are new in SharePoint 2007, and allow you to create a column once and use it on any list or library on the current site and any sites below it. Content types make use of site columns because they, too, can be associated with multiple lists or libraries across several sites.

A more advanced use of content types involves templates known as *page layouts*, which you use to publish only certain types of content on your site. For example, you can create a newsletter article content type so that the web pages reflect your content — in this instance a column for the title, another for the date, and a third for main text body. You can create page layouts via the browser or using SharePoint Designer 2007; after creation, they become available in the Site Actions menu under the Create Pages option. Content types are introduced and explored in Chapter 6.

Sites, Workspaces, and Site Collections

Both the terms *sites* and *workspaces*, and *site collections* all refer to SharePoint sites. These websites, which you can create using available SharePoint templates are also called *team collaboration sites* and they store and share information using Web Parts, lists, and libraries as their various components. The following list explains how they differ:

- ❏ **Sites:** These share information in the form of list items and documents within a team or organization.
- ❏ **Workspaces:** These are more specific to an important document, such as an annual report, on which a team collaborates, or to a significant event, such as a gala or annual business meeting.
- ❏ **Site collections:** These are a group of sites and or workspaces that form a hierarchy with a single top-level website with a collection of subsites, and sub-subsites below it. Figure 1-1 shows a graphical representation of a site collection.

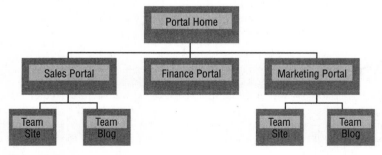

Figure 1-1

One major difference between SharePoint 2007 and SharePoint Portal Server 2003 is related to the default setting of the Collaboration Portal. In SharePoint Portal Server 2003, the portal was completely separate from the site collections beneath it. In SharePoint 2007, the portal is part of the same site collection as the remainder of the sites created beneath it. When designing your portal environment, you can keep the portal and all divisional and collaborative sites within a single site collection. However, if you prefer the SPS 2003 method, you can configure the portal to create new site collections when subsites are created from a special site known as the Sites Directory.

In the first exercise for this book, you create a new site collection based on the Collaboration Portal template, which will be known in all future exercises as the Corporate Intranet site.

Try It Out   **Create a Site Collection**

When learning an application such as SharePoint, it is a good idea to create an area where you can perform exercises without impacting existing environments or users. Therefore, as your first exercise, you create a site collection based on the Collaboration Portal template that will act as the starting location for many of the exercises in this book. This site collection is based on the Collaboration Portal template, which you selected because it closely matches the requirements of most organizations for an intranet site. From this site, you can create many of the content elements such as lists, libraries, and workflows that are required for the next four chapters.

To create a new site collection, you must visit the Central Administration site of your SharePoint environment. If you are unsure what the address for this site is, you should contact your system administrator or the person who installed SharePoint. You may also access the Central Administration site by logging directly into the server and selecting SharePoint 3.0 Central Administration from the Microsoft Office Server option on the Programs menu.

1. Log into the SharePoint Central Administration site for your server farm.

2. Select the Applications tab.

3. Select the Create a Site Collection link from the SharePoint Site Management group of links. You are redirected to a page where you must provide information to create the site.

4. The first item in your list of things to identify is the web application on which you will create the site. Make sure that the web application you select is the correct application. If it is not, you can click the down arrow to the right of the selected web application and click Change Web Application.

Typically, you create most SharePoint sites under the web application that is hosted on port 80 so that end users do not have to see a port number in the address of their sites. For example, a web address of http://servername *is much nicer than* http://servername:32124. *If you are unsure which application to select, ask your system administrator or the person who installed SharePoint.*

5. To create a site, you must provide a title, description, and URL for the site. Name the site **Corporate Intranet Site** and enter the following description:

> **Collaborative portal for practicing exercises within the Beginning SharePoint 2007 book.**

6. For URL name, select sites from the list of paths and enter **intranet**.

If no other sites exist in your web application, you can also create your intranet portal site at the root of the web (such as http://servername)*. Only one site collection can exist at the root of a web.*

7. You have a variety of choices for the site template. As described earlier, the optimal template for a corporate intranet is the Collaborative Portal template. Select that template from the Publishing tab (because it is a publishing site).

8. Enter your own name as the primary site collection administrator.

9. Click the OK button. The process for creating your site takes a few minutes. After it is completed, you are redirected to a page advising you that the process has completed successfully and a URL will be displayed for you to select to visit your site, as shown in Figure 1-2.

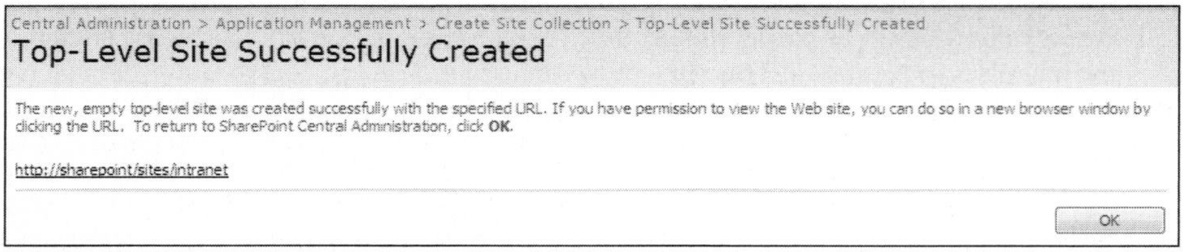

Central Administration > Application Management > Create Site Collection > Top-Level Site Successfully Created

Top-Level Site Successfully Created

The new, empty top-level site was created successfully with the specified URL. If you have permission to view the Web site, you can do so in a new browser window by clicking the URL. To return to SharePoint Central Administration, click **OK**.

http://sharepoint/sites/intranet

OK

Figure 1-2

Enterprise Features

So far, you have examined SharePoint's basic features; however, you've yet to discover components, namely *Enterprise features*, so named because they often represent the functionality that large enterprises require and demand from their collaborative applications. These features also highlight some of the key differences between Windows SharePoint Services and Microsoft Office SharePoint Server.

❑ **Form Services:** *InfoPath* is a forms creation and completion application that is in an important part of the Microsoft Office system. Introduced in 2003, it offers significant integration points for data collection and sharing. In 2003, whenever users completed a form, they were required to have the InfoPath client application installed. *Form Services* makes Microsoft Office InfoPath 2007 forms available via the web browser so you can easily collect and access data, while eliminating the client applications. Chapter 10 explores gives more information on Forms Services.

❑ **Search:** This connects you with the information, people, and processes you need to make informed business decisions. Users' complaints concerning SharePoint 2003's inability to locate information resulted in a greatly improved search engine in the 2007 release, which includes search highlighting. Chapter 14 shows how the search feature accesses multiple systems via a single search engine, and explains how to improve search queries and result relevancy.

❑ **Web Content Management:** With the integration of Microsoft Content Management Server 2002, SharePoint now supports web content creation and publishing. Publishing features ranging from content approval workflow to page layouts and content types which means you can create and publish branded web content without knowing code. You can then host these websites on an intranet environment or an extranet so partners or clients can access information. Chapter 13 shows you how to create and manage web content.

❑ **Excel Services:** Microsoft Excel popularity means many organizations support thousands of spreadsheets full of business information. *Excel Services* lets you work with important data in real time using only the browser. You can publish interactive pivot tables, charts, and spreadsheets to a large audience while protecting your formulas and calculations. Users are given "view-only" rights, which only allows them to see the browser-based version of a report. Chapter 11 covers options for displaying reports in your portals, including those generated from Excel spreadsheets as well as key performance information based on real-time information.

❑ **Business Data Catalog:** Although SharePoint may be your central application, your organization may have legacy business applications. The *Business Data Catalog* (BDC) allows you to connect to these external data sources and display business data via Web Parts, user profiles, or SharePoint lists. Although the BDC does not contain the information from these systems, it acts as the virtual bridge between the alternate system and the user. Chapter 12 discusses the BDC, as well as practical methods for accessing information via the various business data components such as Web Parts and list columns.

❑ **Audiences/Profiles:** SharePoint 2007 can collect user profile information and store it in a centralized database so that various elements in SharePoint can access it and personalize it. *Personalization* targets relevant content to users based on properties of their profiles. Chapter 9 shows you how audiences and personalization provide targeted content to users.

Summary

This chapter provided basic knowledge of the new features available in Microsoft Office SharePoint Server 2007 and how you can use them to service enterprise-level organizations, drive more efficient business processes, and connect people with the information required to make informed business decisions. After reading this chapter, you should also better understand how SharePoint 2007 has been enhanced to address some of the perceived limitations of its predecessor, SharePoint Portal Server 2003. You should also better understand the various SharePoint Products and Technologies that service specific business requirements, including lists, libraries, content types, sites and workspaces, and workflow.

Exercises

1. What is the difference between a team site and a document workspace?

2. Your manager informs you that the organization is currently reviewing the need for a corporate portal. List two reasons to justify why organizations invest in portal technologies.

3. True or False. Microsoft Office SharePoint Server 2007 is the next release of SharePoint Portal Server 2003.

Working with SharePoint Lists

This chapter reviews a very important concept in SharePoint known as *lists*, which you use throughout SharePoint to store and display information. By gaining a solid understanding of how they work early in this book, you can construct highly effective business applications and solutions in later chapters of the book by combining multiple lists with other important SharePoint components.

This chapter focuses mainly on lists basics, describing the various functionalities and features. In Chapter 4, you learn how to customize and manage lists to create working environments that suit your specific business requirements and needs.

This chapter covers the following:

- ❑ A description of what a SharePoint list is
- ❑ A discussion on how you can use lists
- ❑ A detailed description of the type of information that you can store in lists
- ❑ A breakdown of the various default list templates that SharePoint offers
- ❑ A hands-on discussion on how you can work with lists to create and view information

What Is a List?

Virtually everything stored in SharePoint is in some form of a list. Lists can contain a variety of content, from customer contact information to recipes for your favorite dishes. They are similar to databases, and provide reports and views of the information stored in them. They are very easy to construct and require no special tools or knowledge, which makes them an ideal information store for most organizations and teams.

Understanding List Elements

Lists have item, fields, and views. *Items* and *fields* correspond to the rows and columns that you see on grid layout that you often see in spreadsheets or databases. *Views* present list data in a friendlier format that acts very similar to a report.

❑ **Items:** An *item*, or record, is a row in a database. For example, for a list that stores information on customers, each customer may have a unique item in the list, which is also called the *customer row* or *customer record*.

❑ **Fields:** A *field* is a column in a database. You may also see a column referred to as *metadata*, which really contains the details of a row's information. A customer item in a list, for example, contains the phone number, physical address, billing address, and email address.

❑ **Views:** A single list can have multiple views. You create a view to address a user's informational needs relating to list data. A view displays a subset of information from the list, for example customers who have been added during a specific time period. You may also create a view to show all information on a list, but have items displayed in a predefined order.

Discovering SharePoint List Types

SharePoint lists can have the following types of information stored in columns:

❑ **Single Line of Text:** Possibly the most common, because it stores a variety of formats, such as the item's title, names, phone numbers, email addresses, and virtually anything else that you can enter into a single line text box.

❑ **Multiple Lines of Text:** Occasionally, this type of column is useful because it stores larger amounts of information, such as a customer's billing address or background information on the customer. For this column type, you can select whether the information should contain plain, rich, or enhanced text elements, such as bold, italic, pictures, or tables. You can expand this column as you add text to it or you can select how many lines in the box to display initially. When you use this field to collect information from users, it is a good idea to determine the number of lines to display so users will know how much content is expected from them.

❑ **Choice:** When gathering information on an item, you can offer users a selection of values or answers from which to choose. Using the example of a customer list, you may want to find out what type of services the customer purchases from you. If your organization provides only a fixed number of key services, it makes sense to present the user this set of choices to ensure that the field always contains valid information. When creating a choice column, you can select whether to have the choices appear in a drop-down list, as radio buttons, or as check boxes. For check boxes, the user may select more than one item. Alternatively, you can have users fill in their own choices if their items do not appear in the list. This is known as allowing "fill-in choices."

❑ **Number:** You commonly need to associate numerical information with an item so that you can later perform calculations on the information stored in them. You can configure number columns to store numbers that fall within a specific range or percentage values.

❑ **Currency:** This is similar to the number column, but specifically displays financial or monetary values. You can select what type of currency to display and the appropriate format based on region such as $123,000.00 for the United States or £123,000.00 for the United Kingdom.

❑ **Date and Time:** You typically have a list containing dates or times. This might include when an organization first became a customer or the last time it purchased a product. Date columns allow users to enter the date information directly into a text box or select the date from an easy-to-use calendar tool. When configuring a date column, you can control whether to allow only dates or dates with times. You can also select a default value for the date, including a special value that detects "Today's Date" as the user is filling out the item.

❑ **Lookup:** As your SharePoint environment expands, you may have many lists containing important information about things such as projects, products, and employees. In some cases you need to take information from one list and associate it with information from another. In the example of the customers list, you may have a listing of projects that display the name of the customer for which that project is being completed. Because your customers list will contain that information, it makes sense to have a column in the projects list that displays the names of all the customers. Lookup columns encourage users to store information in a single location rather than duplicate items throughout the organization. New in SharePoint 2007 is the ability to select multiple items from a lookup column.

❑ **Yes/No:** This check box column indicates whether an item matches a specific criterion. In the case of the customers list, you may create a Yes/No column named Active. If the customer is active, you select the check box. If the customer is not active, then the check box remains blank.

❑ **Person or Group:** SharePoint 2007 introduces a new type of column that associates specific people or groups of people with an item. Users can select people or groups from the site's membership source (for example, Active Directory) and associate them with items in a list. In the customers list example, you may use this column type to associate an account manager with a customer. Optionally, you can include a display picture along with the account manager's name.

❑ **Hyperlink or Picture:** You can use this column type to enter a website address into a list item to create a hyperlink or display an image located at the source location. In the customer list example, you can use this type of column to display the company's website address or the company's logo.

❑ **Calculated:** Rather than have users manually enter information, you may want to calculate values based on other columns within the list. For this type of column, you can select the names of other columns from the list and identify relationships and formulas. For example, you may have a calculated value that displays how many years the customer has been a client of the organization based on other information in the customer record. You can then select a format for the column.

❑ **Business Data:** This is a tool that accesses enterprise data from other lines of business systems directly from your SharePoint sites. In some cases, you may want to associate business data from the catalog with your list items. For example, you may have a listing of all products in a sales database and instead of recreating it in SharePoint, you can connect to and reuse that information. Using a Business Data column, you can associate a products list with your list so that as you define customers, you can also select which products the customer typically purchases.

For more on the Enterprise feature, see Chapters 1 and 8. Chapter 12 is dedicated to the Business Data Catalog and its various functions.

❑ **Publishing:** Numerous special publishing columns in SharePoint 2007 are specifically intended to create content to display on web pages. You can create these columns on any site that has the Publishing feature enabled.

Chapter 13 is dedicated to the Publishing feature and Web Content Management.

❑ **Audiences:** If a list has audience targeting enabled, this column type is automatically added to it. Audiences are groups of users that you define based on a set of criteria. When you use audiences on list items, the items appear only to members of the audiences associated with the item.

Chapter 9 gives in depth information on audiences and user profiles.

Understanding the Standard List Templates

Now that you understand the basic components of a list, you can look at some of the list templates that are available in SharePoint. Many of these templates address common business scenarios that exist within organizations, such as tracking tasks and sharing contact and meeting information. You should think of these templates as a starting point because you can further customize them to suit the needs of any organization.

More advanced techniques for customizing and managing lists are discussed in Chapter 4.

Understanding and Creating Contact List Columns

In team environments, you commonly need to share contact information. SharePoint provides a very easy-to-use interface just for this purpose that you can create via a template. It's known as a *contacts list*. Rather than storing contact information individually in address books, team members add contacts to a list on a SharePoint site so that the information becomes available to everyone.

A contacts list has the columns shown in the following table. Although you can create or delete columns at any time, the Last Name column is considered the title column, and you cannot remove it from the list. You may rename it if you like, however.

Column Name	Description
Last Name (required)	Single line of text
First Name	Single line of text
Full Name	Single line of text
e-mail Address	Single line of text
Company	Single line of text

Column Name	Description
Job Title	Single line of text
Business Phone	Single line of text
Home Phone	Single line of text
Mobile Phone	Single line of text
Fax Number	Single line of text
Address	Multiple lines of text
City	Single line of text
State/Province	Single line of text
ZIP/Postal Code	Single line of text
Country/Region	Single line of text
Web Page	Hyperlink or picture
Notes	Multiple lines of text
Created By	Person or group
Modified By	Person or group

Adding an item to a contacts list is quite easy and can be done using one of the following methods:

❑ **Clicking New from the toolbar:** You can click this button, shown in Figure 2-1 and then enter all the details for the list manually using a form.

Figure 2-1

❑ **Synchronizing list data from a Microsoft Access database:** By selecting Open with Access from the Actions menu, shown in Figure 2-2, you can create and link an Access database to the SharePoint list so that information you add to the Access database updates to the SharePoint list. This is ideal if more advanced reporting or access requirements exist beyond those that the

SharePoint site can service. This method also provides an excellent option for working offline with SharePoint data.

Figure 2-2

❑ **Synchronizing list data from Outlook:** Not only is a contacts list a great tool for accessing information directly from the site using a browser, but you can also link it to Outlook using the Connect to Outlook item that was shown in Figure 2-2. This is great because business users often prefer to work directly from their email client. Any information entered into the contacts list from Outlook automatically synchronizes back to the SharePoint list. In the previous version of SharePoint, users could import items from their address book into a SharePoint list. In SharePoint 2007, users can create new list items directly from Outlook or drag existing items into the folder so that they are added to the SharePoint list.

Creating Calendar Lists

In addition to sharing contact information, teams often need to share information about important dates, appointments, and meetings. Having a shared calendar that all team members can access improves communication of important things, such as availability, deadlines, and progress.

Earlier versions of SharePoint had a list template known as events. However, the most common use of the template was to create a shared team calendar for tracking date-related information. Therefore, the template has been revamped in 2007 to make it more generic in nature, but far more flexible and functional.

Calendar List Columns

When you create a calendar list, it contains the columns shown in the following table. You can add or remove columns at any time, but you cannot remove the default columns: Title, Start Time, and End Time.

Column Name	Description
Title (required)	Single line of text
Location	Single line of text
Start Time (required)	Date and time
End Time (required)	Date and time
Description	Multiple lines of text
Created By	Person or group
Modified By	Person or group

In addition to these columns, the calendar list has the following special features that are available to you when you create a new item in the list:

❑ **All Day Events check box:** An item in a calendar list may not apply to a specific time of day. For example, a holiday runs all day. When you select this check box, the Start and End Time fields are hidden and automatically set to 12:00 A.M. and 11:59 P.M., respectfully.

❑ **Recurrence:** An event or meeting may occur on a regular basis. You can create a recurrence rule so that list items are created for all subsequent instances from the one original entry. By selecting this check box, you must define how frequently the recurrence takes place and for how long. Figure 2-3 shows the various recurrence options.

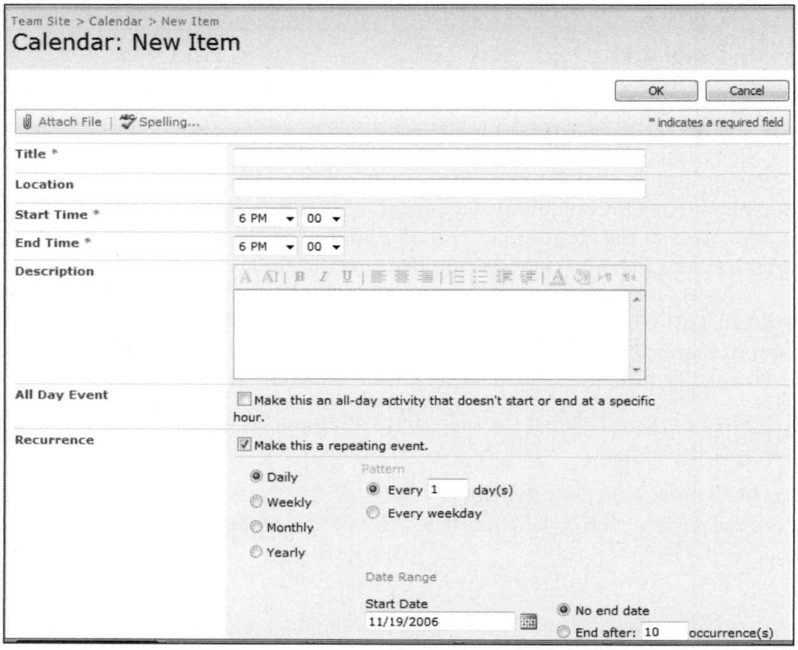

Figure 2-3

❑ **Meeting Workspace:** Your event or special day may require a website specifically created for the event. This website, called a *Workspace*, tracks information and documents related to the event. For example, an upcoming training session Workspace may have draft registration forms and handout materials that a team works on. When you select this check box and save the item, you are redirected to a site creation page where you name the site and select a meeting workspace template.

For more on Workspaces, see Chapter 8.

❑ **Export Event:** Once you have an item added to a list, you can export it as an .ics file that you can save to Outlook or forward to colleagues who cannot access the SharePoint environment. You do this by clicking the Export Event button from the item's properties view, as shown in Figure 2-4.

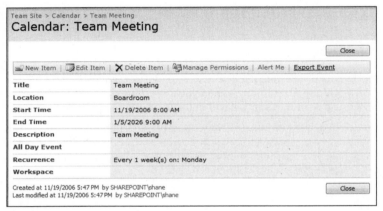

Figure 2-4

Creating a New Event

You use the New button on the List toolbar to create a new event. Like the contacts list, you can connect the calendar list to either Outlook or an Access database through the items listed on the Actions menu. You can also add items to the connected Outlook folder or an Access database and it is automatically added to the SharePoint list. The calendar list features three standard views upon creation:

❑ **Calendar:** This view displays all list information in a month, week, and day calendar format, as shown in Figure 2-5. Users can switch between month, week, and day views of the list items or select a specific date to view all items for the selected day.

❑ **All Items:** This standard list view displays all items (in groups of 100) of the list sorted by their creation date, as shown in Figure 2-6.

❑ **Current Events:** This list view filters out items that have taken place in the past and displays upcoming items in the order that they will take place. See Figure 2-7 for an example.

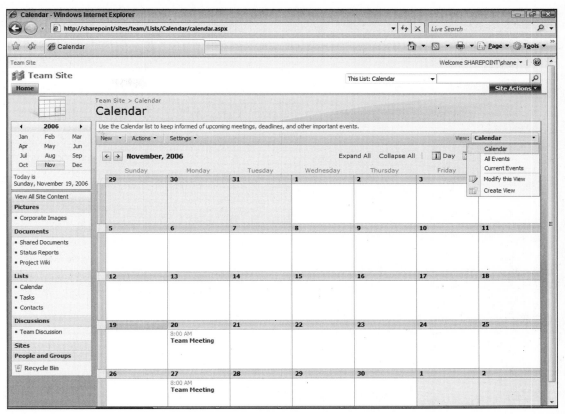

Figure 2-5

Figure 2-6

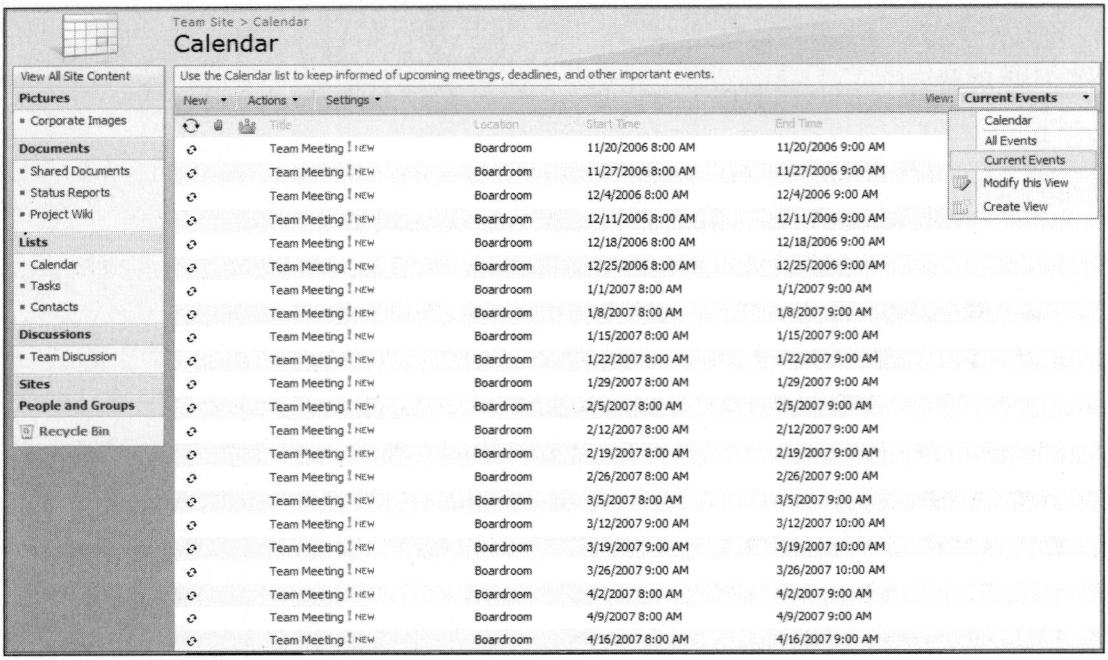

Figure 2-7

Understanding Announcements Lists

Virtually every team needs to track news related to important events and activities. Basically, instead of sending distracting direct email messages to team members, you can use the announcements list to drive members to your site to look for the latest information on key activities and events. Using the announcements list template, site managers can alert team members about key events and milestones related to their business activities, without having to adopt a more formalized news publishing feature.

When you create an announcements list, it contains the columns shown in the following table, but you can add more or remove unwanted columns. Because the Title column is considered a required column, you cannot remove it from the list.

Column Name	Description
Title (required)	Single line of text
Body	Multiple lines of text (enhanced text with pictures and tables)
Expires	Date and time
Created By	Person or group
Modified By	Person or group

The announcements list features two standard views upon creation:

❑ **All Items:** This standard list view displays all items (in groups of 100) in the list sorted by their creation date. Site visitors can access it either from the list itself or a Web Part related to the list.

❑ **Summary:** The announcements list Web Part uses this view to display the item title followed by a segment of the story and the author's name. This view displays the latest stories for which the expiry date has not been specified or has not passed. There is no way to edit the properties or behavior of this view.

Understanding Discussion Boards

Because team members may be collaborating on projects from different geographic locations and have different working schedules, the need for an effective mode of electronic communication is critical. Although email has traditionally played this role, increasingly email proliferation means employees spend more time filtering and sorting through their inboxes. As a result, SharePoint provides a more passive electronic communication. A *threaded discussion* allows an author to post a message, and others to reply to that message through the web interface. Because all the communication occurs on the website, team members can stay informed on decision-making processes without directly participating in a specific thread.

By default, the discussion board contains the columns shown in the following table, but you can add more columns. Because the Subject column is considered the required column, you cannot remove it from the list.

Column Name	Description
Body	Multiple lines of text (enhanced text with pictures and tables)
Subject (required)	Single line of text
Created By	Person or group
Modified By	Person or group

In addition to these columns, there are three unique views, as shown in Figure 2-8. The subject view lists all discussions that are available within the list, whereas the threaded and flat views offer methods for viewing the individual discussions related to a single subject.

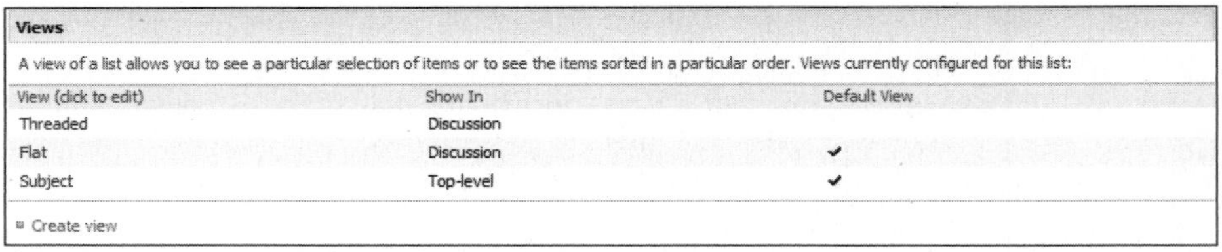

Views		
A view of a list allows you to see a particular selection of items or to see the items sorted in a particular order. Views currently configured for this list:		
View (click to edit)	Show In	Default View
Threaded	Discussion	
Flat	Discussion	✔
Subject	Top-level	✔
▫ Create view		

Figure 2-8

For team members who prefer to control their communications from an email client, you can connect to Outlook in this list template. By clicking Connect to Outlook from the Actions menu of a discussion list, team members can view a new folder specifically for discussion in their Outlook SharePoint lists. Users can make new posts and send replies from Outlook in the very same way that they create a new email message. However, instead of sending a message directly to someone's inbox, the message posts to a central location where everybody can share the information. Figure 2-9 shows an example of a discussion board list item. This view is available by clicking a discussion subject.

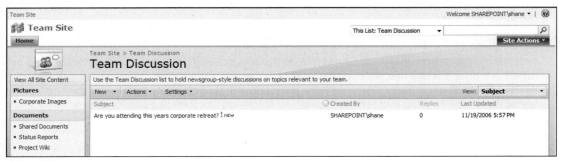

Figure 2-9

Understanding Links Lists

Commonly, working on a project or initiative requires a team to set up website links to share with one another, for example links to third-party information sources. SharePoint provides a list template that makes it easy to share links with team members. Upon creation, the links list has the columns listed in the following table. You can add more columns later, but the URL column is considered a required column and, therefore, you cannot remove it from the list.

Column Name	Description
URL (required)	Hyperlink or picture
Notes	Multiple lines of text
Created By	Person or group
Modified By	Person or group

When adding a new link item to a list, you must specify a URL along with a description. The description gives your URL a title so that the full web address does not display in the list views. When you specify the URL, you can click a link that tests the address to confirm that it is a valid location. You should test your address before you publish it to all your team members.

You can change the link order in case you have a reason to display links in a specific order. For example, while you can list most links in the order they were created in, you may need to ensure the company's public website is listed first. You accomplish this by selecting Change Order from the Actions menu shown in Figure 2-10 and selecting 1 from the Order drop-down list to the right of the company website address. All other items automatically adjust their position based on your selection.

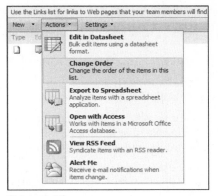

Figure 2-10

Understanding Tasks Lists

Effectively tracking assignments and deadlines is critical for most teams. Using the tasks list template in SharePoint, greatly improved in 2007, you can send automatic email notifications to inform team members of assignments and consolidate information related to the work that you've performed to a single location.

Task List Columns

When you create a tasks list, it has the columns listed in the following table. Although you can add more columns at any time, the Title column is required and you cannot remove it from the list.

Column Name	Description
Title (required)	Single line of text
Priority	Choice
Status	Choice
% Complete	Number
Assigned To	Person or group
Task Group	Person or group
Description	Multiple lines of text
Start Date	Date and time
Due Date	Date and time
Created By	Person or group
Modified By	Person or group

Task List Views

The task list has the following views so team members have relevant and personalized task information:

❑ **All Tasks:** This displays all items (in groups of 100) in the list sorted by their creation date.

❑ **My Tasks:** This personalized view of items is a good default view for team members because it displays the tasks that are likely most relevant to the current user.

❑ **Due Today:** This view features a filtered list of tasks that have a due date equal to the current date. This is an effective choice to display in a Web Part on the main page of site so that all team members are aware of key milestones and critical tasks.

❑ **Active Tasks:** As your task list expands, you need to differentiate between completed tasks and those still in progress. You don't have to remove or delete completed tasks because you may need to refer back to them later. Instead, you can filter out completed tasks and only display active ones. The Active Tasks view only displays items where status is not equal to completed.

❑ **By Assigned To:** As a team leader or manager, you may need to view the assignments of all team members to pinpoint available resources and the progress of key initiatives. This view shows the task sorted by the person assigned to it, as well as the task's status.

❑ **By My Groups:** This is very similar to the By Assigned To view. However, it only displays tasks assigned to groups. Items appear by the group name to which they are assigned.

New Task List Features in SharePoint 2007

There's a lot more you can do with task lists. The new features for SharePoint 2007 help you integrate with Outlook as well as create workflows around task items:

❑ **The template also integrates with Microsoft Outlook.** Many business users are accustomed to how the task functionality in Outlook operated and therefore want SharePoint to support the same ease of use and targeted notification capabilities. Users can connect to Outlook from the Actions menu of the tasks list and create a list in their Outlook folders where they can add new tasks and update existing items directly from within the Outlook interface. All updated items are automatically synchronized back to the SharePoint list.

❑ **A built-in workflow engine enhances the Windows Workflow Foundation.** It features some great solutions for processing common business activities, such as approval, feedback, and content expiration. This is a fantastic addition to the SharePoint environment and is discussed in greater detail in Chapter 5.

❑ **The tasks list integrates with the workflow activities.** As you add users to workflow activities, they are assigned to specific tasks in the site's task list. This integration further highlights how a SharePoint task list can become a user's one-stop source to track and maintain his or her assignment information.

Exploring Project Tasks Lists

The project tasks list is very similar in structure and behavior to the tasks list in the previous section. It has the same columns and most of the same views as well as a special view, called the *Project Tasks* view. A *project task* is a Gantt view that displays a bar for each task indicating status and expected timeline. You can add this view to other list types. SharePoint creates it automatically with the project tasks list to give you a head start in creating visually attractive work breakdown structures that you can apply to just about any project.

Like tasks lists, the project tasks list also features Microsoft Outlook integration and targeted email notifications based on new assignments. However, you cannot associate a project tasks list with a workflow activity. Therefore, users looking to have Gantt chart views of workflow information are advised to use the standard tasks list and create a custom Gantt view.

More information on customizing lists in this manner is described in Chapter 4.

Exploring Issue Lists

Unfortunately, unexpected issues commonly arise when you conduct business or run a project. An *issue* is an event that requires resolution. In a software environment, this may be a bug that someone discovered in the software. In a shipping company, this may be a transportation delay because of a snowstorm. Because issues can have such a huge impact on business operations and the success of an initiative, it is important to effectively track and resolve them. The SharePoint list template for issues provides an easy-to-use method for doing so.

By default, an issue list contains the columns shown in the following table, but you can add columns to meet your needs. Because the Title column is considered the required column, you cannot remove it from the list.

Column Name	Description
Assigned To	Person or group
Issue Status	Choice
Priority	Choice
Description	Multiple lines of text
Category	Choice
Due Date	Date and time
Related Issues	Lookup
Comments	Multiple lines of text
Created By	Person or group
Modified By	Person or group

Because sometimes you cannot resolve one issue until you find a resolution for another issue, the issues list has built-in functionality for tracking related items. In addition, the Comments column of an issues list time stamps and labels each entry that team members make over the duration of the issue. This provides excellent insight into the progress of a specific item.

While the issues list template does support the offline synchronization features of Access, there is no default support for Microsoft Outlook integration.

Exploring Survey Lists

In most organizations, you need to collect information from users on specific programs and events. SharePoint provides a great tool for conducting surveys via the *survey list template*. This template can be highly customized to deliver dynamic surveys to an organization. All data is submitted back to the list and can be viewed in a graphical format or exported to a spreadsheet for additional processing. A new feature in SharePoint 2007 is being able to branch questions based on user's responses. This means you can personalize your survey better than in the previous version.

Creating questions in a SharePoint survey is similar to creating columns with the exception that no default (required) columns exist. Instead, the author must complete a wizard-type interface to create the questions required for the survey.

You can create the following question types, shown in the following table, in a SharePoint survey list.

Column Name	Description
Single line of text	Date and time
Multiple lines of text	Lookup
Choice	Yes/No
Rating Scale (a matrix of choices or a Likert scale)	Page separator (inserts a page break into your survey)
Number	Person or group
Currency ($, ¥, €)	Business data

The survey list template has a unique feature that allows you to create page separators and rating scales to improve a survey form's usability and design. Once you create questions, you can add branching logic to improve the flow of questions and ensure that you're asking the user to answer only the questions that are relevant to them. For example, if a question asks if the user has attended the company social, you can insert branching logic to ensure that, if the user selects no, she can skip questions that focus on the company social and redirect her to the next relevant question.

Working with Lists

Now that you know the various lists that are available in SharePoint, you need an understanding of how you can interact and work with lists to gain the insight you require from a SharePoint site and the information it contains.

Working with List Content

In the next two examples, you learn how to add content to a list as well as make updates to existing content within a list. Because SharePoint lists are only useful if they contain information, it is very important that you understand how to update them effectively.

In SharePoint, a variety of list templates can store just about any type of information or data. In the following example, you walk through the steps of creating a new list item in an existing tasks list. The same steps apply regardless of the list template you use.

Try It Out   **Adding a New Item to a List**

Your boss has just informed you that virtually every document that your company created looks completely different, and that they all have inconsistent fonts, images, and nonstandard logos. Because this inconsistency can portray an unprofessional image to some of your customers, he has asked you to create a standard template that acts as the starting point for all corporate documents. Because you want to ensure that this task gets completed on time, you decide to create a new task item on your SharePoint site.

1.   From the main page of your SharePoint team site, click the Tasks link in the Quick Launch navigation bar.

2.   To create a new task in this tasks list, click the New button on the list toolbar. A page opens that is very similar to a form shown in Figure 2-11.

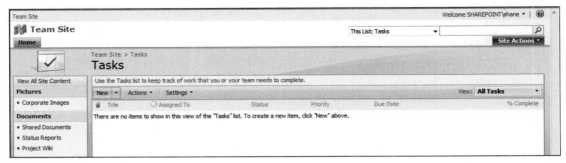

Figure 2-11

3.   Complete the fields shown in Figure 2-12 using the information in the following table.

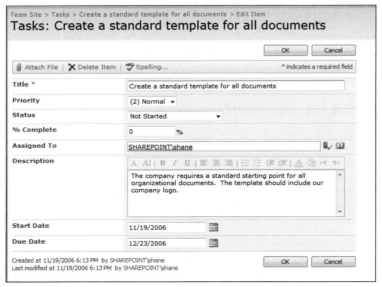

Figure 2-12

Column	Value
Title	Enter **Create a standard template for all documents**.
Priority	Keep the default value of `Normal`.
Status	Keep the default value of `Not Started`.
% Complete	Enter **0**.
Assigned to	Enter **Your Own Name**.
Description	Enter **The company requires a standard starting point for all organizational documents. The template should include our company logo.**
Start Date	By default, the date is the current date. Click the calendar icon and select the date that is one week from today.
Due Date	Click the calendar icon and select the date that is two weeks from today.

4. After you enter all the information, click the OK button. SharePoint creates your new task and returns you to the task list where you can create additional items or modify existing tasks.

How It Works

The content of a list is made up of a series of items. Each item contains a primary column, such as a title, and then usually some additional columns that describe the item. In the previous example, you created a task for the request you received from your boss. The Title column is the primary column, and it describes the subject of the task. All the other columns contain information about that specific task and give descriptive information that better enables you to complete the task on schedule. If you had additional tasks, you would create them in the same manner, and eventually your list would be filled with task information that you could include in various reports.

The previous example focused on creating a new item in a task list. However, you can use the steps to create new items on all lists. Chapter 13, which discusses publishing pages and web content management, shows you additional methods for creating new items.

Try It Out   Editing an Existing Item in a List

After thinking further about your boss's request to create a standard document template for your organization, you decide to do some research. You find several sample templates online that you feel may act as good starting points for your own company's template. You give them to your boss, and he selects one that is a clear favorite. You decide that it's a good idea to associate this sample template with the task you created on your team site.

Once you add a list item to a list, it is fairly common to return to the list and update the item. This is especially true in the case of a task because the status value should change as time progresses. In order for SharePoint to be an effective tool, you should keep all the information contained on the various sites up-to-date.

1. From the main page of your SharePoint team site, click the Tasks link in the Quick Launch navigation bar.

2. Click the title of the task you added for creating a standard document template from the previous example.

3. You now see all the information about your task. Click the Edit Item button on the list toolbar as shown in Figure 2-13.

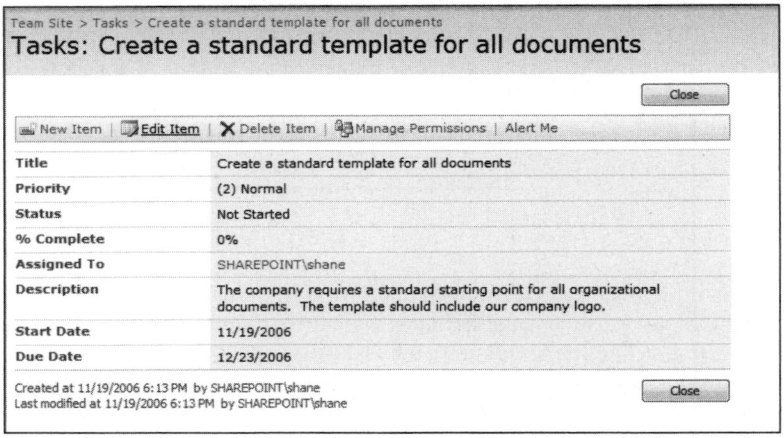

Team Site > Tasks > Create a standard template for all documents

Tasks: Create a standard template for all documents

Close

New Item | Edit Item | Delete Item | Manage Permissions | Alert Me

Title	Create a standard template for all documents
Priority	(2) Normal
Status	Not Started
% Complete	0%
Assigned To	SHAREPOINT\shane
Description	The company requires a standard starting point for all organizational documents. The template should include our company logo.
Start Date	11/19/2006
Due Date	12/23/2006

Created at 11/19/2006 6:13 PM by SHAREPOINT\shane
Last modified at 11/19/2006 6:13 PM by SHAREPOINT\shane

Close

Figure 2-13

4. From the toolbar, click the Attach File button.

5. Click the Browse button. Browse to the location of the resources for this chapter which can be downloaded from www.wrox.com and select the Sample Organizational Template document. Click the Open button.

6. Click OK. The document is added to the list item as an attachment. The file uploads to the SharePoint list and becomes accessible to others who may review the task.

7. Because you have already started working on the task, you should also change the Status field to In Progress and % Complete field to 5. You may also want to change the Start Date to the current date as shown in Figure 2-14.

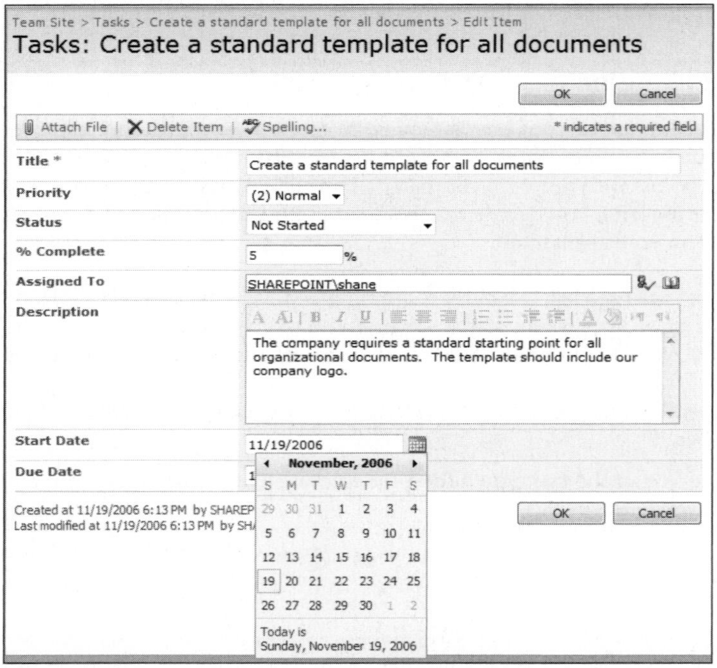

Figure 2-14

8. Click OK to save your changes.

How It Works

In the previous example, you collected additional information related to your task and associated that information with the previously created list item. Rather than saving the sample template on your personal computer, you attached the template to the task so that all other team members have access to the information. Similarly, once you start the task, you should change the status of the task to reflect your progress. This allows other team members (including your boss) to see that you have started the task and they can gain an understanding of your progress. The more teams store accurate and up-to-date information within lists to reflect the actual status, the better team members are informed on the overall progress and status of shared initiatives. This eventually leads to an environment where individual team members spend less time manually reporting status on activities and more time actually completing their work.

Try It Out   Changing the View of a List

As previously explained, views display your list information in a variety of ways to help improve a user's ability to find relevant information. You may notice that over time, lists may start to fill with information as each member of your team begins to add items. To help you find information more easily, you can select from a series of predefined views that display specific reports on the information stored in a list.

1. From the main page of your SharePoint team site, click the Tasks link in the Quick Launch navigation bar.

2. When you first visit a list, the default view of the list displays. In many cases, this is the All Items view, but if you have customized your list, it may be something different.

3. All views are listed in a drop-down box to the right of the list toolbar. Expand the menu and select the My Tasks view from the list as shown in Figure 2-15.

The My Tasks view appears and you should see only your own tasks displayed in the view. This is because the view is filtered to only display items that are assigned to the current user.

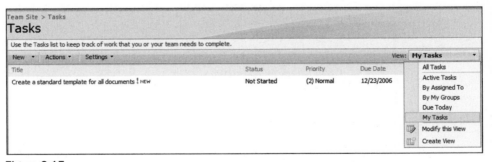

Figure 2-15

How It Works

As you add more and more data to SharePoint lists, it is important that you have methods to organize and access the information in a timely and effective manner. In the previous example, if you accessed a task list on a popular team site, you could have hundreds or even thousands of list items. With such a large amount of information, it's very difficult to quickly identify relevant items in the list. However, through custom views, you create filters that look at the column data and return items that meet specific criteria.

In the example shown, you selected the My Tasks view. The view uses a special property called [me] that identifies the current user and only displays items that have that user's name in the Assigned To column.

Working Offline with List Content

SharePoint 2007 provides mechanisms for working offline on content that is stored in a list or library. If you use Outlook 2007, you can connect specific lists to your profile so that information stored within the list is available as a folder in Outlook. This means you can work directly on task items through Outlook and automatically synchronize your changes back to the list when you reconnect. This keeps SharePoint list information up-to-date, even when you are away from the office or disconnected from the network. If a conflict exists, you receive a notification and you have a choice on how you want to resolve the conflict.

1. From the main page of your SharePoint team site, click the Tasks link in the Quick Launch navigation bar.

2. From the list toolbar, click the small arrow to the right of the Actions menu item. This expands the menu to display all the available actions for working with this list.

3. Select Connect to Outlook, which is shown in Figure 2-2.

4. Outlook opens, and a small message appears asking you to confirm that you want to connect to the SharePoint list. Click the Yes button to confirm the action. You should now see a listing of any lists that were available within your SharePoint site within an Outlook folder.

5. Select your task for creating a standard document template. A window appears as shown in Figure 2-16.

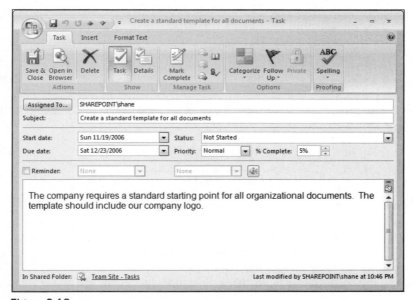

Figure 2-16

6. Update your task to mark it as complete using the values shown in Figure 2-16, and click the Save and Close button. When you return to your SharePoint site, you should see that the task is marked as complete.

Tracking List Content Updates

As teams make updates to SharePoint lists, you'll need to stay in tune with these updates and keep track of any progress. SharePoint provides a couple of different methods for tracking list updates:

❑ A subscription-based service allows you to create a rule on the list so you are automatically notified of changes. This functionality is greatly improved in SharePoint 2007 because it supports more choices for receiving notifications and creating alerts. Previously, when working with file shares or other tools for managing information, team members placed a document in a location and then sent an email to other team members stating the document's location, thus running the risk of people never receiving the information, or being distracted by the constant and unnecessary email messages. With the subscription-based service, you give users a way to personalize their notifications.

❑ Each list in SharePoint contains an *RSS*, or *Really Simple Syndication*, feed. Users can select and subscribe to an RSS feed using an appropriate view or application.

Try it Out   Subscribing to an Alert for a List

When you work with SharePoint lists, you want to be notified of changed or added content because receiving this information is less time-consuming than physically visiting every SharePoint site to manually check for new content. SharePoint offers a special Alerts feature, to which you can subscribe and from which you can create lists to keep aware of changes.

By creating alerts, team members can stay up-to-date on the changes to a SharePoint list or library in a manner that is appropriate to their unique work preferences or can receive immediate notifications on items that are of high relevance to them. For example, if you are responsible for responding to trouble tickets submitted to a list, you'll likely want notification as soon as an item is created or edited. However, you may only select a weekly summary report for another list that tracks menu choices for the cafeteria.

1. From the main page of your SharePoint team site, click the Tasks link in the Quick Launch navigation bar.

2. From the list toolbar, click the small arrow to the right of the Actions menu item. This expands the menu to display all the available actions for working with this list.

3. Select Alert Me from the menu (see Figure 2-2). You are then redirected to a page where you can specify details on how you want to receive alerts.

4. Depending on the type of list on which you create an alert, you see different customization options, which are shown in Figure 2-17. If you are working on the tasks, for example, you can specify:

❑ The users who have been subscribed to this alert.

❑ Whether an alert is sent for any changes or for only specific types of change, such as the creation of new items or the deletion or change of existing items.

❑ The type of changes that should trigger an alert, such as an item being marked as complete or the priority level of a task changing.

❑ How often alerts are sent. In some cases, it may be beneficial to receive immediate notification; however, in other cases a daily or weekly summary report is sufficient.

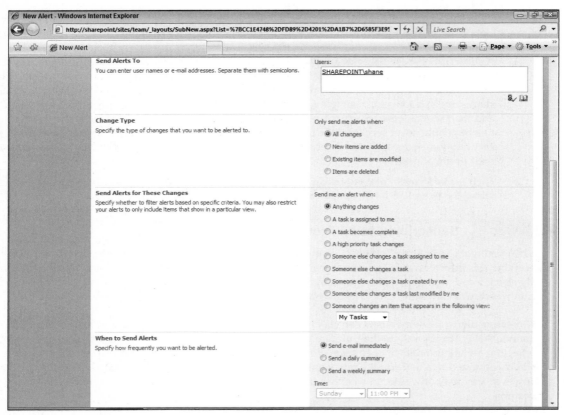

Figure 2-17

Try It Out   Subscribing to an RSS Feed for a List

RSS has become a popular way to deliver and aggregate news and web content to a user's computer. Rather than visiting multiple sites to find and view new content, users can instead subscribe to content via an RSS feed, and the new content downloads periodically. In SharePoint 2007, you can enable RSS feeds on every list and library, thereby making it much easier for users to stay up-to-date. The following example outlines how you can subscribe to an RSS feed associated with a list:

1. From the main page of your SharePoint team site, click the View All Site Content link in the Quick Launch navigation bar. You are redirected to a listing of all lists and libraries for the current site as shown in Figure 2-18.

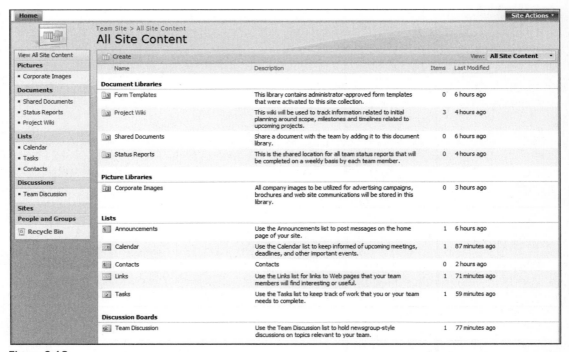

Figure 2-18

2. Click the name of the list for which you want to view an RSS feed.

3. From the list toolbar, click the small arrow to the right of the Actions menu item. This expands the menu to display all the available actions for working with this list.

4. Select View RSS Feed.

5. Select the Subscribe to this RSS feed link to consume the feed in your aggregator, as shown in Figure 2-19.

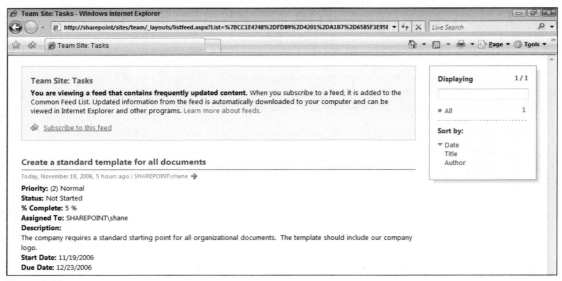

Figure 2-19

6. If you are using Outlook 2007, you can consume the feed and view all updates to your lists directly from your email client. Click the Yes button to add the feed to your Outlook folders or click the Advanced button to configure specific details for the feed, such as the target folder or whether to download attachments.

How It Works

When you select Subscribe to this RSS feed from a specific list or library, you are redirected to a page that displays syndicated content from the list. By subscribing to RSS feeds, you can take a more passive approach to staying up-to-date with information. As new content is added to a list, a new item appears within your RSS aggregator.

Exporting Data to Excel

SharePoint is a fantastic collaborative environment for storing up-to-date information in a centralized store. Editing lists is very similar to editing information in Excel, especially if you are using a datasheet view, but in Excel you can do certain things that are impossible on the browser, such as advanced calculations, data analysis, what-if type analysis, or complex rich formatting. But, you can have the best of both the SharePoint and the Excel worlds; you can create custom views on large amounts of data to filter and display only relevant information. Then, through the Export to Spreadsheet functionality views of list data, you can move data into Excel worksheets to share information or run further analysis.

Try It Out   **Exporting Information to Excel**

The people with whom you collaborate may not have access to the SharePoint environment, but they may be experienced Excel users. Using the Export to Spreadsheet option allows you to provide information to these users while still taking full advantage SharePoint's centrally stored information. Where possible, you should define custom views for commonly required reports that you can generate with the click of a button.

1. From the main page of your SharePoint team site, click the View All Site Content link in the Quick Launch navigation bar.

2. Click the name of the list from which you want to export information to Excel.

3. From the list toolbar, click the small arrow to the right of the Actions menu item. This expands the menu to display all the available actions for working with this list.

4. Click the Export to Spreadsheet menu item (see Figure 2-2). A window appears asking whether you wish to open or save the file.

5. Select the Open button. You may receive a warning about connecting to the selected data connection. This is a security precaution and is expected.

6. If you receive this warning, click the Enable button. Your list view now displays within an Excel workbook, as shown in Figure 2-20. From there you can perform additional calculations, apply styles, print, or email the information to colleagues.

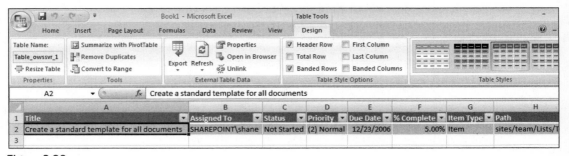

Figure 2-20

Summary

In this chapter, you learned about the basic content storage mechanism in SharePoint called lists. Lists allow you to collect information on a SharePoint site and share it with other team members in a manner that is easy to update and maintain. You learned the following:

❑ Lists contain columns of data that describe an item. Columns can contain a variety of formats of information, such as single line of text, multiple lines of text, date, or numerical data.

❑ You can link some lists such as tasks, project tasks, discussion boards, contacts, and calendar to Outlook to allow users to update and create new content on the SharePoint site directly from their email client. This is convenient for those users who are less familiar and comfortable in a web environment, but very much at ease when they work with their email program.

❑ By linking lists to Outlook, you can create an offline store that you can synchronize later when the SharePoint site is available.

❑ You can link some list templates with an Access database. This also creates an offline store and provides a rich reporting environment for users on data that is stored on the SharePoint site.

❑ SharePoint 2007 has a variety of list templates that you can use to create task assignments, event management, and issue tracking. You can use these templates exactly as they are created, or you can customize them by creating custom views or columns.

❑ You can subscribe to information that is stored within lists via RSS feeds that you associate with the list or via Alerts, which are customizable email notifications that you can define directly from the List toolbar menu.

❑ When you need to share information stored on a SharePoint site with stakeholders who do not have access to the physical environment, you can export SharePoint list views into Excel spreadsheets and save it offline for further analysis or sharing.

This chapter focused mainly on list basics, describing the various functionalities and features. In Chapter 4, you learn how to customize and manage lists to create working environments that suit your specific business requirements and needs.

Exercises

1. If you wanted to receive an email notification every time a new item is added to a list, how would you do that?

2. Describe the difference between a lookup column and a choice column.

3. Describe how you would send a report of information stored in a list to a partner outside your organization that did not have access to your SharePoint list.

4. What are the differences between a tasks list and a projects tasks list?

5. True or False: You can allow users to skip specific questions based on their responses to specific survey questions.

Working with SharePoint Libraries

In this chapter, you discover the magic behind document collaboration: the document library. *Document libraries* allow you to create, store, manage, and collaborate on documents. SharePoint has a variety of them, each designed to allow maximum efficiency when you work with particular types of documents. This chapter discusses the major elements of a document library and walks you through some of the different types of libraries and how you can use them to manage the documents crucial to business operations. The important aspects of document libraries include:

- ❑ Creating and uploading documents
- ❑ Checking documents in and out
- ❑ Managing version history
- ❑ Restoring documents
- ❑ Working with your documents offline
- ❑ Using the different types of document libraries

In Chapter 4, you learn how to customize a template to fit your business needs. You also learn how to customize the properties and features of a document library. This chapter focuses on interacting with document libraries that have been previously created or configured.

Understanding Libraries and Documents

If you want to, you can think of a document library as a Windows file folder, but better. Like folders, libraries act as document storage, but they also store the document's metadata or version history (more about this a little later) that folders do not. Also, folders lend themselves to user personalization in that they may stay on a user's drive or be labeled differently from another user's folder, which leads to inefficiency. You don't encounter this in libraries, which acts as central store, shared across an organization. SharePoint also offers collaboration features that go well beyond the traditional file-sharing techniques that you may have used in the past. Because SharePoint stores lists and libraries in a database rather than the file system, it is arguably more secure, more efficient, and enables more sophisticated document workflow and content management scenarios.

You should remember the following as you work with libraries:

❏ **Storage Types:** You can store a variety of file types, including presentations, images, archives, or spreadsheets. You can store virtually any file type in a SharePoint library as long as the file type has not been added to the Blocked File Types listing.

Managing Blocked File Types

You can view the listing of blocked file types for your SharePoint environment by visiting the Operations tab of your SharePoint Central Administration site for your server farm. Once there, you can find a link to view blocked file types under the Security Configuration group of links.

You can remove items from this list to upload them, via a web application, to SharePoint libraries; however, you should be very careful not to allow certain executables or file types that are security risks or performance issues. It is recommended that you speak with someone familiar with managing security within your network before removing a file type from this list.

Administrators may allow users more or less flexibility for managing certain file types within their personal sites versus their collaborative sites. This may include blocking certain media file formats in the MySites application that may typically be used within the various departmental and team sites for training or reference.

❏ **Metadata Information:** Document libraries have metadata columns for attaching information, such as document owner or status, to the document so that you can tailor it to your corporate practices. Metadata is useful for running searches on documents, which you learn more about in Chapter 14. Users with appropriate permissions can quickly and easily create extra metadata columns, while keeping your methodologies very agile, which is another important asset in today's business environment. In fact, SharePoint document libraries offer many of the same features as the lists that you explored in Chapter 2, such as rows, columns, and views.

❏ **Document Protection:** Documents in libraries are protected by a check in and out feature, which ensures that only one user at a time can edit a document. Later in this chapter, you learn about the various methods available for working with documents in this manner.

❏ **Document History:** Libraries keep a document audit trail, even when multiple people edit the document at the same time. Version history lets you quickly revert to a previously saved version of the document, right from the browser.

❏ **Major and Minor Versions:** While both lists and libraries support versioning of information, document libraries support major and minor versions. *Major versions* are published files that all site users can access, whereas the *minor versions* are files in a draft state that typically only a document's author or members of the approver's group can access.

From the surface, a document library view page, shown in Figure 3-1, looks very similar to that of a list, but with a few additions including:

❑ **Upload menu**: Located on the toolbar, this uploads single or multiple files to the library.

❑ **Windows Explorer type view:** You can see files in the library in this view via the Actions menu.

❑ **Document contextual menu:** This menu has several helpful options including the Send To option, which allows you to copy files to other locations, create collaborative workspaces for a document, or email a document's link to others; the Edit in option, which lets you edit a file in an associated and supported Microsoft Office application; and the Check Out and Check In options, discussed previously.

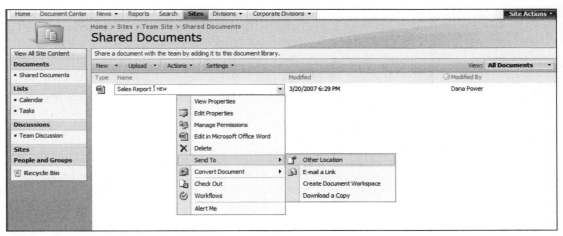

Figure 3-1

You get a chance to see each of these items in action throughout this chapter, starting with basic activities related to creating, uploading, and editing files in a SharePoint library, which are the items you'll learn about next.

> The Try It Outs in this section show you how to perform common library operations using the document library, which you create using the document library template, the most common library type. However, SharePoint has a whole slew of libraries, each designed to store specific content. For example, the picture library stores images and photos and the slide library stores PowerPoint slides. While you can store images and presentations in any library, the picture and slide libraries have content-specific features, such as views for seeing photos and slide shows. For more information on the other library types SharePoint has available, see the section "Understanding SharePoint Library Templates."

Creating and Managing Documents in a Library

Both employees and organizations benefit from SharePoint libraries. Organizations commonly roll out SharePoint 2007 because libraries keep shared documents in a secure system where access, versioning, templates, columns, and content are controlled. From a user's standpoint, creating and managing documents in a library is a simple process. You start by creating a document, with the aid of a template. You then upload a single or multiple documents. When you upload documents in bulk, you may need to edit your documents so that they have the correct metadata.

This section has a series of Try It Outs that walk you through this process, but before you do so, you need to understand the various document templates, shown in the following table, that are available for you to create a document. The obvious purpose of these templates is to start with a blank document or file. You can also use them to create custom templates that help your company to maintain content continuity. For example, you can have a sales proposal document template that contains company elements, such as your company's name, logo, and standard product specifications, as well as elements relating to customer choices, such as sections for recording a customer's requests. Associating this template with the sales team document library allows an account manager to launch a document containing these elements.

With the exception of the first item in the following table, you click the New button in the document library toolbar. The None option starts up the Word application, so it's for situations where you want to work strictly with a Word document outside of SharePoint.

Template	Purpose
None	This starts the Word application and creates an empty Word document.
Microsoft Office Word 97–2003 Document	Creates a blank Word document compatible with versions of Microsoft Office prior to the 2007 release.
Microsoft Office Excel 97–2003 Spreadsheet	Creates a blank Excel spreadsheet compatible with versions of Microsoft Office prior to the 2007 release.
Microsoft Office PowerPoint 97–2003 Presentation	Creates a blank PowerPoint presentation compatible with versions of Microsoft Office prior to the 2007 release.
Microsoft Office Word Document	Creates a new Word document using the new file formats supported only by Microsoft Office 2007.
Microsoft Office Excel Spreadsheet	Creates a new Excel spreadsheet using the new file formats supported only by Microsoft Office 2007.
Microsoft Office PowerPoint Presentation	Creates a new PowerPoint presentation using the new file formats supported only by Microsoft Office 2007.
Microsoft Office OneNote Section	Creates a new OneNote section using the new file formats supported only by Microsoft Office 2007.
Microsoft Office SharePoint Designer Webpage	Creates a standard web page that you can edit using SharePoint Designer.

Template	Purpose
Basic Page	Creates a blank SharePoint web page containing a content editor web part to allow users to add text and basic HTML to the page.
Web Part Page	Creates a blank SharePoint web page with a series of web part zones to support the addition and configuration of multiple web parts in a desired layout.

Try It Out   **Create a New Document from a Document Library**

You can create new documents while working in applications, such as Microsoft Office Word, and then save them to a SharePoint site, or you can create them within SharePoint by selecting the New button from within a document library. By default, each document library has a single blank Word document template associated with it. You are presented with this template as a starting point to create your document. This is the case for any standard document library that you create in a SharePoint site, unless the site manager specifies otherwise or uploads a custom template.

1. From the main page of your team site, click the Shared Documents link from the Quick Launch navigation bar.

2. Click the New button from the toolbar. A blank document opens in Word, as shown in Figure 3-2.

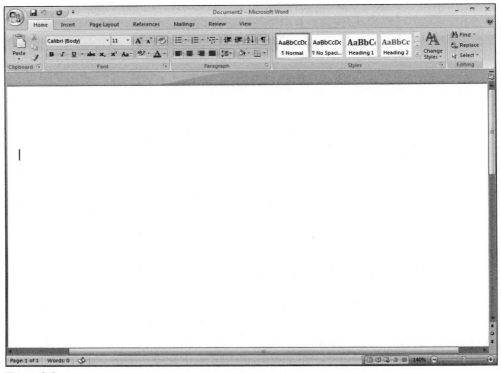

Figure 3-2

Try It Out   Upload a New Document

With SharePoint, uploading previously created documents is as frequent as creating new ones. The following example guides you through the process of uploading a document from your personal computer or network share to a SharePoint document library.

Imagine that you are an account manager for a large technology company, and you want to upload a recently created sales presentation to the team library. In the previous Try It Out, you created a new document from a library. However, you may want to share or manage a document created outside of the SharePoint environment. To accommodate this common situation, SharePoint document libraries support the upload of content to the library from another location.

In this exercise, you browse to the location of a presentation called "Why Our Products are Better.pptx" that is available as part of this chapter's resources and upload it to the Shared Documents library.

1.   Return to the Shared Documents library of your team site, as shown in the last Try It Out.

2.   From the document library toolbar, click the Upload button.

3.   From the Upload Document page, select Browse. The Choose File dialog box appears.

4.   Browse to the location of the "Why Our Products are Better.pptx" file and click Open, as shown in Figure 3-3.

Figure 3-3

5.   Click the OK button. When the page refreshes, you will see the presentation within the document library.

How It Works

When you upload in step 3, you are presented with a standard file-open dialog box from which you can navigate to and select the file. After you select your file and choose OK, your document transfers to the document library and, if applicable, you are prompted to enter any metadata that your document library requires.

Try It Out   **Upload Multiple Documents to a Document Library**

The previous Try It Out works great if you only need to upload a single document to the document library. However, it's less time consuming and more realistic to upload multiple documents to your document library.

1. From the main page of your team site, click the Shared Documents link from the Quick Launch navigation bar.

2. Select Upload ⇨ Upload Multiple Documents from the document library toolbar. The Upload Document page opens, as shown in Figure 3-4.

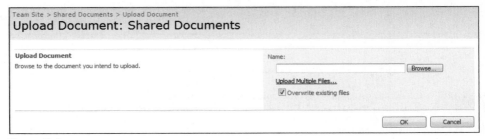

Figure 3-4

3. Select the folder that contains the resource files for this chapter from the left panel, then select the presentation files to upload from the right panel as shown in Figure 3-5. You can only upload items from a single folder at a time.

The default setting when you upload multiple files is to overwrite any files that already have the same name. You can change this by deselecting the Overwrite Existing Files check box. If you select the check box, the file remains selected. As a result, the sales presentation uploaded in the last Try It Out is overwritten by the copy you upload in this exercise.

4. Click the OK button. A message window displays asking you to confirm your wish to upload the documents.

5. Click the OK button to continue.

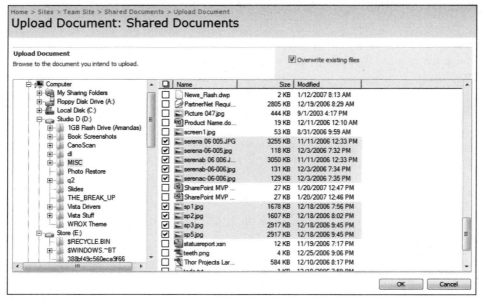

Figure 3-5

Try It Out   Edit a Document Library View in Datasheet Mode

One important thing to remember when uploading files in bulk is that you are not prompted to complete the metadata for each item. Incomplete metadata can negatively impact searches that users perform to locate your documents. If you have to meet a deadline and can't fill in metadata information during the upload, remember to return to the library afterward and do so. The most efficient way is to use the Edit in Datasheet command. This command, which is shown in the following steps, allows you to update document metadata in a manner similar to updating a spreadsheet in Excel.

For more about performing searches in SharePoint, see Chapter 14.

1. From the main page of your team site, click the Shared Documents link from the Quick Launch navigation bar.

2. Select Actions ➪ Edit in Datasheet, as shown in Figure 3-6.

3. Update columns as necessary as shown in Figure 3-7.

4. From the Actions toolbar menu, select Show in Standard View. You may receive a warning stating that you have pending changes or unresolved conflicts. Select Yes that you want to wait for the operation to complete.

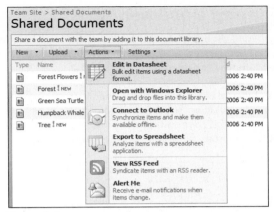

Figure 3-6

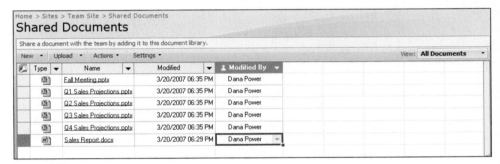

Figure 3-7

How It Works

In this example, you temporarily changed a standard document library view to a datasheet view. This updates to the metadata associated with all documents within your document library. Editing a datasheet view is very similar to completing information within a spreadsheet application and is therefore ideal for occasions where a team member must update in bulk. While you can create views that are always in datasheet mode, you can edit any standard list view in datasheet mode as shown here.

You now know how to create documents within your libraries as well as how to upload documents and update the metadata associated with them. The next section discusses how to update documents that are already in a library.

Updating and Sharing Documents

Your document's life cycle will probably require you to perform updates and edits over time. You can quickly open and edit any document inside its document library via the contextual menu of the item. You have two ways to edit an existing document:

❑ **Via the contextual menu:** Hover your cursor over an item in a library to expose a contextual menu and then select the down arrow. Select Edit in Microsoft Office Word from the list of menu options, as shown in Figure 3-8. You have several other options, such as Edit Properties, which edits the metadata, or View Properties, which displays additional information associated with the document.

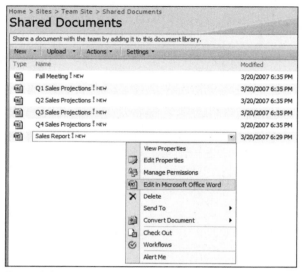

Figure 3-8

❑ **Select an item in a document library.** The associated application opens so you can begin editing.

Obviously, the collaborating often requires that people work on the same document, which can lead to version conflict. For example, if you work on a document, but leave for an extended period of time, another user can make changes to your document that conflict with your version or another user can upload an older version of the document that bears no resemblance to any other document in the department. When you resume your work, you definitely will notice changes, but not necessarily why or how the document changed.

To minimize frustration, instead of editing the document via the contextual menu or from the document library, you can select the Check In/Check Out options. *Checking out* a document locks it so that others can view the last published version, but cannot edit it, until you check the document back in. The Edit Document option also locks the document, but it doesn't save progressive versions of the document so that you can see what changed, why it changed, and who changed it.

The next three Try It Outs cover how to check out and check in a document, either from the SharePoint library, or from a Microsoft Office application, such as Word. The Check In/Check Out feature has the added benefit of allowing you to work offline as you check out. This means you can perform changes away from the office and these changes are placed in the library when you check the document back in. In the last Try It Out, you learn how to send your colleagues notification so that they're aware of the changes you've made to a document.

SharePoint's Check In/Check Out feature is controlled as part of library versioning. To configure and customize the settings for this feature, see Chapter 4.

Try It Out   **Check Out a Document**

Checking out a document greatly reduces the chance of version conflicts because only one person can make changes to the document at a time. The following example shows you how to check out an item from a document library.

1.   Hover your cursor over an item in a document library to expose the contextual menu.

2.   Select the down arrow that appears and then select Check Out, as shown in Figure 3-9. You receive a message informing you that you are about to check out a document, as shown in Figure 3-10. By default, SharePoint temporarily stores your document in your local drafts folder. For this example, the default setting will do.

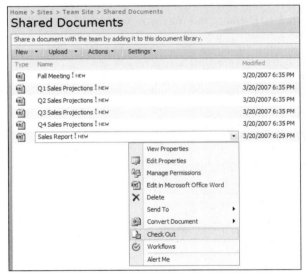

Figure 3-9

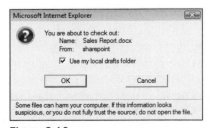

Figure 3-10

3. Click OK to check your document out. The icon to the left of the document name changes to a document with a green arrow next to it, as shown in Figure 3-11.

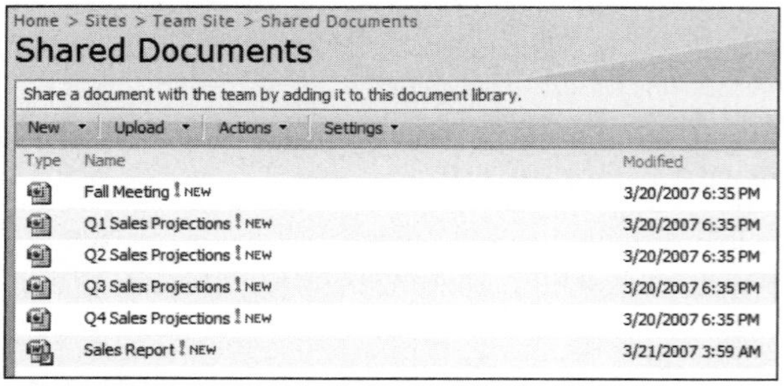

Home > Sites > Team Site > Shared Documents
Shared Documents

Share a document with the team by adding it to this document library.

New ▾ | Upload ▾ | Actions ▾ | Settings ▾

Type	Name	Modified
	Fall Meeting ! NEW	3/20/2007 6:35 PM
	Q1 Sales Projections ! NEW	3/20/2007 6:35 PM
	Q2 Sales Projections ! NEW	3/20/2007 6:35 PM
	Q3 Sales Projections ! NEW	3/20/2007 6:35 PM
	Q4 Sales Projections ! NEW	3/20/2007 6:35 PM
	Sales Report ! NEW	3/21/2007 3:59 AM

Figure 3-11

Try It Out   Check In a Document

After you make changes to your checked out document, you need to check it back in. This creates a new version, complete with your changes, and makes the document available for others to check out. The check in process is very similar to the check out process, but you have the additional option of checking in changes while keeping the document checked out. This means others can see changes you've made so far, but that you can continue working on the document. It's best practice to include comments when checking a document in so that others understand what you did. Comments also create a version history, which makes tracking down problems easier in the future. The following steps show this process:

1. Follow steps 1 and 2 in the "Check Out a Document" Try It Out, but select the Check In option. The Check in window appears as shown in Figure 3-12

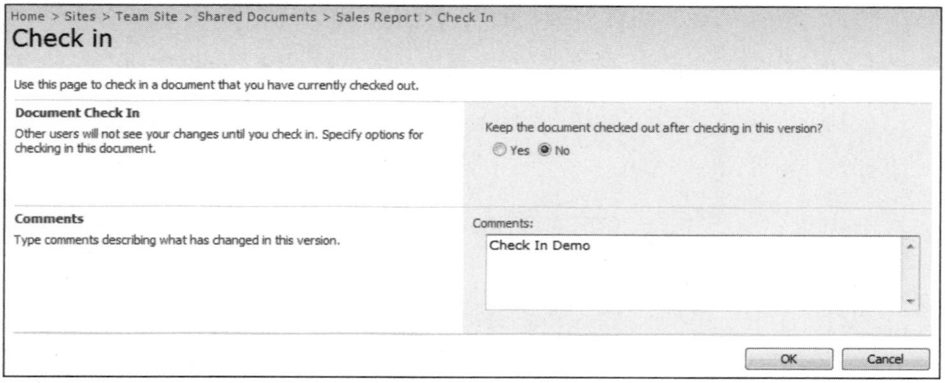

Home > Sites > Team Site > Shared Documents > Sales Report > Check In
Check in

Use this page to check in a document that you have currently checked out.

Document Check In
Other users will not see your changes until you check in. Specify options for checking in this document.

Keep the document checked out after checking in this version?
○ Yes ● No

Comments
Type comments describing what has changed in this version.

Comments:
Check In Demo

OK   Cancel

Figure 3-12

2. To continue working on the document but allow others see your changes, you can select Yes under Keep Document Checked Out After Checking in This Version option. This example assumes that you click No to unlock the document completely for editing by others.

3. Type a reason for your changes to the document in the comments box. For this example, type **Check in demo**.

4. Click the OK button, and the document is checked in.

Try It Out **Check In a Document from a Microsoft Office Application**

If you are editing a document with Microsoft Office application, instead of saving your changes, closing the document, going back to the browser and checking in your document, you can check the document back in straight from the application to cut out some steps. This functionality is only available in Microsoft Office 2007 for Excel and PowerPoint. All other applications require you to check in the document using the SharePoint interface via the browser.

The following steps show you how to check in a document using Word, but they are similar to when you would check in a document in Excel or PowerPoint. Before you perform these steps, you should open a document and check it out from your document library. Checking a document in using the Microsoft Office Word client application has the same effect as checking it in via the browser (shown in the last Try It Out).

1. From Word, select the Office Button on the top-left corner, as shown in Figure 3-13.

Figure 3-13

2. Hover your cursor over the Server button to expose a set of menu options.

3. Select Check In from the list.

4. In the Check In dialog box, add comments describing the changes you have made to your document, as shown in Figure 3-14.

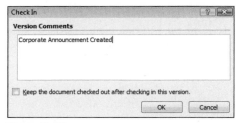

Figure 3-14

You can opt to keep your document checked out after checking in. For more information about this option, see the previous Try It Out. This example leaves the option unselected.

5. Click the OK button.

6. Close the document.

Work Offline with a Document

To this point, the Try It Outs in this section have dealt with checking a document in or out and working with it online, that is, connected to a network. As mentioned previously, you have the option of checking out a document and working offline by saving it to your local drafts folder, which is automatically created the first time you check out and save a document. SharePoint creates a physical copy that you can edit away from the office. When you check a document back in via the browser or through Word using the steps shown in the previous Try It Outs, the offline copy of the document synchronizes and uploads to the document library so that your changes become available to team members.

SharePoint 2007 has multiple methods for working on offline content. Chapter 2 discussed how to connect specific lists to Outlook to make items available offline.

1. Hover your cursor over a document in the library to expose the contextual menu.

2. Select the down arrow.

3. Select Check Out from list of options. A window appears saying that you're about to check out the document (see Figure 3-10).

4. Select the Use My Local Drafts Folder option.

5. Click the OK button.

Send an Email Link of a Document to Others

After uploading or updating a document, you commonly want to share your changes with other team members so that they may review, collaborate, or make their own changes. In the past, this involved opening your email, writing a detailed message to your coworkers informing them of your intention to share a document, attaching the document, and finally sending it. Unfortunately, attaching a document can lead to duplicate files because team members tend to save versions of the document from the email message to their desktop or local drive. This, of course, makes change synchronization and document management very difficult.

SharePoint 2007 bypasses this confusion by allowing you to send an email with a link that directs colleagues to your document on the library. This informs team members of your updates without removing the file from the document management system.

Follow the simple steps outlined below to send a link to your document via email:

1. Hover your cursor over a document in your library to expose the contextual menu.

2. Select the down arrow.

3. From the list of options (see Figure 3-1), select Send To and then select Email a Link. Outlook opens and a pre-populated email with a link to your document appears.

4. Fill in the email addresses to which you want to send the link.

5. Fill in the subject and a brief message.

6. Click the Send button.

Review Document Version History

Imagine working all night on a document and saving your changes to your team's collaborative location, only to have a team member overwrite your document with an older version of the document. For a collaboration team, multiple versions of a single document can translate into lost work and frustration. That's why most organizations mandate a document audit trail, which helps users understand when changes were made and why. SharePoint's Version History option allows you to view this trial as well as restore previous versions if you catch errors or omissions in the active version. If versions before a certain date are in doubt, you can restore the document to a point where you know the information is accurate and relevant. In addition, history can help users investigate when and why things first went wrong.

In the upcoming exercises, you learn how to view the version history related to a document and optionally restore a previous version of a document as the active version.

> *In Chapter 4, you will learn how you can manage the rules around versioning related to a document library.*

Try It Out   **View Document Versions**

SharePoint 2007 stores a document's version history each time a user changes or saves the document. Imagine that while you were away from the office someone made changes to your document that you either were not satisfied with or wanted clarification on. You can visit the version history of the document and review the various versions and associated comments to determine what changes were made. In addition, you may find it useful to review versions of a document to find out what information was published and available to users of the SharePoint site.

1. Hover your cursor over a document in the library to expose the contextual menu.

2. Select the down arrow.

3. Select Version History from the list of options, as shown in Figure 3-15.

Figure 3-15

4.   A list of versions associated with the document displays. Select a version from the list to pre-view it. The version of the document will open for you to review in the associated application.

Try It Out   **Restore a Previous Version of a Document**

Commonly when multiple team members work on a document, they need to revert back to a previous version of the document. This may be because of unwanted changes or just to perform a what-if analysis to see how changes impact a report. With SharePoint 2007, you can easily follow a document's entire audit trail and if need be, restore a previous version of the document by following these steps:

1.   Hover your cursor over a document in the library to expose the contextual menu.

2.   Select the down arrow.

3.   Select Version History from the list of options as shown previously in Figure 3-15. A list of available versions appears, as shown in Figure 3-16.

4.   Hover your cursor over the version you want to restore to expose the document's contextual menu.

Figure 3-16

5. Select the down arrow.

6. Select Restore. You are prompted with a message informing you that you are about to replace the current version of the document with the one you have selected.

7. Click the OK button.

How It Works

When you restore a previous version of a document, the document reverts back to reflect that state of the document and it becomes the current version of the document. The restoration of a document does not overwrite or delete previous versions. Instead, it creates a completely new version within the library. For example, if you view a listing of a document's versions, you may see that there are five versions of the document. If you were to restore version 2.0, then a new version would be created called 6.0. All previous versions would remain unaffected.

Understanding SharePoint Library Templates

So far this chapter has generically referred to libraries as document libraries. However, SharePoint actually has various library types, just as it has various list types. Library variations are generally defined by what you place in them. Once you create your library from the appropriate template, other users can access the library and add content to it. Chapter 4 shows how to create new lists and libraries..In this section, you learn about the features and functions of each so that you can select the proper library for your team. The SharePoint library templates are shown in the following list.

> Up to this point, the chapter examples have used the default document library. However, SharePoint includes other templates for different usage scenarios, such as a picture library that holds image files and the slide library for presentation slides. Although you can store images and presentations in any library, each library has features specific to its content. For example, the picture and slide libraries enable you to view slide shows.

❑ **Document library:** This library stores the majority of documents and files in a SharePoint site and is the most common type of document library created.

❑ **Form library:** You use this template to create libraries that store InfoPath form data and templates. You may use this library to store submitted forms such as purchase requests or status reports created using the Microsoft InfoPath client application or Forms Services.

For more on forms and InfoPath, see Chapter 10.

❑ **Wiki page library:** You use this kind of library for *wiki pages*, which are collaborative web pages that teams use to share information in a highly interactive and less structured environment. This is perfect for storing a Knowledge Base or an FAQ section.

❑ **Picture library:** This library is for sharing photos and images in a collaborative environment. This library uses columns and properties to define images, and has special thumbnail views of the stored files. It's ideal for storing team member photos or your company's logos.

❑ **Translation management document library:** For teams that are creating content for multiple languages, this library helps manage the translation process. This library includes a special workflow process that assigns content to translators.

You use this template with Variations, which controls the translation process. For more information, see Chapter 13.

❑ **Slide library**: You use this library to share PowerPoint presentation slides. Users can upload slides to the library so other users can browse for slides and use them in new presentations. This template works well for teams that are responsible for creating presentations and want a central gallery from which to select the latest slides and information.

❑ **Data connection library:** This library stores trusted data connection information that link SharePoint with documents created using InfoPath or Excel.

❑ **Report library:** This specialized template creates a library that stores spreadsheets and dashboards as part of Excel Services. You use this template to create a location for reporting that would allow business managers to publish spreadsheets to others that could be viewed via the browser and that would hide any protected information from users. This type of library is discussed in Chapter 11 along with Excel Services, because this template type is specific to that feature of SharePoint.

For more on data connections as they relate to InfoPath and Excel, see Chapters 10 and 11.

Document Libraries

Document libraries can store just about any kind of file and are at the center of SharePoint's file sharing and collaboration features. The anatomy of a document library is very similar to a list and includes the following elements:

❑ **File Item:** From Chapter 2, you know that the primary element of a list is an item. Likewise, the primary element of a document library is a file. Most organizations collaborate using Microsoft Office documents (Word, Excel, and PowerPoint) or other common file formats, such as PDF, HTML, or JPEG. Document libraries support just about any file type assuming that an administrator has not explicitly blocked it.

❑ **Columns:** The column types available for lists are also available for document libraries. Depending on what template you select, certain columns may already be created for you. Most libraries share a common set of columns; however, special templates, such as the picture library, contain additional columns such as keywords and image size. You can create additional columns at any time if you have the appropriate rights to the site.

You can find out how to add new columns to a library in Chapter 4.

❑ **Default Views:** Document libraries display their items using two default views.

❑ **All Documents view:** Shows all documents stored within the library in groups of 100 in the following columns:

  ❑ **Document Type:** Displays an icon representing the document's file type

  ❑ **Name:** The file name of the document

  ❑ **Modified:** The date and time the document was last modified

  ❑ **Modified By:** The name of the user that last modified the document linked directly to the user profile or MySite

❑ **The Explorer view:** Shown in Figure 3-17, this displays documents very much like Windows displays files, and is therefore ideal for users familiar with file shares and Windows folders. Users can right-click documents and folders to interact with the system.

❑ **User Defined views:** A user can also create views at any time with the appropriate rights to the site.

For more about creating new views, see Chapter 4.

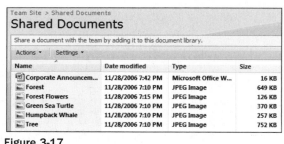

Figure 3-17

Try It Out   Open a Document Library in Windows Explorer

In addition to the Explorer view, you can open a document library in Windows Explorer via the Action menu. This allows you to interact with your library with the usual Windows behaviors, including dragging and dropping content. In the following example, you open a Shared Documents library in Windows Explorer and create a new folder within it called "Product Documentation." Instead of creating a new folder and uploading the documents via the SharePoint browser interface, you open the document library in Windows Explorer and create a new folder. You then copy the files using Copy and Paste commands.

1. From the main page of your team site, click the Shared Documents link from the Quick Launch navigation bar.

2. Select Actions ➪ Open with Windows Explorer from the document library toolbar, as was seen in Figure 3-6.

3. Windows Explorer opens listing the entire contents of your Shared Documents library, as shown in Figure 3-18. Right-click the window and create a new folder called **Product Documentation**.

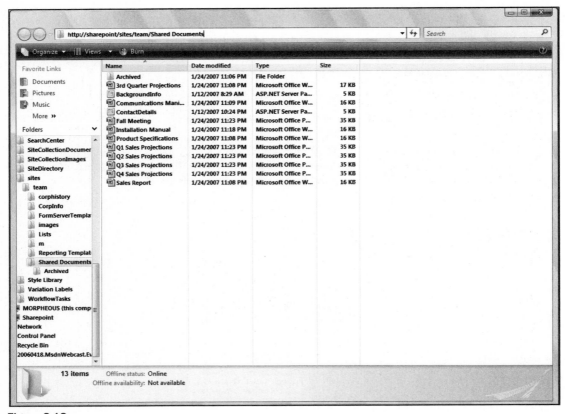

Figure 3-18

4. Copy the contents of the Product Documents folder from the materials for this chapter (go to www.wrox.com). You can copy documents by selecting them, right-clicking, and selecting Copy, or by pressing Ctrl+C.

5. Double-click your newly created folder called "Product Documentation" from within the Windows Explorer view of your document library.

6. Paste the copied documents from Step 4 into the folder by either right-clicking the window and selecting Paste or by pressing Ctrl+V.

When you uploaded multiple documents earlier in the chapter, you had to go back and update the metadata afterward. The same recommendation applies in this situation as well. It is always important to keep the metadata associated with each file up-to-date so that users can easily find the documents either through the available views or search interface.

Form Libraries

Form libraries are special types of libraries that store InfoPath forms. *Microsoft InfoPath* is an application that allows you to collect and share data via highly customizable electronic forms. You can use this application to create form templates that reflect their data collection needs without requiring code or special development skills. The application makes it very easy for business users to craft an electronic form that suits their needs by dragging and dropping form elements onto a page. Users can complete InfoPath forms using either the InfoPath application or via the browser using InfoPath Forms Services, a component of SharePoint 2007 Enterprise Edition. This allows for more advanced reporting on the data contained in multiple forms.

> *For more on InfoPath and Form Services, see Chapter 10.*

Depending on the needs of your organization, you may choose to create either a simple or complex InfoPath form. You can see an example of an InfoPath form in Figure 3-19.

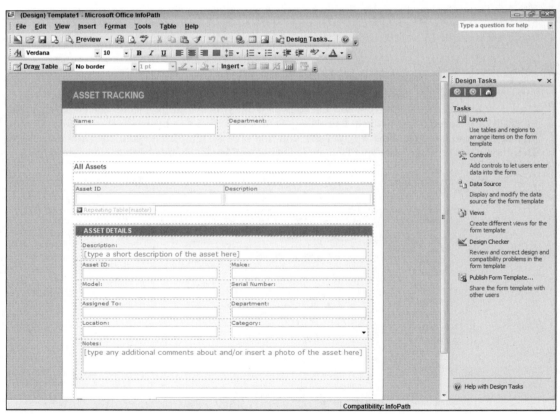

Figure 3-19

You can promote data stored in InfoPath forms to the library so you display the data in views. This gives you more advanced reporting options on the data contained in multiple forms. You might find it advantageous, for example, to create an InfoPath form to collect data from your portal users instead of using standard list functionality because with InfoPath, you can do the following:

❑ Connect to external data sources such as databases, SharePoint lists, or web services to either retrieve or submit data.

❑ Customize the interface in ways not possible using standard lists. This includes performing conditional formatting and filtering value lists based on a user's selection.

❑ Use code to extend forms to provide additional functionality and enhancements related to more complex data calculations or routing.

Traditionally, in order to design or complete an InfoPath form, a user was required to have the InfoPath application installed on her computer. With SharePoint 2007, you can create form templates that users can complete directly using InfoPath Forms Services. In fact, the SharePoint interface takes advantage of InfoPath Forms Services to render forms that users complete to specify workflow rules and approval routing. This is not something that is evident to users of the system but does demonstrate how web-based electronic forms can be embedded within applications to provide better integration within business processes.

Try It Out   Create a Form Library Based on a Form Template

Although Chapter 10 is dedicated to InfoPath and InfoPath Forms Services and it is there that you can learn how to utilize form libraries, you can start with this simple example. Here, you create a simple InfoPath form based on a Microsoft template (a Status Report) and publish it to create a form library. To publish the template to your SharePoint site, you first save the template to your computer or network. This allows you to make edits later from one central location and then publish to sites as required.

1.   Open Microsoft Office InfoPath 2007. The Getting Started window appears, as shown in Figure 3-20.

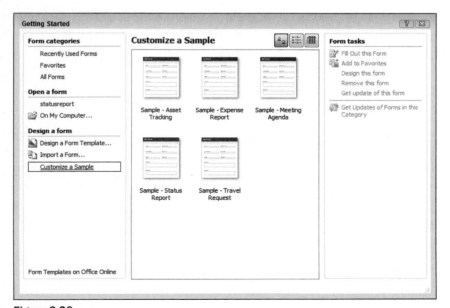

Figure 3-20

2. Click the Customize a Sample link from the Design a Form menu.

3. Select the Sample – Status Report template from the list of sample templates and click the Design This Form link. Your form template opens in Design mode. Typically you perform additional customizations, such as add your company logo and add any extra fields or data sources that you require.

4. Select File ⇨ Publish. A message window appears asking you to save the form. Click the OK button.

5. Save the form to your computer. You can edit this form later, and if necessary, publish it to other locations. When you save the form template locally, the publishing wizard opens.

6. Select the option to publish to a SharePoint Server with or without InfoPath Forms Services, as shown in Figure 3-21, and click Next.

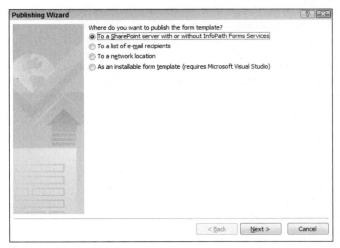

Figure 3-21

7. Enter the URL of your SharePoint Team Site and click Next.

8. Make sure that the options that allow users to fill out the form via the browser are selected. Click Next.

9. Make sure that the options to create a new document library are selected, and click Next.

10. Enter a name and description for your library. In this example, for the name enter **Team Status Reports** and for the description, enter:

> **This is the shared location for all team status reports that will be completed on a weekly basis by each team member.**

11. Click Next.

12. Select which form fields you want to promote as columns to the form library. Click Add.

13. Select emailAddress from the list of fields and click OK.

14. Click Next.

15. Click Publish. A message displays confirming that the form template has been successfully published.

16. Select the check box to open the document library, and click the Close button.

How It Works

SharePoint Server offers many choices when you publish a form template, including publishing directly to a document library, creating a content type, or creating a form to be uploaded by a server administrator. Chapter 11 discusses the last two options. This example creates a document library that will host your form template. The wizard helps you complete document library details including name and description, the columns you want to create as well as the location of the site to which you are publishing. Once you publish the form template in a newly created library called "Team Status Reports," users can go to the library, click the New button, and complete a status report based on your template. This status report can be saved back to the library. If the form template is configured to promote certain fields to library columns upon saving, the information entered into the InfoPath form for those fields are visible when looking at a view of the library.

Familiarize yourself with all the built-in samples as well as the ones on Microsoft Office Online. They provide a great starting point when you want to customize a form for your team.

Wiki Page Libraries

With wikis, a very popular collaborative tool for group sharing and editing content, you can add, edit, or remove web page content in an open and informal manner without following a restrictive editing or approval process. Users can edit wikis using SharePoint's built-in content editor without knowing a special language. Because of the informality and lack of restriction, wiki pages are more inviting for team members to add their experiences and goals.

What's a Wiki?

A *wiki article* or website, is a site where users can freely expand or change the published content, often without registration requirements. Wiki, named for a Hawaiian term meaning "fast," is a popular method for sharing information in a quick and easy-to-use format.

A good example of a wiki is the Wikipedia project (see www.wikipedia.org), which formerly began in January 2001. Wikipedia delivers a free content encyclopedia to which anyone can contribute. The website has grown to become one of the largest content libraries in existence, serving up more than 1.5 million articles, if you're just counting the English ones.

SharePoint 2007 has an option for creating either an entire site to act as a wiki or just a wiki document library within a site:

❑ **A wiki site:** Useful for a technical support team's Knowledge Base or a training department's tips and tricks documentation.

❑ **A wiki document library**: Provides a collaboration tool for planning and sharing ideas around specific operational events. This is illustrated in the next Try It Out.

The next two Try It Outs show how to create a wiki document library as well as how to create a new wiki page.

Try It Out   Create a Wiki Document Library

In this example, you create a wiki document library in your site to brainstorm for ideas for an upcoming project. The wiki page library has special features that allow you to share and publish wiki content pages within a single location. Team members can create these pages around a specific topic or set of topics.

1. From the main page of your team site, select Actions ➪ Create. The Create window appears as shown in Figure 3-22.

2. Select Wiki Page Library from the list of Library types, as shown in Figure 3-22.

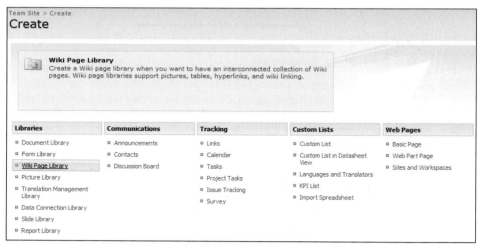

Figure 3-22

3. Enter a name and description for the library. For this example, enter **Project Wiki** for the name and the following for the description:

> **This wiki will be used to track information related to initial planning around scope, milestones, and timelines related to upcoming projects.**

4. Select the Yes option to display the library on the site's Quick Launch navigation bar.

5. Click the Create button.

Figure 3-23 shows an example of a wiki page in the newly created wiki page library. Users can edit the page directly by clicking the Edit button at the top right of the page.

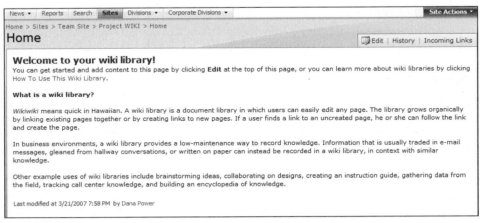

Figure 3-23

Try It Out   Create a New Wiki Page

In addition to editing existing content, users can create new pages. The following example demonstrates how easily you can create new wiki pages within a wiki library so that team members can share information about what they have learned regarding a common topic, such as a new technology (SharePoint). In addition, members can leave notes on topics they would like to learn more about as an invitation for others to provide content.

1. From the main page of your team site, select Project Wiki from the Quick Launch navigation bar.

2. Select Recent Changes ➪ View All Pages.

3. Click the New button.

4. Enter a page name. For this example, enter **SharePoint Learning Project**.

5. For the wiki page content, enter the following to get people started:

> **This is a wiki page to describe new things you have learned related to using SharePoint as well as highlighting new things that you would like to learn.**

6. Click the Create button.

Users of your site can access the page from the Recent Changes menu as shown in Figure 3-24.

Figure 3-24

Picture Libraries

Although document libraries can store just about any file type, in some cases it's better to have a library that caters to a specific file format. Such is the case with the picture library template, which more efficiently displays pictures and images because it includes a thumbnail preview feature. This is an invaluable feature for locating the correct image in a large collection of images.

This next series of Try It Outs demonstrates the features that make the picture library unique. In the first Try It Out, you create a picture library using the picture library template. In the second Try It Out, you upload pictures into the newly created library to simulate a person sharing images with his or her team. In doing so, you see firsthand the unique commands it offers in its menu. These commands are listed in the following table.

Menu Item	Description
Edit	Edits the selected images in a compatible editing tool
Delete	Deletes the selected images from the picture library
Download	Downloads all selected images to the user's computer
Send To	Inserts pictures into an email or document
View Slide Show	Opens a new window to display a slide show of images within library

In the third Try It Out, you act as someone taking images from the library. You download files, and see the picture library's unique options. When you download, you can change the size of your image. You can also change its format to one of the following:

❑ Joint Photographic Experts Group (JPEG)

❑ Tagged Image Format (TIF)

❑ Windows Bitmap (BMP)

❑ Graphics Interchange Format (GIF)

❑ Portable Network Graphics (PNG)

You can also apply one of three sub views to a primary view. These sub views are as follows:

- ❑ **Details:** This updates metadata associated with a file stored in a picture library.
- ❑ **Thumbnails:** This previews images in a thumbnail type view.
- ❑ **Filmstrip:** This previews a larger version of the image within the browser window.

Try It Out   **Create a Picture Library**

In this Try It Out, you create a picture library. This template is unique because it supports image editing, downloading, and previewing. To create a picture library, follow these steps:

1. From the main page of your team site, select Site Actions ➪ Create. The Create window appears (see Figure 3-22).

2. Select Picture Library from the list of Library types. The New window appears, as shown in Figure 3-25.

3. Enter a name for your library. For this example, enter **Company Photos**.

4. Enter the following information for a description:

> **All company images to be utilized for advertising campaigns, brochures, and website communications will be stored in this library.**

5. Select the Yes option to have the library displayed on the Quick Launch, as shown in Figure 3-25.

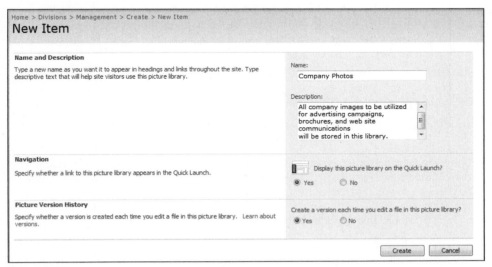

Figure 3-25

6. Select the Yes option to create a version of the file every time you edit it in this library.

7. Click the Create button.

Try It Out   Upload Multiple Images to a Picture Library

When you uploaded in the Try It Out "Upload Multiple Documents to a Document Library," you used the browser interface. The interface in this Try It Out has unique functionality for managing images. You can either upload web-optimized versions of the images or upload the files in their original format. Once the files are uploaded, you can return to your library to view the images.

To identify the differences between the picture template and the standard document library, the following steps have you upload some images into the newly created library:

1. From the main page of your team site, click the link for your Company Photos library from the Quick Launch navigation bar.

2. Select Upload ➪ Select Upload Multiple Pictures. The Microsoft Office Picture Manager opens, as shown in Figure 3-26.

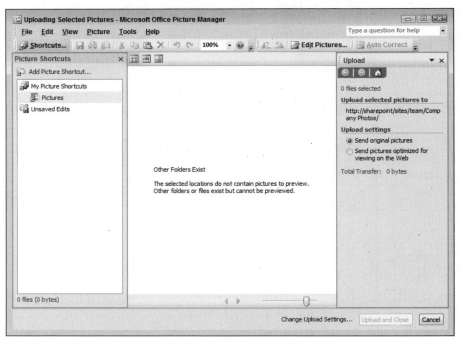

Figure 3-26

3. Click the Add Picture Shortcut link and browse to the Corporate Images folder you downloaded as part of this chapter's resource materials.

4. Select all the images from the folder. You can select multiple items by holding the Ctrl button while you select items.

5. Click the Upload and Close button, as shown in Figure 3-27.

Figure 3-27

6. The Microsoft Office Picture Manager application will close. Select the Go Back to "Corporate Photos" link to return to your picture library.

How It Works

Although this library may look like all other document libraries you've created so far in this chapter, take a close look at the Actions menu shown in Figure 3-28. This menu contains several new items that cater to images.

Figure 3-28

Try It Out   **Download Files from a Picture Library**

To demonstrate how the various picture library menu items work, this example shows you how to select multiple images from a picture library for downloading. In the previous Try It Out, files in the SharePoint library were in the JPEG format. However, when you select the advanced download options in this Try It Out, you can change the format of the downloaded images. You can keep the file in its original format or select another format. The various formats were discussed in the introduction to this section. In addition, you can select a different size for the files and send them to a document instead of downloading them directly as files to your computer. Finally, you can apply sub views to the primary view of your download.

1. From the main page of your team site, click the View All Site Content link from the Quick Launch navigation bar.

2. Select the Corporate Images library from the Pictures group.

3. Select the first two images in the list.

4. Select Actions ➪ Download, as shown in Figure 3-28 in the last Try It Out.

5. Click the Set Advanced Download Options link.

6. Select Graphics Interchange Format (*.gif) from the file format drop-down menu.

7. For the picture size, select custom width and height and specify 640×480.

8. Click the Download button. The Download Pictures window, shown in Figure 3-29, appears prompting you for a location for the images.

9. Select a folder on your computer to store the files in.

10. Select the check box to rename the pictures in the new location and enter a name for the picture. For this example, enter **Corporate Images** for the name.

Figure 3-29

11. Click the Save button.

12. To apply sub views to a primary view, hover your cursor over the All Pictures view from the View Selection box and click Details to update the metadata associated with the image; click Thumbnails to see a preview of the image, as shown in Figure 3-30; or click Filmstrip to preview a larger version of the image in the browser window, as shown in Figure 3-31.

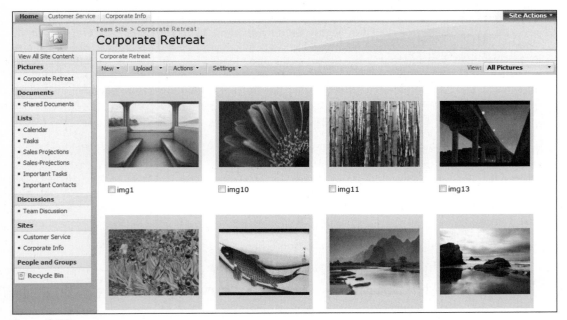

Figure 3-30

Figure 3-31

Translation Management Libraries

Many organizations span multiple geographic regions or must communicate with colleagues using multiple languages. SharePoint addresses this need with its *translation management library*. Although the system does not translate content directly, it lets you customize a workflow to aid in the content translation process.

When you create a translation management library, you have an option for associating the translation management workflow with the document library. This requires you to fill in the workflow process and create a list of languages and translators. When you create a new entry in the translators list (shown in Figure 3-32), you enter the original language, the language into which you want content to be translated, and the user who will act as translator. The translators become the individuals responsible for creating the content in the appropriate languages.

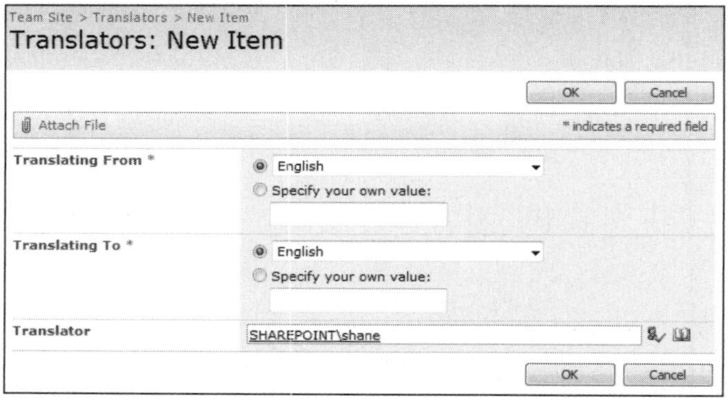

Figure 3-32

Chapter 13 covers web content management and support for multiple languages, and goes into transla-
tion management document library in greater detail.

Data Connection Libraries

Microsoft Office applications, such as Excel and InfoPath, have great built-in support for data connec-
tivity to external sources such as databases, web services, and even SharePoint sites. Traditionally, this
meant that you managed data connections on an individual usage basis. Therefore, every time you
connected to the data source, you needed to define the connection within the file or settings. This often
made it very cumbersome to embed external data into files and subsequently make changes to the
data source or file. For example, it might seem logical to use a SharePoint customer list in your
InfoPath forms any time that you wanted to display a listing of customer names. But to do this, you
would need to create a data connection within your form template each time you wanted to include
customer information.

If you later decided to move your SharePoint list to another location or add new columns, in order to
have the changes updated within your InfoPath form, you would have to go back into each form template and update the settings.

The Microsoft Office 2007 release solves the cumbersome connection dilemma of past versions by allowing you to create data connection files. These Universal Data Connection (UDC) files contain all the connection settings applicable to the data source and usage scenario. Therefore, instead of specifying the
connection settings in each of your form templates, you save the connection settings as a file and have
your form templates point directly to this file, as shown in Figure 3-33. When you do this, making
changes to a single file updates multiple templates.

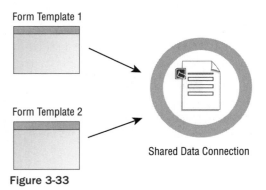

Figure 3-33

In Chapters 10 and 11, you work in greater detail with data connections. These chapters have specific
examples of how beneficial data connection files can be and how you can store them centrally in a data
connection library.

Slide Libraries

Because PowerPoint presentations are a common way for members of an organization to communicate, companies generally produce, deliver, and store presentations in large quantities. Unfortunately, the sheer quantity can cause the following issues:

❑ **Duplicated work:** Because individuals are seldom aware of a fellow colleague's work, there is very little reuse of information.

❑ **Outdated material:** Duplicated material across many locations means that an individual is more likely to grab an outdated presentation or present the wrong version of a presentation. This can lead to miscommunication of objectives or performance.

❑ **Inconsistent presentation:** Depending on who creates a presentation and what their interpretation of the content is, an organization may encounter company-wide inconsistencies in how data is presented to customers, partners, and other important stakeholders.

For these reasons, many organizations try to standardize how information is presented. SharePoint 2007 offers a unique method for consolidating presentation information that encourages users to share slide content.

The slide library template in SharePoint allows authors to upload slides to a library where other team members can view them. The following Try It Outs show you how to address these issues and by doing so help reduce duplicate efforts while protecting the quality and integrity of your organization's presentations. First, you learn how to upload a presentation to a slide library. You then create a new presentation in the library, and then update a presentation based on corrections to a source slide.

Try It Out   **Upload a Presentation to a Slide Library**

In the following example, you upload a presentation to a slide library so that it can be converted to individual slides that other team members can use.

1. From the main page of your team site, select Site Actions ➪ Create.

2. Select Slide Library from the list of library types.

3. For the name of your slide library, enter **Team Presentations** and select to have the library display on the Quick Launch navigation bar.

4. Select the options that enable versioning on the slide library.

5. Click the Create button.

6. Select Publish Slides from the Upload menu of the library toolbar, as shown in Figure 3-34. Microsoft Office PowerPoint 2007 opens and requires you to locate the presentation from which you want to upload slides to the slide library.

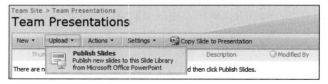

Figure 3-34

7. Locate the presentation named "2007-2008 Financial Performance Report" from the downloaded resources for this chapter (these are located on www.wrox.com) and select the Open button. A publishing window, shown in Figure 3-35, lists all the slides available for upload from the selected presentation.

8. Click the Select All button, as shown in Figure 3-35, and click the Publish button.

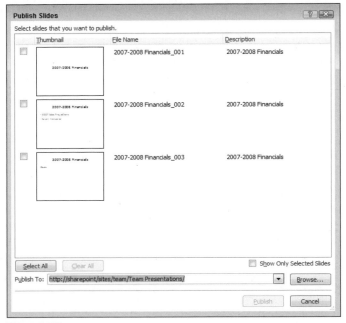

Figure3-35

How It Works

This process is noticeably different than uploading a standard document to a document library because slide libraries can accept individual slides rather than a complete presentation. Although this exercise had you upload all the slides in a presentation, the interface that appeared in step 8 during the upload process allows you to select individual slides. Once you click the Publish button in step 8, a status bar indicates where you are in the upload process. Depending on how many slides you've selected, this process may take a few minutes. While each slide of the presentation contains a metadata field from the original presentation, you can treat them as individual files.

Try It Out   **Create a New Presentation Using a Slide Library**

You can create a new presentation using slides from multiple presentations. This example shows how to create a new presentation based on the slides available in a slide library. In addition to creating a new presentation, you can add slides to an existing presentation. This is ideal for a situation where you are creating a new presentation and you want to add a slide to represent content that has been used previously in a presentation or perhaps want to present content from a standardized slide.

1. From the main page of your team site, click the Team Presentations link from the Quick Launch navigation bar.

2. Select the first, second, and third slides from the library's All Slides view.

3. Click the Copy Slide to Presentation toolbar button.

4. Select Copy to a New Presentation.

5. Select the Tell Me When This Slide Changes option, as shown in Figure 3-36.

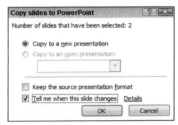

Figure 3-36

6. Click the OK button.

How It Works

SharePoint takes the individual slides that you select and turns them into a new presentation after you click OK in step 6. In step 5, you selected the Tell Me When This Slide Changes option, which means that you are notified whenever someone updates the source slides. Keeping slides connected to the library ensures that presentations always contain the most relevant and updated information. However, synchronization is not automatic. This is actually good because you never want to change the content of an important document without first reviewing the changes or considering the impact. Also, for archiving reasons, you may want to view a presentation as it was presented, and you have no need for updated data once a presentation is made. For example, if you plan to give a presentation discussing a team's performance over a period of time, you may want to know when source slides are updated in the library, but once you deliver the presentation, there is no need to change content.

Try It Out   Update a Presentation Based on Source Slide Updates

This Try It Out assumes that when you created a presentation with slides from the slide library that you selected the Tell Me When This Slide Changes option. As mentioned in the last Try It Out, if someone makes changes to the slides in the library, SharePoint notifies you of the change when you open the presentation. The following steps show you how to update the slide. First, you simulate a slide change, by changing a library slide that you selected for your presentation in the last Try It Out. You then open the presentation and update the slide in your presentation.

1. From the main page of your team site, click the Team Presentations link from the Quick Launch navigation bar.

2. Hover your cursor over the first slide in the library and select the Edit in Microsoft Office PowerPoint menu item.

3. Make a change to the slide by changing the title value to **Updated Title**.

4. Click the Save button.

5. Click the Close Application button.

6. Open the presentation you created in the previous Try It Out called "Create a New Presentation Using a Slide Library." A notification window appears advising you that the presentation contains slides that are connected to a slide library.

7. Click the Check button to check for slide changes. Because in step 3 you made a change to a slide in the presentation from the previous example, you receive a notification that one slide has been updated, as shown in Figure 3-37. You have a choice of either replacing the slide completely (Replace) or appending the changes made to the slide to the affected slide (Replace All).

8. Select the Replace button.

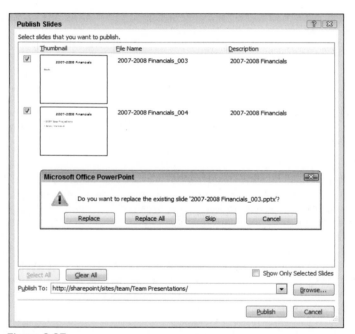

Figure 3-37

9. Click the Yes button.

Summary

This chapter discussed document collaboration in a team environment and then detailed the benefits and pitfalls of managing a single document with multiple editors. Things to remember about this chapter are as follows:

❑ SharePoint's library feature enables you to create, store, and manage your documents from a central location.

❑ Document libraries let you track a variety of different types of information. It is the most common type of SharePoint library.

❑ SharePoint also offers you libraries that are for a specific type of file or information and has templates to create these libraries, including InfoPath form data, images and pictures, Excel spreadsheets for browser-based reporting and dashboards, data connection files, and presentation slides.

Throughout this chapter, you looked at the ways that a user can interact with document libraries and the content within them. In Chapter 4, you take a deeper look at customizing libraries along with lists to suit more specific needs your organization might have.

Exercises

1. Your project manager informs you that the version of the document you submitted for approval was not correct and that the version that was sent earlier in the week is more appropriate. How do you remedy the situation?

2. Your manager assigns your team a series of presentations for an upcoming conference. How can your team most efficiently collaborate on various slides?

3. You've been given the task of archiving an old document. Currently, these documents are stored in a common file share. What is the best method of mass-copying these documents to a document library?

4. You need to change the metadata information for multiple documents. What is the fastest way to change the metadata of a particular column for multiple documents?

Managing and Customizing Lists and Libraries

The previous two chapters discussed how to use lists and libraries in their most basic format, and SharePoint has some great templates you can use. However, your information and sharing needs may require something different, in which case, you can customize specific components so that they better address those needs. When you customize SharePoint elements to more closely reflect business practices and processes, users can focus on their jobs instead of working harder or around an ill-fitting tool. This chapter shows you how to customize both lists and libraries. Many of the examples use the term *list* to describe both lists and libraries because anything that you can do to a list, you can also apply to a document library.

This chapter reviews the following:

❑   Specific reasons for customizing a SharePoint list or library

❑   Best practices for creating business elements

❑   Examples of working with list-centric columns and site columns

❑   The various types of views available in SharePoint and best practices related to creating them

❑   Working with list and document templates

After reading this chapter, you should feel comfortable taking a specific list or library template and customizing it to suit your specific needs. You should also understand the steps and value associated with adding your custom list to the central list of templates so that teams and users can benefit from your customization efforts.

Creating an Environment that Reflects Your Business

Information is not very useful if it is disorganized and hard to find. Traditionally, electronic documents are stored in a file system consisting of folders and subfolders, often many levels deep. In computer lingo, this is often called a *tree structure*. You create the document tree according to your needs or whims, and then you share it with your associates. However, they may not understand your organizational approach, and so may have difficulty finding documents in your folders. For example, you may have a folder for each city in your territory, and within each city folder, folders for your customers in that city. In each customer folder, you store project specifications, statements of work, proposals, project status reports, and other documents related to that customer. But what if an associate simply wants a list of the current project status reports for all of your customers? This is pretty hard to get because status reports are scattered throughout your document tree.

This example shows the major limitation of using the file system to share documents: Because you have only one way to organize and categorize information, you must develop a system in advance that is useful for everyone, and which usually results in a compromise that no one wants. And once you choose a folder structure, it may become both difficult to change and difficult to teach to others.

With SharePoint, you can associate a great deal of information with documents by using standard and custom list columns. For example, you can customize a list to attach the information shown in the following table to each document:

Column Name	Column Type	Values
Document Status	Choice	Not Started In Progress In Review Final Draft
Client	Lookup	Lookup to title column from Clients list
Project	Lookup	Lookup to title column from Projects list
Project Type	Lookup	Lookup to title column from a Project Categories list
Due Date	Date and time	
Assigned to	People or group	
Owner	People or group	

With file sharing, it's difficult to store this information and have it easily associated with a specific document. However, with SharePoint, you simply add columns to the document list. By capturing the appropriate information in the list, your associates can search and view the document library in the ways they prefer. For example, one colleague might search for projects by client, while another might search by author.

Once you recognize trends in how your team searches for documents, you can create custom views to match the most popular search criteria. For example, if users frequently search for documents assigned to them for review, you can create a view that displays a list of documents that have been assigned to the current user, and you can even sort the list in the order in which they are due. With custom list fields and views, SharePoint takes you out of the restricted world of file sharing and into a multidimensional world where each of your associates can see your documents in the most appropriate way.

Best Practices for Building a Dynamic System for Managing Content

In this section, you learn the best practices to ensure that your SharePoint site offers the maximum value to your organization based on the customizations that you implement. This is an important consideration because the right customizations can make your site user-friendly and efficient, while the wrong ones can make data entry burdensome and can cause user confusion.

Ensure that Your Changes Add Value

When you design an information system for your team to use for sharing and managing content, remember that your changes should add value; changes should make the system easier to use and the information simple and intuitive to find.

You can identify what adds value by familiarizing yourself with the information goals of team members and site users:

❑ Hold meetings or send questionnaires to gather information on users' frustration points.

❑ From these discussions, create a list of problems that you need to address.

❑ Rank and prioritize the list based on the number of people who are affected and the productivity impact they experience because of the issues.

❑ Look at how SharePoint lists and libraries can improve the situation. For example, if people have a difficult time finding documents created during a specific time frame, you can create views that filter and sort documents based on when they were completed.

Follow Similar Processes and Practices

When you create additional columns and views to your lists, follow similar rules in each situation. The more consistency you create within the environment, the more unified and intuitive the experience will be for the users:

❑ A column that describes the status of a list item or document should offer the user consistent choices. If you use a certain set of status values for one list or library, use the same for all other lists and libraries. Do not use values such as "Not Started," "In Progress," and "In Review" in one location and then use completely different values to represent the same type of information elsewhere.

❑ If you start creating custom views, offer some level of standardization, such as consistent ordering and sorting of columns based on the type of information you're presenting.

Provide Guides and Descriptions

Have you ever been asked to complete a task without receiving a clear explanation of what was required of you? If so, then you probably understand how frustrating completing forms and column values in SharePoint can be for your users if you do not offer good descriptions and guidelines for defining specific items. If users are unsure about what information you are asking for, they are highly likely to provide less than optimal information. Giving users clear direction will result in them entering the information you want into the system.

Working with Columns

It's time to look deeper into what columns are and how you can effectively use them to define and organize information within your SharePoint sites. By carefully planning the various components of your site, you can build an environment that a user will successfully adopt. This section first discusses what a column is and then shows you how to create a column, which is also called a *list-centric column*, or a column that is attached to a single list. Like the lists and libraries discussed in the first three chapters of this book, columns have different types, and you'll examine the various column types that you have available to you. Next, you learn what a site column is and then examine when to use a list-centric column versus when to use a site column.

What Is a Column?

A *column* is an element of information that describes an item on a SharePoint site. In some cases, the item may be an event, a company, or a task; in other cases, it may be a document, a web page, or a business form. In SharePoint, any content stored in a list or library is considered an *item*. No matter what the actual item is, columns provide a great way to further define and organize information beyond what is available via titles or folders.

Defining information effectively is a key reason you use SharePoint. Therefore, you may need to add new columns to define the various list and library items. For example, you can add a column to track document status to a document library so users can easily identify a document's current state strictly by looking at its properties rather than making an assumption or asking the author directly. This is called a list-centric column, and you will learn to create one in the next Try It Out.

You may hear people describe columns as *metadata* or *properties of an item*. As described in Chapter 2, *metadata* is essentially information about information. In the case of a document, metadata is information that describes the document such as its status, owner, or due date. A single document might have multiple metadata values because quite often there are many things to describe about a document. When you design or change an information environment, you should understand what content is stored within the site and what people will need to know about it.

Try It Out   **Create a Column**

In this example, you create a column for a technical documentation library so business users can track the status of technology-related documents, such as user manuals and training presentations. Therefore, you need to create a team site and a document library called "Documentation" inside it. Because you do not want users to enter just any value for status, you provide a list of common choices. This example assumes you require a choice column that allows the selection of a document's status, such as Alpha, Beta, or Final Release, in a document library.

1.   Select Settings on your Lists toolbar.

2.   Select Create Column from the drop-down menu, as shown in Figure 4-1. The Create Column window appears as shown in Figure 4-2.

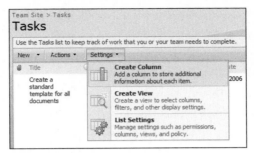

Figure 4-1

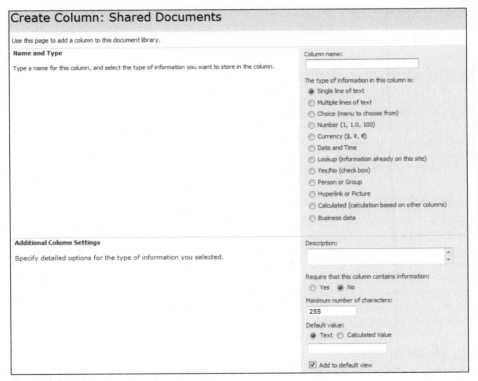

Figure 4-2

3. In the Column Name field, type **Document Status**.

4. For the column type, select the Choice (Menu to Choose from) option.

5. In the Description field, type **This column contains the document status**.

6. For the Require That This Column Contains Information option, select Yes. This ensures that all documents are flagged with a status upon saving.

7. In the Choices field, type on separate lines **Alpha**, **Beta**, and **Final Release**.

8.   In the Display Choices Using field, select Drop-Down Menu.

9.   Ensure that the Allow Fill in Choices option is set to the default of No because you do not want the user to create his own status labels.

10.   Remove the text from the Default Value field.

11.   You can leave Add to Default View selected.

12.   Click the OK button to save your changes.

How It Works

In steps 6 through 9, you create a choice column. A *choice column*, one of several column types, gives users a list of values from which to select in an intuitive manner, such as a set of radio buttons or a drop-down menu. The remaining column types are discussed in the next section.

Exploring Column Types

Chapter 2 discussed the different types of data that you can store in a column at a higher level. This section looks even deeper at the types of columns you can have in SharePoint, and discusses some of the various customization options that exist with them. In the "Create a Column" Try It Out you just completed, you selected a Choice column type to collect information from a drop-down menu, but you have other options at your disposal. At the end of this section, the "Change the Order of Columns on a List" Try It Out shows you how to reorder the columns of a list to make them more user-friendly.

Single Line of Text

Virtually every list starts with the *Single Line of Text* column type, possibly the most commonly used within SharePoint lists, as its primary or title column. When creating a Single Line of Text column, you have very few options for customization, as you can see from Figure 4-2 earlier in the chapter. However, you can select whether the column is required or optional. You can also limit the number of characters that a user can enter to prevent users from entering unnecessary data in a column. For example, this type of column limits users to entering ten digits for a phone number or five digits for a zip code. The final customization option is to specify a default value, which users can enter manually or which you can allow SharePoint to calculate.

Multiple Lines of Text

A *Multiple Lines of Text* column type has a variety of configuration options, shown in Figure 4-3. As with other columns, you can specify whether the column is required and enter a description that tells users what information to complete.

Because this column allows a variable amount of text, you can specify how many lines the field should display when users complete the information. You should give users plenty of space for situations where you expect them to enter a great deal of data; the size gives users a visual cue of how much information you want them to enter. For example, if the column is for a mailing address, three or four lines should be acceptable. However, if the column is for background information on a customer, you may want to provide at least 25.

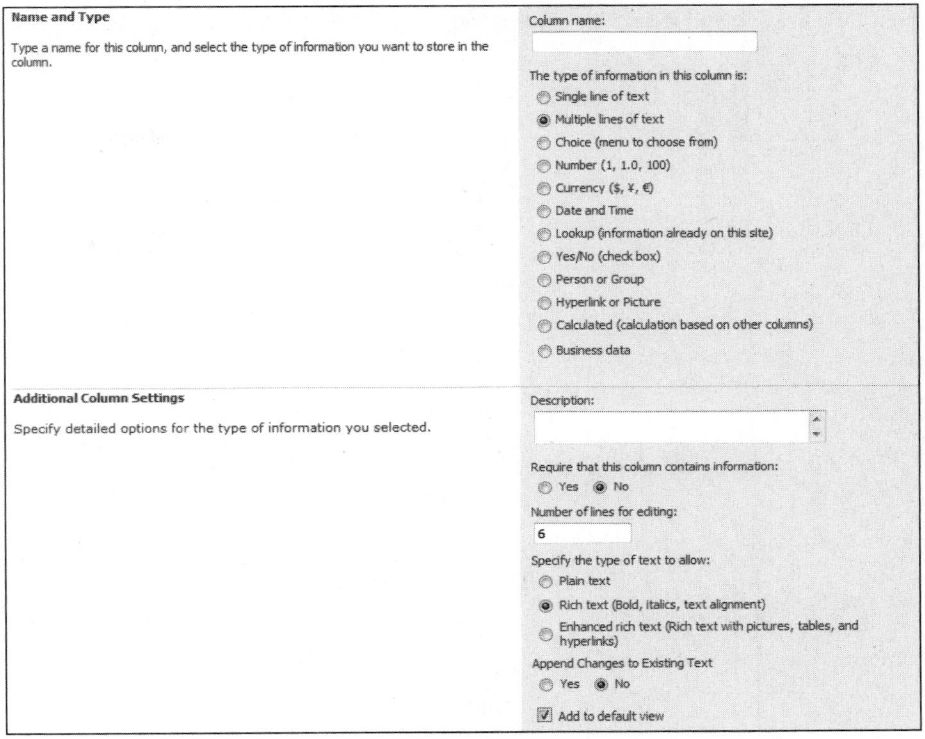

Figure 4-3

The Multiple Lines of Text column has more advanced formatting options than most other columns, including the following:

❑ **Plain Text:** Most appropriate for scenarios where no special formatting is required, such as in the example of a mailing address.

❑ **Rich Text:** Users can format the text using the Rich Text Editor, shown in Figure 4-4, which is ideal when users input a larger amount of text that doesn't have specially formatted elements, such as tables or pictures but may require some formatting and text alignment. You select this for notes and comments related to an item.

❑ **Enhanced Text:** Allows your users to add images, tables, and hyperlink elements to the column via the Advanced List Text Editor, as shown in Figure 4-5. This format is ideal for article body columns in an announcements list or employee biography content columns.

SharePoint 2007 has a new option called Append Changes to Existing Text. This feature keeps a running log of changes and additions to the list item and is great for situations where you need to track progress on a task or document changes. To use this feature, you must have versioning enabled on the list because each change is stored within a specific version of the item.

For more information on versioning, see Chapter 3.

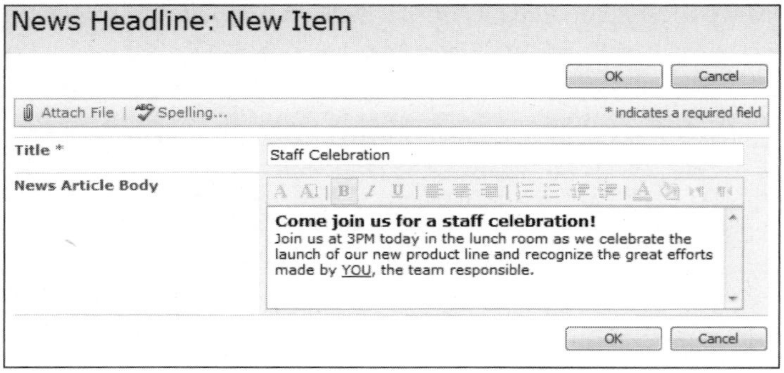

Figure 4-4

Figure 4-5

Choice

The *Choice* column allows a site manager to define a list of values from which a user can select, as shown in Figure 4-6. As with other columns, you can specify whether the column is required and enter a description that serves as an aid to users as they complete the information.

Figure 4-6

You enter all values by placing each value on a separate line. Users see this as a drop-down list, a set of radio buttons, or a series of check boxes. A drop-down list or set of radio buttons means users can only select one option, while check boxes allow them to select more than one item from the list of values. You can also specify whether users can fill in their own item if an appropriate value does not appear in the list, which is great if you want users to enter exceptional values. For example, you may have a survey list that collects information on preferences for the next company social. You may offer a set list of locations and then have an option that allows users to enter suggestions for a location.

As with the Single Line of Text, you can also include a default value from the list of choices or have the default value calculated. In cases where you are making a choice column a required field for a list, it's best not to specify a default value because users may accidentally forget to specify the value and the default selected item is then saved. By not specifying a default value, you can enforce the selection of an item, which ensures the information entered into the list is accurate. For example, if you are required to give users a choice of whether information is confidential or public in a list or library, it would not be wise to set either choice as the default value because you would want the user to think about their selection and pick the right option.

Number

A *Number* column is pretty simple in customization options, as shown in Figure 4-7, but is extremely useful in many lists because it's helpful for calculations or reporting.

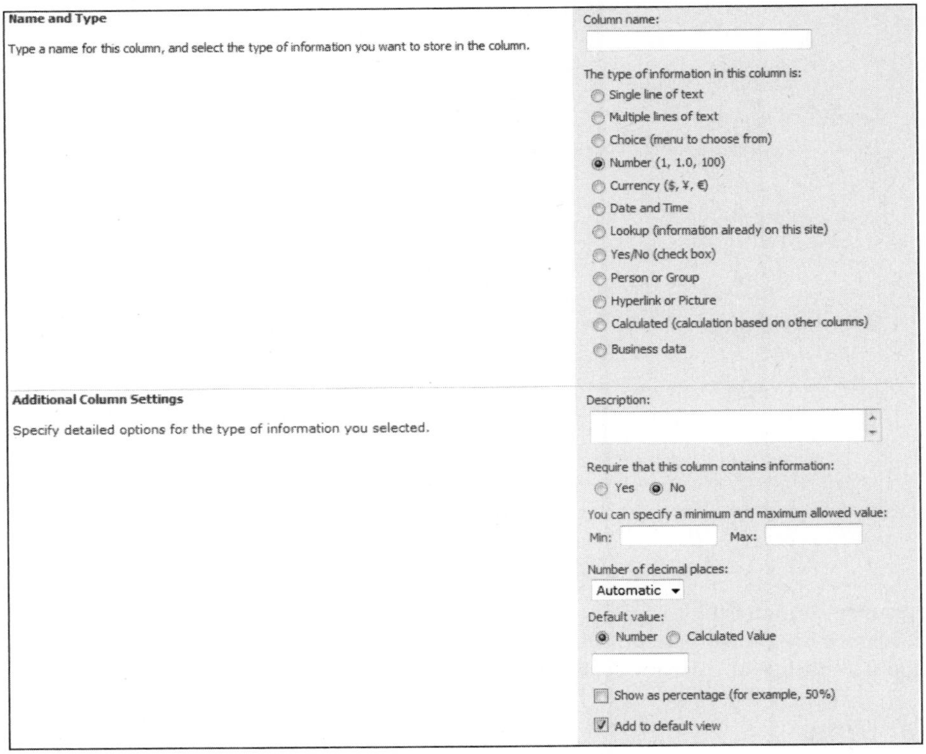

Figure 4-7

You can make a Number column either required or optional. You may specify an allowed range of numbers that users can enter. For example, if you have a column to represent a user's rating of an item, you can have a minimum value of 1 and a maximum of 10. You can also configure a column to display a specific number of decimal places or percentage value regardless of the format a person uses to enter the information. As with some of the previous examples, you may select a default or calculated value for your column.

Currency

A *Currency* column has the same customization options as the Number column type with one addition, as shown in Figure 4-8.

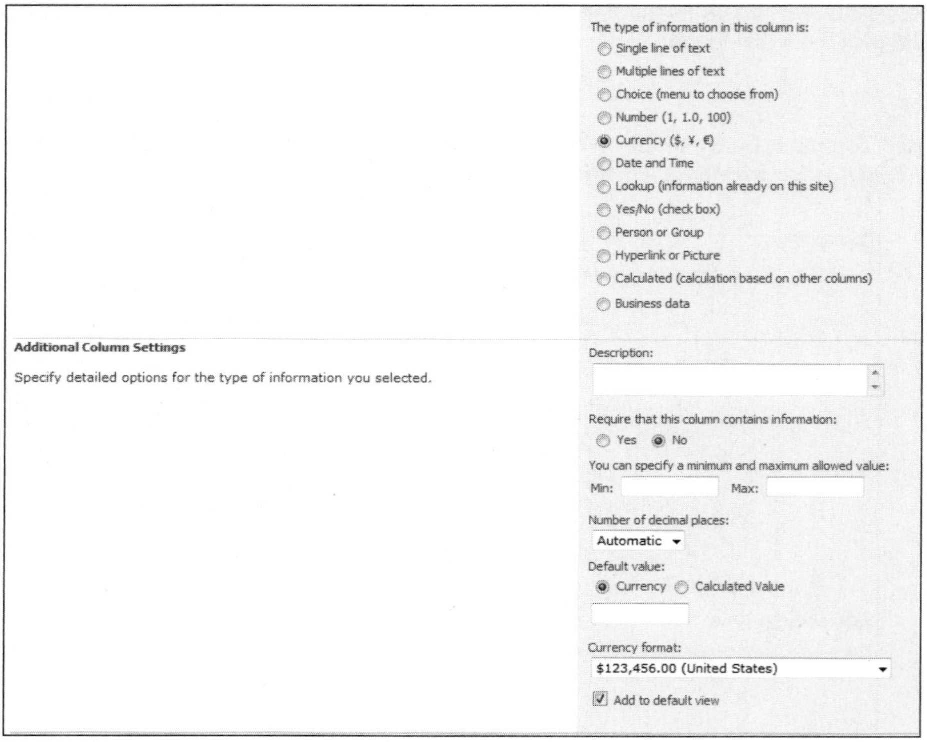

The type of information in this column is:
- Single line of text
- Multiple lines of text
- Choice (menu to choose from)
- Number (1, 1.0, 100)
- ● Currency ($, ¥, €)
- Date and Time
- Lookup (information already on this site)
- Yes/No (check box)
- Person or Group
- Hyperlink or Picture
- Calculated (calculation based on other columns)
- Business data

Additional Column Settings

Specify detailed options for the type of information you selected.

Description:

Require that this column contains information:
- Yes ● No

You can specify a minimum and maximum allowed value:
Min: Max:

Number of decimal places:
Automatic ▾

Default value:
- ● Currency Calculated Value

Currency format:
$123,456.00 (United States) ▾

☑ Add to default view

Figure 4-8

The Currency column enables a user to specify the regional format in which the data displays, such as $150,000.00 for the United States or £150,000.00 for the United Kingdom. There is no direct link between the regional setting and currency exchange rates.

Date and Time

You may need to add columns containing date and time information because many of the items you track in a list have some level of time relevance, such as a due date, start date, finish date, or completion date. In fact, every list has *Date and Time* columns for tracking when an item was created or last modified.

Beyond the options that determine whether this column is required and that add a description, you can have the column display as only a date or a time value. Time values are particularly useful if you intend to display your list information in a daily calendar view or if you define details on events, such as meetings or appointments.

You also have a few choices for displaying a default value — either no value, the current date, or a specific date, as shown in Figure 4-9. So, if you have a list where users submit requests, you can select Today's Date as the default value for a column called "Request Date." This reduces the amount of user entry and lets you accurately determine when a user submitted a request.

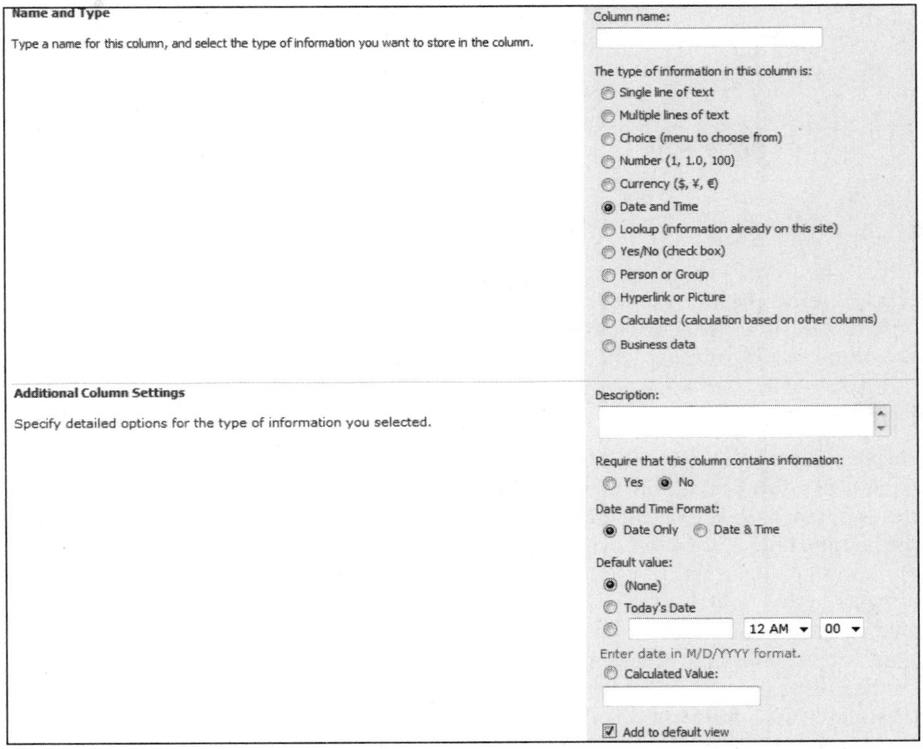

Figure 4-9

As with previously described columns, you can create a calculated value for a date column. This is useful if you are setting a value such as the default due date for an item. In that case, you may select the default value as [today] + 7, which sets the value to a week past the current date.

Lookup

A *Lookup column* is very similar to a Choice column because it supplies users with a set of predefined values for a column. The advantage is that you can point it to another list on the site and thus create more dynamic list values. This is better than storing all the values as a static property of the column because users update the list as part of normal business operations. For example, if you have a customer list, it's unrealistic for a site manager to constantly log in and change a list column's properties each time a company acquires a new customer. Instead you can have this column point to a centralized customer list that those closest to the business operations can maintain. The new customer name would then automatically appear as a value in the column as soon as the centralized customer list updates.

In addition to selecting the list and column that the Lookup column uses to display data, site managers can configure the column so that users can select multiple values for a list, as shown in Figure 4-10.

Figure 4-10

Yes/No

A *Yes/No* column type is essentially a check box column that defines whether an item meets a specific criteria item. For example, this type of column can designate whether an item displays on the main page of a SharePoint site, or whether an item is active. The primary configuration option when defining a Yes/No column is determining whether the default value should be selected or unselected.

Person or Group

The *Person or Group* column is ideal for assigning ownership of an item or personalizing the display of data to users of a list. Besides the usual determination of whether to make the column required or to add a description, you have the option of selecting multiple items, which allows you to assign a single task to multiple people. In fact, for a tasks list, the Assigned To column is based on the Person or Group column type.

You can also assign this column type to a group. For example, you can create a group called "Project Managers," create a task list and assign it to all members of the Project Managers group. This is far more efficient than assigning a task to each member individually, especially if you had 800 members in this group. You have the added option of defining whether a person from this column is drawn from the list of all users or a SharePoint group, which is useful if you want to have an Assigned To column to represent who should review the document next. Because only those with approval rights should be reviewing items, it may make sense to specify that only members of the Approvers SharePoint site group be assigned to the column.

Your final customization option involves how the information displays. You can have the person identified by a variety of personal profile properties including display name, email address, and job title.

Hyperlink or Picture

This column offers very little from a customization perspective beyond specifying whether the item is required, but does offer one significant attribute. You can format the URL of the item as either a web address that users can click to open, or as a picture that displays as a thumbnail. See Figure 4-11 for an example.

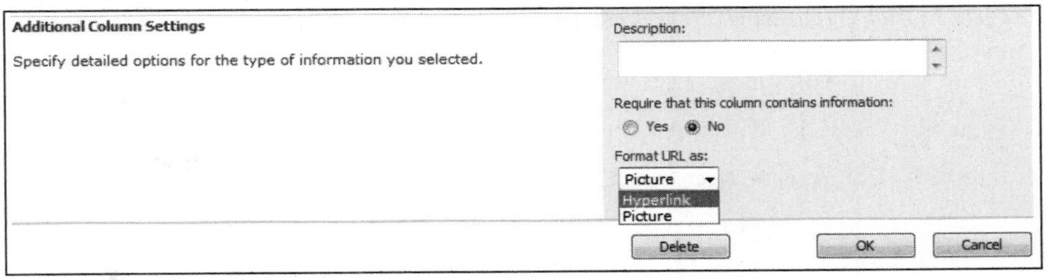

Figure 4-11

Other column types such as Audiences and Business Data are covered in greater detail in Chapters 9 and 12.

Try It Out   Change the Order of Columns on a List

When you create a list or library column, it is added to the list in the order in which it was created. The form fields reflect this order — an order which is not always the most logical flow for entering information. If, for example, you have the columns First Name and Email Address on your list and later want to also add a Last Name column, Last Name will show up as the last item on the form. A more logical scenario is displaying First Name, and then Last Name, and finally Email Address.

Because the order in which your columns display can make it easier for users to find and enter information into a list item, SharePoint offers an intuitive way to do it. The following example walks you through reordering the columns of a list to make the metadata more user-friendly. Although this example uses a list, you can apply the same methodology to reordering columns of a document library. You reorder the columns of the list so that the first and last names display at the top of the new item form versus being spread out, as shown in Figure 4-12.

Figure 4-12

97

See Chapter 2 for more details on the differences between a form and a column.

1. From your Lists toolbar, select Settings.

2. Select List Settings from the drop-down menu.

3. From the Columns section, select Column Ordering.

4. By changing the drop-down selections, you can easily reorder columns into a more logical sequence as shown in Figure 4-13.

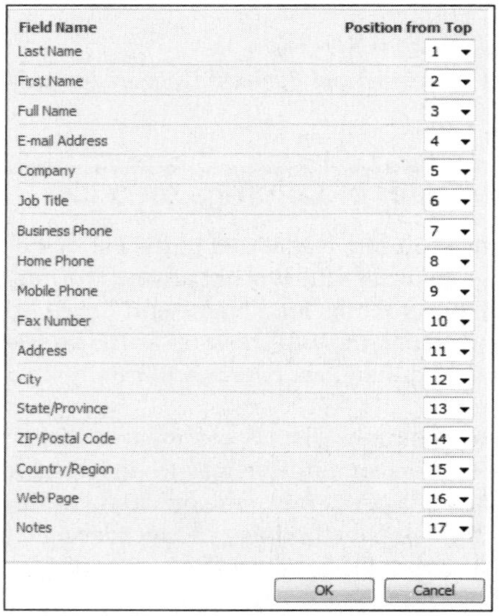

Field Name	Position from Top
Last Name	1
First Name	2
Full Name	3
E-mail Address	4
Company	5
Job Title	6
Business Phone	7
Home Phone	8
Mobile Phone	9
Fax Number	10
Address	11
City	12
State/Province	13
ZIP/Postal Code	14
Country/Region	15
Web Page	16
Notes	17

OK   Cancel

Figure 4-13

5. When you are satisfied with your new order, click OK.

What Are Site Columns?

So far, all examples in this chapter have been limited to creating a column for a list or library. But you can associate the information for a single list with multiple lists. For example, for a column that defines customers, you commonly associate a customer's name with items from multiple lists and libraries. Because the steps for creating a suitable customer list are somewhat time-consuming, it's inefficient to reproduce the column on each list with which you want to associate client information. Instead, you can create what is known as a *site column*, which makes a column available to all sites and subsites. Generally speaking, if many lists will use your column at all levels of a corporate intranet or portal, you should create it at the top-level site of a site collection. This makes the site column available on all sites throughout the site collection.

A site column may be relevant only to a specific division or team. In that case, you may want to create the column only on the divisional site itself. It will still be available to all lists within that site and all sites below it; however, it will not be listed under the Available Site columns for the other subsites within the site collection.

It's important to consider where to place site columns in order to ensure that the organization gets optimal use of this shared feature. This is discussed later in Chapter 6.

The next two Try It Outs show you how to create a site column as well as how to add a site column to a list.

Try It Out   Create a Site Column

In the "Create a Column" Try It Out, you learned how to create a list-centric column. This Try It Out walks you through creating a site column within the central gallery of columns so that it can later be used by multiple lists with a site and its subsites. For this example, you create the site column so that it holds all the regions in which an organization has a presence. Because you want to ensure that your column is available to the maximum number of sites in your intranet, you create it at the very top level of your site collection.

1.   From the top level of your site collection, select Site Actions ➪ Site Settings, as shown in Figure 4-14.

Figure 4-14

2.   From the Galleries section, select Site Columns. SharePoint presents you with a wide range of preexisting site columns, which are good starting points.

3.   Click Create from the toolbar. The Create Column window appears as previously shown in Figure 4-2.

4.   Give the site column a name. This example uses the name **Corporate Regions**.

5.   Select the Choice (menu to choose from) option as the type of information in this column.

6.   To better organize your site columns you can choose a group for your site column. You can create a custom group for your custom site columns. To do this select New Group, and type **Classification Columns** in the field provided.

7. In Additional Column Settings, shown in Figure 4-15, type a description for the column type. For this example, type **This is a list of regions our organization has offices in**.

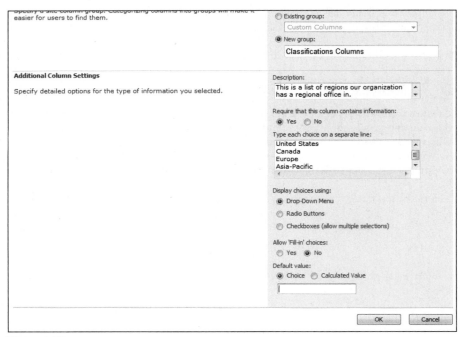

Figure 4-15

8. Because regional association with content is required, select Yes for Require That This Column Contains Information.

9. In the area under Type Each Choice On a Separate Line, type the various choices. For this example, enter **United States**, **Canada**, **Europe** and **Asia-Pacific**.

10. Select Drop-Down Menu as the Display Choices Using option. This should be the default.

11. Select No for Allow "Fill-In" Choices. This should be the default.

12. Remove the text from the Default Value field.

13. Click OK. You can now add your site column to all lists and libraries throughout your site collection.

How It Works

Now, when users add a list item, they are required to select a region from this list of choices. If you want to update the region choices available in your site column, you can return to the site column gallery to edit your column. In addition to the previous selection options, you also see a new check box that allows you to update all lists and libraries using this site column to include your changes.

So, you can update a large number of lists to accommodate a change in your organization from one single location. As you accumulate more and more lists and libraries, this valuable feature becomes more powerful and is a great timesaver.

Try It Out   Add a Site Column to a List

The previous example guided you though creating a new site column. You can now use this site column on any list or library on your site collection. This saves you the time and energy required to recreate list-centric columns. The following example guides you through the process of attaching a site column to a list or library. Instead of creating a column on the list from scratch, you add an existing site column to the list. The steps for doing so are considerably easier, and future updates to the column properties can be streamlined and rolled out to all lists from a single location. As you add site columns to a list, they become fields that users are required to fill out as they add list items.

1.   Select Settings ⇨ List Setting from your Tasks list toolbar.

2.   Select Add from Existing Site Columns from the Columns section.

3.   Select the Classification Columns group. As mentioned previously, site columns are organized by groups. Once you select a group, you see a list of site columns associated with that group.

4.   Select the site column you created earlier called Corporate Regions and select Add. You see the site column appear in the Columns to Add field of the screen, as shown in Figure 4-16. You can remove site columns by selecting the appropriate item in the Columns to Add area and clicking Remove.

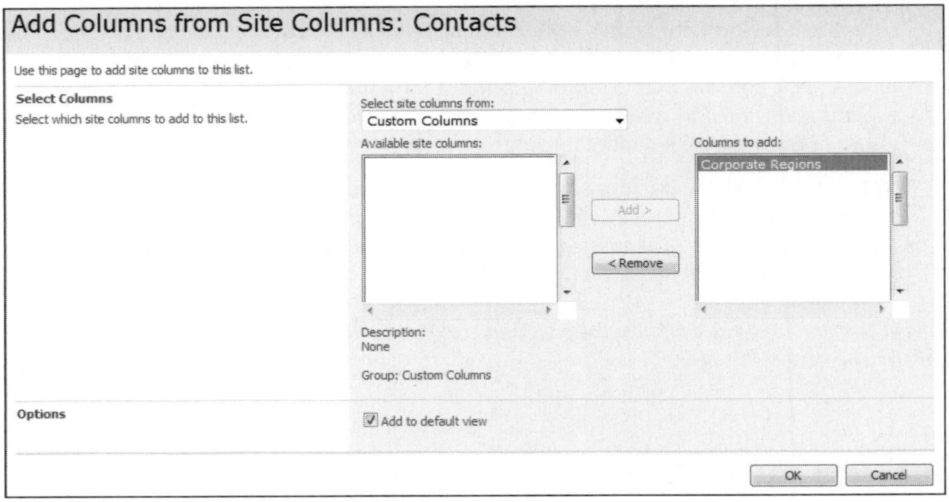

Figure 4-16

5.   Make sure the Add to Default View option is selected and click OK.

How It Works

As you can see in Figure 4-17, the site column is now added to your list and users must select a region when they add an item. Most organizations like to enforce a standard set of required items that users must complete on lists and libraries, such as Owner or Status. Based on this methodology, an organization can create a site column for each type of information it wants to enforce and then reuse this column on all lists and libraries throughout the site collection. This greatly reduces the amount of maintenance.

Figure 4-17

When to Use a List-Centric Column versus a Site Column

Now that you can create list-centric columns and site columns, it's important to understand when to use each one. Although it's tempting to create a site column for everything and make it accessible to everyone, remember the following:

❑ **List-centric columns:** You use this column for specific column types or when you don't want the column to appear in a column gallery. Some column types are only relevant for a specific list and only clutter the site column gallery for all other users and usage scenarios. For example, a software development team's issue list may have a column that tracks whether a client called about an application bug or feature request and that column isn't appropriate for any other list or site. Or, a column may contain important data that should not be shared with the entire organization, such as manually entered items or information from the business data catalog. In either of these cases, it's more appropriate to create a column that is attached to a single list.

❑ **Site columns:** These are more appropriate for information that you want to associate with multiple lists. You also use a site column to ensure that there is consistency in how a column is configured. Because you create the column once and it's placed in a central gallery for others to reuse, you save time and effort.

Global elements, such as workflow templates and content types also use site columns. This is discussed in later chapters of this book.

Creating and Customizing Views

In Chapters 2 and 3, you read how both lists and libraries can contain views. A *view* basically displays the information about a list in different ways. Some views display all the items in the list, while others show specific items based on their properties or metadata values. Every list has at least one view, and SharePoint offers five views: Standard, Datasheet, Calendar, Gantt, and Access. You can customize these SharePoint views to quickly find relevant information. Imagine opening the telephone book and having it display only the numbers that are relevant to you. That's the type of flexibility you have with a custom view. The following examples guide you through the basics of setting up the views available with SharePoint 2007.

This section goes deeper into what views are. You learn the different types of views as well as how to use them effectively:

❑ You start by setting up the Standard view. The Try It Out that accompanies this section also shows how to select a view, once you create it. The method for displaying a view is the same regardless of the type of view that you create. Therefore, the rest of this chapter assumes that you'll use one of these methods whenever you select a view for a list.

❑ Next, you work your way through setting up a Gantt, Calendar, and Datasheet view. You also create a view based on an existing view.

❑ Finally, you learn how to work with an Access view, which essentially lets you combine the best aspects of SharePoint and Access.

Working with the Standard View

Because the Standard view is the most common view type and because it has so many elements that follow, this section details the various elements of the Standard view. You then get an opportunity to create a Standard view in a Try It Out.

❑ **View Name:** The name that displays in a drop-down menu of views associated with each list. When you create a view name, be specific so that users can clearly identify the unique nature of each view. For example, "Grouped by Status" communicates that all items are grouped together based on their status values.

❑ **Default View Selection:** Defines the default view for a list. This view appears first whenever a user visits the specific list or library.

❑ **View Audience:** When you create a view, you can make it either a personal or public view. A personal view is only available to its creator in the drop-down list of views. However, it does not have any specific security applied to it. Personal views are ideal if your list is for administration purposes and of no value to others. All users can see a shared view in the View selection drop down associated with a list.

❑ **Column Selection:** You must select which column displays in your view and specify their relative position from the left in the view. When you specify the position of a single column, all other columns automatically adjust their position.

❑ **Sort Order:** You can select up to two columns by which items in the list are sorted. Sort order can be either ascending (A to Z) or descending (Z to A).

❑ **Filter:** You can customize a view by defining the items that display based on specific column values or properties. You first select a column from the drop-down list, and specify a rule so that only items that meet your criteria display in the view. You can add up to 10 filter rules for a single view.

❑ **Group By:** Because views can quite often contain a large amount of information, SharePoint allows you to group up to two columns of similar items together. The first column acts as a parent item, and the second as a child of the parent. For example, you can group a task list by "Project" and then by "Assigned To." This allows users to see a report of all tasks grouped first by the project name and then by each person to which the tasks are assigned.

❑ **Totals:** For numerical columns, it's beneficial to display total values for all your items. These might be the sum, average, or standard deviation of all items in a view or group. For other columns, the total value is useful to display the number of items in a view or group by selecting Count.

❑ **Style:** Depending on your presentation requirements, you can select a style for your view. For example, you may select "Newsletter, No Lines" for a plain view of items in a list or "Boxed" to display items in a series of rectangular boxes. Take a few minutes to try out each view style so that you can familiarize yourself with the options that are the most appropriate choice for your views.

❑ **Folders:** In a list or library, folders organize items or documents. However, you may not want to show folders for a particular view. Instead, you can show items that meet specific criteria, regardless of their folder location. For example, if you have 10 layers of folders in your document library and you want to view all documents associated with a specific project, rather than manually clicking through the various levels of folders, you can create a custom view that displays items with no folders that gives a complete listing of all documents that meet your criteria in a single level. No additional clicks are required.

❑ **Item Limit:** For performance reasons, you commonly may only want to display a specific number of items; for example, it's not very efficient to display 10,000 documents in a single view, but groups of 100 may be more beneficial. In fact, the All Items view for most lists display items in groups of 100 by default.

❑ In other cases, you may want to limit the number of items to a goal number and display them to meet a criterion. For example, you may want to show the last 25 documents that have been added to a library. You first sort the view by either the created or modified date in descending order. You then specify the limit for the view to be 25 items.

❑ **Mobile:** When creating or editing a view, you can select whether it is a Mobile view. A Mobile view is one that is suitable for access from a device such as a cell phone or PDA. Many of the user-interface elements such as tables and images that would typically be seen via a standard browser are left out of these views. Only views that are public views can be created as Mobile views.

Try It Out   Create and Display a Standard View

By sorting, filtering, and grouping the columns of metadata, SharePoint can display the contents of a list in a personalized way, one that is directly relevant to the information you want to see. This is particularly useful when you have lists shared across an organization, or when you have large lists. For this Try It Out, you will sort items in a task list by their due date so that items appear in the order in which they need to be responded. In addition, you create a view for members at the Canadian office, which involves displaying items only where the Corporate Regions column has "Canada" specified.

1. From your Tasks list toolbar, select Settings ➪ Create View (the menu path is shown in Figure 4-1). The Create View window appears.

2. Select the Standard View option.

3. Give your view a user-friendly name. For this example, type **Canadian Tasks**.

4. You can make your view the default by selecting the check box directly under your view name.

5. Select a view audience. You may want to make your view personal or share it with other users.

6. Select the columns you want to display in your view from the Columns section.

7. You may choose to sort your items by a particular column by selecting up to two columns to sort by from the Sort section, as shown in Figure 4-18.

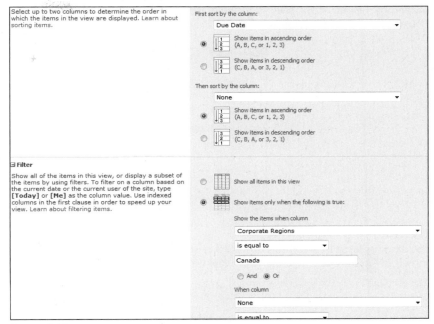

Figure 4-18

8. You can also filter the display of items based on the columns meeting a set of conditions, which you can set in the Filter section. In this example, you are filtering where the Corporate Regions column has a value of "Canada," (also shown in Figure 4-18). This will ensure that only Canadian items are returned in the view.

9. You may choose to group your items by a particular column in ascending or descending order by specifying this in the Group by section. In this situation, you will group items by their status.

10. When tracking things such as numerical data, you may make minor calculations using the Totals section.

11. Select a view style from the Styles section to control how your data will be presented.

12. Select whether you want to display items in folders from the Folders section.

13. You may invoke paging by selecting a maximum number of items to display on one page in the Item Limit section.

14. SharePoint 2007 enables more accessible list views. If you want to make your view a Mobile view, select it from the Mobile option.

How It Works

Once you create a view, you have two ways to display it:

❑ You can display it within a Web Part using the task pane user interface for modifying Web Part properties. Under Views, select your view from the drop-down list and then click Apply and OK, as shown in Figure 4-19.

Figure 4-19

❑ You can display it in the Views drop-down menu, which is on the far right of your list toolbar, shown in Figure 4-20. Selecting your view initiates data filtering.

Figure 4-20

The method for selecting a view is the same regardless of the type of view that you create. Therefore, the rest of this chapter assumes that you use one of these methods whenever you select a view for a list.

Setting up a Gantt, Calendar, or Datasheet view

This section deals with setting up three specialized views that SharePoint has to offer:

❑ **Gantt view:** This view displays a graphical representation of tasks and how they are progressing over time. It gives you a clear picture of how a project or task is evolving at a glance, and helps you easily identify bottlenecks in the process. For many small teams, the Gantt chart view is the ideal solution for managing and reporting a project. This particular view is a big hit with resource managers who need to track how tasks are evolving and give updated status reports to an executive team.

❑ **Calendar view:** Allows you to create a daily, weekly, or monthly view of your data.

❑ **Datasheet view:** This view gives you a spreadsheet-like view of your data, very similar to an Excel spreadsheet. This view is particularly useful when you want to customize multiple columns of data.

In addition to showing you how to set up these views, this section also has a Try It Out that shows you how to create a view based on an existing view. This is particularly useful when you have columns that are similar, but with slightly different requirements.

Try It Out   Create a Gantt View

When configuring a Gantt view, you must select a start and end date. Based on this elapsed time and the percentage of the task completed, SharePoint can calculate a graphical representation of how things are progressing. The following steps enable you to get started using the Gantt view:

1. From your Tasks list toolbar, select Settings ⇨ Create View (the menu path is shown in Figure 4-1). The Create View window appears.

2. Select the Gantt View option.

3. Select your name and other configuration settings as discussed in the "Create and Display a Standard View" Try It Out.

4. For a Gantt view, you must select a start and end date.

5. Click OK.

Try It Out   Create a Calendar View

This view allows you to move back and forth between months, add tasks to your calendar, and even connect your calendar to Outlook, a familiar interface for managing calendars. To connect your Calendar view to Outlook, select Connect to Outlook from the Actions menu of your Lists toolbar. Figure 4-21 shows an example of a Calendar view. The following steps walk you through setting up the Calendar view.

1. From the list toolbar, select Settings ⇨ Create View (the menu path is shown in Figure 4-1). The Create View window appears.

2. Select the Calendar View option.

3. Select your name and other configuration settings as discussed in the "Create and Display a Standard View" Try It Out.

4. For the Calendar view, you must select a default scope to have your calendar default to a daily, weekly, or monthly view as well as a time interval for adding items to your calendar.

5. Click OK.

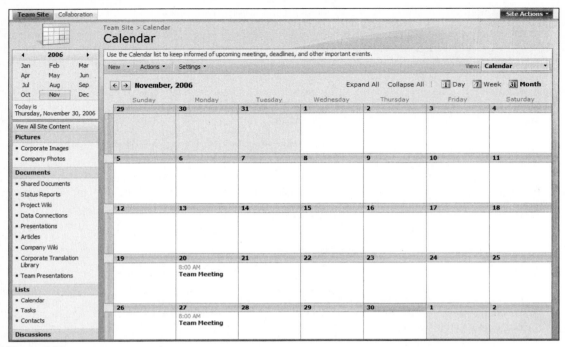

Figure 4-21

Try It Out   Create a Datasheet View

The *Datasheet view* gives you a spreadsheet view much like Excel, but allows for much easier and faster mass updates and data customization. Figure 4-22 shows the Datasheet view.

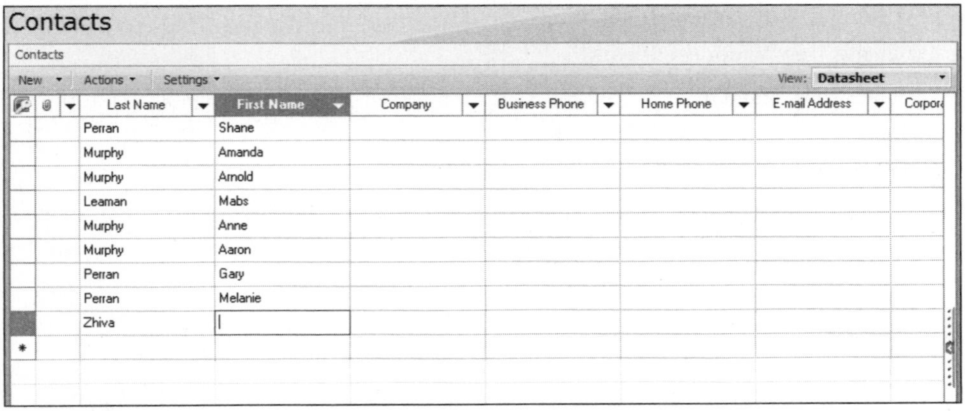

Figure 4-22

The following steps will help guide you through creating the Datasheet view.

1. From your list toolbar, select Settings ⇨ Create View (the menu path is shown in Figure 4-1). The Create View window appears.

2. Select the Datasheet View option.

3. Select your name and other configuration settings as discussed in the "Create and Display a Standard View" Try It Out.

4. Click OK.

How It Works

After creating and selecting your Datasheet view (see the "Create and Display a Standard View" Try It Out to display the view), you are presented with a spreadsheet-like view of your list's data. With this spreadsheet, an ActiveX control, you can select multiple columns at the same time and subsequently customize them. This is a big timesaver, particularly if you are dealing with large amounts of list data.

Try It Out   Create a View Based on an Existing View

In some situations, a single list or library may contain multiple views that are similar but have slight differences to meet specific information requirements. Instead of creating each new view from scratch, you can use a particular view as a starting point and slightly alter it to meet your needs.

Each time you add a new view to a list, it appears in the Start from an Existing View section in the Create View window. Selecting one of these views generates a view based on the filtering, sorting, and metadata columns of the existing view. This saves you time and helps you efficiently customize views. By creating a starting point, you can reuse this view to minimize your efforts for all remaining views for the list. You can also think of using this method as a way to give structure because it acts as a template for displaying common components.

The following steps guide you through creating new views based on an existing one:

1. From the Tasks list toolbar, select Settings ⇨ Create View (the menu path is shown in Figure 4-1). The Create View window appears, as shown in Figure 4-23.

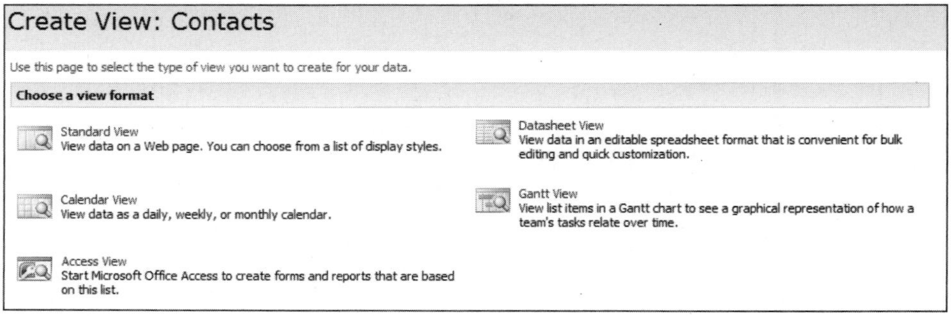

Figure 4-23

2. Below the listed options is the Start from an Existing View heading with any views currently available for your list. Select a task view from which to start building your custom view. For this example, select the Canadian Tasks view.

3. Select your name and other configuration settings as discussed in the "Create and Display a Standard View" Try It Out.

4. Click OK.

Working with Access Views

SharePoint 2007 introduces some great new functionality for working with Access. As discussed in Chapter 2, you can now link many of the lists in SharePoint to an Access database. This makes offline data available and allows you to synchronize data. In addition, Access provides reports and forms that are not available using a browser. By creating an Access view for a list, you gain all the advantages of Access's reporting functionality and you also have information stored in a central secured online store such as SharePoint.

Try It Out   Create an Access View for a List

In this example, you give the interface that displays your SharePoint lists more flexibility and options by creating an Access view. To do so, you export data from the list to an Access database, which creates a more advanced view for entering and updating the data. This example uses the Split Form view so that users can see details of selected individual records as well as update items by simply typing into the datasheet.

1. From your Contacts list toolbar, select Settings ⇨ Create View (the menu path is shown in Figure 4-1). The Create View window appears, as shown previously in Figure 4-23.

2. From the list of view choices, select Access View. A dialog box appears, as shown in Figure 4-24.

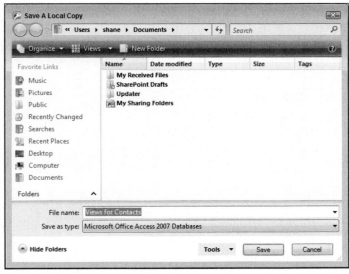

Figure 4-24

3. Select a file name, browse to the location where you want to store the Access information, and click Save. The Create Access View window appears, shown in Figure 4-25, requiring information on the type of view that you want to create for your list. You have a variety of options.

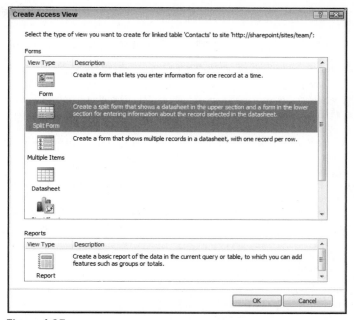

Figure 4-25

4. Select a view type. This example uses the Split Form view. Click OK. An Access view opens with a single item list view form and a Datasheet view. You can enter data into the Datasheet view or Form view.

5. When you finish entering or viewing your data, click the Publish to SharePoint Site button just below the top menu bar of the Access application, as shown in Figure 4-26. If this is your first time saving the Access database back to SharePoint, you are requested to identify a save location for the database.

Figure 4-26

How It Works

Once you complete your edits, a copy of your Access database is saved back to the SharePoint site so that other users can access the created views and reports.

Working with Custom Lists and Libraries

Chapter 2 detailed the various SharePoint 2007 list templates, which are ideal for creating a list that you want to modify or customize to suit your team's or your individual needs. However, you may need to create a list where no existing template can serve as a starting point. This, of course, involves creating a custom list and defining all the columns and views from scratch. This section first introduces all the basic skills you need to create a custom list: how to create a list, how to make that list a template so that you don't have to repeat work, and then how to load that template into a gallery for team use.

Once you have list customization basics under your belt, you learn about *versioning* items in SharePoint — you can modify either list items or documents, and save each iteration as a specific version. Certain customization options are unique to document library environments and do not apply exactly the same to a list. Next, you learn how to associate a custom document template with a library. This helps standardize the documents that your company uses to create various memos, procedures, and processes.

Custom List Basics

As you create a column within a list or library, think about what information users need about the item or how they may need to view the item. For example, if you are responsible for creating a centralized listing of projects, you may ask users the following questions:

❑   What are the active projects on which the organization is working?

❑   Are the projects running on a schedule?

❑   Who are the primary contacts or project managers associated with each project?

❑   What is the project background, and what are the primary deliverables from the project team?

❑   Who is the client for whom the project is being completed?

Using the information from these questions, you can accurately create a custom list featuring the appropriate columns and views. In cases where you intend to have multiple lists for the same subject matter within an organization, you should plan the details out in the beginning, create the list, and then save the list as a template for reuse by others. This reduces the amount of repetitive work you or your team will need to perform.

The following series of Try It Outs illustrate how to work with a custom list or library. In the first Try It Out, you create a custom list with specific columns to track a project. The second Try It Out shows you how to save the list or library as a template so that others can use your work. Finally, in the last Try It Out, you see how to save the template to a gallery so that others can view and use it.

Try It Out   Create a Custom List

In this example, you create a list to represent all the projects for an organization. Based on your meetings with Project Management Office (PMO), you determine that you must implement a project list containing the columns for the project status, due date, project manager, project summary, and client. To track project information, the PMO must have this information on active projects. By clicking the project name, more detailed information on the summary should be available.

To meet these requirements, you create a list based on the Custom List template, which has just a single column called Title. To this, you must add five list-centric columns. In a real-life project, you might want to make some of these site columns so other lists and sites can use these columns. However, for simplicity's sake, this example uses the list column model. Next, you create a custom view on your list based on the information requirements of your stakeholders. Because the PMO requested a listing of all active projects, you create a filtered view to show projects with a project status value of In Progress.

Follow these steps to create the custom list:

1. From the main page of the site where you want to create your projects list, select Site Actions ➪ Create.

2. From the Custom Lists category, select Custom List.

3. Enter **Projects** for the list name, and provide a description.

4. Select Yes for display on the Quick Launch navigation bar.

5. Click the Create button to continue. Your list is created with a single column for title.

6. From the toolbar, select Settings ➪ List Settings (as previously shown in Figure 4-1).

7. From the Columns section, click the link to create a new column. The Create Column window appears, similar to what is shown in Figure 4-2.

8. Enter the following details for your column:

Property	Details
Name	Project status
Column Type	Choice
Description	Please specify the current status of your project.
Require That This Column Contains Information	Yes
Choice Values	Not Started In Progress Complete Halted
Display Choices Using	Radio buttons
Default Value	Leave blank

9. Click OK to create your column.

10. From the Columns section, click the link to create a new column.

11. Enter the following details for your column. Note that once you select the Date and Time option, your settings look a lot like those shown earlier in Figure 4-9.

Property	Details
Name	Project due date
Column Type	Date and time
Description	Please enter the date your project is scheduled to be complete.
Require That This Column Contains Information	Yes
Date and Time Format	Date only
Default Value	(none)

12. Click OK to create your column.

13. From the Columns section, click the link to create a new column.

14. Enter the following details for your column:

Property	Details
Name	Project manager
Column Type	Person or group
Description	Please specify the Project Manager for this project.
Require That This Column Contains Information	Yes
Allow Multiple Sections	No
Allow Selection of	People only
Choose From	All users
Show Field	Name (with presence)

15. Click OK to create your column.

16. From the Columns section, click the link to create a new column.

17. Enter the following details for your column:

Property	Details
Name	Project summary
Column Type	Multiple Lines of Text
Description	Describe the project by providing some background information and outlining the deliverables.
Require That This Column Contains Information	Yes
Number of lines for editing	25
Type of Text to Allow	Enhanced rich text (rich text with pictures, tables, and hyperlinks)
Append Changes to Existing Text	No

18. Click OK to create your column.

19. From the Columns section, click the link to create a new column.

20. Enter the following details for your column:

Property	Details
Name	Client
Column Type	Choice
Description	Specify the client name
Require That This Column Contains Information	Yes
Choice Values	Customer A Customer B Customer C
Display Choices Using	Drop-down menu
Allow Fill-In Choices	No
Default Value	Leave blank

21. Click OK to create your column.

22. From the Views section, click the link to create a new view.

23. Select Standard View.

24. Specify the following details for your view:

Property	Details
View Name	
Audience	
Display Columns and Order	Select to display the columns in the following order: Attachments Title (linked to item with Edit menu) Project Manager Project Due Date Client
Sort	Due Date (in ascending order)
Filter	Show items when Project Status is equal to In Progress.
Group By	None

25. Click OK to create your view.

How It Works

This view includes information that is short enough for the user to view on the interface, which in this case is the Project Manager, Client, and Due Date. Because the information in the Project Summary tends to be lengthy, you omit it from the initial view, but set things up so that the users can click the Project Title column and be redirected to a details page that contains the Project Summary. After you create this view, you can allow others to use it as a template, as illustrated in the next Try It Out.

Try It Out   Save a List as a Template

Once your list is complete, members of your organization can use it. You may even want to save the list as a template so that others can use it as a starting point in the future rather than repeating all the steps you took to create this list — the last Try It Out showed just how involved this process is! Follow these steps to save a list or library as a template:

1. From the list toolbar, select Settings ➪ List Settings (the menu path is shown in Figure 4-1). The Customize Tasks window appears, as shown in Figure 4-27.

2. From the Permissions and Management category, select the Save List as Template link. A window appears for you to enter information about your template.

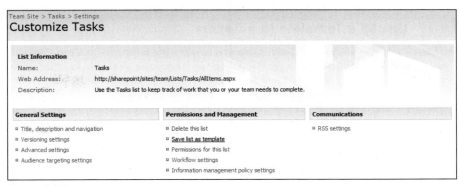

Figure 4-27

3. Specify a display name, file name, and description for the list template. You may also optionally select to include list content in the template if specific list items should be saved with the template.

4. Click OK to complete the operation.

How It Works

When you save your list as a template, it appears in the site as an option under the Custom Lists column, shown in Figure 4-28, whenever a user creates a new list.

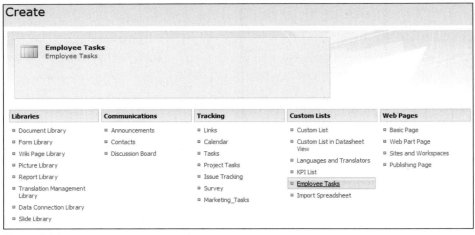

Figure 4-28

Try It Out   Upload a Template to a Gallery

Each site has its own list template gallery. After you create a list template on a separate site collection or server, you may want to upload it to a central gallery so it becomes available to other users when they create a new list. The following steps detail how to upload an existing list template to a new location.

1. From the resource materials website, download the file clients.stp.

2. From the top level of your site collection, select Site Actions ⇨ Site Settings (the menu path was previously shown in Figure 4-14). The Site Settings window appears as shown in Figure 4-29.

3. From the Galleries category, select the Site Templates link.

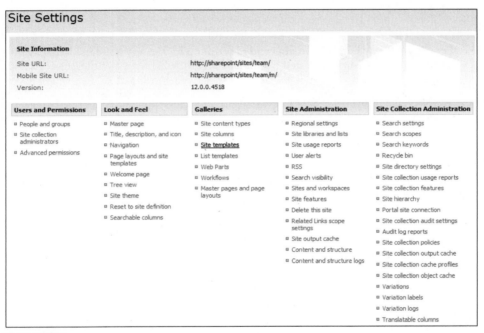

Figure 4-29

4. Click the Upload button from the toolbar.

5. Browse to the location where you saved the clients.stp file.

6. Click OK to upload the template.

How It Works

Once uploaded to the gallery, the template can be used by other users as a starting point for a new list. This same process applies to custom document library templates. You will review a very similar process for managing site templates in Chapter 8.

Managing Version Control

Items in SharePoint can be *versioned*. This means that as you modify either list items or documents, SharePoint saves iterations as specific versions. This allows users to revisit a previous version of an item or even track how something changes over time. To make this functionality available, you must enable versioning on the list or library.

Certain customization options are unique to a document library environment and do not apply exactly the same to a list. When you enable the document version history creation on the *library*, you have the following choices for how to store the versions:

❑ **Major version:** This is considered the same as a published version of a document. Over the life of a key organizational document, a site admin is more concerned with a previous major version of a document rather than the minor versions that show specific iterations of the document's creation or modification. You can limit the number of major versions that are retained. This is useful particularly for libraries where documents are fairly large in size and change very seldom.

❑ **Minor version:** This is an iteration of the document while in draft mode. This is helpful for scenarios where many people must work on a document before it publishes to the entire organization. Each time a user works on the document and saves it, SharePoint creates a new minor version. However for long-term editing purposes, the minor version is not as relevant.

❑ **Check in and check out:** Instead of making this feature optional for users, you can require that all documents be checked out before users can edit them. This provides a greater level of control in the editing process.

You can enable versions on lists as well as document libraries. However in a list, there is no concept of major and minor versions. Nor can a user limit the number of versions of a document that are stored.

The next Try It Out shows you how to enable document versioning.

Try It Out   Enable Document Versioning

In this example, you set options so that a maximum of 10 major versions are saved and stored in your library. Once more than 10 versions are created, the older versions are no longer kept. To enable version control on a document library, follow these steps:

1. From the main page of your site, select View All Site Content from the Quick Launch navigation bar. The All Site Content window appears, as shown in Figure 4-30.

2. Select the library for which you want to enable versioning by clicking the hyperlink for its name.

3. Select Settings ➪ Document Library Settings from the toolbar menu.

4. Select Versioning Settings from the General Settings category. The Document Library Versioning Settings window appears, as shown in Figure 4-31.

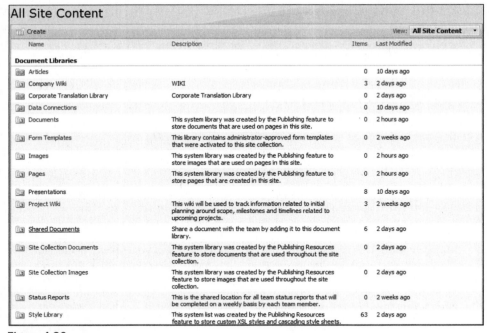

Figure 4-30

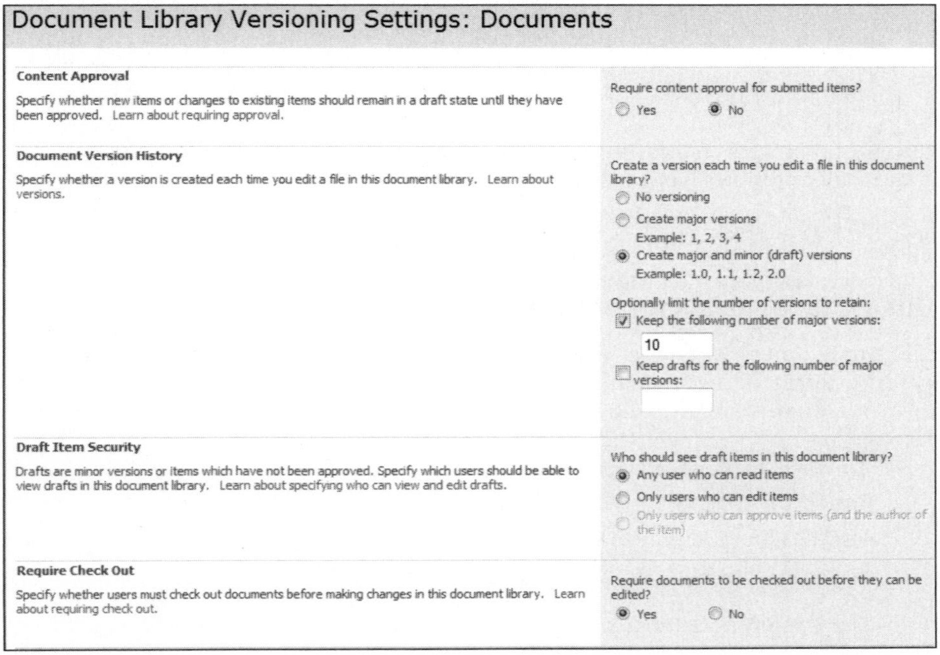

Document Library Versioning Settings: Documents

Content Approval

Specify whether new items or changes to existing items should remain in a draft state until they have been approved.   Learn about requiring approval.

Require content approval for submitted items?
○ Yes   ● No

Document Version History

Specify whether a version is created each time you edit a file in this document library.   Learn about versions.

Create a version each time you edit a file in this document library?
○ No versioning
○ Create major versions
　Example: 1, 2, 3, 4
● Create major and minor (draft) versions
　Example: 1.0, 1.1, 1.2, 2.0

Optionally limit the number of versions to retain:
☑ Keep the following number of major versions:

　10

☐ Keep drafts for the following number of major versions:

Draft Item Security

Drafts are minor versions or items which have not been approved. Specify which users should be able to view drafts in this document library.   Learn about specifying who can view and edit drafts.

Who should see draft items in this document library?
● Any user who can read items
○ Only users who can edit items
○ Only users who can approve items (and the author of the item)

Require Check Out

Specify whether users must check out documents before making changes in this document library.   Learn about requiring check out.

Require documents to be checked out before they can be edited?
● Yes   ○ No

Figure 4-31

5. Select the Create Major and Minor (Draft) Versions option from the Document Version History section.

6. Select the Keep the Following Number of Major Versions check box and enter **10** into the text box.

7. From the Require Check Out options, select Yes.

8. Click OK.

Managing Document Templates

When you create a document library, you are asked to select the document template that will be associated with the library by default. This association does not affect what type of documents you can store in a library, but instead determines the type of file that gets created when a user selects the New button from the Document Library toolbar. The choice of templates to select from includes:

- ❑ Word 1997–2003 Document
- ❑ Excel 1997–2003 Spreadsheet
- ❑ PowerPoint 1997–2003 Presentation
- ❑ Word Document
- ❑ Excel Spreadsheet
- ❑ PowerPoint Presentation
- ❑ OneNote Section
- ❑ SharePoint Designer Web Page
- ❑ Basic Page
- ❑ Web Part Page

When you customize a SharePoint site, the goal is to implement elements that encourage reuse and standardization. If you want to use a document library to store sales presentations, it's a good idea to associate the standard organizational template for sales presentations with the library so that the New button generates a blank presentation that users can then customize and use for their own purposes.

In cases where you have a document, such as a Word file containing your company's logo or letterhead, and you would want to use that as the default document template. Another common example is an Excel spreadsheet containing the fields and calculations needed for a report that users often create when in the document library.

You have three ways to associate a document template with a document library:

- ❑ **Edit the template directly and save the changes.** This is most appropriate where an existing template already exists. However it's not practical if you already have a standard organizational template available.

❏ **Upload the template to a specific location and change the URL.** In this case, you change the URL for the document library template to point to the new location. This is appropriate if you have a single location with multiple templates already, or you may want to have the document template associated with more than one document library. This method is explored in the next Try It Out.

❏ **Give your template the file name of** template.doc **and upload it to the Forms folder of the document library.** When you do this, you are prompted to overwrite the existing template, as shown in Figure 4-32. This is best for situations where you have an existing template but you only want to associate it with a single document library.

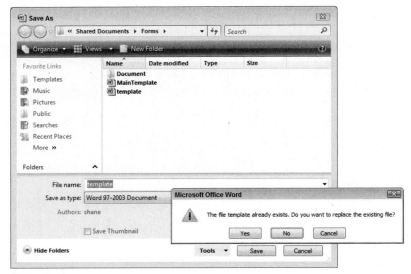

Figure 4-32

Try It Out   Associate a Custom Document Template with a Library by Changing the URL

For this example, you upload your template to a specific location and change the URL to point to a new location.

1. From the main page of your site, select View All Site Content from the Quick Launch navigation bar.

2. Select the library for which you want to enable versioning by clicking the hyperlink for its name.

3. Select Settings ➪ Document Library Settings. The Customize Shared Documents window appears, as shown in Figure 4-33.

4. Under General Settings, select the Advanced Settings link. The Document Library Advanced Settings window appears as shown in Figure 4-34.

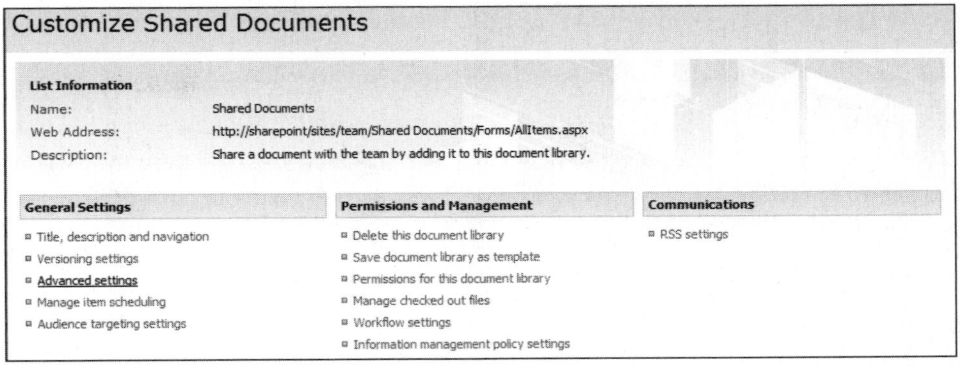

Customize Shared Documents

List Information

Name: Shared Documents

Web Address: http://sharepoint/sites/team/Shared Documents/Forms/AllItems.aspx

Description: Share a document with the team by adding it to this document library.

General Settings	Permissions and Management	Communications
▫ Title, description and navigation	▫ Delete this document library	▫ RSS settings
▫ Versioning settings	▫ Save document library as template	
▫ Advanced settings	▫ Permissions for this document library	
▫ Manage item scheduling	▫ Manage checked out files	
▫ Audience targeting settings	▫ Workflow settings	
	▫ Information management policy settings	

Figure 4-33

Team Site > Shared Documents > Settings > Advanced Settings

Document Library Advanced Settings: Shared Documents

Content Types

Specify whether to allow the management of content types on this document library. Each content type will appear on the new button and can have a unique set of columns, workflows and other behaviors.

Allow management of content types?
- ○ Yes
- ● No

Document Template

Type the address of a template to use as the basis for all new files created in this document library. When multiple content types are enabled, this setting is managed on a per content type basis. Learn how to set up a template for a library.

Template URL:

Shared Documents/Forms/template.doc
(Edit Template)

Browser-enabled Documents

Specify how to display documents that are enabled for opening both in a browser and a client application. If the client application is unavailable, these documents will always be displayed as Web pages in the browser.

Opening browser-enabled documents
- ● Open in the client application
- ○ Display as a Web page

Custom Send To Destination

Type the name and URL for a custom Send To destination that you want to appear on the context menu for this list. It is recommended that you choose a short name for the destination.

Destination name: (For example, Team Library)

URL:

Folders

Specify whether the "New Folder" command appears on the New menu. Changing this setting does not affect existing folders.

Display "New Folder" command on the New menu?
- ● Yes
- ○ No

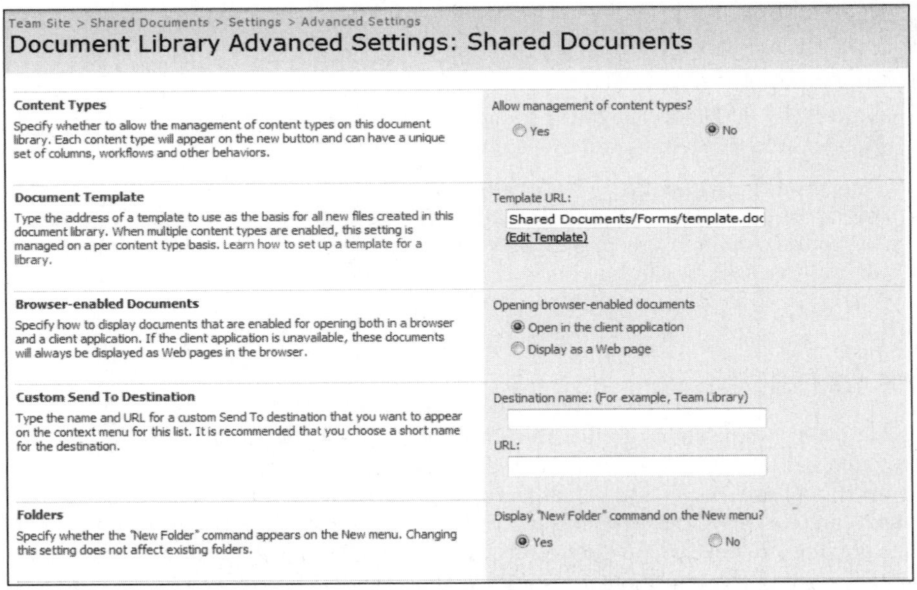

Figure 4-34

5. Under the Document Template section, you can select one of two options:

❑ Select the URL to the location of the new document template. This is useful if you have a central library of templates located on the site.

❑ Select the Edit Template hyperlink. This opens the existing template so that you can customize it by adding all the necessary elements.

6. Save your changes to the document, and close it when you finish.

7. Click OK to complete the operation.

Summary

This chapter discussed how to customize column types and views that are associated with lists and libraries. From it, you learned the following:

❑ The advantages of creating a work environment that more closely reflects the users' actual business activities. By customizing SharePoint to operate in accordance with common business processes, users can focus more on their specific work duties rather than on technology. However, it is always important to remember not to over-customize. You should only implement changes that offer value to the business and operational environment.

❑ The types of columns that you can create in SharePoint 2007 and their specific configuration alternatives. Understanding what is possible from a configuration perspective is a key element in recognizing the appropriate customization approach.

❑ The importance of a list-centric column versus a site column. Unlike list-centric columns that you must manually create on every single list in which they appear, site columns are stored in a central gallery on a SharePoint site, and are available for use on all lists and libraries of the current site and each site below it.

❑ The various view types in SharePoint and the process for creating each. This included some new view types in SharePoint 2007 such as the Gantt view and Access views, which help provide a greater level of presentation to a standard SharePoint list.

❑ The importance of working with your stakeholders to gain an understanding of their specific needs for information on specific subject areas. You then discovered how you can take all the concepts covered in this chapter to create a completely customized list in SharePoint, comprised of multiple custom columns and a custom view that can address those needs.

Exercises

You've just been assigned to customize the SharePoint site for your company's sales team. The team has struggled with having a central location that stores all information related to its various opportunities, contacts, meetings, and tasks. It has had a SharePoint site for a few months; however, the team has expressed some concerns that information is too difficult to find. The following exercises focus on ways in which you need to develop the site to become a more useful tool for the sales team.

1. After conducting a planning workshop with some members of the sales team, you determine that while the sales manager wants to see all information stored in a single location, the actual sales team members struggle with seeing too much information. As a result, it takes sales team members longer than necessary to look up contact phone numbers. The sales team prefers to only see contacts from their own region. What can you do to make both groups happy?

2. Whenever a sales person views the central list of contacts, he wants to see specific contacts which he himself has added. How would you accomplish that?

3. The sales manager wants to see a list of all opportunities that are in the pipeline for his staff. Because he has some concerns about the length of time certain sales staff members are taking to close their leads, he wants to visually identify leads that have the longest duration from the initial point of contact to the expected date of sale. What can you suggest to help address this situation?

Working with Workflow

Most businesses have processes related to specific activities and, typically, the steps of these processes are documented in procedures in a predictable manner. *Workflow* involves the various tasks that employees must complete on a business activity, and these tasks often occur in a specific order. A workflow could be something completely nontechnical, such as washing your car; however, it usually involves some level of interaction with technology mixed with human activity. Workflows in SharePoint generally focus on a specific document or list item. However, it is important to remember that the actual document may be representative of a much larger human-based process such as applying for a job or requesting vacation time.

In the 2003 release, SharePoint did not include an automated workflow engine. For many organizations, this meant purchasing third-party software solutions to get automated business process management. However, in 2007, SharePoint comes with support for automated workflow solutions built upon the *Windows Workflow Foundation*, which is Microsoft's platform for workflow development and tools. Because it is a development platform, it can be extended and customized to meet the needs of most organizations if the available solutions do not.

Because it parallels business processes and natural human activity, workflow is an important part of document management. When used correctly, it can meld automation and tasks that rely heavily on people, allowing your team to track a project's progress and keeping team members informed of their duties. In this chapter, you learn about the various levels of workflow in SharePoint 2007 including:

- ❑　A discussion of what workflow is
- ❑　The various types of workflow solutions in SharePoint 2007
- ❑　A hands-on review of the different workflow templates available in SharePoint Server
- ❑　Examples of how to create a custom workflow solution using SharePoint Designer

Types of Workflow Solutions

The expansion of workflow support in SharePoint 2007 based on the Windows Workflow Foundation provides many alternatives for organizations looking to automate business activities and drive processes through use of the SharePoint environment. To best understand how workflow can help your organization, you need to understand some basic concepts. First, you need to understand the differences between a serial and parallel workflow. You also need to understand the three different ways to create a workflow template, which you will use to build your workflow. Finally, you need understand the process behind workflow creation. Before you delve into all of this, the following explains the difference between a serial and parallel workflow:

❏ A *serial workflow* is one that allows users to participate one at a time. An example of this is an employee requesting vacation leave. The employee submits a request to his or her supervisor. The request is approved and sent to a departmental or human resources manager, and then sent to accounting or the payroll manager. Each step requires some sort of input before the next step can take place, and no steps can be interchanged.

❏ In a *parallel workflow*, multiple users can participate at the same time with individual steps being less structured and defined. An example of this is a review process where a research and development team creates a report, which is circulated around to all departmental managers for feedback and suggestions. Managers from each division can respond in whatever order they prefer, or choose not to participate. Once research and development receives an adequate amount of feedback, their team updates the report and publishes it.

Understanding the Workflow Templates

In this section, you learn about the various SharePoint workflow templates that you can adapt to your workflow. Note that if your internal processes require a specific set of activities and/or notifications that the SharePoint templates don't support, you can develop a custom workflow template using either SharePoint Designer or Custom Development. You use SharePoint Designer when the workflow centers around a specific list or library, and you do not need to reuse the template for another location. You would consider custom development if the SharePoint Designer templates don't work for you or you want to reuse the template in any list or library.

Microsoft Office SharePoint Templates

One of Microsoft Office SharePoint Server's greatest features is not available in Windows SharePoint Services — a set of workflow templates for team collaboration, content publishing, and document management. You can use these templates to create a workflow and then further customize them to suit your needs. Four templates are usually assigned to a specific document library:

❏ **Collect Feedback:** For workflows in which you want to receive feedback around specific documents or items. Although you can use this for completed items, its common use is for documents in draft form or projects in progress. This is ideal for draft material, applications, or special requests.

❏ **Collect Signatures**: For workflows that result in an approval in the form of a signature. This workflow template is designed to allow for electronic signatures in the documents via a compatible Microsoft Office application.

❏ **Approval:** For workflows that require a review team or manager to review and approve an item or document.

❏ **Disposition Approval**: For workflows that must determine how or when content will expire.

Custom List-Based Workflows Created with SharePoint Designer

For situations where you need to create a unique workflow that interacts exclusively with a single list or library and don't want to reuse this template anywhere else, you can use SharePoint Designer. *SharePoint Designer* has an intuitive wizard-type design tool that content owners and web designers use to create multi-step and interactive workflows. An example of such a workflow might be the purchasing process for your organization. You may track all purchase requests via a single list that the purchasing department manages. Using SharePoint Designer, you can create a workflow that features more customizable actions and messages than would be available using a standard SharePoint template. You can add custom messages to send to different users based on the value of a certain column. For example, if the purchase request was for something computer-related, an email might go to the head of the Information Technology group containing details on the type of computer purchase required.

SharePoint Designer is a great tool for extending and customizing the SharePoint environment; however, like any development tool, it should only be used by those with some basic design and development skills, and all custom activities should be planned and approved by business users before implementation. Later in this chapter in the "Custom Workflows with SharePoint Designer" section, you see how to use SharePoint Designer to create a workflow.

Global Workflow Templates Created by Developers

Although the SharePoint templates provide an excellent foundation for most common business activities that organizations conduct, they might not meet your needs. If you want to create additional templates beyond what SharePoint offers, you can do so using development tools and the Windows Workflow Foundation. Unlike the SharePoint Designer workflows that you will create, you can reuse these templates with any list, document library, or content type directly via the interface.

For more information on lists and document libraries, see Chapters 2 and 3. For more information on content types, see Chapter 6.

This book does not cover specific examples on creating custom workflow templates using development techniques with Visual Studio .NET.

Understanding the Workflow Creation Process

Now, you're ready to understand the basic process for creating a workflow. This process involves naming your workflow to distinguish it from other similar workflows created from the same template and associated with the same document library. You then associate your workflow with a list of tasks. Finally, you can view task history to make sure that team members are following through on what they are assigned.

Naming and Creating Workflows

When you add a workflow to a document library, you must give it a name to distinguish it from other workflows created from the same template that are tied to the same document library. For example, you can have two workflows, one for management approval and the other for document approval. The management approval workflow may be a serial workflow assigned to a departmental manager and only required for document types of strategic importance; the document approval workflow may be a simple approval process that requires members of a reviewers' group to sign off on a document before it becomes available to the rest of the team, or the review group may need to sign off on the document so that management can review it. Alternatively, you might have two workflows based on the same template that manage different document updates — one for new documents and one for existing documents that need to be edited.

Creating and Assigning a Task List

Once you have a name, you associate your workflow with a tasks list. This means you can create and assign individual tasks to users so they can complete the steps of a workflow action. To use the management approval process as an example, a division manager would be assigned a task in the tasks list of the site whenever a new document is created. If the task list is configured to send email notifications, she receives an email notifying of the task assignment. She can view task details directly from the email message, review the linked document, and launch her task for updates directly from the email message, as shown in Figure 5-1. If she does not respond to the task when she receives the initial email notification, the task is marked as incomplete on her task list until the approval decision is made.

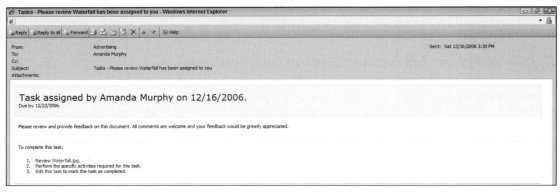

Figure 5-1

Viewing History and Tracking Progress

You can associate a history list with each workflow process to track the progress of specific activities. You view this history directly from the individual document, as shown in Figure 5-2.

You can view a history for every individual workflow process to which a document is assigned and see a listing of active tasks in addition to specific steps that have been completed on the workflow process to date. This information helps you track the progress of a specific request. Users can add comments throughout the workflow process as part of the history to explain delays or difficulties associated with a specific document.

Using Workflow Templates

To understand how to effectively use SharePoint workflow templates, this section gives you some hands-on experience. Here, you learn about the various SharePoint workflow templates and how to use each one. You create a new team site within an existing corporate intranet site collection based on the collaboration publishing site template. This gives you a location to create and practice the various workflow templates. You create this site as part of the next Try It Out and use it in the rest of the exercises in the chapter.

Advertising Team > Advertising Concepts > Workflow Status
Workflow Status: Concept Review and Feedback

Workflow Information

Initiator:	Shane Perran	Document:	Discover NL Brochure
Started:	12/20/2006 7:50 PM	Status:	In Progress
Last run:	12/20/2006 7:50 PM		

▫ Update active tasks
▫ Add or update reviewers
▫ Cancel this workflow

If an error occurs or this workflow stops responding, it can be terminated. Terminating the workflow will set its status to Canceled and will delete all tasks created by the workflow.
▫ Terminate this workflow now.

Tasks

The following tasks have been assigned to the participants in this workflow. Click a task to edit it. You can also view these tasks in the list Tasks.

Assigned To	Title	Due Date	Status	Outcome
Shane Perran	Please review Discover NL Brochure ! NEW	12/28/2006	Not Started	
SHAREPOINT\amandam	Please review Discover NL Brochure ! NEW	12/28/2006	Not Started	

Workflow History

▫ View workflow reports
The following events have occurred in this workflow.

Date Occurred	Event Type	User ID	Description	Outcome
12/20/2006 7:50 PM	Workflow Initiated	Shane Perran	Concept Review and Feedback was started. Participants: Shane Perran, SHAREPOINT\amandam	
12/20/2006 7:50 PM	Task Created	Shane Perran	Task created for Shane Perran. Due by: 12/28/2006 12:00:00 AM	
12/20/2006 7:50 PM	Task Created	Shane Perran	Task created for SHAREPOINT\amandam. Due by: 12/28/2006 12:00:00 AM	

Figure 5-2

Collect Feedback Workflow

At the completion of a project, or when a specific item or document is in the process of being produced, team members may want feedback from other team members or management. For example, an advertising group may be working on a new ad campaign for a travel resort, where it has come up with new concepts for the brochure and print advertising materials. Team members can upload their work to the SharePoint site and submit them for colleagues to review to generate feedback. SharePoint stores all feedback in the workflow history so that the group can update its documents in response to colleagues' edits. But this workflow isn't just for draft materials feedback; it's also useful for document libraries that contain applications or special requests.

The first Try It Out reflects the fact that many materials in the concept stage do not necessarily follow the same goals from start to finish, but instead reshape and reform based on the feedback. Therefore, it is more effective to keep all items in this stage of the process in a single location. In the second Try It Out, you find out how to manually start the workflow process related to a document in a library, which involves assigning tasks and reviewers. After you've launched a workflow, you can still add more reviewers and tasks that you've accidentally overlooked or in cases where a reviewer goes on vacation and you want to reallocate tasks. The third and fourth Try It Outs cover how to add a reviewer to an existing workflow and then how to reassign an existing workflow task to another user.

Try It Out   **Associate a Feedback Workflow Template with a Document Library**

In this example, you create a new team site for an advertising department to help facilitate and encourage communication around a new marketing campaign. For the promotional material to be successful, the team needs to examine all possible interpretations the content might have. To help this collaborative feedback process, you associate the workflow template with a document library.

First, you create a new collaborative team site for the advertising team and a new library for storing materials for initial conceptual and pre-release states. You will then enter document library settings to configure your workflow. For example, you will set the workflow to launch upon an author's request. You could select to have the request launch immediately, but in this example, there could be a lag time between the document's submission and review. You also do not specify the reviewers for the document because the document owners may want to specify this information when launching the workflow. You will create this workflow as a parallel workflow because you want to assign multiple people at once to allow document owners to receive feedback from more than one person at a time. You associate the workflow tasks with the default task list so that you can store all tasks for the advertising team in a single list. This cuts down on the number of locations you are required to review and update later in the process. Using views and filters, you can accomplish any additional separation of tasks.

Finally, you will associate a history list with your workflow so you can track all activity related to your document in a single location. This allows team members to view feedback as well as the current status of the material.

1. From your Corporate Intranet site, select Sites from the top navigation menu.

    For more on setting up a Corporate Intranet site using a collaboration publishing template, see Chapter 8.

2. Select the Create Site tab. The New SharePoint Site window appears, as shown in Figure 5-3.

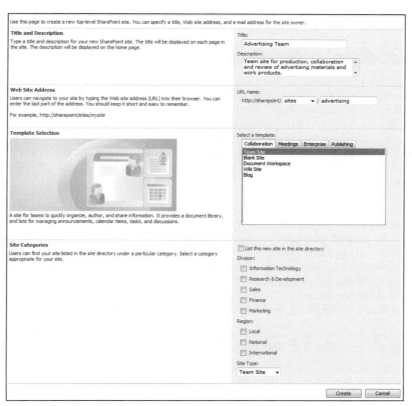

Figure 5-3

3. Type a title and description for the site. For this example, enter **Advertising Team** and for the description enter the following:

> **Team site for production, collaboration, and review of advertising materials and work products.**

4. Enter a URL for the site. For this example, enter **advertising**.

5. Select the Team Site template from the Collaboration tab.

6. Retain all other default settings and click the Create button. Your site is created, and you are redirected to it.

7. Within your new team site, you want to create a new document library for storing advertising materials that are still in the concept stage. Select Create from the Site Actions menu.

8. Select Document Library.

9. For the properties of your document library, specify the following:

Property	Value
Name	Advertising Concepts
Description	Document library for storing in progress concepts and materials related to upcoming campaigns
Display this item in Quick Launch?	Yes
Create a version each time you edit a file in this document library?	Yes
Document Template	Microsoft Office Word document

10. Click the Create button.

11. Select Document Library Settings from the Settings toolbar menu. The Document Library Settings page appears.

12. Select Workflow Settings. The Workflow Settings page appears.

13. Select the Collect Feedback template for the Workflow activity as shown in Figure 5-4.

14. Enter a name for the workflow. For this example, enter **Concept Review and Feedback**.

15. For Task List and History List, retain the default list name settings.

16. For Start Options, select the Allow This Workflow to be Manually Started by an Authenticated User with Edit Items Permissions option.

17. Click the Next button. You are redirected to the next page of the workflow creation process.

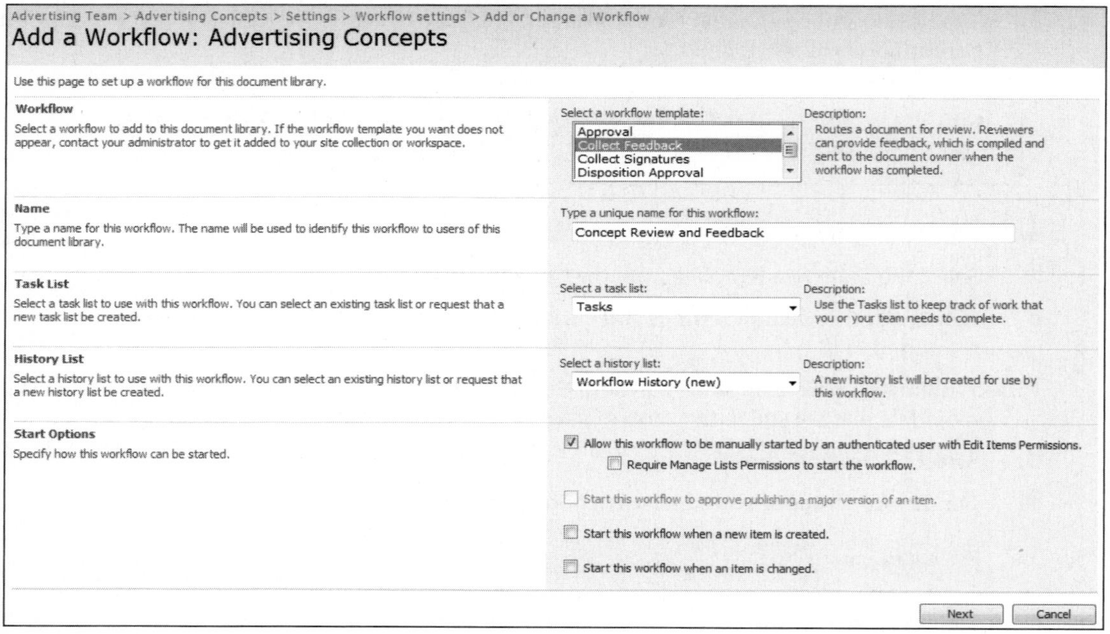

Figure 5-4

18. For the workflow tasks, select to assign tasks to All Participants Simultaneously (Parallel) and retain the selection to allow users to Reassign the Task and Request Changes.

19. Do not specify any names for the Reviewers field.

20. Enter the following for a message:

> **Please review and provide feedback on this document. All comments are welcome and your feedback would be greatly appreciated.**

21. Click the OK button at the bottom of the page to save your workflow settings for the Advertising Concepts library.

Try It Out   Launch a Feedback Workflow Instance

In this exercise, you upload new content to the Advertising Concepts document library that you created in the previous Try It Out. This new campaign is for tourists who are considering traveling to Newfoundland and Labrador on Canada's east coast. You upload a new brochure that the company wants to give to travel agencies throughout the world. The brochure is in the early stages, and your team needs feedback on the layout, text, and images. For this reason, you launch an instance of the Concept Review and Feedback workflow that you created in the last Try It Out. When you created this workflow in the last example, you did not specify the reviewers. This is so that the user launching the workflow could select the reviewers.

By default, the message related to this workflow process is the same as the one you selected to configure the workflow. You can change this message to suit the specific objective of this review. For example, you can say you're looking for input on the layout of the brochure so that the reviewers know what is required of them.

In this example, you select a due date to receive feedback by a certain deadline. By default, the task list associated with the workflow process sends an email message to reviewers when they are assigned to a task. Setting a due date ensures that the assigned reviewers will receive an email reminder if their task is not marked as complete by the deadline.

1. From the Advertising Concepts document library created in the previous example, select Upload from the toolbar.

2. Browse the location of resources for this chapter that you downloaded from the website and select the "Discover NL Brochure" document for upload.

3. Click the OK button.

4. Hover your cursor over the document in the document library to expose the drop-down menu shown in Figure 5-5.

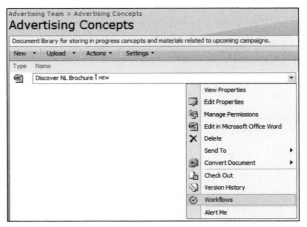

Figure 5-5

5. Select Workflows.

6. Select Concept Review and Feedback from the list of three workflows available from within this library.

7. Enter the names of people who you would like to review the document. Select at least two users. If you do not know the exact names of the users, you can select the Reviews button to perform a search and selection.

8. For Due Date, select a day that is approximately one week from the current date.

9. For the Notify Others field, enter your own name.

10. Click the Start button.

11. Select the Tasks list from the Quick Launch navigation bar.

How It Works

Once you successfully launched the workflow, you can jump to the Tasks list of the site and view individual tasks assigned to each of the reviewers. Reviewers receive tasks and email notifications. In addition, on the due date, you receive an email telling you what team members are assigned to the workflow task with a link to view the current status of the workflow activity. An example of the email message is shown in Figure 5-6.

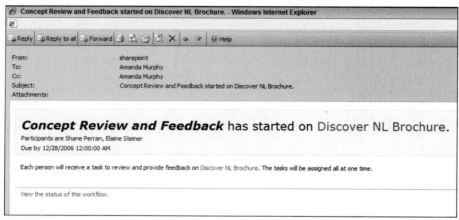

Figure 5-6

Try It Out   **Add a Reviewer to an Existing Workflow Activity**

In this example, you learn how to add new reviewers to an existing document. To do this, you return to the workflow interface associated with the document. Notice that you can no longer select a new instance of the Concept Review and Feedback workflow process because it is already associated with your document and you can only have one instance of a specific workflow activity running on a document at a time. However, you can launch different workflow activities from the same document while another is running.

Adding a new user is very similar to the process you used for originally setting up the workflow activity. You can either enter the name of the user directly into the field, or you can select the To button to search and select specific users from the server's address book.

As you add a new reviewer to the existing workflow process, note that the due date information is already there. You could set a unique due date for this reviewer; however, you generally keep the existing due date specified for the activity to keep the workflow on the original schedule.

1. From your Advertising Concepts document library, hover you cursor over the Discover NL Brochure that you uploaded in the previous Try It Out, and select Workflows from the drop-down menu.

2. From the running workflows section of the page, select Concept Review and Feedback. The Workflow Status window appears, as shown in Figure 5-7.

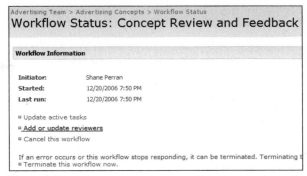

Figure 5-7

3. From the Workflow Information section, select the Add or Update Reviewers link.

4. Enter your own name in the To field so that you can assign yourself as a reviewer of the document.

5. Click the Update button.

How It Works

A new task is created for you in the workflow's task list. An email message is also generated automatically and sent to you to notify you of the new assignment. An example of this message is shown in Figure 5-8.

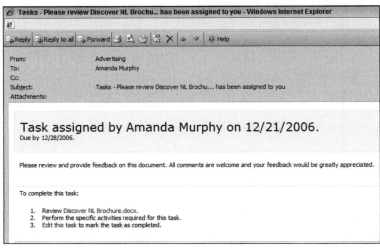

Figure 5-8

From the task assignment notification email, you can click a link to jump directly to the document you have been assigned to review. Alternatively, you can select a link to edit the details of the assigned task.

Try It Out   Assign a Workflow Task to Another User

What if, after assigning someone to a task, you must reassign it to someone else? Perhaps you are unqualified to complete the task or maybe you will be out of the office and unable to complete your assignment. The following example illustrates how to reassign a task when you discover that another member of your team is better suited to give feedback on the travel campaign created in the first Try It Out.

By selecting the reassign task link, you can either assign a task back to the workflow owner or another person. You might select the owner when you feel that you cannot complete the assigned task and you do not know who the best person is to suggest. In this case, the owner receives a notification and can ask someone else to complete the task. For this example, you change the task assignment to another person because you have a specific individual in mind to take over responsibility on the task.

To start this process, you use the email message that was generated as a result of the last Try It Out as follows:

1.   From the notification email you received related to the task assignment from the previous exercise, click the Edit This Task button from the menu bar. A new window appears.

2.   Select the Reassign Task hyperlink at bottom of the page. A window appears, as shown in Figure 5-9.

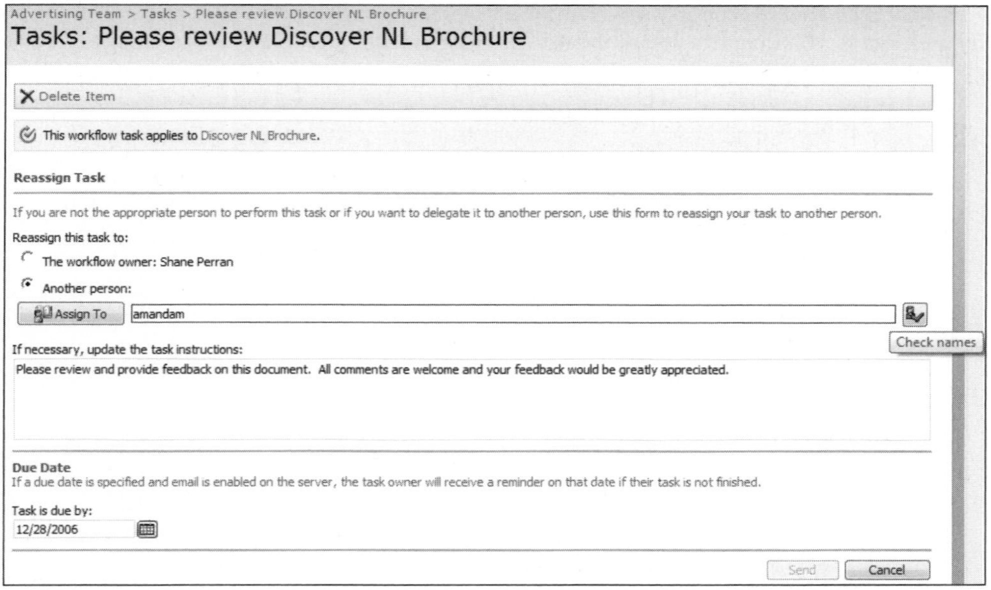

Figure 5-9

3. Click the option that assigns the task to another person, and enter the name of the person to whom you want to assign the task. Click the Check Names button on the right to associate the name you entered with the correct user account.

4. For the task message, change the message to read as follows:

> **Please review this document and provide feedback by the assigned deadline. Based on your specific experience with this customer, I feel you would be able to provide excellent insight on our approach with this campaign.**

5. Click the Send button.

How It Works

After you complete the task reassignment, you should return to the All Items view of the task list. This list now shows that the task is assigned to the new person. In addition, if you return to the Advertising Concepts library and select the Concept Review and Feedback status link associated with the document, you see that the workflow history is updated to display the task delegation along with the reassignment message you had entered. An example of this is shown in Figure 5-10.

Workflow History				
≡ View workflow reports				
The following events have occurred in this workflow.				
Date Occurred	Event Type	User ID	Description	Outcome
4/26/2007 3:46 PM	Workflow Initiated	Amanda Murphy	Concept Review and Feedback was started. Participants: Benjamin Walker, Elaine Steiner	
4/26/2007 3:46 PM	Task Created	Amanda Murphy	Task created for Benjamin Walker. Due by: 5/3/2007 12:00:00 AM	
4/26/2007 3:46 PM	Task Created	Amanda Murphy	Task created for Elaine Steiner. Due by: 5/3/2007 12:00:00 AM	
4/26/2007 3:46 PM	Task Created	Amanda Murphy	Task created for Amanda Murphy. Due by: 5/3/2007 12:00:00 AM	
4/26/2007 3:46 PM	Comment	Amanda Murphy	Participants for Concept Review and Feedback on Discover NL Brochure were updated by Amanda Murphy. New participants: Amanda Murphy	
4/26/2007 3:48 PM	Task Completed	Amanda Murphy	Task assigned to Amanda Murphy was delegated by Amanda Murphy. Comments: Please review this document and provide feedback by the assigned deadline. Based on your specific experience with this customer, I feel you would be able to provide excellent ins...	Delegated by Amanda Murphy to Shane Perran
4/26/2007 3:48 PM	Task Created	Amanda Murphy	Task created for Shane Perran. Due by: 5/3/2007 12:00:00 AM	

Figure 5-10

Collect Signatures Workflow

For legal or internal reasons, you may need to have a person of authority sign off on a document or request. For that reason, SharePoint offers a workflow template to collect signatures that you can launch from within a Microsoft Office client application such as Word, Excel, or PowerPoint. By allowing users to sign the document directly, you maintain the document's integrity and have the benefits of storing the document in the central document management system. In addition, when you use a custom workflow process, you can launch a new activity that can move or send the document to a new location or recipient for further processing.

The fact that this workflow template works only with Microsoft Office applications makes the template different from the other templates in this chapter; you cannot select workflows based on this template from the document's drop-down menu and then initiate a Collect Signatures workflow as you did with the Collect Feedback workflow, nor can you configure a document library to have this workflow initiated automatically whenever someone adds a new document. The workflow instance can only be launched from the Microsoft Office application.

This section has three Try It Outs to familiarize you with the Collect Signatures workflow. In the next Try It Out, you configure a document library for the Collect Signatures workflow so that you can later use it to gather signatures from your advertising account managers for new client agreements generated from the site. In the second Try It Out, you add a signature line to a document template so that a manager can sign off on the document. Once you add a template that supports a handwritten or digital signature to the document library, you can create new documents from that template and launch the workflow process, as illustrated in the final Try It Out. The user can sign the document using Ink. *Ink* is special functionality built in to Microsoft Office applications to support the use of signing, annotating, and drawing with a digital pen such as one that might be used with a Tablet PC.

Try It Out **Associate a Collect Signatures Workflow Template with a Document Library**

The Collect Signatures workflow template allows certain Microsoft Office applications to accept user signatures in documents that have a signature line. In the next exercise, you modify a Word document template to include a signature line where an Account Manager would sign to accept a client agreement. You then upload this template to the document library so that you can use it in a later example to collect a signature as part of the workflow process.

1. From the home page of the Advertising Team site, select Site Actions ➪ Create.

2. Select Document Library from the Libraries group. You are redirected to the document library creation page.

3. Type the document library name and a description. For this example, type **Client Agreements** for the document library name and enter the following description:

> **Use this library to create new client agreements based on a standard template and organize existing agreements.**

4. Select Yes to display the document library on the Quick Launch navigation bar.

5. Select Yes to create a new version every time you edit the document.

6. For Document Template, select Microsoft Office Word Document from the drop-down. You could also select a different template if you wanted; however, in this example you are working with a Word template.

7. Click the Create button. Your document library is created, and you are redirected to it.

8. Select Settings ➪ Document Library Settings. You are redirected to the Document Library Settings page.

9. Select Workflow Settings from the Permissions and Management options to go to the Add a Workflow window, shown in Figure 5-11.

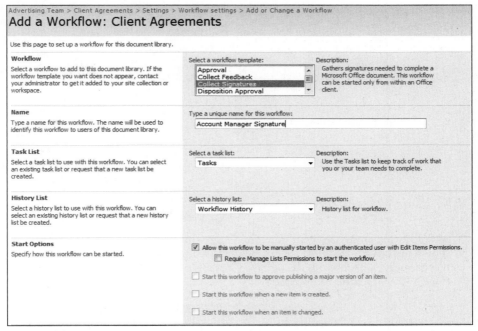

Figure 5-11

10. Select the Collect Signatures workflow template.

11. Enter a workflow name. For this example, enter **Account Manager Signature**.

12. Click the OK button at the bottom of the page to complete the workflow creation process.

Try It Out   **Add a Signature Line to a Document Template**

In this example, you modify a Word document template by inserting a signature line so your Account Manager can sign his signature on client agreements. You then upload this new document template to the Client Agreements document library so that you can have users sign it as part of the Account Manager Signature workflow process that is based upon the Collect Signatures workflow template.

To complete this example, you need the document included as part of this chapter's resources called clientagreement.docx.

1. Open the document stored within this chapter's resources called clientagreement.docx in Microsoft Word 2007.

2. Place the cursor at the very bottom of the document.

3. Select the Insert tab from the Ribbon. A menu appears, as shown in Figure 5-12.

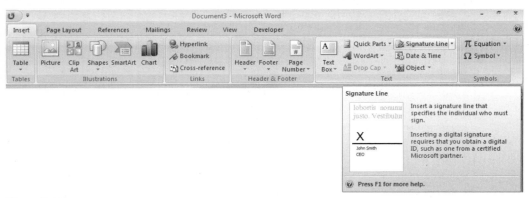

Figure 5-12

4. Select the Signature Line item from the Text group. The Signature Setup dialog box appears, as shown in Figure 5-13. If this is your first time using this option, you may also see a warning window appear before this dialog box. Click OK on the warning window so that you can continue to the Signature Setup window.

Figure 5-13

5. Enter the title of the person who will be providing the signature in the Suggested Signer's Title field. For this example, enter **Account Manager**. You could also optionally prepopulate the name of the person who would be signing the document, which would insert their name underneath the signature line in the document.

6. Select the check box to Allow the Signer to Add Comments in the Sign Dialog box.

7. Check the "Show Sign Date" box.

8. Click the OK button.

9. Save changes to the document.

10. Return to the Client Agreements document library on the Advertising Team site and select Open with Windows Explorer from the Actions menu.

11. Double-click the Forms folder. If you do not see the Forms Folder, you may need to turn on the ability to view Hidden Files and Folders in your Windows Explorer settings.

12. Copy the clientagreement.docx file into the Forms folder.

13. Close the Windows Explorer view window and return to the document library of the Advertising Team site.

14. Select Settings ⇨ Document Library Settings.

15. Select Advanced settings. The Document Library Advanced Settings window appears, as shown in Figure 5-14.

Advertising Team > Client Agreements > Settings > Advanced Settings

Document Library Advanced Settings: Client Agreements

Content Types Specify whether to allow the management of content types on this document library. Each content type will appear on the new button and can have a unique set of columns, workflows and other behaviors.	Allow management of content types? ○ Yes ◉ No
Document Template Type the address of a template to use as the basis for all new files created in this document library. When multiple content types are enabled, this setting is managed on a per content type basis. Learn how to set up a template for a library.	Template URL: greements/Forms/clientagreement.docx (Edit Template)
Browser-enabled Documents Specify how to display documents that are enabled for opening both in a browser and a client application. If the client application is unavailable, these documents will always be displayed as Web pages in the browser.	Opening browser-enabled documents ◉ Open in the client application ○ Display as a Web page

Figure 5-14

16. For Template URL, change the end portion of the URL from template.dotx to clientagreement.docx.

17. Click the OK button. You have now changed the document template associated with your library to your custom signature template.

Try It Out   **Launch a Collect Signatures Workflow from a Document**

In this example, you create a new document based upon the custom client agreement template you created in the last Try It Out. As the person responsible for the users' SharePoint experiences, it's effective and timesaving to associate document templates with libraries that contain the elements that users need so they can focus on creating new content rather than recreating everything from scratch. For this example, having templates that contain the most common and shared elements of a typical agreement allows clients to receive a signed and completed agreement much sooner than if the account manager had to create the agreement from scratch, and eliminates the chances for human error associated with element omissions. Once you save the client agreement and it's ready for signing, you launch the Account Manager Signature workflow process. This opens a new window requesting further information to complete the workflow process, such as who the required signer is.

1. From the toolbar of your Client Agreement document library, click the New button. You may receive a dialog warning box. If so, click the OK button to continue.

2. A new blank client agreement opens for you to complete. Once you have made the desired changes to the document, click the Office button to expose the menu shown in Figure 5-15.

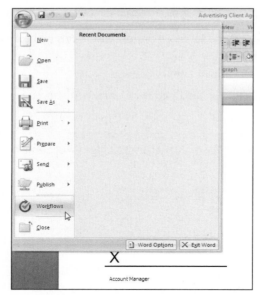

Figure 5-15

3. Select Workflows. You will receive a warning stating that the document must be saved.

If the Workflows option does not appear in the menu as shown in the figure, you may not be using a version of Microsoft Word 2007 that supports this SharePoint integration feature. This feature is only available in Enterprise versions of the application.

4. Click Yes to save the document.

5. Enter the file name for the file. For this example, enter **Client 123456.** Click the Save button.

6. From the listing of available workflow processes, find the Account Manager Signature workflow process and click the Start button.

7. Enter the username of the person that you want to sign the document as shown in Figure 5-16 and click the Start button.

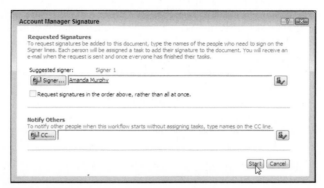

Figure 5-16

How It Works

Once you specify the signers for a document, those users receive an email message requesting their signature on the document. An example of that email message is shown in Figure 5-17.

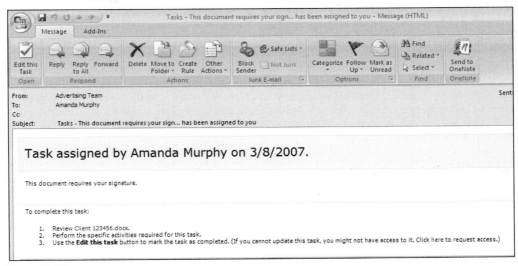

Figure 5-17

In addition, SharePoint creates a task in the central team task list to notify users that their input is required. From either the email message or the task, signers can click a link to open the document and to access a special interface, allowing them to upload an image of their signature or sign the document using Microsoft Office's built-in Ink functionality. An example of this interface is seen in Figure 5-18.

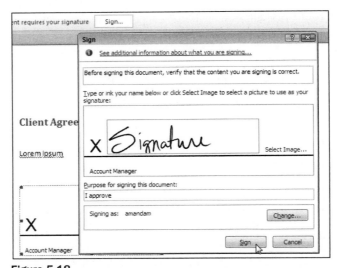

Figure 5-18

Approval Workflow

Commonly, when you collaborate with others on a document, you must obtain approval from other colleagues or a superior, which in SharePoint 2007 means using the Approval workflow. With this workflow, you can assign content to specific team members for review and the document is pending until they approve it. Like the previous workflow templates, the Approval template supports integration with a tasks list as well as Workflow History, and you can make the process either serial or parallel.

This section presents three Try It Outs to explore the Approval workflow. For the first Try It Out, you configure the Client Agreements document library to launch an approval workflow process every time a new agreement is added. New agreements require an Account Manager's approval before they are official or active so that the approver can identify any required change. In the second Try It Out, you see how to handle change requests in the event that your approvers find mistakes or edits on the document under consideration. The final Try It Out shows you how to remove an approval workflow once you decide it is no longer necessary.

Try It Out   Associate an Approval Workflow with a Document Library

In this example, you add a new workflow to the Client Agreement document library to track the approval of specific client agreements. You decide whether the process is serial or parallel. For a parallel process, any one member of the approving group can complete the approval process. Alternatively, the document can be approved only after a specific number of members approve it. For example, if you have five managers in the Approvers group, you can designate that you only need three managers to approve the document to complete the process.

For the purposes of this example, you specify that the request for approval be sent to the site's built-in Approvers group — the Account Managers group — but in real life, you can associate the Approvers group with another site group.

1. From the toolbar of the Client Agreements library, select Settings ➪ Document Library Settings.

2. Select Workflow settings from the Permissions and Management options. The Change Workflow Settings window appears, as shown in Figure 5-19.

3. Click the Add a Workflow link. You are redirected to an Add a Workflow page.

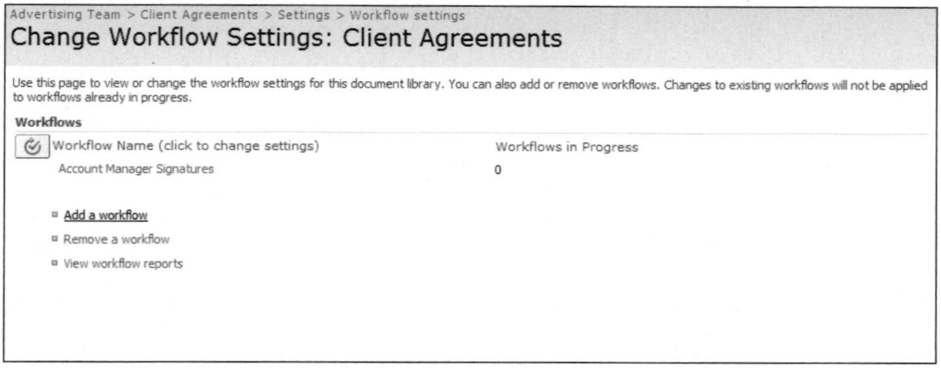

Advertising Team > Client Agreements > Settings > Workflow settings
Change Workflow Settings: Client Agreements

Use this page to view or change the workflow settings for this document library. You can also add or remove workflows. Changes to existing workflows will not be applied to workflows already in progress.

Workflows

Workflow Name (click to change settings)	Workflows in Progress
Account Manager Signatures	0

▫ **Add a workflow**
▫ Remove a workflow
▫ View workflow reports

Figure 5-19

4. Select Approval for the workflow template.

5. Enter a unique name of the workflow. For this example, enter **Account Manager Approval**.

6. Select the check box to start this workflow when a new item is created.

7. Click the Next button. You are redirected to a page where additional details are specified related to your new workflow.

8. Select to Assign Tasks to All Participants Simultaneously (Parallel).

9. Keep the check boxes selected to all workflow participants to reassign the task to another person and request a change before completing the task.

10. In the Default Workflow Start Values section, click the Approvers button. The Add Recipients – Webpage Dialog appears, as shown in Figure 5-20.

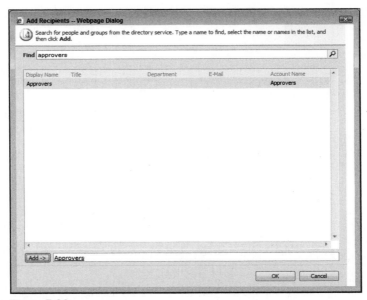

Figure 5-20

11. In the Find Box, search for Approvers.

12. Select the Approvers group that is returned and click the Add button.

13. Click the OK button.

14. Enter the following message to be included with each request:

> **Please review and approve this new client agreement.**

15. Click the OK button.

Try It Out   Request a Change in an Active Workflow

Commonly, for a document to be approved, you need to correct errors, typos, or generally edit the material. For this reason, SharePoint supports changes you make to your active approval workflow. In this example, an account manager notices a spelling error in a customer's name. The incorrect spelling would make the client agreement invalid or offend the customer.

1. From the Client Agreements document library, click the New button.

2. Save the document as **Client 123457.docx**.

3. Close the document.

4. Click the Tasks link in the Quick Launch navigation bar. The Tasks list appears, as shown in Figure 5-21.

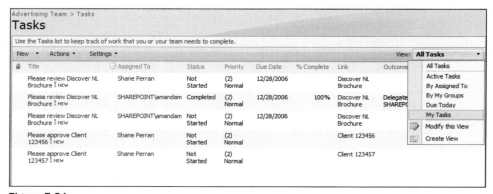

Figure 5-21

5. Change the view of the Tasks list to My Tasks.

6. Select the Task named "Please approve Client 123457."

7. Select the Request a Change link. The task's Request a Change window appears, as shown in Figure 5-22.

8. In the Type Your Request text box, enter a description of your request. For this example, enter the following:

> **The client's name is spelled incorrectly. Please verify correct spelling of name and resubmit for approval.**

9. Set the due date to be one day from the current date.

10. Click the Send button.

11. Select the new task created called "A change has been requested on Client 123457."

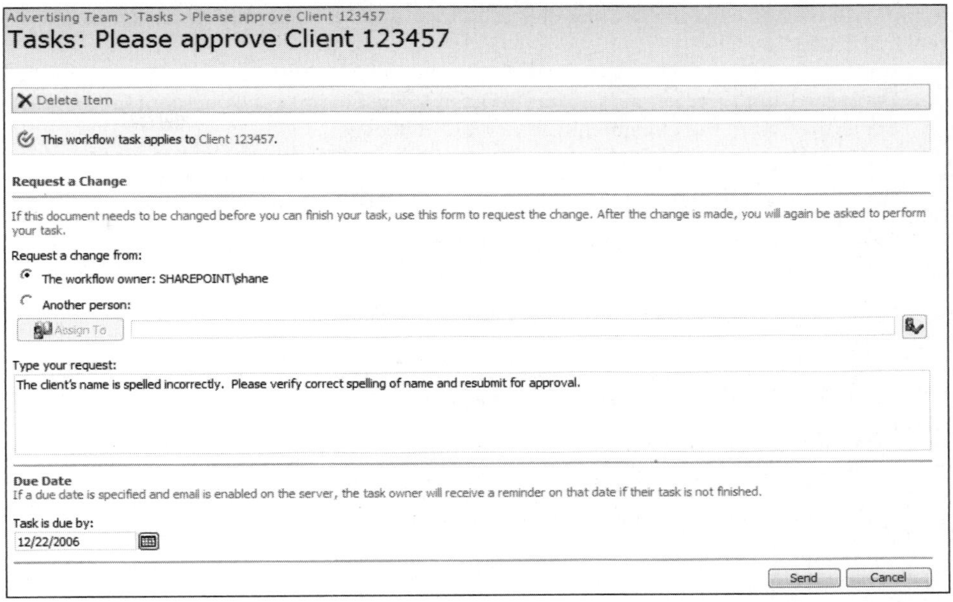

Advertising Team > Tasks > Please approve Client 123457

Tasks: Please approve Client 123457

✕ Delete Item

⊘ This workflow task applies to Client 123457.

Request a Change

If this document needs to be changed before you can finish your task, use this form to request the change. After the change is made, you will again be asked to perform your task.

Request a change from:

⦿ The workflow owner: SHAREPOINT\shane

○ Another person:

[📇 Assign To] [_____] 📇

Type your request:

The client's name is spelled incorrectly. Please verify correct spelling of name and resubmit for approval.

Due Date

If a due date is specified and email is enabled on the server, the task owner will receive a reminder on that date if their task is not finished.

Task is due by:

12/22/2006 [📅]

[Send] [Cancel]

Figure 5-22

12. Enter the following for a response:

> **This has been resolved. Sorry for mistake.**

13. Click the Send Response button.

How It Works

When a change was requested, the original task that was created for the approver was marked as complete and a new task was created for the document's author. Once the author makes the requested change and marks the task as complete, the workflow engine reinitiates the original approval request and creates a new task for the approver to either approve or reject. SharePoint automatically delegates tasks to ensure that no items "slip through the cracks" and that people are continuously aware of what actions are required of them.

Try It Out **Remove a Workflow from a Library**

In some cases, after adding a workflow process to a library, list, or content type, you may later decide that it isn't necessary. In an earlier Try It Out in this section, you associated a Collect Signatures workflow process and an approval workflow process with our Client Agreements document library, but you now discover that because the account managers essentially approved the client agreement by signing it, the workflow for approving the document within the library is no longer necessary, so you need to remove this process.

1. From the Client Agreements library toolbar, select Settings ➪ Document Library Settings. You are redirected to the Document Library Settings page.

2. Select Workflow Settings from the Permissions and Management options. You are redirected to the workflow settings page for the Client Agreements library.

3. Select the Remove a Workflow link. The Remove Workflows window appears as shown in Figure 5-23.

4. For the Account Manager Approval workflow, select the Remove option.

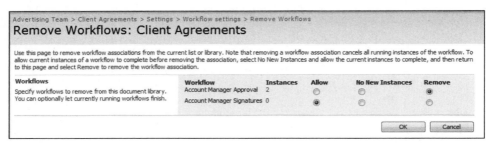

Figure 5-23

5. Click the OK button. Your workflow is permanently removed from the document library. If you decide later that you want to use the workflow again, you must recreate it.

Translation Management Workflow

The *translation management library* is a special workflow template for managing processes related to the translation of documents and content into other languages. Although you can use SharePoint 2007 to create a portal that supports content in multiple languages using variations, which is something you'll learn about in Chapter 13, many organizations initially create content in a single language and assign it to translators or content specialists to create the information in alternate languages. This process has a series of common steps no matter how the organization operates.

Step	Activity
Step One	The production and development team creates a product specification document in English.
Step Two	Management reviews the document and approves it for release.
Step Three	The English version of the document is published to the portal site.
Step Four	A copy of the document is emailed or delivered to a translator for replication in French.
Step Five	The French version of the document is published to the portal site.

Steps 1 through 3 are very similar to some of the collecting feedback and approval workflow scenarios discussed earlier in this chapter related to collecting feedback or approval related to content with the added process of translating content in another language.

The next three Try It Outs show you how to work with the Translation Management workflow. In the first Try It Out, you create a translation management library so your advertising team can generate advertisements and brochures in multiple languages. The second Try It Out shows you how to configure a translator list so you can translate content from English to Spanish and French. In the third Try It Out, you upload a document and launch the translation management workflow process. This assigns the document to translators, so the content can be converted to Spanish and French.

Try It Out   Create a Translation Management Document Library

As you create a new translation management library, you are automatically walked through a series of steps that allow you to configure a property on the Creation page. In the other Try It Outs in this chapter, when you added a workflow to a document library, you had to configure the properties of the workflow as a completely separate step. However, because the translation management library is very much dependent on the workflow template for translation management, you create the library and configure the workflow together.

In the following example, you create new lists to track tasks and the workflow history. In previous workflows, you used a single task and history list to minimize the number of locations storing workflow activities and information, but in this example, because the translation process is completely separate from all other activities taking place on the site, you create a separate task and history list.

To follow the next example, you must use a site template that has the Translation Management feature enabled. The team site for this example should have this feature activated by default. If the site you are using does not have a translation management library option available, you may need to activate the Translation Management Library site feature in the Site Features section of the Site Settings of the site, as shown in Figure 5-24.

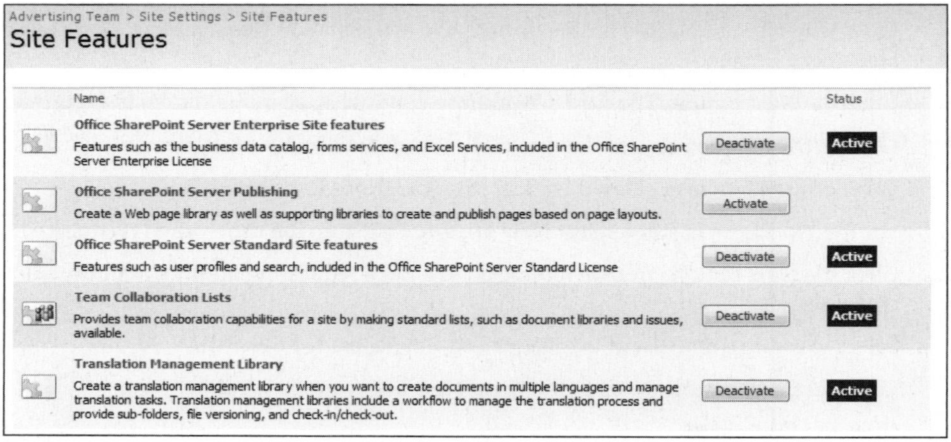

Figure 5-24

1. From the home page of the Advertising Team site, select Site Actions ⇨ Create. The Create window appears as shown in Figure 5-25.

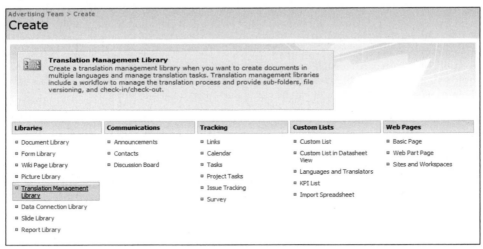

Figure 5-25

2. Select the Translation Management Library link from the Libraries group. You are redirected to the library creation page.

3. Enter **Advertising Materials** for the library name and enter the following for a description:

> **A location for storing published versions of advertising materials in both English and Spanish languages.**

4. Ensure that Yes is selected for the option Add a Translation Management Workflow to this Document Library.

5. Click the Next button. The Add a Workflow window appears, as shown in Figure 5-26.

6. Change the unique name of the workflow to **Advertisement Management**.

7. For the Tasks list, select New Task List from the drop-down menu.

8. For the Workflow History, select New History List from the drop-down menu.

9. Click the Next button. You are redirected to a page requesting additional information for the workflow.

10. Select to create a new list of languages and translators for this workflow.

11. Unselect the check box to open the translators list in a new window.

12. Click the OK button.

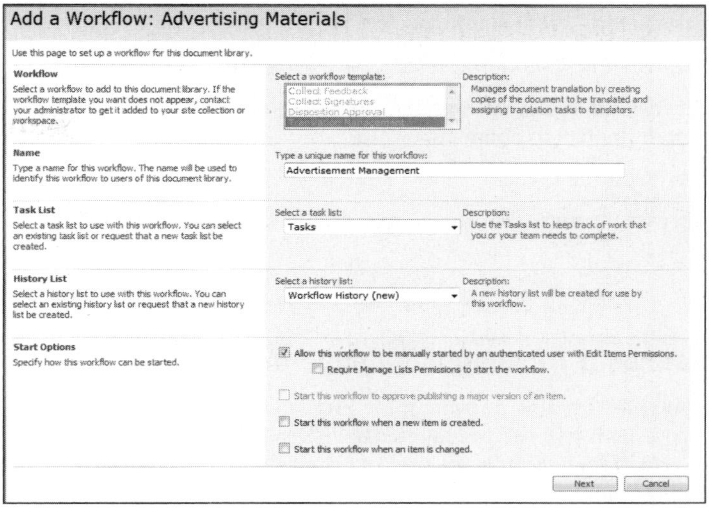

Add a Workflow: Advertising Materials

Use this page to set up a workflow for this document library.

Workflow
Select a workflow to add to this document library. If the workflow template you want does not appear, contact your administrator to get it added to your site collection or workspace.

Select a workflow template:
Collect Feedback
Collect Signatures
Disposition Approval

Description:
Manages document translation by creating copies of the document to be translated and assigning translation tasks to translators.

Name
Type a name for this workflow. The name will be used to identify this workflow to users of this document library.

Type a unique name for this workflow:
Advertisement Management

Task List
Select a task list to use with this workflow. You can select an existing task list or request that a new task list be created.

Select a task list:
Tasks

Description:
Use the Tasks list to keep track of work that you or your team needs to complete.

History List
Select a history list to use with this workflow. You can select an existing history list or request that a new history list be created.

Select a history list:
Workflow History (new)

Description:
A new history list will be created for use by this workflow.

Start Options
Specify how this workflow can be started.

☑ Allow this workflow to be manually started by an authenticated user with Edit Items Permissions.
☐ Require Manage Lists Permissions to start the workflow.

☐ Start this workflow to approve publishing a major version of an item.

☐ Start this workflow when a new item is created.

☐ Start this workflow when an item is changed.

[Next] [Cancel]

Figure 5-26

Try It Out   Configure a List of Translators and Languages

The translator list identifies and tracks the individuals responsible for translating content from one language to another. The workflow process refers to this list when it needs to determine for which user(s) to create the task for translating content from one language to another. For this example, you want to automate the process so that English content can be translated to Spanish and French. You, therefore, create a translator list item for each language to which a document is translated.

1. Select View All Site Content from the Quick Launch navigation bar.

2. Select the Translators list.

3. Click the New button. The Translators: New Item window appears, as shown in Figure 5-27.

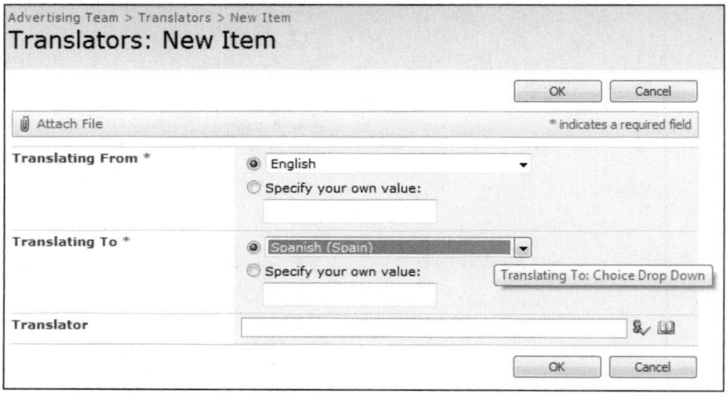

Advertising Team > Translators > New Item
Translators: New Item

[OK] [Cancel]

📎 Attach File   * indicates a required field

Translating From *
  ● English
  ○ Specify your own value:

Translating To *
  ● Spanish (Spain)
  ○ Specify your own value:
        Translating To: Choice Drop Down

Translator

[OK] [Cancel]

Figure 5-27

4. For the Translating From column, select English.

5. For the Translating To column, select Spanish (Spain).

6. For the Translator, select the name of a user on your site who is responsible for translating the content from English to Spanish.

7. Click the OK button.

8. Repeat steps 3 through 7 for each additional language you wish to translate content for such as French.

Try It Out   **Launch a Translation Management Workflow**

In this example, you create a new document (an English advertisement for a client) in your document library. The advertisement will run in magazines in North America and, therefore, should be available in English, Spanish, and French. Your team speaks primarily English, so the team creates content in that language first and lets language specialists translate it into the other languages. To do this, you save the document in English. You then launch the workflow process. Two new versions of the document are created — one for French and one for Spanish — and a task is in the Advertisement Translation Tasks list. From this list, the team can assign the translator for each language.

1. From the Advertising Materials document library, click the New button from the toolbar. This launches a new document, as shown in Figure 5-28.

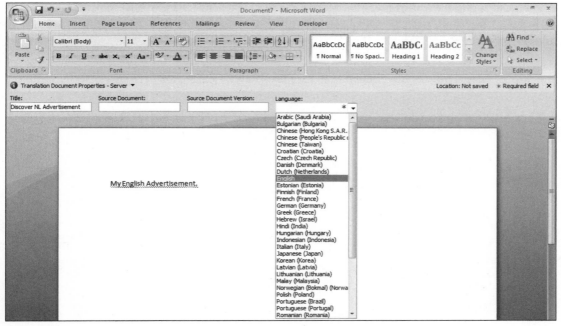

Figure 5-28

2. Enter the following text in the document:

> **My English Advertisement.**

3. In the Document Information Panel, enter a title and select English for the language of the document. This example uses **Discover NL Advertisement** for title.

4. Save the document as **Discover NL Advertisement.docx** and close the document.

5. Hover your cursor over the document and select workflows from the drop-down menu as you did in Figure 5-7.

6. Select the Advertisement Management workflow.

7. For Due Date, select a date that is one week from the current date.

8. Enter the following message to include with your request:

> **Please translate this advertisement into the appropriate language.**

9. Click the Send button.

How It Works

When you return to the Advertisement Materials document library, shown in Figure 5-29, you see three copies of the document. The Translation Status for the French and Spanish versions of the document is automatically set to Not Started. The documents for French and Spanish are copies of the English documents and act as placeholders until they are translated by the assigned translators. You also see that the Advertisement Translation workflow process has a status of In Progress.

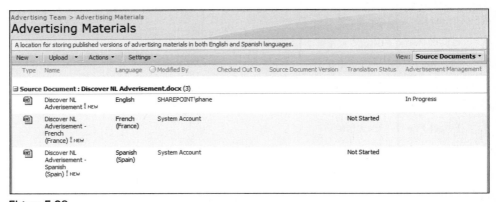

Figure 5-29

Custom Workflows with SharePoint Designer

Although the templates you've seen thus far are quite useful for most processes your organization may have, you may find you need a workflow process that closely matches a unique business activity. You can do this using the SharePoint Designer application. This requires you to download the .NET Framework 3.0 from the Microsoft site. This framework features the Windows Workflow Foundation elements required to create a custom workflow solution.

For example, in the following Try It Out, you find there is no easy way to transition an advertising concept to production material. You therefore need to create a new column in the document library to flag client-approved concepts that are ready to become production material. Rather than create a custom view that flags items, you decide it's easier to copy the documents directly into the document library that stores production materials. From there, you can launch other SharePoint workflow processes, such as translation management.

Try It Out   **Create a Custom Workflow Solution in SharePoint Designer**

For this example, you need to create a process to promote a concept document to a production material. You use SharePoint Designer with its easy-to-use wizard tool to create a custom workflow to first copy the approved concept material from the concept library to the production library, and then notify account managers of the update. SharePoint populates the document's name in the message area of the automatically generated email message. This makes it easier for the account managers to identify what content they need to convert. You can add more lookup fields to include a direct link to the library so users can jump directly to the item from their email message. When you finish creating the workflow, you upload it to the Advertising site and associate it with the Advertising Concept document library. From there, you can run the process by creating a new document, setting the Production material column to Yes and launching the workflow.

1.   From the Advertising Concepts document library, choose Settings ➪ Create Column.

2.   Enter **Production Material** for the column name.

3.   For column type, select Choice.

4.   Enter Yes and No as choice values.

5.   Select Radio Buttons as the display choice.

6.   Set the default value to No.

7.   Click the OK button. You are returned to the Advertising Concepts document library.

8.   Open SharePoint Designer.

9.   Select File ➪ Open Site.

10.   Enter the URL of the advertising team site.

11.   Select File ➪ New ➪ Workflow as shown in Figure 5-30.

   Note if you do not see the Workflow option in your menu, you may need to download and install the .NET Framework 3.0 from the Microsoft site.

12.   Name your workflow **Production Material Promotion**.

Figure 5-30

13. Select the Advertising Concepts library for the list to which the workflow should be attached.

14. Click the Next button. The Workflow Designer window changes, as shown in Figure 5-31.

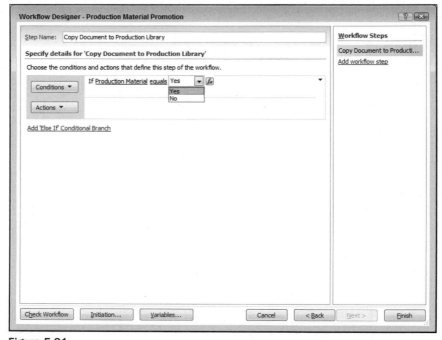

Figure 5-31

15. For Step Name, enter **Copy Document to Production Library**.

16. Select Conditions ⇨ Compare Advertising Concepts field.

17. Click the field link and select Production Material.

18. Select the value field as shown in Figure 5-31, and select Yes.

19. Select Actions ⇨ Copy List Item.

20. Click the first This List link. Select Current Item as shown in Figure 5-32, and click the OK button.

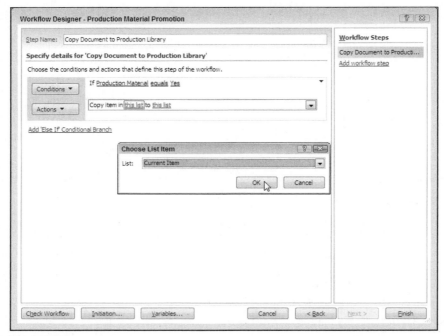

Figure 5-32

21. Click the second This List link. Select the Advertising Materials library.

22. Select the Add Workflow Step link.

23. For Step Name, enter **Notify Account Managers**.

24. From the Actions menu, select Send an Email.

25. Select the This Message link.

26. Click the address book to the right of the To field.

27. Select the Approvers group and click the Add button.

28. Click the OK button.

29. For Subject, enter the following:

> **New Advertising Material Available**

30. Click in the message body window and select the Add Lookup to Body button.

31. For Source, select Current Item, and for Field select Name.

32. Click the OK button.

33. Enter the following message after the lookup field as shown in Figure 5-33.

Figure 5-33

> **has been added to the Advertising Materials library for your use.**

34. Click the OK button.

35. Click the Finish button.

36. To test your workflow, create a new document in the Advertising Concepts library and set the Production Material field to Yes. Then from the workflow menu, select the Production Material Promotion workflow and click the Start button.

Summary

In this chapter, you saw how you can support and sometimes automate various business processes using SharePoint 2007's workflow capabilities. You can define workflow as the various tasks, and the order in which those tasks occur, related to a business activity that your team must complete. Although most SharePoint workflows are generally based around specific documents or list items, they can represent much larger human-based processes and actions. After reading this chapter, you should know the following:

❑ When defining a workflow process, you can select users or groups for specific activities. By doing so, tasks are created for these users.

❑ Workflow processes can be either serial or parallel. A serial workflow is one that only allows users to participate one at a time, whereas a parallel workflow may involve multiple participants at a given stage in an undefined order.

❑ SharePoint provides a number of templates that you can configure to suit your company's process and that you can associate with various content elements such as lists and libraries. These workflow processes include common activities related to content approval, feedback, or collecting signatures.

❑ You can also create custom templates using the Windows Workflow Foundation, Visual Studio 2005, or SharePoint Designer, if you are familiar with these programs. You can only assign workflows you create using SharePoint Designer to a single list or library; other central components, such as content types, which are discussed in the next chapter, cannot leverage them.

❑ The translation management template assigns and delegates tasks related to translating documents, and you associate this template with a document library. This workflow has a special list called Translators that stores information the system requires to identify for which languages documents should be created and to whom the workflow should assign translation tasks. When you upload a document to a translation management library, you specify a language. When the workflow launches, it copies the source document and creates new versions as placeholders for the translated versions.

This chapter demonstrated just a small amount of what is possible using workflow in SharePoint 2007 by looking at the usage scenarios of a small advertising team. It is recommended that you take some time to familiarize yourself with the various templates and customization alternatives so that you can effectively support your organization's business process management needs.

Exercises

1. What is the difference between an Approval Workflow template and the Collect Signatures workflow template?

2. True or False: You can create a custom workflow in SharePoint Designer for use across all sites in a site collection.

3. Explain the difference between a serial and parallel workflow process.

4. What two lists are required on a site that has workflow enabled on a document library?

5. Explain what happens when a change is requested during an approval workflow activity.

Working with Content Types

Thus far, this book has discussed components that can help you organize information in a SharePoint site. You should now know how to create lists and libraries, and assign metadata values to content items. You should also know how to associate business processes with lists and libraries so that you can track, review, and approve items in a consistent and automatic manner. Using this functionality in your work environment means that you spend more time doing actual work, rather than searching in disorganized filing systems.

This chapter takes the concepts discussed thus far and brings them together to create an information management package that ties to your content. It covers topics including:

- ❑ What a content type is and why it is such an important part of SharePoint 2007
- ❑ The various content types you can create
- ❑ Hands-on examples of creating the major content types
- ❑ Best practices for creating and managing content types for your organization

After reading this chapter, you should feel comfortable creating content types suitable for efficiently managing the information that is vital to your organization.

Content Types Overview

A *content type* represents a group of informational items in your organization that share common properties. You can define these properties, which include name, description, a grouping category, to meet your business needs. In addition, you can adjust the properties associated with templates, workflow, site columns, and policy management as well as the settings for the document information panel. You can change these properties at any time and optionally apply those changes to your entire environment.

> *For more on the various content properties and what they do, see the section "The Anatomy of a Content Type."*

SharePoint offers several content types that provide solid foundations for all future content types. You can select one of these content types and use it to create your content type in the central gallery, where you can then apply it to multiple lists and libraries throughout a site collection. By creating new content types, you can apply rules and properties to customize information and tie it to your business activities. Once you define your content type, you can create a new item by selecting the appropriate template from a drop-down menu presented by the New command on your library toolbar (see Figure 6-1). This chapter discusses the various elements of a content type as well as some of the configuration and customization alternatives of the most common content types.

Figure 6-1

Storing Custom Content Type

It's important where you store a custom content type in the site hierarchy. If you use it throughout your organization in many sites, you should store it in the content type gallery of the top-level site. For more specialized content, you might create content that will apply to a specific site and its subsites.

Most organizations have company rules for storing documents that ensure that documents adhere to the corporate culture and procedures. Such practices are becoming more and more commonplace with initiatives related to new regulatory requirements such as the Sarbanes-Oxley Act that requires a greater level of accountability regarding information and auditing.

When you create a content type, you must select a parent, from which it will automatically inherit any existing settings for a template, workflow, or metadata columns. You should consider the content types you need for your organization and then identify any relations they may have with each other or inheritances that they share so that you can place similar content types into groups. Using the same parent for each of these content types means you can filter based on the parent and include information from all child content types. For example, to manage your workflow, you company may need a general leave request form that reflects each division. You can create a standard leave request content type and then create each divisional content type using it as the template. All metadata and the form template become automatically associated with each divisional content type; however, you can define a unique workflow process for each child content type to allow different departmental managers to approve requests. You can easily update the form; because each divisional content type is based on the same parent, edits to the parent copy down into each child.

In Chapter 7, you review how certain Web Parts support filtering based on content type.

To show you how to use content types, this section presents two Try It Outs. In the first, you see how to create a new content type, and in the second, you see how to edit one of the content types that SharePoint has to offer to suit your needs.

Try It Out   Create a New Content Type

You need to manage your company's sales proposals in a more organized fashion as well as provide more automated support to the sales team during the proposal creation stage. This includes giving them access to a standard proposal template as well as an automated review and approval workflow process. To reach your goal, you must first create the initial shell of the content type, which you can later modify to include elements such as templates, standard metadata, and workflow processes. In this example, you create a financial report content type based on the document parent content type, and place it in a group.

1. From the top level of your site collection, select Site Actions ➪ Site Settings. A Site Settings window appears. If the top-level site is a publishing site such as a collaboration portal, you may also have to select Modify All Settings.

2. Under the Galleries section, select Site Content Types.

3. Click the Create button. The New Site Content Type screen appears, as shown in Figure 6-2.

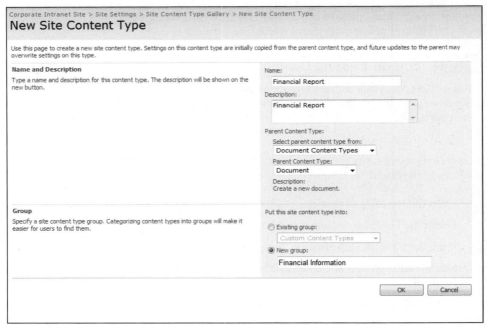

Figure 6-2

4. In the Name field, type a name for the content type. For this example, use **Financial Report**.

5. In the Description field, type a description for the content type. For this example, use **Financial Report (Spreadsheet)**.

6. From the Select Parent Content Type From drop-down menu, select the group name for the content type on which you are basing your new content type. For this example, select Document Content Types.

7. From the Parent Content Type drop-down menu, select the name of the content type on which you are basing your content type. All new content types must have a parent, so typically you will select a parent that contains a similar template, a similar workflow process, or similar metadata columns to the item you are creating. For this example, use the Document content type.

8. From the Put This Site Content Type Into section, select either an Existing Group or create a New Group. In this example, use a new group name called **Financial Information.**

9. Click the OK button to create the custom content type.

How It Works

Site content types allow you to manage multiple document types and templates from a single location. Once you have created a content type and associated it with a group, it becomes available in your list of site content types, which can then be associated with a particular library. Your content type is then accessible via your library's New drop-down menu (see Figure 6-1).

Try It Out   **Edit an Existing Content Type**

SharePoint offers many site content types that are preconfigured to support a variety of business situations. To save time, you can use one of these existing content types as a starting point and edit it to suit your own particular organizational needs. Editing an existing content type is easy. Just follow these steps:

In steps 6 through 14, you are creating a column to add to your content type. For more on creating columns in SharePoint, see Chapter 4.

1. From the top level of your site collection, select Site Actions ➪ Site Settings.

2. Under the Galleries section, select Site Content Types.

3. From the Financial Information Types section, select Financial Report.

4. Select Add from new site column. The New Site Column window appears, as shown in Figure 6-3.

5. In the Column Name field, type **Owner**.

6. From the Type of Information in This Column section, select Person or Group.

7. Create a new group for site columns called "Standard Classifications."

8. Select Yes for Require That This Column Contains Information.

9. In the Update All Content Types Inheriting from This Type, leave the default value of Yes selected. This ensures that any list or library to which you've added your content type will update automatically.

10. Click the OK button to update the content type.

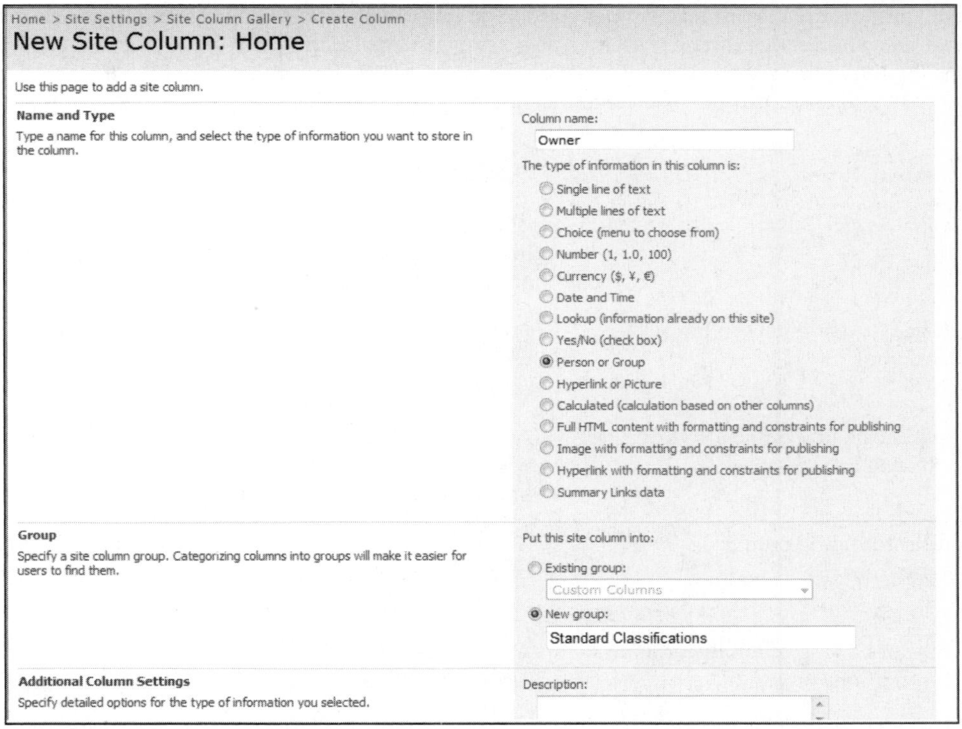

Figure 6-3

How It Works

For step 4, in the Columns section you will notice there is only one piece of metadata: Title. Most companies require you to supply a document owner. Note that when you select Yes in step 9 and create a new metadata column for this site content type, SharePoint automatically updates all lists and libraries already using the content type (provided the option is selected). This is a fast and effective way enforcing simple rules across multiple lists or libraries.

Base Content Types

SharePoint offers a repertoire of content types that address the basic business needs. These are organized into groups according to their purpose. This section details each of these built-in content groups and types.

Business Intelligence Content Types

SharePoint 2007 introduces powerful features that organize, track, and display data from a variety of sources so you can monitor the status of your business. This section discusses the business intelligence content types, and Chapter 11 describes the useful set of business reporting tools included in this latest version of SharePoint. The content types in the following table are available as part of the Business Intelligence group. The indicator types contain columns that collect business intelligence information from a data source so it can be presented as a key performance indicator (KPI) or in a report. By creating a new content type based on one of these base content types, you can augment the information that is gathered by default. You can also customize the dashboard and report types to meet your needs.

Content Type	Description
Dashboard	A special type of web page geared toward the display of business intelligence reports. This content type can be created from a Reports library.
Indicator using data in Excel workbook	A key performance indicator based on information stored within an Excel workbook. This type of indicator can be created from a KPI list.
Indicator using data in SQL Server 2005 Analysis Services	A key performance indicator based on information stored within SQL Server 2005 Analysis Services. This type of indicator can be created from a KPI list.
Indicator using data in SharePoint list	A key performance indicator based on information stored within a SharePoint list. This type of indicator can be created from a KPI list.
Indicator using manually entered information	A key performance indicator based on information entered directly into an item in a KPI list.
Report	An Excel document page for the browser-based display of spreadsheet information. Content authors create content in this type by uploading a spreadsheet to a reports library or creating a new spreadsheet from the library.

Document Content Types

You'll probably use the document types frequently in your SharePoint sites because the typical site functions as a document repository and viewing system for your team. The following document types are built into SharePoint, some of which will be explored throughout this book:

Content Type	Description
Basic Page	A very simple web page containing a single rich text editor.
Document	The parent content type for many other collaborative content types including basic page, Dublin core columns, form, and picture. Possibly one of the most common and popular content types.

Content Type	Description
Dublin Core Columns	Based on the Document content type but contains many standard columns to conform with the requirements for the popular classification system known as *Dublin Core*.
Form	Based on the Document content type and is specifically designed to support the use of InfoPath. See Chapter 10 for more on forms.
Link to a Document	In some cases, a document may be stored in one location and linked from another library. This content type helps support such scenarios by creating a record or row in a document library that references the document located in the other location.
Picture	Based on the document content type and is the primary content type associated with a Picture library.
Web Part Page	A web page with a number of Web Part zones for the use of Web Parts. These web pages can come in a variety of layouts and templates.

Folder Content Types

You use this type for folders and discussion boards in SharePoint. Because individual discussions in SharePoint are stored within folders, it is appropriate that the base content type is affiliated with the Folder Content Types group.

The following base content types are available as part of the Folder Content Types group:

Content Type	Description
Folder	Expanded in SharePoint 2007 to support columns and metadata like any other element stored within a list or library. Unlike other content types, the folder does not support workflow or information management policies.
Discussion	Based on the folder content type, supports workflow and information management policy settings as well as custom metadata. This type of content type is associated with a Discussion list, which was discussed in Chapter 2.

List Content Types

An important SharePoint 2007 feature is easily creating and storing information in lists. Lists can hold any information from a simple To-Do list, to a more complex resource tracking list. You can now take full advantage of content types by creating a base content type for each primary list template. Each content type in turn has a set of associated metadata columns that represent the information that will be stored in the list.

The following base content types are what SharePoint has to offer as part of the List Content Types group. This section also presents two Try It Outs that show how to create a new content type based on the SharePoint Issues content type. You basically tweak this content type so you can use it in your company. In the second Try It Out, you see what happens when you add a column to a parent content type.

You can apply the processes illustrated in this section to virtually every other content type in the chapter to make your own custom content types.

Content Type	Description
Announcement	Based on the Item content type, is used for tracking simple news updates for a team. This content type is associated with an Announcements list, which was covered in Chapter 2.
Contact	Based on an Item content type and contains the columns required to share contact information. This content type is associated with the Contacts list, which was covered in Chapter 2.
Far East Contact	Very similar to the Contact content type but contains special columns related to Phonetic information. We do not cover this content type in this book.
Issues	Contains columns for tracking problems that may arise within a collaborative or work environment. This content type is associated with the Issues list, which was covered in Chapter 2.
Item	A parent content type of the Document content type and many list items. It is created by default with a single column for Title.
Message	Contains common columns required for content similar to that used in a discussion list item such as message subject, body, and email sender.
Task	Based on an Item content type and contains the columns required to share task information. This content type is associated with the Tasks list, which was covered in Chapter 2.

Try It Out   Create a New Content Type Based on Issue Content Type

Imagine that you work for a software company. The Issues content type contains many of the settings that you want to track bugs or problems in your software applications. However, each team has slightly different workflow processes to manage and respond to the issues that users report on the various software applications. To accommodate this, you create content types based on the Issue content type and customize the workflow processes associated with each to match the team.

In the following steps, you create a content type that has all the settings as an Issue content type. You accomplish this by setting the Issue content type as the parent type.

1.   From the main page of your site, select Site Actions ➪ Site Settings.

2.   Under the Galleries section, select Site Content Types.

3.   Click the Create button from the toolbar.

4.   In the Name field, type **Technology Issues**.

5.   In the Description field, type **Issues related to technology**.

6. From the Select Parent Content Type From drop-down menu, select List Content Types.

7. From the Parent Content Type drop-down menu, select Issues.

8. From the Put This Site Content Type Into section, select New Group.

9. In the New Group field, type **Divisional Issue Tracking**.

10. Click the OK button to complete the creation of your new content type.

Try It Out **Add a Column to a Parent Content Type**

Whenever you select a content type as a parent of a new content type, all site columns are automatically added to the new content type. Similarly, if you add a new custom column to the base Issues content type, you can optionally add that column to all content types inheriting from that type. For example, if you add a new column to the Issues content type for cost so that you can track what the expected costs of responding to the issue might be, you can also add that column to your Technology Issues content types. In this example, you create a new column on the base issue content type called Billing Information.

1. From the main page of your site, select Site Actions ⇨ Site Settings.

2. Under the Galleries section, select Site Content Types.

3. From the List Content Types group, select Issues.

4. From the Columns section, select Add from Existing Site Columns. The Add Columns to Site Content Type window appears, as shown in Figure 6-4.

5. From the Select Columns From drop-down menu, select Core Task and Issues Columns.

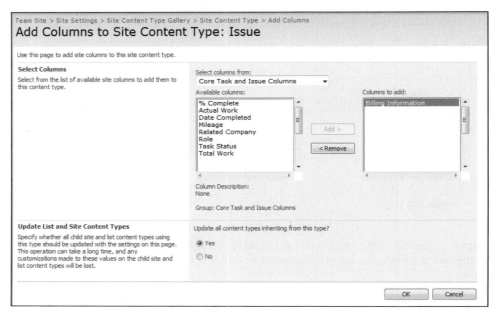

Figure 6-4

6. Select the Billing Information column from the Available columns field and click the Add button.

7. Ensure that Yes is selected for the Update All Content Types Inheriting from This Type value.

8. Click the OK button to complete the addition of the new column.

How It Works

The Technologies Issues content type that you create in the "Create a New Content Type Based on Issue Content Type" Try It Out, updates to include the Billing Information field.

Page Layout Content Types

One of the most significant advancements of SharePoint 2007 is the integration of Microsoft Content Management Server into the platform under the name *Web Content Management* (WCM). This great functionality allows users to create content for a site directly from the browser without having any special web development knowledge or skills.

Most sites have unique types of pages in them. For example, you might have a main page, a generic subpage, and a newsletter page. Each page type, in turn, has specific content elements that make them unique to the site. For example, the Newsletter page likely has a Title, Newsletter Body, and Published Date. A Page Layout content type defines these unique content elements by attaching site columns to your content type. You can later use this content type to create a *Page Layout*, which is a special type of template page that users can use to create new pages in a site. Figure 6-5 shows some of the default page templates that exist as choices when creating a new page from a Page Layout.

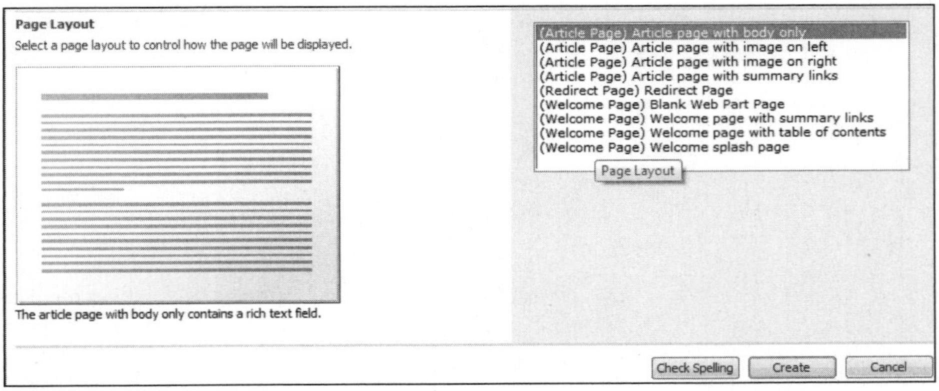

Page Layout
Select a page layout to control how the page will be displayed.

(Article Page) Article page with body only
(Article Page) Article page with image on left
(Article Page) Article page with image on right
(Article Page) Article page with summary links
(Redirect Page) Redirect Page
(Welcome Page) Blank Web Part Page
(Welcome Page) Welcome page with summary links
(Welcome Page) Welcome page with table of contents
(Welcome Page) Welcome splash page

Page Layout

The article page with body only contains a rich text field.

Check Spelling   Create   Cancel

Figure 6-5

In essence, a Page Layout content type has the same relationship to a page in a site that a Document content type has to a document in a document library. It is a template combined with site columns and rules.

The following base content types are available as part of the Page Layout Content Types group:

Content Type	Description
Article Page	Contains many of the common properties that a page should have, including elements used for publishing such as scheduling date and others that are used for content display such as page content. As shown in Figure 6-5, several page layouts exist based on the Article Page template.
Redirect Page	A page layout that is intended for the creation of pages that will redirect visitors and readers to another location.
Welcome Page	Contains a number of columns for the display and publishing of content.

Chapter 13 discusses Page Layout content types in much greater detail, including how to make and manage these special components.

Publishing Content Types

Besides offering a feature for content approval, WCM lets you publish information both automatically via workflow and manually. Another WCM-related content type group in SharePoint 2007 is *Publishing content types*. The base publishing content types provide the structure for all major web publishing components. The following base content types are available as part of the Publishing Content Types group:

❑ **Page:** A system parent content type uses the page layout content types (see the section "Page Layout Content Types") as a parent. This content type contains many columns related to the creation of publishing content.

❑ **Page Layout:** A system parent content type used for publishing content in the site collection.

❑ **Publishing Master Page:** A system content type used for publishing content in the site collection.

Page layouts are template pages that are explored in Chapter 13, as are Master pages. Because Publishing content types are the key to creating websites using SharePoint 2007, Chapter 13 discusses them in much greater detail.

Special Content Types

The content type group called *Special content types* allows users to upload documents regardless of content type to a library. It offers no special customization characteristics and is intended for use in situations where the content type is unknown or not important.

The Anatomy of a Content Type

The magic of SharePoint is making its various pieces fit your business situation, and nowhere is that more evident than in content types. Content types all have properties, the basic ones being the name, description, and grouping category. In addition, you have properties associated with templates, workflow, site columns, and policy management as well as settings for the document information panel. You can define and redefine these properties to fit your business situations, but to do that, you need an understanding of how to work with them. For example, you can change a content type name to reflect a change in process, but it's important for you to make the name consistent and intuitive when you redefine it. In this section, you learn about the various content type properties and how to work with them.

Name and Description

Because the name displays on all the buttons and labels associated with the content, you should assign a clear and descriptive name. For example, users should intuitively know what name to select when they click the button for creating a new item in a document library. You should consider who will work with this content type and make sure that they understand exactly what they are creating when they select a name. This is especially critical when you work with the automated workflows, templates, and policies. For example, if your company sells multiple product lines related to aerospace and transportation, and you create a content type that contains the proposal template, approval process, and metadata related to a specific marine product line, consider using a name that clearly defines. Naming it "sales document" or "marine product documents" would not be as appropriate as "marine sales proposal."

As with all other SharePoint content elements, a good description helps communicate the purpose and intended use of a content type. By concisely stating what the content type is, users will more easily fill in information, modify settings, or select a content type for inclusion with a list or library.

Parent Content Type

To easily change properties, you can define hierarchical relationships between two content types. In SharePoint, the *parent content type* defines the properties for a child content type, which, in turn, inherits all the parent's properties. For example, going back to the marine sales proposals scenario, you can create a new content type called "Marine Documents," which has specific site columns and metadata that you want to apply to all marine-related documents. By making Marine Documents as the parent content type for the Marine Sales Proposals content type, all content types associated with the "Marine Documents" content will automatically inherit all the parent content type's columns. Likewise, if you later need to add a new site column to all marine content types, you simply add columns to the Marine Documents parent content type to automatically have them added to the children of the content type. Figure 6-6 shows how you assign a parent content type during the creation process. Parent content types create better consistency across all common content types as well as improve design efficiency and individual component maintenance.

Group

You can organize your various customized content types by grouping them. As you create or edit a content type, you must specify a group name — either an existing group name or a custom group. Instituting some standards for groups provides a solid base for expanding and organizing content types as you create them. For example, using the Marine Sales Proposals as an example, it may be appropriate to associate the content type with a custom group called "Marine Sales Documents" that can store all content types related to the marine product line.

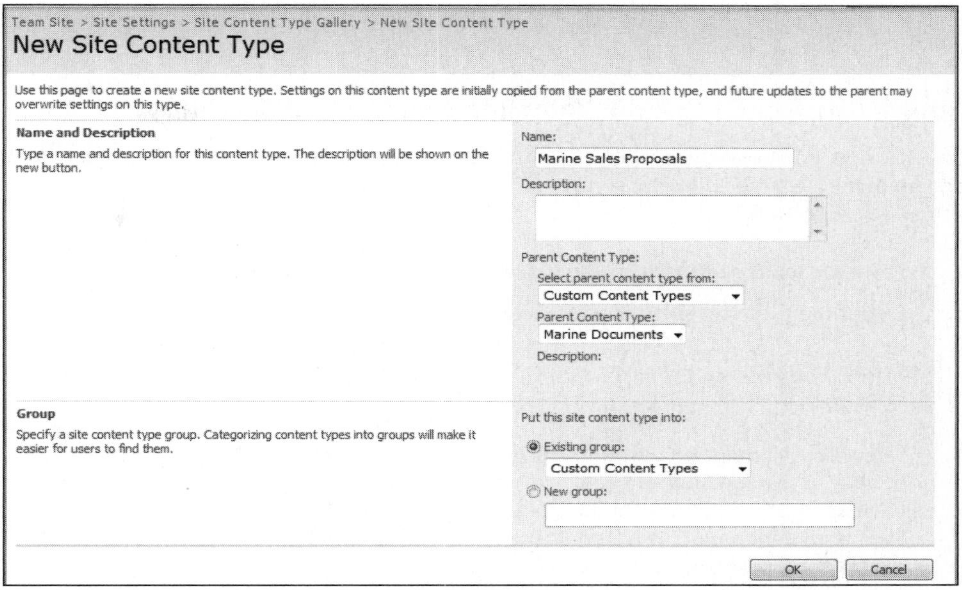

Team Site > Site Settings > Site Content Type Gallery > New Site Content Type
New Site Content Type

Use this page to create a new site content type. Settings on this content type are initially copied from the parent content type, and future updates to the parent may overwrite settings on this type.

Name and Description

Type a name and description for this content type. The description will be shown on the new button.

Name:

Marine Sales Proposals

Description:

Parent Content Type:

Select parent content type from:

Custom Content Types

Parent Content Type:

Marine Documents

Description:

Group

Specify a site content type group. Categorizing content types into groups will make it easier for users to find them.

Put this site content type into:

◉ Existing group:

Custom Content Types

○ New group:

OK   Cancel

Figure 6-6

Template

When you associate document templates with a content type, you can better control the quality of the data that you collect. You can base the template on a variety of file formats including Word documents, Excel spreadsheets, InfoPath forms, and custom web pages. You can either upload a custom template to the content type, or you can point to a template stored at another location. If you want to point to an existing template, be sure that all members using the content type can access the location of the template. For example, if you create a sales proposal content type and a document template for sales proposals already exists on the sales team site, make sure that the people who create content based on your newly created content type have access to that sales team site.

For Microsoft Office files, such as Word and Excel, updating or changing the document template associated with a content type has no effect on items that users have already created and that are stored in the document library. This is because of the way these files relate to a template. In Word, a document template is primarily only relevant for the initial creation of the document. However, for content types based on InfoPath or publishing templates such as page layouts, changing the template associated with the content type updates the existing documents to display the information as detailed in the template. This will become clearer when you explore those content types in greater detail later in this book.

Chapter 4 discussed how you can associate custom document templates with a document library. This association means that users can automatically generate documents based on that template by clicking the New Item button for a document library, a feature available in the previous version of SharePoint. With SharePoint 2007's introduction of content types, you now have more than one item in the New Item menu (see Figure 6-1), which gives you a single document repository to store several different types of information and simplify how people access materials. To do this with your process, see the following Try It Out.

Try It Out   Upload a Custom Template to a Content Type

In this example, you go to the properties of an existing content type and upload a custom template. Users can then select this template using the New Item button from a document library that has the content type associated with it.

1. From the main page of your site, select Site Actions ➪ Site Settings.

2. Under the Galleries section, select Site content types.

If your content type was created on a top-level site, you need to go to the top-level site settings to edit the content type directly.

3. Select your content type from the list. Use the Group Selection box on the right-hand side of the toolbar to display only the group of which your content type is a member. This is helpful if you have a large number of content types on your site. In this example, you select the Financial Report content type that is part of the Financial Information group. The Site Content Type page for the content appears, as shown in Figure 6-7.

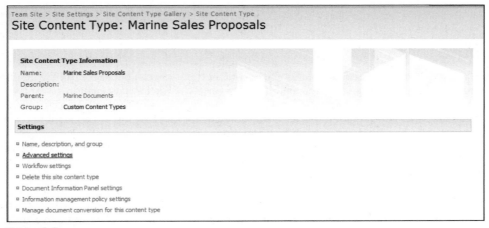

Figure 6-7

4. Select Advanced Settings from the Settings group.

5. Select Upload a New Document Template, and click the Browse button to locate your custom template. Please note that it is not necessary to have your document saved as a template file (.dotx or .dot).

6. When you have the appropriate file selected, click the Open button.

7. Click the OK button to complete the operation.

Workflow

Creating important documents often requires the creator to follow an equally important business process. This process ensures that everyone involved in the collaboration activity is doing their part and communicating properly. When people follow processes without the aid of automated tools, they often encounter or create roadblocks because of distractions and other duties. For example, if a sales manager completes an important sales proposal and sends it to a colleague or supervisor for feedback with an email notification, that colleague may not immediately respond because of another task or emergency and as a result, the request gets buried into an inbox or lost in the shuffle. This is a common situation because many people struggle to keep up with email and daily responsibilities. Unfortunately, this means missed deadlines, frustration between team members, missed opportunities, and it may ultimately impact the overall operations of the company.

By assigning a workflow template with a content type, you can define a realistic series of tasks with built-in reminders for a specific business activity so that workers can focus on duties. For example, in the previous scenario, whenever a salesperson creates a sales proposal, he can send it to the sales team or a supervisor for feedback with tasks and deadlines automatically created so that the request for feedback is less likely to be lost. Even if the sales team supervisor does forget the task, the system will send reminder messages to the supervisor until the task is complete. This means that the salesperson doesn't have to follow up on the task.

Depending on the parent content type you select when you define your custom content type, you may already have workflows enabled. If these workflow processes do not apply, you can remove them, but be careful not to remove a workflow that is important to the operations of a specific content type. By updating the workflow settings of a parent, you can optionally update any content types that are inherited from that content type.

Adding a custom workflow to a content type is a fairly simple process and similar to adding a workflow to a document library or list as described in Chapter 5. The advantage here, however, is that you typically have to define the process only once and it is applied to multiple document libraries that utilize that content type. If you add multiple content types to a single library, each content type can have its own unique workflow or set of processes that are independent of the others.

Try It Out   Define a Custom Workflow for a Content Type

Assigning a custom workflow with a content type is very similar to assigning a workflow to a document library. In the following example, you associate an approval workflow with an existing content type.

   1.   From the main page of your site, select Site Actions ⇨ Site Settings.

   2.   Under the Galleries section, select Site Content Types.

   If your content type was created on a top-level site, you need to go to the top-level site settings to edit the content type directly.

   3.   Select your content type from the list. Use the Group Selection box on the right-hand side of the toolbar to filter the list to display only the group containing your content type. This is a helpful tip if you have a large number of content types on your site. In this example, use the Financial Report content type that is part of the Financial Information group. The Site Content Type window appears.

4. Under the Settings section, select Workflow settings.

5. Select the Add a Workflow link. The available templates for a workflow are listed in the Workflow Templates box, as shown in Figure 6-8.

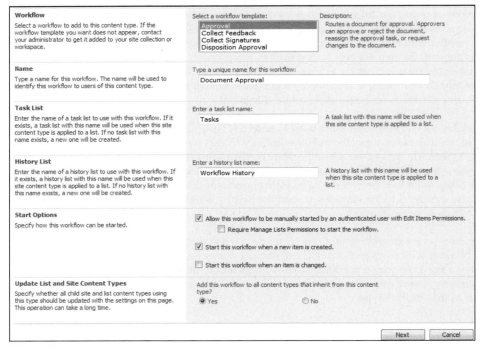

Figure 6-8

6. Select the Approval template.

7. Specify a name for the workflow such as **Document Approval**.

8. Because you can associate workflow processes with a tasks list to help manage the assignment information and duties, the next step is to select which task list to use. By default, a task list is suggested. However, you can specify a name for a new task list, and SharePoint will create one for you if this name hasn't already been used. For this example, use the default value of **Tasks**.

9. The workflow activities can be associated and tracked in a history list. By default, a name of "Workflow History" is selected.

10. For Start Option, you want the workflow to launch whenever you create a new item. Select Start This Workflow When a New Item Is Created check box.

11. Click Next to continue. A window similar to Figure 6-9 appears.

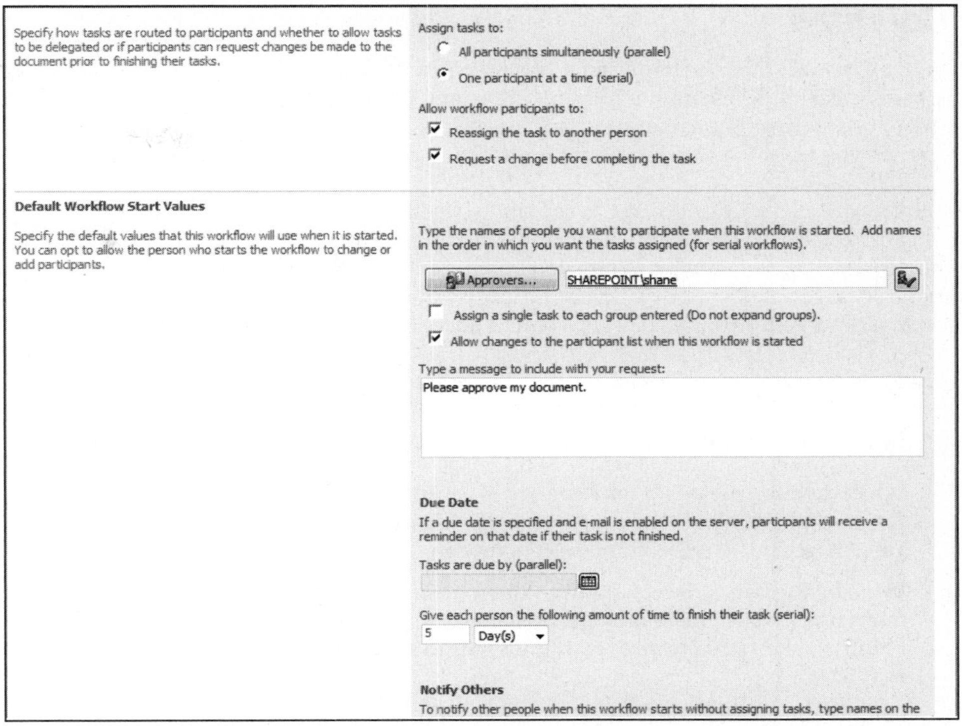

Specify how tasks are routed to participants and whether to allow tasks to be delegated or if participants can request changes be made to the document prior to finishing their tasks.

Assign tasks to:
- ○ All participants simultaneously (parallel)
- ● One participant at a time (serial)

Allow workflow participants to:
- ☑ Reassign the task to another person
- ☑ Request a change before completing the task

Default Workflow Start Values

Specify the default values that this workflow will use when it is started. You can opt to allow the person who starts the workflow to change or add participants.

Type the names of people you want to participate when this workflow is started. Add names in the order in which you want the tasks assigned (for serial workflows).

[📇 Approvers...] SHAREPOINT\shane

- ☐ Assign a single task to each group entered (Do not expand groups).
- ☑ Allow changes to the participant list when this workflow is started

Type a message to include with your request:

Please approve my document.

Due Date

If a due date is specified and e-mail is enabled on the server, participants will receive a reminder on that date if their task is not finished.

Tasks are due by (parallel):

Give each person the following amount of time to finish their task (serial):
5   Day(s) ▼

Notify Others

To notify other people when this workflow starts without assigning tasks, type names on the

Figure 6-9

12. In the Workflow Tasks section, select to assign tasks to one participant at a time.

13. Click the Approvers button. The Add recipients window appears.

14. Enter your first name, and click the magnifying glass button. A listing of results is displayed. Select your own name from the list of results, and click the Add button.

15. Click the OK button to close the Add recipients window.

16. Enter 5 in the text box for number of days to complete task.

17. In the Complete the Workflow section, unselect the Document Is Rejected check box.

18. Click the OK button to save your changes.

How It Works

The workflow activity you created will launch whenever a new item is created based on that content type, and a task will be created for you because you selected your own name as an approver for the serial workflow. The due date for the task will be five days from the point the document is created. If you do not complete the task by the assigned date, you will receive a reminder.

Site Columns

In Chapter 4, you learned the importance of site columns when creating standard metadata properties for lists and libraries. To recap, site columns are stored in a central gallery on each site, and any list or library can use them on the same site or any site below it. Site columns provide standardization and ease of use when you want to share important information across multiple lists, libraries, or sites.

Site columns are also very important in content types. Because content types are created and stored in a central gallery, all associated components must be centralized as well. Therefore, you can only associate site columns with a content type. When you add a content type to a library, the required site columns are automatically associated with that library for use by the content type. You can create custom views on the columns, and Web Parts, such as the content query Web Part, and you can apply advanced filtering.

Web Parts are explained in Chapter 7.

Remember the following when working with site columns:

❑   When defining metadata for a content type, you can use existing site columns or create new site columns directly from the content type Settings page. When you use existing site columns, you are redirected to a site column selection page.

❑   By using the Group Selection drop-down menu, you can filter the list of site columns to a more manageable size. This is why group names are very important, and why you should make them intuitive when you create site columns (see the section "Name and Description" earlier in the chapter).

❑   Once you select the site columns you want, you click the Add button to move them from the left-hand list box to the right-hand list box.

❑   You can remove an item you may have added accidentally by selecting it from the box on the right and clicking the Remove button.

❑   You can update all content types that inherit from the current content type with the new columns you selected. For example, if you have a content type "Human Resources Document" that is the parent to the other content types "Policies and Procedures" and "Leave Request Form," by selecting the Yes option in the Update List and Site Content Types section, a site column for "Division" that is added to the Human Resources Document is also added to Policies and Procedures and Leave Request Form content types.

You can also create a new site column as you create a content type. Even though you're creating the site column from the administration interface of the specific content type, SharePoint still adds it to the central gallery of the site, making it available to other content types, lists and libraries on the current site, and sites below.

Document Information Panel Settings

Whenever you associate a document with a document library or content type, columns appear when the document is first saved or checked in. This is the *document information panel*, which asks you to complete metadata, as shown in Figure 6-10, and which is the subject of the next Try It Out.

For more on the Check In/Check Out process, see Chapter 3.

Figure 6-10

To manage the Document Information Panel settings of a content type, you must do the following:

1. Select Document Information Panel Settings from the content type Administration page.

2. You can then change the template associated with the panel or have the document information panel always display for the user whenever the document is opened or initially saved.

It's advantageous to display the panel when a user opens the document when you consider the metadata associated with a document is critical and/or when it is subject to change throughout the lifecycle of the document — for example, project lead, percentage complete, schedule, and budget status. It is up to the document owners to maintain the relevance and accuracy of this information. By presenting users with the document information panel each time they open the document, they are far more likely to update any column values.

Try It Out   **Create a Custom Document Information Panel**

A custom document information panel is useful when you need to attract attention to specific elements or add custom text to guide users in the completion of important metadata related to an item. You can customize the document information panel directly from the content type administration area using InfoPath. Although InfoPath is covered in greater detail in Chapter 10, the following walk-through does not require a great deal of familiarity with the tool.

These steps require that you download the logo.jpg file from www.wrox.com.

1. From the main page of your site, select Site Actions ⇨ Site Settings.

2. Under the Galleries section, select Site Content Types.

If your content type was created on a top-level site, you need to go to the top-level site settings to edit the content type directly.

3. Select your Financial Report content type from the list. Use the Group Selection box on the right-hand side of the toolbar to filter the list to display only the Financial Information group. This is helpful if you have a large number of content types on your site. A Site Content Type window appears, as previously shown in Figure 6-7.

4. Select Document Information Panel Settings.

5. From the Document Information Panel Template Settings section, select Create a New Custom Template.

6. The InfoPath client application opens on your system and displays a Data Source Wizard, as shown in Figure 6-11. Click the Finish button. An InfoPath form appears in Design view, as shown in Figure 6-12.

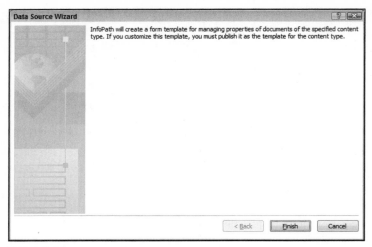

Figure 6-11

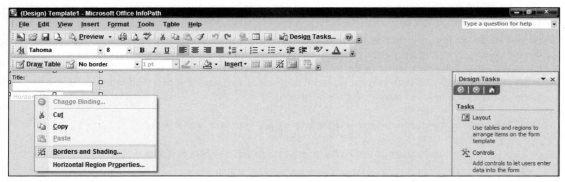

Figure 6-12

7. Click on the words `Horizontal Region` to select each entire form field.

8. Right-click and select Borders and Shading (shown in Figure 6-14).

9. Select the Shading tab, and select the color yellow from the list.

10. Click the OK button.

11. After you have adjusted the background color for each form field, you should add a line break below the form fields. To do this, select the words `Horizontal Region` for the last field, press the right arrow button on your keyboard and then press Return. From the menu, select Insert ➪ Picture ➪ From File.

12. From the resources folder for this chapter that you downloaded from the Wrox website, select logo.jpg and click the Insert button. Your image should now display within your custom panel as shown in Figure 6-13.

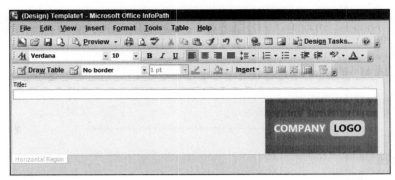

Figure 6-13

13. Select your image and click the right-hand justification icon to align your image.

14. Click the Save button.

15. You may receive a reminder message telling you to publish the form when you finish your edits. Click the OK button to continue.

16. Save your custom template to a location either on your computer or within your network.

17. Click File, and then Publish. The Publishing Wizard appears, as shown in Figure 6-14, with the document information panel item selected by default.

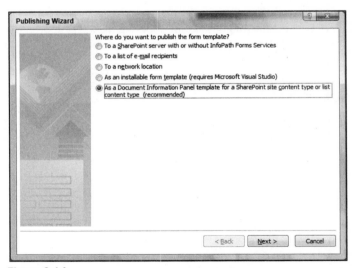

Figure 6-14

18. Click the Next button. All the required settings will be automatically detected by the wizard.

19. A final screen displays with the URL of the site and content type name. Click the Publish button to complete the process.

20. Click the Close button on the publishing window and close the InfoPath application. You can click the Go Back to the Document Information Panel Settings Page link to return to your settings page.

21. Select the check box for Always Show Document Information Panel on Document Open and Initial Save for This Content Type.

22. Click the OK button to save your changes.

How It Works

In the previous example, you created a custom information panel for your content type that displays a unique color background and custom logo. While it may not be considered best practice to implement bright colors into your user interface, his example demonstrated how easy it is to use InfoPath to customize your organization's document information panels. Once you create a single custom panel, you can reuse it for other content types by pointing to it from the Document Information Panel settings of your other content types. You would do this by selecting Use Existing Custom Template (URL, UNC, or URN) from the Document Information Panel settings instead of creating a new template as you did previously.

You enabled a check box in Step 21 on your content type so that the document information panel always appears whenever your content type is opened within a Microsoft Office application such as Word or Excel. By displaying the panel whenever the document is opened, users treat the panel as a form that they must update before closing the document. If an item is required, it will have to be completed or added before the document is closed. However, if a required column is already specified but outdated, having the values front and center while someone is working on the document should help reduce the probability of them closing the document without updating the latest information. There is no way to force someone to update a column if a value already exists, so communicating the importance of keeping information up-to-date to your team is still important.

Policy Management

Another great feature of content types is how they define certain policies and behaviors around how they are managed. Because content of a specific type quite often has the same requirements for retention and management, it is beneficial to define a set of policies around a content type and have those inherited by all documents that are created from it.

You can configure the items in relation to a content type's information policies:

Policy Item	Description
Administrative Description	Provide some background information to users who are responsible for managing the policies related to the content type.
Policy Statement	A customizable message that appears when users open documents associated with the content type. A message bar appears at the top of the document in an Information Management Policy box. Users can click a Details button to view all the details related to the policy message. By using a policy statement, content type owners can ensure that users have all the information they need concerning the important policies related to specific content.

Policy Item	Description
Labels	Ensures that important properties or messages are printed with documents related to a specific content type, such as confidential or a specific non-calculated document property. Content type owners can customize the presentation of the label by choosing font formatting and size.
Auditing	By enabling auditing on a content type, the following activities related to documents associated with the content type are tracked: ❑ Opening or downloading documents, viewing items in lists, or viewing item properties ❑ Editing items ❑ Checking out or checking in items ❑ Moving or copying items to another location in the site ❑ Deleting or restoring items
Expiration	Allows you to control the life span of specific types of content. You can configure content types to automatically be deleted after a certain time period based on a document property. Alternatively, you can launch a workflow that gives the user a final chance to review the document before it is archived or deleted. This method is recommended in situations where you have no formal requirement for deleting content automatically because it provides the greatest level of flexibility.
Barcodes	This automatically inserts an auto-generated barcode into documents of a specific content type. You can also prompt users to insert barcodes when they use specific Microsoft Office client applications.

Try It Out   Configure an Expiration Policy on a Content Type

Configuring a policy is a fairly intuitive process as you will see in the following example, where you create an Expiration policy. You can only have a single expiration policy per individual content type. Once you complete your configuration, individual documents that are created related to that content type will expire two years after their last modification date. If someone modifies the document, the timer resets, and the document has another two years before it expires.

1. From the main page of your site, select Site Actions ➪ Site Settings.

2. Under the Galleries section, select Site Content Types.

   If your content type was created on a top-level site, you need to go to the to- level site settings to edit the content type directly.

3. Select your content type from the list.

4. Select the Workflow Settings link. A listing of all workflow templates associated with the content type displays. The Change Workflow Settings window appears, as shown in Figure 6-15.

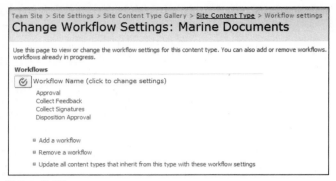

Figure 6-15

5. If the Disposition approval workflow is not listed, select Add a Workflow. Select the disposition approval workflow from the template list; enter **Disposition Approval** for the unique workflow name. Scroll to bottom of page and click the OK button.

6. Select Site Content Type from the navigation trail over the title of the page (see Figure 6-15) to return to the Site Content Type window, shown in Figure 6-16.

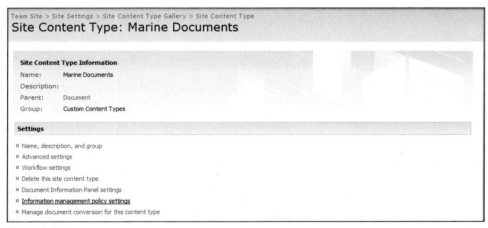

Figure 6-16

7. Under the Settings section, select Information Management Policy Settings.

8. Select Define a Policy and click the OK button. The Edit Policy window appears, as shown in Figure 6-17.

9. Select the check box for Enable Expiration.

10. Select the option for the retention period being a time period based on the item's properties.

11. Select modified from the field drop-down box and enter **2** into the text field for years.

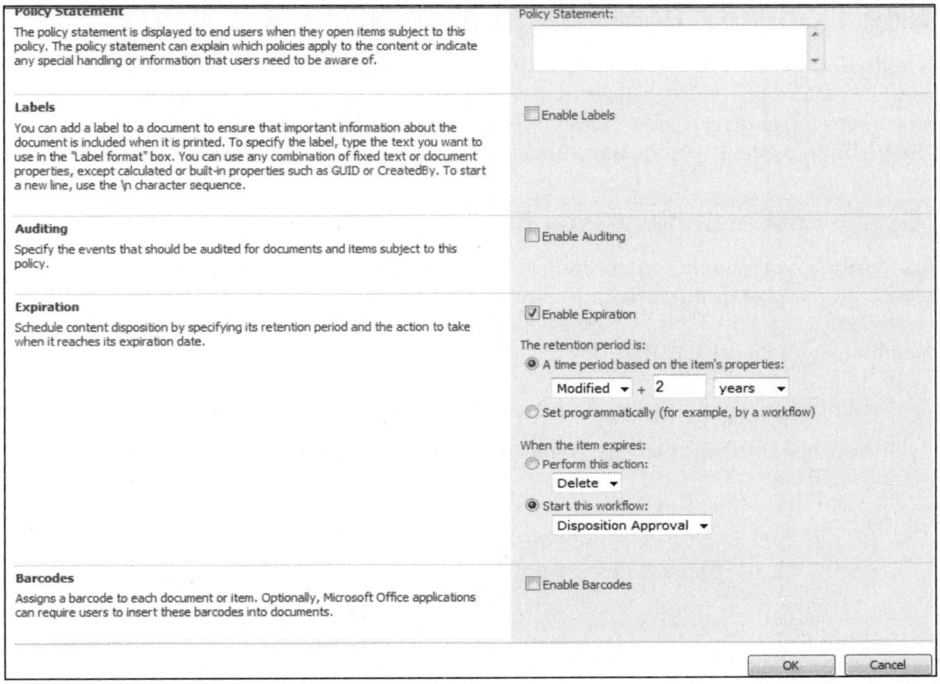

Figure 6-17

12. Select the Start This Workflow action and select the Disposition Approval workflow.

13. Click the OK button to complete the configuration of expiration settings.

How It Works

When a document reaches the time period for content expiration, you may not want your documents to be automatically deleted. Instead, for this example, you created a rule that triggers a workflow process. When you specify that a workflow process should start, you must reference a configured workflow activity. Because there was no content expiration type workflow associated with the content type already, you configured a disposition approval workflow on the content type before you started configuring the expiration policy. Only workflow activities that you have associated with the current content type display in the list of available templates when you are configuring an expiration rule.

Managing Content Types

An important aspect of managing a SharePoint site or environment is to understand how to combine and manage the information that a team or group shares. In this section, you discover some of the common management tasks that ensure that users in your organization can easily share and use your content types.

Enabling Content Type Management on a Library

While many things have changed in the 2007 version of SharePoint Products and Technologies, Microsoft has maintained a consistent experience for users moving from one version to another. For this reason, content types unavailable in previous versions are not enabled on a document library by default. Luckily, enabling content type management on a library is easy, as the next Try It Out demonstrates.

Try It Out   **Enable Content Type Management on a Library**

For this example, you enable content management on a previously created document library. Once you do so, you can manage multiple unique content types and their associated elements from the document library settings page. Until this feature is enabled on a document library, the functionality related to content type management are hidden.

1.   Select the document library on which you want to enable Content Type Management.

2.   From your document toolbar, select Settings ⇨ Document Library Settings, as shown in Figure 6-18.

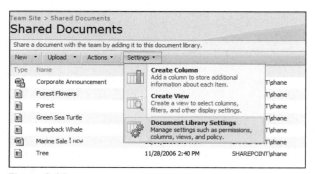

Figure 6-18

3.   Select Advanced Settings from the General Settings section of the Customize page. The Advanced Settings window appears, as shown in Figure 6-19.

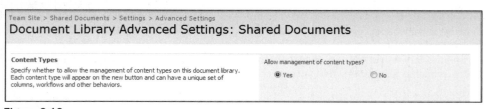

Figure 6-19

4.   In the Allow Management of Content Types section, select the Yes option.

5.   Click the OK button.

How It Works

SharePoint supplies several default content types based on common business patterns such as announcements, tasks, and issues. In addition, any Site content types that you have created on the current site or a parent site will also be available for you to add to your document library. See Figure 6-20 for a view of the administrative page of a document library after content types have been enabled and added to the library.

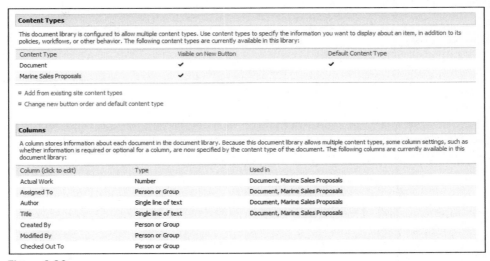

Content Types

This document library is configured to allow multiple content types. Use content types to specify the information you want to display about an item, in addition to its policies, workflows, or other behavior. The following content types are currently available in this library:

Content Type	Visible on New Button	Default Content Type
Document	✔	✔
Marine Sales Proposals	✔	

▫ Add from existing site content types
▫ Change new button order and default content type

Columns

A column stores information about each document in the document library. Because this document library allows multiple content types, some column settings, such as whether information is required or optional for a column, are now specified by the content type of the document. The following columns are currently available in this document library:

Column (click to edit)	Type	Used in
Actual Work	Number	Document, Marine Sales Proposals
Assigned To	Person or Group	Document, Marine Sales Proposals
Author	Single line of text	Document, Marine Sales Proposals
Title	Single line of text	Document, Marine Sales Proposals
Created By	Person or Group	
Modified By	Person or Group	
Checked Out To	Person or Group	

Figure 6-20

Managing Multiple Content Types in a Library

Today's technology requires working with various types of content, which means managing many document templates, business processes, and information policies. Previous versions of SharePoint Products and Technologies meant you could only associate a single document template with a document library, so you had to have a large number of document libraries just to accommodate unique document templates and classification requirements. By associating multiple content types with a document library in SharePoint 2007 (shown in the next Try It Out), however, you can freely manage all important information from a single location. These can be different types of templates using the same format, or completely different applications such as Excel, InfoPath, PowerPoint, or Word. This means you can save a tremendous amount of time because you can edit and share multiple types of documents from the same location.

Try It Out   **Associate Multiple Content Types with a Library**

You can set up multiple content types on a single library by following these steps:

1.   From the document library on which you want to enable multiple content types, select Settings ➪ Document Library Settings.

2. From the Content Types section, select Add from Existing Site Content Types.

3. To make content types easier to locate and associate, SharePoint places them in groups. Select Document Content Types from the Select Parent Content Type From drop-down menu, as shown in Figure 6-21.

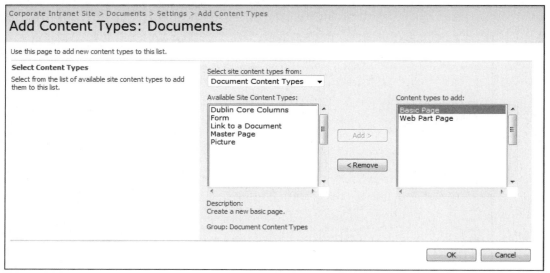

Figure 6-21

4. From Available Site Content Types, select Basic Page and Web Part Page and then click Add.

You can hold the Ctrl or Shift keys to make multiple selections.

5. Click the OK button to complete the process.

How It Works

When you associate multiple content types with a document library, they become available in the drop-down menu of the New item on your document library toolbar where you can select the type of document you want to create. For example, you might have a content type for Meeting Minutes associated with a Word template and a Financial Report content type associated with an Excel spreadsheet, as shown in Figure 6-22.

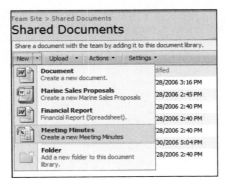

Figure 6-22

Customizing List or Library Views Based on Specific Content Types

Although managing and creating multiple types of content from a single list or library is a powerful feature, it can also make things difficult to manage. As information builds up in the library, you should identify what views and reports your users will require and create custom views that only display items from a specific content type. A *view* is a way of displaying a customized subset of items from a larger set of items in a list or library.

For example, a document library on a project management site might contain a variety of project artifacts such as project plans, scope documents, and status reports. Each of these categories represents unique content types. The following Try It Out shows how to configure a custom view.

Try It Out   **Configure a Custom View Based on Content Type**

One of the most powerful features of tagging items with metadata is creating custom views of content so that only a subset of the documents displays based on certain criteria being met. In this example, you create a custom view that only displays items from a specific content type.

1.   Following the steps previously outlined in "Create a New Content Type" Try It Out at the beginning of the chapter, create a content type called Project Scope Document and associate a Word document as a template.

2.   Associate your Project Scopes Document content type with a document library as discussed in the "Associate Multiple Content Types with a Library" Try It Out.

3.   From the document library's toolbar, select Settings ➪ Create View, as shown in Figure 6-23.

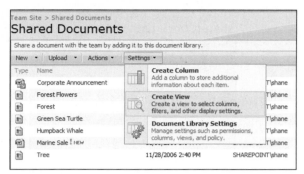

Figure 6-23

4. From Choose a View format, select Standard View.

5. In the View Name section, type **Project Scope Documents**.

6. Scroll down to the Filter section and select Content Type from the Show Items drop-down menu.

7. In the field below Is Equal To, select Project Scope Document as shown in Figure 6-24.

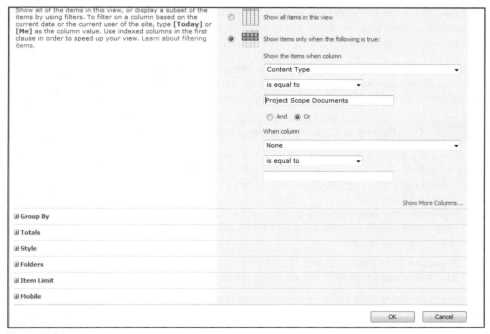

Figure 6-24

8. Scroll to the bottom and click the OK button.

How It Works

After creating a view, it becomes available in the View drop-down menu on your document library tool-bar. Selecting the Project Scope Documents view will show only the items created using the Project Scope Documents content type. See Figure 6-25.

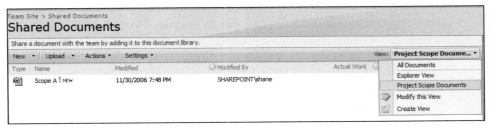

Figure 6-25

Summary

This chapter discussed the very important SharePoint 2007 feature known as content types. *Content types* allow you to package and manage elements such as templates, workflow processes, policies, and meta-data columns into a single reusable component. You can then associate these components with lists and libraries throughout a site collection. Users can then make edits centrally to the site content type gallery, and changes can be updated in all existing content types. After reading this chapter, you should know the following:

❑   The default groups of content types include: Business Intelligence, Document content types, Folder content types, List content types, Page Layout content types, Publishing content types, and Special content types

❑   Every new content type must have a parent content type from which it inherits its settings. You can extend the parent content type to suit your business requirements.

❑   You can associate a content type with a custom template, workflow processes, and site columns. You can also create information management policies to control what information display when an item is opened or printed. You can also configure rules to determine when it must expire.

❑   Some content types are very basic in nature and do not require configuration. However, other content types may be more heavily regulated and controlled.

❑   A single document library or list can host multiple content types. This allows users to work from a single repository for related content. However, when managing multiple content types and large amounts of data within a single library, consider using custom views to maintain an acceptable level of usability for users. Information should always be well organized and easy to find.

Exercises

1. True or False. You can only associate one document template with a document library.

2. Imagine you are responsible for ensuring that all documents created and printed within your organization have the words Private and Confidential on them. What are your options for making this happen, and which would provide the best results?

3. People in your company have complained that recent job postings are being published on the corporate intranet website with typos and grammatical errors. Your management team demands a certain level of professionalism in any content that division posts. What are some steps you can take to ensure that future job postings are reviewed prior to publishing?

Working with Web Parts

You can think of *Web Parts* as the blocks you use to build a team or portal site. Essentially, they are modules or applications that you retrieve from a site's gallery and add to a web page. Every time you create a list or document library, SharePoint creates a corresponding Web Part, which you can drag onto a Web Part page to view the contents of that list or library. Web Parts can be as simple as something that tracks the statistics of your favorite local sports team or as complex as a multitier support system that monitors life-saving medical equipment.

While SharePoint 2007 has Web Parts ready for your use, you can also create your own Web Parts using ASP.NET. For example, if you need a special module on your site that allows users to submit, update, and review support incidents from a central tracking application, you may develop a Web Part for that purpose.

In this chapter, you learn the following:

- ❑   What a Web Part is and what it consists of
- ❑   How to add, move, connect and customize Web Parts
- ❑   What Web Parts are available to you, and how you can use them in your business tasks

The Anatomy of a Web Part Page

Perhaps one of the most important things to note about Web Parts is that you can only add them to a special type of page known as a Web Part page. A *Web Part page* usually consists of Web Part *zones*, or areas where you add Web Parts. The layout template you select will determine the layout of the zones on the page, but you generally have a header, columns for the middle sections, and footer. Figure 7-1 shows an example of a Web Part page that has a header, footer, and three columns in the middle section.

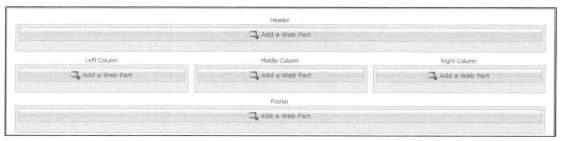

Figure 7-1

Although each Web Part can act independently of all others on the page, you can also connect or organize them in a fashion that best suits your business or purpose. You can place content in the different zones in any manner you desire, but here are some suggestions on how each zone may be used for the Web Part page layout template shown in Figure 7-1:

❏ **Header zone:** Perfect for the company name and logo or title of the web page. You can also place category or regional links here — for example, the different regions of a company that has global interests, links that go to a page with a different language, or links to a specific category of a product. This zone is also a good location for general welcome and instructional text for the site.

❏ **Middle zones:** For the main content of your web page. Middle zones can contain the content on which you want the user's attention to focus, such as a list or library. You can use left or right column for links related to the content in the center column or additional information related to the content in the center column.

❏ **Footer zone:** Good for web page creator credits, commands such as "print page," or general links such as "Contact Us," "About Our Company," or links to privacy and security policy.

There are a few important things to note about Web Part zones:

❏ You will not see a Web Part zone unless Web Part has been added to it. Therefore, if you only want to see Web Parts in the middle zones, you can leave the header and footer zones empty and users of the site will not be able to see those zones when they visit the page. Also, if you have two or three zones, but only add content to one zone, the column with content will take up the entire page. Figure 7-2 shows an example of this. The Shared Document library was added to the middle column Web Part zone. However, because no content existed in either of the other zones, they are not visible on the page and the Shared Documents library takes up the entire page.

Team Site > Shared Documents > BackgroundInfo

BackgroundInfo

Shared Documents

Type	Name	Modified By
	BackgroundInfo ! NEW	SHAREPOINT\shane

⊞ Add new document

Figure 7-2

❑ The Web Part pages have special features that help you build the page by adding content. These features, outlined in more detail in the section "Web Parts Basics," let you browse and search for Web Parts, import and export them, and drag them from zone to zone.

❑ SharePoint offers several Web Part page templates. For example, virtually every site template has a single Web Part page that represents the home page or the default.aspx page. Site managers can create additional pages and store them in a document library so other users can view content and data.

❑ Before you select a template, it's a good idea to sketch how you want content to appear on the page, and then select the Web Part page layout that best fits your sketch. Your final layout should present information so that it's easy to read, uncluttered, and minimizes page scrolling.

In the next Try It Out, you create a new Web Part page in an existing team site.

Try It Out   Create a Web Part Page

In this example, you create a new Web Part page, which is very similar to creating other content elements, such as document libraries, lists, or sites. You select one of the layout templates SharePoint has to offer. Once you select a layout template for a page, you really can't change it later. Therefore, it's best to select a layout that will allow you the greatest level of flexibility for growth and expansion.

1. From the main page of a standard team site, select Site Actions ➪ Create. The Create window appears, as shown in Figure 7-3.

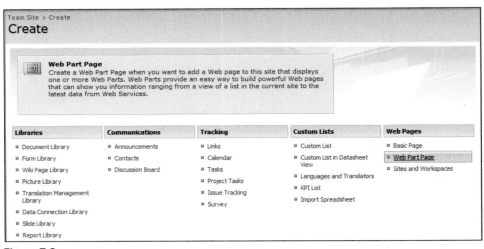

Figure 7-3

2. Select Web Part Page from the Web Pages group.

3. Enter a name for the Web Part page. For this example, enter **backgroundinfo**.

4. Browse through each of the available layout templates and select one that will fit your content. For this example, select the header, footer, three columns layout.

4. Select the Shared Documents library.

5. Click the Create button. A web page appears with a header, footer, and three columns as shown in Figure 7-1.

How It Works

Once you create a Web Part page, you can add Web Parts to the various zones. The layout adjusts as you add content.

Web Parts Basics

In this section, you learn the basics of working with Web Parts — operations common to most Web Parts. As mentioned earlier, you add Web Parts, stored in a site's Web Part gallery, to a Web Part page. Users with appropriate permissions can access this gallery by entering the Edit mode for a Web Part page where they can add Web Parts to a Web Part page in one of the clearly marked Web Part zones. You can enter Edit mode by selecting Edit Page from the Site Actions menu. Figure 7-4 shows an example of a page in Edit mode.

Figure 7-4

From this mode, you can do the following:

❑   **Add Web Parts to a Web Part zone:** Web Parts can be added to the page by clicking an Add a Web Part button available at the top of each Web Part zone. Doing so opens a Web Part selection window displaying a categorized listing of Web Parts.

❑   **Drag Web Parts from zone to zone:** Web Parts can be moved from one Web Part zone to another by simply selecting the title bar of a Web Part and dragging it to the desired zone.

❑   **Change properties of a Web Part:** When a Web Part page is in Edit mode, an Edit button appears on the right-hand side of each Web Part title bar. By selecting this button, the Web Parts property pane appears. From this pane, you can make changes to the configuration, appearance, or behavior of the Web Part. You may also change the location of the Web Part using this pane.

❑ **Export a Web Part:** You can export some Web Parts from a page and reuse and import them on another page. When a Web Part is exported, all settings for the Web Part are retained and saved in a file that can later be imported to another SharePoint page or site.

To learn what the different SharePoint Web Parts are and how to use them, see the next section, "Using the Various SharePoint Web Parts."

In addition, when adding a Web Part to a zone from the Web Part selection window, you have the option of entering the Advanced Web Part gallery, shown in Figure 7-5. From this gallery, you can do the following:

Figure 7-5

❑ **Browse for Web Parts:** You can browse the available galleries of the site and server in an intuitive manner. In Figure 7-5, you can see three galleries:

❑ *Closed Web Parts* include any Web Parts previously added to the page but that a user with the appropriate permissions has closed. When a Web Part is closed, it no longer appears on the page, but only in this gallery.

❑ *Site Gallery Web Parts* are Web Parts that SharePoint offers as well as any Web Parts unique to the site, such as list- and library-related Web Parts. See the next section, "Using the Various SharePoint Web Parts" for more information.

❑ *Server Gallery Web Parts* are those custom Web Parts installed on the server that have either been developed or purchased separately to meet a specific need of the organization.

❑ **Import Web Parts to a page:** You can import Web Parts to a page from another location, such as your desktop or a network share. To import a Web Part, you must select Import from the menu at the top of the tool pane, as shown later in this chapter in Figure 7-15.

❑ **Search for Web Parts:** As a Web Part gallery grows, it becomes tedious to browse through the Web Part listings. Therefore, SharePoint has a search function in the Advanced Web Part tool pane specifically for searching for Web Parts across all galleries. This is helpful if you are unsure in which gallery a Web Part is available.

The next few Try It Outs focus on some of the features just discussed so you can understand how each works and how you can manage activities related to your Web Parts. The first Try It Out has you working with the Content Editor Web Part to add and format content. You then learn, in the second Try It Out, how to tailor to your Web Part to meet your corporate culture; each Web Part has properties and attributes that you can use to modify a Web Part's title bar, border, height, and width. In the third Try It Out, you use the Edit mode to drag Web Parts above or below other Web Parts in the same zone, or to a completely different zone.

No matter what the technology, it's always best to make things reusable. SharePoint helps you recycle Web Parts by allowing you to export them as single portable files with a .DWP or .WEBPART extension. You learn how to export in the fourth Try It Out in this section. You can then use the fifth and final Try It Out to import a Web Part to another site.

Try It Out   Add a Web Part to a Page

In this example, you add the Content Editor Web Part to the backgroundinfo.aspx page you created in the "Create a Web Part Page" Try It Out. This Web Part allows you to add free-form text related to your company. Because you haven't added any content, when you first place the Web Part to the Web Part zone, you'll see instructions on configuring the Web Part. Your next action is to launch the Web Part Tool Pane so you can change the Web Part's appearance, layout, and content. The Content Editor Web Part has buttons that allow you to edit content either in a rich-text editor or a source editor. This Try It Out demonstrates both options.

1. From the home page of your team site, select the Shared Documents library from the Quick Launch navigation bar.

2. Select the backgroundinfo.aspx page you created in the previous Try It Out.

3. Select Site Actions ➪ Edit Page. The Web Part Zones on the page should now be clearly visible, as shown in Figure 7-6.

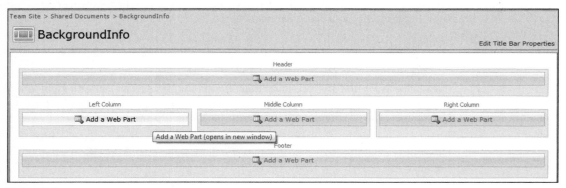

Figure 7-6

4. Select the Add a Web Part link from the Left Column Web Part zone. The Add Web Parts – Webpage Dialog window appears, as shown in Figure 7-7.

5. Locate the Content Editor Web Part from the Miscellaneous group.

6. Click the Add button. Your Web Part becomes visible on the page.

7. Click the Open the Tool Pane link. The Web Part Tool Pane appears on the right side of the window.

8. Click the HTML button from the pane. A HTML editor appears as shown in Figure 7-8.

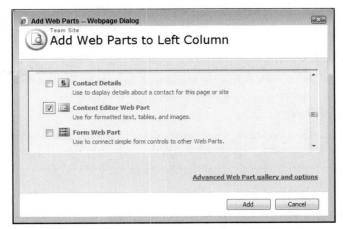

Figure 7-7

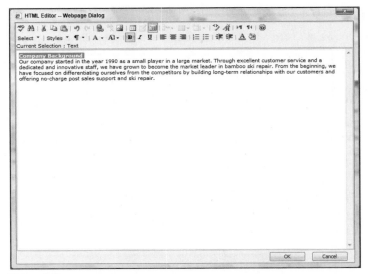

Figure 7-8

9. Enter the following text into the window.

> **Company Background**
>
> **Our company started in the year 1990 as a small player in a large market. Through excellent customer service and a dedicated and innovative staff, we have grown to become the market leader in bamboo ski repair.**
>
> **From the beginning, we have focused on differentiating ourselves from the competitors by building long-term relationships with our customers and offering no-charge post sales support and ski repair.**

10. Select the words `company background` and click the Bold button from the Editor toolbar.

11. Click the OK button.

12. Click the Source Editor button from the Content Editor Web Part pane.

13. Enter the following code below the last line of the content in the editor:

> **Committed to Service**
>
> **If, for any reason, a customer is not satisfied with their ski purchase, we will refund their money 100 percent, no questions asked.**

14. Click the Save button.

15. Click the Apply and OK buttons at the bottom of the Web Part tool pane.

How It Works

As this example shows, you can add a content editor to a page to allow users to add content. Most business users will prefer the rich-text editor because it has buttons similar to the formatting buttons you find in Word. Users familiar with HTML may prefer the source editor.

Try It Out   Modify the Appearance of a Web Part

Every Web Part has a set of customizable features such as Appearance, which you can modify via the Web Part Properties tool pane. By selecting the Modify option from a contextual menu, you can change the Web Part's title, height and width, and chrome. *Chrome* refers to the appearance of the interface, so changing the chrome type will alter things like the Web Part's border and title bar.

1. Open the backgroundinfo.aspx page from the previous Try It Out.

2. Select the down arrow on the right-hand side of the Content Editor Web Part title bar to open the contextual menu, shown in Figure 7-9.

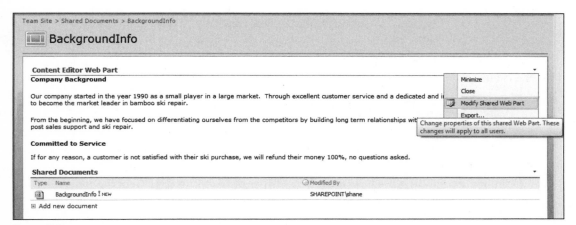

Figure 7-9

3. From the list of available options, select Modify Shared Web Part.

4. From the Web Part tool pane, locate and expand the appearance section, as shown in Figure 7-10.

Figure 7-10

5. In the Title field, type a title for the Web Part. For this example, type **Corporate History**.

6. Leave the height, width, and chrome state at the default settings.

7. For Chrome Type, select Title and Border.

8. Click the OK button. You'll notice that your Web Part has a border and title.

Try It Out   **Move a Web Part to a New Web Part Zone**

As discussed earlier, Web Parts have zones, into and out of which you can move Web Parts to alter the look of your page. To do this, you enter the Edit mode, and drag the Web Part above or below Web Parts in the same zone or to a different zone. This demonstrates a Web Part's flexibility; in the past, you had to make significant code updates to make simple layout changes to a page, but by using Web Parts, you can move content modules anywhere on the page by just a few simple actions.

1. Select Site Actions ➪ Edit Page. Your page is now in Edit mode, as shown in Figure 7-11.

2. Click the title bar of a Web Part and then drag and drop it from one zone to another or within the same zone, just as long as the Web Part stays in a zone. You cannot drag a Web Part to an area of the page that doesn't have a Web Part zone.

Figure 7-11

Try It Out   Export a Web Part from a Page

You may find it useful to reuse an already configured Web Part on another site, particularly when the Web Part contains specialized content and customizations that would be difficult to recreate. SharePoint allows you to export Web Parts as single portable file (.DWP or .WEBPART), which you can then easily move to another site. With this feature, SharePoint prompts you to name and save the file you want to export to a location on your hard drive.

1. Select Site Actions ➪ Edit Page.

2. Locate the Web Part you want to export. In this case, you use the Content Editor Web Part you used in the last Try it Out, which is called Corporate History.

3. Click the Edit button on the toolbar to make the contextual menu appear.

4. From the contextual menu, select Export as shown in Figure 7-12.

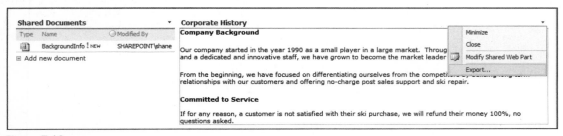

Figure 7-12

5. Click Save. The Save As window appears, as shown in Figure 7-13. You are prompted to name and save your Web Part. Save the Web Part with the name Corporate_History and place it on your desktop. You should save this with a .DWP extension.

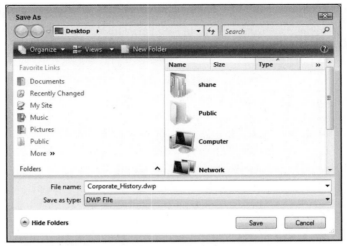

Figure 7-13

How It Works

Some other more complex Web Parts may be with a .WEBPART extension, instead of the .DWP in this exercise, but the purpose is the same. SharePoint automatically determines which format should be used. You can later import this file to a different site using the steps in the next Try It Out.

Try It Out   Import a Web Part to a Page

Once you export a Web Part, you can import it to any site you want using the Import command in Edit mode. This command lets you browse through the exported Web Part so you can import them into your Sites Web Part gallery, which you can view in the Web Part tool pane. From there, it's a simple matter of dragging the Web Part to your page.

In the case of the Content Editor Web Part, you could import the .DWP file to any SharePoint server regardless of location because no references existed to data sources or special assemblies. When working with Web Parts that connect or display data from specific locations, it may be necessary to ensure that the data is accessible from the new location.

1. Select Site Actions ⇨ Create. You are redirected to the SharePoint creation page.

2. Select Sites and Workspaces from the Web Pages group.

3. Enter a title for the site. For this example, use **Corporate Information**.

4.   Enter a URL name for the Web Part and select a blank site template. For this example, enter **corpinfo** for the URL name.

5.   Click the Create button. Your new page is created, and you are redirected to it.

6.   Select Site Actions ➪ Edit Page to enter Edit mode for your page.

7.   Select Add a Web Part from any of the Web Part zones. The Add Web Parts – Webpage Dialog appears, as shown in Figure 7-14.

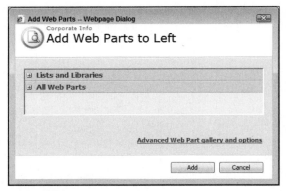

Figure 7-14

8.   From the bottom right of the dialog window now exposed, select Advanced Web Part Gallery and Options. The Add Web Parts tool pane should now be available at the far right of your screen, as shown in Figure 7-15.

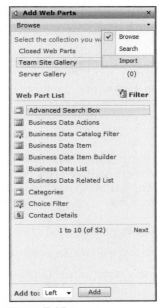

Figure 7-15

9. From the top of the tool pane, select Browse.

10. A menu appears displaying options for Import and Search; select Import. The pane changes to show an Import section with a Browse button, as shown in Figure 7-16.

11. Select the Browse button. The Choose File window, also shown in Figure 7-16, appears allowing you to locate the Web Part you want to import.

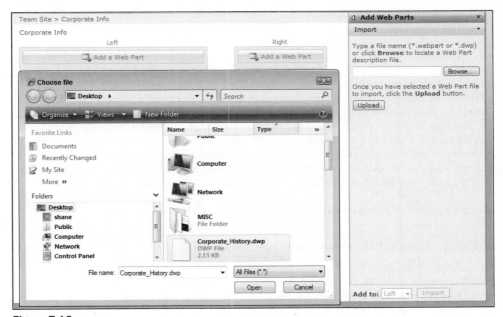

Figure 7-16

12. Browse to your desktop and locate the Corporate History.DWP file you exported in the previous Try It Out. When you have the file selected, click the Open button in the Choose File window to complete the operation.

13. Click the Upload button on the pane. You see a list of imported Web Parts. You are now free to drag these into a Web Part zone.

Using the Various SharePoint Web Parts

Now that you know the basics of working with Web Parts, it's time to find out what Web Parts SharePoint has to offer. Each SharePoint Web Part is designed to aid in the display of content or information on your website. Some Web Parts display information based on the SharePoint site or environment, such as the Table of Contents Web Part, which is a navigational tool to display links to sites, lists, and libraries. Other Web Parts, such as the Content Editor Web Part you used in the previous section, can be configured to include content that users enter. Then there are Web Parts that work in combination with other Web Parts to control how a page displays information, such as the Filter Web Parts.

The previous section discussed operations that were common to most Web Parts. This section introduces each of the different Web Parts as well as some of the unique characteristics of each.

List and Library Web Parts

Some of SharePoint's best collaborative features are the lists and libraries where teams can store and organize documents. Each time you create a list or library, SharePoint creates a corresponding Web Part in the gallery so you can place a view of the list or library on any Web Part page. This empowers you to channel information to key locations of your site where they make the most sense. For example, you may have a custom page on your site for reporting outstanding tasks. Therefore, you can add a Web Part of the tasks list to this page so users can view what tasks they should focus on next.

List and library Web Parts allow you to select views and display toolbars in order to access the information that you need. In Chapter 4, you learned how to create custom views to address your requirements for information display. In this section, you learn how you can use the List and Library Web Parts to display these views on any page you want. The first Try It Out shows you how to change the view of a List Web Part so the user can see only the information he or she needs. In addition, each List View Web Part has a toolbar associated with it to help you work with list data and settings. The toolbar has multiple states. The Full Toolbar exposes all the key functionality such as RSS feeds, Connect to Outlook, Export Spreadsheet, and Alert Creation as well as List Settings and Column or View creation. The Summary Toolbar allows users to add a new item to the list directly from the Web Part. You also have the option of not having a toolbar at all. You may select that option in cases where the page is intended primarily for reporting or viewing information and no interaction is expected or desired from viewers.

For more on lists and libraries and how to manage them, see Chapters 2 through 4.

Try It Out   Change the View of a List Web Part

In this example, you add a Web Part to a page that is associated with the Tasks list of your team site. For every list or library on your site, SharePoint creates a Web Part to display the data associated with that list. For example, a default team site template contains several preconfigured lists and libraries such as a tasks list, links list, and Shared Documents library, and each has a corresponding Web Part in the Web Part gallery. So, if you create a tasks list called "Team Tasks," a new Web Part appears in the site's gallery called "Team Tasks." You can add this Web Part to any Web Part page to display items from that list on the page.

You can have the available views associated with a list display in the Web Part. For example, you can have users see all tasks assigned to them, as well as those assigned to the entire team for the current day. You can, therefore, add the Tasks list to the page twice and select the appropriate view in each instance of the Web Part to suit your requirements.

1. From the home page of a team site, select Site Actions ⇨ Edit Page. The site zones appear, as previously shown in Figure 7-6.

2. Click the Add a Web Part button from the left Web Part zone. The Web Part Selection window appears.

3. Select the Tasks List Web Part.

4. Click the Add button. An instance of the Tasks List Web Part is added to your page.

5. From the toolbar, select the Tasks Web Part's Edit button.

6. Select Modify Shared Web Part to expose the Web Part Properties tool pane.

7. From the Selected View drop-down menu, select My Tasks as shown in Figure 7-17.

Figure 7-17

8. Expand the Appearance group of the Web Part properties.

9. Change the Title to **My Personal Tasks**.

10. Click Apply.

11. Click the OK button on the Web Part Properties tool pane to close it.

How It Works

In this Try It Out, you select the My Tasks view and then change the title of the Web Part to describe the view to be displayed. This informs users that they are viewing a subset of the data available in the list and not the default view of All Items. When you click OK in step 11, notice that your List View Web Part has changed slightly. You can use this same process for custom views you create for any list or library.

Try It Out   **Change the Toolbar of a List Web Part**

As mentioned previously, List Web Parts have an associated toolbar that offers users quick access to list data and settings. You can change these toolbars to offer more or less functionality depending on the properties you set. Your choices include Full, Summary, and No Toolbar. Before you change a toolbar that goes to a List Web Part, you should consider how users interact with the data stored in Web Parts. If you expect that the users will interact heavily with content and updates, they may need the Full toolbar.

1. Select the down arrow on the right side of the title bar of the Tasks Web Part and click Modify Shared Web Part.

2. From the Toolbar Type option, select Full Toolbar, an example of which is shown in Figure 7-18. You also have options for a Summary toolbar (as shown in Figure 7-19) and No Toolbar.

Figure 7-18

Figure 7-19

3. In some cases, it may be most appropriate to show No Toolbar in the Web Part at all. The next example reviews the steps for changing the toolbar display option on a Web Part.

4. Click the OK button to close the tool pane. Notice your Web Part now has a toolbar exposing some key functionality allowing you to interact even further with your list data.

Business Data Web Parts

Although SharePoint is an excellent data repository, a typical company keeps much of its operational and historical data in other systems such as SAP, PeopleSoft, Oracle, and custom line-of-business (LOB) applications. These are usually called *back-end systems*, and they often run on mainframe or midrange computers and have been in place for many years. Because it may be impractical to reengineer them to use SharePoint for data storage but there is still a need to extract their data for reports, KPIs, and other SharePoint collaboration features, SharePoint's offers the Business Data Catalog (BDC). BDC lets you access data from these other data sources via specialized Web Parts, lists, and libraries.

The *Business Data Web Parts* are a group of powerful Web Parts that allow you connect to and interact with important business data from various sources ranging from Excel workbooks data sources connected through the BDC. The Business Data Web Parts consist of the following Web Parts:

Web Part	Description
Business Data Actions	Displays a list of actions from the BDC that allow you to view or interact with business data. For example, you may be able to email a customer by selecting an action from a Web Part displaying information about the customer.
Business Data Item	Displays information related to a single item from a data source in the BDC. For example, you may be able to view details of a customer's invoice in a Web Part.
Business Data Item Builder	Used only on business data profile pages, this Web Part creates a business data item from parameters on the query string and then provides it to other Web Parts.
Business Data List	Displays a list of items from a data source in the BDC. An example of this might be a listing of customers.
Business Data Related List	Displays a list of items as they pertain to child parent relationships from a data source in the BDC. An example of this is a listing of orders made by a single customer that had been selected in a Business Data List Web Part.
Excel Web Access	Allows you to interact with an Excel workbook as a web page. This is helpful for displaying financial or numerical reports based on information stored in a spreadsheet by displaying it directly in a Web Part.
iView	A special Business Data Web Part used to display iViews from SAP portals.
WSRP Consumer	A special Business Data Web Part used to display portals from websites using WSRP 1.1.

Each of the business data Web Parts (excluding the iView and WSRP consumer Web Parts) is covered in detail in Chapters 12 and 13.

Content Rollup Web Parts

Content rollup Web Parts allow you to gather information from multiple subsites within a site collection and then create a "rolled-up" view of that information in a single location. Commonly a user might place these Web Parts on a personal site, such as *My Site*. On a My Site, users can track tasks assigned to them from all sites in the site collection. Content rollup Web Parts are also particularly helpful when you have multiple divisions or teams in your business. Rollups allow each division to have a presence on the corporate intranet, while allowing users to roll up information so that they can view only the divisions that they need. The content rollup Web Parts include the following:

Web Part	Description
Colleague Tracker	Displays a list of your colleagues and any recent changes they have made to their profile. For example, if someone you have specified as a colleague changes positions in the organization and updated his title, you would see information displayed in the Colleague Tracker Web Part.
Colleagues	Displays links to the colleagues a user has shared with you. By clicking a link, you are redirected to the personal site of that user.
Get Started with My Site	This Web Part displays tips and tricks to get a user familiar with using a My Site. This Web Part is an administrative Web Part that is part of each My Site when it is created.
In Common Between Us	When viewing another user's My Site, this Web Part displays things in common between you and the site owner based on information in your user profiles. For example, if you view the site of a user who attended the same university as you, you see this highlighted in the Web Part.
Memberships	This Web Part displays your site and distribution list memberships.
My Links	Displays a list of your links that you have added to the My Links list on your My Site.
My Pictures	Displays pictures from your picture library with an option to view them as a slide show.
My Workspaces	Displays a list of subsites created under your My Site.
Recent Blog Posts	Displays the recent user blog posts.
SharePoint Documents	Displays documents authored by the user where the user is a site member.
Site Aggregator	Also called *My SharePoint Sites* on your My Site, you can add this Web Part to any site to display a combined view of documents and tasks that are related to the current user across a number of sites. A user can add sites by creating tabs in the Web Part for each of the sites they frequent often (see the next Try It Out).

Try It Out   **Using the Site Aggregator Web Part**

As you begin creating your team sites, you need a way to help organize these sites. The Site Aggregator Web Part puts the sites you frequently use at your fingertips so that accessing documents you create and assigned tasks is a breeze. The Site Aggregator Web Part collects documents and tasks from sites that you specify in the Web Part by entering a URL or creating a tab. In this Try It Out, you add the Site Aggregator Web Part to a page and create a new tab in the Web Part for the Advertising Team site. This allows members of the team site to directly access documents and tasks in completely separate sites directly from the Web Part on the team site.

1. Select Site Actions ⇨ Edit Page. The page appears in Edit mode.

2. Select Add a Web Part in the zone you want to display your Web Part.

3. In the Content Rollup Web Parts section, select the check box next to the Site Aggregator Web Part.

4. Click the Add button. The Site Aggregator Web Part is added to the page.

5. To add a new Site tab to the Site Aggregator, select New Site Tab. The Web Part refreshes and contains a form where you can enter the name and description of a site.

6. Enter the URL of the advertising site you created in Chapter 5. If you do not remember that URL or did not complete the exercises, enter the URL of a site that contains multiple documents that have been created by you and tasks that are assigned to you.

7. Change the title for the tab to **Advertising Documents**.

8. Click the Create button.

How It Works

When you create a new tab, you specify the URL of a SharePoint site and the site's name is automatically populated. This means that the Web Part connects and recognizes the site. Once you save the tab, you see a listing of documents and tasks in the Web Part, as shown in Figure 7-20.

Figure 7-20

These Web Parts are stored on the advertising site but accessible via the Web Part for your convenience. This Web Part will display a personalized list of documents and tasks to each visitor to the team site. Users commonly place this on a My Site so they can add tabs for the sites they frequent so they can easily access documents and tasks in a single location. You will also likely notice that the location for some documents may be different. This is because the Web Part is displaying documents from multiple document libraries. This is an example of the rollup capabilities of the Web Part.

Dashboard Web Parts

Key performance indicators (KPI) are business metrics that organizations use to monitor their current state of growth and activity. Executives determine how well their company is doing by comparing KPIs against predetermined business goals. Because the company's future course of action may largely depend on this comparison, executives demand reports that accurately show KPIs. SharePoint uses KPI in its Dashboard Web Parts to give you a visual indication of how well or poorly your business activities are progressing. Part of this visualization comes from the ranges that you set for icons that act as warning indicators. A green icon indicates that the KPI is on target. A yellow icon means that the KPI is at the lower end of the target, and the red icon KPI warns that the KPI is severely below target.

Dashboard Web Parts include the following:

Web Part	Description
Key Performance Indicators	A list of status indicators that measure your organization's progress toward goals.
KPI Details	A single status indicator that may derive data sources, such as SharePoint Lists, Excel Workbooks, and SQL Server 2005 Analysis Services KPIs.

In this section, you work through a Try It Out to see how to use the Key Performance Indicator Web Part. In Chapter 11, which discusses Excel Services, you learn how to actually create a KPI list as part of a business scorecard, which is basically a list of various KPIs versus a company's targets.

Try It Out   Using the Key Performance Indicator Web Part

To start this Try It Out, you must first create key performance indicators in a list on a team site so that you can display the data in a Web Part. Although you can create key performance indicators based on multiple data sources, in this case you create a KPI using manually entered data.

For more on lists, see Chapters 2 and 4. For more on KPIs as they relate to Excel Services, see Chapter 11.

To get a sense of how KPIs work, you set your first quarter sales item goal as 1,000 units and specify the current indicator value as 950. You then set values for when warning icons will appear. For this example, the yellow range is between 900 and 1,000 and any items below 900 will display a red warning symbol.

Next, you add the KPI Web Part to your page by configuring the Web Part to a list, in this case a sales projections list. When configuring the KPI List Web Part, you may select between the various display templates that impact the shape and format of the icons. These are Checkboxes, Flat, and Traffic Lights.

1. Select Site Actions ⇨ Create from your team site.

2. Select KPI List from the Custom Lists Column.

3. Enter a list name. For this example, enter **Sales Projections**.

4. Click the Create button.

5. Click the drop-down arrow on the New Menu Item of the KPI list toolbar and select the Indicator Using Manually Entered Information option, as shown in Figure 7-21. You are redirected to an Indicator Creation page, as shown in Figure 7-22.

Figure 7-21

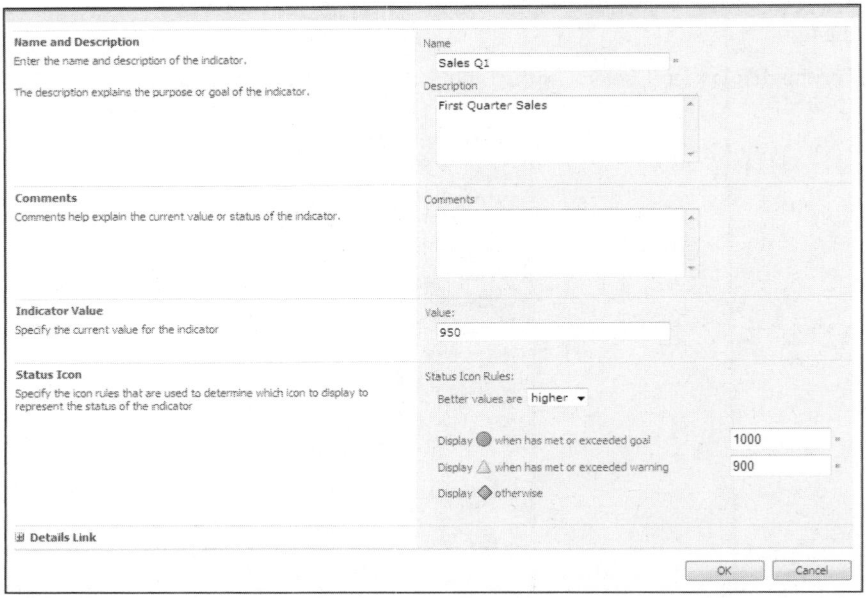

Figure 7-22

6. Give your indicator a name and description. For this example, type **Sales Q1** for the name and **First Quarter Sales** for the description.

7. For indicator value, enter **950**.

8. Enter the values at which you want your green and yellow indicator icons to appear. Note that the red icon appears anytime the value is below whatever you specify for the yellow icon (in this case below 900) so you do not have to enter a value for the red icon. For this example, use the following table to enter these values:

Value Name	Entered Value
Status Icon section	Select the Better Values Are Higher option.
Green Icon	Type **1000**.
Yellow Icon	Type **900**.

9. Click the OK button. Your KPI is created in the list.

10. From the home page of your team site, select Site Actions ⇨ Edit Page. The page reloads in Edit mode.

11. Select Add a Web Part in the zone you want to display the Web Part.

12. From the Dashboard Web Parts section, select the check box next to Key Performance Indicator Web Part and then click Add.

13. Click the Open the Tool Pane link to configure the Web Part link displayed inside the Web Part.

14. Click the icon to the right of the Indicator List field.

15. Select the Sales Projects list. Note: You may need to select the team site from the options on the left.

16. For the display icon, select Traffic Lights, as shown in Figure 7-23.

Figure 7-23

17. Click Apply, and then OK on the Web Part tool pane.

How It Works

Because your current value is 950, you can expect to see a yellow indicator. As long as you keep your KPI items updated over time, the visual indicators will remain accurate and executives can make informed business decisions.

Filter Web Parts

As an organization grows, inevitably so does the amount of information revolving around it, resulting in users wasting time sifting through data to find what they need. *Filters* ensure that the right information goes to the appropriate users. They both instantly reduce the amount of information that displays within connected Web Parts and return relevant information to end users. SharePoint offers several filters for users to access data. With the exception of the Filter Actions Web Part, all the Web Parts in the following table filter Web Part content using the method indicated. The Filter Action Web Part filters actions only.

Web Parts can be connected to one another so that one Web Part provides values to filter the display of information on the other Web Part. For example, one Web Part may contain a listing of customers, which is connected to another Web Part that displays a listing of orders. When a user selects a customer from the first Web Part, the orders list will refresh to display only orders that contain the customer's name. Filter Web Parts expand on your options for connecting Web Parts by providing you with more options on how data can be filtered in the Web Parts.

Web Part	How It Filters
Business Data Catalog Filter	Uses a list of values from the BDC.
Choice Filter	Uses a list of values that the page author enters.
Current User Filter	Identifies properties of the current users to filter information on the page.
Date Filter	Allows the user to enter or pick a date that filters information on the page.
Filter Actions	This filter Actions
Page Field Filter	Uses information about the current page to filter information in a Web Part.
Query String (URL) Filter	Uses values passed via the query string.
SharePoint List Filter	Uses a list of values from an Office SharePoint Server list.
SQL Server 2005 Analysis Services Filter	Uses SQL Server 2005 Analysis Services Cubes.
Text Filter	Allows the user to enter text values.

You can use the Current User Filter Web Part to display information from other Web Parts or data that is relevant to the current user. Upon recognizing the user, the system generates content based on a field that contains either the current user's username (example: domain\user) or a specific user profile property such as Name or Email Address.

When you connect two Web Parts, they share information between them in order to filter content. In this particular Try It Out, you connect the Current User Filter Web Part to a standard Tasks List Web Part to filter the tasks list so that users only see items assigned to them. You start by first creating a list that displays in a List Web Part. Although this exercise uses the Tasks list, you can apply the same process to any list or library that contains a column with user profile information. For example, if your document library has a column for Reviewer that uses the Person or Group column type, then you can connect that column to a Current User Filter Web Part.

In this example, you use the Summary toolbar to add sample data to your list. In the "Change the View of a List Web Part" Try It Out, you learned that you can customize the toolbar on a Web Part by choosing either the Summary, Full, or No toolbar options. By leaving the default toolbar choice of Summary in this example, users can add content directly from the Web Part instead of visiting the list page. This toolbar is only displayed to users who have the permissions to create new content.

Once you add the Current User Filter Web Part to the page, you define what type of information it should look for in the connected Web Part. By default, the search is for the current username column, which has information in the domain\user format. However, the type of information you seek may be in a person- or group-based column. If so, you must select a profile property compatible with the format of the information in the column. In this example, you select the Name column because it is the same information that displays within the Assigned To column of your List Web Part.

1.   From your team site, select Site Actions ➪ Create. You are redirected to the SharePoint content creation page.

2.   From the Tracking column, select Tasks.

3.   In the Name field, type **Important Tasks**.

4.   Click the Create button. Your new Tasks list is created, and you are redirected to the List page.

5.   Return to the main page of your site and select Site Actions ➪ Edit Page. The main page reloads in Edit mode.

6.   Select Add a Web Part in the left Web Part zone. The Web Part Selection window appears.

7.   In the Lists and Libraries section, select the check box next to the Important Tasks Web Part, and then click the Add button. The main page reloads with the new Web Part added to the left Web Part zone.

8.   Click the Exit Edit Mode link.

9.   To ensure that you have some actual data to filter, you add a couple of sample tasks directly from the Web Part. Click the Add a New Item link from Summary toolbar. The Important Tasks: New Item window appears, as shown in Figure 7-24.

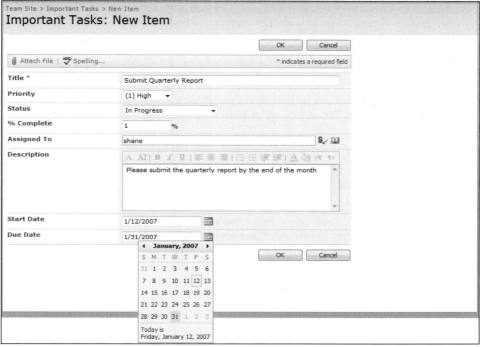

Figure 7-24

10.   Enter information for the new task. For this example, use the following table to enter values:

Value Name	Entered Value
Title	Type **Submit Quarterly Report**.
Priority	Select (1) High from the drop-down menu.
Status	Select In Progress from the drop-down menu.
% Complete	Type **1**.
Assigned To	Type your name here.
Description	Type **Please submit the quarterly report by the end of the month**.
Start Date	Leave as the current day.
End Date	Select the last day of the current month.

11.   Click the OK button.

12. Repeat the steps for at least one other task, ensuring that it's assigned to another user. This exercise assigns Amanda Murphy with the task of updating the January sales figures. Now that you have a list and data to filter, you can add the Current User Filter Web Part to the page.

13. Select Site Actions ➪ Edit Page. The page reloads in Edit mode.

14. Select Add a Web Part from the Right zone. The Web Part selection window appears.

15. From the Filters Web Parts section, select the check box next to the Current User Filter Web Part and then select Add. The main page reloads with the current user filter Web Part added to the page.

This Web Part is not visible on the page to users. It is used to filter data in the Tasks List Web Part.

16. From the Current User Filter Web Part, select Edit ➪ Modify Shared Web Part. The Web Part tool pane appears.

17. In the Select Value to Provide section of the Web Part properties tool pane, select the radio button for SharePoint Profile Value for Current User, as shown in Figure 7-25.

Figure 7-25

18. Select Name from the drop-down menu.

19. Click the Apply button. The main page refreshes to contain your latest changes.

20. Select Current User Filter Web Part Edit Menu ➪ Connections ➪ Send Filter Values to ➪ Important Tasks. The Web Part Connection Definition window appears.

21. In the Consumer Field Name drop-down menu, select Assigned To.

22. Click the Finish button. Your Web Parts are now connected.

23. Click the Exit Edit Mode link. Your Web Parts do not display only tasks for which you are listed in the Assigned To column.

How It Works

When the Web Parts are connected, the requested values are filtered based on the specified criteria. In this case, only information relevant to the current user is visible. Adding the other Filter Web Parts follows a similar process to that which is listed in the previous Try It Out; however, the type of information that will be filtered may be slightly different.

Miscellaneous Web Parts

The *Miscellaneous Web Parts* feature a group of Web Parts that are designed to meet a number of unique needs and can be customized to display custom information or data. Some of these Web Parts such as the Content Editor, Form, and Image Web Parts have existed in previous versions of SharePoint, but others are new or significantly enhanced, as shown in the following table:

Web Part	Description
Contact Details	Displays information about a contact for the page or site.
Content Editor Web Part	Places rich text, tables, or images directly on to a page.
Form Web Part	Connects simple form controls to other Web Parts.
Image Web Part	Displays a single image.
Page Viewer Web Part	Displays linked content such as a file, folder, or web page. This content is separated from the rest of the page.
Relevant Documents	Displays documents relevant to the current user.
Site Users	Displays a list of the users of the current site and their online status.
User Tasks	Displays tasks assigned to the current user.
XML Web Part	Use this for XML and XSL Transformation.

Some examples of the new Web Parts include relevant documents and user tasks, which roll up information from multiple locations into a single Web Part. These Web Parts take advantage of personalization and content rollup in order to minimize the locations where users are required to visit to see relevant information. In the next example, you use the Relevant Documents Web Part to demonstrate some of its rollup and customization capabilities.

Try It Out   Using the Relevant Documents Web Part

In this Try It Out, you add the Relevant Documents Web Part to the main page of a team site. As team members visit your site, they will see a listing of documents relevant to them across all existing document libraries. A site manager has three display options for this Web Part: The site can display documents that the user last modified, that the user created, or that the user currently has checked out. Although a custom view of a library would accomplish the same thing, the Relevant Documents Web Part can display documents on the site regardless of their location. The Data category has an option that allows you to display a hyperlinked location to where the document is actually stored.

A good use of this Web Part is to place it in the right-hand corner of a fairly active team site with the title "Items Checked Out to Me." When documents are buried in folders and spread across multiple libraries, users may not know they still have documents checked out, and showing a quick list of checked out items is beneficial. This saves the user the significant time it would take to navigate down through multiple levels to find their working documents.

1. Select Site Actions ⇨ Edit Page. The page appears in Edit mode.

2. Select Add a Web Part and then select Relevant Documents from the Miscellaneous group.

3. Click the Add button. The main page reloads with your Web Part added to the page in the desired zone.

4. Select the Edit button on the Web Part title bar and select the Modify Shared Web Part from the drop-down menu that appears. The Web Part tool pane opens.

5. Expand the Data category at the very bottom of Web Part tool pane.

6. Select the check boxes for Include Documents Created By Me and Include Documents Checked Out To Me, as shown in Figure 7-26.

Figure 7-26

7. Change the maximum number of items shown to 15 so that up to 15 items will be display in the Web Part.

8. Click Apply, and then OK save the Web Part tool pane changes. The Web Part reloads to display up to 15 items that have been created by you or are checked out to you.

Outlook Web Access Web Parts

With more and more organizations taking advantage of the rich email capabilities of Exchange Server 2003 and 2007's Outlook Web Access, it's no surprise that SharePoint offers Outlook Web Access Web Parts. The various Web Parts are: Calendar, Contacts, Inbox, Mail Folder, and Tasks list. These Web Parts allow you to see what's going on in Outlook without exiting SharePoint.

Note that these Web Parts only work if you're using Outlook Web Access or Exchange Server 2003 or later.

In the next Try It Out, you learn how to add two of these Outlook Web Access Web Parts to a personal site to view your Outlook Calendar and Tasks. By default, the My Calendar Web Part should already exist on your personal site. However, if for some reason it has been removed, you need to add it back to complete this exercise using the method described in the previous Try It Out for adding a Web Part to a page.

The following Try It Outs focus on the Calendar and Task Web Parts; however, the same processes can be used to add the other Outlook Web Access Web Parts to a page. The only difference will be the view of information that is displayed.

Try It Out — View Outlook Calendar and Tasks from Your Personal Site

Once SharePoint is rolled out to users, it usually becomes the application that is always open either in the browser or dashboard so that they can perform their work. Naturally, then, users need an area where they can track their personal email, appointments, or tasks. The Outlook Web Access Web Parts give them this capability, and they can easily configure it by simply defining the mail server address (if not already populated), the mailbox name (if not already populated), and a preferred view (if applicable).

In this example, you add the Exchange Calendar and Tasks List Web Parts to a user's personal SharePoint site so that any items that these parts can access become available each time they visit it. The My Site can be customized based on the user's wishes. The Calendar Web Part can display either a monthly view, weekly view, or daily view. The Tasks Web Part can sort things either by their due date or strictly by subject. Users also commonly display their inbox so that they can access email directly from their My Site. This is particularly helpful for mobile or remote workers who log into the SharePoint interface to access information in a web-based environment. Having their email messages embedded within their site provides instant accessibility and ease of use.

1. Click the My Site link from anywhere within your SharePoint environment. By default, in the top right-hand corner the My Calendar Web Part should appear, as shown in Figure 7-27.

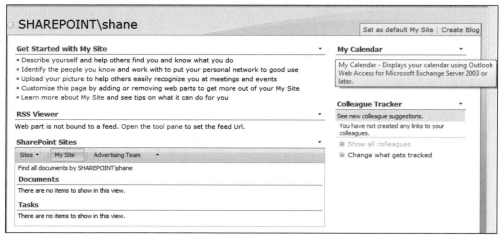

Figure 7-27

2. Click the Open the Tool Pane link from within the Web Part. The Web Part tool pane appears.

3. Enter the web address for your Exchange 2003 or 2007 mail server. If you are unsure of the address, see your mail server administrator.

4. The value of your mailbox should be already specified. If not, enter your email address.

5. Click the Apply, and then OK. The page reloads containing your configured Web Part.

6. Select Site Actions ⇨ Edit Page. The page is displayed in Edit mode.

7. Select Add a Web Part from the Middle Right Zone. The Web Part Select window appears.

8. From the Outlook Web Access group, select My Tasks.

9. Click the Add button.

10. Click the Open the Tool Pane link from within the Web Part.

11. Specify the web address for your Exchange 2003 or 2007 mail server.

12. Select By Due Date for the view.

13. Click Apply, and then OK. Your Web Parts are displayed on your My Site containing information directly from Outlook Web Access.

Search Web Parts

While SharePoint easily channels important information to relevant audiences, you still may have to search for information. To make searching for information as easy as possible, SharePoint 2007 has made significant improvements to the Search capabilities, not the least of which includes Search Web Parts.

The Search feature and related Web Parts are reviewed in detail in Chapter 14, which is dedicated to the topic of search and search interface customization. In this chapter, you configure some of the following Web Parts to create a customizable search interface. While some of the display properties of the Web Parts may be slightly different, many common features exist between them from a configuration standpoint.

The Search Web Parts include those in the following table:

Web Part	Description
Advanced Search Box	For parameterized searches based on properties and combinations of words.
People Search Box	Used to search people.
People Search Core Results	Displays the people search results and the properties associated with them.
Search Actions Links	Displays the search action links.
Search Best Bets	Displays the special term and high confidence results.
Search Box	Searches documents and items.
Search Core Results	Displays the search results and the properties associated with them.
Search High Confidence Results	Displays keywords, best bets, and high confidence results.
Search Paging	Displays links used to navigate pages containing search results.
Search Statistics	Displays the search statistics, such as the number of results shown on the current page, total number of results, and the time it took to search.
Search Summary	Displays the "Did You Mean" portion of the search terms.

Site Directory Web Parts

As a SharePoint environment grows and expands, so do the number of sites and site collections. To prevent users from getting lost in their own environment, SharePoint has a special site template for a site directory where you can categorize your sites in an intuitive fashion. Multiple categories, hierarchy rollups, and a centralized sites list allow users to avoid browsing through an entire navigation tree to find what they need. The following table shows the Site Directory Web Parts:

Web Part	Description
Categories	Displays a list of categories from the Site Directory.
Sites in Category	Displays a list of sites in the Site Directory.
Top Sites	Displays a list of the top sites in the Site Directory.

In the next Try It Out, instead of adding one of these Web Parts to another site, you modify the categories Web Part directly from the Site Directory. As explained in Chapter 8, the Site Directory is a site that can be created on its own or is part of the Collaboration Portal template. This demonstrates how you can further customize and extend existing embedded Web Parts.

Try It Out   **Modify the Settings of a Site Directory Web Part**

The Site Directory offers several tabbed pages, with each page containing a Web Part that you can further customize or extend. If desired, a site manager can add new Web Parts to these pages or create additional tabs. In this Try It Out, you modify an existing Categories Web Part in the Site Directory to change some of the presentation features. You use some of the pre-built styles available in SharePoint 2007.

1. Go to the top-level site of Corporate Intranet site based on the Collaboration Portal template.

2. Select Sites from the top navigation to visit the Site Directory of that portal.

3. Select Site Actions ➪ Edit Page. The page reloads in Edit mode.

4. From the Categories Web Part, select Edit ➪ Modify Shared Web Part. The Web Part tool pane appears.

5. Expand the Presentation group. The Web Part tool pane is displayed.

6. Enter or change the options to suit your needs. For this example, use the following table to change options or fields:

Value Name	Entered Value
Header Text	Type **Browse Our Sites by Category**.
Header Style	Change to Centered.
Number of display columns	Change from 2 to 3.
Level 1 Style	Select Vertical with Boxed Title.
Level 2 Style	Select Vertical with Small Title.
Level 3 Style	Leave as Vertical.

7. Click Apply and OK to preview your changes, which should resemble Figure 7-28.

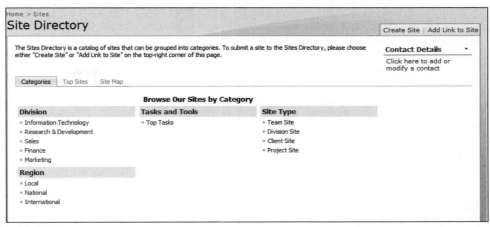

Figure 7-28

Default Web Parts

Each site you create has default Web Parts that serve various functions, such as content rollup, information display, or navigation. Some of these Web Parts are key elements for making SharePoint pages useful and intuitive to users. The following table shows the default Web Parts and their purpose:

Web Part	Description
Content Query	Displays content located throughout the site collection based on criteria a user specifies in a customizable query.
I need to...	Launches tasks for users based on common activities they might complete from the portal or other web-based locations outside of SharePoint. This Web Part is tied to the top tasks property in the Sites Directory. Whenever a URL is added to the Site Directory with the Top Tasks check box selected, it appears in this Web Part.
RSS Viewer	Retrieves information from an RSS source and displays it on a web page.
Summary Link	Displays links to web pages and sites both within and outside the SharePoint environment. You can group and style these links and associate them with images or icons.
Table of Contents	Used in the Site Map tab of the Site Directory, this Web Part can be added to any page to display the site hierarchy from a fixed or dynamic location.
This Week in Pictures	Displays an image from a picture library and a link to a slide version of the library.

The Content Query Web Part, shown in the first Try It Out, is the most versatile because it rolls up content so that you can display information on a page from any location in a site collection. You can roll up content based on its List Type, Content Type, or on site column values.

For more on lists, columns, and content types, see Chapters 2, 4, and 6.

In SharePoint, you use the Summary Links Web Part to aggregate and display information more easily than in previous versions, where content authors manually published links to a portal area (and where an author's focus on content meant this important step was skipped). The Summary Links Web Part creates direct links to content and groups them based on a common heading.

The Content Query Web Part can be configured to display certain types of content and then automatically searches through a site collection to display links to items. This is a common form of something called *content aggregation*, which is the process of consolidating information in a single location from multiple locations. For example, someone on your team is probably responsible for recording and later storing meeting minutes, and everyone on the team knows where on the site these are located, but management or stakeholders wanting to keep abreast of certain projects may not know where to look. Rather than relying on the content author to publish a link to the minutes for each meeting, the portal administrator can add a Content Query Web Part to search for all meeting minutes throughout the site collection. In the next exercise, you walk through how that process can be done by adding a Content Query Web Part to a management site, which pulls documents from all over the site collection that uses a unique content type.

Besides allowing aggregators to view content from an RSS feed, SharePoint has a Web Part that displays RSS-enabled content directly from SharePoint. In the second Try It Out, you add an RSS Viewer Web Part to the main page of your corporate portal to display news and updates from outside the company.

Try It Out   Using the Content Query Web Part

In this Try It Out, you see that no matter where you add a Web Part, it can pull information from any location in the site collection. You can run a query on the entire site collection, or limit it to specific subsites or lists and filter based on list types, metadata properties, or content types. To filter using metadata properties, the property should be a site column accessible from where you have the Web Part. For example, if you have a column at the top-level site of your site collection (http://servername), it can filter a Content Query Web Part on or below that site. If you have the column on a subsite further down in the site collection (http://servername/divisions/marketing/branding), that column would only be available for filtering on that site and subsites.

In this Try It Out, you select the document's content type that is the same as most documents you store in the site collection. You also select the option for all child content types, which means that any documents based on your selected content type display in the Web Part. Because you can potentially retrieve every single document in the organization, you limit the query, in this case a maximum of 25 items. By default, the sort order is based on when the documents were created and sorted in descending order. This means that for this Try It Out, you see the last 25 documents created in the site collection.

You have various options for displaying content in the Web Part, including how to style the group name and item details. In addition, you can specify how many columns appear in the Web Part. If you anticipate a large amount of data or several groups, presenting the information in multiple columns makes it easier for the end user to read. For the group heading, you use a dynamic property of <site>, which shows each item grouped by the site on which it resides. This is particularly helpful in situations where a company may have team meetings displayed in a single Web Part. By grouping items by the site, meeting minutes display under the site name, which clearly differentiates each team.

The last thing you do in this Try It Out is enable an RSS feed on the Web Part. Thus, users who subscribe to the query can view new items in their RSS aggregator as they appear in the Web Part. For example, because Microsoft Outlook 2007 supports the content aggregated from an RSS feed, users can subscribe to this Web Part and, as new items appear in the Web Part, they also appear in the user's Outlook folder.

1. From the home page of a Corporate Intranet site collection based on the Collaboration Portal template, select Site Actions ⇨ Create Site. The site creation page appears.

2. Create the site using the following settings:

Item	Value
Title	Divisions
Description	Corporate Divisional Portal Sites
URL Name	Divisions
Template	Publishing Site (from the Publishing tab)
Permissions	Use same permissions as parent site
Use top link bar of parent site	Yes

3. Click the Create button. A new site is created, and it acts as the parent site of all divisional pages.

4. Create a Management portal site to serve as a location where managers can work together and aggregate content. Select Site Actions ⇨ Create Site. The Site Creation window appears.

5. Create the site using the following settings:

Item	Value
Title	Management
Description	Management Portal Site
URL Name	Mgmt
Template	Publishing Site (from the Publishing tab)
Permissions	Use unique permissions
Use top link bar of parent site	Yes

6. Click the Create button.

7. Click the OK button to accept the site groups that are automatically created for the new site.

8. Add a Web Part that aggregates content from the site collection and displays it at the top level of the site collection. From the top level of the site collection, select Edit Page.

9. From the left column Web Part zone, select Add a Web Part.

10. From the Default group, select the Content Query Web Part and click the Add button. The Content Query Web Part appears on the page in the left column Web Part zone.

11. Select Modify Shared Web Part from the Edit menu of the Web Part. The Web Part tool pane appears.

12. Expand the Query category as shown in Figure 7-29. Notice that the default selection shows items from the entire site collection. You should keep this option selected because you want to display content that is stored anywhere in the site collection.

Figure 7-29

13. For List Type, select Document Library.

14. Select the content type that you want to display in the Web Part. In most cases, you should have a custom content type to reflect the data you want to display such as Meeting Minutes, Financial Reports, or Sales Proposals. Because the goal of this Try It Out is to demonstrate how the Web Part is configured, you select the Document Content Types group and the content type "Document" as shown in Figure 7-29.

15. Select the Include Child Content Types check box.

16. Expand the Presentation category.

17. For the Grouping and Sorting settings, group the items by <site> and display them in 2 columns.

18. Select the check box to limit the number of items displayed to 25.

19. For Styles, use the Banded style for the group name and make the item style a bulleted title.

20. Enable a Feed for the Web Part. For Feed Title, enter **Latest Documents**.

21. Select Apply, and then OK to save your changes. The Web Part refreshes on the page, displaying items grouped by their site with an RSS icon in the bottom.

Try It Out   **Use the RSS Viewer Web Part**

RSS (Really Simple Syndication) is a popular method for aggregating content from various sources and displays them in a client application such as Outlook or a web application such as SharePoint. In the last Try It Out, you added a Web Part that consumes an RSS feed so users can view headlines for items newly added to a source location. You can use an RSS feed to display news headlines from a central news site within SharePoint or from a major news network site such as www.cnn.com or www.msn.com.

1. Return to the management site created in the previous Try It Out.

2. Select Edit Page from either the Page Editing toolbar or the Site Actions menu. The page reloads in Edit mode.

3. Select Add a Web Part from the Right column. The Web Part Selection window appears.

4. Select RSS Viewer from the Default group, and click the Add button. The page reloads containing the RSS Web Part.

5. Click the Open the Tool Pane link that is displayed in the Web Part. The Web Part tool pane appears, as shown in Figure 7-30.

Figure 7-30

6. Specify an RSS Feed URL.

If you do not know what RSS feed to supply, try visiting any major news site or weblog. You can often find RSS feeds by looking for the words RSS or XML, or by looking for an orange icon. You can also view an RSS feed for any list or library in SharePoint as well as select Web Parts such as the Content Query Web Part that was configured in the previous Try It Out.

7. Set the feed limit to 10.

8. Select Apply, and then OK. Your page should refresh with an updated Web Part, as shown in Figure 7-31.

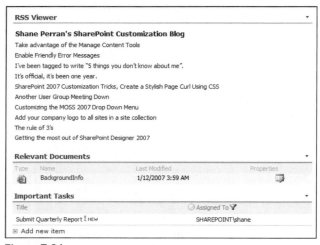

Figure 7-31

The Data View Web Part

The Data View Web Part can display data from a variety of sources including but not limited to SharePoint lists, databases, Web Services, or Line-of-Business (LOB) applications. You can use the Data View Web Part to transform the default XML (CAML) list data to XSL, and thus customize the look and feel of an otherwise relatively flat list data. For example, you can display your data in a decorative table, complete with vibrant colors and background images, or give your titles a more stylish font. The Data View Web Part is far from limited to simple layout or colors; in fact, its uses are far-reaching when dealing with dynamic data. You can use the Data View Web Part to connect to a database or web service, as well as write code to perform advanced calculations of information.

Because this book is intended to demonstrate some basic uses of the Web Parts, chapters do not cover the advanced usage of this Web Part. The Data View Web Part requires that you use SharePoint Designer 2007 and as such, it's recommended that you have a seasoned developer familiar with the software perform the work that this Web Part requires.

Try It Out   Converting from List View to Data View

As mentioned before, the Data view Web Part performs XSL transformation on the XML data, thus converting it to a more customizable template-based format. This allows you to edit the data in a what-you-see-is-what-you-get (WYSIWYG) editor. In this Try It Out, you use the WYSIWYG editing system to change the color of the row displaying the list data, which would otherwise be white.

When you save the document, you receive a warning that you are customizing the page and breaking its relationship with the site definition. It is generally a good idea to create your data views on a temporary page, export them using the method described earlier in this chapter, and then import them back into a page that is still connected to the site definition. This helps reduce the number of pages in your site collection that are not connected to the site definition.

For more on importing and exporting a page, see the section "Web Parts Basics."

In this Try It Out, you start by creating a basic contact list on a team site. You then add the List Web Part to the site using the process demonstrated in "Add a Web Part to a Page" Try it Out earlier in this chapter.

1. To create a basic contact list on a team site, select Site Actions ⇨ View all Site Content.

2. Select Create from the toolbar.

3. Select Contacts from the Communications column.

4. In the name field, enter **Important Contacts** and then click Create.

5. To add the List Web Part to a new Web Part page, select Site Actions ⇨ Create.

6. Select Web Part Page from the Web Pages group.

7. Name the page **ContactDetails.aspx**, select the Full Page, Vertical layout template, and select that you want to save the page in your Shared Documents library.

8. Click the Add a Web Part button from the Full Page Web Part zone.

9. Under Lists and Libraries, select the check box next to Important Contacts and then click Add. Notice that your list is added to the page.

10. Create three new contact items in your list by adding contact information for three of your team members. The process for adding content to a list was described in Chapter 2.

11. To convert the basic List Web Part to a Data view, you need to connect to the site using SharePoint Designer 2007. Open the SharePoint Designer application.

12. Select File ⇨ Open Site and type the URL of your site.

13. Open the page containing your List Web Part and switch to Design view.

14. Select the List Web Part by clicking on it once.

15. Right-click and select Convert to XSLT Data View.

16. Select the entire second row (to select, click in an end column and drag your mouse along the entire row) to display your data as shown in Figure 7-32.

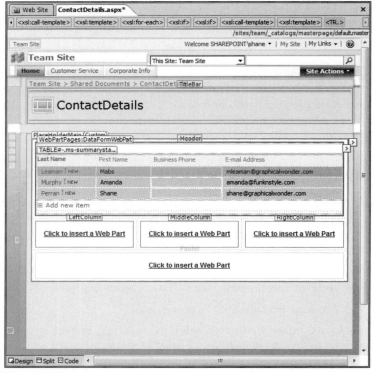

Figure 7-32

17. Right-click and select Cell Properties.

18. Click Background Color and change it to Blue.

19. Click Apply, and then OK to set your changes.

20. Save your document. When prompted with a warning that you are about to customize the page, click OK. When you are redirected back to your page, notice the data column has changed to blue. Adding a new item to the list yields another row of data with the same look.

Summary

Because Web Parts are such an integral part of SharePoint and are used, to some degree, in every chapter in this book, this chapter discusses the various Web Parts that can help your team with any business problem. In this chapter, you learned the following:

❑   Web Parts are applications that you can only add to a Web Part page that allow users to interact with the site. SharePoint has various Web Parts, which were discussed in detail, and you can create your own using ASP.NET.

❑   Web Part pages have a Web Part tool pane where you can select and modify Web Part properties. You add Web Parts to zones by dragging and dropping them to different positions within a zone, or by dragging them to completely separate zones on the page. You learned the basics of adding Web Parts, customizing the title and border, and importing or exporting them from one page or site to another.

❑   Each time you create a list or library, a corresponding Web Part is added to the Web Part Gallery. You can use this gallery later to add content to the page and display the data in the list or library. You can modify the view of a List or Library Web Part to display metadata columns and quickly channel information to your users.

❑   The Business Data Web Parts let you access important business information from a variety of data sources.

❑   Content rollup Web Parts gather data from multiple subsites, rolling the results up to a single location, making it easier to consume data from multiple sources.

❑   Filter Web Parts filter the data displayed in Web Parts based on the properties of the page.

❑   Search Web Parts aid in quickly searching for information.

❑   Outlook Web Access Web Parts help you view email while working within your team collaboration sites.

❑   Dashboard Web Parts display Key Performance Indicators, which visually measure progress toward business goals.

❑   Miscellaneous Web Parts perform a variety of common tasks.

❑   Site Directory Web Parts help you organize your team sites in an intuitive hierarchy.

❑   Default Web Parts are special Web Parts that cover a number of functional areas to display content, aggregate it from other locations, or improve how you can navigate to other areas of the site.

❑   The Data View Web Part can customize the default XML (CAML) based list data, transforming it into a more customizable friendly XSL format.

Exercises

1.   You get an email from marketing informing you that the executive team would like to add a list of key contacts to the main page of the corporate intranet. What do you do?

2. It's requested that you move the main news Web Part from the small right column to a more prominent section of the home page of the human resources team's collaboration site. How can you make this happen?

3. Sales makes a change in its division so that all current tasks displayed on the home page of the team site via a Web Part must also display which of the two team leads is responsible for the task. How can you modify the Web Part to display who the team lead is?

4. During a meeting, an executive asks if you can display a listing of all upcoming events for the organization. What is your answer?

5. The creative department recently analyzed their team site and think that the site would be more appealing if they added some background colors to the list Web Parts. How do you achieve this?

Working with Sites and Workspaces

So far in this book, there's been discussion about all the components and modules that make up the various sites and workspaces in SharePoint. Now, it's time to look more specifically at the sites themselves. In SharePoint, the *site* is the primary container or location for content on which a team collaborates. A SharePoint environment may only contain a few sites or thousands. This chapter discusses some of the different templates as well as the common usage scenarios of each.

In this chapter you learn the following:

❑   What the difference is between a site, workspace, and site collection

❑   How you can customize a SharePoint to achieve a particular look and feel

❑   The SharePoint site templates server and common uses for each

❑   The options you have for users to navigate across various sites within a site collection

After finishing this chapter, you should feel comfortable selecting the most appropriate template for creating a site. While the chapter discusses each site template in moderate detail, you may want to take the time to create a test environment with each of the primary site templates for reference and practice.

Understanding Sites and Site Collections

When a company haphazardly stores information, a system becomes people-dependent. You see an increase in storage locations, such as personal drives, network file shares, or removable media. Different people will catalog information using different methods, resulting in co-workers relying on each other to find information — a serious loss in productivity. When a company uses SharePoint to store, share, and collaborate in a central location, it becomes more dependent on an organizational system, and workers become more productive.

To help you tap into the organizational power of SharePoint, this section helps you understand what a site, site collection, and a workspace are, and shows you how to create a site collection of your own.

What Is a Site?

SharePoint organizes pages, lists, libraries, and other components into *sites*. Each site typically contains information with a common theme, such as an intranet site for a project team or an extranet site for collaboration with business partners. From a web browser perspective, a SharePoint site is simply a website.

By gathering related information in SharePoint sites, organizations can adopt consistent procedures and practices concerning content management. Users no longer have to wait for others to supply them with "inside information" such as the location of shared files. Instead, information access becomes more "self serve," resulting in more efficient work patterns.

What Is a Site Collection?

A *site collection* is a group of sites organized into a tree structure. A site can either be a subsite or a top-level site that stores the common templates and components for the entire group of sites below it. A *sub-site* has a parent and may also have additional sites below it. An individual site, whether it is a top-level site or a subsite, can have its own security and access profile. Similarly, a subsite may be configured to inherit the access rules of its parent site. In an organization's SharePoint structure, every site in an intranet may be in a single site collection, or multiple site collections may exist to distinguish between groups. Today's workplaces often use site collections to represent their various divisions and projects. Typically, each division has its own top-level site, with subsites representing projects assigned to a division. The subsites have lists and libraries where teams can share information and collaborate on the project.

> *For more on the basics of sites, workspaces, and site collections, including a helpful diagram, see Chapter 1.*

To build a site collection, the first Try It Out in this section has you creating the site collection's top level using the Collaboration portal template. Then, in the second Try It Out, you see how to add subsites to this top level, using the team site template.

> *For more on the team site template, see the section "Understanding and Working with the SharePoint Site Templates," which discusses each template in greater detail.*

Try It Out   Create a Site Collection

SharePoint revolves around creating team collaboration sites, each having its own unique lists and document libraries where teams can store, share, and collaborate on a particular project. Site collections, which have a top level and subsites below it, are a way of creating a group of these sites, with individual sites collectively representing a particular business unit in an organization. In the following steps, you create a top-level site collection using the Collaboration portal template.

1.   From the Central Administration site, select Application Management. The Application Management window appears.

2. From the SharePoint Site Management section shown in Figure 8-1, select the Create Site Collection link. The Create Site Collection window appears, as shown in Figure 8-2.

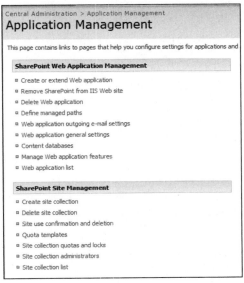

Figure 8-1

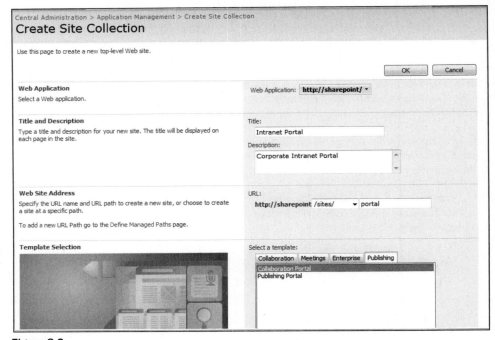

Figure 8-2

3. From the Web Application section, select where you want to create your site collection.

4. In the Title field, type a title for your site collection. For this example, use **Intranet Portal**.

5. In the Description field, type a description for your site collection. For this example, use **Corporate Intranet Portal**.

6. In the URL field, type the URL address for your site collection. For this example, type **portal**.

7. From the Select a Template section, click the Publishing tab and select Collaboration Portal.

8. Select a primary and secondary administrator for your site collection. In this example, select yourself and another member of your team as the site collection administrator.

9. Click the OK button.

How It Works

The top-level site of your site collection is created. This top-level site then becomes the umbrella under which you can create all subsites, and you can use what you created in this exercise to create other sites throughout the exercises in this chapter. Collaboration portal template is a great starting point for a Corporate Intranet site collection because it contains many of the elements and subsites that are useful in a collaborative corporate environment. In step 8, it is best practice to set a primary and secondary administrator for your site collection. This person or these people can then add users and permissions for all items and subsites within the site collection.

Try It Out   Create a New Site Using the Team Site Template

In the following steps, you create a site containing the common elements that a collaborative team site requires. You can then either further customize it or begin using it right away. As you create this site, you have to decide how users will navigate on the site and what security settings the site will have. In this example, you select the Use Same Permissions as Parent Site option. This means all subsites will inherit this parent site's security settings. You can always change these later using the Use Unique Permissions option. You will also select to use the same navigation as the parent site, which means the top navigation links will be the same on both sites. The top navigation links are often referred to as the *global navigation*.

Changing the navigation settings is described later in this chapter. Chapter 9 discusses how to use the Unique Permissions options as well as how to define security settings. For more on the various elements of a team site template, see the section "Understanding and Working with the SharePoint Site Templates."

1. From the main page of your Intranet Portal Site, select Sites from the global navigation. This brings you to the site directory for your portal, which is the most appropriate place to create a new subsite.

2. Click the Create Site link as shown in Figure 8-3. The New SharePoint Site window appears, as shown in Figure 8-4.

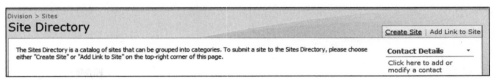

Figure 8-3

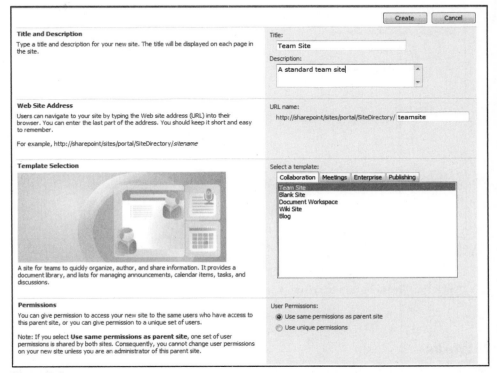

Figure 8-4

3. Give your site a Title, Description, and URL Name.

4. Under User Permissions, select the Use Same Permissions as Parent Site option. Doing so will result in the new site you are creating to inherit the same security settings and groups of the site above it. This option creates less administration because permissions will only need to be managed from a single location.

5. From the Select a Template section, select Team Site from the Collaboration tab.

6. Select the check box to add the site to the Site Directory, as shown in Figure 8-5, and select the appropriate site categories that describe your site.

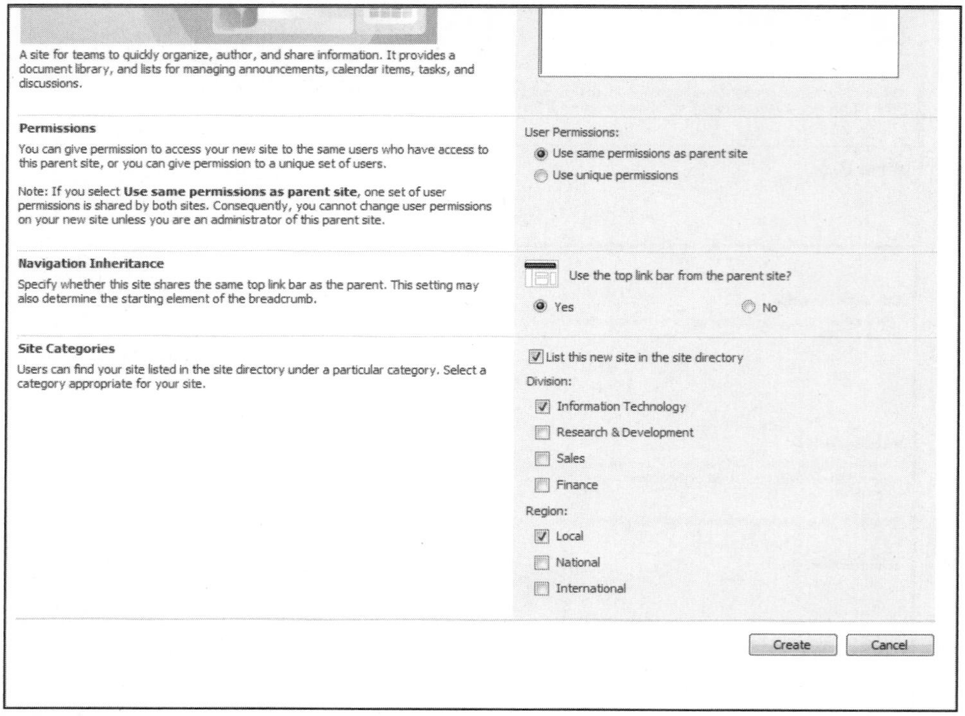

A site for teams to quickly organize, author, and share information. It provides a document library, and lists for managing announcements, calendar items, tasks, and discussions.

Permissions

You can give permission to access your new site to the same users who have access to this parent site, or you can give permission to a unique set of users.

Note: If you select **Use same permissions as parent site**, one set of user permissions is shared by both sites. Consequently, you cannot change user permissions on your new site unless you are an administrator of this parent site.

User Permissions:
- ◉ Use same permissions as parent site
- ○ Use unique permissions

Navigation Inheritance

Specify whether this site shares the same top link bar as the parent. This setting may also determine the starting element of the breadcrumb.

Use the top link bar from the parent site?
- ◉ Yes   ○ No

Site Categories

Users can find your site listed in the site directory under a particular category. Select a category appropriate for your site.

☑ List this new site in the site directory

Division:
- ☑ Information Technology
- ☐ Research & Development
- ☐ Sales
- ☐ Finance

Region:
- ☑ Local
- ☐ National
- ☐ International

[Create]   [Cancel]

Figure 8-5

7. Click the Create button to create your site.

How It Works

For step 6, depending on how the site directory is customized, you may have a variety of different options from which to select. By defining your site well, you ensure that others can find your site more easily.

What Is a Workspace?

Organizations today rely on documents, such as sales projections and market analysis, to make key business decisions and adapt to an ever-changing marketplace. These documents are often the product of several meetings and input from several executive decision makers. To make collaborating on these documents as efficient as possible, you can create a workspace. A *workspace* is a special type of site that empowers teams to collaborate on specific documents or events. A workspace, like other site templates, can contain lists and libraries and use Web Parts, but is generally created around the collaboration of a single document or event. SharePoint has special templates to support these activities.

The processes for creating workspaces based on documents and meetings is discussed later in the chapter.

Site Management Overview

As you create a new SharePoint environment, you should consider how to organize its sites so that users can easily access what they need. Important questions that you should consider include:

- ❑ What primary sites should be part of this environment?
- ❑ What users should have access to each site and what are the user's needs and requirements?
- ❑ What site templates will be used for each site?
- ❑ Should site permissions be inherited or should they be unique for each site?
- ❑ Will any sites share any components, such as content types or site columns?
- ❑ Should the users see a different navigation interface at each site level, or should this be consistent throughout the hierarchy?
- ❑ Should all sites in the hierarchy have the same look and feel, or will sites have their own color schemes and branding?

The answers for these questions may vary depending on the situation, so there's not really a set of rules on how to create a SharePoint site hierarchy. However, by taking the answers to the questions under consideration, you can determine the best approach to build around whatever situation you encounter.

When designing a SharePoint environment, draw out the site hierarchy's primary structure. You can use drawing tools, such as Microsoft Visio or something as simple as a sketch, to help you through the planning stage. From there, you can add information such as what templates to use, where you should define permissions, or where you should create content elements such as content types. You can also determine the environment's trends and requirements. An example is shown in Figure 8-6. Although SharePoint is very flexible when you want to change something, identifying the core structure of a SharePoint environment early in the game has a positive effect on the environment's growth and prevents costly reworks and downtime later on.

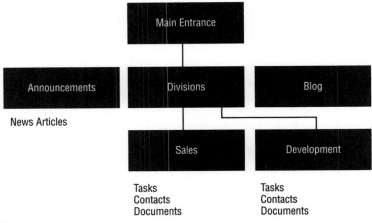

Figure 8-6

This section shows you how to create a site that a user can easily navigate to find the information that they need and which is relevant to them. First, you learn how to add the navigation that best suits your site. You then set the regional features so that your site reflects the region for which you created it. These features include such things as the calendar the site uses, the workweek, and time zone. Finally, you learn how to enable features on your site.

Creating Navigation

Navigation is one of the most important parts of any site. As a user, you need a clear and easy path to the information you require, and as a site designer it is equally important to supply your users with a single consistent navigation experience so that they can become familiar with it. As a general rule, you need to answer a few key questions concerning your site's navigation menu:

❑　Where am I?

❑　Where can I go?

❑　Where have I been?

SharePoint offers several built-in navigation menus and items, and allows you to tailor things to your environment so that users are never lost when they look for information.

As mentioned in the section the "Understanding Sites and Site Collections," a site collection has a top-level site and several subsites below it. To give users a single consistent navigation experience, the site can inherit the current (side) or global (top) navigation of the site directly above it. You can do this during or after you create a site (see the next Try it Out to find out how). You have several navigation options:

❑　**The tree view:** Most users are comfortable navigating in their Windows operating system (Windows 98, Windows XP, and now Windows Vista). Therefore, the most widely adopted web navigation form is the tree view. By default, all sites come with a Quick Launch bar (see Figure 8-9), which displays your lists, libraries, and subsites in a logical way. Should you have a large number of items in this menu, you may not want to display this flat listing and instead enable the tree view.

❑　**The breadcrumb trail:** The breadcrumb trail is basically links that show each level you have traveled in the site hierarchy to get to your current location (see Figure 8-7 for an example of this). You can select links to step back a level in the hierarchy. In the figure, by selecting the Team Site link, which is the parent site of a weblog site, you can navigate directly (back) to the team site without going through menus to do so.

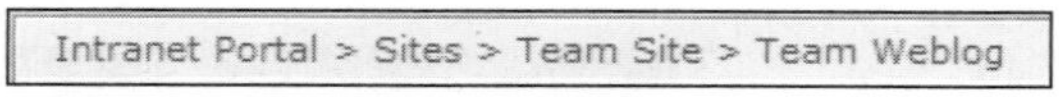

> Intranet Portal > Sites > Team Site > Team Weblog

Figure 8-7

To get you started creating your navigation system, the next Try It Out shows you how to create a site that inherits its parent's navigation. When navigation is *inherited*, the same links display on the subsite that are displayed on the parent site. For example if the top link bar of the parent site has links for Home, Document Center, Search, and Sites, these links are mirrored on the subsite. In the Try It Out that follows this one, you learn how to create a tree view navigation.

Try It Out   **Inherit Navigation of Parent Site**

To give users a single consistent navigation experience, SharePoint allows you to inherit the current (side) or global (top) navigation of the site directly above it, known as the *parent site*, so that it will display the same items. Follow these simple steps to inherit the navigation from the parent site. The example assumes you have already created a subsite as was done in the earlier Try it Out called "Create a New Site Using the Team Site Template."

1.   From your team site, select Site Actions ➪ Site Settings.

2.   Click the Navigation link from the Look and Feel section. You are presented with a page allowing you to customize navigation. See Figure 8-8.

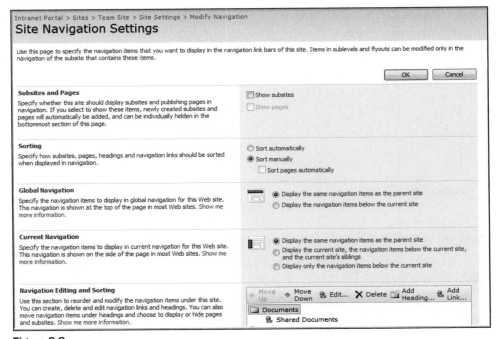

Figure 8-8

3.   The Subsites and Pages section has options for having subsites, or in the case of a publishing site, created pages, show up in the navigation menu. For this exercise, leave it with the default of nothing selected.

4.   The Sorting section has options for sorting navigation items manually or automatically. You can leave the default setting of Sort Manually.

5.   From the Global Navigation section, you can decide whether your site will inherit the global navigation from the parent site. The Global Navigation is the top navigation menu displaying any subsites you create or, in the case of a publishing site, pages or sites you create. Leave it as the default, which is to inherit from the parent site.

6. From the Current Navigation section, you can decide whether your site will inherit the current navigation menu from the parent site. The current navigation is the Quick Launch bar (mentioned earlier), which has a left-side navigation menu that displays any lists or libraries you create and can also display subsites. Change this option to display the same navigation options as the parent site.

How It Works

You now have an interface available allowing you to edit and sort the navigation options. See Figure 8-9.

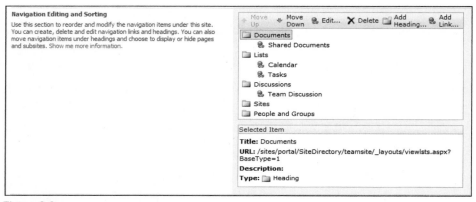

Figure 8-9

Try It Out   Enable a Tree View Navigation in Quick Launch

A tree view allows you to quickly access files by expanding or collapsing layers of the file structure, creating a way to quickly drill down to the files you require. With SharePoint 2007, you can create a tree view navigation of the site hierarchy by following a few easy steps. Please note that for the following exercise to work correctly, the site should not inherit the parent site's current navigation. If, for this exercise, you use the team site where you modified the navigation in the previous Try it Out, you need to change the navigation using the steps in the previous Try It Out to either the your site's siblings or the items below your site.

1. Select Site Actions ⇨ Site Settings.

2. Click the Tree View link from the Look and Feel section. The Tree View window appears, as shown in Figure 8-10.

3. Select the Enable Tree View check box.

4. Click the OK button.

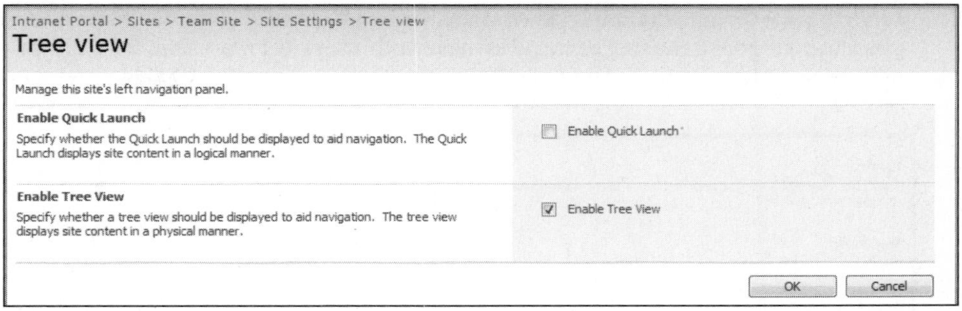

Intranet Portal > Sites > Team Site > Site Settings > Tree view

Tree view

Manage this site's left navigation panel.

Enable Quick Launch

Specify whether the Quick Launch should be displayed to aid navigation. The Quick Launch displays site content in a logical manner.

☐ Enable Quick Launch

Enable Tree View

Specify whether a tree view should be displayed to aid navigation. The tree view displays site content in a physical manner.

☑ Enable Tree View

[OK] [Cancel]

Figure 8-10

How It Works

When you enable the tree view navigation, you turn on an expandable and collapsible menu that shows you the physical site hierarchy in a more compact form, allowing even easier navigation of all lists, libraries, and subsites. You can see an example of a tree view navigation in Figure 8-11.

Figure 8-11

Using Regional Settings

In some cases, the regional settings on your site may need to be different than those specified on the server by default. For example, you might want to open up your site to a division located in a different region and time zone, or perhaps a division that has a different workweek than you. In these situations, you can modify the regional settings of a site to better suit the users.

Try It Out   **Change the Regional Settings of a Site**

Regional settings include such things as locale, time zone, and calendar type. Changing the regional settings of a site can be done in a few simple steps.

1.   Select Site Actions ➪ Site Settings.

2. From the Site Administration section, select Regional Settings. From the Regional Settings page, you can configure a number of items to make your users feel more familiar with the interface and display of content. See Figure 8-12.

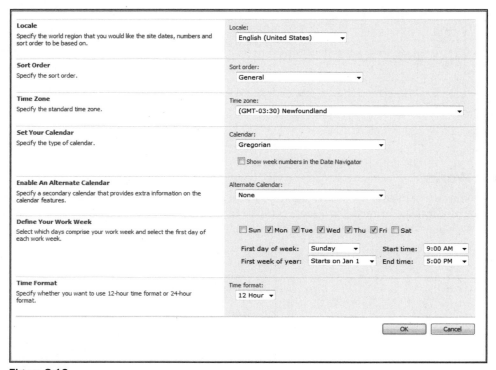

Figure 8-12

3. In the Locale section, you can select a region on which to base numbers, calendars, and sort order. This example uses English (United States).

4. You can set the Sort Order based on common settings for a particular region or language by selecting it from the drop-down menu. For this example, use General.

5. You can set the Time Zone so that time stamps are displayed to use in a time zone that is familiar and relevant to them. This example assumes the people using the site are from Newfoundland, Canada. From the drop-down menu, select (GMT -3:30) Newfoundland.

6. Some cultures use a different calendar. This example uses Gregorian. Ensure that the Show Week Numbers in Date Navigator is unselected.

7. You can choose to specify an alternate calendar, but for this example you can leave the default selection of None.

8. Sometimes people work slightly different days, and as such you can select the workweek to suit. For this example, use Monday to Friday, 9:00 A.M. to 5:00 P.M.

9. For Time Format, you can choose a 12-hour or 24-hour format. This example uses 12 Hour.

10. Select the OK button.

How It Works

Your site now reflects the regional settings for which you created it. Users can also personalize regional settings to reflect their preferences by selecting My Settings from the Welcome drop-down menu, as shown in Figure 8-13.

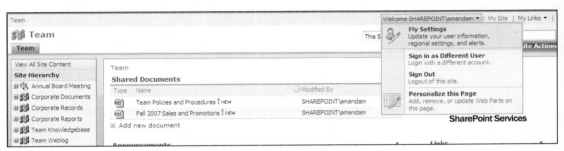

Figure 8-13

Enabling Features

SharePoint 2007 introduces the concept of *features*, which you can think of as bundles of functionality that you can switch on or off with a single click. For example, you can turn a regular collaborative team site into a publishing site to take advantage of Web Content Management (WCM) functionality. You can enable features on a per site basis or on a site collection. With the help of a developer, you can create your own features, combining different types of functionality to meet even the most diverse site demands and extending a site's functional abilities.

> *In Chapter 13, you learn in detail about WCM and all it can do. In the following Try It Out, you simply enable the Publishing feature on a collaborative site, in this case a team site.*

Try It Out   Enable Publishing Features

SharePoint 2007 is the new home of the platform formerly known as Content Management Server. The collective functionality, WCM, gives users a rich web content publishing experience. Certain site templates under the Publishing tab have this functionality when you create them. Other sites, such as the team site or sites underneath the Collaborative tab, do not. Through the magic of features, you can turn a standard team site into a content publishing site by following these simple steps:

1. Select Site Actions ⇨ Site Settings.

2. Click the Site Features link from the Site Administration section.. The Site Features window appears, as shown in Figure 8-14.

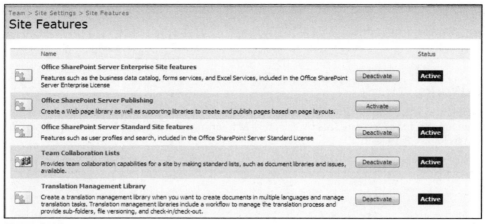

Figure 8-14

3. From the list of available features, locate and activate Office SharePoint Server Publishing.

How It Works

When you go back to your site, you now notice a new set of functionality on the Site Actions tab, such as Create Page option, shown in Figure 8-15, which SharePoint added when you enabled the Publishing feature on the site.

Figure 8-15

Enabling the Publishing feature also creates a Pages library, along with several other supporting libraries, which means you can do more with your site, such as set rules for publishing pages via workflow — something discussed in Chapter 5. Also, when you select Site Actions ➪ Create Page, the Create Page window shown in Figure 8-16 allows you to select or create new pages based on page layouts.

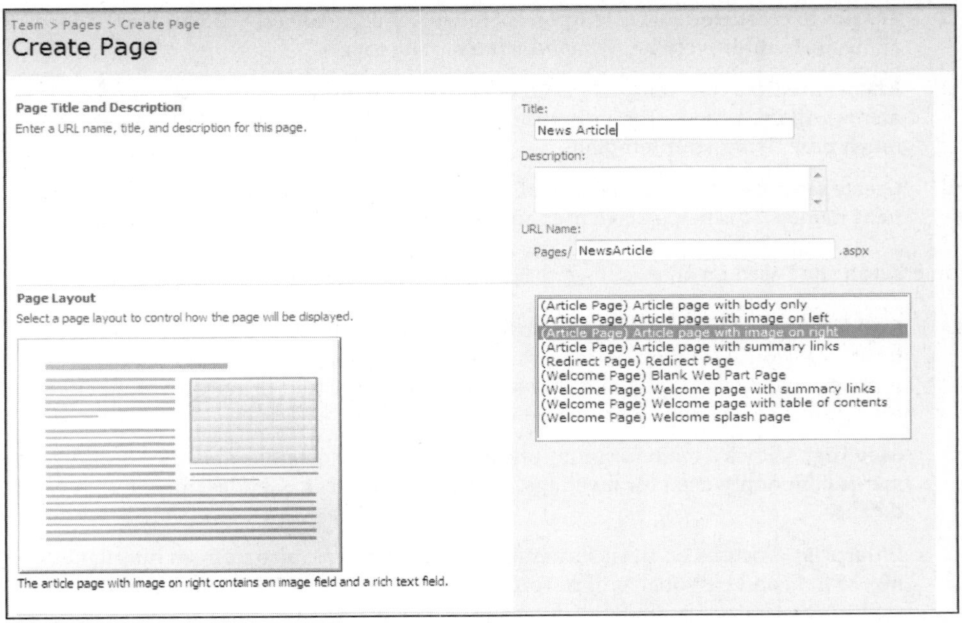

Figure 8-16

Understanding and Working with the SharePoint Site Templates

In SharePoint, whenever you create a new site, you start with a template, which has predefined components including a home page, lists and libraries, customized Web Parts, features, and content types that anticipate how you will use the site and that reflect its possible requirements. It's left to you to determine your requirements (as mentioned in the section "Site Management Overview"). So which template should you choose? Obviously, to cut down on work, the key is to select a template with as many of the components you need for your situation. You can then modify it to fit your requirements and save it to use on future sites. For example, to create a site template for your company's projects, you can start with the team site template, which has built-in management components, and then add a list that tracks timelines and milestones for the project, as well as content types for project management and reporting. You can then save your site as a template and call it **Standard Project Management Site** so users will have all the elements they need to work on the site.

If you are responsible for a SharePoint site, remember the following timesaving tips in creating customized templates for your site:

❑ **Identify the key templates your organization will need.** Anticipating your users' needs prevents them from creating their own templates.

❑ **Try not to create too many templates.** Too many templates are difficult to manage, and will not aid users in intuitively knowing which template to use.

❑ **Make sure that your template is an adequate starting point.** Having too few or too many elements will frustrate a user and cause them to either create their own template or spend too much time fixing your template.

❑ **Create sites from a consistent set of templates with common interface elements and component names**. This helps drive user adoption and overall acceptance of the environment.

If you create a site based on an existing site template, SharePoint offers several template categories:

❑ **Collaboration:** Helps teams work toward a common goal or share information on a common topic in a central location. Sites from these templates are very active because team members perform their daily work on them. These templates are geared heavily for team environments featuring storage locations for documents, blog posts, or wiki pages.

❑ **Meeting:** Allows a team to communicate on a specific event or meeting. Templates have elements commonly used for meetings, such as lists to track agendas, meeting minutes, or location details.

❑ **Enterprise:** Focuses on the information organizations require from an intranet, such as reporting, search, and personalization. You can use them on their own or through other templates, such as the Collaboration Publishing site, which is the corporate intranet starting template.

❑ **Publishing:** For publishing information on either an intranet or Internet. These templates have specific workflow processes enabled so you can create content and have it reviewed and approved before it's visible to others in the organization. In addition, certain features make publishing images and information much easier for non-developers and content owners.

❑ **Custom:** You save modifications you make to the other templates in this table as templates. These serve as excellent starting points for future sites. Once you create them, these templates appear under the Custom tab, as shown in Figure 8-17.

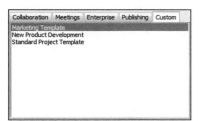

Figure 8-17

The following sections cover each category of templates and help identify which template you should use as a starting point for creating your business solutions.

Working with Collaboration Templates and Sites

In SharePoint, the term *collaboration* is often used to describe sites and activities that focus on the sharing of information. SharePoint offers five sites under its Collaboration Sites tab that encourage and facilitate information sharing, which in turn improves how teams work together. These sites include:

❏ **Team Site**: Contains many of the common elements used by teams including document library, tasks list, and links list.

❏ **Blank Site**: Starts with no list or libraries and can be a clean slate for a team looking to create a collaborative site with the items that are unique to it.

❏ **Document Workspace**: Used by the system to generate a workspace based on a document and can also be created by a site manager.

❏ **Blog**: A simple news site that allows certain users to post stories and other users to respond to their ideas by posting comments.

❏ **Wiki Site**: *Wiki* stands for the term "quick" and provides an informal location for teams to collaborate around a common idea without requiring formalized processes for content editing or reviewing.

This section discusses each site and how to work with them to create the collaboration site that's right for you.

Team Site

You created a site using this template when you followed the steps in the "Create a New Site Using the Team Site Template" Try It Out earlier in the chapter. The *Team Site template* contains the elements that teams need in a collaborative work environment, including the following that help schedule, organize information, and communicate:

Category	Elements
Home Page Web Parts	Announcements Web Part Calendar Web Part Links Web Part Site Image Web Part
Libraries	Form Templates Shared Documents
Lists	Announcements Calendar Links Tasks Team Discussion

Blank Site

The *Blank Site template* is suited for those who require a collaborative area for their team, but don't want all the items in the team site template or perhaps want a slightly different configuration than the team

249

site. This template doesn't contain lists or libraries. The only Web Part in the home page is the Site Image Web Part, which has the Windows SharePoint Services logo as shown in Figure 8-18.

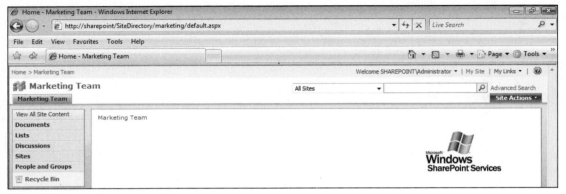

Figure 8-18

If you want to create a team template from scratch, or if you want to create your own lists and libraries and other elements, this template is ideal for your purposes. The process for creating a blank site is exactly the same as that for a team site (see the "Create a New Site Using the Team Site Template" Try It Out earlier in the chapter).

Document Workspace

The team site and blank site templates are perfect for environments where people collaborate regularly on a specific project or customer. But what if your group needs to collaborate on a very specific document or deliverable that has its own set of communication and collaboration requirements?

The *document workspace* has collaboration lists and functionality related to the development of a specific document. You can create this site using the steps in the "Create a New Site Using the Team Site Template" Try It Out. You can also create a document workspace from a document or file that resides in a document library, as shown in the next Try It Out.

When you generate a document workspace using either of the aforementioned methods, team members can create tasks and participate in discussions to complete the document. They can also upload files, such as research papers or guidelines, to the workspace to aid in the document's development. Once the team finalizes the document, you can publish it back to the original source location.

The next two Try It Outs show you how to create a document workspace as well as how to publish the document from that workspace back to its original location.

Try It Out   Create a Document Workspace from a Document

In the following example, you create a new document in the team site. This team site was created in the "Create a New Site Using the Team Site Template" Try It Out. From this new document, called "Sales Proposal" — an important opportunity for a company's sales team — you will create a document workspace where users can collaborate. On the team site, sales team members can only upload and review documents within the site. However, you can configure the document workspace to allow members to perform more administrative functions and duties. Because their involvement is much higher, they can add content, create views, participate in discussions, and share information required to develop the proposal.

1. From the main page of the team site you created in the "Create a New Site Using the Team Site Template" Try It Out, click the Shared Documents link from the Quick Launch bar.

2. Click the New button from the toolbar. Word opens a blank document.

3. Save the blank document in the document library as **Sales Proposal.doc**, as shown in Figure 8-19.

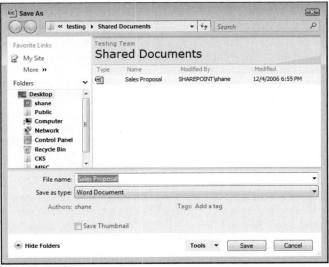

Figure 8-19

4. Close the document.

5. Hover your mouse over the Sales Proposal document and click the menu that appears. Select Send to ➪ Create Document Workspace, as shown in Figure 8-20.

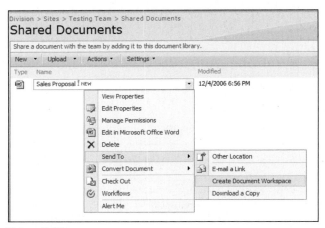

Figure 8-20

6.   You are redirected to a screen that displays the name and location of your document workspace. Click the OK button to complete the creation of your workspace.

How It Works

Although you can name your document whatever you want, for this example, the new "Sales Proposal" document represents a sales opportunity where work centers around the document's development. A document workspace is ideal for this development because team members can collaborate independently of the day-to-day operations on the team site. You created a copy of the document in the document workspace, so edits to this copy of the document aren't visible or available from the original location. However, the previous version of the document is still located in the source document library until you publish the altered workspace copy back to the document library.

Try It Out   **Publish a Document Back to the Source Location from a Document Workspace**

For this Try It Out, you can assume that developing the proposal from the "Create a Document Workspace from a Document" Try It Out is complete and users have made changes to the sales proposal in the document workspace. You can now publish the document back to the team site for others to view by following these steps:

1.   From the Shared Documents library of the document workspace created in the "Create a Document Workspace from a Document" Try It Out, hover your mouse over the Sales Proposal document and select Edit in Microsoft Office Word from the drop-down menu, as shown in Figure 8-21.

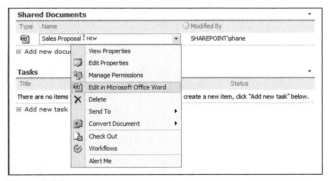

Figure 8-21

2.   Enter the following text into the document:

> **This is a sales proposal for a very important project.**

3.   Save your changes and close the document.

4. Hover your mouse over the Sales Proposal document and click the menu that appears and select Send to ➪ Publish to Source Location as shown in Figure 8-22. You are redirected to a page where you are advised that you are about to overwrite the file stored in the Shared Documents library of your team site with the version from your document workspace.

Figure 8-22

5. Click the OK button to complete the operation.

6. You receive a message confirming that the operation was successful, as shown in Figure 8-23. Click the OK button.

Figure 8-23

7. You are returned to the home page of the document workspace.

8. Click the link in the very top left of your screen to return to the home page of your team site. This top left navigation as shown in Figure 8-24 is known as the breadcrumb trail.

Figure 8-24

9. Click Sales Proposal.doc from the Shared Documents library of your team site to view the changes made from the document workspace.

How It Works

From the Shared Documents library of the document workspace, a special action appears on the document's menu as was shown in Figure 8-23 so users can publish a copy of the document back to the team site so that it can be viewed there. This does not affect either the document or the workspace in which it resides.

The document workspace remains accessible to its members for historical reference even after the document is complete. In addition, members can use the workspace for later edits to the document. There is no immediate need to delete the workspace, and it will remain in the same location and be available to the site members unless changes are made to its configuration.

Blog

A *blog*, or *weblog*, is a user-generated site where an author (or authors) post(s) a journal or set of articles. The site becomes a running commentary on the blog's subject matter because users are encouraged to respond and share information on whatever's posted. A *post* is the original journal entry or article that the author(s) places on the blog. *Comments* are responses from other users who read the entry or article. Because users can respond to the original post or any subsequent comments and because authors can respond to other user's comments, blogs are very collaborative in nature. They are extremely easy to use and therefore a popular choice for users who want to share information and experiences with others.

You may choose to use a blog over the other collaborative sites you have reviewed if you want to post news or journal-type entries and receive comments back from others. In a corporate environment, an author might place an article, technical paper, or proposal on the blog so that peers can comment on it. This helps the author refine the document before presenting it to an important audience, client, or manager. In addition, all content posted to the blog is available via an RSS feed. In Chapter 2, you looked at how every list or library in SharePoint offers an RSS feed. While RSS is available throughout SharePoint 2007, it has specific relevance in the world of blogs where the technology has become widely adopted.

The blog site template has many special built-in features and components that are unavailable in other SharePoint site templates, but that allow users to easily manage weblogs without any special technical knowledge or skills. Some key elements of the blog template are as follows:

Element	Description
Posts	The primary content element of a weblog. This is the either an initial set of articles, or something users write as part of their involvement with the blog. The columns for this list include title, body, and category. Additional columns define the post, including the number of comments, published date, Created By, and Modified By values.
Comments	Support conversations around a topic or article. Users visit a blog and complete a form that associates their comment with a specific post. By default, comments posted on an article appear immediately. However, you can enable content approval so that the blog's author can review items before posting them to the site.

Element	Description
Categories	Blogs can have numerous posts and comments. Therefore, authors can assign posts a category. Readers can select a category from a list on the blog's navigation and view all posts assigned to that category. By default, a blog has three categories upon creation. Users should customize this list to represent the content they intend to publish.
Other Blogs	Also called *blogroll*. This is a list of links to other blogs that an author places on his or her blog so readers can access other sites. These blogs are either recommended by the author or contain similar content. Blogs owe some of their success to blogrolls that interlink weblog authors to create a larger community focused on an issue. SharePoint has an easy mechanism for collecting a list of links to other blogs by using a standard links list.
Links	Commonly, blog authors include links to other websites related to the subject matter of the blog. By default, the blog site in SharePoint has three items already included within the links list to help users more easily navigate to the photos library and post archive sections of the site.
Photos	Blog authors can share photos with their readers. They may embed specific images within the blog posts themselves or may just have a photo library where users can browse a group of images. The Blog template in SharePoint contains a Photo Library to allow for the easy publishing and sharing of photos.

In the next four Try It Outs, you get a chance to see a blog site in action. You create the blog site, and then you customize it to fit the topics you intend to discuss on the site. You also learn both how to create a new blog post as well as leave comments on the post.

Try It Out   Create a Blog Site

In this example, you create a site based on the blog site template. This site will contain elements that are common to most weblogs including posts, categories, comments, and links. The site will inherit the permissions of the team site you created in the Try It Out "Create a New Site Using the Team Site Template" earlier in the chapter.

1.   From the main page of your team site, select Site Actions ➪ Create Site, as shown in Figure 8-25. If you do not see this option, you can select Create and then select Sites and Workspaces from the Web Pages category.

Figure 8-25

2. Enter the following information:

Title	Team Weblog
Description	This weblog will be a location for team members to share information about things they have learned.
URL	Weblog
Site Template	Blog
User Permissions	Use same permissions as parent site.

3. For the navigation options, select Yes to use the same top link bar as the parent site, as shown in Figure 8-26.

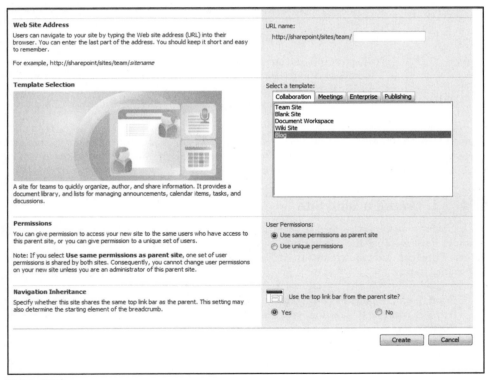

Figure 8-26

4. Click the Create button to create your site.

Try It Out   **Customize the Blog Template**

Before your team can start posting articles to the blog, it is a good idea to customize it to fit the content that you intend to post there. For example, you need to customize the categories list to feature topics that are relevant to the blog.

In the following example, you replace the sample items in a Category list with actual topics that will be written about on the team weblog. Assume that the intention of the blog is to share knowledge that team members collect as they learn how to use the new technologies of SharePoint and InfoPath. You need to change the Category list to include these topics. By default, only one category may be assigned to a single blog post. However, because the Category column on the posts list is a lookup column to another list, you can change the properties to allow multiple selections.

1. From the home page of your blog site, click the Categories link from the Quick Launch bar as shown in Figure 8-27. You are redirected to the Categories list default view.

Figure 8-27

2. Because the Categories list is the same as all other SharePoint lists, you should edit the items in a manner that allows for easy and fast updates across multiple items. For this, you use the Datasheet view. From the Actions item on the toolbar, select Edit in Datasheet. The screen changes to show the items displayed in a Datasheet view.

3. Select the three existing sample categories and select the Delete button on your keyboard. A message asks if you want to send the rows to the site Recycle Bin, as shown in Figure 8-28. Click OK.

Figure 8-28

4. Enter the following items into the list for categories by typing into the Datasheet view:

- ❑ SharePoint
- ❑ Office
- ❑ InfoPath

5. Click the Team Weblog link, which is over the word "Categories" on the top left of the window as shown in Figure 8-29 to return to the home page of your weblog site.

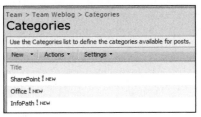

Figure 8-29

6. Click the Manage Posts link from the Admin Links Web Part of your site. You are redirected to the default view of your posts list.

7. Select Settings ⇨ List Settings on the toolbar. You are redirected to the List Settings Admin page.

8. From the Columns section of the Admin page, select the Category hyperlink. The Change Column: Posts window appears.

9. Select the Allow Multiple Values check box as shown in Figure 8-30.

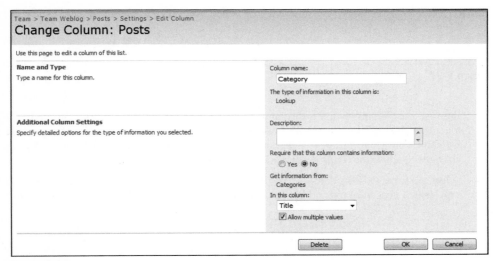

Figure 8-30

10. Click the OK button to save your changes.

How It Works

Besides changing the items in the category list (steps 3 and 4), in steps 8 and 9 you edited the properties of the Category column on the posts list so that users can assign multiple topics to a single post. This is a good example of how you can take the basic template and change it to better suit your needs.

Try It Out   **Create a New Blog Entry**

Now that you know how to create and customize a blog site, it's time to add actual content to it so that others can respond to it. The new post you create describes something that you've learned so far in this chapter about working with the Blog Site template.

1.   From the home page of your blog site, click the Create a Post link from the Admin Links Web Part as shown in Figure 8-31. The Posts: New Item window appears, as shown in Figure 8-32.

Intranet Portal > Sites > Team Site > Team Weblog

3/14/2007

Welcome to your Blog!

To begin using your site, click **Create a Post** under Admin Links to the right.

What is a Blog?

A Blog is a site designed to help you share information. Blogs can be used as news sites, journals, diaries, team sites, and more. It is your place on the World Wide Web.

Blogs are typically displayed in reverse chronological order (newest entries first), and consist of frequent short postings. With this Blog, it is also possible for your site visitors to comment on your postings.

In business, Blogs can be used as a team communication tool. Keep team members in touch by providing a central place for links, relevant news, and even gossip.

Posted at 3:20 PM by SHAREPOINT\Administrator | Permalink | Email this Post | Comments (0)

Admin Links

- Create a post
- Manage posts
- Manage comments
- All content
- Set blog permissions
- Launch blog program to post

Figure 8-31

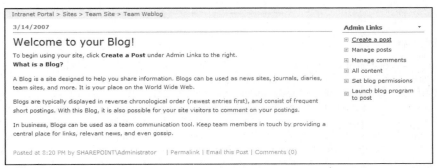

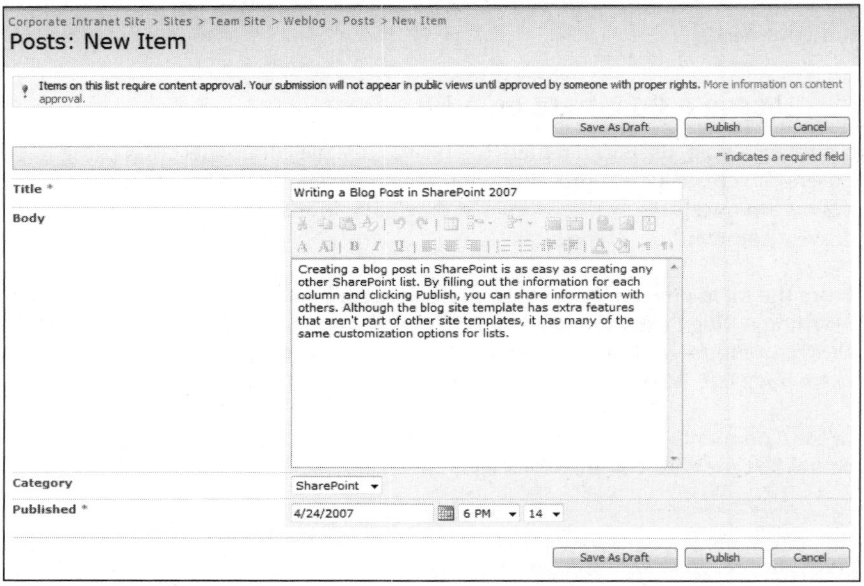

Figure 8-32

2. Enter Writing a Blog Post in SharePoint 2007 as the title of your post.

3. For the body of your post, enter the following text:

> **Creating a blog post in SharePoint is as easy as creating any other SharePoint list. By filling out the information for each column and clicking Publish, you can share information with others. Although the blog site template has extra features that aren't part of other site templates, it has many of the same customization options for lists.**

4. For the category, select the SharePoint item from the drop-down menu and click the Add button.

5. Click the Publish button to save your post and make it available for others to view.

How It Works

This process is very similar to creating other list items in SharePoint. You added the SharePoint category because your entry was about SharePoint. If the post had also featured information on InfoPath or Office, you could have included those categories as well. When you clicked Publish in step 5, the post becomes available on the main page. In step 5, you also have the option of saving the post as a draft. This makes the approval status of the post "pending." By default when a blog site is created, the Posts list has content approval enabled. Because content approval is enabled on the Posts list, only items that are approved will display on the home page. Only users who have permission to approve items, or the original author of a post, can see items saved as drafts. When you created this blog site, you chose to inherit permissions from the parent site. Therefore, any user who has permission to approve content on the team site will also be allowed to approve posts made on the blog site. In Chapter 9, you learn in more detail some of the various groups that exist within a SharePoint and how permissions can be managed to suit your needs.

Try It Out   **Leave a Comment on a Blog Post**

Once you publish a post, users can review the post and leave comments concerning it. In a team environment, users can create a post outlining what they have learned related to a specific subject and others can post follow-up questions or resources that they have found. In the following example, you see how a user can leave a comment on a blog post.

1. From the main page of the weblog site, select the heading of your previous blog post titled "Writing a Blog Post in SharePoint 2007," as shown in Figure 8-33. You are redirected to a page, shown in Figure 8-34, which displays the entire article along with any comments that other users have left. Below the comments is a form for you to leave your own comment.

2. In the Comments form on the page, enter the title **Follow Up Question** and then enter the below text for your comment's body:

> **Will comments appear immediately or do they have to be approved by the site author?**

Figure 8-33

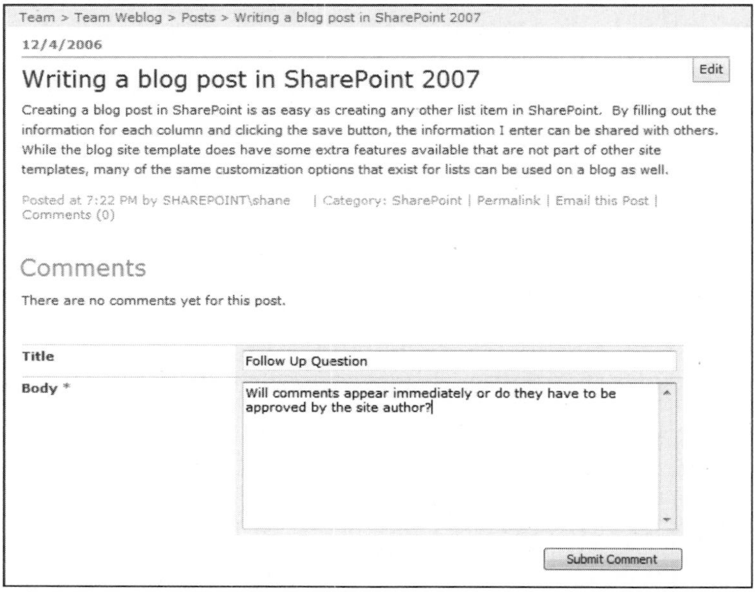

Figure 8-34

3. Click the Submit Comment button.

How It Works

This example showed another user commenting on a blog post; however, it is not uncommon for the blog author to use the same Comment feature to reply to questions or comments left by others. By default, comments posted to the site are automatically approved. However, because comments are stored in a standard SharePoint list, you can enable content approval to allow authors the opportunity to review comments before they appear for others to see. You can enable content approval on a list or library from within the Version History settings of a list, as shown in Figure 8-35.

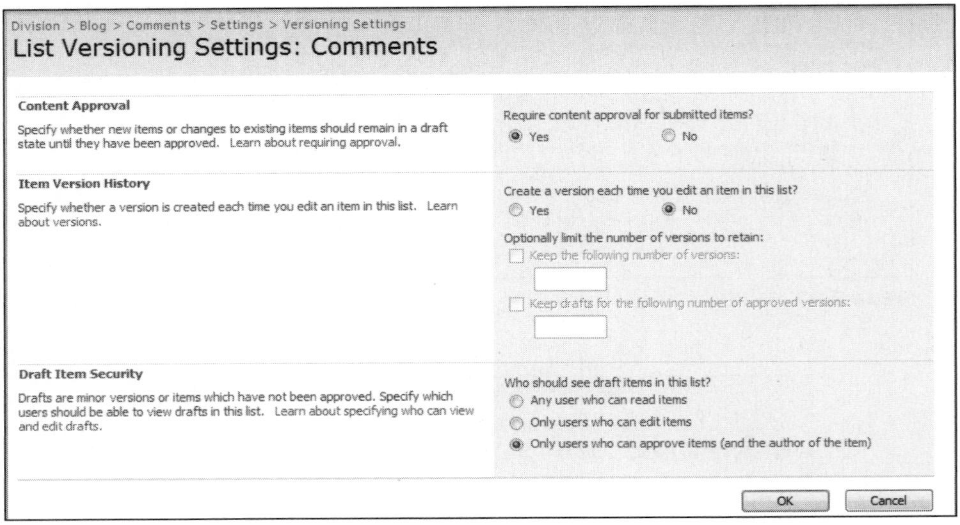

Figure 8-35

Wiki

Besides blogs, *wikis* are a new popular tool that enables users to share and edit content in SharePoint. Whereas a blog is a running commentary on a particular subject, on a wiki site a user can literally change web page content. An extremely popular global online site, Wikipedia (www.wikipedia.com), demonstrates just how powerful the wiki concept can be as an information repository.

Because users edit wikis with SharePoint's built-in Content Editor, they require no HTML or code experience. In a corporate environment, a wiki site encourages collaboration and brainstorming without the restrictions of a formal content editing or approval process. This makes wikis ideal for mapping out new ideas or for collaborating on an upcoming project, which users can later move to more formalized documents and policies. Because you can quickly create new content that is indexed and easy to navigate, you can set up information in a Frequently Asked Questions (FAQ) or a KnowledgeBase format.

A KnowledgeBase is a collection of information related to a topic or group of topics that provides good reference to other users. You may have a KnowledgeBase related to a product line that addresses many of the common support and sales scenarios that may arise. By using a wiki, it is easy for team members to keep the KnowledgeBase up to date as new scenarios or circumstances surface.

In SharePoint 2007, you can create either a wiki site or a wiki document library. A wiki site is ideal for a technical support team's KnowledgeBase or human resources' policies and procedures. A wiki document library provides the same collaboration features of a site within a single library. This is helpful in situations where there is not expected to be a large amount of information collected, and team members can benefit from using the wiki directly on an existing collaborative site.

To show you just how powerful a tool wikis are, the next two Try It Outs illustrate how to create a wiki site, and then how to edit a wiki page.

Try It Out   Create a Wiki Site

In Chapter 3, you learned how to create a wiki document library, and in this Try it Out you will look at the steps related to creating a dedicated site for a wiki. A common use for a wiki site is to collect information concerning a specific topic in a central location. In this example, you create a subsite below your team site to store solutions for problems stemming from a new process.

For more information on the team site template, see the "Create a New Site Using the Team Site Template" Try It Out earlier in the chapter.

1.   From the main page of your team site, select Site Actions ➪ Create Site, as shown in Figure 8-36.

Figure 8-36

2.   Enter the following information or select the following options:

Title	Team KnowledgeBase
Description	This wiki site stores common solutions to problems encountered from the new process.
URL	Kb
Site Template	Wiki Site
User Permissions	Use same permissions as parent site.

3. For the navigation options, select Yes to use the top link bar of the parent site as shown in Figure 8-37.

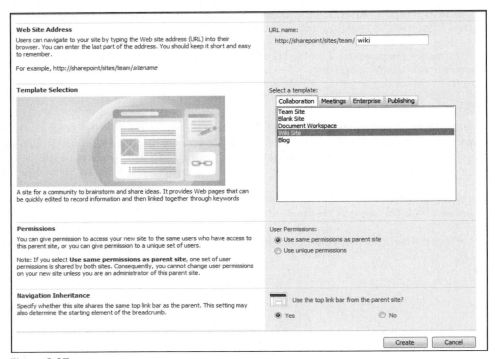

Figure 8-37

4. Click the Create button to create your site.

How It Works

Your wiki site is created with a page containing instructions and placeholder content. You can edit the page to include content more suitable to your topic. In addition, you can add other pages by clicking the New button on the Pages library.

Try It Out   Edit a Wiki Page

In this example you see how easy it is to update content on a wiki page without knowing code. All edits to wiki pages are versioned. A History button also exists to view the different versions of the pages and explicitly what content was edited, removed, or added. Changes are conveniently color-coded with gray representing deleted content and yellow representing added content.

1. From the wiki site's home page, click the Edit link as shown in Figure 8-38. The wiki content appears as shown in Figure 8-39.

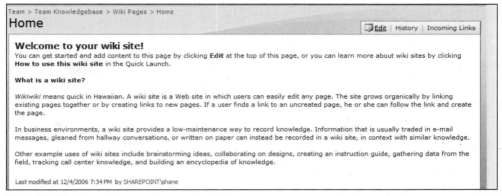

Figure 8-38

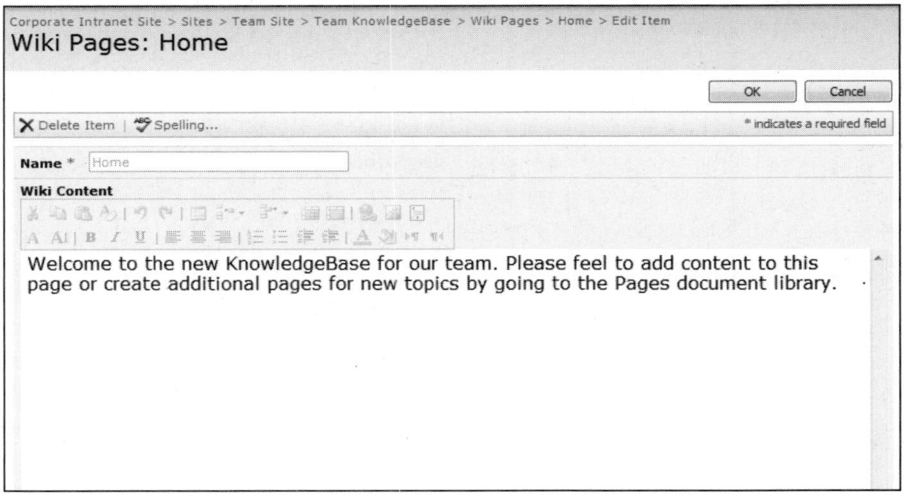

Figure 8-39

2. Select the existing page content, and click the Delete button.

3. Enter the following text:

> **Welcome to the new knowledgebase for our team. Please feel free to add content to this page or create additional pages for new topics by going to the Pages document library.**

4. Click the OK button.

When you return to the page, your new content appears. Click the History button to view the differences between the current version and previous versions.

Meeting Templates

As previously mentioned, SharePoint has special workspaces to allow collaboration and communication about meetings. Because most businesses revolve around meetings, there are a variety of templates for various meeting types as well as the information that team members need both to prepare for them and to store items discussed at them.

SharePoint has five meeting workspace templates:

Site Template	Content Elements
Basic Meeting Workspace	Objectives Agenda Attendees Document Library
Blank Meeting Workspace	Empty
Decision Meeting Workspace	Objectives Attendees Agenda Document Library Tasks Decisions
Social Meeting Workspace	Attendees Directions Things to Bring Discussion Board Picture Library
Multipage Meeting Workspace	Objective Agenda Attendees

Each meeting workspace lets you create new content elements and multiple pages so that you can adapt your meeting documents to your business requirements.

You have two methods for creating a meeting workspace:

❑　Follow the same process that you use for creating all other subsites as described earlier when creating a team site, blog site, and wiki site.

❑　Create a meeting workspace related to a specific event in an Events list, as shown in the following Try It Out.

Try It Out   **Create a Meeting Workspace from an Item in a Calendar List**

Because meeting workspaces are often tied to Events or Calendar list items that are listed already on a SharePoint site, it makes sense to use the Calendar list item to create a meeting workspace within the same process, as shown in the following steps. By creating an item based on an event in a calendar list, SharePoint creates an automatic link between the item in the site calendar and the meeting workspace so users can easily navigate between both items.

1. From the home page of your team site created earlier in the "Create a New Site Using the Team Site Template" Try It Out, click the Calendar link from the Quick Launch bar. If you do not see a calendar link on your Quick Launch bar, you may select the list from the View All Site Content page of your site.

2. Select New Item as shown in Figure 8-40. The Calendar: New Item window appears as shown in Figure 8-41.

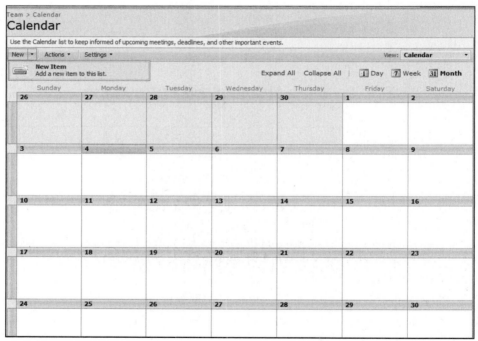

Figure 8-40

3. Enter a title for the meeting. For this example, use **Annual Board Meeting**.

4. For the Location, enter a room or floor number and room description. For this example, use **7th Floor Board Room**.

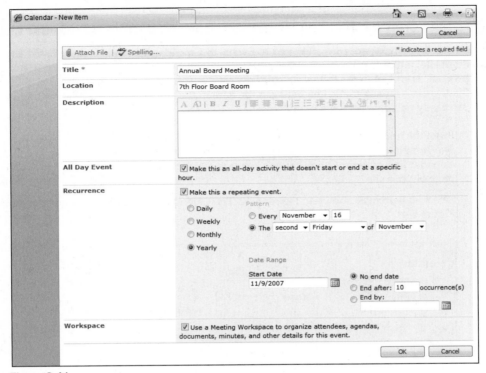

Figure 8-41

5. Select the check box to make the item an All-Day activity.

6. Select a date for the event. For this example, use **November 16, 2007** as the Start and End Time.

7. Select the check box to Make This a Repeating Event.

8. Specify that the event should repeat on an annual basis on the second Friday of November starting on November 9, 2007, as shown in Figure 8-41.

9. Select the check box to create a meeting workspace.

10. Click the OK button. A meeting workspace creation page appears.

11. Change the URL to **abm** (Annual Board Meeting) rather than the default value based on the title of the site.

12. Click the OK button. The Template Selection window appears, as shown in Figure 8-42.

13. Select the Basic Meeting Workspace template.

14. Click the OK button.

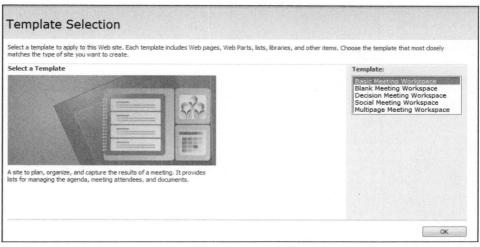

Figure 8-42

How It Works

In this example, you chose to make your meeting an all-day event. This is suitable for events that are expected to take up the entire day. An example of this might be a holiday or vacation day. In some cases, such as the Annual Board Meeting example in the previous Try It Out, you might select that something is an All-Day Event to remove any references to specific hours and to let others know that they should attend for the entire day. If you do not select All-Day Event, you will be required to specify a time interval for which the event will take place. In the case of a two-hour meeting that started at 8 A.M., you would enter **8 A.M.** for the start time and **10 A.M.** for the end time.

You could also have not made this item repeat if the meeting was a one-time occurrence. In that case, you skip step 8. In step 11, you change the URL to **abm** because it is a much shorter form of "Annual Board Meeting" and will make the URL more attractive and simple to users. Figure 8-43 shows an example of the meeting workspace home page.

Enterprise Templates

Larger organizations can have information dispersed or spread across many locations. SharePoint includes templates to address ways in which information such as reports, records, and official documents can be published and shared with others. Collaboration and meeting sites are great tools for teams and groups of individuals to work together toward a common goal. However, many organizations also require sites and templates to address the need to strictly share information in a view-only format for everyone in the organization or larger groups of people.

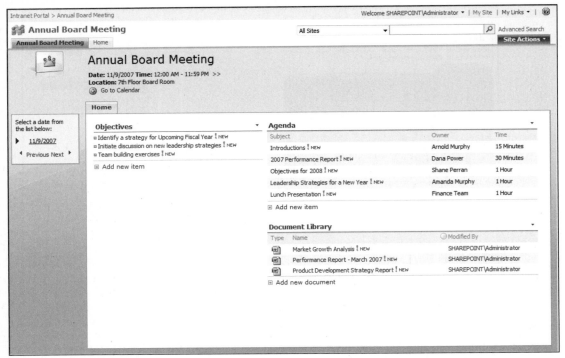

Figure 8-43

For example, the sales and marketing team of your company may have their own collaborative site using the team site template described in an earlier example. In this site, they will share documents and collaborate on the creation of reports and proposals. However, in some cases they may want to take a single report and publish it to a location where it can be viewed by the entire organization. It may not be practical to expect or allow the entire organization to find that report on their collaborative site because of access restrictions. Therefore, they may use an enterprise template such as the Report Center to publish the file to a site specifically tailored for such information display.

The next few sections provide a description of the some of the different templates that exist under the Enterprise category in SharePoint.

Document Center

The *Document Center* is a site template that is a part of the Collaboration publishing template described in the next section of this chapter. You can use this template to create a document center site within any site collection so that you can organize documents within the portal. It has an announcement list, task list and document library. Web Parts are available to display content from these lists and other lists within the site. Figure 8-44 shows an example of the Document Center.

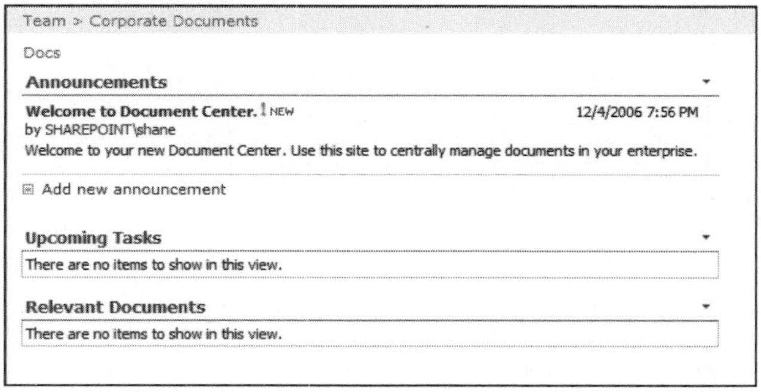

Figure 8-44

Because this site can potentially contain numerous documents over the course of time, having an easy method for users to identify content relevant to them is very important. Therefore, the Web Part on the main page of the site displays any documents that a user last modified or checked out. Because this site uses the Relevant Documents Web Part, it may not always be necessary to store all documents in a single document library. You could create multiple document libraries, and content is displayed to users from the single Web Part. You would do this if you have multiple unique topics on which different users or groups would be publishing information. By separating the content in multiple libraries, you could customize each library to suit the specific storage requirements of each type of information as well as change permissions to suit unique management needs or rights.

In Chapter 9, you learn how you can change permissions related to a single library or list to be unique from the site in which they are contained.

Report Center

The *Report Center* is a part of the Collaboration publishing template. You use it within any other site collection as long as you enable the Publishing feature for that site collection. Instructions for enabling features on a site collection are given later in this chapter. Using the sample data and instructions that are part of the Report Center site template shown in Figure 8-45, a site manager can create a reporting portal to display worksheets and other business applications.

Chapter 11 discusses report centers, Excel Services, performance indicator information, and other business reporting features.

Records Center

SharePoint 2007 enables users to assign rules and policies to certain types of content in order to consistently manage and control the access, expiry, and deletion of important corporate records. This is an area of major concern for many large organizations that store customers' personal information or manage information that has specific access and retention rights. Healthcare, insurance, and government agencies are just a few examples of the types of organizations that have requirements for effective record management. Effective handling of such information is not only critical for historical reference or corporate protection, but may also be required by law. Using these policies, you can track content within special repositories to maintain the integrity of your documents in a formalized and controlled manner. The Records Center has several lists and libraries that help control and store records and managed content. Figure 8-46 shows an example of a Records Center site upon initial creation.

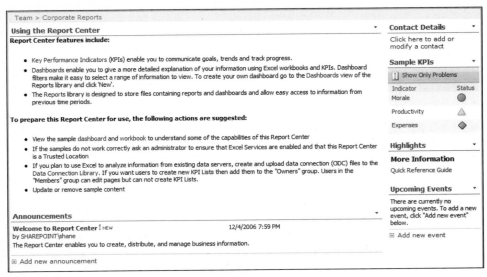

Figure 8-45

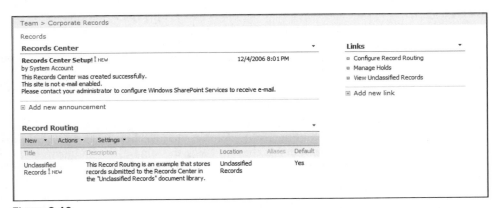

Figure 8-46

Chapter 6 discusses the various information management policies you can create.

News

Common to most organizations is the need to share news and announcements about important internal and industry-related events. The *News template* is designed to easily create news content articles that can be published for others to share. News stories can be created by content owners by selecting Create Page from the Site Actions menu, and will be automatically listed in a customized Content Query Web Part at the top of the news page. In addition, any previous news articles can be viewed by clicking the Browse News Archive link at the right of the page, as shown in Figure 8-47.

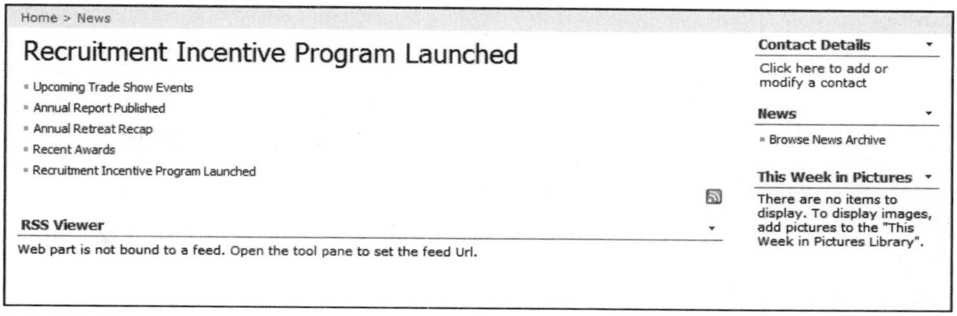

Figure 8-47

In addition, this template comes configured with an RSS Viewer Web Part that was introduced in Chapter 7 and can provide a great way to display news articles from other non-SharePoint sources such as major news sites or industry publications.

Site Directory

Contained within the Collaboration publishing site template is the *Site Directory template* that organizes sites created within a site collection and is therefore very important for many corporate intranet scenarios. You can add more site directories to a corporate intranet in cases where you need to track many sites, each with unique properties.

The Site Directory template has a special list called *sites* that stores metadata and information about sites within a site collection. This becomes critical when a corporation needs to maintain a good level of organization as it creates more and more sites. By default, SharePoint provides a few columns to track information such as:

- ❑ **Region**: The region a site represents.
- ❑ **Division**: The division for which the site was created.
- ❑ **Owner**: Which member of the organization is considered the owner of the site.

You can create additional columns to further define the sites. In fact, whenever you create a new corporate intranet site, you should go to the Site directory and customize the columns of the Sites list so that newly created sites are properly categorized and organized.

By default in SharePoint 2007, you can only create subsites in the site collection. This differs from SharePoint Portal Server 2003 where you can create new site collections instead. Creating a new site collection is a good idea for large deployment where the top-level sites have different sets of templates and components and won't share content with other sites. You can create new collections in SharePoint 2007, but you need to configure things differently from both the central administration site and the Corporate Intranet site collection.

Site columns and content types (which were described in Chapters 4 and 6 respectively) cannot be shared across site collections. As well, certain Web Parts that we looked at in Chapter 7 such as the Content Query Web Part only display content from a single site collection. Therefore, if you anticipate a need to standardize content types, metadata, and display information using the Content Query Web Part, a single site collection may be more appropriate. If you anticipate a larger scale deployment where sites would require their own unique templates, content types, and metadata without much need for displaying content from other sites, then multiple site collections may be more appropriate.

The next two Try It Outs show you how to customize the site list in the Site Directory as well as how to configure the Site Directory to create site collections rather than standard subsites. This is a good idea for large deployments where most top-level sites are expected to use a completely unique set of templates and components and have few requirements for cross-site content sharing.

Try It Out   Customize the Sites List of the Site Directory

In this example, you edit the Sites list so that it contains a special column called Site Type, which will distinguish whether a site is for a team, division, client, or project. You also modify the Division category to include a choice for Marketing.

1. From the home page of your corporate intranet site, click the Sites link from the top link bar.

2. Click the View All Site Content link on the Quick Launch bar.

3. Click the Sites link from the Lists section, as shown in Figure 8-48. You are redirected to a list displaying links to sites that have been created in your site collection and added to the Site Directory.

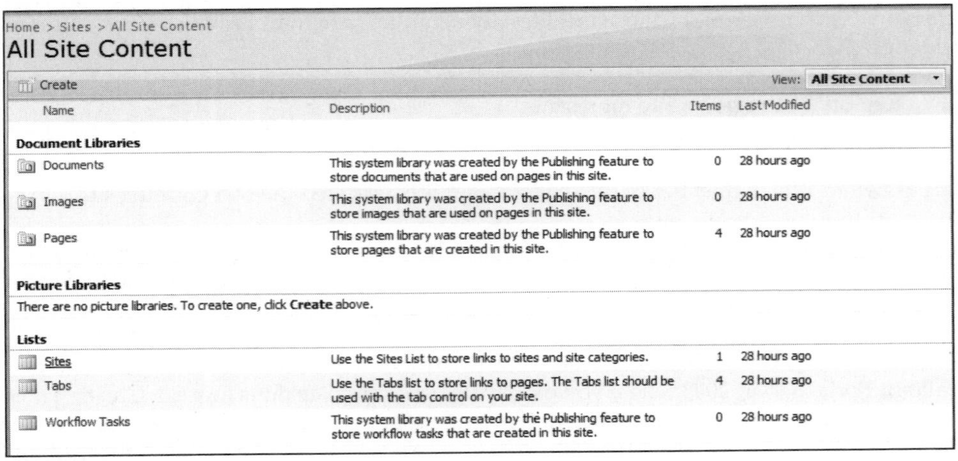

Figure 8-48

4. Select Settings ⇨ List Settings on the toolbar. You are redirected to the List Administration page.

5. From the Columns section, click the Division column link. You are redirected to the Settings page for the Division column.

6. From the Additional Column Settings section, update the choice value list to include Marketing, as shown in Figure 8-49.

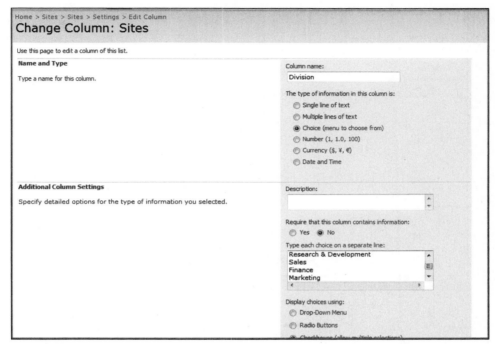

Figure 8-49

7. Click the OK button. You return to the List Administration page.

8. Click the Create Column link from the Columns section.

9. In the Column Name field, enter a name for your column. For this example, enter **Site Type**.

10. Select Choice, as shown in Figure 8-50, for the type of column.

11. For Require That This Column Contains Information field, select Yes.

12. In the Choice field, enter the values that you want users to be able to select concerning an item. For this example, enter **Team Site**, **Division Site**, **Client Site**, and **Project Site**.

13. Select Radio Buttons for the display choice.

14. Remove the default value so that it is blank.

15. Click the OK button.

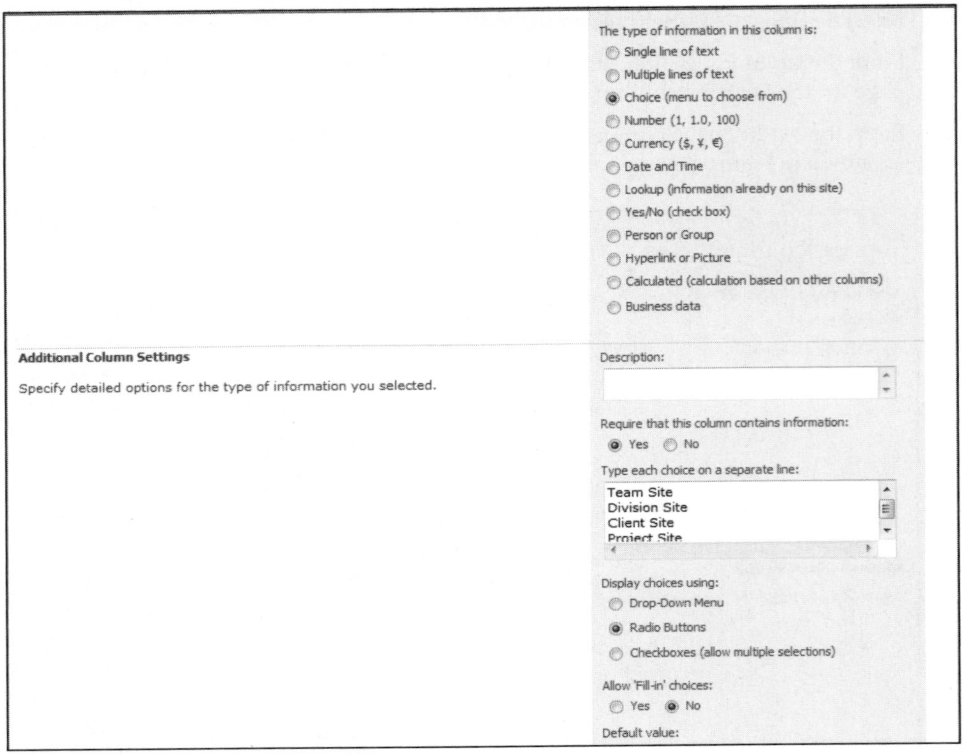

The type of information in this column is:

- Single line of text
- Multiple lines of text
- Choice (menu to choose from)
- Number (1, 1.0, 100)
- Currency ($, ¥, €)
- Date and Time
- Lookup (information already on this site)
- Yes/No (check box)
- Person or Group
- Hyperlink or Picture
- Calculated (calculation based on other columns)
- Business data

Additional Column Settings

Specify detailed options for the type of information you selected.

Description:

Require that this column contains information:
- Yes - No

Type each choice on a separate line:

```
Team Site
Division Site
Client Site
Project Site
```

Display choices using:
- Drop-Down Menu
- Radio Buttons
- Checkboxes (allow multiple selections)

Allow 'Fill-in' choices:
- Yes - No

Default value:

Figure 8-50

How It Works

Your customization of the Sites list for this example will better capture information on sites in the site collection. Now, whenever users create a new site, they will have the option to select Marketing as a choice for the division and will be required to specify whether the site is intended for tracking information related to a team, division, project, or client.

Try It Out   Configuring the Site Directory to Create Site Collections

In the following example, you create site collections from the Site Directory instead of subsites. To do this, you first enable self-service site creation within the Central Administration site. You then return to the primary site collection that contains the Site Directory and modify the Site Directory settings so that site collections are created from that location. In the previous Try It Out, you created a site collection by visiting the Central Administration site. Now, you create the same site collection from the Site Directory.

You would enable the creation of site collections from the Site Directory if you were managing a SharePoint environment where different departments or divisions were very unique and therefore did not share the same templates, content types, security settings, or site columns. For example, imagine you were managing a SharePoint implementation for a large multinational company that created several unique product lines that operated with completely separate management teams, departments, and staff. Each group would not be required to share information with one another or display content from one another's sites. In this situation, it may be more beneficial to allow for each main product line to have its own site collection. Another example might be where a large government organization has implemented SharePoint, and each key organizational unit would have a requirement to operate independently from the other. For example, there would be no requirement to display federal healthcare forms and policies on the same site as the federal department related to military and defense.

1.   Log into the Central Administration site of your SharePoint environment.

The Central Administration site is a unique site collection and has tighter access requirements than your standard portal site. If you do not have access, contact your server administrator to assist with this step. Also, the Central Administration site is usually hosted on a different port than your corporate portal, so it is a good idea to add the link to your My Links list under an Admin group.

2.   Select the Application Management tab.

3.   Click the Self-Service Site Management link from the Application Security section, as shown in Figure 8-51. You are redirected to the Self-Service Site Management page, as shown in Figure 8-52.

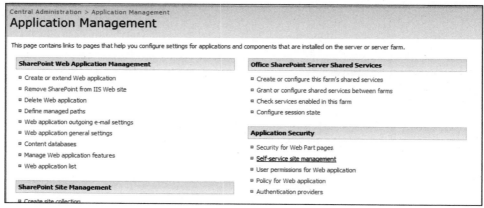

Figure 8-51

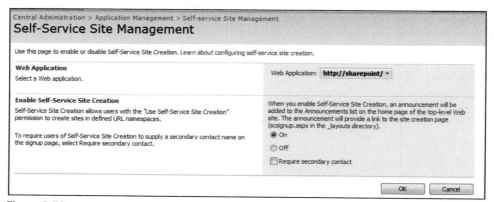

Figure 8-52

4. Select your web application from the drop-down list. Generally most portals are hosted under port 80. If you are unsure which application is correct, check with your system administrator.

5. Under Enable Self-Service Site Creation, select On.

6. Click the OK button.

7. Return to your corporate intranet site and select Site Actions ⇨ Modify All Site Settings.

8. Select Site Directory Settings from the Site Collection Administration section.

9. Select the check box for Create New Site Collections from Site Directory, as shown in Figure 8-53.

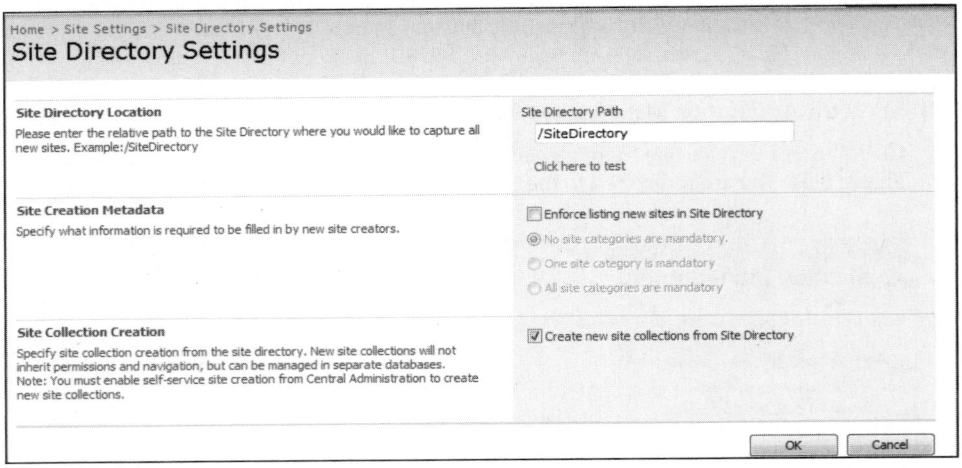

Figure 8-53

10. Click the OK button.

Search Center

You can create a Search Center using one of two templates. In SharePoint 2007, one template has been revamped to include common search tabs such as People or All Sites if you want them; an example of this shown in Figure 8-54. The advantage of tabs is that you can predefine certain search types that a user may want to conduct and have a page dedicated specifically to that topic. For example, by selecting the People tab, any queries you enter will only search the user profiles of people within your organization.

Because the searching for information is so important, this topic is covered in great detail in Chapter 14.

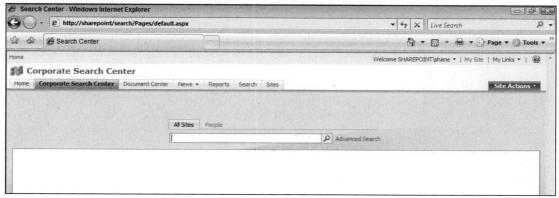

Figure 8-54

Publishing Templates

When creating a new site collection, users have the ability to select either Collaboration Portal or Publishing Portal from the Publishing tab. These sites are not available as subsites because of their unique content and usage scenarios. Instead, they can only be selected when creating a new site collection.

Collaboration Portal

As discussed earlier in this chapter, the Collaboration publishing template is the standard starting point for most intranet portal sites in 2007. This site template features a top-level site and five subsites based on sites created from the previously reviewed Enterprise template category including:

- ❑ Document Center
- ❑ News
- ❑ Reports
- ❑ Search
- ❑ Sites

The Collaboration site template comes with the publishing feature enabled so that all changes made to the content of each portal page must be checked in, published, and approved. Because this template is generally used to reflect the communication needs of an organization, the content displayed is generally more tightly managed than what is shared at the team and divisional level.

Publishing Portal

The *Publishing Portal site* gives you a starting point for the type of site you would typically see when browsing the Internet. This is sometimes referred to as an *Internet facing website*. It contains lists and libraries to store web content and workflows, including a workflow for approving created or modified content. Figure 8-55 shows an example of a publishing portal.

Figure 8-55

Chapter 13 details the features and functionality related to managing Internet facing websites and web content management as well as how it works as part of the Publishing Portal site template.

Creating Custom Templates

As mentioned previously, the templates discussed in this chapter so far may only give you some of the elements you need for an effective collaboration or communication site. To create a site for your situation, you can use an existing template and then create the additional elements you need. Once you have a site that works for you, you can save your site as a template for future use. Corporations commonly do this to create uniform sites and to save time and effort when creating new sites.

Try It Out   Save a Site as Template

In this example, you create a team site and add another library to store team photos — a requirement expressed by management. Rather than having each person with a team site manually create a photo library, you add the library to a site and then save that site as a template for the other teams to use.

1. Return to your team site that was created earlier in this chapter in the "Create a New Site Using the Team Site Template" Try It Out.

2. Select Site Actions ⇨ Create. You are redirected to the List and Library template selection page.

3. Select Picture Library from the Libraries section.

4. Enter **Shared Photos** for the library name.

5. Select Yes for the Create a Version Every Time You Edit a File in This Picture library item.

6. Click the Create button. You are redirected to your newly created Picture Library.

7. Select Site Actions ⇨ Site Settings. You are redirected to the Site Administration page.

·8. Click the Save Site as Template link from the Look and Feel section, as shown in Figure 8-56. You are redirected to a page where you must define the details of your site template, shown in Figure 8-57.

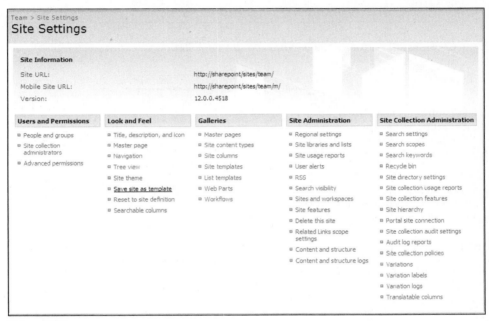

Figure 8-56

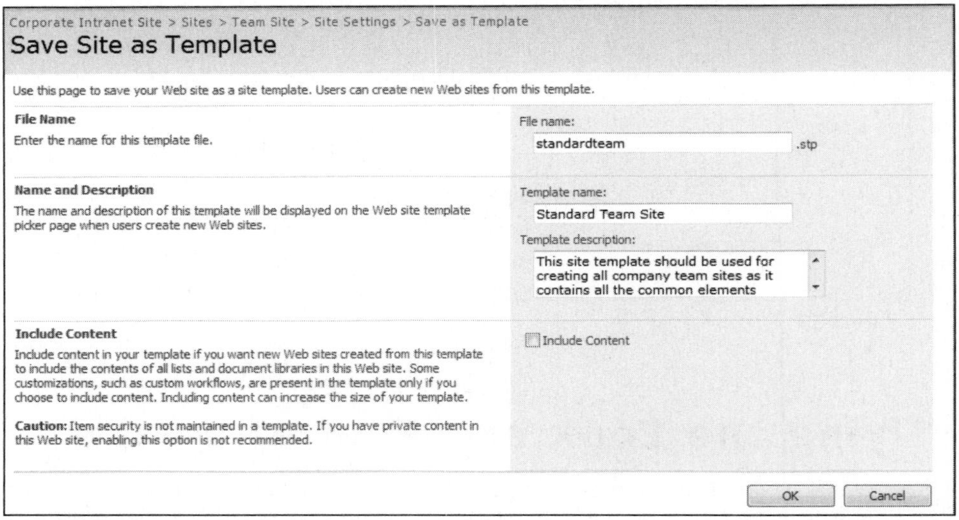

Figure 8-57

8. Enter a file name for the template. For this example, enter **standardteam**.

9. Enter a template name for the template. For this example, enter **Standard Team Site**.

10. Enter a description of the template. For this example, enter the following:

> **This site template should be used for creating all company team sites as it contains all the common elements required, including a picture library.**

11. Click the OK button. You are redirected to a page stating that your site template has been saved successfully.

How It Works

Now users can use that template when creating their sites by selecting it from the Custom tab as shown in Figure 8-58.

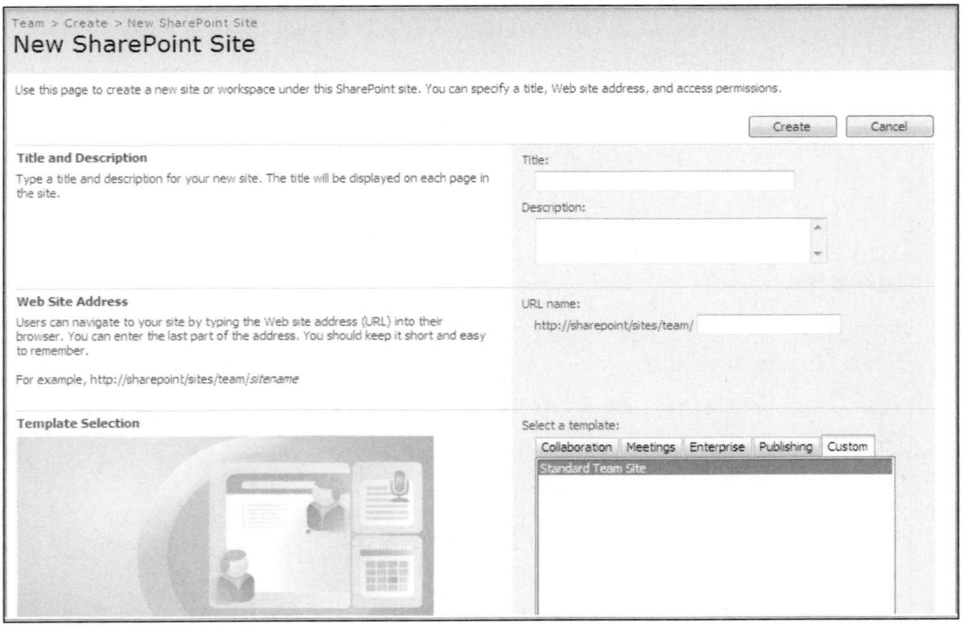

Figure 8-58

Modifying the Look and Feel of a Site

While SharePoint comes with templates that give your site a certain look and feel, many organizations, divisions, or teams may want to customize or change the look and feel of their site to match their own unique requirements or preferences. In this section, you learn some of the alternatives that exist in SharePoint for doing so, including the use of themes and master pages.

Using Themes

You can customize your sites using *Cascading Style Sheets* (CSS), which allow you to separate the presentation aspects of a site from your content and HTML. SharePoint takes advantage of style sheets in many ways, one of the most notable being themes. SharePoint themes control the color scheme of a site, things like the background color of a menu item or toolbar. See Figure 8-59 for an example of a site with a Theme applied.

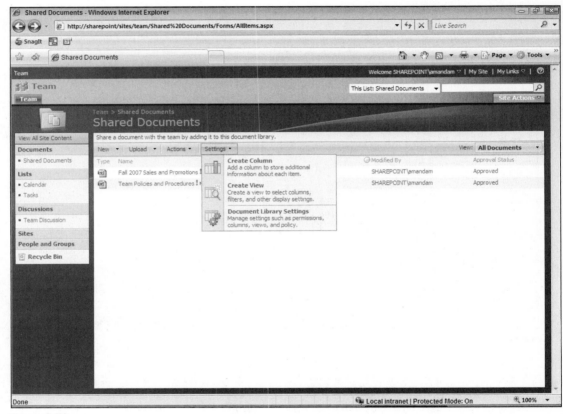

Figure 8-59

Try It Out   Apply a Theme

Themes are used to brand your site to suit a corporate color scheme without the risk of disturbing the layout.

1.   Select Site Actions ➪ Site Settings.

2. Click the Site Theme link from the Look and Feel section.

3. Select Wheat from the list of available themes.

4. Click the OK button. You will notice a significant color change in your site elements. See Figure 8-60.

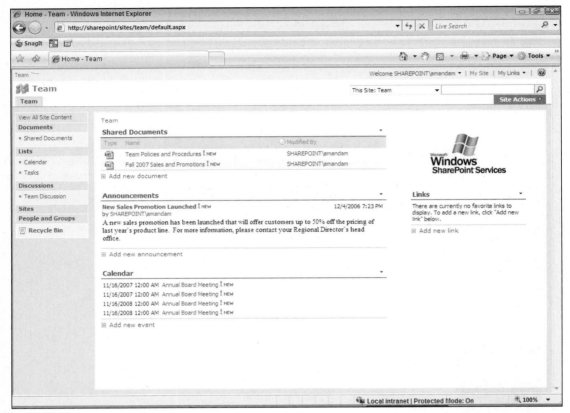

Figure 8-60

When applying themes to your site, be careful to use only those that enhance or add value to your site, and do not prevent your team members from viewing information. Some themes apply dark background colors and fonts, which can make things difficult for users to view.

How It Works

When you apply a theme to a site, the style sheet associated with the theme overrides the default style sheet and subsequently changes the look and feel of your site. This quick and easy method of customization is a temporary change and applies only until you select a new theme to the site.

Understanding Master Pages

Because SharePoint 2007 is built on ASP.NET 2.0, it takes advantage of the master pages technology. *Master Pages* allow you to control common elements such as the layout and navigation for an entire site from a single "master" page. The idea is that a single page controls the layout, navigation, and content placeholders. Content pages, which also have content controls that plug content into the placeholders, inherit the look of the master page. Using master pages, you can select a single look and feel template for your site collection at the top level and reset all sites below it to inherit this look and feel. This is a major advantage to companies that go through regular changes to their corporate standard or brand. In earlier versions of SharePoint, a site manager would have to update the look and feel of each site individually, which would be a time-consuming and challenging operation.

When a page is requested via the browser, the content and master pages merge, displaying a single page. Master pages in SharePoint are stored in the Master Pages Gallery you access via the Site Settings page as shown in Figure 8-61.

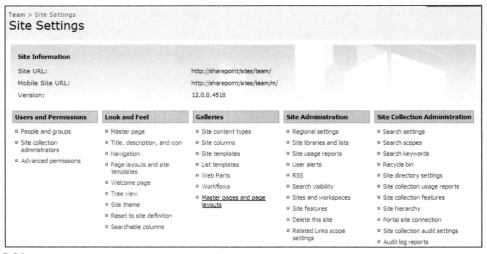

Figure 8-61

You would customize a master page to create a custom layout for your site. The most common application for customizing master pages is SharePoint Designer. Chapter 13 reviews how you can select a new master page and apply it to your sites and all subsites.

Try It Out   Restore to Site Template

All sites are originally created based on a single set of files, commonly referred to as a *site definition*. After creating your site, you have the option of customizing your pages and modifying the layout to better suit your needs. In the event you want to revert back to the old look and feel, you can do so using SharePoint 2007 UI.

To reset a page or entire site to its default look and feel, follow these easy steps:

1. Select Site Actions ⇨ Site Settings.

2. Click the Reset to Site Definition link from the Look and Feel section.

3. You can reset a particular page by specifying the URL, or you can choose to reset all pages within the site to the default look and feel. See Figure 8-62.

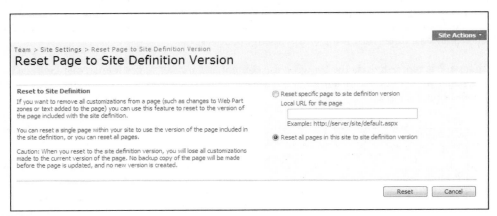

Figure 8-62

4. Select the Reset All Pages option.

5. Click the OK button.

How It Works

When you revert a site to its default state, SharePoint makes a snapshot version of your altered master page before the reversion. This means you can later go back to the altered master page.

Summary

This chapter discussed the key feature of SharePoint — the site.

❑ It discussed the differences between a site, a site collection, and a workspace. It then looked at the various templates and usage scenarios of each. The five categories of site templates are Collaboration, Meeting, Enterprise, Publishing, and Custom.

❑ Your choice of a site template depends on your requirements. In addition, you can create your own set of templates to suit your needs. Establishing a set of common templates reduces the confusion of having each site owner create all the required elements on his or her own, and provides a consistent interface and environment. This helps drive user adoption, learning, and acceptance.

❑ The chapter then turned to alternatives within sites that control elements, such as the navigation and regional settings. You can also enable features to extend the functionality of your site. Using features, you can transform a standard team site to contain more advanced functionality, such as web content publishing and approval. By familiarizing yourself with the various templates and the features that are available with each, you can make decisions on what features you can enable to improve the user experience and functionality of your sites.

❑ You can use master pages to customize your site, but if the changes you make aren't desirable, you can restore the site to its original state. This protects your site from unwanted changes.

Exercises

1. Describe the difference between a site and a site collection.

2. You have been asked to create a corporate portal for your company. What would be the appropriate site template to use to create the site?

3. There is a growing need within your division to share more information between employees so that they can get to know each other better and stay on track with developments in their various projects and activities. What tool can you use to empower them to share more information with their peers and receive feedback on posted topics?

4. You have a site requirement that contains a document library, announcements list, tasks list, shared calendar, issues list, and discussion board. How would you go about creating that site?

User Management, Audiences, and Profiles

So far in this book, you've read a lot about how to work with SharePoint content and the various components you can create and customize. Unfortunately, none of your work with these topics means anything unless your users can quickly access that content — and configuring access to that information has a lot to do with how much of it there is and where it's located. Just because users have access to content does not mean that they have a requirement to see the content. It's important to evaluate the content that will be stored in your information system and determine how users will need to access and view it. You may need to do this by asking some important questions: Do you have too little information? Do you have so much information that a user can't wade through it? Where is your information located? Do you have one location or do you have information in a hierarchy? Can users easily access the information they need to perform their jobs? Is the content they view relevant to them?

In this chapter, you learn about the following:

❑ The difference between user access and personalization

❑ The different permission levels in a SharePoint site

❑ SharePoint site groups and the built-in ones you can use

❑ How to update user profile information manually and automatically

❑ How to create audiences based on specific memberships or profile properties

❑ How to target information and Web Parts to specific audiences

After reading this chapter, you should feel comfortable planning and implementing changes to your SharePoint environment to ensure that users can access content relevant to them.

Understanding User Access Management and Personalization

Before you learn how to manage access to any SharePoint site, you need to understand two very important concepts in SharePoint related to the users who connect to your sites:

❑   The difference between access management and personalization

❑   How users log in to a SharePoint site

Understanding these concepts helps you learn how to effectively manage a site, protect the site's integrity from users who shouldn't have access to certain information, and make the user experience as productive and problem-free as possible.

What Is the Difference Between User Access Management and Personalization?

Imagine you work for a company where users from around the globe share information related to their various business activities. There are different divisions such as Sales, Marketing, Finance, and Legal. Members of a specific division can log in to their portal site and stay up-to-date on projects and initiatives as well as work with others in their divisions and teams. For this to happen effectively, you must configure the SharePoint environment to support the following:

❑   **User access management:** There are rules that determine what a user can do on a site. To ensure that users can access only the content they need to perform their work, you apply permissions to each divisional site. Within a specific division, users may have different roles and privileges. For example, some users only view content, while others can add or approve new content.

❑   **Personalization:** Ensures that content is relevant to the users of a site. You use personalization and audience features to do this. *Personalization* allows users to view only content that applies to them. You may accomplish this by providing them with the ability to customize the interface to display only items that are relevant to them, or it may mean creating certain views that only display items where their username is displayed in a specific column, such as the Assigned to column. In some cases, you may want to target specific content elements such as a document, list item, or Web Part to members of a role. Through *audiences*, you can identify the groups of people that would find information relevant as you publish it. Perhaps in the Sales division, for example, certain promotions and sales procedures are only relevant for the North American region, and distracting to sales personnel from the other regions. Therefore, when publishing these promotional documents, the content manager would select a North American audience.

Before you try to personalize content, it's very important that you solidify the underlying content access. With that in mind, the chapter covers user access features of SharePoint 2007 first, and then discusses audiences and other personalization features in greater detail.

How Do Users Log In to a SharePoint Site?

SharePoint 2007 greatly improved its interface to address alternate authentication providers, user switching, and security trimming. Before delving into these improvements, you need to understand how a user logs in to a site. When users click a link or enter the web address of a SharePoint site, they are either logged into the site automatically because they may already be authenticated to the site, or they are prompted for a username and password via a dialog box or form. In some cases, there may be no need for authentication because the site is configured for anonymous access. This chapter primarily reviews scenarios where the user is connecting in an authenticated environment.

Once users are logged into the site, they will see only content and user-interface elements that they have been given permission to view. The content that users view and edit is determined by their SharePoint site group membership. *Site groups* are specific roles in SharePoint that determine what a user can do within a site.

For more on the different site groups, see the section "Working with Site Groups and Permission Levels."

Most organizations using SharePoint in a corporate or enterprise setting, such as an intranet, will use Active Directory to manage user profiles and determine how users log in to the network, which is also known as the *authentication process*. Since SharePoint 2003, Active Directory has been used to authenticate users and build user profiles using basic personalization features. This means that if your organization uses Active Directory, SharePoint becomes a great browser-based tool in which to work because a user who logs in to the domain does not typically need to enter credentials again to access a SharePoint site. This is because when the system administrator configured the SharePoint server, it was added as a member of your Active Directory domain. Therefore, when you enter your username and password to connect to the network, the SharePoint environment recognizes you as a member and therefore does not require you to specify your username and password again. In addition, SharePoint allows you to connect to sites based on your site group membership and retains your permissions as you access various other Windows-based systems such as file shares or printers. Most users prefer this type of experience because it can be tedious and confusing to manage both multiple usernames and passwords.

A site manager can add specific Active Directory users to a site group by typing his name or email address into the site membership interface. See Figure 9-1 for an example of how this can work.

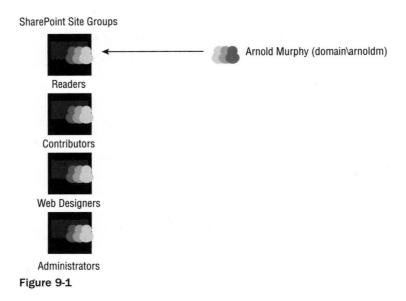

SharePoint Site Groups

Readers

Arnold Murphy (domain\arnoldm)

Contributors

Web Designers

Administrators

Figure 9-1

However, in organizations with thousands of users, it's more realistic to add Active Directory security groups to a SharePoint site group. This not only reduces administrative overhead when you first set up a site, but also means the site's membership stays up-to-date as new users join or leave the organization. As you add users to the Active Directory security group, they are automatically assigned to the SharePoint site group that has been associated with the security group, as shown in Figure 9-2.

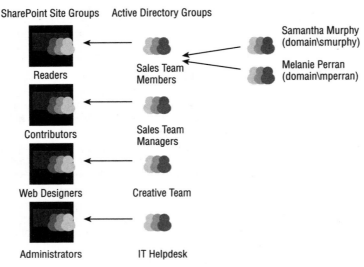

Figure 9-2

The rest of this chapter looks at specific access and authentication examples based on an underlying assumption that Active Directory is the primary membership store.

Other Authentication Methods

In SharePoint 2007, you can connect your membership database to stores aside from Active Directory or Windows. In fact, because SharePoint is built on the .NET 2.0 Framework, any membership provider that you can use in ASP.NET 2.0 can control access to the SharePoint environment using forms-based authentication.

Although Active Directory and other membership provider services, such as a SQL Server database or custom application, provide some great benefits to SharePoint 2007, you're not required to use them. In fact, users can log on to SharePoint sites if they have a local user accounts on the server.

Although enabling forms-based authentication is beyond the scope of this book, you can use custom membership databases as well as existing non-Active Directory connections. For more information, see *Professional SharePoint 2007 Development*

Try It Out   Sign In as a Different User

In this example, you've already logged in to a site with a user account and need to sign in as a different user with a different set of credentials. Depending on how your organization is using SharePoint, you may have entered login information when you first accessed the site, or you may have automatically logged in because your organization is using Active Directory.

Follow these steps to sign in as a different user:

1.   From the home page of your Intranet Portal site collection created in Chapter 8, click the Welcome link as shown in Figure 9-3.

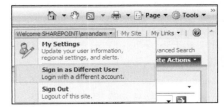

Figure 9-3

2.   Select Sign in as Different User. A login box appears.

3.   Enter the credentials of the user you want to log in as.

4.   Click the OK button. You now see the name of the user you logged in as in the welcome menu.

How It Works

Signing in as a different user is a new capability for SharePoint 2007 — previous versions of the application, especially those associated with Active Directory, did not support it. This capability is important when you start applying special access settings or configurations to your environment and you need to validate your configurations by logging in under test user accounts. For example, if the members of the reader group for your site should not have access to a specific document library, you can set up a test user account in the reader group and log in as that user to confirm that the library is not accessible. Also, if you support an environment and users claim that they cannot perform a specific action or see a particular menu item, you can log in as a test user with the same access rights as that user to troubleshoot the problem.

Managing Access in SharePoint

As your SharePoint environment starts to become populated with important business documents, it's important to manage access properly. Users who require information to do their jobs should be able to easily locate and then access information. In cases where you have sensitive information on the portal, it's crucial that only users who have a business requirement to access it have the rights to do so. Because

SharePoint will become a central storage location for important business information, it is critical that this information be protected. This means locking out those who could cause harm to the system or should not have access to information.

Understanding the SharePoint Membership Groups

A SharePoint site group defines the specific roles and permissions for users. By default, SharePoint has several groups, which vary depending on the type of site you create and the type of activities users perform on that site. The following list shows the different types of site groups that SharePoint has to offer and explains the purpose of each:

❑ **Site Members:** Members can view, add, edit, or delete content in existing site elements, such as lists and document libraries. In a collaborative setting, team members in this group generally have no reason to create new instances of lists or libraries but participate by constantly adding and reading existing content. This is the group that most closely resembles the "Contributor" role from WSS version 2 and SharePoint Portal Server 2003.

❑ **Viewers:** Members can only view pages, documents, and list items and have limited options in the File drop-down menu (see Figure 9-4). If an application exists to handle file viewing, members of this group can access files via that application. For example, if a member of a group opens a spreadsheet stored in a reports library using Excel Services, that person can view the spreadsheet through the browser rather than via Excel.

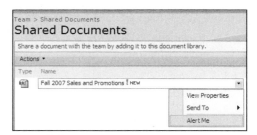

Figure 9-4

❑ **Site Visitors:** Users in this site group have read-only access to site content. This group most closely resembles the "Reader" role from WSS v2 and SharePoint Portal Server 2003.

❑ **Site Owners:** Member have complete control over a specific SharePoint site. Members can create new content elements and subsites, and specify access and permissions for other users. This most closely resembles the "Administrator" role from WSS v2 and SharePoint Portal Server 2003.

❑ **Designers:** This represents users who contribute and approve content, create new content elements, and customize the site's presentation through page templates and style sheets. This group is specific to sites that have the Publishing feature enabled.

❑ **Hierarchy Managers:** Members can create new lists, edit pages, and add content to existing lists, but also create and manage subsites. This group most closely resembles the "Web Designer" role from WSS v2 and SharePoint Portal Server 2003.

❑ **Approvers:** Members have permission to edit, create, and approve content. Members of this group can decide whether to approve or reject documents or list items. Items pending content approval are not seen by users unless this group, or someone with equal rights, approves it.

❑ **Restricted Readers:** Members of this group can access the latest versions of published content but cannot view the historical versions or view any information on who has access to the content.

❑ **Quick Deploy Users:** Specific to the content deployment functionality, members can publish content using the Quick Deploy method. Typically only a site owner can do this.

The Quick Deploy User makes use of the content deployment functionality of SharePoint 2007, which is a function of the Publishing feature and Web Content Management (WCM), discussed in Chapter 13.

Working with Site Groups and Permission Levels

Now that you have an understanding of the various SharePoint 2007 site groups, let's take a look at some of the ways you can manage access to the content stored with sites by working with the site groups and permission levels. This section looks at how you can create your own site groups as well as change the access rights of a user by adding them to a site group or changing their existing permissions. You also learn how to control how users request access changes related to your site.

If the site groups listed in the previous section do not meet your specific requirements, you can create your own groups with the specific rights and permissions. For example, if you want a group where users can view, add, and edit content, but you don't want them to delete content, you can create a site group called "Limited Member" with that restriction. Although you can edit the permissions level of a standard group, this is generally not recommended unless you intend to do so for the group across all sites in your server farm. Minor changes to the default settings can be difficult to identify later as the environment grows and may lead to improper assumptions on who has access to do what. In cases where you require a slight modification to an existing site group, it's better to copy the group and make the changes to the copied version.

In the next set of Try It Outs, you create a group that is very similar to the Members group; however, you name it "Limited Membership" to identify that it was slightly different than the default Members group. You then add the new team members to your site groups. If you find later that you need to change permissions on a group or user that you've already created, or totally delete a user altogether, you learn to do so in the third and fourth Try It Outs. In the last Try It Out of the section, you find out how to enable access to a site when a user requests it.

Try It Out   Create a New Site Group

In this example, you create the specific permission level, which allows users to create new content and edit existing content but prevents them from deleting documents. Existing permission levels do not separate content editing from content deleting. You will notice that selecting the rights to edit content automatically enables the rights to view items and pages because these additional abilities are required to edit content. Once you define a permissions level, you can create a new site group to use it. Separating the group and a permissions level allows one or more groups to use a single set of permissions, which gives you greater flexibility and control and is therefore the recommended practice when defining new permissions.

This example assumes that the team site is using unique permissions from the parent site. What this means is that any user who has access to the parent site, will not have access to the team site unless he is added as a user to the team site. If the permissions of your team site were inherited from the parent site, then any user who had access to the parent site would have the same access to the team site. If you do not have a site that uses unique permissions, it is recommended that you create a new site from the Site Directory of your Intranet Portal site collection using the steps discussed in Chapter 8 and select Unique Permissions during the creation process.

1. From the main page of your team site, select Site Actions ⇨ Site Settings.

2. Select the Advanced Permissions link under the Users and Permissions section, as shown in Figure 9-5. You are redirected to the Permissions page.

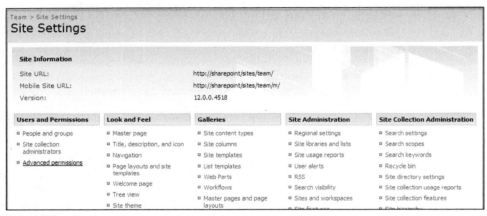

Figure 9-5

3. Select Settings ⇨ Permission Levels from the toolbar. You are redirected to the Permission Levels page.

    If you do not see the Settings menu on the toolbar of the Permissions page in step 3, it is likely that your site is inheriting permissions. You can select Actions ⇨ Edit Permissions to change from inherited permissions to unique permissions. Doing so copies any users and groups from the parent into the team site. Therefore, if any users or groups that had access to the parent but you did not want them to have access to the team site, you must remove them later. If your team site was configured to inherit permissions from the parent site, you also need to select Edit Permissions Levels prior to completing Step 4. This also breaks any associations with the permission levels from the parent site.

4. Select the Edit Permissions Level button. A window appears saying that you are about to create custom groups and custom permissions for the site. Select the OK button to continue. The toolbar changes to reflect the custom permission levels for the site.

5. Select the Contribute permission level. You are redirected to a page that lists all rights associated with the Contribute permission level.

6. Scroll to bottom of page and click the Copy Permission Level button. You are redirected to a page where you must define your new Permission Level as shown in Figure 9-6.

7. Type a name and description in the Name field for your new permission level. For this example, enter **Limited Contribute**. In the description field, enter the following text:

> **Can view, add and update but cannot delete content.**

Name and Description

Type a name and description for your permission level. The name is shown on the permissions page. The name and description are shown on the add users page.

Name:

Limited Contribute

Description:

Can view, add and update but cannot delete content.

Permissions

Choose which permissions to include in the new permission level. You can keep the permissions from the original permission level or make changes. Use the **Select All** checkbox to assign all user permissions to the permission level.

Select the permissions to include in this permission level.
☐ **Select All**

List Permissions
☐ Manage Lists - Create and delete lists, add or remove columns in a list, and add or remove public views of a list.
☐ Override Check Out - Discard or check in a document which is checked out to another user.
☑ Add Items - Add items to lists, add documents to document libraries, and add Web discussion comments.
☑ Edit Items - Edit items in lists, edit documents in document libraries, edit Web discussion comments in documents, and customize Web Part Pages in document libraries.
☐ Delete Items - Delete items from a list, documents from a document library, and Web discussion comments in documents.
☑ View Items - View items in lists, documents in document libraries, and view Web discussion comments.
☐ Approve Items - Approve a minor version of a list item or document.
☑ Open Items - View the source of documents with server-side file handlers.
☑ View Versions - View past versions of a list item or document.
☐ Delete Versions - Delete past versions of a list item or document.
☑ Create Alerts - Create e-mail alerts.
☑ View Application Pages - View forms, views, and application pages. Enumerate lists.

Site Permissions
☐ Manage Permissions - Create and change permission levels on the Web site and assign permissions to users and groups.
☐ View Usage Data - View reports on Web site usage.

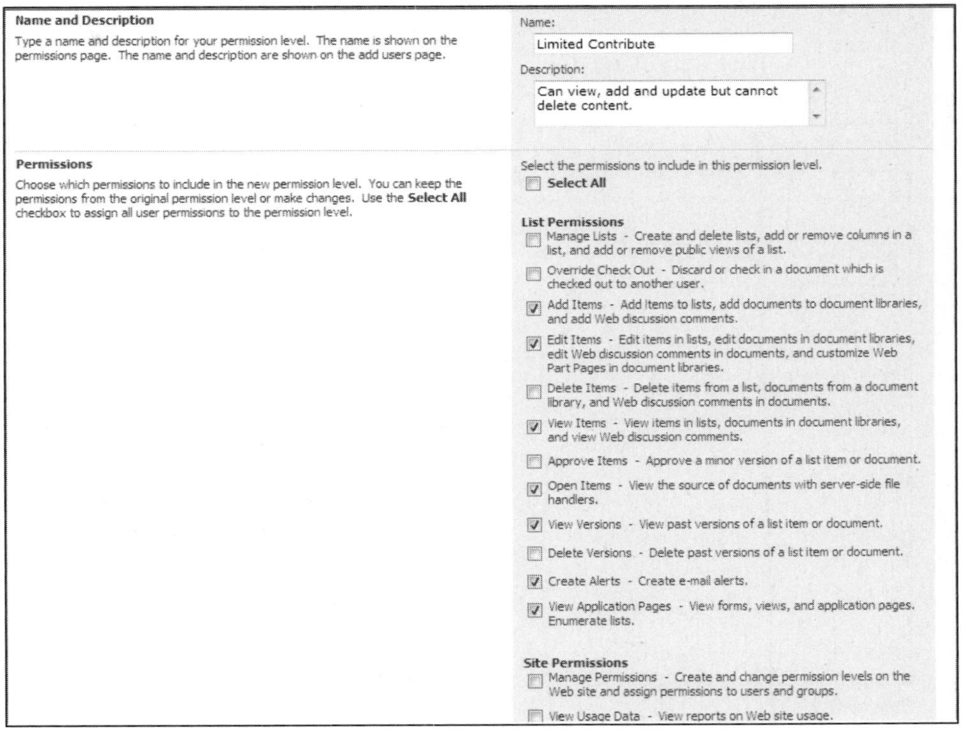

Figure 9-6

8. Unselect the Delete Items and Delete Versions check boxes under List Permissions, as shown in Figure 9-6.

9. Click the Create button.

10. Select Permissions from the navigation breadcrumb above the words "Permission Levels."

11. Select New ⇨ New Group from the toolbar. The new group creation window appears.

12. Type a name for your new site group. For this example, use **Limited Membership**.

13. In the About Me field, enter the following:

> **Use this group to give people limited contribute permissions to the SharePoint Site. Members of this group will not have the ability to delete content.**

14. Select yourself as the owner of this group. This should be the default setting.

15. For the Group Settings section (see Figure 9-7), keep the default settings that only group members can view the membership of the group, and only the group owner can edit the actual membership of group.

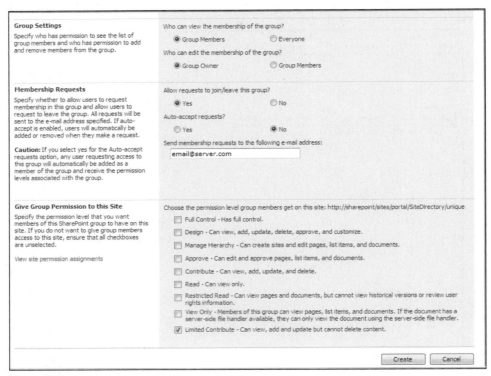

Figure 9-7

16. Under the Membership Requests section, select Yes for Allow Requests To Join/Leave This Group and enter your own email address to receive the requests. Select No for Auto-Accept Requests.

17. For the Group Permission to this site, select the Limited Contribute option.

18. Click the Create button. Your new site group is created based on the permission level you specified.

How It Works

When you create your group, you automatically become a member because you are the creator. Although members of the new group cannot delete content, you can still do so because of your membership in other site groups, such as Site Owners.

The next step is to add new team members to your site groups. You do this in the next Try It Out.

Add a User to a Site Group

In this example, all members of the Local Administrators group become site owners for your site. You can do this either by assigning each individual or by using security groups in Active Directory. When possible, doing the latter is preferable. In most organizations, Active Directory security groups represent an organization's job roles, such as sales manager or support representative, and are kept up-to-date with the organization's access requirements for those roles.

In this example, you specify a security group from your own Active Directory or SharePoint server and give it full control over the site. The process for adding a user or group to a site group is exactly the same.

You may run into situations where the people responsible for managing a SharePoint environment may not be experts in the Active Directory group structure that another administrative group establishes. To prevent this, whenever two groups plan a new SharePoint environment or site collection, they should consult each other to ensure that permissions are assigned in a way that benefits the entire organization and minimizes administrative overhead.

1.   From the main page of your team site, select Site Actions ➪ Site Settings.

2.   Select the People and Groups link under the Users and Permissions category.

3.   Select New ➪ Add Users from the toolbar. The Add Users window appears, as shown in Figure 9-8.

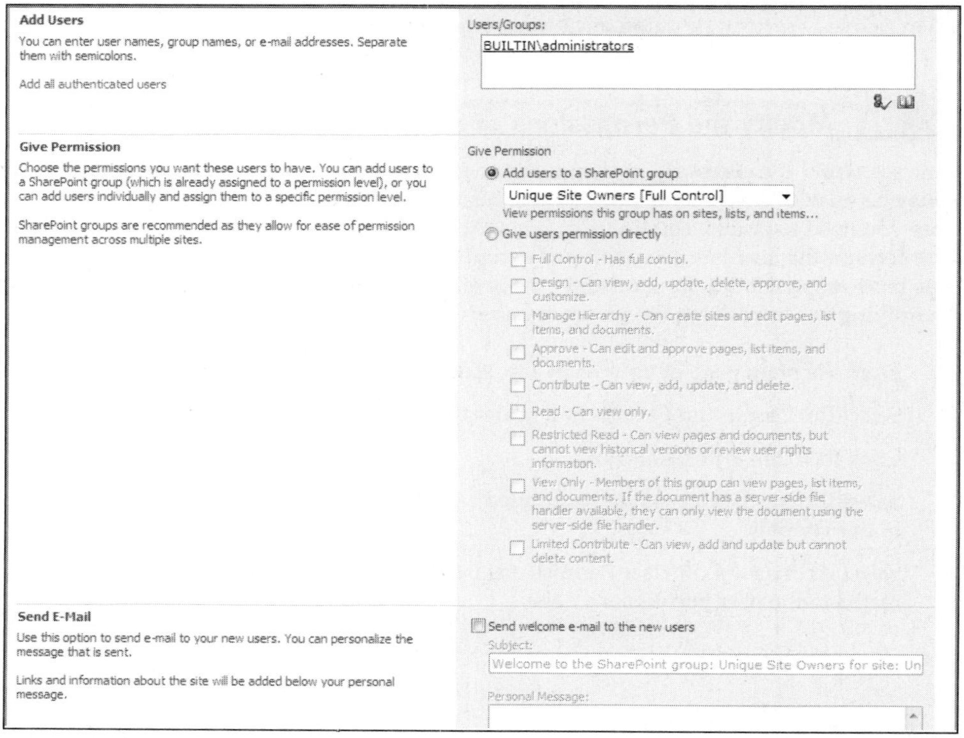

Add Users

You can enter user names, group names, or e-mail addresses. Separate them with semicolons.

Add all authenticated users

Users/Groups:

BUILTIN\administrators

Give Permission

Choose the permissions you want these users to have. You can add users to a SharePoint group (which is already assigned to a permission level), or you can add users individually and assign them to a specific permission level.

SharePoint groups are recommended as they allow for ease of permission management across multiple sites.

Give Permission

⦿ Add users to a SharePoint group

Unique Site Owners [Full Control] ▾

View permissions this group has on sites, lists, and items...

◯ Give users permission directly

☐ Full Control - Has full control.

☐ Design - Can view, add, update, delete, approve, and customize.

☐ Manage Hierarchy - Can create sites and edit pages, list items, and documents.

☐ Approve - Can edit and approve pages, list items, and documents.

☐ Contribute - Can view, add, update, and delete.

☐ Read - Can view only.

☐ Restricted Read - Can view pages and documents, but cannot view historical versions or review user rights information.

☐ View Only - Members of this group can view pages, list items, and documents. If the document has a server-side file handler available, they can only view the document using the server-side file handler.

☐ Limited Contribute - Can view, add and update but cannot delete content.

Send E-Mail

Use this option to send e-mail to your new users. You can personalize the message that is sent.

Links and information about the site will be added below your personal message.

☐ Send welcome e-mail to the new users

Subject:

Welcome to the SharePoint group: Unique Site Owners for site: Un

Personal Message:

Figure 9-8

4. Add the name of the group you want to add to the site to the Users/Groups box and click the check names icon. This icon verifies that you entered a proper name in the box. If you do not know the exact name of the user or group you are adding, you can click the Browse icon to perform a search of the membership directory. This example uses "administrators," which is a local administrative group on the SharePoint Server.

5. In the Give Permissions section, you can either assign your users to a site group or select a permissions level. This example assigns the administrators to the Site Owner group.

6. You can send an email to let users know you have added them to the SharePoint site as part of the selected group. In this example, you have left the box unchecked. If you were adding a user, the email address would likely be automatically populated. Typically when you specify a group, this information is not available on the server so you can either manually enter an alias or distribution list address for the group or leave it blank. This approach requires you to notify the users that they have been added via alternate means.

7. Click the OK button.

How It Works

If you checked the option in step 6, the users receive an email letting them know that you've added them to the SharePoint site. Using Active Directory groups ensures that as new employees are added to an appropriate role, they are automatically provided access to the SharePoint sites with which those groups have been associated. For example, if the Sales Manager Active Directory security group is added to the Member site group of the sales site, then whenever an employee is added to the sales manager security group in Active Directory, he automatically becomes a member on the Sales site in SharePoint. This provides a more seamless access management environment and helps standardize access across groups.

Try It Out   Modify the Permissions of an Existing User or Group

In some scenarios, it's necessary to change the specific rights that a single user or site group has on a site. This may be related to a direct request from a business manager, a change in requirements or perhaps because you need to grant a certain user rights to a workspace beyond what he or she currently has. This may be because the user has demonstrated exceptional skills and would make a good candidate to assume more responsibility for managing the SharePoint site. In the next example, you see the process for identifying and modifying the group membership and site permissions of a single user.

1. From the main page of your team site, select Site Actions ⇨ Site Settings.

2. Select the People and Groups link under the Users and Permissions category.

3. Click the Site Permissions link.

4. Select the check box next to the Limited Membership group you created in a previous Try it Out in this chapter.

5. Select Actions ⇨ Edit User Permissions from the toolbar, as shown in Figure 9-9. You are redirected to the user permissions page.

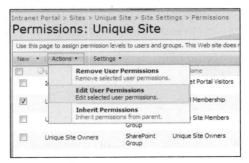

Figure 9-9

6. Because the requirements for the Limited Membership group have changed, you must now grant all members of that group the permission to Approve content. Select the Approve permission level.

7. Click the OK button. You are returned to the Site Permission page.

How It Works

When you review the list of users, you'll notice how the Limited Membership group now has Approve and Limited Contribute rights under the Permissions column, as shown in Figure 9-10.

```
Intranet Portal > Sites > Unique Site > Site Settings > Permissions
Permissions: Unique Site

Use this page to assign permission levels to users and groups. This Web site does not inherit permissions from its parent.

New  ▼  |  Actions ▼  |  Settings ▼
```

	Users/Groups	Type	User Name	Permissions
☐	Intranet Portal Visitors	SharePoint Group	Intranet Portal Visitors	Read
☐	Limited Membership	SharePoint Group	Limited Membership	Approve, Limited Contribute
☐	Unique Site Members	SharePoint Group	Unique Site Members	Contribute
☐	Unique Site Owners	SharePoint Group	Unique Site Owners	Full Control

Figure 9-10

You may later need to reduce a user's or group's permission to limit his access. This process is very similar to the previous steps, but you would remove the user from his current site group membership and add him to another group with fewer privileges.

Try It Out   Remove a User from a Site Collection

Rather than elevate or reduce a user's or group's access as shown in the last Try It Out, you may need to remove him completely from the site. This may be necessary if, for example, the user transfers to another division, or to a new position where his current access to site is no longer necessary. Alternatively, the scope of a project may change, which might lock a site so that only a few users still have access. In the following example, you look at what steps are required to remove a user from a site collection.

1. From the main page of your team site, select Site Actions ➪ Site Settings.

2. Select the People and Groups link under the Users and Permissions category.

3. Click the All People link.

4. Select the check box next to the user's name that you want to remove from your site collection.

5. Select Actions ➪ Delete Users from Site Collection from the toolbar, as shown in Figure 9-11.

Figure 9-11

Note that you cannot delete anyone that is listed as the owner of a site collection because that user has built-in rights, and it is generally not good practice to remove owners of a site collection without ensuring that someone else has filled the role.

6. You are prompted with a message in a pop-up window asking you to confirm that you want to remove the selected user from the site collection. Click the OK button. The page refreshes, and your selected user is removed from the site collection.

How It Works

In previous versions of SharePoint, removing a user meant removing his or her name from all files that he or she created or modified. This caused obvious problems for companies that needed to retain these files. This problem was rectified in SharePoint 2007. If you remove a user from the site on which he or she currently has tasks assigned, you need to manually reassign these tasks to other team members. For this reason, it's a good idea to review any task lists before removing a user.

For more about task columns, see Chapter 2. For more on assigning a workflow task to another user, see Chapter 5.

Try It Out   **Enable Membership or Site Access Requests**

So far, you've seen tasks that you, a site owner, can complete to assign access to team members or groups. However, certain situations may require that users request access to a site. For example, a user might click a hyperlink to a site of which he or she is not a member. SharePoint has a built-in access management feature that allows users to request access via the web interface by clicking a Request Access link. In the following example, you see how a user can request access to a site.

1. From the main page of your team site, select Site Actions ⇨ Site Settings.

2. Select the People and Groups link under the Users and Permissions section.

3. Click the Site Permissions link.

4. Select Settings ⇨ Access Requests. You are redirected to a page for enabling access request on the site.

    If you do not see this item in the Settings menu, your server may not be configured to send email. You can change this by having your system administrator configure the outgoing email settings from the Operations tab of the SharePoint Central Administration site.

5. Select the check box to enable access requests, and enter your own email address as shown in Figure 9-12.

Figure 9-12

6. Click the OK button.

How It Works

Once a user clicks the link, he or she can input a message and click a Send Request button as shown in Figure 9-13. The advantages to this include the following:

❑   **Users can request access without having to access another tool or interface.** The system automatically provides all the information that is required to effectively address the request and routes the request to the appropriate individual responsible for the site. This is the person (or group of people) associated with the email address specified in the previous steps. This saves both parties valuable time and is a benefit in large organizations that use ticket tracking systems to give such access.

❑   **Users requesting access do not know who is responsible for the site.** It discourages people from going around a defined methodology and using more direct access request methods such as telephone or manual email, which could be potentially more time-consuming and distracting.

Figure 9-13

Understanding the Different Levels of Access in SharePoint

Everything you've learned so far has been related to controlling access and rights on a SharePoint site. However, SharePoint 2007 also supports permissions management on the list and item level. This means that while a user may contribute to his team's collaborative site, he may only be a reader for a particular document library or even a single document on a library. This section discusses the different levels of access that you can have on a SharePoint site.

Site Level Access

Each example thus far in this chapter has applied to managing access at the site level because, by default, this is the level where access is defined. From a restriction standpoint, you do not want to over-complicate access — and you want to keep things simple unless your requirements dictate it.

When you work on a site level, you need to determine whether you want a subsite to inherit permissions from a parent site or not. Your decision generally depends on your requirements:

❑ **Inheriting permissions:** When you inherit permissions from a parent site, you create a scenario in which any user who has permission to the parent site will have the same permissions and rights on the child site. This cuts down on the tasks and effort associated with managing permissions and creates a consistent access experience for all users.

❑ **Creating unique permissions:** Creating a site with unique permissions allows you to manage permissions and access to your child site, independent of the settings specified for the parent site. Therefore, a user who can add content on the parent site may not necessarily have access to the child site. Users perform different roles from site to site. This means that you'll have to spend more time setting up and managing the site, but you will have greater flexibility in meeting the access requirements of each individual team. Sometimes it's beneficial to give users greater access rights on a subsite than they have in a parent. For example, in a sales proposal document workspace, members of the sales team may be able to create lists and libraries to aid in their production of the proposal, whereas on the sales team site they may only have permissions to add content to existing lists.

I = Inherited From Parent / U = Unique Permissions

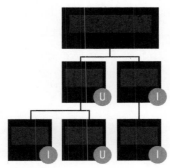

Figure 9-14

Try It Out   **Stop Inheriting Permissions from a Parent Site**

You may have created a site and selected the option to inherit permissions from the parent, but at a later time, realize you need to manage the site's permissions independently of the parent site. The following example uses the weblog site that you created in Chapter 8 and assumes that the weblog has different usage patterns from your team collaboration site; the people most responsible for creating and managing content have very limited permissions on the team site. You change the permissions settings on the site, which copies all site groups and users from the parent into the weblog site so that you can manage them separately.

Remember that if users have permissions on the parent site and you do not want them to have access to the weblog, you must remove them after breaking the inheritance because SharePoint copies the permissions, groups, and users from the parent into the child. You don't have to do this if you do not select to inherit permissions when you first create the site. In that case, once the site is created, it has a blank set of permissions, and no users of the parent have access to the site unless explicitly given access. The exception, of course, is a site collection administrator or site owner on the parent site.

If you did not create a weblog under your team site in Chapter 8, you can create any subsite on your team site that inherits the permissions of parent. The same steps apply regardless of what site template you use.

These steps walk you though the process for breaking the permissions inheritance from a parent site.

1. From the main page of your team weblog site, select Site Actions ⇨ Site Settings.

2. Select the Advanced Permissions link under the Users and Permissions category.

3. Select Actions ⇨ Edit Permissions from the toolbar, as shown in Figure 9-15. You receive a warning window, shown in Figure 9-16, that says you are about to stop inheriting from the parent and that any changes you make to the parent will no longer affect this site.

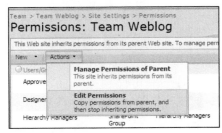

Figure 9-15

Figure 9-16

4. Click the OK button to continue.

How It Works

You now see a message above the toolbar stating:

> **Use this page to assign permission levels to users and groups. This web site does not inherit permissions from its parent.**

List or Library Level Access

Sometimes a list or library on a team site requires a different set of permissions than the rest of the site. For example, a document library containing sensitive financial performance reports should not be shared with everyone who has access to the site. You could create a separate site to store this information, but it's easier to simply adjust the permissions on the library so that a subset of users can access the library. Another example is where only certain users can edit a specific list or library in which team members can only view content. For example, only a manager can create new items on an Announcements list for a team, but team members can contribute to list and libraries on the rest of the site.

Try It Out   Assign Unique Permissions to a List

In the following example, you modify the permissions on an announcements list so that only members of the Approvers group can create new content. Even though all other site members can add content to other lists, it is important that you restrict the Announcements to only allow Approver members to add new items. To accomplish this, you must stop inheriting permissions on the Announcements list from the site. Similar to the scenario in the previous Try It Out, when you stop inheriting permissions for a list from a site, all rights get copied from the site into the list, so you must update the settings to reflect your requirements. For this exercise, you use the team site you created in the last Try It Out that has unique permissions from its parent.

1.   From the main page of your team site, select the Announcements title link from the Announcements Web Part.

   It might be more direct to click the title of a list Web Part to go to default view of a list than to navigate there using the View All Site Content link.

2.   Select Settings ⇨ List Settings. The Customize Announcements window appears, as shown in Figure 9-17.

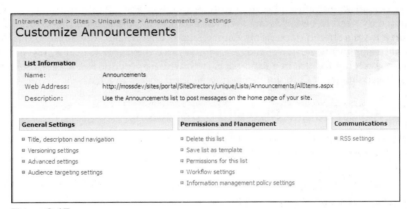

Figure 9-17

3.   Select the Permissions for this List link under the Permissions and Management category. The Permissions page for the Announcements list appears.

4.   Select Actions ⇨ Edit Permissions from the toolbar. You receive a warning, shown in Figure 9-18, that you are about to disconnect from the permissions of the parent site.

Figure 9-18

5. Click the OK button to continue.

6. Click the Select All check box to select each group. Then unselect the Approvers group.

7. Select Actions ⇨ Edit User Permissions from the toolbar.

8. Select Read from the list of permissions.

9. Click the OK button.

How It Works

When you disconnect from the permissions of the site, all rights and users are copied to the permissions scheme for the Announcements list. Therefore, you must edit the rights of each group and user so that they can only read items. You selected every group and changed their rights to Read-Only, but then deselected the Approvers group so that members could edit content. Note that the Site Owners group can still add content, and you cannot remove this group from a specific list or library.

Item Level Access

By default, access to an individual list item is inherited from the list or library in which it resides. However, you may need to better define this. For example, a policies and procedures document that's stored within a team's shared documents library means anyone can contribute and add contents; however, for legal reasons, only certain managers should have the rights to edit it. You can restrict access in one document, even if it resides in a list or library to which everyone has access, as shown in the next Try It Out. In a second Try It Out, you learn how to limit access to a list.

Try It Out   Assign Unique Rights to a Document

In this example, you create a new document and restrict the rights so that only members of the Approvers group have the access to edit the document.

1. From the main page of your team site, select Shared Documents from the Quick Launch bar.

2. Select New from the Document Library toolbar.

3. Save the document with a file name of **Team Policies and Procedures.doc**.

4. Hover your mouse over the document and select the Manage Permissions item from the drop-down menu, as shown in Figure 9-19. The Manage Permissions page for the document appears.

5. Select Actions ⇨ Edit Permissions from the toolbar.

6. Click the Select All check box to select each group. Then unselect the Approvers group.

7. Select Actions ⇨ Edit User Permissions from the toolbar.

8. Select Read from the list of permissions.

9. Click the OK button.

Figure 9-19

How It Works

In this example, you created a new document that has slightly different requirements over all other documents in the library, rather than placing it in a unique location. It's far more effective to manage the rights of this document independent of the library and make the required changes on an item-by-item basis.

Try It Out   Customize Item Level Access Rights on a List

You can uniquely apply permissions to documents or list items in the same way as the last Try It Out. However, lists also have a unique function that allows for a site manager to determine which users can view or edit their own items or the items of others. For example, it may be helpful to allow team members to view each other's appointments. However, a user should not be allowed to edit appointments belonging to a coworker. In the following example, you modify the default settings of the Calendar list so that users can view, but not edit, a coworker's items. You can do this on SharePoint lists, but not with documents stored within document libraries.

1. From the main page of your team site, select Calendar from the Quick Launch bar.

2. Select Settings ➪ List Settings.

3. Click the Advanced Settings link. The List Advanced Settings window appears, as shown in Figure 9-20.

4. In the Item-Level Permissions section, for Read Access, keep the default value that users can view all items.

5. In the Item-level Permissions section, for Edit Access, select that users can edit only their own appointments.

6. Click the OK button.

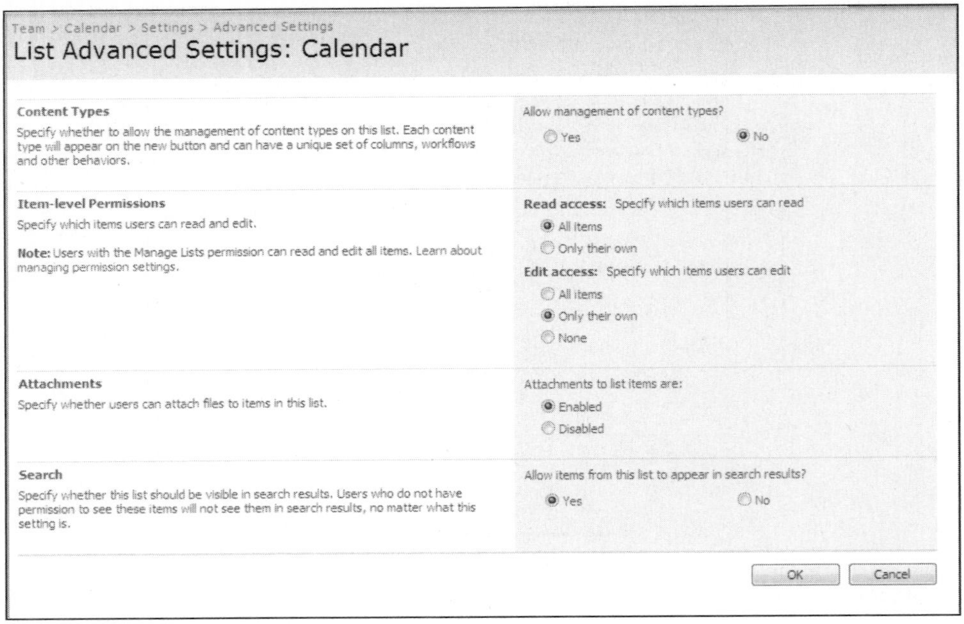

Figure 9-20

Understanding User Profiles

SharePoint 2007 has a special database that can store information about the users of the system called the *user profile database*. This database contains properties and metadata about each user of the system in a very similar manner that you can store information describing a document in a document library. User profile information is useful for storing contact information and biographies of the different users of the system for information-sharing purposes, but you can also use it for more advanced purposes, such as content targeting and personalization via audiences (discussed in a later section of this chapter).

While SharePoint 2007 can import profiles from other sources, this chapter assumes that Active Directory is your primary profile source because it is the most common membership store for organizations using this application. SharePoint collects common profile properties from Active Directory including Name, Email Address, Phone Number, Manager, and Address. SharePoint can also import custom profile properties such as skills, languages, and employee ID.

While SharePoint 2003 can only collect user profile information from Active Directory, SharePoint 2007 can obtain it from the following sources:

❑   Active Directory
❑   Other LDAP servers

❑ Business data catalog applications

❑ User-defined properties

Adding and Updating User Profiles

User profiles are not required for an organization to implement SharePoint; however, they allow you to personalize information, including profile information to share with coworkers. For example, each SharePoint user can create a My Site site; he or she can store personal or shared files, view organizational content, write a personal weblog, and maintain his or her own profile properties. You can create a personal site by selecting the My Site link from the top right of the screen from any page or site in the portal, as shown in Figure 9-21.

Figure 9-21

Each My Site has a public view that displays user information where you can place basic personal facts as well as relevant organizational information. By sharing more details on personal sites and profiles, workers can get to know each other better, which helps in situations where employees work for the same company but in different buildings.

Despite a great potential for quickly finding out about another user when you use My Site, it's always important to be aware of how much information you share about yourself and to ensure that any content posted in your personal site or profile is appropriate for your corporate setting.

From the Public Profile page, you can view a variety of information about an employee including:

❑ An image of the employee

❑ Contact information

❑ Documents that the employee has shared

❑ Information on who the employee reports to and any other employees who report to them

❑ Things that the employee has in common with you based on profile properties such as languages, skills, or schools

❑ Shared links

❑ Colleagues

Because profile properties are indexed and searchable, you can search for a specific property and find a list of people who have that property assigned to them. For example, if you are a manager looking for a computer programmer with ASP.NET experience to build a custom Web Part for your SharePoint site, you can use the People search scope to search for ASP.NET to receive a list of people in your organization who have that skill. By clicking their names, you are redirected to their personal sites where you can find out who their manager is (in cause you want to contact the manager) and what previous projects the employees have worked on.

For more on using the People search scope, see Chapter 14.

Although you can import some profile properties from primary membership systems such as Active Directory, users can update others themselves via their My Site. This helps keep information up-to-date and relevant. The server administrator decides what profile properties a user can update. A user can also select from the following choices on who can view information that is stored in specific properties:

- ❑ Everyone
- ❑ My Colleagues
- ❑ My Workgroup
- ❑ My Manager
- ❑ Only Me

For example, something such as skills or schools would be shared with everyone while a home phone number would only be viewable to a manager. The following Try It Outs illustrate how users can update their own profile properties via their personal site. In the event you have a specific detail that you want a user to provide on the site, for example specific professional experience, certification, or attended business seminars, you can add a new user profile property.

Try It Out   Update Personal Profile Information

In this example, you update all profile properties that you have access to edit, noting that you cannot edit some profile properties such as those of your manager. Generally, the information that you cannot edit is imported from a central directory or application dedicated to storing such information.

Updating profile properties is only a small function of what you can do from their personal sites. But it's a great way to familiarize yourself with your personal site and will keep your personal information up-to-date. All information entered into a user's profile is saved and not overwritten by the regular Active Directory scheduled imports (discussed in an upcoming section of this chapter).

1. From the home page of your corporate site, click the My Site link from the top-right navigation bar.
2. Select the My Profile tab from the site's navigation.
3. Click the Edit Details link, as shown in Figure 9-22. The Edits detail window appears, as shown in Figure 9-23.

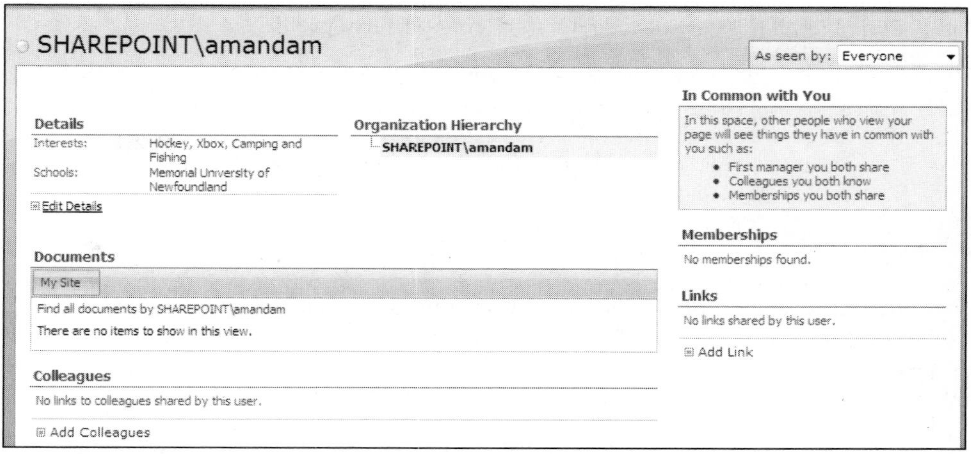

Figure 9-22

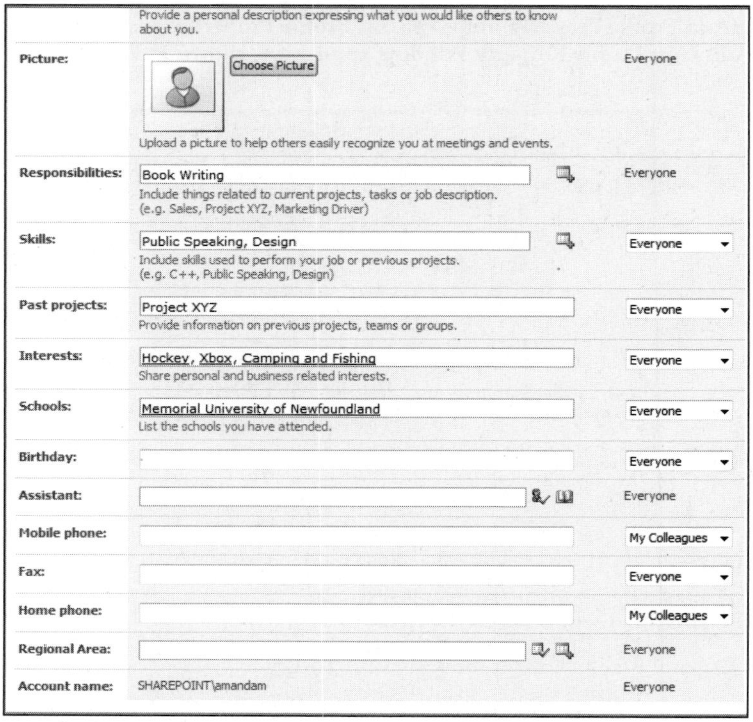

Figure 9-23

4. Complete all missing information from your personal profile.

5. For the Home Phone field, change the Show to drop-down value to My Manager.

6. Click Save and Close.

Add a New User Profile Property

In the last example, you updated common profile properties. In addition to those properties, you can add new profile properties that users can update on their own. For example, you can add a property to allow users to specify what certifications they have attained, as the following steps show. Because users may have more than one certification, you should allow for multiple values. Because not every user may want to specify that information, you can make it optional.

1. From the main page of the Central Administration site, select the link for the Shared Services Administration site from the left-hand navigation menu.

2. From the User Profiles and My Sites section, select User Profiles and Properties.

3. Select Add Profile Property from the User Profile Properties section near the bottom of the page. The Add User Profile Property Window appears, as shown in Figure 9-24.

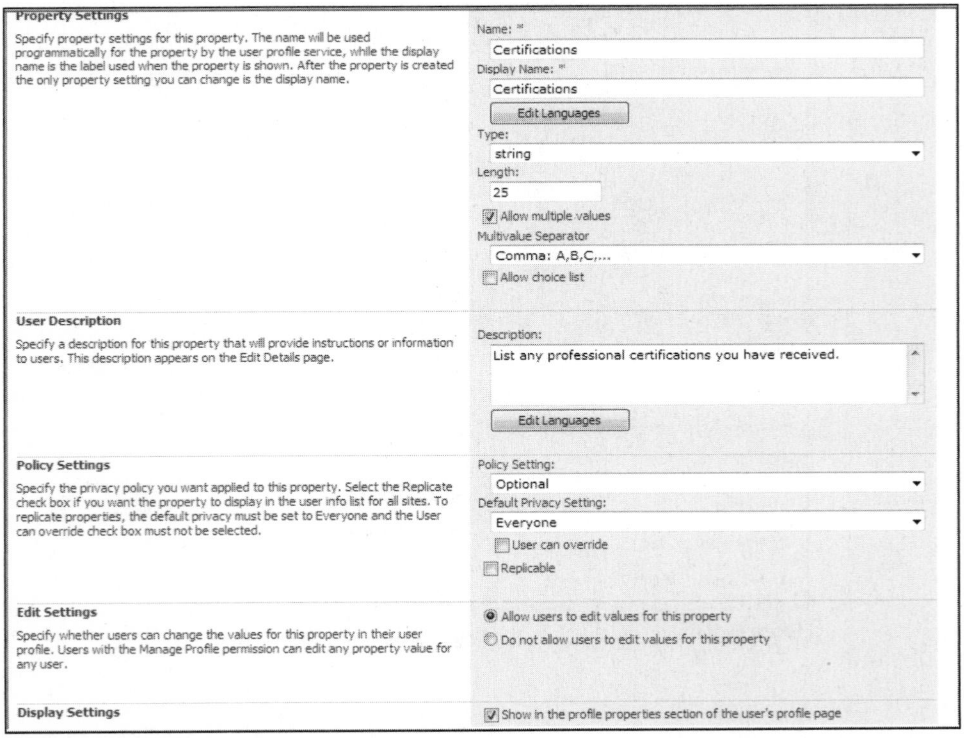

Figure 9-24

4.   Complete the information as follows:

Item	Value
Name	Certifications
Display Name	Certifications
Allow Multiple Values	Yes
Description	List any professional certifications you have received.
Policy Settings	Optional
Default Privacy Setting	Everyone
Edit Settings	Allow users to edit values for this property
Display Settings	Select these three options: Show in the Profile Properties Section of the User's Profile Page Select Show on the Edit Details Page Show Changes in the Colleague Tracker Web Part
Search Settings	Select the Indexed box

5.   Click the OK button.

6.   Click the My Site link from the top-right navigation bar.

7.   Select the My Profile tab from the site's navigation.

8.   Click the Edit Details link.

9.   Scroll to the bottom until you see the custom property you created for Certifications. Update this with any certifications you have attained, and click the Save and Close button.

How It Works

In this example, you specify that the property should be indexed because this may be a value for which someone might want to search. For example, when a business manager prepares to launch a major new project for an upcoming product launch, she may want to search for someone who has a project management certification such as PMP. By searching for this item, she can find employees with this qualification and review their experience on past projects to discover who might be a perfect match to manage this new project.

Configuring Profile Updates

You import user profiles into SharePoint on a scheduled basis and can do so from single or multiple sources. In cases where you are importing profile information from more than one database, you must have a master connection, which is either Active Directory or another LDAP server and a secondary connection, which is a Business Data Catalog application.

You configure profile imports on the Shared Services Administration site. You can access this site from the side navigation available in the Central Administration site. If you do not have access to visit this site, speak to your server administrator for assistance.

If your server is a member of a domain, it automatically associates with that domain in the profile settings. However, profiles are not imported until a server administrator configures the import process. If no domain connection exists, you must create a new connection under the View Import Connections link of the User Profiles and Properties section, as shown in Figure 9-25.

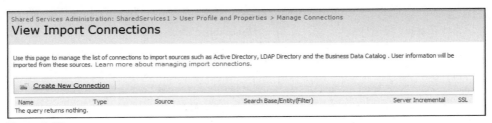

Figure 9-25

From User Profiles and My Sites section of the Shared Services Administration site, you may specify permissions for a variety of personalization services, such as:

- ❑ Create personal site
- ❑ Use personal features
- ❑ Manage user profiles
- ❑ Manage audiences
- ❑ Manage permissions
- ❑ Manage usage analytics

Working with Audiences

An *audience* is a special group to which content is targeted so that only people in that audience see it. A user becomes a part of an audience based on profile properties or membership to a distribution list or SharePoint site. Audience content targeting should not be confused with access. Just because a user cannot see an item does not necessarily mean that he does not have access to the item. An audience may exist for members of an organization that work out of a certain region such as Canada. Therefore, by assigning the audience to an announcement related to a special event taking place at the Canadian office, it will only be seen by members of that audience. The following sections give some examples of how you can use audiences.

You can configure certain Web Parts such as the Content Query Web Part, discussed in Chapter 7, to support audience filtering. This means that when you display multiple items in a Web Part, users will see only those that are targeted to them. Figures 9-26 and 9-27 demonstrate examples of filtering list information by audience via a Content Query Web Part. Figure 9-26 is what the team site looks like to a member of the sales team audience, which can view the Sales Strategy document because it's targeted to their audience. Figure 9-27 shows the same site page as viewed by someone who is not a member of the sales team audience. Notice the user does not see the Sales Strategy document even though it exists in the library.

Figure 9-26

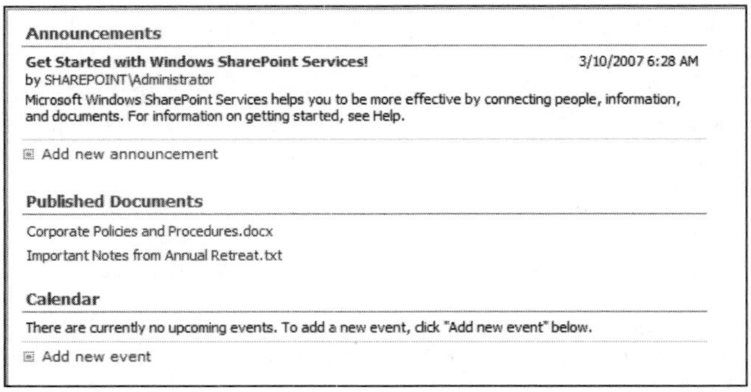

Figure 9-27

If the user who isn't in the sales team audience were to click the Shared Documents library, he or she can still see the document listed in the view as shown in Figure 9-28. This is because the Content Query Web Part filters so that items only display to targeted audiences and the standard list Web Parts do not. All Web Parts, however, allow you to target the contents of an entire Web Part to an audience.

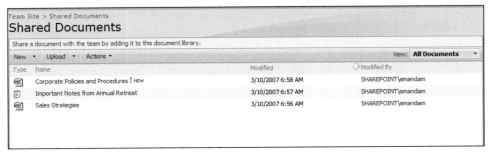

Figure 9-28

Membership-Based Audiences

More than likely, your organization has already made significant investments to Active Directory, which groups people based on their roles as well as the organization's communication requirements. So instead of creating audiences, which you need to manage and maintain as an extra layer in the SharePoint environment, you can take advantage of existing objects, such as Windows Distribution Lists or Security Groups. In fact, your organization probably has a distribution list on your Exchange mail server for the sales team that keeps them informed of product updates and sales promotions. You can use the distribution list as an audience and target content from the SharePoint environment directly to the audience's members. As announcements are added to the corporate portal, the audience can see and thus view the latest news upon login. If the organization is fairly busy and generates numerous new announcements each day, the use of audiences helps users "separate the wheat from the chaff."

The next three Try It Outs show you the process of managing a membership-based audience. In the first Try It Out, you design a rule that creates an audience using a distribution list in Active Directory, specify the audience's membership criteria, and compile it. The second Try It Out shows you how to target an item to your newly created audience so your audience can keep up-to-date on new promotions and other information via a central portal page. This is useful for sales teams who, because they travel and work remotely, have limited time and need to view content directly related to them. The third Try It Out shows you how to target specific list items, documents, or even entire Web Part content to an audience by creating audiences based on membership to SharePoint site groups.

Try It Out   Create an Audience Based on a Distribution List

In this example, you use an existing group (created for a sales team) to create your audience. You first design a rule that creates an audience from a distribution list in Active Directory. You then specify the audience's membership criteria and compile it. Compiling involves a search through the Active Directory membership pool for users who meet the criteria that the audience specifies. You can run the compilation process manually, as shown in this Try It Out, or you can schedule a compilation. It is a good idea to run the compilation schedule on a regular basis to ensure that your audience's memberships stay up-to-date.

This example assumes that a distribution list or security group exists in your company's Active Directory for a sales team. If such a group does not exist, identify a group that does exist and change the naming of the audience to match.

1. From the Central Administration site, select the link on the left-hand navigation for the Shared Services Administration site. The name of this link may vary depending on what the administrator named it during its configuration. If you do not know the location of the Shared Services Administration site, ask your server administrator.

2. Select the Audiences link from the Audiences group.

3. Select Create Audience.

4. Enter a name for your audience. For this example, use **Sales Team** for the name of the audience.

5. Enter a description for the audience. For this example, enter the following for the description:

> **This is an audience that represents all members of the global sales team.**

6. Enter your own name for the owner of the audience.

7. Select the option to include users who satisfy all of the rules.

8. Click the OK button.

9. Because this audience is based on a distribution list (or Windows Security Group), select User for Operand on the Add Audience Rule window, shown in Figure 9-29.

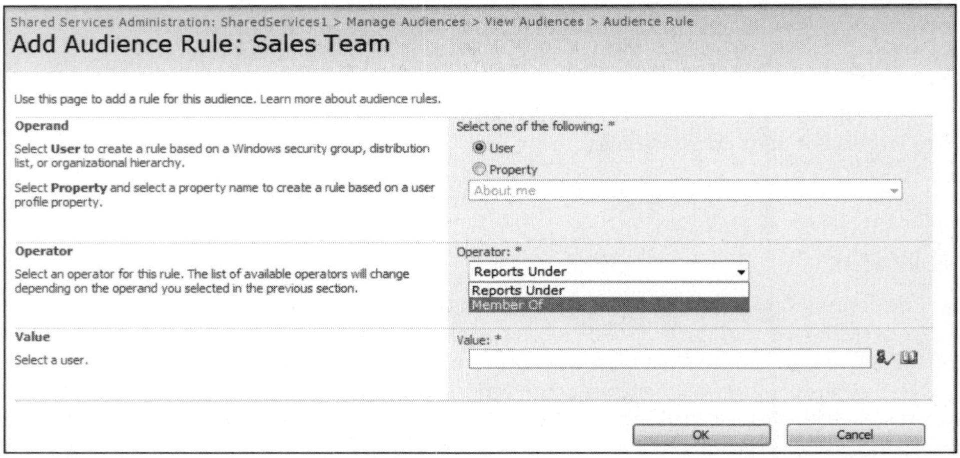

Figure 9-29

10. Select Member Of from the Operator drop-down menu.

11. Click the Browse button next to the Value box. The Select Security Group or Distribution List dialog box appears, as seen in Figure 9-30.

12. In the Find box, type the word **sales**.

13. Select the distribution list that represents your company's sales team.

14. Click the Add button.

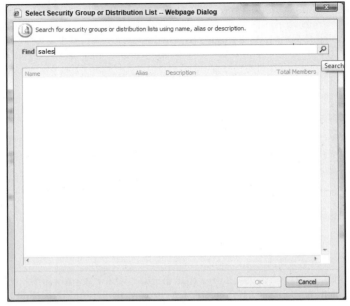

Figure 9-30

15. Click the OK button.

16. Select the Compile Audience link to run a system scan for members of your portal that meet the criteria of your audience rules.

How It Works

When the compilation is complete, any user who is a member of the distribution list for Sales becomes a member of your new audience. As new sales people join the organization, they are added to this group automatically as part of the existing processes for new hires. This also results in the new members being added to the Sales audience whenever compilation is scheduled. You can specify the schedule by which audiences are compiled by clicking Specify Compilation Schedule from the Manage Audiences option. If your organization experiences a lot of changes to user profiles or membership, you may consider a more frequent compilation schedule such as once per day. If changes are less common, a weekly compilation may be acceptable.

Try It Out   **Targeting a List Item to a Specific Audience**

Once you create the sales team audience, you can target specific news and announcements directly to it. This allows them to keep up-to-date on new promotions and sales tactics when they visit a central portal page that contains a Web Part that supports the use of audiences. Other team members cannot view the announcement in this example when they visit the same page, although they still have access rights to view it if they want to. This page may contain updates for many other groups and divisions so by effectively using audiences to target content to users based on their roles, you help ensure that content is limited to only what is relevant to users.

1. From the main page of your team site, select the Announcements link from the Announcements List Web Part.

2. Select Setting ⇨ List Settings from the toolbar.

3. Select Audience Targeting Settings.

4. Select the check box to Enable Audience Targeting.

5. Click the OK button.

6. Click the Announcements link from the breadcrumb navigation trail.

7. Click the New Item button.

8. Enter the following information into the list item form:

Column	Value
Title	New Sales Promotion Launched.
Body	A new sales promotion has been launched that will offer customers up to 50% off the pricing of last year's product line. For more information, please contact your Regional Director's head office.
Expires	Select a date one month from the current date.

9. For the Target Audiences column, select the Browse button. The Select Audiences dialog appears.

10. Search for and select the sales team audience you created in the previous Try It Out from the Global Audiences and click the Add button, as shown in Figure 9-31.

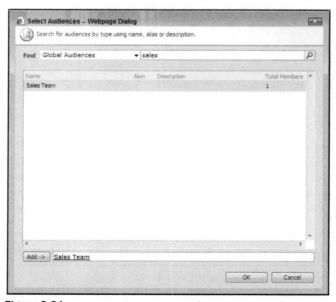

Figure 9-31

11. Click the OK button to complete your audience selection.

12. Click the OK button to save the announcement to the list.

How It Works

Once you have configured audiences for the list, you can add a Content Query Web Part to the main page of your team site and query the announcements list using the method described in Chapter 7. You can then select the option to apply audience filtering as shown in Figure 9-32.

Figure 9-32

Try It Out   Target a Web Part to an Audience

You can target specific list items, documents, or even entire Web Part content to an audience. In this example, you target a list Web Part that displays items that are pending approval to the SharePoint site group responsible for approving content. By adding the Web Part to the main page with a listing of all pending items as the default view, Approvers are more likely to respond in a timely manner. An example of this is a Web Part on the main page of a site that highlights items pending approval. Because these items are only relevant to members of the Approvers group, you select this audience on the Web Part to ensure that only they can see the Web Part on the main page. While other team members can still access the documents, no action is required from them so the Web Part would only be a distraction.

1. From the main page of your team site, select Shared Documents from the Quick Launch bar.

2. Select Settings ➪ Document Library Settings from the toolbar. You are redirected to the administration page for the document library.

3. Select Versioning Settings. You are redirected to the library's Version History Settings page.

4. Select Yes for Require Content Approval for Submitted Items.

5. Click the OK button.

6. Return to the main page of your site by clicking the Team Site link in the navigational breadcrumb trail.

7. Select Site Actions ➪ Edit Page.

8. Click the Add a Web Part button from the left-hand Web Part zone. The Add Web Parts to Left window appears, as shown in Figure 9-33.

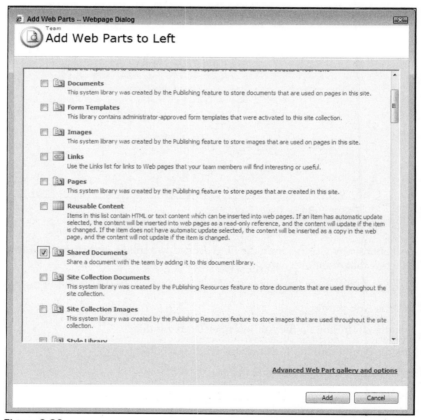

Figure 9-33

9. Select the Shared Documents Web Part, and click the Add button.

10. Click the Edit button for the Shared Documents Web Part, and select Modify Shared Web Part.

11. Select the Approve/Reject Items view. You may receive a pop-up window warning that you may lose changes made to the view. Click OK to continue.

12. Expand the Advanced properties pane.

13. From the Target Audiences field at the very bottom of the Web Part pane, select the Browse button. The Select Audiences dialog box appears, as shown in Figure 9-34.

Figure 9-34

14. Select SharePoint Groups from the Find drop-down menu, and click the Search icon to the right of the box that resembles a magnifying glass.

15. A listing of all SharePoint groups for the current site is displayed. Select the Approvers group.

16. Click the Add button.

17. Click the OK button on the Audience selection window.

18. Click the Apply, and then OK buttons on the Web Part.

19. Click Exit Edit Mode on the main page.

How It Works

In this example, the pending status of documents is of no interest to team members other than the Approvers group. To other members, it might be distracting and take up valuable real estate. Sometimes by effectively using audiences on Web Parts, you can fit a greater deal of content on a page, yet avoid unnecessary clutter on each user's screen by limiting the number of Web Parts he or she sees.

Profile Property-Based Audiences

All examples of the audience creation process so far have been based on either Active Directory- or SharePoint-based groups. This chapter now discusses how audiences are created based on properties from the user profiles. When you consider that the profile can not only contain information from your Active Directory (or another LDAP server), but also from other business applications, such as a human resources or financial database, the possibilities of how specific you can target content are endless. By using personal profile properties, you can make audiences very detailed to the point of defining audiences for specific topics. For example, you can create a profile property called News and Promotions that has a value list from which users can select via their profile to identify what products they want to receive promotional updates on.

In the following example, you see how to create an audience based on the property you created earlier in the chapter for certifications in the Try It Out for "Add a New User Profile Property." If you recall, this field gives users a place to update their own certifications from their My Site. However, it is equally as possible for you to automatically update this profile property from an external system, such as Active Directory or a Central Human Resources database.

Try It Out   Create an Audience Based on Profile Information

In this example, you create a rules-based audience that checks the certifications profile property and compiles the members who have a project management certification. Because this is an audience where you expect membership changes over time, you will base membership on a profile property that you know users will keep up-to-date on their own, instead of manually identifying and updating membership within a specific Active Directory group, distribution list, or site group.

1.   From the Shared Services Administration site, select the Audiences link from the Audiences section.

2.   Select Create Audience. The Create Audience window appears, as shown in Figure 9-35.

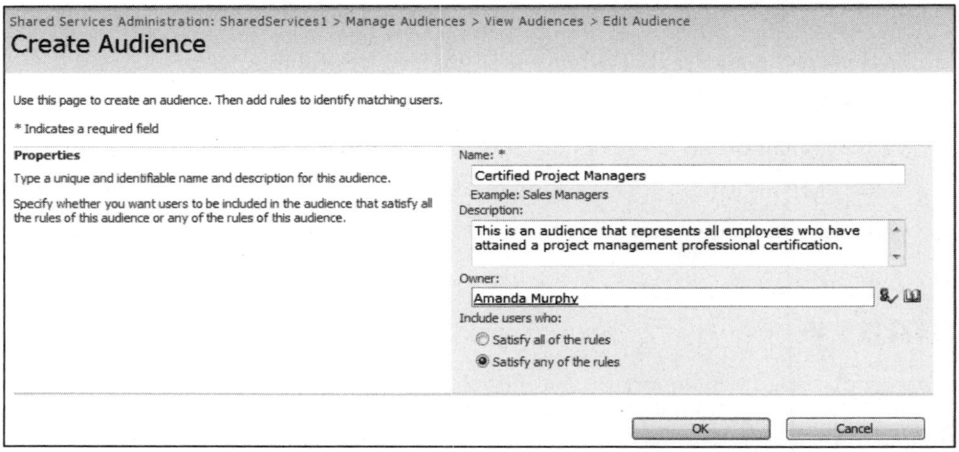

Shared Services Administration: SharedServices1 > Manage Audiences > View Audiences > Edit Audience

Create Audience

Use this page to create an audience. Then add rules to identify matching users.

* Indicates a required field

Properties

Type a unique and identifiable name and description for this audience.

Specify whether you want users to be included in the audience that satisfy all the rules of this audience or any of the rules of this audience.

Name: *
Certified Project Managers

Example: Sales Managers
Description:
This is an audience that represents all employees who have attained a project management professional certification.

Owner:
Amanda Murphy

Include users who:
○ Satisfy all of the rules
● Satisfy any of the rules

[OK]   [Cancel]

Figure 9-35

3. Enter a name for the audience. For this example, use **Certified Project Managers**.

4. Enter a description for the audience. For this example, enter the following:

> **This is an audience that represents all employees who have attained a project management professional certification.**

6. Enter your own name for the owner of the audience.

7. Select the option to include users who satisfy any of the rules.

8. Click the OK button. The Add Audience Rule window appears, as shown in Figure 9-36.

Figure 9-36

9. Because this audience is based on a user property, select Property for Operand.

10. Select the Certifications profile property from the drop-down menu.

10. Select Contains from the Operator drop-down menu.

11. Enter **PMP** for value.

12. Click the OK button.

Summary

This chapter discussed two important concepts related to information management: user access and personalization. User access is how you can control who can view, edit, or create content in a SharePoint environment. You can define access on the site level, document library, or list level through permission levels and site groups. For lists, you can also define rules on what content users can read or edit at the item level.

As a general rule, you should use existing Active Directory groups and objects when you assign permissions to specific roles in a SharePoint group. In most organizations, Active Directory is kept up-to-date as employees change positions, leave, or are hired. By creating a relationship between Active Directory and SharePoint site groups, you automatically keep user membership current without relying on manual updates

Personalization in SharePoint is delivered via features such as user profiles, audiences, and My Sites. When you use personalization features, users become exposed only to content that is relevant to them. Profile properties and My Sites also help encourage users to learn more about each other and interact with one another. In many organizations, users do not connect with one another because of a lack of awareness of what they have in common with one another or who has what skills.

When defining personal profile properties, users can determine if everyone, their colleagues, their manager, workgroups, or only the user can view information. This helps create a network of professional and personal information sharing that is controlled and secure so that users feel comfortable sharing specific details and know that these details will only be shared with the appropriate audience.

This chapter also discussed how you can create audiences to identify groups of users that share common profile properties, group memberships, or characteristics. Once an audience is created, content from the SharePoint site can be targeted at them. The more audiences are used for content, the more relevant the user experience becomes.

Exercises

1. Explain the difference between a SharePoint site group and an audience.

2. True or False: By targeting content to users, you can ensure that only the right people have access to view items.

3. What are the three different types of audiences that you can create in SharePoint 2007?

4. What are the different levels of access that you can control in SharePoint?

5. Explain from what source you can import user profile information.

Working with Forms Services

An important aspect of working in a business environment and collaborating with others is the collection of information. A common challenge is to identify ways to make this process more efficient and effective. One solution is to collect information in a form that contains pre-configured fields for the data you want to receive. This ensures that all the required information is collected, and it also helps consolidate information that can be used for comparison or calculations. For example, by collecting feedback from your customers on their satisfaction level with your services, you can identify trends or averages in their responses. If the average of all customer satisfaction ratings is 4.5 out of 5, and a customer submits a rating of 3 out of 5, it is easy to see that the response is below average. If all customer feedback were submitted verbally or via a less structured format such as email, it would be more difficult to compare results in a calculated manner.

Forms simplify the task of gathering important information. In Microsoft Office, you can use InfoPath to create electronic forms that you can then publish to team members and others. InfoPath is straightforward enough that nonprogrammers can use it for a simple forms creation system, yet flexible enough for programmers to create sophisticated forms-based applications.

When InfoPath was released in 2003, in order for someone to view or complete a form, the user had to install the InfoPath application on his computer. In 2007, a new server product, *InfoPath Forms Services*, was released that allows you to publish form templates to a web server for users to complete and view directly through the browser. SharePoint has built-in support for InfoPath Forms Services in the Enterprise version of the product.

As you read this chapter, you find out the following:

❑   When you should consider using InfoPath over the data collection techniques available with SharePoint 2007

❑   How to create a new form template and publish it to SharePoint for others to complete

❑   What different types of publishing options are available for form templates

❑   How to use data connections within an InfoPath form template

❑   How to create form template parts for reuse

After reading this chapter, you should feel comfortable identifying scenarios where the use of InfoPath forms would be beneficial for your organization for the collection of information from various key stakeholders.

What Is InfoPath?

InfoPath is an application that integrates with SharePoint to collect and present data. InfoPath forms are XML-based documents that you can design to help collect data in ways that SharePoint interface cannot. While InfoPath can be used on its own, it truly excels as a data collection tool when combined with SharePoint. Some ways of using InfoPath within an organization include:

❑ **Team reports:** Team members can create weekly status reports from which the team's manager can create a single report, which tracks the team's progress. This involves creating a form template that features fields related to weekly activities and publishing it to a shared location, such as a team site. Every week, the manager can access a special view that displays all the forms and then she can merge them into a single document. This consolidation reduces the amount of work that a manager must perform each week. She can even customize that single document to present to her own management team.

❑ **Data connections:** Sales people can use forms to report on customer information from a centralized database containing details on the customer and previous purchases. They can also attach a document with a record of meetings and communication with the customer so that colleagues can access this later. Again, you must create a form template and store it on a centralized team site, but this template features special data connections that display customer data directly from the database. This reduces duplicate data by eliminating the need to recreate this content in SharePoint because it already exists in the database, improves data access, and allows the sales team to make accurate decisions. With InfoPath, you can also submit information to other data systems via a web service, which means that you don't have to enter data into two separate systems.

❑ **Customer web forms:** Customers can visit a web page and complete an electronic form to request information on a company's products and services. The form is submitted securely to a location, and the customer is supplied with the requested information. A new feature of InfoPath is the ability to create forms that customers can view and edit via the browser. These forms can be hosted on a website via InfoPath Forms Services.

This chapter discusses how you can create, edit, or view forms, including browser-based forms in the "Creating and Customizing an InfoPath Form" section of this site.

❑ **Employee feedback:** A human resources department can get feedback from employees on new policies and procedures. To help control the collection of feedback, the department sends a form embedded in an Outlook email message. Employees can complete the form and send it directly back to the human resources SharePoint site where the information is collected and analyzed. Employees can keep a copy of their submitted information in a folder in Outlook for later reference.

What's New in InfoPath?

The 2007 version of InfoPath is much improved over the last one; with InfoPath 2007, you can use a browser to work with forms even if you haven't installed the InfoPath application — 2003 wouldn't let you work with forms unless you had InfoPath installed. Browser-based forms are possible via InfoPath Forms Services, which is available with the Enterprise release of SharePoint 2007.

Other great features released in this new version include:

❑ Improved support for the management of multiple data connections

❑ The ability to create reusable form components known as *template parts*

❑ A design checker that determines if your form is compatible with previous versions of the application as well as the browser

❑ New data controls such as the combo box and multiple selection list box

❑ The ability to embed InfoPath forms within custom applications and websites

❑ Improved ability to centralize templates in a single location

Creating and Customizing an InfoPath Form

You use InfoPath in situations when you need to improve how information is shared or collected in your organization. One of the primary advantages of using InfoPath is that the interface can be made very simple and intuitive for users to add and complete information. An example of a typical InfoPath form is shown in Figure 10-1.

Before a user can complete an InfoPath form, you must start with a form template, which someone using the InfoPath application designs. You then have to publish the template to a location where users can complete the form by adding information. Each time a user completes and saves the form, a new file is created. For example, if you take the example of the weekly status reports described in the introduction of this chapter, a single form template exists that contains all the required and optional fields that the form should contain. This form template would be published to the SharePoint site using a method similar to that described in Chapter 4 for document libraries or Chapter 6 for content types. Each team member would then click the New button on the Library toolbar to open a new instance of the form. Once the form is completed, the team member would save it to the library and create a new form data file. If five members are on a team, then each week five new form data files are created in the library as the team members create their status reports. However, there would only be one form template file for the status reports.

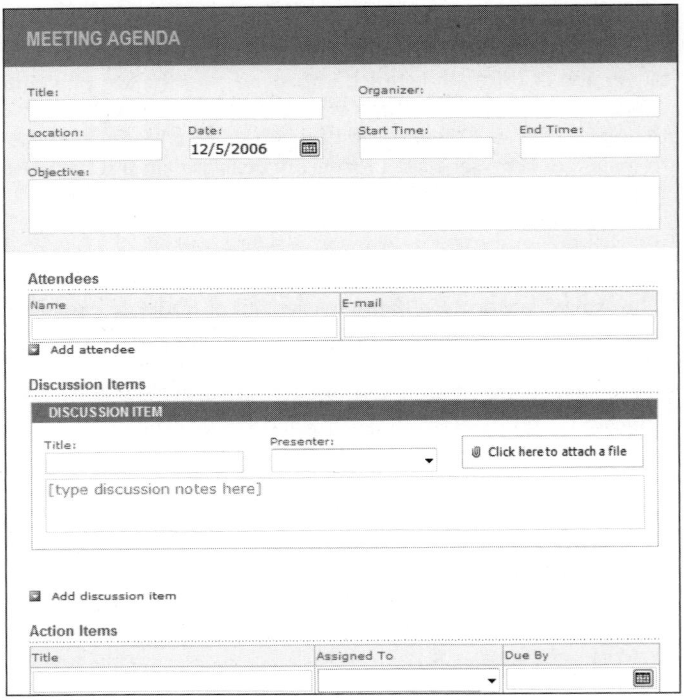

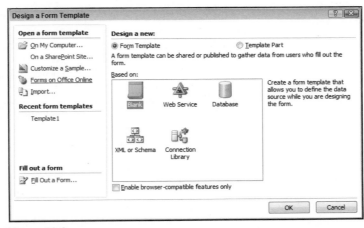

Figure 10-1

To get started with using InfoPath, you must first create or design a form template. InfoPath has several sample form templates that you can customize to suit your data collection requirements. It's always a good idea to view the sample form templates to see if any represent the business activity you are trying to support before you start developing a template from scratch. You should also check the Microsoft Office Online template galleries, which you can access directly via the Forms on Office Online link from the application's Start menu as shown in Figure 10-2.

Figure 10-2

In the first Try It Out in this section, you open an existing sample template in Design view and modify a field to make it more appropriate for your organization. You can also make modifications to the form to give it a look and feel that is more appropriate for your organization. This may include adding a company logo to the various form views or adopting a color scheme that matches that of other company documents and interfaces. The second Try It Out in this section illustrates how to do this.

Try It Out   Creating an InfoPath Form

Using a starting point to create a form gives you more time to focus on tailoring the form to fit your needs. In this example, you modify the existing Meeting Agenda form template to include the names of staff members who typically organize your meetings. You also make this a mandatory field because, in your company, every meeting should have an identified meeting organizer. Giving users a list of values rather than a standard text box reduces the amount of time it takes users to complete the form. The list of values also allows you to build special views in the SharePoint library so you can filter them via the meeting organizer. For example, this Try It Out allows for Amanda Murphy to select or create a view that only displays meetings that she organizes.

1.   Open the InfoPath application.

2.   From the Getting Started window, click the Customize a Sample link from the Design a Form action group, as shown in Figure 10-3.

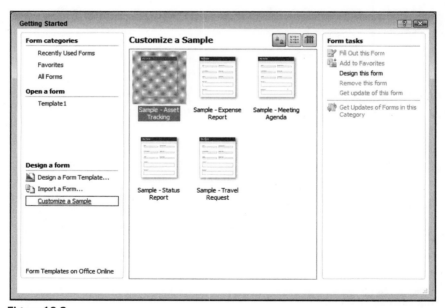

Figure 10-3

3. Select the Sample – Meeting Agenda template.

4. From the Form Tasks list on the right-hand side of the window, click the Design This Form link. Your form opens in design mode.

5. Click to select the Organizer field.

6. Click the right mouse button and select Change To, and then Drop-Down List Box from the menu as shown in Figure 10-4. Notice that the Organizer field changes from a standard text box to a drop-down list box.

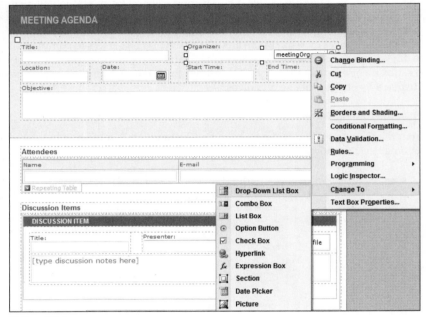

Figure 10-4

7. Click the right mouse button again and this time select Drop-Down List Box Properties. The Drop-Down List Box Properties dialog box appears, as shown in Figure 10-5.

8. Select the check box for Cannot Be Blank under the Validation and Rules section.

9. From the List Box Entries section, click the Add button. The Add Choice dialog box appears.

10. Enter a name for the team organizer. For this example, enter **Amanda Murphy** in the Value and Display Name fields. By entering the text for the Value field first, it is automatically added to the Display Name field.

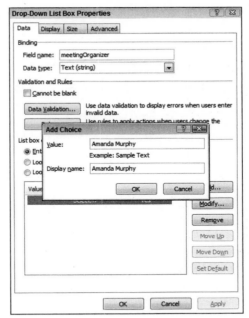

Figure 10-5

11. Click the OK button. You will now see Amanda Murphy as a value listed in the properties of the field.

12. Repeat this process by clicking the Add button again and entering another team organizer. In this case, enter **Shane** Perran as a value for the drop-down list, and then again enter your own name as a value.

13. Click the Apply button.

14. Click the OK button.

15. Select File ➪ Save As. You receive a message window advising you that you will need to publish the form template to make it available to other people.

16. Click the OK button to accept the message and continue.

17. Save the file on your computer in the location containing the resource files for this chapter. Give the form template a file name of **meetingagenda.xsn**.

18. Click the Preview button from the toolbar.

How It Works

Your form opens in preview mode, as shown in Figure 10-6.

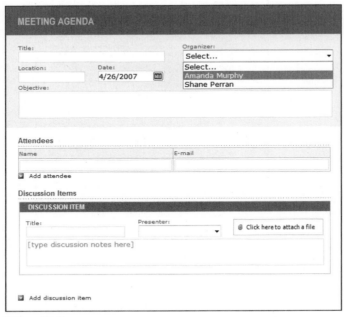

Figure 10-6

You now see that the Organizer field is a drop-down list box featuring the names you had entered in the previous steps.

| Try It Out | **Customize the Look and Feel of a Form Template** |

In this example, you add your company's logo to the form template so that it appears whenever users view or print the form. Branding forms and document templates help create a more professional image for your forms and can help customers identify you as a company. Also, it's good to have a standardized template with a logo for conducting business activities so that people can clearly identify the official company template.

For this example, you make slight look-and-feel changes to the form template. Note that any alterations you make should be reviewed with the appropriate departments — usually communications or marketing. If these departments do not exist in your organization, consider reviewing changes with stakeholders. By allowing others to participate in the design and planning stages, you can increase the probability of solid end-user adoption because you are more likely to directly address their needs and requirements.

1. Open the form template designed in the previous example called meetingagenda.xsn.

2. Click the header of the form just to the right of the words "meeting agenda" and click the right mouse button.

3. Select Split Cells as shown in Figure 10-7. A dialog box appears requesting information on the format you want to create for your table.

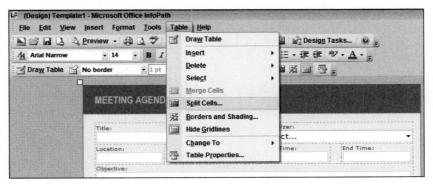

Figure 10-7

4. Enter **2** for the number of columns, keep the value of 1 for number of rows, and click the OK button. The table is reformatted as specified.

5. Click in the right-hand column of the header. Choose Insert ➪ Picture ➪ From File, as shown in Figure 10-8. A file selection window appears.

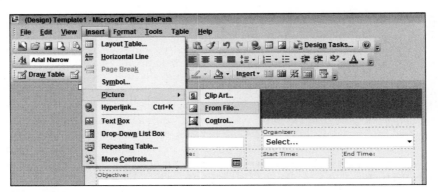

Figure 10-8

6. Browse to the resource files from this chapter and select companylogo.jpg.

7. Click the Insert button.

8. Chose Format ➪ Background Color. The View Properties dialog box appears with the General tab selected, as shown in Figure 10-9.

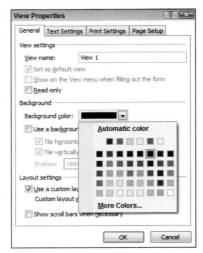

Figure 10-9

9. Select the color blue and ensure that the check box to Use a Background Picture is not selected.
10. Click the OK button.

Using the Design Tasks Pane

In InfoPath, the Design Tasks pane shown in Figure 10-10 contains the most common design activities and concepts related to customizing or developing a form template. By clicking any of these items, you expand the configuration options for that item in the pane. The items on the pane represent the process you follow when you create a form template. You start with a blank form template, and it launches with no data source. As you add controls to the form in Design mode, fields appear in the form's data source to support the use of these controls. Next, you can create various views for the form, which are similar to those discussed in Chapter 4 related to lists and libraries, but in this case are specifically located in the form. You can basically create a set of criteria that displays your data in different ways, depending on what you want to collect or represent. You then check your design to make sure that it's compatible in the browser where it will operate. Some field types are not suitable for use in a web browser, so when you create a form for the browser, it is important to include only elements that are supported. InfoPath has a Design Checker mode that helps support you with this. Finally, you publish your form template so that others can use it and so that you can begin collecting data.

The Task pane is generally opened by default when you first start the InfoPath application in Design mode. Otherwise, you can access it by selecting Design Tasks from the View menu. Because you will spend most of your time using this pane as you create a form template, this section is entirely devoted to the pane's many items, which include Layout, Controls, Data Source, Views, Design Checker, and Publish Form Template.

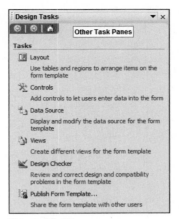

Figure 10-10

To learn how to create and publish a form template, see the next section, "Working with Form Templates."

If you are not creating your form from an existing file, you should take time to plan it out. By considering your information requirements in advance and sketching a form out on paper, you can determine what your form and data source elements should be before you even start creating the form template.

Layout

The Layout task pane item allows you to create tabular layouts in your form to control how information is presented. Quite often, in order to create a form that contains multiple columns of information, you need a table to effectively organize everything. From the Layouts section of the task pane, you can:

❑ Insert predefined table rows and columns.

❑ Insert a custom table.

❑ Modify cells, rows, and columns within an existing table.

❑ Insert special layout controls such as horizontal or scrolling regions.

In Figure 10-11, you can see the contents of the Layouts section of the Design Tasks pane. Notice that in addition to using one of the table options listed in the pane, you can also create a custom table to suit your specific needs.

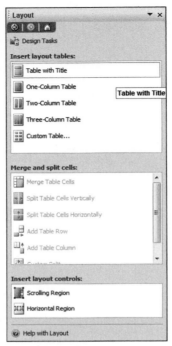

Figure 10-11

Controls

Once you lay out a form and define its overall structure, the next step is to add the fields that the form will contain. InfoPath offers a variety of controls that can be used to effectively collect and display information in a form including text boxes, rich-text boxes, selection list boxes, data pickers, check boxes, option buttons, buttons, and sections.

Adding controls is closely linked to creating a data source, which is covered in the next section. You can start with a blank form template and create the data source by adding controls to the form. As you add a control to the form, an item is created automatically in the data source to represent that control. You can add controls either by dragging them from the Design pane to the area you want them to appear on the form, or by selecting the area in the form and double-clicking the control in the Design pane. You should name your fields as you add the controls. You can rename a field by either double-clicking it or right-clicking the field and selecting Properties. The name cannot contain spaces and should be intuitive. When you open the Properties dialog box, you will see other aspects of the field that you can customize, such as default values, display options, or selection values. Each type of control has its own set of unique attributes and properties.

Text Box

A text box can hold all sorts of information types such as Name, Phone Number, or Currency. When you edit the properties of a text box, you can determine what format the information should be stored as by selecting the Data Type. When designing a form using this field type, you can have default values populated based on a user's selection for other fields. InfoPath also supports the use of customizable rules that allow you to perform actions such as show a dialog box message or set a field's value based on the user's selection of an item or activity within the form. You may also include placeholder text that demonstrates to a user the type of information that the field should contain or how they can complete the item. Some of the options related to the text box control are listed in Figure 10-12, including some of the formatting and display alternatives:

Figure 10-12

❑ **Auto complete**: This option suggests words or phrases to a user as she is completing a form based on previously entered options. Sometimes Auto Complete can make the process for filling out a form easier for the users. However, it is not typically appropriate for forms where information entered may be of a sensitive or confidential nature.

❑ **Spell check**: This enables spell checking on content stored in the field.

❑ **Multi line**: This option allows you to specify whether a text box can include paragraph breaks or if text can wrap. This is helpful for situations where the text may exceed a single line. If you do select multi line, you can determine whether the control should allow scrolling or expand to display the text when it exceeds a single line.

❑ **Text box limit**: This option allows you to specify the number of characters a field can contain. You may use this option when accepting information, such as a phone number or social security number, whereby the number of characters is limited to a fixed number.

❑ **Conditional formatting**: In some cases, based on the value that is entered in text box or in another field, you can choose how to display a field. For example, if the number of items ordered in a form exceeds the value in another field for the number of items available, you may select to have the order field highlighted in red. Also, you can use conditional formatting to hide certain fields based on the selection of another field.

❑ **Placeholder text:** You can use placeholder text to include suggestions in a text box or field to represent the text a user might enter or provide instruction on how he or she should complete a field. For example, for a name field, you might have placeholder text that states "Enter Name Here." As soon as a user clicks the field, the text is erased. You cannot use placeholder text for forms that you intend to publish to Forms Server for access via the browser. Only use the Placeholder Text feature for forms users will complete. Users must have the InfoPath application installed on their computers.

Rich-Text Box

You use the rich-text box to collect more detailed information from a user, such as a description or background information. This field type or control has many of the same customization features as the text box including spell check, placeholder, conditional formatting, and wrapped text. When customizing this field type, your user can apply certain levels of formatting directly in the field, such as including images, rich text, or tables. Note that if you intend to publish your form to a Forms Server or SharePoint environment so that users can access it on a browser, your form may only support certain levels of formatting. Therefore, to make your form accessible via the browser, you should select Enable Browser-Compatible Settings Only, as shown in Figure 10-13.

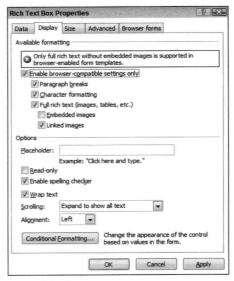

Figure 10-13

Selection List Boxes

Selection list box field controls include drop-down list box, combo box, list boxes, and multiple selection list boxes. Depending on the type of information you are collecting from your users and whether you intend to make the form available in the browser, your implementation choices may vary:

❑ **Drop-down list box:** This type of box allows users to select from fixed sets of values. If there are many items, you may select a drop-down list box to save room because it only shows one item until the user clicks a down arrow. Too many items can negatively impact a user experience, so consider applying a filter so that only a relevant set of items display based on a user's selection in another field — for example, if the user enters the United States as his country, a field for State or Province selection could be filtered to only display states because there is no requirement to display provinces. The drop-down list box can be used in browser-enabled forms.

❑ **Standard list box:** This option allows users to select from a fixed set of values. The items display in a listing box and are viewable all at once. This is different from the drop-down box for that reason and is typically only suitable when you have less than ten or so values. Otherwise, the control will take up a large amount of space, and selecting from too large a set of values may be difficult for some readers. The standard list box can be used in browser-enabled forms.

❑ **Combo box:** The combo box is very similar in presentation to the drop-down list box; however, it also allows users to enter their own values in a list. Therefore, if the item they want to select is not listed in the drop-down list, they can type in their own value. This field cannot be used in a browser-enabled form.

❑ **Multiple selection list box:** The multiple selection list box is similar to the standard list box, but contains check boxes for each item and can also optionally allow users to enter their own values into the list. This field cannot be used in a browser-enabled form.

Date Picker

This feature helps a user select a date, which is especially helpful when you have regional variations in date formats. For example, 05/06/07 can represent a completely different day in Canada than it would in the United States. It's also helpful to select the correct dates when they are critical to travel plans, or when the user may not know the exact date of something — for example, when they are planning meetings that occur the third Monday of every month. An example of the Date Picker control as seen by an end user on the completed form is shown in Figure 10-14.

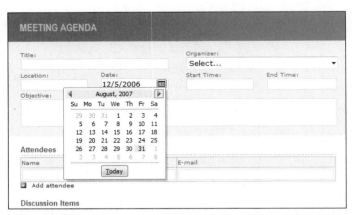

Figure 10-14

You can configure the Date Picker to contain certain default values including special functions, such as today (), which sets the default date to the current date of when the user is completing the form.

Check Box

In many of the exercises in this book, you selected a check box to enable an option for an application. The same logic applies in a form template. You can have a single check box to provide a Yes or No type answer to a question. For example, if a check box were associated with a to-do list, a blank box would indicate that the task has not been completed, whereas a selected check box would indicate that the task was completed. Alternatively, you have check boxes that allow a user to select one or more items from a group of choices, as shown in Figure 10-15. While each choice is an individual field, you can group the check boxes together in a section or table for data organization purposes.

Figure 10-15

Option Button

The option button gives users a choice between items. Instead of allowing users to select more than one item, you give them a list of choices and allow them to select only one of them. In Figure 10-16, a user can select only a single size when ordering their pizza.

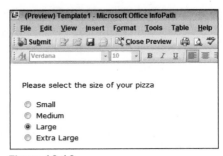

Figure 10-16

You select how many choices you want to give the user, and you assign each option button a unique ID that makes it easy for you to identify the user's selection.

Button

You can add a button to launch a new activity or series of rules on a form. When the user clicks the button, the activity or rule triggers. You can use buttons to launch several actions including:

❑　Change views in a form.

- ❑ Submit to a data connection.

- ❑ Retrieve information from a data connection.

- ❑ Launch a new form template.

- ❑ Launch a message window or display box.

- ❑ Set the value for a field in the form.

- ❑ Close a form.

By implementing rules in combination with special conditions, a simple form template can become a dynamic application and drive specific business processes in a way that is very intuitive and easy to use.

Sections

Sections give elements structure, and are therefore important when you design a form's data source and display needs. You can add, remove, or hide sections within a form template. As shown in Figure 10-17, you can select to have a section initially excluded from the form or added by a user. You may choose to hide a section if you want to have portions of your form only appear based on a user's response to a question. For example, if you have a set of questions in your form related to what pizza toppings a user wants on their pizza, you might choose to hide those questions, if in a previous answer the user selected that he wanted to order hamburgers.

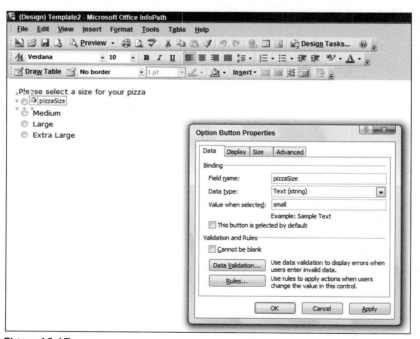

Figure 10-17

It is generally a good idea to add sections to your form templates to group information that is similar or related. You should name sections appropriately so that you can better identify a set of related fields within the form's data source.

Other Controls

The previously listed field types are just a few of the standard controls available for use in an InfoPath form. Additional control types include:

- ❑ **Tables:** You can include tables in your form for users to complete. Each table can contain a number of fields and may include repeating rows so that users can add more information or items to the table as required.

- ❑ **Master/Detail:** In some cases, you may have two controls or sections whereby the selection in one will dictate the detail displayed in another. An example of this might be a product category list and a product details listing. If a user selects a category, the details listing should be reformatted to display only the items related to the selected category.

- ❑ **Lists:** A list can be a more informal control that allows a user to add a bulleted or numbered list in his response. You may include a list in a form that asks a user to submit ideas for a new product or accomplishments for a particular time period.

- ❑ **File Attachment:** It may be appropriate or beneficial to have a user attach a file to his form instance. This file becomes embedded in the form document and others can access it later when reviewing the form.

- ❑ **Picture:** This control allows you to create a field that will either upload and embed a picture in the form, or link to a picture stored elsewhere.

- ❑ **Ink Picture:** For users with a drawing tablet or Tablet PC, InfoPath has built-in support of Ink, which allows a user to write directly into a form with a digital pen. This field supports the drawing of an image directly within the form.

- ❑ **Hyperlink:** This control allows you to insert a hyperlink into the form whereby you can specify the link to a location and display text.

- ❑ **Expression Box:** For more advanced users, this control can be used to enter an XPath expression that can perform advanced calculations on data stored in the form. The results of the calculation are displayed in the form.

- ❑ **Vertical Label:** For design purposes, you may want to have a vertical label added to your form. This control presents the form designer with a text box within which text can be added. This text displays vertically on the form.

- ❑ **Regions or Groups:** Similar to sections, regions and groups are organizational elements that can be added to pages to support fields or text.

Data Source

The primary data source of your InfoPath form is basically the skeletal information structure of your form. In order to have a field in the form, it must be tied to an element in the data source. When you create your form by adding controls, data source elements are automatically added in the primary data source for you. You can also have secondary data sources, such as external data connections that you can use to display information in the form. For example, you may have a secondary data source that is a database. You can drag information from your database onto the form and select which fields or controls should be used to display the information.

As previously described in the last section, the data source is very closely tied to the controls. You should name your fields as you add the controls. This will automatically update the data source. The name cannot contain spaces and should be intuitive. You can also add groups, tables, or sections in your form's data source so that you can easily track elements or items that are related to one another.

The primary data source of a form can be imported based on an XML file or data connection. This approach is more advanced whereby a formalized data structure is imported into the form and then controls are added to the form to represent the data. If you are not creating your data source from a data connection or XML schema file, you should take time to plan it out. Consider your information requirements, and sketch a form out on paper. By considering what some of the information requirements are in advance, you can generate a good idea on what your data elements should be before you even start creating the form template.

> When you remove a control from a form's view, you do not remove the field from your data source. Views are discussed in the next section.

In addition to the primary data source of a form template, additional data sources become available as new data connections are added to the form. An example of this is shown in Figure 10-18.

Figure 10-18

Similar to the behavior of the primary data source, you can drag elements within a secondary data source onto the page. This can help provide some data reporting from external data sources within the form itself. You can add items either as sections or tables and then format them as required. For example, in a form template that tracks information about a customer, the primary data source of the form may contain items such as the customer's phone number, company name, and email address. And you might create a secondary data source that connects to the orders database. You can drag information from this secondary data source onto the form to show a salesperson all the products the customer has purchased.

Views

In Chapter 4, you saw how to create custom views for lists and libraries to display different records and columns from a single data source. With InfoPath, you can also create multiple views from a single form. The views can act either as reports or pages in a form where they can represent completely unique steps related to the completion of a process. For example, you can have a form template with four different views: one for customer requests, a second that logs troubleshooting issues that an employee must resolve, a third that tracks correspondence with customer, and the final that tracks customer's comments on the level of service they've received.

Views can be created from the Design pane by selecting Add a New View from the Actions list. When a view is created, it is blank. The Form Designer must drag layout elements such as tables onto the form and add controls as needed. A single field can be added to multiple views. For example, you may have a field for customer name. You can add this field to every view in your form. You can also change unique characteristics related to the presentation of the field on each view. While the data remains the same, the presentation of a field on each view can be slightly different. For example, on one page the customer's name may appear in large bold letters, and on another it may appear in a drop-down box. However, the data of the field remains the same. Therefore, if "Graphical Wonder" is listed as the customer in one view, it will also be listed on all other views in that field.

You can use buttons on views to toggle between each of the available views. In some cases, multiple views and buttons can be implemented on a form to collect information from a user in steps. You essentially add a button to a view that, when selected, will launch another view using the Rules capabilities of buttons. This replicates the experience of a wizard and can help simplify the experience of the user as she completes the operation. If you don't use custom buttons, you can have users switch between various form views within the InfoPath application using the View menu, as shown in Figure 10-19.

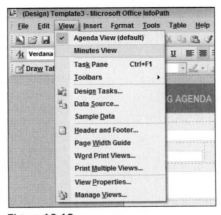

Figure 10-19

Design Checker

As previously stated, not all form controls are supported for use within browser-based forms. Therefore, you need to consider who the audience for your form will be and how they will access the form. If the form has to be available for use on the browser, careful consideration is required to ensure that the experience is positive. This may seem like a lot to understand if you are just getting used to creating these forms. Therefore, a Design Checker exists with the InfoPath application to guide you by highlighting anything you may have in your form that would not be compatible with the browser or previous versions of InfoPath.

If you decide that a form should be browser compatible after you have already begun the form design process, you can change the setting by selecting the Compatibility item under Form Options, as shown in Figure 10-20.

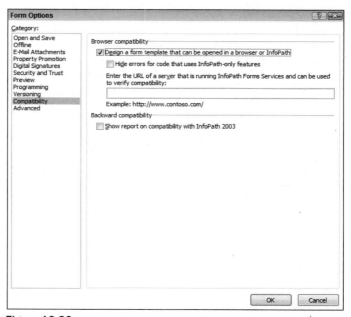

Figure 10-20

Another option in this same interface is a URL to test whether the form will be compatible with the destination SharePoint Server. By specifying a URL, the Design Checker displays alerts and messages indicating items in your form that may affect compatibility with either the browser or older versions of the application.

Publishing a Form Template

You can always save a template in a location for your personal use and to edit further, but to make your form available to others you need to publish the template to a central location. You can publish an InfoPath form template to any of the following locations:

❑   A SharePoint Server with InfoPath Forms Services (supports use of browser-based forms)

❑ A SharePoint Server without InfoPath Forms Services (does not support browser-based forms)

❑ A shared network location such as a file share

❑ A list of email recipients (requires Outlook 2007)

❑ An installable form template

Depending on the environment in which you are working and what tools you have available, you may select either one of these options when completing the Publishing Wizard.

In the next section, "Working with Form Templates," you walk through examples of publishing an InfoPath form to a SharePoint Server, including directly publishing to a document library, creating an InfoPath Form content type, and uploading an administrator approved form template.

If you publish your form template to any of these locations, you must save a local copy of the template on your computer. If later you want to make updates to the form template, you can make them to your local copy and complete the Publishing Wizard to update your form template in its shared location. However, you should be confident that no edits were performed directly on the template in its shared location. If there are, then you may overwrite them by publishing an older version of the form. It is a good idea to identify and define development policies and procedures related to your organization's custom InfoPath forms to ensure that such situations do not occur.

Working with Form Templates

Now that you know the design-related functions of an InfoPath form template, you can start creating some actual form templates that can help you collect and view information. This section discusses creating a new form template, and then addresses some options for publishing and customizing the form to further meet the business requirements.

Designing a New Form

Before you can begin creating a new form, you need to figure out the form's requirements. This might involve gathering information from the group or sponsors who are requesting the form. However you gather the information, you should know the following:

❑ What types of information should the form collect?

❑ How should you present the information, and what special rules are there for submitting the information? For example, you can create Name and Email fields because they are required to contact employees after they submit feedback.

❑ How should you format the Data field? For example, you may apply special formatting or filtering that disables other fields based on a user's input in another field. This is helpful to ensure that users only have to deal with the fields they are required to complete.

Once you have the information that you need, it's time to do the actual work of creating the form template.

Although there are many steps in the next Try It Out, they represent a small portion of the steps required to create the most basic of electronic forms. In the second Try It Out of this section, you look at the new functionality of InfoPath 2007 related to creating reusable template components called *template parts*.

Try It Out   **Design a New Form Template**

For this example, you first set up the layout of the form. This helps mold the canvas for how the form will look. It is also recommended that prior to opening the InfoPath application you should always sketch out how you want the form to look on a piece of paper. This is something that can be helpful for collecting feedback from your sponsors prior to starting any development work. As you see in the exercise, sometimes there can be many steps to creating even the most basic of forms. Therefore, it is always a good idea to have a solid roadmap before you even start.

Once the layout is defined, you begin adding controls and creating the data source. In this situation, every time you add a new control to the page, it creates a new data source field. You name the fields as you go along to keep things organized and easy to follow. This is very important as forms become more complex and large numbers of fields are created.

1. Open the InfoPath application.

2. From the Getting Started window, select Design a Form Template from the Design a Form action group.

3. Specify that you want to design a new Form Template based on a Blank data source.

4. Select the check box for Enable Browser-Compatible Features Only, as shown in Figure 10-21.

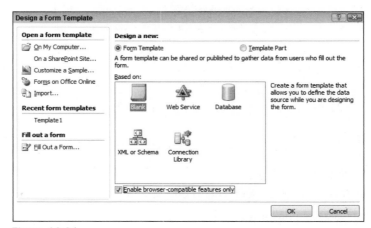

Figure 10-21

5. Click the OK button. A new blank form view appears.

6. From the Design Tasks pane, select Layout.

7. Click to select Table with Title. A table appears in the form template featuring a placeholder title and text.

8. Click the row containing the form's title and change it to read **Feedback** Form.

9. Click the row below the title and select the Three Column Table item from the Layouts task pane.

10. Select the left-hand column, click the right mouse button, and select Table Properties as shown in Figure 10-22.

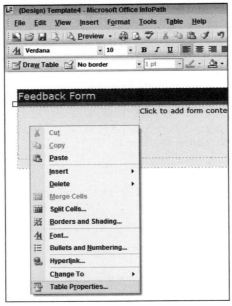

Figure 10-22

11. Select the Row tab.

12. For Size, change the value to Automatically Set Row Height.

13. Select the Column tab.

14. Enter **300** px for the column width of the left-hand column.

15. Click the Next Column button.

16. Enter **50** px for the column width of the center column.

17. Click the Next Column button.

18. Enter **300** px for the column width of the right-hand column.

19. Click the Apply button.

20. Click the OK button. You will notice that your table is now formatted with two wide columns on each side with a smaller column in the middle.

21. Select the Design Tasks hyperlink at the top of the Layout task pane, as shown in Figure 10-23.

22. Click the Controls link.

23. Click in the left-hand column of the table.

Figure 10-23

24. Type the word **Name** and press Enter.

25. From the Controls task pane, click the text box. Note that if you click the text box with the cursor already positioned in the table, the control is automatically added where you have specified. Otherwise, you can drag the control to your desired location.

26. Double-click the control to expose its properties, as shown in Figure 10-24. Enter **employeeName** as the Field Name.

Figure 10-24

27. Select the Cannot Be Blank check box.

28. Click the Apply button and then the OK button.

29. Select the right-hand column of the form table.

30. Type the words **Email Address** and press Enter.

31. From the Controls task pane, click on the text box.

32. Double-click the control to expose its properties. Enter **employeeEmail** as the Field Name.

33. Select the Cannot Be Blank check box.

34. Click the Apply button and then the OK button. If the Email Address control is still selected, click the right arrow on your keyboard.

35. Click the Table menu item and select Insert and then Rows Below. A new row is added to the table. Repeat this step once more to add another row. This separates the fields a bit visually, which should make it easier for end users to fill out.

36. Select the last row in the table with your mouse to highlight each column.

37. Click Table ⇨ Merge Cells as shown in Figure 10-25.

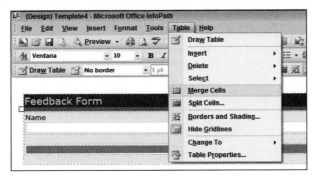

Figure 10-25

38. In the newly merged row, shown in Figure 10-26, enter the text **Tell Us What You Think** and press Enter.

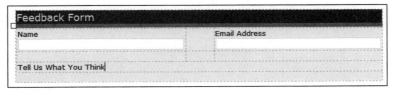

Figure 10-26

39. From the Controls task pane, click on the rich text box.

40. Double-click the control to expose its properties. Enter **employeeFeedback** as the Field Name.

41. Click the Apply button and then the OK button.

42. Click File ⇨ Save As.

43. You receive a message window advising you that you will need to publish the form template to make it available to other people. Click the OK button to accept the message and continue.

44. Save the file on your computer in the location containing the resource files for this chapter. Give the form template a file name of `employeefeedback.xsn`.

45. Click the Preview button to see how your form will be viewed by all users.

How It Works

After you finish adding fields and save the form, you preview it. Figure 10-27 demonstrates that the Name and Email Address have a special character within them that communicates to the user that the fields are required.

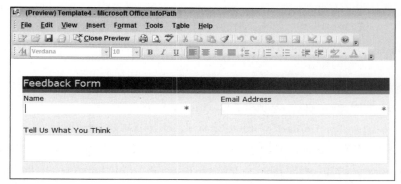

Figure 10-27

Try It Out   Create a Template Part

In the last example, you looked at the process for creating an entire form template. However, a fantastic new feature in InfoPath 2007 is the ability to create reusable components called template parts. A *template part* is a section or group of controls that may have specific fields, data connections, or customizations that could be potentially reused across multiple form templates. For example, consider a common contact form. It generally contains a name, email address, phone number, and address. In fact, many other forms also contain this information. Therefore, it's beneficial to create template parts containing each of those items so that they can be easily added in the future to all other forms requiring those components.

In the next example, you walk through the process of creating a template part in InfoPath 2007.

1. Open the InfoPath application.

2. From the Getting Started window, select Design a Form Template from the Design a Form action group.

3. Specify that you want to design a template part based on a blank data source, as shown in Figure 10-28. You will also design this template part to be supported in the browser.

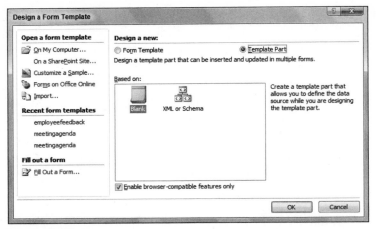

Figure 10-28

4. Click the OK button.

5. From the Controls task pane, select that you want to add a section.

6. Double-click the section on the form to expose its properties.

7. Name the section **ContactInformation** and click the OK button.

8. Click inside the section and click the Three-Column Table from the Layout task pane.

9. Change the width of the table columns to be wider within both the left- and right-hand columns.

10. Add four new text box fields to your form, as shown in Figure 10-29, to represent the name, phone number, email address, and street address fields.

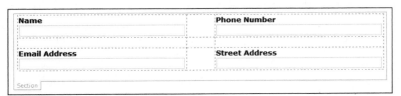

Figure 10-29

11. When you finish your designing and customization, select File ➪ Save As.

12. Save the template part within your resource files for this chapter using the name **ContactInformation.xtp**.

13. Click the Save button.

14. From the File menu, select that you wish to Design a Form Template.

15. Select that you want to design a form template based on a blank data source and click OK.

16. Click the Add or Remove Custom Controls link below the Controls task pane.

17. Click the Add button. The Add Custom Control Wizard dialog box appears, as shown in Figure 10-30.

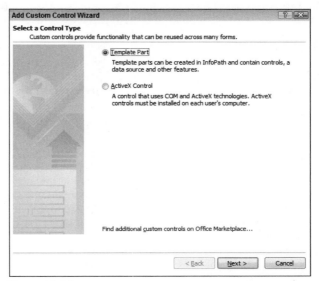

Figure 10-30

18. Select the Template Part option.

19. Click the Next button.

20. Browse to the location of the file you saved as part of step 12. Select the ContactInformation.xtp file and click Open.

21. Click the Finish and then Close buttons to complete the import process. Click the OK button to close the Add or Remove Custom Controls window.

22. Your new template part appears in the Controls task pane under the Custom category whenever you create a new form template. You can select it to add the fields for contact information to your new form template.

How It Works

Sometimes when creating form templates, you begin to recognize that certain elements appear in multiple form templates. Other times you may find that it requires a significant amount of effort to configure a set of fields and controls to behave the way you require. Therefore, it may be advantageous to wrap the elements into a single package that contains all the customizations and configurations required to reuse it again with very little effort.

In the previous example, you took a set of fields that were contained in many different form templates and created a template part out of them. Once a template part has been added to a control list, it will show up under custom controls whenever you open the InfoPath application. Adding the template part control is exactly the same as adding a single control to a form.

The advantage of using template parts can be calculated by identifying the total amount of time to re-create the form fields and their customizations, and then multiplying that number by the number of times you anticipate the fields would be required or used in a form. This number can be considerably high for common usage scenarios and form elements.

If you work in a team environment where multiple people are creating form templates, it is a good idea to share all the created template parts by storing them in a central location. This should increase the potential benefits of creating template parts because it will likely result in a higher reuse number.

Publishing a Form Template to a Library

In the previous example, you created a very simple form for users to fill out to provide feedback to a communications group within an organization. Once a form template is created, it must be published to a location where users can fill it out. As previously mentioned in the introduction of this chapter, SharePoint includes support for *InfoPath Forms Services*, a server feature that allows for users to complete InfoPath Forms via the browser so they do not require the InfoPath application. In order for a site to support this functionality, this Enterprise feature must be activated on the site collection and the site to which the form is being published.

In the first Try it Out in this section, you learn the process for creating a new SharePoint site with the InfoPath Form Services features enabled so that the form template can be made available to users from either the InfoPath application or a browser. For this example, you create a new SharePoint site using the blank template named "Communications." Creating a new site is not a requirement for pub-lishing a new form template; however, because you will be adding very specific lists for use by this form, you will create a brand-new site from which to work. Once the site is created with the appropriate feature enabled, you explore the process for publishing a form template to a document library in the sec-ond Try It Out. Then finally, in the last Try It Out of this section, you learn how to configure a document library to ensure that all users have the same editing experience, and specify that the form is opened as a web page in a browser regardless of whether the user has the InfoPath application installed on their computer.

Try It Out   Activate the Form Services Feature

InfoPath Form Services is an Enterprise feature that is not enabled by default on the Blank Site template used to create the communications site. Therefore, before you attempt to publish the form template out for your users to complete via the browser, you have to enable the Enterprise feature that controls InfoPath Forms Services. You first enable the feature on the site collection and then on the individual site to which you plan to publish your form.

   1.   From your Corporate Intranet site, go to the Sites directory and create a new site using the Blank Site template with Unique Permissions. Give the new site a URL of **http://servername/ sitedirectory/communications**.

   2.   Go to the Site Settings page of the new site and select Go to Top-Level Site Settings. Then select Site Collection Features from the Site Collection Administration links.

3. Click the Activate button for the Office SharePoint Server Enterprise Site Collection features. You may notice that the feature is already activated. If this is the case, then continue to next step without making a change.

4. Return to the Site Settings page of your new communications site and select Site Features from the Site Administration links.

5. Click the Activate button for the Office SharePoint Server Enterprise Site features.

Try It Out   **Publish a Form Template to a Document Library**

Now that your site is prepared to host the form template, you will publish it to a document library on the site as part of the form publishing process. This is the first of three publishing options available in InfoPath for publishing to a SharePoint Server and is the least complex. The other more advanced options are explored in the last section of this chapter.

Publishing a form template to a document library is most appropriate if you only have to make the form available in a single location and have no need to associate the form with a content type or multiple sites.

1. Open the InfoPath application.

2. From the Getting Started window, select Design a Form Template.

3. Select On My Computer from the Open a Form Template group. Browse to the location where you saved the employeefeedback.xsn template from a previous example and click Open. Alternatively, the form may be listed in the Recent Form Template section.

4. From the Design Tasks pane, select Publish Form Template.

5. A wizard appears asking where you want to publish the form. Select To a SharePoint Server with or without InfoPath Forms Services.

6. Click the Next button.

7. Enter the URL of the communications site you created in the previous Try It Out.

8. Click the Next button.

9. Select the check box to Enable This Form to Be Filled Out by Using a Browser, as shown in Figure 10-31.

10. Keep the default selection of Document Library for what you want to create or modify.

11. Click the Next button.

12. Keep the default selection to Create a New Document Library and click the Next button.

13. Enter **Feedback Form** for the name of the library.

14. For Description, enter the following:

> **Electronic form for collecting feedback from employees on new communications website.**

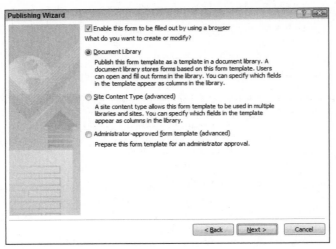

Figure 10-31

15. Click the Next button.

16. Click the Add button and add each of the fields contained in the form so that they can be promoted to columns in the library. You will have to repeat the process for each field.

17. Click the Next button.

18. Click the Publish button.

19. Once your form is published to the document library, you can click the Open This Form in the Browser link to view the form in its published state.

How It Works

In this example, you created a new document library on the communications sites as part of the form publishing process. This document library has the form template associated with it so that whenever a user enters the site and clicks the New button, the form is launched. If the user has InfoPath on his computer system, the form opens in the application. If the user does not have the application installed, it is launched from in the browser.

During the publishing process, you chose to promote specific fields within your form template to become columns within your document library. This allows you to see the contents of the forms in a view in the library without having to open each form individually. This makes it possible to create custom reports on data stored within a document library.

Try It Out   **Force a Form to Open as a Web Page**

In this next exercise, you will review how you can change the setting on the document library to enforce everyone to open the form within a browser. In some situations, this technique will be used to ensure that all users have a consistent experience when completing forms. It also helps control the interface so that only items exposed within a specific view are displayed to the user.

1.   From the main page of your communications site, click the View All Site Content link.

2.   Click the Feedback Form link to enter the document library.

3.   Select Settings ⇨ Form Library Settings from the Library toolbar.

4.   Click the Advanced Settings link.

5.   For the Opening Browser-Enabled Documents value, select Display as a Web Page, as shown in Figure 10-32.

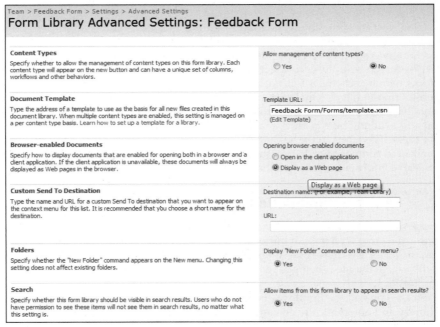

Figure 10-32

6.   Click the OK button.

7.   Return to the document library by clicking the Feedback Form link in the breadcrumb trail.

8.   Click the New button from the Document Library toolbar.

How It Works

As previously described, in some situations it may be necessary to ensure that all users open a form as a web page regardless of whether they have the InfoPath application installed. In this exercise, you modified the properties of the document library to ensure that all browser-enabled documents, including InfoPath forms, are opened in the browser.

Now that you have published your form template to the site, users can come in and complete the form template. When they are done, they can save the form back to the library using the toolbar buttons. However, after giving it some consideration, you have decided that it would be nice to have a Submit button added to the form that will save the document back to the library and name it automatically. This is the subject of the next section.

Customizing a Form Template

Once a template has been created and published to a library, it can still be edited and enhanced to further address business needs. As a form designer, you should consult with business users to identify ways in which the form can evolve to better suit their needs. This may include improving how data is submitted or saved to a library as well as how the form is presented to users.

In this section, you are going to review some of the enhancements and changes you can make to a form template that might make it a more effective tool for a team. In the first Try It Out, you look at how you can add a button to a form as well as submit a data connection that will save the form to a destination library without requiring a user to select Save As from the File menu. These approaches helps ensure that a proper naming scheme is followed for saved forms because the name can be derived from form data upon submission. It also makes the user experience better for those completing the form because they do not have to bother with understanding the details of where and how they should save the form. Once you add a Submit button, there may no longer be a need to expose the Save buttons on the form's toolbar to users. Therefore, in the second Try It Out of this section, you learn how the form's toolbar can be customized to suit your needs. You then look at how a data connection can be added to a form template to retrieve information from another content source.

Try It Out   Add a Submit Button to a Form Template

In some cases, rather than having a user select File ⇨ Save As and manually name their form file, it's more appropriate to offer a Submit button at the bottom of the form that the user can select when she completes the form. This makes the submission process easier because the user does not have to be concerned with where the file is being saved and what the file name will be.

In this exercise, you edit the Employee Feedback form to include a Submit button that will save the file to your library and automatically generate a name based on information stored within the form.

1. Open the employeefeedback.xsn template in Design mode from the location saved to your computer.

2. Select the bottom row of the table containing the form's fields.

3. Select Insert ⇨ Rows Below from the Table menu, as shown in Figure 10-33.

4. From the Design Tasks pane, select the Controls.

5. Click in the new row you created, and then select the button control from the Controls task pane.

6. Select the button and click the right mouse button. Select the Button Properties item from menu. The button properties dialog box appears.

7. Select Submit from the Action drop-down list.

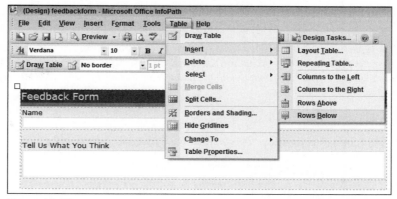

Figure 10-33

8. Click the Submit Options button.

9. Select the check box to Allow Users to Submit This Form.

10. From the Destination drop-down list, select SharePoint Document Library.

11. Click the Add button to identify what document library you want users to submit to.

12. Enter the URL for the document library you created for feedback forms. If you are unsure of the exact URL, visit the document library and copy the URL.

13. For the File Name field, click the fx button to the right of the field.

14. Enter the following into the Formula field as shown in Figure 10-34:

```
concat(employeeName, " - ", now())
```

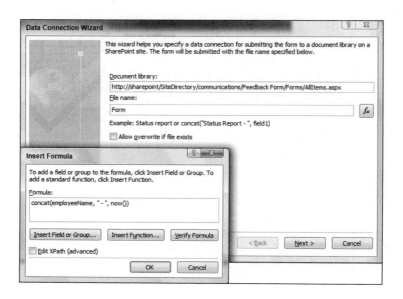

Figure 10-34

*Rather than typing employeeName, you should try clicking the Insert Field or Group button and select
the field from the list. This is the optimal method for selecting fields from your form or a data source.
Also ensure that you include the commas and quotation marks when entering your formula or you may
receive an error.*

15.   Click the OK button.

16.   Select the check box to Allow Overwrite if File Exists, as shown in Figure 10-35.

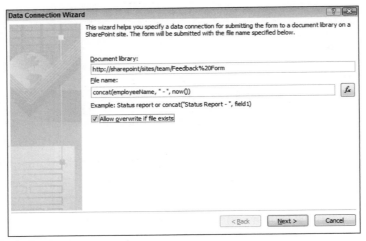

Figure 10-35

17.   Click the Next button.

18.   Click the Finish button.

19.   Unselect the option to have the submit option displayed on the toolbar and menu.

20.   Click the Advanced button.

21.   Change the drop-down list value for After Submit to be Close the Form.

22.   Click the OK button.

23.   Click the Apply button.

24.   Click the OK button.

25.   Click the Save button from the File menu to ensure that your changes are saved.

How It Works

In this example, you made a modification to the form template to allow users to more easily submit their
changes to the document library. Previously you had to rely on users to click the Save As button from

the toolbar or menu. From that point, users were required to name the file on their own. This could lead to major inconsistencies in naming practices and the ability to easily identify specific differences between forms.

You implemented a Submit button on the form. You could use several different methods to submit the form, including Web Services or email. However, in this situation, because all completed forms are being saved to the same document library you are using to launch the form, it makes sense to use the Submit to Document Library option.

In addition to specifying where you can submit a form, you can select how the form should be named, whether items with the same name should be overwritten, along with what actions take place once the form is submitted. In this situation, you chose to name the forms based on the name of the employee submitting the form in addition to a special set of characters, which define the exact time the form was submitted. While this does not create a visually appealing file name, you can be sure that it will be very easy to identify who submitted each form, and you can ensure that file names will be unique. You also determined that if a file was updated and resubmitted, then the existing form record should be overwritten rather than creating a completely new record.

Your final customization choice when defining the Submit option was that you set the form to close upon submission. Given the type of form created, this sort of action seems most appropriate.

Try It Out   Customize the Forms Services Toolbar

Typically once such an update is made to a local copy of the form template, the changes should be immediately published to the SharePoint document library again. However, there is still another set of changes that need to be made to the form to make it more usable and intuitive. Figure 10-36 shows what the form looks like in its current form.

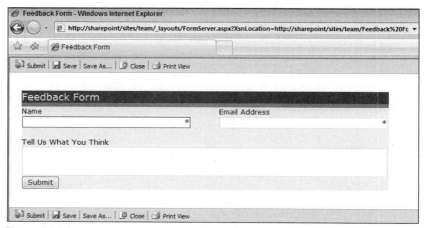

Figure 10-36

The users now have to choose between the custom Submit button, a Save button, and a Save As button. This can lead to some users selecting to save their forms using their own naming structure, and thereby eliminates any benefits associated with a standardized naming scheme that has been introduced with the custom button. Most important, for a very simple form you are offering users far too many choices. This leads to confusion and possibly even frustration. So in this example, you customize the toolbar that is automatically added to the Forms Services forms to only display the Print View option because this is something that users might find useful. In addition, because your form is fairly simple and small in size, you will remove the Footer toolbar because you don't need it in this form.

1. Return to your local copy of the Employee Feedback template featuring the changes implemented in the previous example.

2. Select Form Options from the Tools menu.

3. Unselect the option to display the toolbar at the bottom of the form.

4. Unselect all commands except Print View, as shown in Figure 10-37.

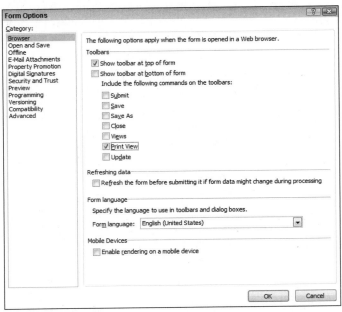

Figure 10-37

5. Click the OK button.

6. Publish the latest version of your form to the SharePoint site using the methods described earlier in this chapter.

How It Works

In this example, you used the Form Options menu to customize what commands display in a toolbar to users when they view the form via the browser. You did this to simplify the interface so that users can easily identify what they should select when it comes time for them to submit their information to the site. As in most cases, it is far more important for users to focus on the information they are submitting rather than the steps they are taking to submit it.

Try It Out   Add a Data Connection to a Form Template

So far, you have reviewed how to create a custom template that supports browser-based viewing and editing. You created a data connection in the form template to allow for the form to be submitted to the document library using a standardized naming scheme. However, you can also use data connections to display information in a form from an external data source, such as a database, web service, or SharePoint site.

In the next example, you discover how data entry can be made easier by allowing information to be pulled directly from a central source. For this example you will use the user information list from your site collection. If for some reason you are unable to query that list, you can create a custom list on your site containing a field for Employee Name and Work Email Address and use that list as a data source.

1. Return to your local copy of the Employee Feedback template featuring the changes implemented in the previous example.

2. Select the employeeName field from the form's Design view and click the right mouse button.

3. Select Change To, and then Drop-Down List Box. The field is transformed into a drop-down list box.

4. Double-click on the field to display its properties. The properties window appears.

5. From the List Box Entries section, select the Look Up Values from an External Data Source option, as shown in Figure 10-38.

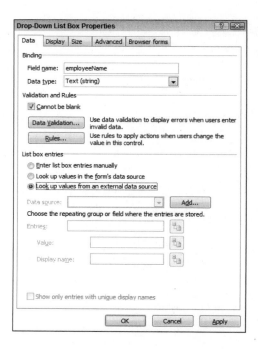

Figure 10-38

6. Click the Add button to launch the Data Connection Creation Wizard.

7. Select the Create a New Connection To option button, and select Receive Data.

8. Click the Next button.

9. Select SharePoint List or Library, and click the Next button.

10. Enter the URL of the top-level site of your site collection. A listing of all lists in that site are returned.

11. Select the User Information list.

12. Click the Next button.

13. Select the Name and Work Email fields, and click the Next button.

14. Select the check box to store a copy of the data in the form template.

15. Click the Next button.

16. Retain the default settings for the data connection name and synchronization settings, as shown in Figure 10-39.

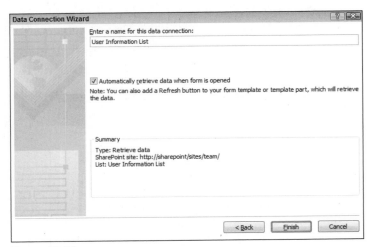

Figure 10-39

17. Click the Finish button.

18. Click the button to the right of the Entries field.

19. Expand the groups and select the Name field, as shown in Figure 10-40.

20. Click the OK button.

21. Click the Apply, and then OK button.

22. Double-click the employeeEmail field to manage its properties.

23. Click the fx button to the right of the Default Value field.

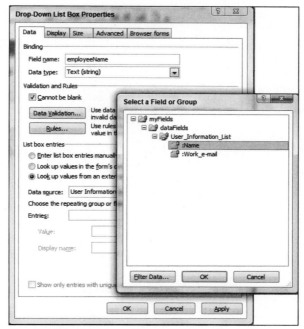

Figure 10-40

24. Click the Insert Field or Group button.

25. From the Data Source drop-down list, select User Information List (Secondary), as shown in Figure 10-41.

Figure 10-41

26.   Expand the Data Fields group along with user_information_list group to view available fields.

27.   Select the work_e-mail field.

28.   Click the Filter Data button.

29.   Click the Add button to create a new rule for the filtering.

30.   Select Name for the left-hand drop-down list.

31.   For the right-hand drop-down list, select Use a Field or Group.

32.   Change the data source back to Main and select employeeName, as shown in Figure 10-42.

Figure 10-42

33.   Click the OK button on all open windows to commit changes.

34.   Click the Save button from the toolbar to ensure that your changes are committed to the template.

How It Works

When you first created your feedback form, you allowed users to enter whatever they wanted into the User Name field. As a result, you had mixed results because sometimes users would enter their first name and not their last, or enter their employee user ID, or, in a rush, would make a typo or misspell their name. This makes reporting on the data difficult. Instead of allowing users to enter their name in a text box, you decided to let them select their name from a drop-down list of choices. In addition, rather than manually maintaining this list of users, you would draw the value list from an external data source. In this case, it made sense to look up the users who were members of the communications site because these were the users you would be collecting information from directly.

In addition to a requirement to standardize the data that was being entered for name, you recognized a need to reduce and simplify the data entry experience of users as they were completing the form. For example, it seemed somewhat ridiculous to some users to specify their email address because they were logged in to the network as registered users. Therefore, the organization should already have an email address associated with them. You did not want to just strictly remove the field because your goal might be to later email all users who complete the form. Therefore, you decided that it would be useful to retain the Email Address field but have its value auto-populated based on the selection of a user's name.

You therefore added a new data connection to the form template that looked up the user information list of the site collection. You specified that the information contained in this list should be available within the form itself. This allows you to open and interact with the external data when you are offline or detached from the network. A cached local copy of the data will be available to users while they are offline. From the data connection you selected the name and work email fields to be added to the form's secondary data source.

Once the data connection was configured, you connected the drop-down list box to the data connection. By default, all names are returned and displayed in the drop-down list box. If required, additional filtering can be applied to display only a certain subset of users. You then configured the default value of your email address to be the email address specified for the user on the team site who had the same name as the value selected for employeeName within the form.

When you click the Preview button after making the changes, you should see the names of users from your communications site displayed in the drop-down list box. As you select a user, you should see that user's email address appear in the Email Address field of the form. If you do not, the user may not have a specified email address within her SharePoint user profile.

Once you finish your updates, it will be necessary to publish these changes to the SharePoint Server again to update the template associated with the library.

Advanced Form Publishing Options

In the section "Publishing a Form Template to a Library," you learned how a form template is published to a single document library. This approach is suitable for scenarios where a form is only required in a single location and where multiple groups or sites do not reuse the form. However, you may need to make a form template available to multiple sites in a site collection or multiple site collections. In each of these cases you can choose one of the advanced form publishing options.

For scenarios where you want to publish a form template to multiple sites or libraries in the same site collection, the optimal publishing choice is to publish as a Content Type. In Chapter 6, you learned how content types can be associated with multiple libraries and locations in a single site collection. In Chapter 7, you discovered how Web Parts, such as the Content Query Web Part, can be used to display rollups of content from multiple locations based on a single content type. So in the case of a feedback form that is deployed to multiple sites, you can add a single Web Part to a page that displays all instances of the form across all sites in a site collection. In the first Try It Out of this section, you publish your employee feedback form template to be a content type so that it can be added to multiple libraries. Because the data connection is added to submit your form to a central location, you do not have to worry about users saving the form data in multiple locations.

In some situations, you may have a single form template that you want to make available in multiple site collections. In this case, you would choose to upload your template as an Administrator-Approved form template via the Central Administration site. From there, form templates can be activated to site collections from one central location. This method is also the only supported choice for advanced form templates containing custom code or highly complex data connections. In the second Try it Out of this section, you walk through the process of uploading a form template to the Central Administration site and activating it out to a site collection.

Try It Out **Publish a Form Template as a Content Type**

You now know how to publish a form template directly to a SharePoint document library. The next step to look at is the process for creating a content type by publishing a form template. For this example, you use the same form created in the previous section for Feedback. However, you open it in Design view and choose a different publishing location and type. You will publish the form template as a content type so that you can deploy it to multiple sites in the site collection.

1. Open the Feedback Form template in Design mode from the local version you saved on your computer.

2. From the Design Tasks pane, select Publish Form Template.

3. Select To a SharePoint Server, with or without InfoPath Forms Services as the destination type.

4. Click the Next button.

5. Enter the URL of your Corporate Intranet portal (such as http://servername).

6. Select the check box to Enable This Form to Be Filled Out by Using a Browser.

7. Select Site Content Type (Advanced).

8. Click the Next button.

9. Select the Create a New Content Type option, as shown in Figure 10-43.

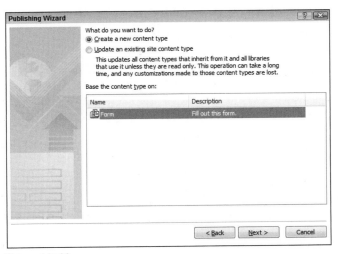

Figure 10-43

10. Click the Next button.

11. For the name of the content type, specify **Employee Feedback Forms** and enter the following for the description:

> **This content type is an electronic form for collecting feedback from employees on various communication methods and promotions. All content submitted using this content type will be directed to the communications site.**

12. Click the Next button.

13. Click the Browse button to specify a location where the form template can be stored within the site collection.

14. Select the Form Templates document library and click the Open button.

15. Enter the name in the File name field as **employeefeedback.xsn**.

16. Click the Save button.

17. Click the Next button.

18. Verify that the appropriate fields have been selected to be promoted as columns to document libraries within the site collection, and click the Next button.

19. Click the Publish button. You receive a confirmation indicating that the form template was successfully published.

20. Click the Close button to complete the wizard.

How It Works

After reviewing the number of responses you receive from the feedback form, you notice that not enough people were coming to the site to complete the form. Therefore, you decide it makes more sense to push the form template out to other sites in the site collection because quite often users are more inclined to complete a form from their own workspace rather than take the time to visit other workspaces. One of the primary advantages of a content type is being able to add a single content type to multiple locations throughout a site collection. Using the previously explored method of publishing directly to a document library, the form template could only be pushed out and associated with a single library. There would be no way to add it to other libraries without republishing it manually in a series of redundant and unrelated processes. Because the submit and receive data connections are still associated with the form, even if the template is added to a document library in another site, completed forms will still be submitted directly to the specified document library on the communications team site.

To add the InfoPath content type to a document library on other sites, you use the same process as was explored in Chapter 4. Similarly, you can apply all the same features available to content types to this form template including the association of workflow processes, information policies, as well as additional site columns.

Try It Out   Publish a Form Template as an Administrator-Approved Template

You may have a single form template that you are required to share with users across multiple site collections or a form template that was created using advanced development techniques and custom code. For each of these situations, you are required to use the Administrator-Approved Upload technique as described in this example. The example shows how to publish a form template to an administrative area of the portal so that it can be activated and published out to multiple site collections. You typically use this method for more complex forms that contain custom code, advanced functionality, or must be created as content types across more than one site collection. In this example, you use one of the sample forms available with InfoPath to keep things simple, but recognize that this is the method most commonly used for custom-developed complex forms.

1. Open the InfoPath application.

2. From the Getting Started window, select Customize a Sample from the Design a Form action group.

3. Select the Sample – Expense report template.

4. From the Form Tasks action list, select Design This Form.

5. Select Publish Form Template from the Design Tasks pane. A window may appear advising you to save the form template. If you do, click OK to continue.

6. Save the file locally to the folder containing all resource files for this chapter. Name the file **expenseformtemplate.xsn**. Once you save the form, the publishing wizard window appears.

7. Select To a SharePoint Server with or without InfoPath Forms Services as the destination type.

8. Click the Next button.

9. Enter the URL of your Corporate Intranet portal.

10. Click the Next button.

11. Select the Administrator-Approved Form Template (Advanced) option, as shown in Figure 10-44.

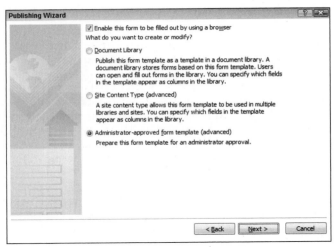

Figure 10-44

12. Click the Next button.

13. You are now required to save the file to a location from where an administrator can upload it. Typically you would place the form template on the server or in a network location both you and the administrator have access to. Save a copy of the form template to the Chapter Resources folder using the name **ExpenseForm.xsn**.

14. Click the Next button.

15. Select any fields from the form that you want displayed in document libraries as columns and click the Next button.

16. Click the Publish button. You receive a confirmation indicating that the form template was successfully published.

17. Click the Close button to complete the wizard.

18. Go to the Central Administration site for your SharePoint Server.

19. Select the Application Management tab.

20. Click the Upload Form Template link from the InfoPath Forms Services group, as shown in Figure 10-45. The form upload window appears.

Figure 10-45

21. Browse to the location where you saved the ExpenseForm.xsn template in step 13. Select the form and click Open. You are returned to the form upload window.

22. Click the Upload button. You receive a success message.

23. Click the OK button.

24. The final step in this process is to activate the form template out to a site collection. Hover your cursor over the form's name in the list of form templates and select Activate to Site Collection from the drop-down menu as shown in Figure 10-46.

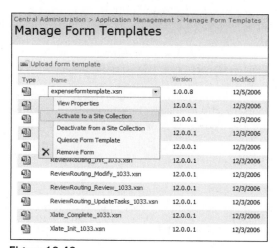

Figure 10-46

25. Select your Corporate Intranet site collection as the Activation Location. You may need to change the default value to do this.

26. Click the OK button.

How It Works

In this exercise, to publish the form template, you first have to save it locally as is required for publishing all form templates. Next, you define where you want to publish the template. You then had to save the form a second time. The most common reason for this second save is that in many organizations, the person creating the form is not necessarily the person with the rights to perform the upload operation. Instead, they will save the form template to a shared location on the network where a server farm administrator can access the form and complete the operation.

Once you complete the Publishing Wizard, the form is prepped for upload. However, the upload has to take place from the SharePoint Central Administration site. From there, the form template is uploaded from the shared location. Once it is uploaded, it was then activated out to the site collections where you intend to use the form. The activation process creates a content type within the site collection using the Microsoft Office InfoPath group name.

Summary

This chapter discussed how a Microsoft Office application for creating electronic forms can be used and integrated with SharePoint using InfoPath Forms Services.

You looked at how InfoPath has evolved since its last release, including support for browser editing and viewing of form data as well as enhanced support for external data connections and controls.

You learned about the various design level tasks and elements associated with an InfoPath form including its layout, controls, data source, design check, and publishing functions. You saw some of the standard controls you can add to a form, as well as what some of the publishing possibilities are for a form template.

This chapter offered several step-by-step examples showing how to create form templates and use them within SharePoint.

After reading this chapter, you should feel comfortable planning, designing, and developing InfoPath form templates that can map directly to specific business activities within your organization and improve the efficiency and effectiveness in how information is collected from users.

Exercises

1. Explain the reasons why you would decide to create a form that supports editing in the browser.

2. Explain the different scenarios by which you can publish a form template.

3. Describe a template part.

4. Explain the difference between a control and a data source element.

5. True or False. InfoPath cannot submit to a data connection. It can only retrieve information.

Working with Excel Services

Microsoft Excel is a familiar application that many companies use for data entry and reporting. However, Excel was originally designed for desktop use, and so it is difficult to share a spreadsheet among several users who are collaborating on a project. Typically, the owner of the spreadsheet places it in a shared folder on a file server so that other team members can retrieve, modify, and update it. While this approach can work, it requires a great deal of diligence to maintain the spreadsheet's integrity; the owner has no way to prevent a user from intentionally or accidentally changing a formula or a key parameter in the spreadsheet, or protect parameters that are based on confidential or highly sensitive data. A work-around is to hide formulas by saving documents in alternate formats, such as JPEG or HTML, which restricts access to formulas but prevents users from interacting with reports and performing simple what-if type scenarios. SharePoint 2007 addresses this issue by introducing Excel Services, a feature that enables spreadsheet collaboration in ways that are much more secure and robust than simple file sharing.

This chapter reviews the following:

- ❑ How to share information within organizations using Excel
- ❑ How to access and interact with Excel reports via the browser using Excel Services
- ❑ What the process is for publishing Excel workbooks to SharePoint
- ❑ How to create a data connection file and upload it to SharePoint
- ❑ How to use key performance indicators in SharePoint
- ❑ How to create interactive Dashboards using Excel Services

After reading this chapter, you should feel comfortable with what Excel Services is and how it may benefit your organization. You should know the steps for creating your own reporting site for the sharing of business reports in a manner that makes important information available to users while still protecting any confidential details related to formulas or calculations.

Excel Services Overview

Excel Services allows you to publish spreadsheets and workbooks to a server in a controlled environment, where users can access calculated data and reports directly from the browser, but where you can set controls to limit the data users can see and safeguard confidential elements, such as formulas or connection details. This means users don't have to have the Excel application on their computer to view, create, and author spreadsheets.

Users can also view a *snapshot* of the file in Excel, which protects source file and formulas but limits the user to a read-only view of the calculated data. Excel Services also lets users interact with pivot table reports; reports have filtering and sorting functions so users can generate a view to meet their requirements. For example, rather than creating individual reports for each project manager on the progress of your individual projects, you can create a single project status report, where users can filter results based on time, project manager, and project name. This means you can serve a greater audience with a single report, while still providing a useful tool to project managers so they can generate reports of their own.

This section reviews the various features of Excel Services including a special template called the *Report Center* that contains many of the elements available in SharePoint to create an interactive reporting environment.

The Report Center

SharePoint 2007 has a built-in site template containing many of the common elements that an organization might use to create a centralized reporting site called the *Report Center*. Using preconfigured elements saves you time as you build your organization's reporting environment. In this section, you learn the components that make up this site template and the steps for creating a centralized reporting portal site for your organization. The Report Center contains the following elements by default:

❑ **Instructional Information**: These are instructions in the Web Parts of the home page of the site. To help you get started, this information tells you how to effectively use the elements available in the Report Center template.

❑ **Key Performance Indicators (KPIs):** Many organizations set goals for certain operational or strategic aspects of the business and then track progress against them using real-time information. The Report Center template features a KPI list containing sample content and a Web Part to display graphically the current status of the organization at meeting those goals. KPIs can be created based on manual information or by connecting to another information system using a data connection.

❑ **Sample Dashboard and Associated Data:** A *Dashboard* is a web page containing multiple reports and graphical indicators in an easy-to-consume format. Dashboards can combine all the key reporting elements available in SharePoint.

❑ **Sample Reports:** The Report Center contains a sample Excel document to demonstrate how a single spreadsheet can be viewed via the browser as a single report or within Web Parts in a Dashboard. The sample report contains a *pivot table*, which is a tabular report that allows for a high level of interaction by containing filter fields and customizable fields allowing users to drag, drop, and filter information on the fly.

❑   **Data Connection Library:** Sometimes reports can feature information from other information systems such as a database. These information systems are called *data sources*. Using Excel 2007, users can connect to these data sources to include information directly in their spreadsheets. Rather than having every user create his own data connection for each file for which he wants to include information from a data source, a data connection library can be used as a central repository for data connection files.

The five Try It Outs in this section walk you through using the Report Center. First, you create a performance reporting site using the Report Center template that acts as the base location for many of the examples you complete in this chapter. Once you create the Report Center, it's critical that you add it to the Trusted File Locations of the SharePoint environment, which you commonly do through the Shared Services Administration site. If you don't perform this step, users will be unable to access the site. In the third Try It Out, you see how an Excel workbook will display in the site and perform in the browser by viewing the workbook sample that is provided as part of the Report Center site. This exercise shows that you can have users view and manipulate data in Read-Only mode without them seeing sensitive information or formulas. Next, you edit data in the sample spreadsheet using Excel and view these changes in the browser with versioning to see how History is affected. Only a select group of users in your environment will have Edit access to the workbooks, while the majority of users will be limited to either Read-Only access of copies of the workbooks, snapshots, or strictly viewing the files through the browser. For the final Try It Out, you see the various ways in which users with Read or View access to the files can interact with the workbooks.

Try It Out   Create a Report Center Site

In this example, you create a new site within a site collection. This becomes your central location for shared corporate reports. Although this site will contain many elements that are useful for your organization as a dynamic reporting portal, it will require a significant amount of customization and configuration before you can mold it to your corporate needs.

> *Whenever a site collection is created from the Collaboration portal site template, it contains a Report Center site template already. In this example, your new site becomes something on which you build future exercises. You can create this site within any site collection. For more information on site templates, see Chapter 8.*

For this exercise, you give your site unique permissions. Once you have properly configured your site, you may want to give others access to it. Also given the nature of this site and the type of content that you will make available, you will likely want to manage permissions independent of all other primary intranet sites.

1.   From the home page of your Corporate Intranet site, select Site Actions ➪ Create Site.

2.   Give your site a title. For this example, type **Performance** for the title.

3.   Enter a description for your site. For this example, enter the following:

> **Central performance reporting site.**

4.   Name the URL for the site. For this example, use **performance**.

5.   For the Template selection, click the Enterprise tab and select Report Center.

6. For Permissions, select Unique Permissions until everything is configured.

7. For Navigation Inheritance, select Yes.

8. Click the Create button.

9. Click the OK button to accept the default site groups for the site. You are redirected to a new site, as shown in Figure 11-1.

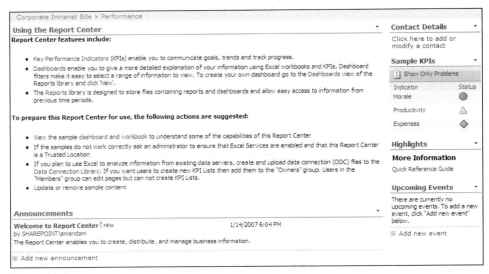

Figure 11-1

How It Works

The site will contain instructional information on how you can get started, as well as sample reports and Dashboards that you can extend or review for ideas on presenting information. Before users can access reports, such as the sample Dashboard, you need to add the site to the Trusted File Locations in the Central Excel Services settings — the subject of the next Try It Out. Otherwise, users may receive "access denied" errors when they click Sample from the Quick Launch bar, as shown in Figure 11-2.

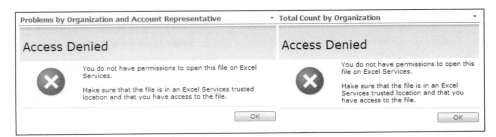

Figure 11-2

Try It Out   Add Report Center to Trusted File Location

In this example, you add the site you created in the last Try It Out to the Trusted File Locations of the SharePoint Server Farm for Excel Services. You cannot load or access an Excel Services workbook in the browser unless you store it in a location that the system trusts. When specifying a location, you may select from one of the following choices:

❑   **Windows SharePoint Services Location**: Select this option when the location is a SharePoint site.

❑   **File Share**: Select this option if the location is a shared file folder location on your network.

❑   **Web Server Address**: Select this option if the location is a web address other than a SharePoint site.

When you specify the address of your SharePoint site, you can list the exact URL of your Performance site, but for this example you list the top-level site of the site collection, which allows you to create more Excel Services-based sites within the site collection in the future and have it automatically recognized as a trusted location.

1.   From the Central Administration site of your SharePoint environment, click the name of the Shared Services Administration site that controls your settings for Excel Services.

2.   Select Trusted File Locations from the Excel Services Settings group.

3.   Click the Add Trusted File Location button from the toolbar.

4.   Enter the address of your site collection into the Address field.

5.   For Location Type, select Windows SharePoint Services.

6.   Select the check box to trust children. This ensures that all future sites you add to this site collection are automatically added to the trusted sites location.

7.   For workbook properties, change the maximum supported size to 8. This helps you manage the server's overall performance by limiting the size of the workbooks that are added. You can identify the optimal size based on your server farm's configuration and available resources, as well as by consulting with business users to determine the average size of a workbook.

8.   Click the OK button.

How It Works

When you return to your performance site now and select the Sample link from the Quick Launch bar, the sample Dashboard should display as shown in Figure 11-3. If not, you may need to close any active browser sessions that are connected to the site and reload the site in a new browser session to refresh any security settings.

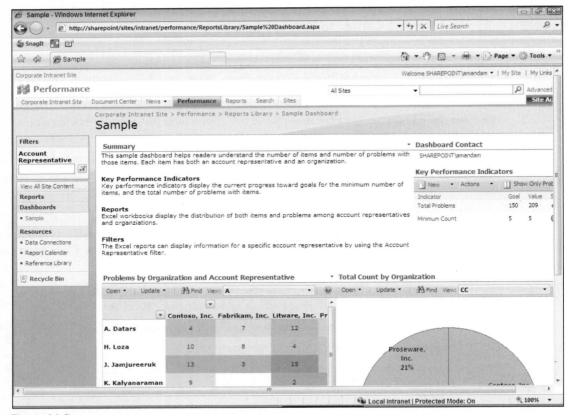

Figure 11-3

Try It Out   Interact with Excel Services Workbook

In this example, you load a sample workbook from the sample Reports document library for the performance site. Even if you have the Excel client application installed, the sample automatically loads in the browser. You see the report in a series of views, each of which are individual sheets in the workbook; you can switch between views by selecting a different view in a drop-down menu. You can update data to retrieve the latest workbook version and recalculate values available since the last time the owner uploaded the report. Multiple simultaneous launches of the same reports do not affect server performance because the server will cache much of the data. Users can filter or change the sort order of the data so they can create pivot-type reports. Pivot reports have a larger amount of data and allow users to drill down to details.

1. Notice that the Quick Launch bar of a site created from the Report Center site template is slightly different than the other standard site templates. Click the Reports heading.

2. Click the SampleWorkbook file in the library that exists when the site is created from the Report Center template. The workbook opens in the browser displaying the default view of the report as shown in Figure 11-4.

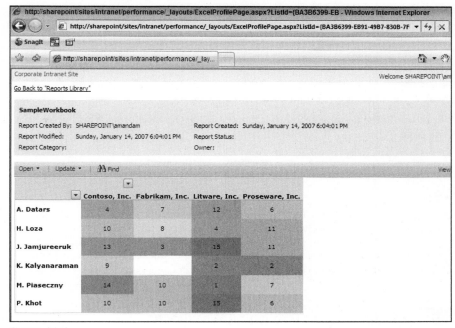

Figure 11-4

3. Expand the Update menu item to view the available actions for this workbook. From this area, you can update any connections or recalculate the figures that are in the workbook.

4. From the row above the company names, select the down arrow to expand the Filter and Sort menu. Select the Filter menu item. The Filter dialog box appears, as shown in Figure 11-5.

Figure 11-5

5. Unselect the check box next to Select All. This clears all other check boxes next to the company names. Select the check boxes for only Contoso, Inc. and Fabrikam, Inc.

6. Click the OK button. The report only displays information for each of the companies that you selected in step 5.

7. From the View drop-down menu on the right, select CC. The report once again changes to display a pie chart report from the same workbook.

8. To return to the document library, click the Go Back to Reports Library link at the top left of the page.

How It Works

You'll notice that you cannot view formulas or specific connection details and that data is presented in a read-only format. Users with Reader rights can open a complete copy of the spreadsheet in Excel on their local drive to make changes, but the source file remains unaffected. If a user has rights beyond View Item, he or she can also open the file using the client application either as the complete workbook or a snapshot. Users with rights to edit the file can do so in Excel within SharePoint as well as change formulas.

Try It Out   Edit an Existing Publishing Workbook

For this exercise, you walk through the steps of editing the sample workbook that was published as a major version to a Reports Library. As discussed in Chapter 3, when a file is published as a major version, it becomes available to all users of a site. Changes can be made to the file and then republished. You will make changes to data in the published sample spreadsheet using Excel and then view these changes in the browser. To demonstrate the versioning settings of the library, you will restore the file to its original version.

1. From the home page of your performance site, select View All Site Content from the Quick Launch bar.

2. Select the Reports Library.

3. Hover your mouse over the SampleWorkbook document to expose the contextual menu and select the Edit in Microsoft Office Excel option.

4. If you receive a warning that the file may not be safe, select the OK button. Your worksheet opens with the various views seen through the browser in Figure 11-3, consolidated on a single page.

5. Review the values shown in the cell range of A1:E8, as shown in Figure 11-6. The values you receive will likely be different than those shown in the figure.

6. Scroll over to Column S. If you select a cell such as S2 in this column, you notice that you can see the formula that drives the collection of data for the workbook. The Rand() function returns a random integer, and the formula converts the integer to a number by multiplying it by 100. The returned value is then rounded to a specific number of digits. Change the formula to something different such as:

```
=ROUND(RAND()*100,4)
```

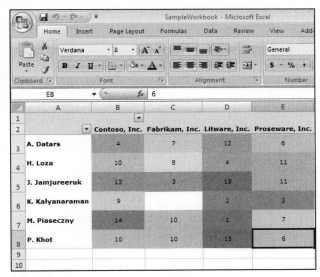

Figure 11-6

7. Copy the formula down to each of the cells in the column by dragging the bottom-right corner of the selection box over those cells, as shown in Figure 11-7.

P	Q	R	S	T
1		2	3	4
Contoso, Inc.	M. Piaseczny	9	3.8778	
Contoso, Inc.	H. Loza	12	75.151	
Contoso, Inc.	A. Datars	52	30.0942	
Contoso, Inc.	P. Khot	18	51.4693	
Contoso, Inc.	K. Kalyanaraman	90	24.6364	
Contoso, Inc.	M. Piaseczny	32	81.0658	
Contoso, Inc.	H. Loza	71	41.5928	
Contoso, Inc.	A. Datars	4	86.9523	
Contoso, Inc.	J. Jamjureeruk	32	40.0717	
Contoso, Inc.	P. Khot	1	97.8621	
Contoso, Inc.	M. Piaseczny	89	62.2056	
Contoso, Inc.	J. Jamjureeruk	0	2.9393	
Contoso, Inc.	A. Datars	41	98.2189	
Litware, Inc.	K. Kalyanaraman	3	4.9506	
Litware, Inc.	J. Jamjureeruk	21	99.3435	
Litware, Inc.	M. Piaseczny	77	88.3634	
Litware, Inc.	A. Datars	35	82.3157	
Litware, Inc.	H. Loza	76	40.2391	
Litware, Inc.	P. Khot	7	25.8526	
Litware, Inc.	P. Khot	46	85.1606	
Litware, Inc.	H. Loza	69	93.6682	
Litware, Inc.	J. Jamjureeruk	98	4	

Figure 11-7

8. Repeat the same process for Column R.

9. Select the Data tab in the Excel Ribbon.

10. Click the Refresh All button. The data should update and the values will be different than those in step 5. See Figure 11-8 for an example.

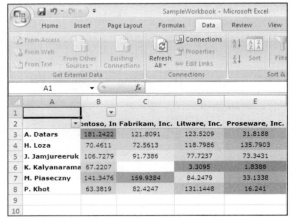

Figure 11-8

11. Select the down arrow of the Filter and Sort control just below the B column label. Unselect Litware, Inc. as a value to display in the report and click the OK button on the filter options box.

12. Close the document.

13. You are prompted to save your changes. Select the Yes button.

14. Click the name of the document. The spreadsheet opens in the browser showing the data with four decimal places as changed upon your edits. Also notice that the Litware, Inc. values are still filtered out of the report.

15. Click the Go Back to "Reports Library" link.

16. Hover your mouse over the SampleWorkbook document to expose the contextual menu. Select the Version History item from the menu.

17. Hover your mouse over Version 0.1 to expose the contextual menu and click Restore. The original version of your document is restored. If you return to the document library and click the workbook, you should see the workbook in its original format showing items rounded off with no decimal places. You will also see that Litware, Inc. is displayed again by default when the report loads.

For more on viewing a document's history, see Chapter 3.

When reviewing the version history of the document, you'll notice that the document is still in draft mode and has not been published as a major version. To publish the document, you must select Publish a Major Version from the contextual menu of the report from within the document library. This makes the document available for other users who have limited rights such as Read or View.

Try It Out   **View a Snapshot of a Report in Excel**

In this Try It Out, you add a new user to the site with the View Only right and complete the exercise logged in to the site as that user. Members with the View Only right can view pages and documents but only via the browser or as a snapshot. As mentioned earlier, a snapshot is a subset of the original workbook that allows limited-rights users to interact with the workbook without giving them access to formulas or data connections.

Before you can do these steps, you need to do the following:

❑   Make sure you publish the SampleWorkbook document as a major version by selecting the Publish as Major Version option from the document's contextual menu.

❑   Add a test user to the site by assigning them the View Only right under the Site Permissions settings.

❑   Sign in as the test user by selecting Sign In as Different User from the Welcome menu.

For more information on adding a user to a SharePoint site and signing in a different user, see the appropriate Try It Out sections in Chapter 9.

In this exercise, you first open a snapshot of the sample workbook from within the report itself and then open it directly from the library. This approach is useful if a limited-access user can open the actual workbook, but wants to perform what-if analysis. You then log in to the performance site as a user with limited access. For users with the View Only option, the only way to access reports is through the server-rendered versions or Excel Snapshots. These users can access the data but not the logic or calculations that are going on in the background to present the data.

1.   From the home page of your performance site, click the Reports link from the Quick Launch bar.

2.   Hover your mouse over the SampleWorkbook document to expose the contextual menu.

3.   Select Snapshot in Excel.

4.   You may receive a security warning asking you to confirm you trust the location. Click the OK button to continue loading the application. The various views of the report open in Excel as separate sheets.

5.   Enter a value of **100** into cell B3. The cell updates. However, if you try to save the document, you receive a warning that the document is only open as a read-only document. You can optionally save a copy of the document locally; however, you cannot save the document back to the server.

6.   Close the document without saving changes.

How It Works

You notice that when you select to view the snapshot of the document, a browser-based version of the spreadsheet opens as well. From the browser you have the ability to refresh data connections, filter data, and open a snapshot from that location as well.

To complete the remaining exercises in this chapter, make sure you log back in to the performance site as yourself rather than the limited access user from this example.

Publishing a Workbook to SharePoint

So far, you've looked at ways you can interact with existing workbooks that had been added to your performance site as sample data. Now, it's time to publish your own workbooks to a SharePoint site. You have two ways to publish a workbook:

❏ Uploading the workbook using the upload methods in a SharePoint document library. In cases where you need to publish the work of a colleague or someone outside the company, this is more appropriate.

❏ Publishing the workbook directly from Excel. This is usually more efficient to do as part of your creation processes.

In the next couple of exercises, you get a chance perform both of these methods. For this first method, shown in the first Try It Out, you want others to access the data of a document but not the calculations or connection details. You upload the workbook to the Report Center, but once it is uploaded, you can restrict access to View-Only. In the second Try It Out, you publish directly from Excel to the SharePoint site. This approach may be more realistic for scenarios where you are creating the document in Excel and want to make it available to others in the organization immediately.

Try It Out   **Upload a Workbook to a Document Library**

As the SharePoint manager for your company, you receive a request from the company's accountant to publish financial projections to the Corporate Performance portal so that employees can stay up-to-date on goals and objectives for the next five years, which are expected to be critical for growth in the global marketplace. You upload the report using the same procedure for adding a document to a document library that you explored in Chapter 3, during which you are prompted to fill in content that's associated with the Report content type. This information is displayed to users in the default view of the library.

Once you upload the document, you set permissions so that all site visitors have the View Item right, which allows users to view the document in the browser or a report snapshot in Excel. For users to view the document, you need to publish it as a major version. By default, the Reports Library has major and minor versioning enabled. Therefore, the majority of users will not be able to see the document in the library while it is in draft mode or saved as a minor version. When you publish the report as a major version, it would be available to all users.

1.   From the Reports Library of your performance site, select the Upload button from the toolbar.

2. Browse to the location of the resource materials for this chapter (www.wrox.com) and select the file titled 5-year financial plan.xlsx.

3. Click the OK button.

4. Ensure that Report is selected as the Content Type.

5. Enter a title and description for the document. For this example, enter **5-year financial plan** and the following for description:

This report highlights our organization's goals and objectives for the next five years.

---

6. Select the check box to save to report history.

7. Enter your own name for the report owner. In a real-life scenario, you would likely select the Accountant as the owner because this is the person whom users would contact if they had any questions related to the report.

8. Select Category 1 for the Report Category. You can customize this column to suit your organization's specific categories using the same method for updating any standard list column, as shown in Chapter 4.

9. For Report Status, select Preliminary.

10. Click the OK button. You are returned to the Reports Library.

11. Hover your mouse over the document and select Manage Permissions from the document's contextual menu.

12. Select Actions ➪ Edit Permissions. A dialog box appears, click the OK button to continue.

13. Select the Performance Members and Performance Visitors groups, and select Actions ➪ Edit User Permissions.

14. Select the View Only right from the list of permissions, and click the OK button.

15. Return to the Reports Library and select Publish a Major Version from the document's contextual menu. You can add comments to the document to describe the current version and click the OK button.

16. Click the name of the document (in this case, 5-year financial plan.xlsx) to open the report.

How It Works

The document opens in the browser, as shown in Figure 11-9. Users can access the data of a document but not the calculations or connection details.

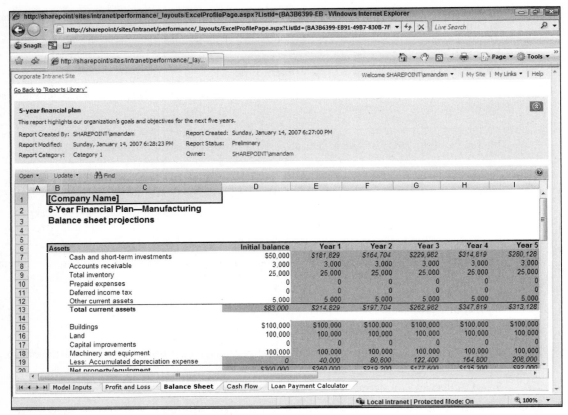

Figure 11-9

Try It Out	**Publish a Workbook from Excel**

You have just finished creating a pivot table report outlining performance on a recent project that your team has completed. You want to publish a chart from the workbook to your performance site to share the information with others. Because you have the document saved on your computer, you will publish the document directly from the application. During this process, you opt to publish the document to an Excel Services location. You do this by selecting the Excel Services option from the Server tab of the Office Button menu.

From the Excel Service Options menu, you can select what information is published to the Reports Library. Because you are interested in sharing only the chart information from the server, you select only that sheet from the list of available sheets. All other sheets are still accessible for the Chart view, but those sheets are not accessible via Excel Services. You publish a major version to ensure that the document is available to other users of the site.

1. Open the file Project Performance.xls from the resources associated with this chapter (see www.wrox.com).

2. Click the Office Button to expose the contextual menu.

3. Click Publish ➪ Excel Services.

4. Click the Excel Services Options button. The Excel Services Options dialog box appears as shown in Figure 11-10.

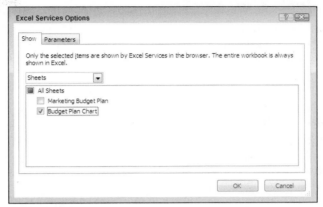

Figure 11-10

5. From the Show drop-down menu, select Sheets and select only the Budget Plan Chart sheet.

6. Click the OK button.

7. For the file name, and enter the URL of your performance site.

8. Select the Reports Library.

9. Save your report in the library, keeping the check box selected to Open in Excel Services.

10. For Document Type, ensure that Report is selected and click the OK button. The report is published to the document library and opens automatically, displaying the chart as shown in Figure 11-11.

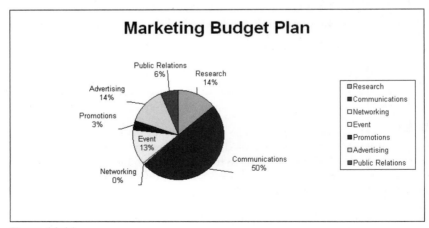

Figure 11-11

11. Return to the library and select Publish a Major Version from the document's contextual menu.

Excel Web Access Web Part

Sometimes you don't want to display an entire spreadsheet in a separate view, but a portion of it within a page that contains other information. You may do this to emphasize a certain aspect of the information, or you may need to show a larger picture of information and the spreadsheet data represents a single piece of a puzzle. To support those situations, you use Excel Services to expose the Excel Web Access Web Part.

Try It Out   Display a Workbook in a Web Part

Once you finish publishing your project's performance to the Reports Library (see the last several Try It Outs), the chart becomes available for others to see whenever they click the report. However, you want to add a Web Part to the performance site's main page so users can view the chart as soon as they visit the site. This helps your team follow its progress. In this example, you see how to display specific worksheets in an Excel Services Web Part. To do this, you must add an Excel Web Access Web Part to the main page of your performance website. You must then connect it to a workbook.

1. From the home page of your performance site, select Site Actions ➪ Edit Page.

2. From the top-left zone, select Add a Web Part.

3. Select the Excel Web Access Web Part from the Business Data group and click the Add button. The page refreshes to show an unconfigured Excel Web Access Web Part displayed in the top-left zone.

4. Click the link displayed in the Web Part to open the tool pane.

5. Click the icon to the right of the Workbook field to launch the File Selection box. Double-click the Reports Library and then double-click the Project Performance report.

6. From the Toolbar and Title Bar options, select None for the Type of Toolbar.

7. For the Toolbar Menu Command, unselect each of the four check boxes Display as Options.

8. Click Apply, and then OK to save the Web Part settings.

9. Publish the page to finalized changes and make the page available to all users.

How It Works

By selecting the icon next to the Workbook field, you can browse to the location where your workbook is stored. You can determine the level of interactivity that users can have with the workbook by selecting what toolbar displays and whether users have the ability to refresh collections or recalculate data. When you perform step 9, you are redirected to the published version of the page that looks similar to Figure 11-12.

Figure 11-12

Data Connections

Excel has built-in support for data connections so that reports can display real-time information from business applications and information systems. This support is available for workbooks that you publish to Excel Services as well. By generating reports directly from business data, you ensure that the information is up-to-date and accurate versus if the information was manually entered into a workbook. Entering manual information can be very time-consuming and in some cases may be prone to error. Reports created based on external data connections to key business applications mean you reduce the amount of effort users have to dedicate to produce reports and help minimize the requirement for manual entry which can sometimes lead to errors.

Although previously Microsoft Office applications such as Excel and InfoPath supported data connections, users had to create their own individual data connections for each report or document. Chapter 10 looked at the creation of InfoPath forms. This meant repeating work to maintain similar information.

Using SharePoint 2007, you can create a data connection library that has a shared repository of data connection files, which multiple reports and documents can share. If you need to make a change to the data source, you only need to update one file rather than every single report.

Although a data connection library is similar to all other document libraries in SharePoint, you don't manage documents; instead, the items are special files that contain information about specific business applications and how to connect to them to pull information. The next three Try It Outs show you how to navigate around data connections. For a data connection library to provide information to Excel Services documents as a trusted source, you must first add it as a trusted data connection source within the Shared Services Administration site, which you learn to do in the first Try It Out. Once you identify the data connection library as a trusted location, the second Try It Out shows you how users can upload their spreadsheets, reports, and business documents. In the last Try It Out, you see how to add an existing data connection file to a document.

Try It Out   Add a Trusted Data Connection Library

Before you can start using a central data connection library on your site for the storage of data connection files for your Excel Services documents, you must first add it as a trusted data connection library within Excel Services. In the previous Try It Outs, you created a reporting site for tracking performance of your organization. For this example, you add your performance site's data connection library as a trusted library within your Excel Services environment. You use the data connections from this library for a workbook in an upcoming example.

1. Go to the SharePoint Central Administration site for your SharePoint environment.

2. Click the link to the Shared Services Administration site from the side navigation.

3. From the Excel Services Settings group, select Trusted Data Connections Libraries.

4. Click the Add Trusted Data Connection Library button from the toolbar.

5. Enter the address of the data connection library from your performance site.

6. Enter the following for a description:

> **Location for storage of shared data connections related to documents stored within the performance reporting site.**

7. Click the OK button.

How It Works

The page refreshes with your data connection library URL listed as a trusted connection, as shown in Figure 11-13.

Because data connections from your library will be called from within Excel Services documents, it is important that a system administrator verifies and trusts them. This acts as a security measure to ensure that files do not call unsafe locations that may not be secure or may contain untrusted files or information.

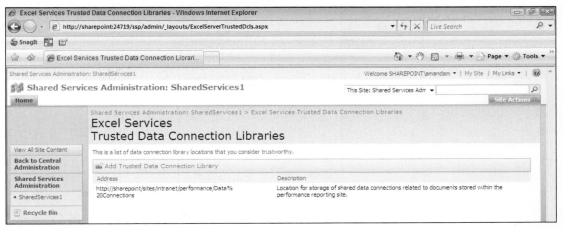

Figure 11-13

Try It Out	Upload a Data Connection File to SharePoint

In this exercise, you create an Access database that business users use to collect and track important sales information. Once created, you construct a data connection file for it from Excel using the standard Data Connection tab commands. You then save it in a local file system folder as a .UDC file. You can take that file and upload it to a data connection library in SharePoint so that it's available for use for other files in the future.

You start by creating a sales pipeline database using Access. Access is just one example of a data source that you can connect to via Excel. Other sources may include an Excel document, website, SQL database, Oracle database, or OLAP cube (OLAP stands for on-line analytical processing). The exercise went with an Access database because you more than likely have the templates to easily create such a source. Using the Data tab, you can add data connections to a workbook with just a few clicks and then add them to a local folder where you store other data connections. Of course, it's more efficient to have a central location where you can share data connection files with others, so you upload the connection file to a shared repository on the performance site.

1. Open Microsoft Office Access 2007.

2. From the Template Categories group, select Local Templates and then select the Sales Pipeline Database template.

3. Click the Create button. Your sales database will be created.

4. Close the Access application and open Microsoft Office Excel 2007.

5. Select the Data tab from within Excel.

6. From the Get External Data group of commands, select From Access to allow yourself to select an Access data source for information to display in your spreadsheet.

7. Browse to and select the Access database you created in the previous steps.

8. Select the customers table and click the OK button. The Import Data dialog box appears as shown in Figure 11-14.

Figure 11-14

9. Select the option to display a table of data within the existing worksheet using the settings and click the OK button.

10. Close the Excel document without saving your changes. Even though you are closing the workbook that you had created, the data connection file still exists in your My Data Sources folder with your Documents folder.

If you are running Microsoft Windows Vista, data connection files are stored in a My Data Sources folder that is automatically generated in your Documents folder as soon as you create your first data connection. If you are running Microsoft Windows XP, the same folder is created for you automatically in your My Documents folder.

11. Go to the home page of your performance site and select Data Connections from the Quick Launch bar.

12. Click the Upload button.

13. Browse to your My Data Sources folder and select the data connection file for your sales pipeline database and click the OK button.

14. For Content Type, select Office Data Connection File.

15. Enter **sales** and **customers** as keywords to help make the file easy for others to find.

16. Click the OK button.

17. Hover your mouse over the document to expose the file's contextual menu.

18. Select Approve/Reject.

19. Select Approved from the list of approval choices and click the OK button.

How It Works

Because of the Content Approval setting on the data connection library, you had to get the file approved before you could share it. This is the default setting for this library when created as part of the Report Center site. You can change content approval settings from the Version History settings of a library.

Try It Out   **Use a Data Connection File from a SharePoint Library**

In this example, you create a new spreadsheet and add an existing data connection from the centralized library of data connections. Because you have added this data connection library to your SharePoint server farm's trusted data connection libraries in the first Try It Out of this section, this location is a suitable place for storing all connections to key business applications.

1. Open Excel and launch a blank workbook.

2. Select the Data tab to access information from business applications.

3. From the Connections group, select the Connections button.

4. Because you started with a blank workbook, no existing connections are present. Instead you add a connection from the performance reporting site's data connection library. To do this, click the Add button.

5. Because the data connection you are looking for is probably not displayed on the list of connections that appears, select the Browse for More button.

6. Type the URL of your performance reporting site and click the Open button.

7. Select the Data Connections library from the list of content that is available on your site.

8. Select the Sales Pipeline Customers.odc file that is displayed in the library and click the Open button.

9. Click the Close button to close the Workbook Connections window. Now, when you click the Existing Connections window, you will be able to access your Sales Pipeline database.

How It Works

Your connection is now ready for use within your new spreadsheet. This approach encourages users to share data connection files. It minimizes the effort of creating reports and maximizes control over what data sources are used. If later you make changes to the Sales Pipeline database customer table, you will only need to update one file to maintain accurate information within the various reports.

Business Scorecards

Business scorecards evaluate how an organization is functioning across key performance areas or business targets that are based on current activities and other information. They show business goals as well as the real-time measurement of activities related to those goals. SharePoint 2007 supports performance indicators that use data from business activities and applications to give a clear visual indication of how an organization is progressing toward its goals. It accomplishes this using *KPI list templates* that generate the information and specialized Web Parts, which construct graphs of the generated information.

This section discusses how you can work with SharePoint to display KPIs for your organization using the KPI lists and Web Parts available in SharePoint. The KPI lists and Web Parts can be an important element in any reporting solution or Dashboard.

Creating a KPI List

SharePoint has several data sources that generate key performance indicators, including those in the following table:

Source	Description
SharePoint List	Generates performance information based on a team's day-to-day operations and activities. To generate a KPI from a SharePoint list, you first select the list, and then the view that contains the data. You must calculate the data for the KPI.
Excel Workbook	Because many organizations use Excel for reporting, it is a viable location for up-to-date information on performance. To create an indicator using Excel Services information, you point to a published workbook and select the cell location for the indicator value. This is useful for exporting information from business applications.
SQL Server Analysis Services 2005	Possibly the most robust and dynamic of all data sources. To create a KPI item based on SQL Analysis Services, you must have an existing data connection file within your data source that defines the connection.
Manually Entered Information	Sometimes, the information you want to use to generate a KPI may not be accessible via any digital file or information system and therefore you must enter values into KPI fields manually. This option is explored in the next Try it Out.

In the next two exercises, you create KPI information in a SharePoint list both manually and using SharePoint data. To complete your examples, you use the Sample KPI list that is created automatically with the performance site. You will notice that you can place information from multiple KPI types in a single list.

Try It Out   Create a KPI List Using Manually Entered Data

As the health and workplace safety officer, you track the overall safety of your company's work environment. You receive accident reports and log them in a KPI List item in SharePoint. At the end of each week, you manually update the list to show the current number of accidents versus the organization's monthly goal. Given the large size of your organization, the average number of accidents is two per month, and may vary from a worker slipping on a slick floor to a construction accident on a work site. Recently, the CEO announced a company-wide goal to completely eliminate workplace accidents, and you were asked to report progress to all employees. To do this, you create a KPI based on your manually entered information. Because your organization does not have an official application that tracks workplace accidents, you have no central tool from which to generate the information and instead must update it in the list item as workers report incidents to you via telephone, email, or fax.

1. From the home page of the performance site, click the View All Site Content link from the Quick Launch bar. You are redirected to the All Site Content page.

2. Select the Sample KPIs list. You are redirected to a view page for the KPI list.

3. Click the down arrow next to the New button and select the Indicator Using Manually Entered Information menu item. The Sample KPIs – New Item window appears, as shown in Figure 11-15.

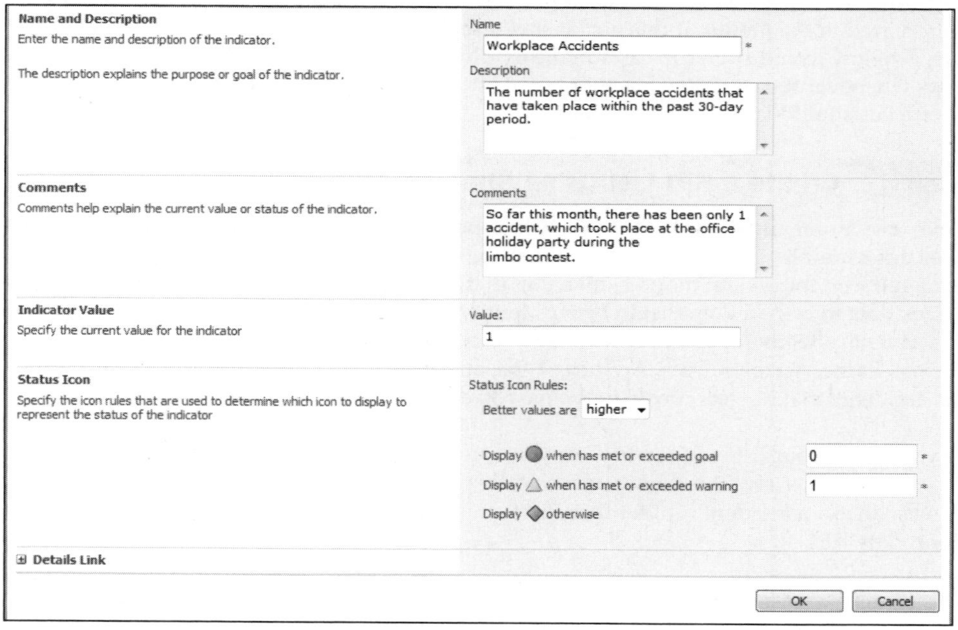

Figure 11-15

4. Type a name and description for your indicator. For this example, enter **Workplace Accidents Per Month** and enter the following for description:

> **The number of workplace accidents that have taken place within the past 30-day period.**

5. Enter comments to explain the current value or indicator status. For this example, enter the following:

> **So far this month, there has been only 1 accident, which took place at the office holiday party during the limbo contest.**

6. For Indicator Value, select 1, which is the current number of accidents for the month.

7. For Status Icon Rules, select that better results are lower because you prefer fewer accidents per month than the defined average target.

8. For the green icon, enter a value of **0** and for the yellow icon, enter a value of **1,** as shown in Figure 11-15.

9. Click the OK button.

How It Works

When you select 0 as the target goal in step 8, this reflects the company's goal to have no workplace accidents reported in the month. If this goal is met, users see a green icon. If a single workplace accident occurs, a yellow icon displays to caution the employees, but this icon isn't as critical as a red icon, which appears whenever the company has more than one workplace accident. This icon indicates that company officials should launch an investigation.

Try It Out   Create a KPI List Using SharePoint Data

You may encounter situations where it's more appropriate to track KPI information from a SharePoint list. For this example, you are again the workplace safety officer as in the last Try It Out; however, after seeing a red icon for several months, meaning that the company hasn't reached its goal of zero accidents, you track data in a SharePoint list to better identify trends in an effort to prevent future incidents. To track accidents effectively, you decide to create a custom list that contains the following: Accident ID, Employee Name, Accident Date, Accident Type, and Accident Details. In addition, you want a view to report accidents that have occurred in the past 30 days.

Once you create your list, you can replace your previous manual indicator with a new one that references your custom view. This view automatically reflects any new data so your KPI now remains up-to-date. As soon as an accident is older than 30 days, it no longer displays in the view and is no longer referenced by KPI.

1. From the performance site, select View All Site Content from the Quick Launch bar. You are redirected to the All Site Content page.

2. Select the Create button from the toolbar to be brought to site's Create page.

3. Select the option for a custom list for your accident report because no existing template contains the columns or views that you will require. You are redirected to the Custom List Creation page.

4. Enter a list name and description for the list name. For this example, enter **Workplace Accidents** and the following for description:

> **Detailed listing of all workplace accidents by date and type.**

5. Select not to display the list on the Quick Launch bar and click the Create button. Your Workplace Accidents list is created and you are redirected to it.

6. Select Settings ⇨ List Settings from the drop-down menu. You are redirected to the List Settings page.

7. Create the following columns using the column types and properties defined here:

Column Name	Column Type	Special Properties
Accident ID	Single Line of Text	Rename the existing title column to Accident ID.
Employee Name	Person or Group	None.
Accident Date	Date and Time	Select Date Only for format and set the default value to today's date because most accidents are reported immediately.
Accident Type	Choice	Enter the following as values for a drop-down: Construction Site Plant Machinery Transportation Forbidden Limbo Contests
Accident Details	Multiple Lines of Text	None.

8. Once you create these columns, you need to create a custom view on the list that displays the accidents that have occurred in the past 30 days. To do this, you must create a view with the following properties:

Property	Details
Name	Past 30 Days.
Default View	Yes.
View Audience	Public.
Filter	Show items when the Accident Date column is greater than or equal to [today] -30.
Totals	Display Count total for Accident ID.

9. To create some sample data to generate your KPI from, enter an item in the list for an accident involving an employee for the current date related to a limbo contest. Then enter an item in the list for an accident two months ago related to a construction site accident and a different employee.

When you save your second item, you'll likely notice that it does not appear in your view because the view selected will only show items for Past 30 Days.

10. Select View All Site Content from the Quick Launch bar.

11. Select Sample KPIs.

12. Hover your mouse over your Workplace Accidents Per Month indicator and click Delete from the drop-down menu.

13. Click the OK button on the pop-up message window to confirm you want to delete the indicator.

14. Select Indicator using data in a SharePoint list from the New Item menu.

15. Enter a name and description for the indicator. For this example, enter **Workplace Accidents Per Month** and enter the following for description:

> **The number of workplace accidents that have taken place within the past 30-day period.**

16. Click the icon to the right of the SharePoint List URL text box.

17. Select your Workplace Accidents List as the source list and select the Past 30 Days as the view.

18. For Value Calculation, select Number of List Items in the View.

19. For Status Icon Rules, select that Better Values Are Lower.

20. Enter **0** for the green icon and **1** for the yellow icon as you did in the previous Try It Out, and click the OK button. You are returned to the Sample KPI list where you see your new indicator has a yellow icon because your list contains one record for the current month.

21. Return to your list by clicking Workplace Accidents from the View All Site Content page and add a new record for the current date to reflect another workplace accident.

22. Return to the Sample KPIs list by selecting it from the Quick Launch bar to see that the indicator is now showing a red icon because of the latest accident, as seen in Figure 11-16.

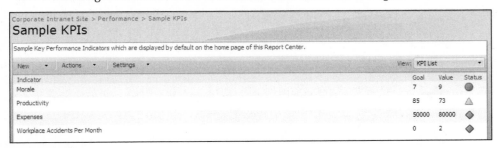

Figure 11-16

How It Works

By creating a custom list, you create automated updates to the KPI and increase the amount of detail you receive on specific workplace accidents. When users click the KPI item, they are redirected to a details page, such as the one shown in Figure 11-17. This shows the current status of indicator and the records it is referencing.

Figure 11-17

Using KPI Web Parts to Display Performance Data

Once an organization accumulates KPI data within lists, it can make this information available to various users using Web Parts. SharePoint 2007 offers two Web Parts for referencing and displaying KPI information:

Web Part	Description
Key Performance Indicators	Use this Web Part to display a listing of KPIs from a list.
KPI Details	Use this Web Part to display the details of a single KPI.

To demonstrate how both Web Parts operate, in the next Try It Out you add both to a new Dashboard page. This page displays KPI data and details relating to the Workplace Accidents KPI you created in the section "Creating a KPI List." A *Dashboard page* contains a report Web Part, such as KPIs and Excel Web Access, so users can access information on a specific indicator.

Try It Out   Create a Dashboard Page

In this example, you create a new Dashboard page to display the content you've created throughout this chapter. Using a combination of Web Parts (such as the Content Editor and related link), specific Dashboard Web Parts (such as the KPI Web Parts), and Excel Web Access Web Parts, you can create an interactive and dynamic Dashboard for others in your organization.

The example adds the two KPI Web Parts to the page. The Key Performance Indicators Web Part displays a simple listing of KPIs drawn directly from the Sample KPIs list. The KPI Details Web Part lets you select a single key performance indicator and display detail related to it, such as its current status and a link to the data from which it was generated. Using the Related Links Web Part, you can also point to supplementary materials or documents that may be of interest to the viewer. You finally add an Excel Web Access Chart Web Part.

1. From the main page of your Performance site, click the Dashboards link from the Quick Launch bar. You are taken to the Dashboards view of the Reports library.

2. Select New Item ⇨ Dashboard Page. You are brought to a Dashboard creation page as shown in Figure 11-18.

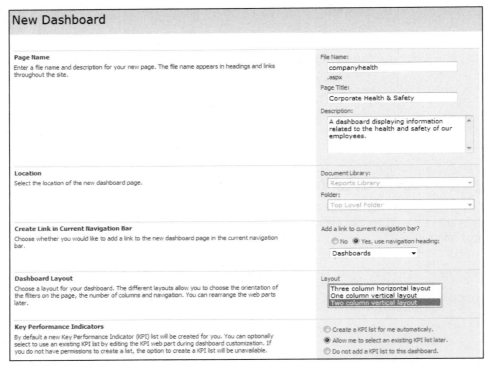

Figure 11-18

3. Enter a file name and page title for the Dashboard page. For this example, enter **companyhealth** and then **Corporate Health & Safety** for page title.

4. Enter a description for the Dashboard. For this example, enter the following text:

> **A dashboard displaying information related to the health and safety of our employees.**

5. Select the option to add a link to the current navigation bar under the Dashboards heading.

6. Select Two Column Vertical Layout for the page.

7. Because the KPI list and data are already created, select the Allow Me to Select an Existing KPI List Later option.

8. Click the OK button. You are redirected to an uncustomized version of your new Dashboard page containing many of the Web Parts commonly used in a Dashboard page, including KPI Web Parts and the Excel Access Web Parts. There is also a basic Content Editor Web Part to allow you to write a summary of the purpose of the Dashboard to viewers.

9. Click the Open the Tool Pane link in the Content Editor Web Part to enter the following text:

> **The goal of this Dashboard is to provide you with the information you need to monitor and review the number of workplace accidents that have taken place over the past 30 days as well as view trends related to overall health of the company based on its performance on projects and overall satisfaction levels of employees.**

10. Click the Open the Tool Pane link from within the Key Performance Indicators Web Part.

11. Select the icon next to the Indicator List text box. This allows you to select the Sample KPIs list from the site's lists and libraries.

12. From the Change Icon drop-down menu, select Checkmarks.

13. Change the title of the Web Part to **Overall Company Health and Safety** and click Apply, and then OK on the Web Part. The page displays the Sample KPIs in the Web Part.

14. Select Site Actions ➪ Edit Page from the toolbar to make additional changes.

15. Click Add a Web Part to the middle right zone.

16. Select the KPI Details Web Part, and click the Add button.

17. Click the Open the Tool Pane link for the KPI Details Web Part. The KPI Details pane appears as shown in Figure 11-19.

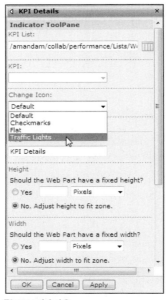

Figure 11-19

18.   Select the icon next to the KPI List field, and select the Sample KPI list.

19.   Select Workplace Accidents as the KPI to display and select Traffic Lights as the Icon Type to show within the Web Part.

20.   For the Web Part Title, enter **Workplace Accidents This Month**.

21.   Click Apply, and then OK on the Web Part to save changes. The page displays the details of your Workplace Accidents KPI.

22.   Next, you create a link to the Workplace Accidents list from the Related Information Web Part. Click the New Group item from the Web Part toolbar and enter **Performance Details** as the group name. Click OK to add your heading.

23.   Click New Link from the Web Part and enter **Workplace Accidents Details** as the title. Browse to the location of the workplace accidents list by clicking the Browse button to the right of the link URL field.

24.   For Style, select Bulleted Title.

25.   Click the OK button to save your link within the Web Part.

26.   Select the Click Here to Open tool pane link from the Excel Access Web Part [1] item on the page.

27.   Click the icon next to the Workbook field and browse to the Project Performance workbook you uploaded to the Reports Library in a previous example. Click the OK button to save your selection.

28.   Click Apply, and then OK on the Web Part.

29.   Drag the Web Part to the top-left zone underneath the summary.

30.   For the Web Part in the bottom-right zone, select Delete from the Edit menu. Click the OK button to confirm your action.

31.   Click the Publish button to save the changes to your Dashboard and make them available for others.

How It Works

The page looks similar to Figure 11-20 when you are complete.

Because the Dashboard gives a very visual consolidation of information, charts can often provide the update that users require in a format that is easy to follow.

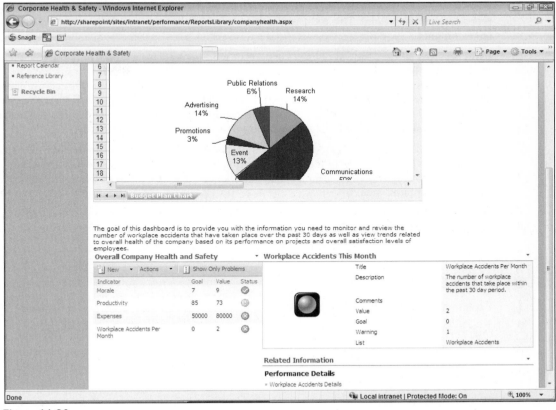

Figure 11-20

Summary

In this chapter, you discovered Excel Service's features in SharePoint Server including key performance indicators (KPIs) and Dashboard reporting. You also learned the following:

❑ Because companies have a large amount of data in spreadsheets, users are familiar with Excel as a client application and prefer to use it for reporting because it supports calculations, data connections, and interactivity.

❑ Companies need employees to access information related to performing duties and making decisions. However, they do not need to provide too much information to generate duplicate reports, or to release confidential or proprietary information. As workbooks begin to pile up on local drives, network shares, and even SharePoint sites, greater risks appear related to an organization's ability to achieve these goals.

❑   Excel Services supports publishing business data stored in spreadsheets to a centralized repository on SharePoint. This reduces duplicate workbooks from emails or uncontrolled environments.

❑   Excel Services renders browser-based versions of workbooks. This exposes only the calculated data and not the formulas or calculations themselves, and controls the access users have to shared reports. These workbooks are stored in a central library where only a limited number of resources have Edit capabilities. Those with Read or View Only capabilities can view the information they need, interact with the report by filtering, sorting or refreshing details, and perform what-if analysis or advanced calculations without affecting the data's integrity.

❑   SharePoint's KPIs generate scorecard-type reports based on important business data. You can generate KPIs from a variety of locations including SQL Server Analysis Services, Excel, or even a SharePoint list. In some cases, it may also be beneficial to create a KPI based on manually tracked and entered data.

❑   You can use SharePoint's specialized Reporting Web Parts to create interactive Dashboards. These dashboards provide personalized information to business users and decision makers.

Exercises

1.   Explain three benefits to using Excel Services for your organization's data reporting needs.

2.   True or False. When a workbook is published to a Reports Library, no one can change it.

3.   Your manager informs you that whenever team members access the newly created Dashboard, they receive an access denied error message and cannot see the individual reports. What's the likely cause for this?

Working with the
Business Data Catalog

Although SharePoint is an excellent data repository, a typical company keeps much of its operational and historical data in other systems such as SAP, PeopleSoft, Oracle, and custom line-of-business (LOB) applications. These are often called *back-end systems*; they often run on mainframe or midrange computers and have been in place for many years. It would be impractical to re-engineer them to use SharePoint for data storage, but you need to extract their data for reports, KPIs (discussed in Chapter 11), and other aspects of SharePoint collaboration.

The *Business Data Catalog* (BDC) is a new SharePoint feature that enables users to access data from these other data sources via specialized Web Parts and in lists and libraries. Throughout this chapter, you find out:

❑ What the BDC is and how you can use it for organizations

❑ What various roles are associated with the BDC

❑ How to use the various BDC Web Parts to display business data on pages within a SharePoint site

❑ How to display and associate business data within a list

❑ How to manage and control access to business data within a BDC application

This chapter prepares a user who is responsible for displaying business data on the SharePoint site to interact with and expose the information he or she needs.

> Note that this chapter does not supply the information that a developer or data specialist requires to define the application for import into the Business Data Catalog or to develop custom applications that interact with the Business Data Catalog. You can find more information on those tasks, including samples, in the Microsoft Office SharePoint Server 2007 SDK located at msdn.microsoft.com.

Business Data Catalog Overview

Increasingly, organizations are under pressure to become more efficient, and part of this is enabling employees to make accelerated and accurate decisions based on business data. Complex schedules and initiatives require that workers spend less time looking for information and more time using it to effectively perform and complete tasks.

So far in this book, you've seen the various ways to input information into SharePoint and make it available to others. A business may have its information stored in places like SharePoint and file shares, as well as in business applications or databases. This data is very tightly tied to the business' core operations and can offer the greatest insight into an organization's true fiscal health. Therefore, a good way to improve a business process is to start with how it accesses its information and what business applications it uses to do this. This section discusses what the Business Data Catalog is and what some of the key roles related to its use and configuration are.

What Is the Business Data Catalog?

The BDC is a new shared service that enables users to access data from back-end business applications on their SharePoint sites via Web Parts, lists, search, or as part of their user profiles. While the BDC does not store the data directly, it defines business applications and supports the access of the content in real time via web services or database connections. In some cases, the BDC may feature complementary information to that which is stored in SharePoint. For example, an organization may use Active Directory for its authentication service and to store basic user profile information. However, the Human Resources central tracking database may contain much richer details, which you can store in user profiles and which would be highly useful for audience creation and personalization.

> *The basic concepts of Web Parts were introduced in Chapter 7 and user profiles in Chapter 9. You explore the topic of search in greater detail in Chapter 14.*

The Business Data Web Parts support the display and interaction of business information from those back-end systems, making it possible for users to view up-to-date information immediately from their working environment. These Web Parts allow users to search for information, drill down for more detailed information, or view predefined reports. Figure 12-1 demonstrates how a single web page can display information from an external system in a Business Data Web Part.

The Business Data column support makes it easier to associate documents and list items with global entities such as products, customers, and employees, which may be tracked in separate applications. In addition to mapping business data information to documents and list items, the BDC lets you map business data information to user profile properties. This allows organizations to connect their user profile store to business applications that contain richer and more relevant data related to employees. In doing so, organizations improve the personalization services available in SharePoint and reduce the information duplication or manual entry.

Consider an example of a guitar manufacturing company that is running SharePoint internally to track and store documents and content related to their business. They may also use a custom application for storing details related to their product line including each product's pricing, description, images, and specifications. Because this application is tightly integrated with the manufacturing process, it makes sense for the existing process to continue managing and updating that information. However, by using the BDC, users can view information about each product directly from SharePoint. This improves the overall product education level among employees and encourages a greater sense of self service related to finding information.

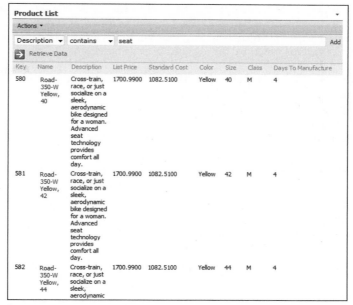

Figure 12-1

Primary Roles for the BDC

People filling key roles in an organization support and use the BDC. Although a single person may fill these roles, typically these roles are filled by specialists who excel in their own subject area. The following sections discuss the various roles and their purpose related to the BDC.

Application Definition Author

To make an application's data accessible via the BDC, a user who is familiar with the data source's structure and API must create an application definition file. An *application definition file* contains information about the system that is being connected to and describes how the data is structured and can be accessed. Typically, the person responsible for creating the file is called the *application definition author*, and he or she has skills similar to that of a database developer. While no programming is required, the user should be familiar with XML and database development tasks to properly define the application.

This book does not show how to create an application definition file; the Try It Outs assume that an application already exists in the BDC. To define applications illustrated in the Try It Outs, the authors used the AdventureWorksDW SQL Server 2005 Sample. You can find this sample as part of the Microsoft Office SharePoint Server 2007 SDK on the MSDN website (http://msdn2.microsoft.com/en-us/library/ms494876.aspx). If you want to complete the Try It Outs and do not have the required sample applications, you may instead opt to use information from your organization's own business applications.

Business Analyst or Site Manager

In most organizations, the *business analyst* or *site manager* is an expert in an organization's information systems and, more importantly, in preparing the SharePoint environment to support these needs. The analyst's general responsibilities are to recognize what features a system lacks and give requirements to a developer to fill those gaps. This person is also likely to know what experience a person filling a role must have to interface with the business's various applications. Depending on the organization, the business analyst has various functions during the life of a SharePoint site:

❑ **BDC and SharePoint site definition:** The business analyst often works with a SharePoint administrator (discussed a little later in this chapter) and application definition authors to identify and define an organization's needs concerning a specific business application. The business analyst identifies how to make the information available with the SharePoint environment to complement how users work and how they need to access business data.

❑ **Web Part configuration:** Once an application is defined in the BDC and displayed in SharePoint via Web Parts, columns, search, or user profile properties, the business analyst works with site managers to configure the system's Web Parts to support previously defined requirements.

❑ **Site management and maintenance:** Usually, the business analyst is also the same individual responsible for managing the SharePoint environment. Because the business Web Parts can display lists of data from the source application or individual records, the SharePoint site manager may connect multiple Web Parts on a single page. This allows users to essentially drill into the data so the information on the page changes as they select records in connected Web Parts.

❑ **Business data and SharePoint content integration:** The business analyst or SharePoint site manager may use columns from a list or library to look up business data in an application. This creates a tight bond between business data and SharePoint content, eliminates data duplication, and improves how users search and report on information.

Developer

When the various SharePoint features do not provide an organization the access and integration to the business application data it needs, a developer can build custom applications to interface with and extend the BDC features. Although custom development activities are beyond the scope of this book, you should understand that BDC features, though extensive, can be further expanded using custom development and applications.

Administrator

The SharePoint administrator is responsible for importing the application definition file and controlling access to the application and its entities. The administrator is also responsible for deploying any applications that developers create. Once the application definition file is imported and access is established, the information from the application becomes available throughout SharePoint sites for use in the Web Parts, search, and columns.

The introduction of this chapter discussed how the BDC may be used to connect to a Human Resources database to provide additional information to the user profile database. Once the HR database application file is defined, the administrator would import the definition file, and then configure the application as a secondary user profile property source.

Configuring a BDC Application

Before you can begin working with a BDC to solve your data-related problems, you need to configure an application. This involves first importing the application definition file into the SharePoint system so users can view specific information elements, known as *entities*, and interact with these items using predefined actions. An *entity* is a business data item that represents an aspect of the business's operations such as a customer, product, or supplier. A single application usually contains information about multiple entities.

You then create a*ctions*, which allow you to interact with your business application's information. You might include these actions in the application definition file before you import it into SharePoint, or you can add them at a later time; however, if you add an action after the import, you may need to reimport the application definition file.

Finally, you're ready to add users to the BDC so that they can use the application, and to assign them the appropriate permissions.

Importing the Application Definition File

As previously mentioned, an application definition author creates an application definition file. This user is someone who typically has skills similar to that of a database developer and possibly has some knowledge of the business application to which the business must connect. The application definition file controls the various entities, relationships, filters, and actions required to connect to the external system through the SharePoint application.

The BDC does not contain business data but instead defines the business data application so that users can connect to it to view and generate information. Once the author creates an application definition file, the administrator can import the file via the Shared Services Administration site of the SharePoint environment using the following process:

1. Go to your Shared Services Administration site, which is accessible from the left-hand navigation menu of your Central Administration site.

2. Click the Import Application Definition link from the Business Data Catalog section, as shown in Figure 12-2.

3. Browse to the location of your Application Definition file and click Import.

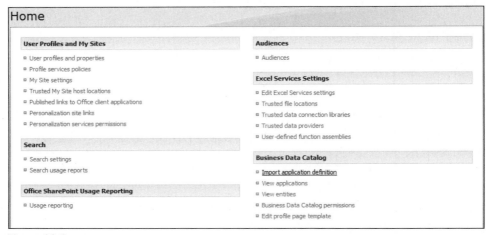

Figure 12-2

Viewing Entities

As mentioned before, an entity is a business data item that represents an aspect of the business's operations, such as a customer, product, or supplier, with a single application containing information about multiple entities. For example, a line-of-business application that tracks a company's products, prices, and sales would be a single application in the BDC. However, that application could have unique entities for the products, categories, customer sales, and sales personnel. Relationships may exist between entities, such as the one that exists between a sale and a product.

In an application, an entity is defined by *entity details*, which are all the properties the entity contains and the relationship an entity has with other entities.

Try It Out   View Entity Details

In this example, you will view details on an entity through the SharePoint interface. To do this, you visit the Shared Services Administration site of the portal because the BDC is a shared service. To view properties of a particular entity, such as permissions, filters, and relationships, you view the details of the application.

1. Go to the Shared Services Administration site.

2. Click the View Applications link from the Business Data Catalog section.

3. Click the application for which you want to view the entity information.

4. Hover your cursor over the Entity name and select View Entity, as shown in Figure 12-3.

5. From the details page of an entity you can view the properties, actions, filters, and relationships of the entity, as shown in Figure 12-4.

Figure 12-3

Figure 12-4

Understanding Actions

As mentioned earlier, you use actions to interact with your business application information via SharePoint's Web Parts and built-in components. You can use actions to launch other applications, such as web-based interfaces, details pages, or activities such as email or search. If you have a business application that stores information about your customers, you can have an action associated with the application that launches an email message to the customer whose information you are viewing or another action that launches a page containing all their orders. By default, a View Profile action exists for BDC applications, which launches a new page containing the Business Item Web Part and details about the specific item. This View Profile action could be used in your customer application as an easy method for looking up customer contact information via SharePoint.

If the application supports it, you can create custom actions to write information back to the source application. An example of this might be if a customer service representative added information about a customer support call from SharePoint to the customer's information in the business application. However, the actions may simply launch a URL that triggers a specific lookup or activity based on a parameter specified by the action. In the case of the customer service representative, they may select an action that shows a listing of all previous support calls from the customer.

You can add actions to an application definition file either before you import or afterward. If you do the latter, the administrator may need to delete the application's definition file from the BDC and reimport the updated version of the application definition file.

Application Permissions

Once you've configured the BDC, it's time to add users to it so they can begin using it. Also, for each application and its associated entities, you can set permissions to control how the user accesses the application and to manage properties related to it. The different levels of permission that you can assign to an application are listed as follows:

- ❑ **Edit:** Users can import application definitions and update or delete objects in an application or entity.
- ❑ **Execute:** Users can view instances of an entity that has finder methods.
- ❑ **Select in Clients:** Users can select an entity or object in a Web Part, column, or any other client.
- ❑ **Set Permissions:** Users can set permissions across all objects.

In the first of the two Try It Outs in this section, you learn how to add a new user to the BDC application. In the second Try It Out, you learn how to manage permissions on an entity.

| Try It Out | Add a User to an Application |

In this example, you add a new user to a BDC application, a process that is very similar to that of adding a user to a site (a topic we explored in Chapter 9). You specify the name and select the appropriate rights for the user and save your changes. Once you specify permissions, you must copy those rights down to the individual entities for that application.

1. Go to the Shared Services Administration site.

2. Click the View Applications link from the Business Data Catalog section. The Business Data Catalog Applications window appears.

3. Hover your cursor over the application name to expose the contextual menu and select Manage Permissions, as shown in Figure 12-5. The permissions for the application window appear.

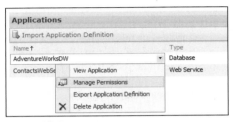

Figure 12-5

4. Click the Add Users/Groups button from the toolbar.

5. Enter the username or group name you want to add.

6. Select the rights you want to give the user or group.

7. Click the Save button. The Manage Permissions window appears.

8. Click the Copy All Permissions to Descendants link, as shown in Figure 12-6. A dialog box appears asking you to confirm. Click the OK button to complete the action.

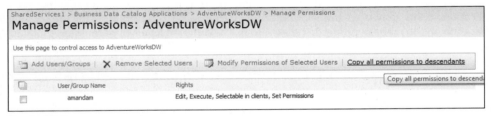

Figure 12-6

Try It Out   Manage Permissions on an Entity

In this example, you modify the existing rights of a user for an application entity. In the last Try It Out, you set the rights for the application and copied all rights to the descendants of the application, which included the associated entities. However, you may need to set unique permissions on entities that do not directly inherit permissions from that of the application. To do this, you select the entity directly from the global list of entities or from the application itself and then select Manage Permissions. Any permission changes can remain unique to that single entity or be copied to any descendants.

1. Go to the Shared Services Administration site.

2. Click the View Entities link from the Business Data Catalog section. You are directed to a page listing all available entities.

3. Click the name of the entity for which you want to edit. The View Entity window appears, as shown in Figure 12-7.

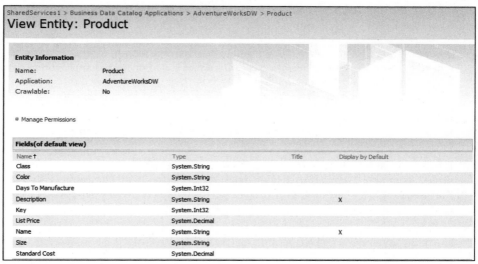

Figure 12-7

4. Click the Manage Permissions link.

5. Select a username or group for which you want to modify permissions.

6. Click the Modify Permissions of Selected Users button from the toolbar.

7. Make the desired changes to the permissions of the users by selecting or unselecting rights.

8. Click the Save button.

Working with Web Parts and Lists in the BDC

Once you have defined an application in the BDC per the discussion in the last section, SharePoint users can access it from within interface elements, such as Web Parts and list columns. You discover how to work with these items in this section.

Chapter 7 discusses how important Web Parts are to a SharePoint site for displaying information users need to do their jobs. One of the Web Part groups introduced in that chapter was the Business Data group, which has a specialized set of Web Parts that interact and connect with one another so users have a rich reporting environment. The Business Data Web Parts give you a way to display business information on your SharePoint site and allow users to interact with it to filter and generate more information.

If you had a business application in the BDC that contained all your customer service information, you could use Web Parts to see a listing of customers, search for customer information, view customer details, or see a listing of orders related to a selected customer. All of this is possible using one or more of the following Web Parts:

❑ **Business Data List Web Part**: Allows you to display information from a business application related to a specific entity. This information may be based on a predefined filter so that users automatically see a list when viewing the Web Part, or it may be based on searches that the user conducts within the Web Part.

❑ **Related Business Data List Web Part**: Connects to another Web Part, such as the Business Data List Web Part to show more information related to a selected item such as product subcategories or customer invoices.

❑ **Business Item Web Part**: You can use this on its own to display a single item, but often it is connected to another Web Part to display details of a selected item. For example, you can use a Business Item Web Part to display invoice details based on a user's selection of a customer invoice from a Related Business Data List Web Part.

You review each of these Web Parts in the upcoming sections of this chapter.

As the person responsible for managing your organization's SharePoint environment, it's important for you to meet with your business users to define what applications contain the data they need to perform their jobs more effectively, and then create an interface that supports their goals and objectives. By familiarizing yourself with the various Web Parts and their capabilities, you become better equipped to make good recommendations and implementation choices on how best to empower your business users.

Business Data List Web Part

The Business Data List Web Part is very similar to a Datasheet View or the List View Web Parts explored in Chapter 7. It can display a business application's information in a table view. However, unlike a List Web Part, it can facilitate real-time drill-down searching and information filtering, and can generate reports based on user requirements.

The next four Try It Outs show you everything you need to know to set up a Business Data List Web Part. In the first Try It Out, you configure the Web Part by defining which business application and entity the Web Part will connect to. In addition, you can set limits to the number of items that are returned or what properties are displayed. In the second Try It Out, you use the Web Part to search for a specific item, which involves defining criteria for your search. In the third Try It Out, you see how to launch an action from a Web Part. In the final Try it Out of this section, you learn how to customize the Web Part view based on user requirements or preferences.

| Try It Out | Configure the Business Data List Web Part |

In this example, you add the Business Data List Web Part to the customer service team site so that members of the site can easily retrieve information about products. You then select what business data entity you want to display in the Web Part. Because your goal is to provide users with quick and easy access to detailed product information, you add the product entity so that users can perform lookups on specific products directly from their SharePoint site.

1. From your corporate intranet portal, create a new site from the Sites directory called "Customer Service" using the blank site template. The blank site template was introduced in Chapter 8 as one of the collaborative site templates.

2. Choose Site Actions ⇨ Edit Page. The page reloads in Edit mode.

3. Click the Add a Web Part link from the left Web Part zone. The Web Part selection window appears, as shown in Figure 12-8.

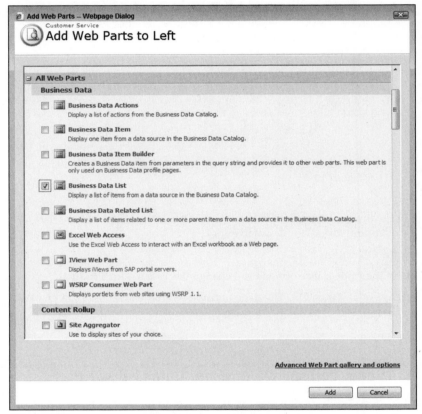

Figure 12-8

4. Select the Business Data List Web Part from the Business Data section.

5. Click the Add button. The Web Part Selection window closes, and the page reloads with the Web Part you selected added to the left Web Part zone.

6. Click the Open Tool Pane link in the Business Data List Web Part.

7. Click the Browse button. The Business Data Type Picker – Webpage Dialog appears, as shown in Figure 12-9.

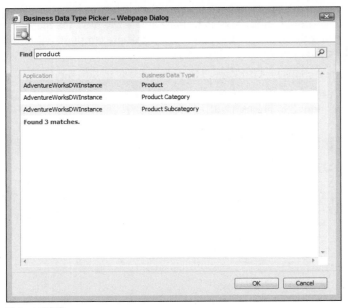

Figure 12-9

8. Select the Business Data list you want to display. In Figure 12-9, you select the Products list from the AdventureWorks Sample database.

9. Click the OK button.

10. Expand the Appearance options and change the Title to **Our Products**.

11. Click Apply, and then OK. The page refreshes with the Business Data List Web Part configured on the page.

Try It Out   **Display Items in the Business Data List Web Part**

In this example, you use the search capabilities of the Business Data List Web Part to locate product details on a bike stand that your company produces. First, you select the Name property from the drop-down list and enter a value that you expect the product name contains. You can include additional criteria in your search by clicking the Add button and defining new rules. Once you define the criteria of the search query, you select the Retrieve Data button, which returns a filtered set of results meeting your criteria.

1. From the main page of your customer service page, select a property from the drop-down list in the Our Products Web Part you configured in the last exercise, as shown in Figure 12-10. In this example, you perform a search using the Name property.

2. For the text value, select Contains.

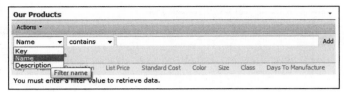

Figure 12-10

3. Type a value into the search box that will likely return the items for which you are looking. In this example, search for items that contain the word **Bike**.

4. Click the Add link.

5. Add another test value to further refine your search. This example selects where the description contained the word `stand` because you want to search for a bike stand.

6. Click the Retrieve Data button. Results are returned similar to what appears in Figure 12-11.

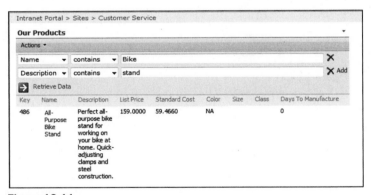

Figure 12-11

| Try It Out | **Launch an Action from a Business Item** |

In this example, you conduct a search for an item with a specific phrase or word in the product name. From the listing of returned results, a subset of details should display in the Web Part. The details of what displays in the Web Part are selected by the site manger, and you review how this is done in the next Try It Out. Sometimes to keep the display of information simple and easy to read, you should have only a small amount of data display in the Web Part. For example, for a product, you might only display the product name and price columns. To view more details on a specific product, you would want to be able to click a link to see all the information. In the Business Data List Web Part, you can use the View Profile action to do this.

1. Return to the home page of your customer service site. Use the Business Data List Web Part that you added to the page in the previous Try It Out to perform a search. This example will perform a search for where the product name contains "HL."

2. From the returned results, select an item and hover your cursor over the item name to expand the contextual menu.

3. Select the View Profile action as shown in Figure 12-12.

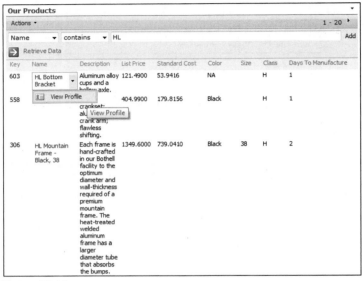

Figure 12-12

Try It Out   Change the View of the Business Data List Web Part

By default, all columns related to the data source display in the Web Part. In this Try It Out, you edit the properties of the Business Data List Web Part so that you change what details display, including the number of items. When determining how many items display on the site, remember that the more you select, the more time it takes to load them on the page. Obviously, pulling too much data from the data source will result in delays.

The process of selecting what properties display in the Web Part is very similar to creating a view on a list, which you learned about in Chapter 4. You select the check boxes of the items you want to display in the view and then identify the order in which they are listed from left to right. You should only include the items that users are likely to need. Using actions, users can view the complete profile of an item (see the previous Try It Out); therefore, you should only include those properties most relevant to users. For example, if you were showing product information, you may only include details related to the product that users would often look up, such as name, description, and price.

1. From the main page of your customer service site created in a previous Try It Out, select the menu arrow on the "Our Products" Web Part and then Modify Shared Web Part. The page and Web Part reload in edit mode.

2. Select Edit View as shown in Figure 12-13. You are redirected to a page where you may edit details of the view.

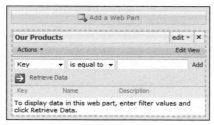

Figure 12-13

3. Select Retrieve All Items.

4. Unselect the columns you do not need displayed in the view, as shown in Figure 12-14.

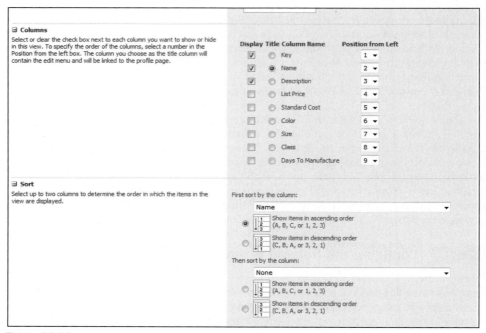

Figure 12-14

5. For the Pages section, select to return items in groups of 10.

6. Click the OK button.

How It Works

Because specific queries can potentially return large amounts of data, the Web Part supports the grouping of results so that only a limited number of items display at a time. Users can use the arrows next to the results grouping to view the next set of items in the list. Figure 12-15 shows an example of this..

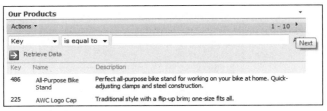

Figure 12-15

Related Business Data List Web Part

As mentioned in the section "Viewing Entities," entities store information concerning how they relate to other application entities. The SharePoint site manager can use the Related Business Data List Web Part to create a drill-down or dynamically driven reporting experience for site visitors. As a user selects an item in one Web Part, another Web Part can automatically filter to display more details related to the initial selection. For example, if the Business Data List Web Part displays a listing of customers, you can use the Related Business Data List Web Part to display a related listing of invoices.

In the first of the two Try It Outs in this section, you walk through the process of adding a related Business Data Web Part to a page along with a Business List Web Part and connecting the two parts so that users can select an item in one and see a related list drawn in the second. To start off the exercise, you create reports your customer service team needs as well as the document library that stores them. You then connect the two Web Parts on the Web Part page. This creates a filtered connection between the two related items. Now when a user visits the page, the selection in one Web Part should change the information that is presented in the other Web Part. In the second Try It Out, you test your creation by selecting items in one Web Part to see how the second one changes.

| Try It Out | Configure the Related Business Data Web Part on a Page |

In this example, you create a new document library on the customer service site for storing custom reports that you want users to access. You select Web Part page as the document template for the library because users will create the majority of report pages by clicking the New menu item directly from the Document Library toolbar. Users can select whichever Web Part page layout they feel best suits their data. A good choice is a multiple column web page of Web Part zones; it allows you to see two Web Parts side by side so that as users change one, they can view the changes on the other.

At first you add a simple Business Data List Web Part containing a list of product categories. In the case of the AdventureWorks database used for this exercise, you only have four product categories. Therefore, it's wise to have all items retrieved by default when users visit the page. After you configure the Business List Web Part containing product categories in the left-hand column, you add the Related Business Data List Web Part to the page to the right-hand column. You will then connect this Web Part to the product subcategories entity. This Web Part, while very similar in display to the previous Web Part, relies on the relationship between two entities to function. By defining the relationship in the Web Part properties, you will notice a message advising that the Web Part must be connected to the product categories list.

1. From your customer service site, select Site Actions ⇨ Create. You are redirected to the content creation page.

2. Select Document Library.

3. Name your document library **Reports**, select to display the library on the Quick Launch bar, and select Web Part Page as the document template.

4. Click the Create button. The page reloads, and you are redirected to your new document library.

5. Select the New button from the Document Library toolbar. The New Web Part Page appears, as shown in Figure 12-16.

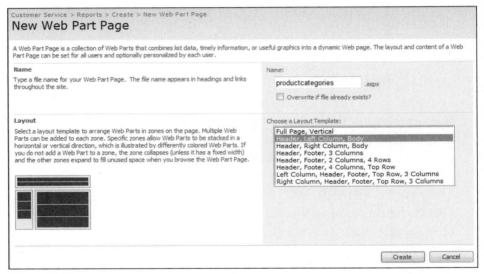

Figure 12-16

6. Enter a name for the Web Part page. For this example, enter **productcategories.aspx**.

7. For the layout template, select Header, Left Column, Body.

8. Click the Create button. The page reloads, and you are redirected to your new Web Part page.

9. From the left column, select Add a Web Part.

10. Select the Business Data List Web Part and click the Add button. The page reloads containing your Web Part. No information is displayed in the Web Part until it has been configured.

11. Click the Open the Tool Pane link to modify the properties of the Web Part.

12. In the Web Part properties pane, for the Type field, click the Browse button. The Business Data Type Picker – Webpage Dialog appears, as shown in Figure 12-17.

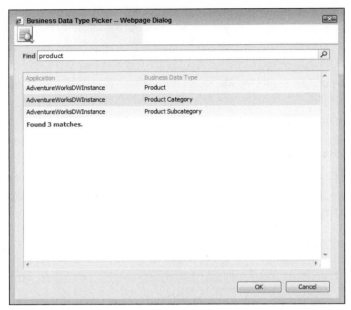

Figure 12-17

13. Select an entity that will be the master list. For example, select the Product Category list from the AdventureWorks DB Sample.

14. Click the OK button. The picker window closes and the selected entity is displayed in the Type field.

15. Click Apply, and then OK. The page refreshes to show the configured Web Part.

16. Click the Edit View link on the Web Part.

17. For Items to Retrieve, select Retrieve All Items.

18. Click the OK button. You are returned to the main page of your customer service site where the Business Data List Web Part displays all items from the selected entity.

19. Select Site Actions ⇨ Edit Page.

20. For the Body Web Part zone, select Add a Web Part.

21. Select Business Data Related List, and click the Add button.

22. Click the Open the Tool Pane link.

23. From the Web Part properties pane, click the Browse button and select the child item from the Business Data Type picker window. For this example, select the Product Subcategory list from the AdventureWorks DB Sample.

24. Click the OK button on the Business Data Type picker window.

25. For Relationship, select the appropriate relationship between the current entity and the entity to which it is related. In this example, select the relationship that is available as the ProductCategorytoProductSubCategory item, as shown in Figure 12-18.

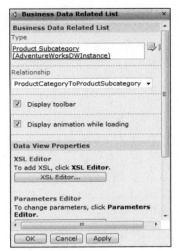

Figure 12-18

26. Click Apply, and then OK on the Web Part properties pane. The page refreshes and displays a message indicating that the related business item Web Part must be connected to a Web Part that provides Product Category.

27. Select the Edit button on the Product Subcategory List Web Part.

28. Select Connections, then Get Related Item From, and then select the Product Category List.

29. Click the Exit Edit Mode link.

Try It Out   **View Related Business Data on a Page**

In this example, you visit the reporting page that contains two connected Web Parts that you created in the last Try It Out. By selecting a product category from the first Web Part, a listing of subcategories returns in the other Web Part. This example demonstrates one possible level of filtering. Realistically, the next step would be to add another related items Web Part to the page so that when a user selects a product subcategory from the second Web Part, a listing of products related to that subcategory displays. More than one instance of a Related Business Data List Web Part can exist on a single page.

1. From the home page of your customer service site, click the Reports link from the Quick Launch bar.

2. Select the productcategories.aspx page. The page appears, as shown in Figure 12-19.

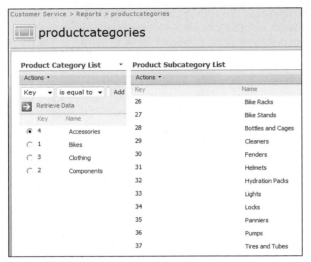

Figure 12-19

3. Select an item in the Product Categories list in the left-hand column. The right-hand column's data adjusts to display the items related to the category you selected.

Business Item Web Part

In the previous Try It Out, you saw how to connect the Related Business Data List Web Part to another business data list to show relevant information based on selection from the master list. With the Business Item Web Part, you can select an item from a Business Data List or Related Business Data List Web Part and the Item Web Part will display the details for the selected item. The Business Item Web Part can be filtered to display only a single item on the page by default, or it can be connected to another Web Part to display details for a selected item. For example, if you had a SharePoint site for tracking information related to a single customer, you might have only their record displayed in a Business Item Web Part on the site. Otherwise, you might connect the Web Part to another so that the details of a user's selection display. For example, if a user selects a specific customer invoice from a business data list, the details of the invoice can display in a Business Item Web Part.

Try It Out   Configure the Business Item Web Part

In this example, you add two Web Parts to a custom Web Part page. The first Web Part is a Business Data List Web Part set to display a listing of items based on a user's query. The second is a connected Web Part that is configured to display details of the selected item. When you combine this feature with the previous Try It Out, you can create reporting pages that allow a team member to select an item from a listing and then drill down via other Web Parts to related items and eventually view the details of a single selected record.

From the properties of a Business Item Web Part, you can determine what actions display on the toolbar of the Web Part. This allows users to launch related business activities and processes directly from the web page when viewing details about a specific item. For example, if your user is viewing a page that contains information about a customer, you can display an action on the toolbar to email the client.

1. From the home page of your customer service site, select the Reports document library from the Quick Launch bar. You are redirected to the Reports document library.

2. Click the New button from the Document Library toolbar. A Web Part page creation screen appears.

3. Enter the page name. For this example, enter **productdetails** for the page name.

4. For page layout, select Left Column, Header, Footer, Top Row, 3 Columns.

5. Click the Create button. Your new Web Part page is created, and you are redirected to it.

6. From the left column, select Add a Web Part. The Web Part selection window appears.

7. Select the Business Data List Web Part.

8. Click the Add button. The Web Part selection window closes, and your Web Part is added to the page.

9. Click the Open Tool Pane link from the Web Part.

10. Select an entity to display in the listing using the method described in previous Try it Outs. In this example, you can use the Product entity from the AdventureWorks sample database.

11. Click the OK button on the Business Data Type picker window once your entity is selected.

12. Unselect the check box next to Display Animation When Loading.

13. Click Apply, and then OK from the Web Part properties pane.

14. Select Edit View on the Web Part. The Edit View window appears, as shown in Figure 12-20.

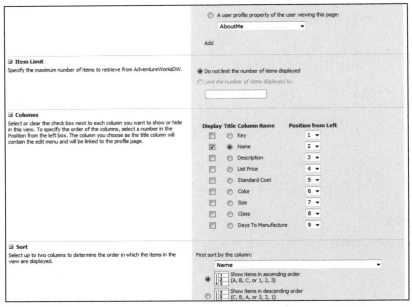

Figure 12-20

15. For Items to Retrieve, maintain the choice of Retrieve Items Specified by the User.

16. For Columns, unselect all items except the primary display name such as Name.

17. Click the OK button. You are returned to your page.

18. Select Site Actions ⇨ Edit Page.

19. From the header Web Part zone, select Add a Web Part.

20. Select Business Data Item.

21. Click the Add button.

22. Click the Open to Tool Pane link from the Business Item Web Part.

23. Once again, select the same entity you used for the other Web Part in step 10. This example, selects Product for the entity, as was done in the previous step.

24. Click the OK button on the Business Data Type picker window once your entity is selected.

25. Click Apply, and then OK from the Web Part. The page refreshes and a message appears in the Web Part suggesting that you connect it to another Web Part.

26. Click the Edit button for the Web Part.

27. Select Connections ⇨ Get Item From ⇨ Product List from the drop-down menu, as shown in Figure 12-21.

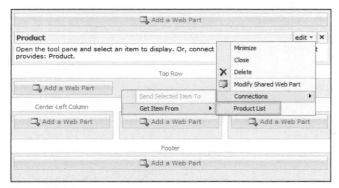

Figure 12-21

28. Click the Exit Edit mode link. Your page is now configured.

How It Works

To test your configuration, conduct a search in the Business Data List Web Part for items that contain HL in the name and select an item from the search results so that you can see the details appear in the Business Data Item Web Part. An example is shown below in Figure 12-22.

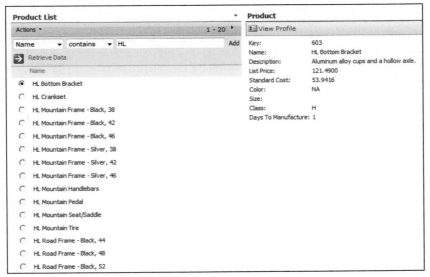

Figure 12-22

Business Data Actions Web Part

You can add the Business Data Actions Web Part to a page to launch actions available for selected or connected items. As previously discussed, entities can contain special actions that users can launch from either the Actions menu of an item or the toolbar of a Web Part. In addition, you can place a Business Data Actions Web Part on a page to enable users to launch actions related to business entities displayed on the current page.

You can add a Business Data Actions Web Part using the same steps as in steps 6 through 8 previously. Properties of the Web Part can then be modified by opening the tool pane, which is described in step 9 of the "Configure the Business Item Web Part" Try It Out.

When modifying the properties of a Business Data Actions Web Part, you must define the entity that the Web Part is referring to. From there, you may select what actions should display and the order in which they are listed. You may choose to display actions as a bulleted list, standard list, or toolbar. In addition, you may select to have new actions displayed within the Web Part automatically. This may result in less administrative overhead as the entities evolve over time.

SharePoint List Integration

While viewing business data via Web Parts in a web page format offers great visibility for most organizations, sometimes users require a deeper integration between business data and existing SharePoint content. For example, if an organization's customer information is stored in a customer relationship management database, it may be more beneficial to have a central listing of customers pulled from the database rather than maintained manually in a SharePoint list.

In a SharePoint list or library, you can create a custom column that pulls data directly from your business application via the BDC. In the next example, you see how to associate specific products with the specification materials and brochures that are uploaded to the customer service center SharePoint site. You base the Products column on product information stored in a business application, such as the AdventureWorks database that you've been using for the examples so far in this chapter. Once that Try it Out is complete, you upload a document to the library and associate business data with the document.

Try It Out   **Create Columns for Business Data in a List**

In this example, you create a new document library to store product-related documentation to help consolidate information for the customer service team. The team has repeatedly asked that it be given the capability to filter or search for a specific product. Typically to associate product names with documents, you create a central SharePoint list and then have a site column or list column point to that product list. However, as it happens, your organization already tracks this information in a central database. Therefore, by creating a business data type column on the library, you can connect to that central products list to allow users to associate product information with the various product documents in SharePoint.

Besides being connected directly to line-of-business application data, an additional advantage that a business data column has over SharePoint lookup columns is having columns known as *related item columns*, which display additional details about the selected item in the list. In this example, you display the description and list price items as columns in the library in addition to the product name. By selecting a product, these columns are automatically populated in the library.

1. From the main page of your customer service site, select Site Actions ⇨ Site Settings. You are redirected to the Site Settings page.

2. Select Site Features. You are redirected to a page containing available site features.

3. For the Office SharePoint Server Enterprise Site Features item, select the Activate button. The Site Features page reloads, and the feature now shows as Activated.

4. Click Site Actions ⇨ Create. You are redirected to the Content Creation page.

5. Select Document Library. You are redirected to a Document Library Creation page.

6. For the title, enter **Product Documentation** and the following for description:

> **Central location for storing materials and documentation related to our products.**

7. Select Yes to display the library on the Quick Launch bar and store version history for each item.

8. For document template, select Microsoft Office Word Document.

9. Click the Create button. Your new document library is created, and you are redirected to it.

10. Select Settings ⇨ Create Column. You are redirected to the Column Creation page.

11. For Column name, enter **Product**.

12. For Column type, select the Business Data option.

13. For Type, click the Browse button and select the entity you want to display and click the OK button. This example uses the Product Entity.

14. In the following drop-down menu, select the field you wish to display from the entity. This example uses Name.

15. Unselect the Display Actions Menu button.

16. You may also select related fields to be displayed, as shown in Figure 12-23. This example uses Description and List price.

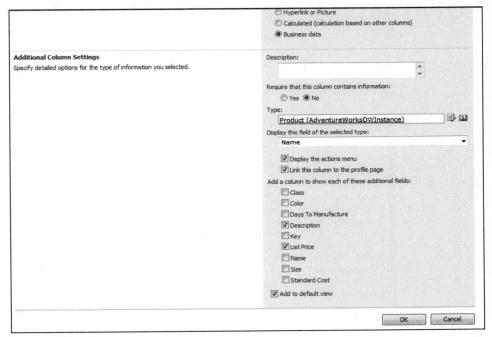

Figure 12-23

17. Select to have the column displayed in Default View.

18. Click the OK button. Your new column is created in the document library.

Try It Out   Associate Business Data with a List Item

In this example, you upload a user manual for a new product that has been added to your company's product line. While the product is extremely new, the product name is automatically available to you when you performed a lookup on the product column. This is because the column connects directly to the production database and pulls the name from the global listing.

1. From the Product Documentation library, select the Upload button. You are redirected to the Upload page.

2. Click browse and locate the HL Touring Handlebars User Manual.doc file from this chapter's resources.

3. Click the OK button.

4. For the Product column, click the Browse button. The Choose Product – Webpage Dialog appears.

5. Conduct a search for a name that is likely in your product listing by typing its name in the find field. Figure 12-24 shows your search for a product name that contains the term "Touring," and your selection of the HL Touring Handlebars product from the AdventureWorks sample database.

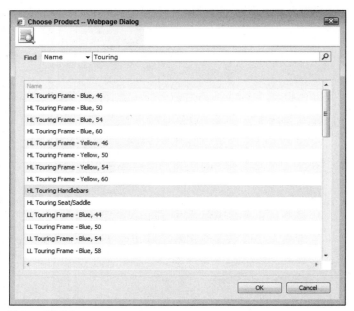

Figure 12-24

6. Click the OK button to select your item.

7. Click the OK button. Your document is uploaded and contains HL Touring Handlebars as the value in the Product column.

How It Works

In Figure 12-25, you see that although you only selected the product name for your library in the example, the values for Description and List Price are also associated with the document because you selected them when you defined the column as additional properties you wanted to display.

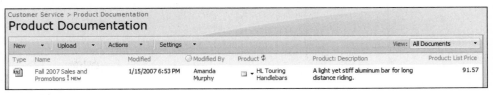

Figure 12-25

Summary

Information empowers employees to work effectively at their jobs, make accurate decisions, and complete their tasks on time. In most organizations, information is often stored in multiple locations and in separate applications. While a goal of an information manager is to consolidate information and make SharePoint a central access point for key business information, sometimes, you have applications that are very tightly integrated with business operations and processes. Therefore, it is not always realistic or advantageous to store this information in SharePoint. Instead, SharePoint can serve as a window into that information, while the original application remains the place where users make all updates and changes to content. In this chapter, you learned the following:

❑   With the Business Data Catalog, business users can use SharePoint to connect to and view information from external business applications. Users can see detailed reports containing data from line-of-business applications or search for information in these external systems.

❑   Throughout this chapter, you learned what some of the key business data Web Parts are and how you can use them independently or together to display important sets of business information to users.

❑   You also learned how to integrate business data with SharePoint lists and libraries. In addition, you learn how to use business data to compliment information stored in SharePoint, such as user profiles as a secondary data source.

❑   You also discovered the key roles that often use the BDC, including the application definition author, business analyst, system administrator, and developer. Each of these user types can play a significant role in ensuring that the right business information is accessible and secured within your SharePoint sites and custom applications.

Exercises

1.   True or False. The Business Data Catalog contains important data from external applications.

2.   Describe the difference between the roles of the application definition author and a developer.

3.   When an application is added to the BDC, can any user with list creation rights add a column to a list that points to the application?

4.   Explain the difference between the Business Data List Web Part and Related Business Data List Web Part.

Getting Started with Web Content Management

With more and more business online, Web Content Management has become increasingly important for businesses. Web Content Management (WCM) is the process of creating and managing web content either on the Internet or an intranet. Where possible, a good web content management system should support a variety of information and provide tools to users for updating this content with minimal effort.

Formerly, a major roadblock to managing web content has been the lack of effective tools, which meant relying on expensive, labor-intensive, and time-consuming processes. But you don't have these roadblocks with SharePoint 2007; in this chapter, you take a look at WCM and how SharePoint 2007 can make business teams and processes more efficient. This chapter covers the following:

❑ What Web Content Management is and how the tools have evolved from CMS 2002

❑ How the tools in SharePoint 2007 can help organizations become more efficient in the WCM space

❑ How to cater to multiple languages using the Variations feature

❑ How to customize the look and feel of your page layouts to enforce brand consistency

❑ How to create your own content types and page layouts

❑ How to enable publishing on your team site

Web Content Management

SharePoint Server 2007 makes business users more independent in their content publishing activities and offers them better collaboration tools. Although Content Management Server (CMS) 2002 addressed the requirements necessary to build a content managed website, you often needed to extend the platform using the Publishing API, known as *PAPI*. SharePoint Server 2007 has both improved most of the Content Management Server 2002's features and reduced the need for development using the API. The following table covers the most common CMS features and their SharePoint 2007 equivalents.

CMS	SharePoint 2007 Equivalent
Content publishing included template galleries, resource galleries, template.	This is now publishing pages, webs, page layouts, image and document libraries.
CMS is no longer supported.	SharePoint is integrated with Windows Workflow Foundation.
CMS supported authoring connector.	SharePoint can convert Microsoft Office System documents to HTML.
Offered template-based rendering feature.	Offers template-based rendering features as well as master pages and page layouts. .ASPX pages are similar to CMS template files.
Channel functionality and postings.	Channel functionality is now in sites or SPWeb properties (that developers can access). Postings are publishing page objects.

So, how can WCM work in your situation? If your company headquarters is in one part of the world, with support teams in other locations, your employees can still collaborate by accessing a company website regardless of location. Website content owners create lists and libraries and supply employees with the materials they need to perform their day-to-day duties. Managers can create and update a tasks list that outlines what the team needs to do and who is responsible. Teams everywhere can log in to the portal and instantly access important information or even create it for someone in another country. Employees can create email alerts on the important lists and libraries so colleagues are instantly notified of new or changed content. Specifically, SharePoint 2007 has the following features for managing and publishing content:

❑ **Page layouts and master pages:** Enforces consistency across your websites and ensures that all new pages that are created follow your corporate brand.

❑ **Creating web pages from the browser:** Allows users without knowledge of HTML code to create web pages that inherit the site's common look and feel.

❑ **Workflows:** Automates the process of publishing or approving content. For example, you might create content for a website and then send it through a workflow system where it is approved and finally published to your website.

❑ **Content versioning:** Ensures that you are always using the most up-to-date versions of your documents and allows you to restore to a previous version by keeping an electronic paper trail as the document evolves.

❑ **Reporting Services:** This is a great way to get a high-level overview of your content.

❑ **Check In/Check Out:** Ensures that multiple people are working on the same up-to-date content so that you can check out and in your documents during editing.

Publishing Features Overview

Publishing refers to the act of creating content such as a new page in your site or modifying content such as a block of text or a picture. By using built-in publishing tools explained throughout this chapter, you can quickly and easily modify your web content without the need for code. With SharePoint 2007's Publishing feature, you can publish web content for pages and content approval workflow material right from the browser or use tools such as the Enhanced Text Editor to edit text right on the page. SharePoint has various templates, such as the Collaboration portal and the Publishing portal, that have the Publishing feature already enabled. However, you can enable the Publishing feature on a regular team site, such as a blank site, at any time to give it the publishing capabilities.

Creating a Publishing Portal

If you are planning to create a site that is going to be highly customized and feature many pages of content, you may select the Publishing portal as the site template for your site collection. Like the Collaboration portal template, you can only select this template as a top-level site within a site collection. In the next example, you create a Publishing portal that acts as sample site for the remainder of this chapter.

See Chapter 1 for a discussion of what a portal is and what it can do for you.

Try It Out	Create a Publishing Portal Site

In this example, you create a new site collection that acts as a host for your company's public Internet site. This site contains news articles, company information pages, as well as information on various ski products and services in multiple languages. In the past, creating a public-facing Internet site required in-depth knowledge of HTML and other related technologies.

1. From the Central Administration site of your SharePoint environment, select the Application Management tab.

2. Select Create Site Collection from the SharePoint Site Management category. The Create Site Collection window appears, as shown in Figure 13-1.

3. Select the appropriate web application for your site collection. This is typically the web application hosted on port 80.

4. Enter a title for your website. For this example, enter **Ski Company Internet**.

5. Enter a description for your website. For this example, enter the following for your description:

> **The Ski Company Internet Website.**

6. For the site URL, ensure that the "sites" path is selected from the drop-down menu and enter **skicompany** for the URL name.

7. Select the Publishing Portal template from the Publishing tab as shown in Figure 13-1.

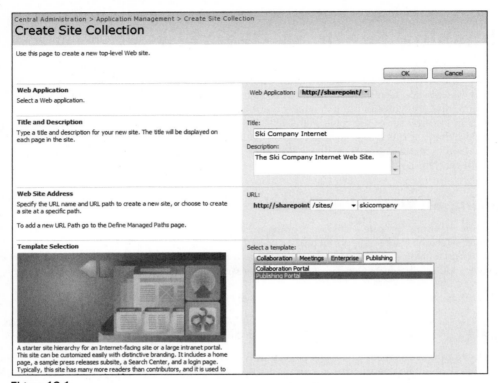

Figure 13-1

8. Select yourself as the Primary Site Collection administrator.

9. Click the OK button.

How It Works

A publishing portal is created with many of the initial lists and libraries that you will need to get started on your website. Figure 13-2 shows an example of how the Internet site will look upon creation.

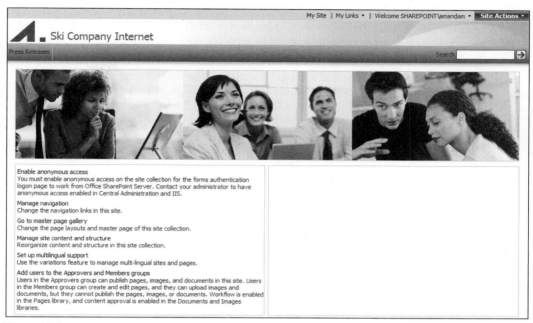

Figure 13-2

The Publishing Portal's Lists and Libraries

As mentioned in the last Try It Out, a publishing portal comes with lists and libraries to get you started, including the ones shown in the following list. In addition to these lists, the site collection contains two subsites for Press Releases and Search. You can create new subsites to represent the various sections of your company website. So although you may think of a company website as a single site, in actual fact it contains multiple subsites. As you create each subsite, the navigation updates to reflect your changes. The navigation controls allow visitors to your site to browse the various sections in a seamless and intuitive manner that does not make them feel as though they are actually visiting multiple sites.

❑ **Documents:** This library stores documents and files to which your website's various content pages link. You can add columns, content types, or views to suit your specific requirements. By default, this has versioning and content approval enabled, as well as columns for the publishing start and end dates. A version of this library is created in each publishing subsite for files and documents unique to that site.

❑ **Form Templates:** Chapter 10 discussed how to activate InfoPath Form templates to a site collection from the Central Administration site. When this happens, a content type is created, and the Form template publishes into the Form Templates library on the top-level site of the site collection. This is a useful location for storing central templates used by InfoPath forms utilized throughout your site collection.

❑ **Images:** This system-generated library stores images for display in the current site that has versioning and content approval enabled. A version of this library is created in each publishing subsite for images unique to the site.

❑ **Pages:** This holds the various pages you create for the content of your website including the default page. It has a series of special content types that allow you to create site content and pages. You can learn more in an upcoming section.

❑ **Site Collection Documents:** This document library acts as a centralized store for documents and files that are required and accessed throughout the site collection. Various publishing controls, such as the Enhanced Text Editor or Publishing hyperlink, can access documents in this library. You can select Site Collection Documents from the left menu when editing either of these controls, as shown in Figure 13-3.

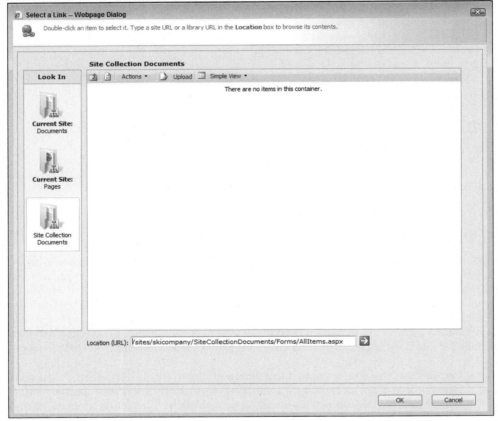

Figure 13-3

❑ **Site Collection Images:** This document library stores the images that a site collection requires. Like the Site Collection Documents library, this is available directly via the interface when you use the various image publishing controls.

❑ **Style Library:** This system-generated library contains many of the style elements that your site requires, including custom XSL styles and CSS files; however, you can also add your own style sheets, which you can reference from within the site collection.

❑ **Content and Structure Reports**: This system list contains special queries within each list item that helps to generate the reports available on a publishing site from the Site Actions menu. Reports are helpful for identifying tasks and content that exists throughout the publishing site collection.

❑ **Reusable Content:** You may need to display content in multiple Web Parts or locations that is pulled from a single centralized source. This system-generated list contains content that you can display within specific Web Parts. You can opt to link it back to the source so that as content updates in the list, the Web Parts also automatically update.

❑ **Workflow Tasks:** This system-generated task list tracks the workflow tasks that are created as a result of the various publishing workflows.

In addition to the seamless navigation experience that SharePoint offers users between sites, it also has support for creating portals in multiple languages. In the next section, you see how to take a company website and configure it so that content users can view it in multiple languages.

Working with Variations

When you design an Internet-facing website or corporate intranet, you may need to present it in multiple languages. This may simply mean providing users access to documents in multiple languages, or you may need all your content — web page and interface elements — in multiple languages. In the latter case, if your content is in one language, such as English, you must translate documents into other languages, but the system should support and manage this process.

SharePoint 2007 introduces the Variations feature, which you can use to create a website hierarchy for content in multiple languages. For example, the site may be where customers from multiple languages can view information about the Company's products and services, or a corporate intranet site where employees live in different regions of the world and need access to information in their primary languages. Although variations do not actually translate the content for you, it starts a workflow that helps you do this work. Basically, you create content in a source language and then provision the content out to other sites, which represent the other required languages. This happens via workflow, which also notifies appropriate users that they are required to perform the translations. Figure 13-4 represents a site hierarchy with support for English and French versions of the website. Besides English and French, Variations can support any other languages, such as Spanish, Japanese, and German.

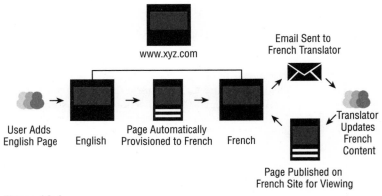

Figure 13-4

In this section, you learn how Variations work, including how to enable this feature. You then learn how to create labels for each language on your site, and then how to manage the workflow so that you have all the pieces you need for a working site with multiple language pages.

How Do Variations Work?

After login, the site version that users see is determined by their preferred language setting in their browser, as shown in Figure 13-5. If for some reason, a user has a requirement to change the site language to something other than their default language, he may do so using the Language Selection control, shown in Figure 13-6. If that page does not exist or is not published yet, he is directed to the next page in the site hierarchy — basically the parent page.

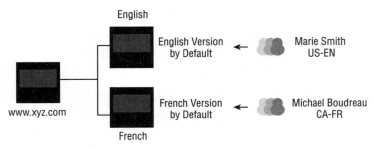

Figure 13-5

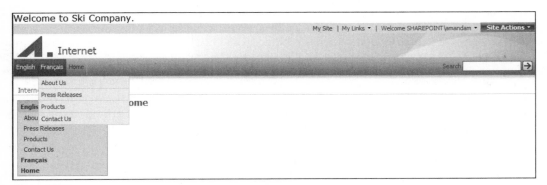

Figure 13-6

For a site to become available in multiple languages, you must first enable the Publishing feature. By default, the Internet-facing publishing site and Collaboration Publishing Site templates have this feature enabled. Enabling variations on a Publishing site, site collection is fairly simple in comparison to the benefit and functionality it provides an organization. In the next example, you configure a site collection to support this feature. You use the Ski Company site for this example.

Try It Out   **Enable Variations on a Site Collection**

Your ski company has customers throughout the United States and Canada, which means you need content in both English and French. To do this, you enable the Variations feature. Because this functionality applies to the entire site collection, you enable this feature from the Site Collection Administration page.

The Variation Settings window has several options. In this example, you start your variations at the root of your site collection, subsequently making English your main language variation. Then you opt to automate the creation of pages for other languages. This means that if you create a new page on the English site, a new page is automatically created in the French site. You then select to recreate any deleted target pages when you republish the source page. You also opt to have Web Part modifications made in one site carry over into the second site. Whether you decide to update Web Parts has to do with the level of Web Part customization you plan to do between languages. For example, if you want unique views available on a product's Web Part for each language, you may opt not to update Web Parts so that the English Web Part doesn't overwrite changes you want on the French Web Part. Finally, you choose to send an email when variation pages have been updated, and choose to share resources with the source variation rather than creating new copies.

1.   From the Ski Company Internet website, select Site Settings and then Modify All Site Settings from the Site Actions menu.

2.   From the Site Collection Administration group, select Variations. The Variation Settings window appears, as shown in Figure 13-7.

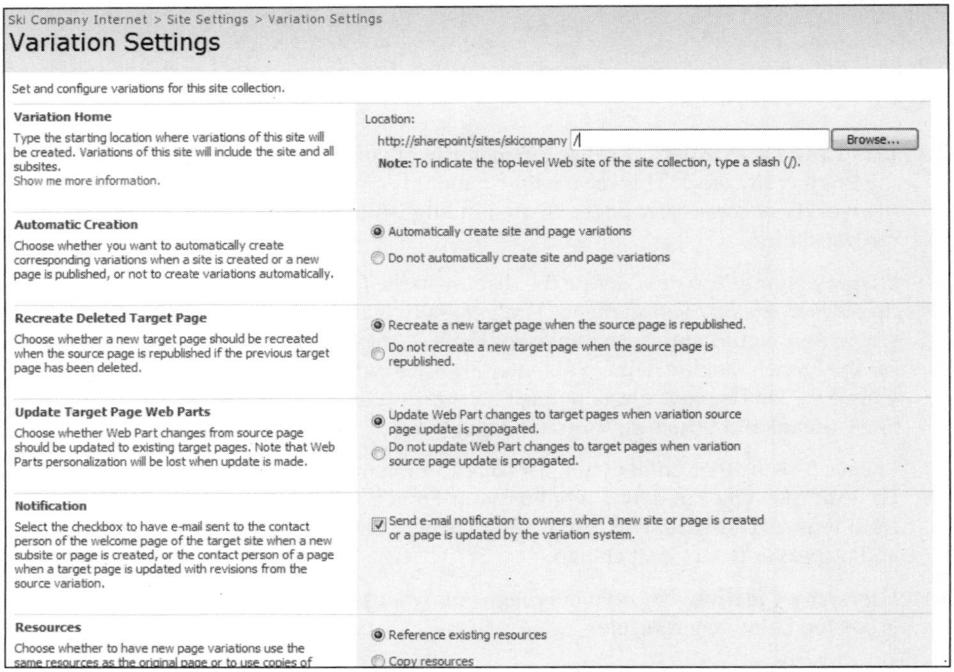

Figure 13-7

3. You must specify the location for your variations to start. In this case, because you want the variations to start at the root of the site collection, you enter /.

4. Select the option to automatically create site and page variations. This ensures that all new sites created in the source site are created in the other languages as well.

5. Select the option to recreate a new target page when the source page is republished.

6. Select the option to update Web Part changes to target pages when variation source page update is propagated.

7. Keep the option checked to send email notification to owners when a new site or page is created or a page is updated by the variation system.

8. Select the option to reference existing resources from the variation pages.

9. Click the OK button.

How It Works

Variations is enabled for your site collections with the options you selected in this exercise. Once you enable Variations, the next step is to create labels to represent the sites for the various languages you want to support. This is the subject of the next section of the chapter.

Understanding Labels

In variations, you create a label for each language you want to represent within the site collection. The label defines the language of the site, the display name, the locale, as well as the hierarchy and source hierarchy.

❑ **Label and Description:** Because the majority of your customers speak English, you start with the English site label. This means that content is created in the English language first, and then the workflow copies any pages created in English to the French site hierarchy and queues them for translation

❑ **Display Name:** You next define the display name for each site hierarchy. This is the name as it displays in the navigation menu. You generally make the display name the name of the language as it would appear to native speakers so they can recognize it and select it. For example, for the French display name, you enter Français, which is the word for "French" in the French language. This is particularly helpful for viewing the structure of the site in reports such as the Site Content and Structure shown in Figure 13-8.

❑ **Locale:** This further tailors your site to reflect the nuances in variations on the same language. For example, you can define whether your French-speaking audience is French Canadian or from France. Likewise, you can distinguish between an English speaker from the United States and a speaker from Great Britain.

❑ **Hierarchy Creation:** For each language you want to represent on your website, a sub hierarchy is created below the root site.

❑ **Source Variation:** You must choose the main language for your variations. This will be the initial language in which all content is created before translation and should be based on the majority of your user's first language.

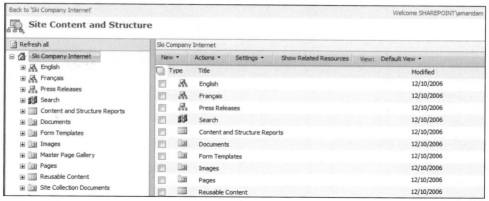

Figure 13-8

Try It Out   Create Labels for Each Language

In this example, you create labels for each of the languages in which you want your Ski Company site available. Each label represents a major language, which in turn represents a unique site hierarchy containing all the elements related to that language. In this example, you make the Ski Company site available in both English and French, but you can expand into other languages later by adding additional labels.

1. Return to the site settings page of your site collection. You may already be there based on completion of the previous exercise.

2. Select Variation Labels from the Site Collection Administration links.

3. Click the New Label button from the toolbar. The Create Variation Label window appears as shown in Figure 13-9.

4. Because the first language you define is English, enter **EN** for the Label name.

5. For Display Name, enter **English**. This is the value that end users see on the site.

6. Specify the locale of the site to be English (United States).

7. Specify the language to be English.

8. For Hierarchy Creation, select Publishing Sites and All Pages.

9. Select the check box to make the current label the source label. A message window appears to advise you that this action cannot be undone. Click OK to continue.

10. For Publishing Site Template, select Publishing Site with Workflow, as shown in Figure 13-9.

11. Click the OK button.

12. Select New Label from the toolbar.

13. Enter **FR** for the Label Name.

14. For Display Name, enter **Français**.

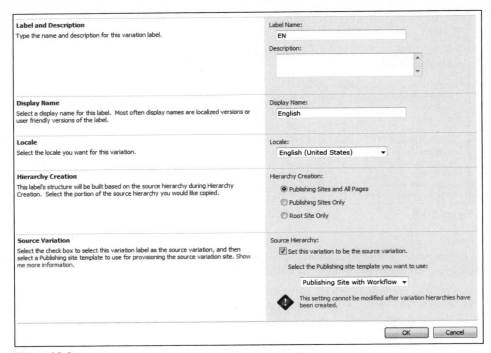

Figure 13-9

15. Specify the locale of the site to be French (Canada). You do this because you expect that many of the French visitors to your site are French Canadian.

16. Specify the language to be French.

17. Click the OK button.

18. From the Variation Labels Management page, click the Create Hierarchies link from the toolbar as shown in Figure 13-10.

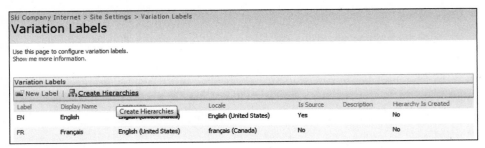

Figure 13-10

How It Works

Depending on the language preference that a user has set in the browser, a user is taken to the site with the appropriate language, which in this example is English. If user defines a language preference that does not exist on the site, she is redirected to the source language.

In this example, although you created labels for two languages, you can still add new languages later. So, if you were to develop a requirement to offer the Ski Company website in Spanish, you could do so by creating a label for Spanish and then clicking the Create Hierarchies link again. Any content contained in your English site, which is the source site, would be copied into the Spanish site and queued for translation.

Managing Translation Workflows

To ensure that pages are translated into the required language of the destination sites as they are created, you can tie your site to a special workflow. As the last two sections showed, pages are automatically created in the language of the source site. The process works something like this: You create content for the source language page. When you check the page in, this automatically launches an approval process. The group that is to approve the page is automatically notified and a task is assigned in their task list. When the source language page is approved, Variations automatically creates the pages for other languages, and email notifications are sent to translators notifying them that new content has been added to their sites. They translate the page to the appropriate language, and upon checking in the page start a second approval process.

This section features three Try It Outs that show you the inner workings of the workflow. In the first Try It Out, you create a new page in the source site, which is English. The page is created in the French site, and both sites go through the content editing and approval stages. In the second Try It Out, you create the site's hierarchy by through a series of subsites that reflect the two main sections of the website:

❑   About Us

❑   Products

Finally, in the third Try It Out, you move the Press Releases site from the root structure of the site into the English version of your site. Once you do this, SharePoint automatically creates a French version of the Press Releases site, just as it did with the Products, About Us, and Custom Contact page from the first and second Try It Outs.

Try It Out	Create a New Page in the Source Site

In this example, you create a contact information page in your English site and check it back into the system to launch an approval workflow. Because you are members of the approvers group, you would normally receive an email notification and task assignment, but for the sake of this example, you can clearly see that the page is pending approval based on the Approve and Reject buttons that were displayed in the toolbar.

> *For more on email notifications, the check-in and check-out process, workflows, and task assignments, see Chapters 3 and 5.*

1.   From the home page of your Ski Company site, select Site Actions ➪ Create Page from the menu.

2. Enter **Contact Us** for the title of the page.

3. From the page templates, click Article Page with Summary Links.

4. Click the Create button. You are redirected to an empty page.

5. Enter some content into the page and select Check In from the Page drop-down menu, as shown in Figure 13-11.

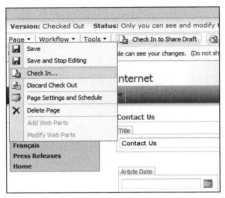

Figure 13-11

6. Select that you want to publish a major version and add some comments, as these will be useful to you and others later when reviewing the page's version history as discussed in Chapter 3.

7. Click the OK button.

8. Click the Start button to launch the approval workflow process.

9. When the page reloads, select the Approve button from the Page Editing toolbar.

10. On the Approval page, select the Approve button. The Contact Us page automatically appears in the navigation.

11. Select the link to visit the French version of the site.

12. Select the Contact Us page link in the French site.

How It Works

Notice the page is in a draft version and not checked in. Upon approval of the English page, the French page for Contact Us is created, and content owners from the French site receive email notifications. They can edit a draft page that the system creates, and then publish the page. Content approval workflows are also launched for this page, and the approvers of this page are notified.

Try It Out   **Create a Site Hierarchy of Publishing Sites**

In this example, you walk through the steps of creating two subsites for your publishing site collection. For the first site, you use the Create Site command from the Site Actions menu, which is the easiest way to create a single site from within a publishing site. Notice that this option along with several others on the Site Actions menu did not exist in the previous examples when you worked on sites without the Publishing feature enabled.

Because you need to create multiple subsites, you should use the Manage Content and Structure interface, shown in this example. From this interface, you can activate many administrative functions such as copying or moving a site, or creating new content. In addition, you can manage security or content across multiple sites very conveniently from this section. The Site Content and Structure window, shown in Figure 13-14, provides a good visual diagram of the entire site collection and its various content elements.

1. From the main page of your newly created Ski Company site, select Site Actions ⇨ Create Site, as shown in Figure 13-12. The New SharePoint Site window appears as shown in Figure 13-13.

Figure 13-12

Figure 13-13

2. Enter a title and URL for the site. For this example, enter **About Us** for the title and **aboutus** for the URL.

3. Select the Publishing Site with Workflow template.

4. Select the option to use the same permissions as parent site.

5. Select the Yes option for Use the Top Link Bar from the Parent Site.

6. Click the Create button. You are redirected to your newly created subsite for About Us.

7. Click the site logo to return to the home page of the top-level site.

8. Select Site Actions ⇨ Manage Content and Structure. The Site Content and Structure window appears, as shown in Figure 13-14.

9. Select New ⇨ Site from the toolbar.

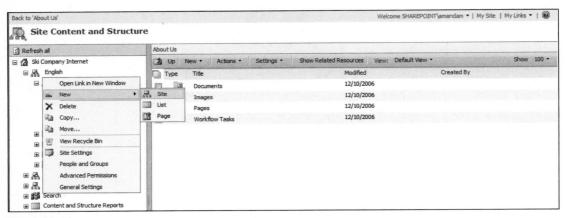

Figure 13-14

10. Repeat steps 2 through 6, but this time, enter **Products** for the Title and **products** for the URL Name in step 2.

How It Works

As you create the new sites, these sites are also created in the French version of your site. The Site Content and Structure view will clearly outline the hierarchy of your site including the multilingual branches

Try It Out   Move a Site Within a Site Collection

From the Manage Content and Structure section, you can perform many administrative functions such as moving sites. In this example, you move the Press Releases site under the English site hierarchy.

1. From the home page of your Ski Company site, select Site Actions ⇨ Manage Content and Structure. The Site Content and Structure window appears.

2. Hover your mouse over the Press Releases site to expose the Administrative drop-down menu.

3. Select the Move option. The Move – Webpage Dialog appears, as shown in Figure 13-15.

4. Select the English site.

Figure 13-15

5. Click the OK button.

How It Works

Figure 13-16 shows how the site hierarchy looks with the creation of the additional subsites in both languages.

Because Variations is enabled, moving the site triggers the creation of the Press Releases site under the French hierarchy. At this point, French content translators can go into the French version of the site and rename pages and update content to reflect the appropriate language.

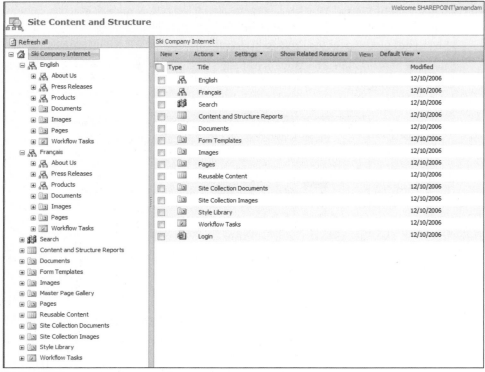

Figure 13-16

Customizing the Look and Feel of a WCM Site

While the tools of Web Content Management in SharePoint 2007 are quite powerful, you'll probably want to customize the look and feel of your site so that it is more in tune with your organization's unique identity. Fortunately, SharePoint 2007 gives you some great options:

❑ **Master pages:** Master pages control the UI or "chrome" elements of a website which are usually shared across all pages — items such as a company logo, navigation menu, or footer. Making a change to the master page subsequently changes all pages that inherit it. This option is commonly used when you want to customize the entire layout of your site.

❑ **Page layout:** This standardizes what and where content displays on a page. A page layout is to the content as the master page is to the UI. You often use page layout to create specific types of content for your site, such as a Newsletter.

❑ **Document conversion:** This basically involves taking a document, such as a Word file or an InfoPath form, and converting it to a web page for display in the browser. You often use this to create browser-based forms from InfoPath.

The real magic of WCM is that content is separate from the pieces you use to change the look of the page. Therefore, you can swap out content, and not change the page appearance or change a site's look and feel without too many extra steps. This section explores each of these options in greater detail so that you know exactly what you're changing and how best to place content to make your business run efficiently.

Master Pages

SharePoint 2007 makes good use of the ASP.NET 2.0 master pages functionality, allowing users to customize the look feel of the portions of a website, such as the navigation menus, headers, and footers that are shared across all pages within a site. The *master pages* allow you to customize a single file and have your changes automatically applied to other pages, called *content pages*, which inherit that master page. The master page and content page are merged to form a single rendered page, which is then presented to the user. This process happens in the background and is seamless to the user.

You can change the master page applied to your WCM websites from the browser quite easily using SharePoint's Master Page Gallery. Although this gallery has several options available, your organization may need something more specific to ensure that your website adheres to a strict corporate brand. In these situations, you can create a custom master page and then upload it to the gallery where it can be applied to content pages. The next two Try It Outs show you how to apply and customize a master page.

Because creating a custom master page requires basic knowledge of both SharePoint Designer 2007 and ASP.NET 2.0, it's recommended that only trained professionals attempt this type of customization work.

Try It Out   **Apply a New Master Page**

In this example, you apply a master page. Basically, you select the master page from the Master Page Gallery, and SharePoint changes the content pages to inherit from this new page and the updated page displays, complete with the look and feel from your selected master page. It is important to note that the form and view pages can inherit a different master page, which you see in this example. For this example, you'll use the Ski Company English site created in the previous section.

1.   From your Ski Company English site, select Site Actions ➪ Site Settings ➪ Modify All Site Settings.

2.   Select Go to Top-Level Site Settings.

3.   From the Look and Feel section, select Master Page. The Site Master Page Settings window appears, as shown in Figure 13-17.

4.   From the Site Master Page section, select a master page from the drop-down menu. For this example, select BlackBand.master.

5.   If you want all subsites to reset to use this master page, you can select the check box. For this exercise, you can leave it unchecked.

6.   From the System Master Page section, select a master page from the drop-down menu (see Figure 13-18). In this example, select Black Band.master. The System master page changes the form and view pages in the site.

7.   Select the Reset Subsites option for this exercise.

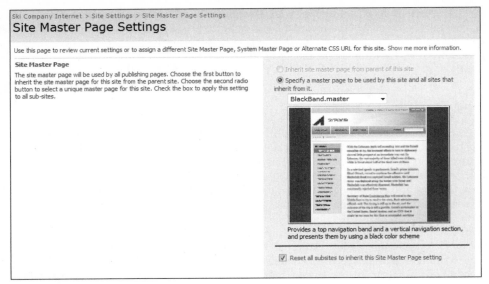

Figure 13-17

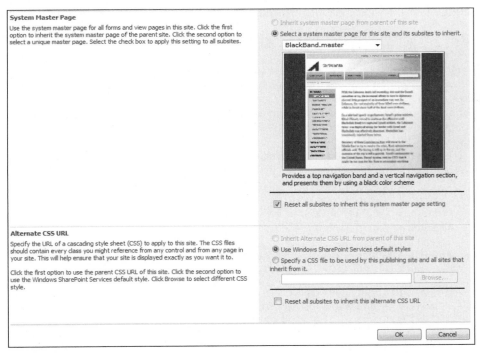

Figure 13-18

8. For even further customization of the look and feel, you can specify an alternate CSS file to overwrite the default out-of-the-box styles, changing the basic colors, backgrounds, and fonts. For this exercise, you can leave the default Windows SharePoint Services default style sheet option selected.

9. Leave the Reset Subsites check box unselected for this example.

10. Click the OK button. Your site reflects the applied master page and has a slightly different look and feel.

Try It Out   Customize a Master Page

Master pages are an ASP.NET 2.0 technology that allows you to separate the presentation and common elements from the content. You can define the common elements, such as navigation menus, headers, and footers in the master page, and then create the content for your site using content pages, which inherit the elements defined in the master page.

As previously noted, creating a custom master page requires basic knowledge of both SharePoint Designer 2007 and ASP.NET 2.0. It's recommended that only trained professionals attempt this type of customization work.

In the following example, you add a message to the BlackBand.master that you applied in the last Try It Out. You add this simple message in the header to welcome the user to your ski company. This message then displays on all content pages to which the master is applied. You can also change or add things such as a company logo or slogan, header graphic, or styling buttons. Note that this exercise requires you to check the master page out and back in again. Also, by default the master page document has content approval workflow enabled.

For more on checking a document in and out, see Chapter 3. For more on workflows, see Chapter 5.

1. Open SharePoint Designer and select File ⇨ Open Site from the menu. The Open Site dialog box appears as shown in Figure 13-19.

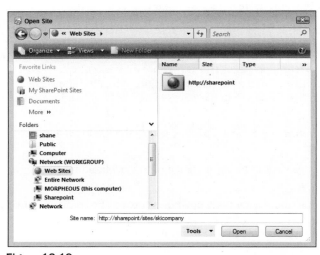

Figure 13-19

2. For the Site Name field, type the URL of the SharePoint site for which you want to customize a master page.

3. Navigate to the Master Page Gallery. You access this from SharePoint Designer by expanding the _catalogs/master page folder in the left window. See Figure 13-20.

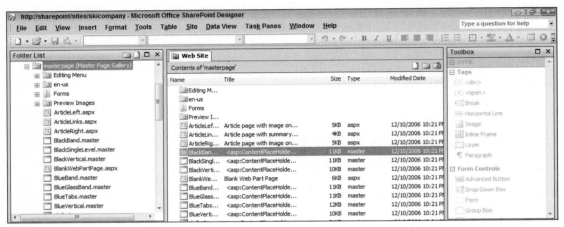

Figure 13-20

In the previous Try It Out, you changed the Ski Company site to use the BlackBand.master page; therefore, this is the page you'll want to edit.

4. Double-click the BlackBand.master page. By default, pages in this library are under source control, so a window appears for you to check out the page. Select Yes for check out and click OK.

5. Switch to Code view by clicking the Code tab at the bottom of the editing area and scrolling down until you see the Table, which has the class MasterContent applied to it.

6. You want the message to display at the very top, so add a table row and column to the top of the table. Copy and paste the following into the top of the table:

```
<tr><td width="100%" colspan="2">Welcome to Ski Company</td></tr>
```

7. Select File ⇨ Save As to save the page. You receive a message telling you that you are about to customize a definition page. This is because all sites start their life cycle from the same master page, which is specified in the site definition. When the site is created, this master page is copied from the file server to the Master Page Gallery to allow you to further customize it at the site level.

8. Click Yes. Notice that an icon appears next to the file in the left menu. This is true of any customized pages.

9. Check the page back in by right-clicking the BlackBand.master page and then selecting Check In.

10. The changes to the master page must be approved by someone with appropriate permissions before going live to the general public. Select Publish a Major Version from Options and click OK. A second prompt displays informing you that this content must be approved. Select Yes to modify the approval. You are transferred to the Master Page Gallery where you can check in and approve newly published items.

11. Notice that the Approval Status Column for the BlackBand.master is in a reading Pending. This means it's waiting to be approved. Hover your mouse over the BlackBand.master file exposing its contextual menu. Select Approve/reject from the list of options. See Figure 13-21.

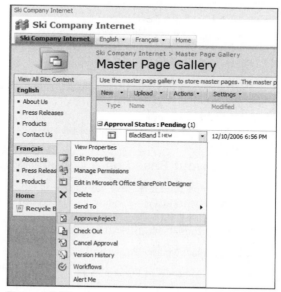

Figure 13-21

12. Ensure that Approved is selected and click OK. The status changes to show the page is approved.

13. Return to the home page.

How It Works

The message you added now displays across the top of the screen as you wanted. The true power of master pages is visible during site maintenance and updates. If you have dozens of content pages in your site and need to make a sweeping change to the navigation menu of these pages, edits to the master page would ripple down through, updating all pages that inherit it.

Page Layouts and Content Types

Page layouts control the type of content that can be created on a page as well as where and how that content displays. Page layouts are built on content types, which were discussed in Chapter 2. A *content type* has one or more metadata columns associated with it, and these metadata columns ultimately control the type of content associated with that particular content type, things such as rich HTML fields or images. You can also place Web Part zones on the page to allow for Web Part placement.

You define page layouts either through SharePoint Designer or via the browser. By default, when you use the browser method, which is described in the first Try It Out in this section, the controls are all added to the page top down, stacked one after another with little control over how the various controls on the page are presented or positioned.

When you require full control over the layout of the page, you can use SharePoint Designer to create the page layout. If you are comfortable editing a page in SharePoint Designer, you can get started by following the steps in the second Try It Out in this section.

> *Because SharePoint Designer 2007 is required, it's recommended that only trained professionals attempt this type of customization.*

In the final Try It Out, you learn how to create a custom page layout.

Try It Out   Create a Page Layout Based on a Content Type

In this example, you have a content type for Marketing Newsletters, which includes columns such as a Title, Date, or Body Text. You create a Marketing Newsletter page layout based on this content type.

1. Select Site Actions ➪ Site Settings ➪ Modify All Site Settings.

2. From the Galleries section, select Master Pages and Page Layouts.

3. Select New ➪ Page Layout, as shown in Figure 13-22.

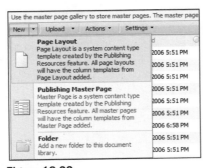

Figure 13-22

4. You must first associate your page layout with a content type. The columns defined in your content type become the content allowed on the page. In the Associated Content Type group, select Page Layout Content Types. Any custom content type groups you may have created become accessible in the menu.

5. Select Content Type Name ➪ Welcome Page.

6. In the Page Layout Title and Description section, type **Marketing** in the URL Name field.

7. In the Title field, type **Marketing Welcome Page**.

8. In the Description field, type **Marketing Division Welcome Page**.

9. Select EN and FR, and click the Add button for the Variations Labels field.

10. Click the OK button.

How It Works

Once you have created a page layout, it becomes visible in the list of Layouts on the Create Page window. You can view this list by clicking Site Actions ➪ Create Page. The Create Page is shown in Figure 13-23.

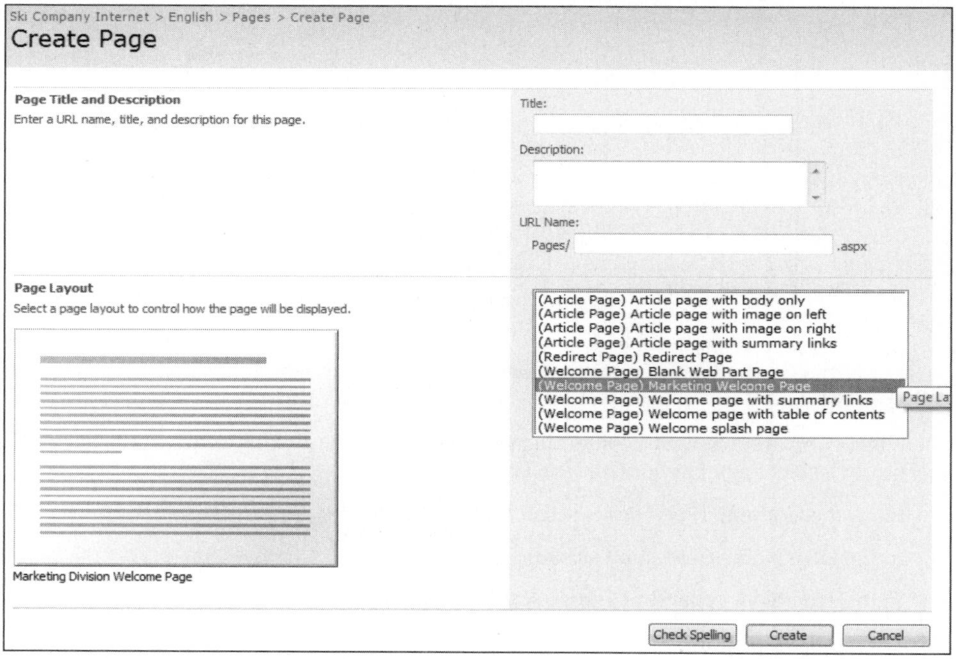

Figure 13-23

Create a Page Layout Using SharePoint Designer 2007

Page layouts set the stage for the type of content you want to allow on a particular page. For example, you might allow someone to place an image and description on a page. These pieces of content are actually columns in the content type on which you built your page layout. These columns are accessible in SharePoint Designer 2007 as content controls in the SharePoint Controls section of the Toolbox.

If the Toolbox is not visible on the right, you can turn it on by selecting Task Panes ➪ Toolbox in the SharePoint Designer toolbar. Using SharePoint Designer, you can place content controls on the page by dragging them from the Toolbox on to the page where you want to display them. It is important to note that the content controls should be placed inside the placeholder labeled "PlaceHolderMain."

1. In SharePoint Designer, select File ➪ New ➪ SharePoint Content tab as shown in Figure 13-24.

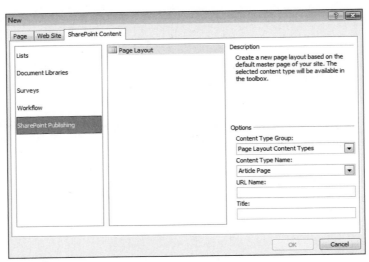

Figure 13-24

2. From the list of available options, select SharePoint Publishing to expose the Page Layout options.

3. For organization reasons, content types are stored in intuitive groups. From the Content Type group, select Page Layout Content Types.

4. From the Content Type Name, select Welcome Page.

5. In the URL Name field, type **skiwelcome**.

6. In the Title field, type **Ski Company Welcome Page**.

7. Click the OK button.

8. Your page layout should open for editing. If not, refresh (F5) and open the Welcome.aspx page. What you have just done is create a blank page layout ready for customization.

9. Enter code view by selecting code at the bottom of the editing window, locate the PlaceHolderMain tag. This is the main content area of the page where you want to make any layout changes as well as accept particular types of content.

10. Add the following table code between the PlaceHolderMain tags. This is the area where you allow content to be created.

```
<table width="100%">
<tr>
<td valign="top"></td>
</tr>
```

```
<tr>
<td valign="top"></td>
</tr>
</table>
```

11. When you create a content type, you attach metadata columns to the content type. These columns are the content you place in your page layout that ultimately becomes the content that the users will add to the page. These columns are visible in the Toolbox under SharePoint Controls, Content Fields.

12. Switch to Design mode by selecting the Design tab at the bottom of the editing window. Select the first row in the table you created. From the Toolbox, locate Page Fields, right-click the Contact Name field, and select Insert to add it to the selected cell of the table.

13. Select the second row in the table you created. From the Toolbox, locate Content Fields, right-click the Page Content field, and select Insert to add it to the selected cell of the table, as shown in Figure 13-25.

Figure 13-25

15. Save the page.

16. Pages in the Master Page library are under source control, and you need to check them out for editing, and check them in and publish them when they are final. Right-click skiwelcome.aspx and choose Check In.

17. Select Publish a Major Version and click OK. Select Yes for Content Approval When Prompted.

18. Hover your mouse over the Welcome.aspx file that is currently pending, and select Approve from the Content menu.

19. Select Approved, and then click the OK button.

How It Works

You can now put your page layouts to work by selecting Site Actions ⇨ Create Page. To create a new page, you must specify a page layout. By selecting the Ski Company Welcome Page that you just created, you generate a page to which you can add a title and page content, just as you specified in the page layout. See Figure 13-26.

Notice that because the page layout also inherits from BlackBand.master, you see the welcome message at the top of the page, which you added in the "Customize a Master Page" Try It Out earlier in the chapter.

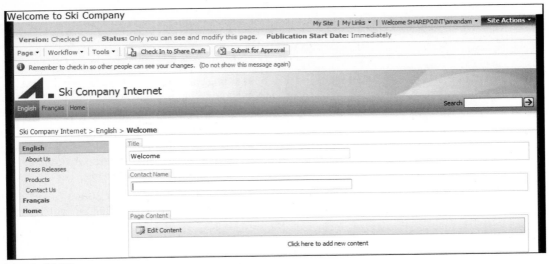

Figure 13-26

Try It Out   Create a Custom Page

In this example, you select a page layout from which you create a custom page. Based on the page layout and master page that it inherits, a page is presented to the user.

1. Select Site Actions ➪ Create Page as shown in Figure 13-27. The Create Page window appears as shown in Figure 13-28.

2. In the Page Title and Description section, type a title for your page. For this example, type **WelcomeSkiCompany**.

3. Type a description for your page. For this example, type **Ski Company Welcome Page**. SharePoint fills in the URL Name field automatically. In this case, it fills in `welcomeskicompany`. You can change this if you want, but for this example leave it as is.

Figure 13-27

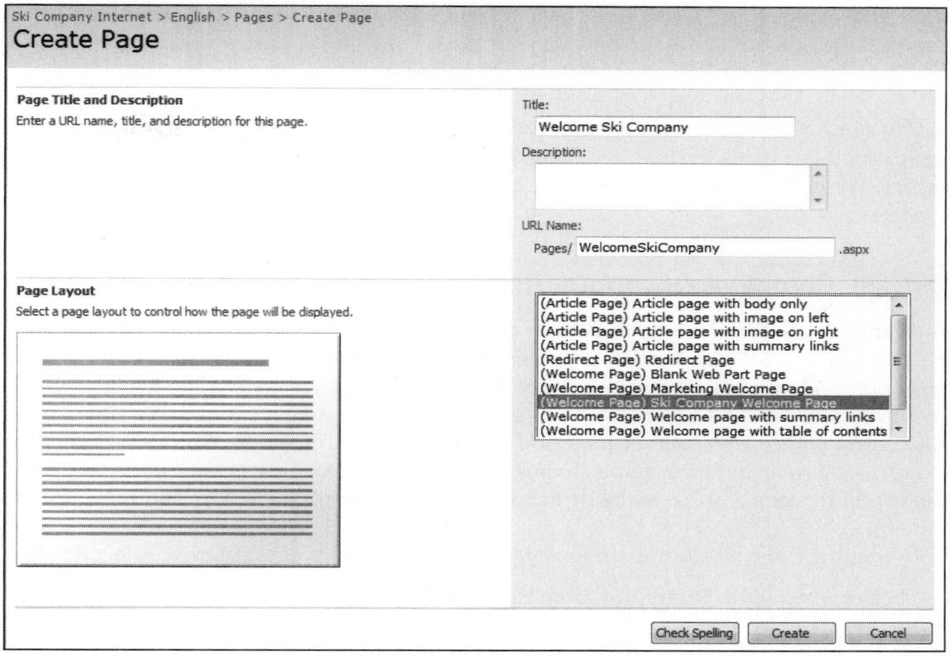

Figure 13-28

5. In the Page Layout section, locate and select (Welcome Page) Ski Company Welcome Page, which you created in the previous section.

6. Click Create. SharePoint creates a custom page based on the Ski Company Welcome Page Layout.

Understanding Document Conversion

Many organizations store a great deal of information in popular file formats, such as Word or InfoPath. Because the information already exists in a format with which users are familiar, it does not always make sense to repeat the authoring process when this content needs to go on a website. Instead, it's faster to create web content directly from these files. Further, if you present this content within the corporate website, you would want to maintain the corporate look and feel. SharePoint 2007 supports a document conversion feature that allows users to create web pages of content directly from specific file types. SharePoint supports document conversion for the following formats:

❑ An InfoPath form to a web page

❑ A Word document to a web page

❑ A Word document with macros to a web page

❑ An XML document to a web page

In addition, developers can write their own converters and install them. This becomes relevant only if you have a large amount of data in files on your SharePoint server that you want to make available as web content while avoiding the publishing or duplication processes.

Before you can convert a document, which you do directly from the document libraries, you must first configure and then enable the feature via the Central Administration site, which is the subject of the first and second Try It Outs in this section. In the third Try It Out, you learn how to convert a document into a web page.

Try It Out   Configure Document Conversion

In this example, you learn how a server farm administrator enables document conversion. You start this process by visiting the Operations Management area of the Central Administration site to ensure that the Load Balancer and Launcher services for document conversions are enabled on the server. You then visit the Document Conversion Configuration page and select the settings required to enable the service. These settings control which server acts as the load balancer server and the interval by which the document conversion timer job runs. In this example, four document converters have been installed on the system, and you can configure each of these to define maximum file size, time-out length, and maximum retries.

1. From the Central Administration site of your SharePoint environment, select the Operations tab.

2. Select Services on Server link from the Topology and Services group.

3. If the Document Conversion Services does not have a status of Started, click the Start link for the Document Conversions Load Balancer Service.

4. Click the Start link for the Document Conversions Launcher Service.

5. Select the server you want to use for the launch server as well as the load balancer server, and click the OK button. The Configure Document Conversions window appears, as shown in Figure 13-29.

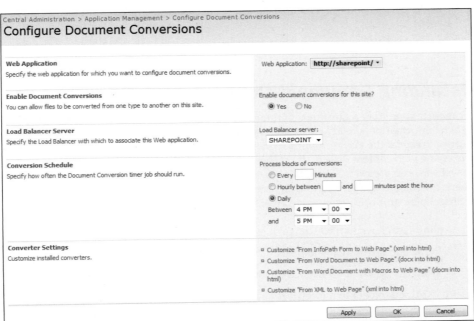

Figure 13-29

If your server is running in a stand-alone configuration, these services may already be running, in which case no action is needed.

6. Select the Application Management tab.

7. From the External Service Connections section, select Document Conversions.

8. Select the appropriate web application from the list. In many cases, the web application you will be working with will be hosted on port 80. Confirm with your server administrator if you are unsure.

9. Select Yes for Enable Document Conversions for This Site.

10. Select the server that will act as the load balancer server. If your server farm is a stand-alone server, the server name may be already populated in the drop-down box.

11. Specify an appropriate interval for the document conversion process to run. Depending on your requirements, your selection here may vary. For an environment that anticipates many documents being converted on a regular basis, the interval may be more frequent. For an environment with few documents and a requirement to ensure optimal performance, the timer job may run less frequently and perhaps be scheduled on a daily basis for when the server does not anticipate a great deal of load.

12. Select the hyperlink for the From Word Document to Web Page.

13. Check the timeout length to 240 seconds.

14. Click the OK button.

15. Click the Apply button.

16. Click the OK button.

How It Works

Once you configure the service on the server, you can enable it on specific content types so that it's available to users in document libraries as an action on the Send to Menu of a document, as shown in Figure 13-30.

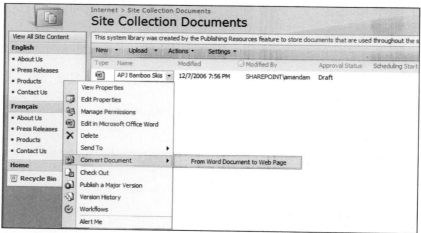

Figure 13-30

Enable Document Conversion on a Content Type

In this example, you configure document conversion on a content type so that users can convert a Word document for your ski company to a web page. The users have a Word document template that they've been using for years to fill out on the company's various products, and it keeps information current. These users have exceptional skills with Word, but very little web publishing or coding skills. By converting the Word document to web content, you allow them keep their familiar tool while converting content to the company's unique look and feel for the web.

1. From your Ski Company site select Site Actions ➪ Site Settings ➪ Modify All Site Settings.

2. If you are not at the top level of your site collection, select Top-Level Site Settings.

3. From the Galleries group, select the Site Content Types.

4. Click the Create button from the toolbar. The New Site Content Type window appears as shown in Figure 13-31.

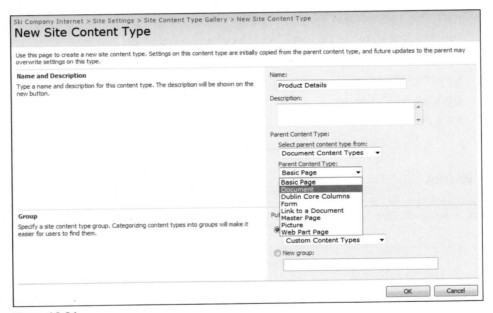

Figure 13-31

5. Type a name for the content type. For this example, enter **Product Details**.

6. Select Document as the parent content type.

7. Enter a group name for the content type. This group name helps organize your content types. For this example, enter **Product Information**.

8. Click the OK button. You are returned to the Site Content Type administration page.

9. Click the Advanced Settings link.

10. Select upload a new document template, and click Browse to locate the file "ski product information.docx" from the resources outlined for this chapter.

11. Click the OK button. You are returned to the Site Content Type administration page.

12. Select Manage Document Conversion for This Content Type. The Manage Document Conversion for Product Details window appears as shown in Figure 13-32.

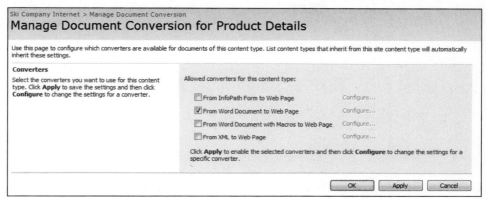

Ski Company Internet > Manage Document Conversion

Manage Document Conversion for Product Details

Use this page to configure which converters are available for documents of this content type. List content types that inherit from this site content type will automatically inherit these settings.

Converters

Select the converters you want to use for this content type. Click **Apply** to save the settings and then click **Configure** to change the settings for a converter.

Allowed converters for this content type:

☐ From InfoPath Form to Web Page   Configure...
☑ From Word Document to Web Page   Configure...
☐ From Word Document with Macros to Web Page   Configure...
☐ From XML to Web Page   Configure...

Click **Apply** to enable the selected converters and then click **Configure** to change the settings for a specific converter.

[OK]   [Apply]   [Cancel]

Figure 13-32

13. Unselect all check boxes except the one for the conversion of a Word Document to a WebPage.

14. Click the Apply button.

15. Click the Configure link to the right of the Word Document to a Web Page item.

16. Select Define Unique Settings for This Content Type.

17. Select the Article page with image on right page layout from the page layout drop-down menu.

18. For field for Converted Document Contents, select Page Content.

19. For the Location section, select the check box to set a default site for creating pages. Because the content you are creating is related to the products site, you need to create all pages there. Click the Browse button to open the Choose Site – Webpage Dialog, as shown in Figure 13-33, and then click the Products site and click the OK button.

20. Keep the default setting for processing, which is Create Pages One at a Time, and Take Users to the Page Once It Is Created.

21. Click the OK button.

22. Select Site Actions ➪ View All Site Content.

23. Select the Site Collection Documents library.

24. Select Settings ➪ Document Library Settings from the toolbar.

25. Select Advanced Settings.

26. Select Yes to allow management of content types.

27. Click the OK button.

Figure 13-33

28. Select the Add from Existing Site Content Types.

29. Select Product Information from the Groups drop-down menu.

30. Click the Add button to add your content type to the library.

31. Click the OK button.

How It Works

In Step 19, you specified that the newly created web pages should be published to the Products Site Pages library regardless of where the documents themselves exist. This means users can create their content in a collaborative area or other area where they have access, and have the pages automatically go to the appropriate site. Because you define the document conversion process at the content-type level, it's convenient for a site administrator to determine the publishing location based on the type of content that is being created; the users creating the content don't have to be concerned with this.

Try It Out   Convert a Document to a Web Page

This example shows you how to convert a document to a web page. This involves creating a document from a document library based on a content type, following the same procedure covered in Chapter 6. Once the content is created, you then convert it to a web page that you can publish to a site.

1. From the main page of your Ski Company site, select Site Actions ➪ View All Site Content.

2. Select the Site Collections Documents library.

3. Select New Product Details Document from the toolbar.

4. Fill in the details for your new product as follows:

Document Section	Details
Product Name	APJ Bamboo Skis.
Product Description	These revolutionary new skis are the latest innovation in cross-country and downhill skiing. Using these skis, you will be able to cover miles of trail without feeling like you left the comfort of your living room.
Price	$1999 USD.

5. Save the file as **APJ Bamboo Skis.docx** and close the document.

6. Close the document, and check it in as a major version of the document using the process reviewed in Chapter 3.

7. Return to the document library. Hover your mouse over the document to expose the menu.

8. Select Send To ➪ Convert Document ➪ From Word Document to Web Page. The Document Conversion window appears as shown in Figure 13-34.

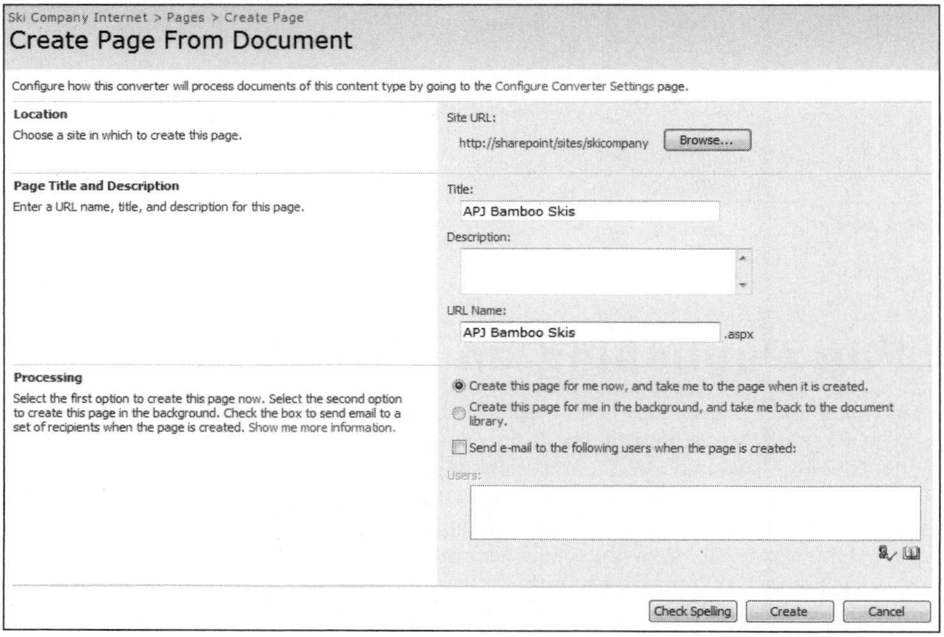

Ski Company Internet > Pages > Create Page

Create Page From Document

Configure how this converter will process documents of this content type by going to the Configure Converter Settings page.

Location
Choose a site in which to create this page.

Site URL:
http://sharepoint/sites/skicompany [Browse...]

Page Title and Description
Enter a URL name, title, and description for this page.

Title:
APJ Bamboo Skis

Description:

URL Name:
APJ Bamboo Skis .aspx

Processing
Select the first option to create this page now. Select the second option to create this page in the background. Check the box to send email to a set of recipients when the page is created. Show me more information.

● Create this page for me now, and take me to the page when it is created.
○ Create this page for me in the background, and take me back to the document library.
☐ Send e-mail to the following users when the page is created:
Users:

[Check Spelling] [Create] [Cancel]

Figure 13-34

9.   Enter a title for the web page. For this example, enter **APJ Bamboo Skis**.

10. Select the Create This Page for Me Now, and Take Me to the Page When It Is Created option.

11. Click the Create button.

How It Works

Figure 13-35 shows how the Word document looks when converted to a web page. Notice how the page automatically appears in the navigation control of the site, and how the URL illustrates how the page is stored in the Pages library of the Products site, even though the original document is located at the top level of the site collection in the Site Collection Documents library.

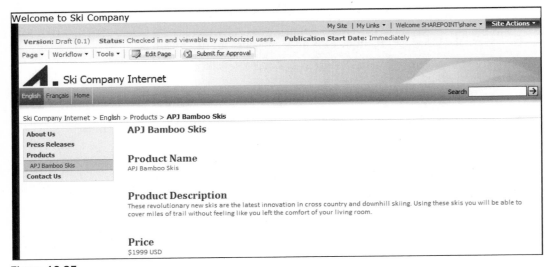

Figure 13-35

Enabling Publishing on a Team Site

So far the examples in this chapter have worked with the Publishing portal site template. This is primarily because this template contains many of the components and elements you need to create a web-facing site. However, you may need to make use of publishing features within a standard team site or workspace, and to do so means you have to enable the Publishing feature, as is demonstrated in the first Try It Out in this section. Switching on the publishing features means you can transform any team site into a publishing site, complete with content approval workflow and new lists and libraries. Figure 13-36 shows a site before the Publishing feature. In Figure 13-37, after the feature is enabled, you see new workflow as well as new elements in the menus and new controls, such as the Create Page option in the Site Actions menu.

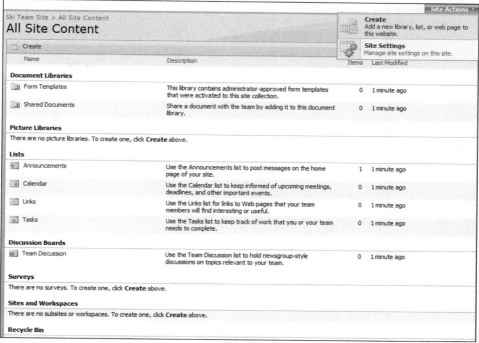

Figure 13-36

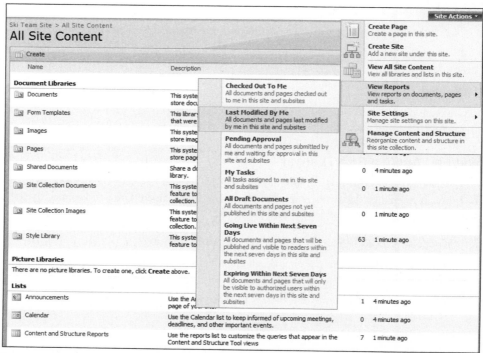

Figure 13-37

In the section "Customizing the Look and Feel of a WCM Site," you learned how the master page can control the appearance of an Internet or intranet portal. This is true for a team collaboration site as well; in addition to master page customizations, SharePoint 2007 makes extensive use of cascading style sheets (CSS) that allow you to make subtle changes to the background colors and fonts on a site. One way CSS is used is through *site themes*. A theme is not permanent; you can change the site again by simply applying another theme, and the new theme will overwrite the already applied theme. The second Try It Out in this section shows you how to apply a theme to a site.

Try It Out   **Enable the Publishing Feature on a Team Site**

In this example, you have a team site that your ski company is using to create content and track progress across various initiatives. However, to track team announcements and news, you decide to enable the Publishing feature on the site. To do this, you visit the Site Settings page for the site and selected Activate for the Publishing feature on both the site collection level and the individual site level.

> *When you enable the Publishing feature on a collaborative site, such as a team site or a blank site, you can no longer save that site as a template. This is something you should be aware of before making the choice to enable specific features or functionality on existing sites.*

1. From the SharePoint Central Administration site, create a new site collection from the Application Management tab using the Team Site template called "Ski Team Site."

2. From the main page of your new team site, select Site Actions ⇨ Site Settings.

3. Select Site Collection Features from the Site Collection Administration links.

4. Click the Activate button next to the Office SharePoint Server Publishing Infrastructure feature.

5. Select Site Features from the Site Administration links of the Site Settings page.

6. Click the Activate button next to the Office SharePoint Server Publishing feature.

How It Works

When you enable the publishing feature, this creates new lists and libraries, automatically adds content approval workflow, and expands the Site Actions menu so that you can create pages.

Try It Out   **Apply a Site Theme**

This example shows you the various site themes that SharePoint has to offer. You can apply these themes via the browser to change the sites colors. To change the theme itself, you need to modify the CSS for the theme using a text editor such as SharePoint Designer.

1. Select Site Actions ⇨ Site Settings ⇨ Modify All Site Settings.

2. Under the Look and Feel section, select Site Theme. The Site Theme window appears as shown in Figure 13-38.

3. Locate and select the name of a theme. In this example, select the theme Verdant.

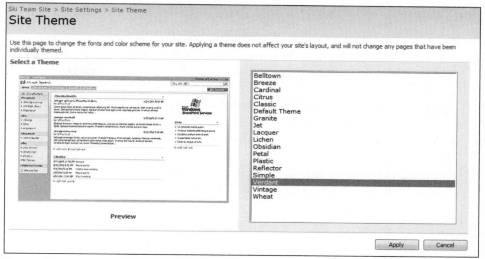

Figure 13-38

4. Click Apply to change the look and feel of your site.

Summary

As your business publishes more and more content online, you need tools to efficiently accomplish this task. This chapter covers one of the biggest additions to SharePoint — Web Content Management (WCM). Using the WCM, users can perform tasks that once required the expertise of a skilled programmer. From this chapter you learned the following:

❑ You can use publishing features to create web content without any web programming skills.

❑ Using content types, you can fully control what content a user creates. These content types can be attached to lists, document libraries, and even web pages.

❑ You can create page layouts based on content types. While content type controls the type of content that you can have on the page, the page layout itself can be customized to position and style the content. Users can later create content or pages in the site based on these Page Layouts.

❑ SharePoint allows you to keep your unique corporate branding using master pages and site themes. By modifying master pages, you customize things such as headers and navigation menus, while themes allow you to change background colors and fonts.

❑ Doing business internationally means having sites that are in multiple languages. SharePoint 2007 can help you set up different calendars and local settings in various languages using Variations, Regional Settings, Resource Files, and Language Packs.

Exercises

1. Your manager informs you that you have been selected to create a website for the communications department on the new Microsoft Office SharePoint Server. The main requirement is to have the site allow nontechnical employees in the communications division to publish monthly newsletters. What do you do?

2. Your organization has recently gone through a rebranding change, and your team must make the corporate intranet reflect these changes. What are your options?

3. True or False. You can enable the Publishing feature after you create a team site.

4. The sales manager says a recent sale requires the implementation of an externally facing customer support portal in two languages, English and French. How do you proceed?

Working with Search

Thus far, this book has covered the various ways you can store and interact with documents and content via SharePoint 2007. Once you configure your system to fit your business requirements, you need to configure the system so that users can easily find the information.

In this chapter, you discover various built-in search features. You then learn what configuration alternatives you, the SharePoint administrator, have on both the site and server level to meet the needs of your organization. Some of the topics covered in this chapter include:

❑ Using the Basic Search interface

❑ Using the Advanced Search interface

❑ Promoting properties for use in advanced search

❑ Using the People Search

❑ Creating custom keywords and best bets for search results

❑ Defining custom content sources

❑ Creating custom search scopes

❑ Working with the various search Web Parts

After reading this chapter, you should feel comfortable managing the search experience available within your SharePoint environment.

Understanding SharePoint Search

The search facilities in SharePoint allow users to easily locate content stored in the various SharePoint sites as well as other external content sources such as file shares, Exchange public folders, and line-of-business (LOB) applications. Before you get started working on some of this chapter's exercises, you need to familiarize yourself with some terms as well as what search features each version of SharePoint has to offer.

So how does a SharePoint search work, exactly? The search must have a *content source*, which are the locations where that SharePoint looks for information when you enter search terms into the SharePoint interface. By default, one content source represents all the sites in the SharePoint environment. However, you can add more content sources so users can search content stored in other locations such as a file share, website, Exchange public folder, or business application.

For SharePoint to search any content, the content must first be indexed. A *content index* combines details on all the information in the content sources. When users perform searches, the index is queried for content that matches the user-entered terms. For a search to be accurate and effective, the system updates the index regularly based on a schedule that you define. A *crawl* is the process by which the SharePoint index is rebuilt or updated to include new information. A *full update* is a complete recrawl of all SharePoint content to update the index. An *incremental update* only reviews items that have changed or been added since the last update. Although SharePoint crawls a number of file types to include content in the documents, the system does not automatically crawl some file types and requires you to install a special tool, called an *iFilter*, to allow the SharePoint search service to index the documents. For example, you must install an iFilter to support PDF document indexing.

SharePoint Services 3.0	SharePoint Server 2007 for Search	SharePoint Server 2007
This is the same as SharePoint Server, with some differences: ❑ You can only index and search SharePoint content. ❑ It does not support keywords and best bets. ❑ It does not support reusing Search Web Parts and creating custom search pages. ❑ There is no Search Center. ❑ It does not support searching user profile information. ❑ It does not support searching of business data.	When an organization requires an enhanced search engine but cannot justify transitioning to SharePoint 2007, they can license SharePoint Server 2007 for Search, which offers the following improvements over WSS 3.0: ❑ Support for custom keywords and best bets. ❑ Support for the Search Center without tabs. ❑ Support for People Search. ❑ Support for multiple content sources (file shares, Exchange folders, external websites, and Lotus Notes).	SharePoint 2007 has the following improvements: ❑ Improved relevance in returned results. ❑ Advanced search for team collaborative sites. ❑ Search results hit highlighting. ❑ Suggested words for misspelled queries. ❑ Features to search more content types. ❑ Customized search query and results pages. ❑ Enhanced support for user profile and people searching. ❑ Features to define content scopes on a global and site level.

To get the most out of your search, you may need to define a content scope or set managed properties. Searching the entire content index or a content source may be too broad of a search. By way of example, if you lose your keys visiting the front lobby of a building and go back to search for them, you limit your search to that lobby, not the entire building. In essence, scopes tell SharePoint what sections of an index to search. You may have scopes that represent smaller subsets of data such as user profiles or the human resources site, that allow users to limit their searches. For managed properties, remember that in Chapter 6 you created site columns as global properties to define documents and list items. You can configure these columns as managed properties so that users can search for documents based on specific content in the Advanced Search interface. For example, if you have a customer site column, you can turn it into a managed property, and when users conduct a search from the Advanced Search interface, they can select Customer from a drop-down list. This refines the search and limits it to items relating to a specific customer.

This book focused specifically on Microsoft Office SharePoint Server 2007, which offers the maximum amount of search functionality over all other versions, including being able to search for business data from LOB systems. The previous table outlines some of the differences between the other versions of SharePoint 2007 that support search and indexing.

Working with the Search Feature

There are multiple ways in which you can interact with and manage searches in SharePoint 2007. The following sections discuss the two most common search interfaces:

- ❑ **Basic Search:** The most common search query where users type simple keywords and phrases that the search uses to find file content, file names and properties.

- ❑ **Advanced Search:** A more detailed search that filters based on properties, file types, and languages. It includes options for how the keywords relate to the search query — for example, if it should search in the order a user enters a phrase or if any of the words should appear.

This section discusses both search interfaces and provides some hands-on experience using both.

Using the Basic Search

Every site in SharePoint has a basic search box in the top-right corner, as shown in Figure 14-1, where users can enter terms or words that allow them to find content. SharePoint searches the titles and column data associated with documents as well as the document itself. Depending on your file format, your administrator may need to install an iFilter, which was discussed in the previous section.

Figure 14-1

To the left of the search box is a drop-down box where you can define a scope for your search. This box has a default scope list that is site-specific and changes depending on where you search for something. For example, by default the drop-down box on a team or portal site home page has the options All Sites, People, and This Site. However, the drop-down box from a View page of a document library or list has the options just mentioned as well as This List: List Name. The following shows the common scope of options for a basic search:

❑ **All Sites:** Searches all sites and content sources in the SharePoint index.

❑ **People:** Searches against user profile properties. This is the same scope that the Employee Finder Web Part uses. For more on Web Parts, see Chapter 7.

❑ **This Site:** Searches for results on the current site only.

You learn how to manage additional scopes later in this chapter in the section "Create Search Scopes." First, you need to become familiar with using the basic search functionality from the perspective of an end user.

To ensure that searches reflect information that should already exist in your environment, you perform searches in this chapter for content created in previous examples in this book. If you no longer have these documents or have not completed all the chapter exercises, use your own search terms to reflect information you know exists in your environment.

Try It Out   Perform a Basic Search for Content

In this example, you perform two basic searches using the words Advertising Materials. For the first search, you type the two words without any quotation marks or special characters. This returns a list of items that show where the words appear together and separately, but in no specific order. For the second search, you place the two words in quotation marks. This limits the results that only show the words together and in the order specified.

1. From the home page of your SharePoint site, enter the words **Advertising Materials** in your search box, as shown in Figure 14-2.

Figure 14-2

2. Click the Search icon to the right of the search box.

3. Select the View by Modified Date option. Notice the number identified for your search results, as shown in Figure 14-3.

4. In the search box, place quotation marks around the words Advertising Materials.

5. Press Enter. Notice the number identified for your search results this time, which are shown in Figure 14-4.

Figure 14-3

Figure 14-4

How It Works

For both searches, you see a list of items in order of relevance that contain the words you have entered, with the words appearing in bolded text. For the first search, all occurrences of the words appear. Selecting the View by Modified Date option in step 3 changes the order so that the most recent item appears first in the list. This is important because for editing purposes, you may need the most up-to-date document instead of the most relevant. For the second search, you have fewer results because the search only lists occurrences when the two words appear together.

Using the Advanced Search

Using quotation marks or changing the result sort order may not be enough when you're typing vague or highly used words. This is especially true if your SharePoint environment has numerous documents — a situation that always yields a large number of results. However, you can refine your search using the Advanced Search feature. Besides being able to type exact phrases for your search criteria, you can specify the type of document you're searching for in the Result Type field (seen in 14-5).

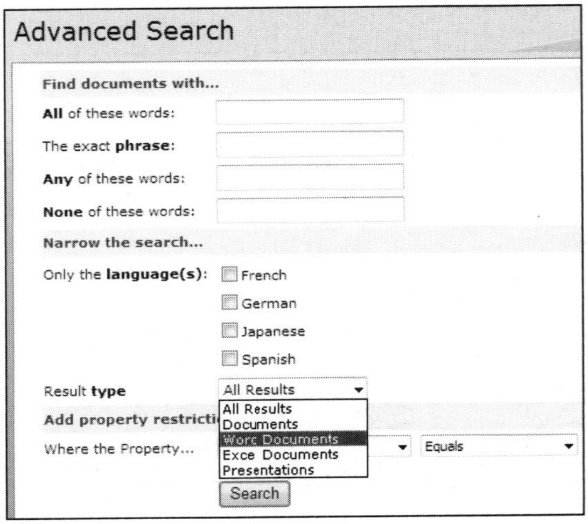

Figure 14-5

When you type something in the Created By field, SharePoint searches through specific column data in document libraries. By default, SharePoint offers the following properties as options:

❑   Author

❑   Description

❑   Name

❑   Size

❑   URL

❑   Created Date

❑   Last Modified Date

❑   Created By

❑   Last Modified By

In addition to these properties, you can create your own properties. This is helpful for locating items in specific columns that are used as properties for multiple lists, libraries, or content types throughout the environment.

In the following exercises, you see the process for promoting these properties to the Advanced Search interface as well as how to work with the Advanced Search feature. In the first Try It Out, you perform an advanced search and then sort for the most recent document. The second Try It Out simulates a scenario where the users must search for documents and content based on the client for which the document was created. This means you need to associate the information with content, which requires a site column as well a central listing of clients that the site column can reference.

Try It Out   Perform an Advanced Search for Content

In this example, you want to find a Word document you created that contains the exact phrase from an advertising campaign for Newfoundland and Labrador. You cannot remember the name or the location of the document, so you use the Advanced Search feature to define what you know about the document and thus increase your odds of finding it.

1.   From the main page of your portal page, click the Advanced Search link to the right of your search box. You are redirected to a page in the Search Center with an interface where you can define search details, as was shown in Figure 14-5.

2.   Enter the following into the available fields:

Field	Value
The Exact Phrase	Experience the thrill of Newfoundland and Labrador.
Result Type	Word documents.
Created By	Enter your own first name.

3.   Click the Search button.

How It Works

By typing the phrase **Experience the thrill of Newfoundland and Labrador** in the box for exact phrase, you eliminated results that contain documents with similar words, such as those that have *Newfoundland* and *Labrador*. However, to further refine your search, you limit the results to include only Word documents that you created.

> To ensure that the experience will be the same for all readers of this book, the next exercise starts by creating a custom property and assigning it to a document library. You then complete the process of mapping the managed property to a crawled property. In order to complete this process, you will require access to the SharePoint Search Administration page as part of the Shared Services admin. If you do not have access to this area, you will have to see your server farm administrator.

Try It Out **Create a Managed Property**

In this example, a property in a site column becomes available to users on an Advanced Search page when you make it a managed property. You first create a site column that references a clients list. This allows site managers to add that column to document libraries, lists, and content types throughout the site collection so they can track content related to specific clients. To validate your configuration, you add test data to the central list and then add the site column to a document library. You can then associate column values with a couple of sample documents so that they can later be returned in your search results when you perform a search using that property.

Next, you start an Incremental Crawl of the SharePoint environment, which searches for any differences in the system since the last crawl. It identifies the new property associated with your sample documents and adds it to a special list called Crawled Properties.

You then go into the Shared Services Administration site of your SharePoint environment to create and define a new managed property. This is the item you will reference from the Advanced Search interface later in the exercise. You add a mapping to the crawled property that you discover during your incremental update related to the client's site column. SharePoint groups all crawled properties based on how they were discovered, and therefore this column was automatically associated with the SharePoint group. More than one crawled property may be associated with a single managed property, if desired.

1. From the home page of the top-level site in your site collection, select View All Site Content.

2. Click the Create button from the toolbar.

3. Select Custom List from the Custom Lists group.

4. Enter **Clients** for the name and the following for a description:

> **This is a central listing of all clients that will be referenced by content stored within this system.**

5. Select No to Display the List on the Quick Launch bar.

6. Click the Create button. Your clients list is created and you are redirected to it.

7. Add two new items to the clients list called **Client A** and **Client B** using the methods described in Chapter 2. These entries will serve as sample data to simulate items that you might have in a real client listing.

8. Select Site Actions ➪ Site Settings. If you are on a publishing site, you may need to select Site Settings ➪ Modify All Site Settings.

9. Select Site Columns.

10. Click the Create button from the toolbar. The Create Column window appears, as shown in Figure 14-6.

11. For Column Name, enter **Clients** and select Lookup (information already on this site) for the Column Type.

12. Select New Group and enter **Global Properties**.

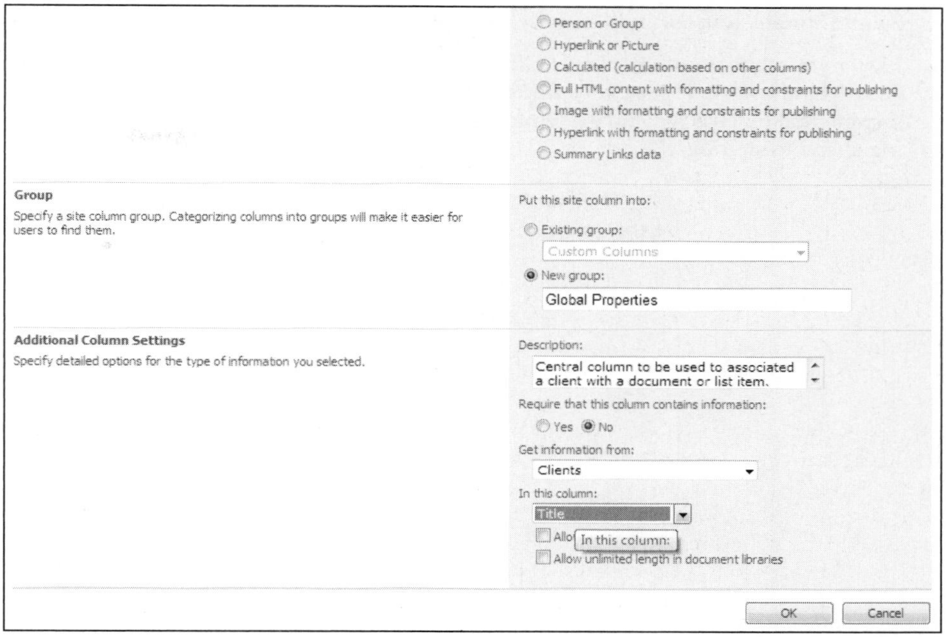

Figure 14-6

13. For Description, enter the following:

> **Central column to be used to associate a client with a document or list item. This column refers to the master clients list.**

14. Select to Get Information from Clients and from the Title Column.

15. Click the OK button.

16. Return to the home page of your top-level site.

17. Click the View All Site Content link.

18. Select the Documents library.

19. Add the Clients site column to the library using the method described in Chapter 6.

20. Upload two documents to the library and associate Client A with one and Client B with the other.

21. Go to the Shared Services Administration site of your SharePoint environment. If you do not know the exact URL of this site, please see your SharePoint farm administrator.

> *This site is also linked from the Central Administration site under the Shared Services Administration heading in the left-hand navigation. The exact name of this link may depend on your system's configuration. If you do not have access to this site, you will need to obtain it to complete this exercise.*

22. Select Search Settings from the Search group.

23. Select Content Sources and Crawl Schedules.

24. Hover your cursor over the Local Office SharePoint Server Sites and select Start Incremental Crawl, as shown in Figure 14-7. Depending on how much content exists on your server, the incremental process may take a while. You should wait for this process to complete before moving ahead to step 29.

Figure 14-7

25. Select Search Settings from the breadcrumb trail.

26. Click the Metadata Property Mappings link, as shown in Figure 14-8.

Figure 14-8

27. Click New Managed Property.

28. Enter the following for the property details:

Field	Value
Property Name	Clients.
Description	Allows for searching based on a property of a client name.
The Type of Information in This Property	Text.
Mappings to Crawled Properties	Include values from all crawled properties mapped.

29. Click the Add Mapping button.

30. Select SharePoint for the category.

31. Type the word **Clients** in the Crawled Property name box and click the Find button.

32. Select the returned property of ows_Clients(Text) as shown in Figure 14-9.

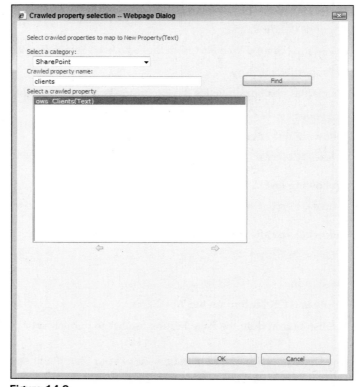

Figure 14-9

33. Click the OK button.

34. Select the check box to allow the property to be used in scopes.

35. Click the OK button.

How It Works

Now that you've created a managed property, you add it to the Advanced Search Web Part so that your team can access it when performing an advanced search.

Try It Out   Add a Managed Property to Advanced Search Web Part

You now add your managed property to the properties associated with the Advanced Search Web Part from the Advanced Search page. The first reference you add defines the property so that when a user selects a check box associated with the client property, the appropriate managed property is searched. The second reference ensures that the results associated with that property displays in the All Results page. Once you finish configuring everything, you rebuild the SharePoint Sites index to ensure that your documents appear in the search results when you perform a test search.

1. Return to the main page of your intranet site.

2. Click the Advanced Search link to the right of the search box.

3. Select Site Actions ➪ Edit Page.

4. Select Edit ➪ Modify Shared Web Part from the Advanced Search Box Web Part.

5. Expand the Properties category.

6. Select the Properties text box and click the Expansion button to the right.

7. Locate the `<PropertyDefs>` tag in the listing box.

8. Place the following line after the `PropertyDefs` tag:

```
<PropertyDef Name="Clients" DataType="text" DisplayName="Client"/>
```

9. Locate the following line in the listing box:

```
<ResultTypes><ResultType DisplayName="All Results" Name="default"><Query/>
```

10. Place the following line after the `<Query/>` tag.

```
<PropertyRef Name="Clients" />
```

12. Click the OK button.

12. Click the Apply and OK buttons on the Web Part.

13. Click the Publish button from the Page Editing toolbar to publish your page as described in Chapter 13.

14. Return to the Shared Services Administration site of your SharePoint environment. Select Search Settings from the Search group.

15. Select Content Sources and Crawl Schedules.

16. Hover your cursor over the Local Office SharePoint Server Sites and select Start Full Crawl, as shown in Figure 14-10.

Figure 14-10

How It Works

When you conduct a new search, you can now visit the Advanced Search interface and select Clients from the Property drop-down list, enter **Client A** as shown in Figure 14-11, and click the Search button.

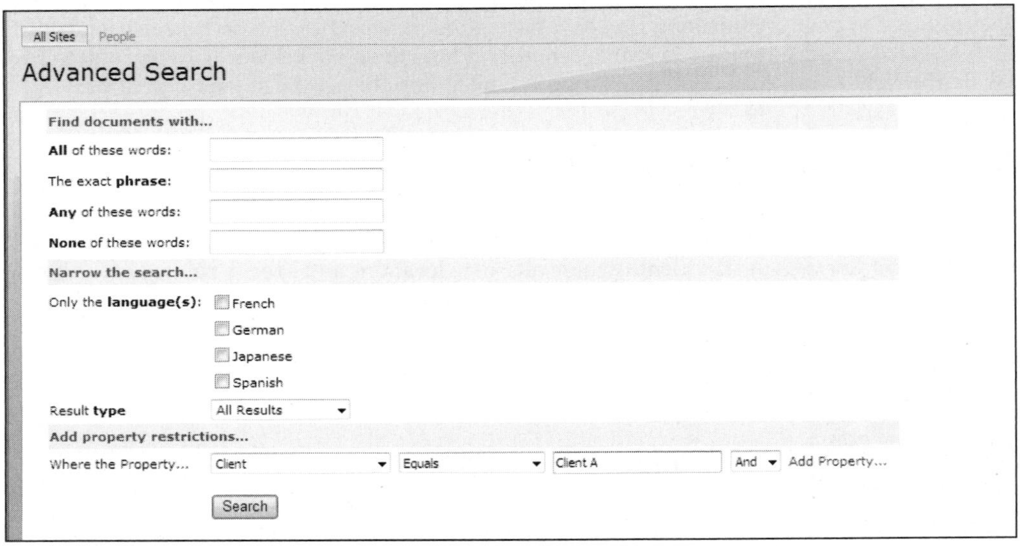

Figure 14-11

You should receive a result that matches the document you uploaded to the document library and specified a value of "Client A" for the Clients site column. Also notice that the list item Client A from the Clients list does not get returned as a result. This is because you have defined the search to be items that specifically have the value Client A as a value for Client.

Customizing and Managing Search

Now that you know how to use a basic and advanced search, it's time to see how you, the SharePoint administrator, can customize and manage the search service. For example, you can create content sources that search for documents across multiple websites or information systems, or create scopes in an existing content source to narrow search queries to a smaller set of data. This section details the process of creating new content sources and scopes to improve a user's search experience. Before you design any customized search, you should query the people who will use it to determine the following:

- ❑ What information storage locations do you want to search for using the SharePoint Search?
- ❑ What file formats will you store in the environment that you want to include in the content index?
- ❑ When you search for people in the organization, what properties do you use?
- ❑ How soon after a document is added to the system should it be available via the search interface?

In this section of the chapter, you learn some of the search customization alternatives SharePoint offers, which in turn will give you tips on how to best address your user's requirements. Because you want to make sure that your search goes to the right location, you learn about content sources, which are the locations that SharePoint looks to when you enter information into the SharePoint search interface. For accurate search results, you need to keep your information up-to-date, which you can do by scheduling regular index updates. Next, you learn how to manage file types so that your searches include the file types relevant to your organization. To allow users to refine searches, this section also explains how to create a search scope, how to use a search center, and how to define keywords so that a user's search will pull up the right information. Finally, you learn how to find the people in your organization.

Create Content Sources

By default, SharePoint has a single content source for all sites on your server. However, SharePoint can index content in other locations, such as file shares, business data, exchange folders, or websites. By creating a content source, you can identify these alternate locations and specify rules, such as how often and when the index will update. You can create content sources from the following locations:

- ❑ SharePoint sites
- ❑ Websites (non-SharePoint)
- ❑ File shares
- ❑ Exchange public folders
- ❑ Lotus Notes
- ❑ Applications via the Business Data Catalog

Depending on your requirements, you may want to separate specific sites or web applications so you have more flexibility for how content is crawled. For example, you can create a separate content source for My Sites that is crawled more regularly than your collaborative team sites. To do this, you remove the MySites web application reference from the Local Office SharePoint Server sites content source and create a new one that points to My Sites. You can then set a unique content crawl schedule for full and incremental updates.

For situations where you have a website that is not based on SharePoint, but that still contains valuable information, you can use the SharePoint search service to crawl content. This is shown in the first Try It Out. The second Try It Out covers situations where an organization transitions from file shares to SharePoint sites, but elects not to move all documents to the SharePoint environment. For example, you may have a large number of documents on a share for historical reference, but the organization doesn't intend to update the documents or control edits so sees no reason to migrate them to SharePoint. Rather than have users adopt a different method for locating these documents, you can index them via the SharePoint Server so that users can perform keyword searches regardless of location.

Try It Out	Create a Content Source Based on Non-SharePoint Websites

In this example, you create a new content source that will allow users of your SharePoint site to search for content contained in your company's Internet-facing website that is not a SharePoint site.

1. Go to the Shared Services Administration site of your SharePoint environment.

2. Select Search Settings. The Configure Search Settings window appears, as shown in Figure 14-12.

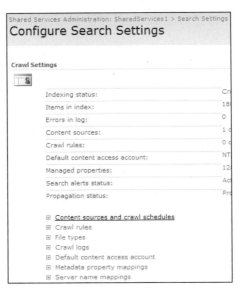

Figure 14-12

3. Click the Content Sources and Crawl Schedules link. You are redirected to the Manage Content Sources page.

4. Click the New Content Source button from the toolbar. The Add Content Source window appears, as shown in Figure 14-13.

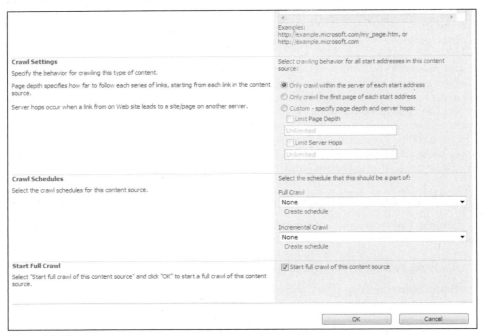

Figure 14-13

5. For the content source name, enter **Corporate** Website.

6. For the type of content to be crawled, select Websites.

7. Enter the web address of your organization's corporate website for the start address.

8. For Crawl Settings, select Only Crawl Within the Server of Each Start Address.

9. Select the check box to start a Full Crawl of content source.

10. Click the OK button.

How It Works

Once you finish these steps, your users can search the company's Internet-facing website. This creates a more unified content discovery experience for all your company's information, both public and private. Other examples of external websites you can index include partner sites or informational sites that contain valuable information related to your line of business.

Try It Out   Create a Content Source Based on File Shares

In this example, you create a new content source that references a file share on the corporate network. This is useful when file shares coexist with a SharePoint environment. In order for the system to crawl the external system such as a file share, the default Content Access Account must have access to that location in order to create the index. This is part of the configuration that is completed when SharePoint is installed and the Search service is configured, which is outside the scope of this chapter.

1. Go to the Shared Services Administration site of your SharePoint environment.

2. Select Search Settings.

3. Select Content Sources and Crawl Schedules. The Manage Content Sources window appears, as shown in Figure 14-14.

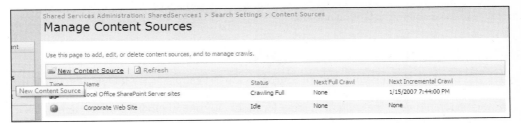

Figure 14-14

4. Click the New Content Source button from the toolbar. The Add Content Source window appears, as shown in Figure 14-15.

Type the URLs from which the search system should start crawling. This includes contents of a file share, such as documents and other files.	\\fileserver\fileshare
	Examples: \\server\directory, or file://server/directory
Crawl Settings Specify the behavior for crawling this type of content. Choose which folders to include in the crawl.	Select crawling behavior for all start addresses in this content source: ⦿ The folder and all subfolders of each start address ◯ The folder of each start address only
Crawl Schedules Select the crawl schedules for this content source.	Select the schedule that this should be a part of: Full Crawl None ▾ Create schedule Incremental Crawl None ▾ Create schedule
Start Full Crawl Select "Start full crawl of this content source" and click "OK" to start a full crawl of this content source.	☐ Start full crawl of this content source
	OK Cancel

Figure 14-15

5. For content source name, enter a name to reflect the file share you are about to reference, such as **Policies** and Procedures.

6. Enter the start address for the file server using the following format:

```
\\fileservername\sharename
```

7. For crawl settings, select the folder and all subfolders of each start address.

8. Select the check box to start a Full Crawl of the content source.

9. Click the OK button.

How It Works

By creating content sources that crawl the file shares, users can take advantage of the SharePoint Search interface to locate all important documents.

Schedule Content Source Updates

When you finished creating your content sources in the last couple of Try It Outs, you opted for a Full Crawl of the content source to start immediately. This process populates the SharePoint index with the appropriate references to the content in those locations. To continue to keep the content index up-to-date, it is important that you schedule regular crawls. This section discusses how to schedule the crawls and manually update the index when required.

SharePoint offers two schedule types:

❑   **Full:** A complete crawl of all content in a content source independent of previous crawls. You should perform this on a content source at least once before an Incremental Crawl can run.

❑   **Incremental:** A crawl of a content source for information updated, changed, or added since the last crawl.

As the SharePoint administrator, you should carefully plan when to schedule crawls involving large content sources. Consult with business users to determine an appropriate time interval in which they expect updated content to be available. It is generally recommended that you run Full Crawls less frequently than Incremental Crawls and that where possible, both crawls should run when there is lower demand on the servers.

The Try It Outs in this section show you how to schedule content source updates. In the first Try It Out, you discover how to schedule an incremental and full update. Alternately, specific changes to the search configuration or content source properties may require you to initiate a manual Full or Incremental Crawl to update to the content index, which is the subject of the second Try It Out. In the third Try It Out, you learn how to reset all crawl content. You may chose to do this in situations where your index becomes corrupt or you make significant content changes at once because of a large migration. While this is not something performed often, it is helpful to know how if the need arises.

Try It Out   **Create a Schedule for Updates to a Content Source**

In this example, you edit your content source to a schedule for the incremental updates. You can use this same process to define a Full Crawl schedule as well. Both processes are managed from the same page.

1.   From the Shared Services Administration site of your SharePoint environment, select Search Settings.

2.   Select Content Sources and Crawl Schedules. The Manage Content Sources window appears, as shown in Figure 14-16.

Figure 14-16

3.   Hover your cursor over the Local Office SharePoint Server Sites content source.

4.   Select Edit. The Edit Content Source window appears, as shown in Figure 14-17.

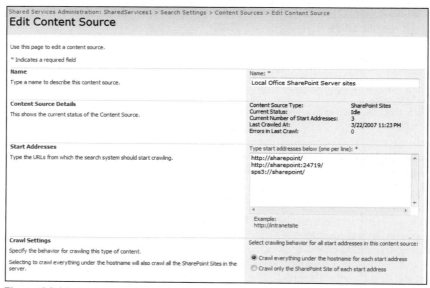

Figure 14-17

5. Under the Incremental Crawl drop-down box, click the Create Schedule link. The Manage Schedules window appears.

6. Select Daily for Type.

7. For the settings, select to run every day at 4:00 AM, as shown in Figure 14-18.

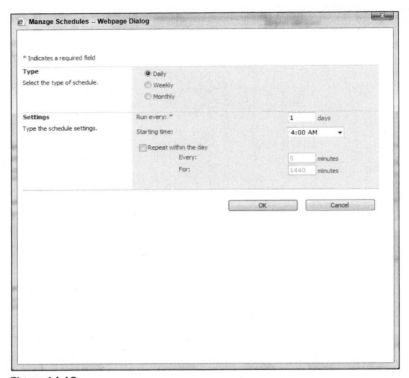

Figure 14-18

8. If desired, select an interval to repeat the crawl process with each day, such as every 60 minutes.

9. Click the OK button on the Manage Schedules window.

10. Click the OK button to save your changes to the content source.

Try It Out   **Initiate a Manual Update of a Content Source**

Some content sources are very slow to change, which means there is no need to run regular crawls. In some cases, you need to make administrative changes to search settings and properties, and require a Full Crawl to properly implement these changes. An example of that was seen in the exercises related to adding properties to the advanced search. In that case, you had to manually update the content source before the next scheduled crawl. Ideally, you should plan to make any major search configurations at the same time and just before a regularly scheduled fill crawl; however, you do have the option of initiating a manual crawl of the content source.

1. From the Shared Services Administration site of your SharePoint environment, select Search Settings.

2. Select Content Sources and Crawl Schedules.

3. Hover your cursor over the Local Office SharePoint Server Sites content source.

4. Select Start Full Crawl, as shown in Figure 14-19.

Figure 14-19

Try It Out   Reset All Crawled Content

One major change in SharePoint 2007 is that now each Shared Service Provider (SSP) has a single content index. Now, all content stored across the various content sources is referenced from a single index. This improves administration functions when you work with multiple content sources. However, when you make major changes to content sources and search settings, or perhaps if you notice a large number of errors in search event logs, you may be required to reset the content index for your SharePoint environment. After this process is complete, you need to manually initiate Full Crawls of various content sources to repopulate the content index. If you do not rebuild the content index, search will be unable to work because the index will be empty. Follow these steps to reset all crawl content:

1. From the Shared Services Administration site of your SharePoint environment, select Search Settings.

2. Select Reset All Crawled Content.

3. Maintain the selection to deactivate all search alerts during the reset, as shown in Figure 14-20. This will avoid any unnecessary alerts being sent to users of the system during this administrative update.

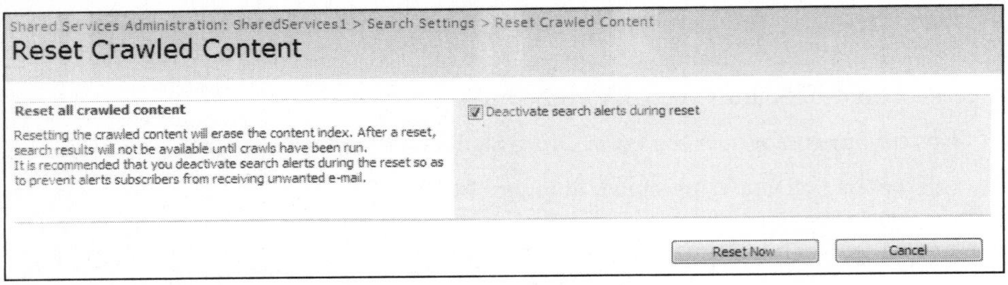

Figure 14-20

4. Click the Reset Now button.

Manage File Types

You may want to index content that is stored in special file formats such as Adobe Acrobat (PDF) or Microsoft OneNote (ONE). To allow users to do this, you as the administrator must associate the file type with the index using the steps in the next Try It Out.

By default, certain file types are automatically crawled to be part of the content index when the application is installed. These are listed for your reference in the following table. Unless someone has made changes to your system's search settings, these types of files automatically appear in the index.

ascx	mht	tiff
asp	mhtml	txt
aspx	Msg	url
doc	mspx	vdx vsd
docm	nsf	vss
docx	odc	vst
dot	pdf	vsx
eml	php	vtx
exch	ppt	xls
htm	pptm	xlsm
html	pptx	xlsx
jhtml	pub	xml
jsp	tif	

Try It Out   Add a File Type to the Content Index

In this example, you add the file extension of PDF to the list of those that you want the system to index. In addition to this process, many file types require custom iFilters to complete indexing of content related to that file type. For example, to have PDFs indexed in your environment, you also need to download and install the PDF iFilter that is available from the Adobe website at www.adobe.com. It is recommended that you check with any vendors you may deal with to see if an iFilter exists for any content you may be storing in SharePoint that is not available in the default listing of file types.

1.   From the Shared Services Administration site of your SharePoint environment, select Search Settings.

2.   Select File Types.

3.   Click the New File Type button from the toolbar. The Add File Type window appears, as shown in Figure 14-21.

Shared Services Administration: SharedServices1 > Search Settings > File Types > Add File Type

Add File Type

* Indicates a required field

File Name Extension

Type the extension of the file type you want to include.

File extension: *

pdf

Examples: doc, html

OK   Cancel

Figure 14-21

4.   Enter the extension of the file type you want to add to the index. For example, Figure 14-21 demonstrates adding the pdf extension, which adds Acrobat PDF files to the index.

5.   Click the OK button.

How It Works

The next time a crawl occurs, the file type you specify in step 4 appears in the index assuming the SharePoint server has all appropriate iFilters installed.

Create Search Scopes

In a previous set of Try It Outs, you learned how to add content sources to a SharePoint environment so that information about the content location could be added to the master index. However, work on a master index is wasted if a user cannot narrow down content on a search, especially when the index encompasses a large amount of content. This is where a search scope comes in handy. A *search scope* is a subsection of the index based on some predetermined rules related to a specific content source, location, or property. You can create scopes that are available throughout all SharePoint site collections or you can instead opt to limit the scope to a single site collection. This section discusses the various scope types and gives some scenarios of how you can use each.

You create rules for search scopes by specifying whether items meeting the criteria of the rule should be included, required, or excluded from the search results. For example, you may create a rule that excludes items that have a published status of expired. Similarly you may create a rule that only includes items stored on the Human Resources site.

To give you an idea of how you can use a search scope, the following list reflects some basic usage scenarios:

- ❑ **Web content:** The graphics department needs to quickly locate images and logos for ads and creative materials. Graphic assets are in a private team site that the communications group manages. The terms the graphic designers use to search for content are very generic ("red car" or "ski slope"), so a query of the entire index may not retrieve relevant results. A special scope is created called "creative assets" so graphic designers can find objects with ease by searching only their area instead of the entire content index. Because the scope is limited to the graphics department, it is created on the site level (the graphics department team site).

- ❑ **Property query:** Your company is a multinational organization with operations in different regions. It has a site column that tracks all documents and content based on the region. This site column appears in the crawled SharePoint properties list as a metadata value once it is associated with a document and is then mapped as a managed property in the same way that you mapped the client property when you made it appear in the Advanced Search interface in a previous Try It Out. When completing this mapping, you made the property available for use in scopes. You can create a scope as either a global or site collection level property so users can search for results based on a region. You can also create regional search pages.

- ❑ **Content source:** Your company's policies and procedures are stored in a file share, which was not moved to SharePoint because content rarely changes and editing access is limited to a small group of people. All employees have read access to the documents. To make the information easy to find, you add the file share as a content source to the SharePoint search index. Although this allows users to search through it, some users will recognize that documents are on the file share. To support these users, you create a custom scope that points specifically at the file share content source. Scopes based on content sources can only be created from the Shared Services Administration site as a global scope.

You can put some of the concepts from these scenarios in the next three Try It Outs. In the next Try It Out, you create a search scope that any site collection in a server farm may use. In the second Try It Out, you help users quickly access a scope by placing it in the site collection's search scope drop-down list. In the last Try It Out, you learn how to narrow a scope to a specific site level.

Try It Out   Global Search Scopes

In this example, you create a custom search scope from the central administration area so you can search via the Shared Service Provider administrative site. This site is where all global search configurations are made.

In the Try It Out "Create a Content Source Based on File Shares," you created a custom content source that pointed to policies and procedures in a file share so that users could easily access them from the central search interface. The scope you are about to create is based on that content source. If you did not create that custom content source, you should create one so you can complete this exercise.

1. From the Shared Services Administration site of your SharePoint environment, select Search Settings.

2. From the scopes section, select View Scopes.

3. Click the New Scope link. The Create Scope window appears, as shown in Figure 14-22.

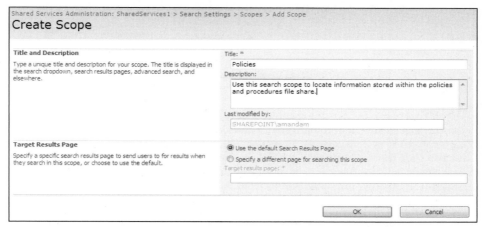

Figure 14-22

4. Enter a name and description of the scope. In this example, enter **Policies** for the name of your search scope and the following text for description.

> **Use this search scope to locate information stored within the policies and procedures file share.**

5. Select the Use the Default Search Results Page option.

6. Click the OK button.

7. Click the Add Rules link that appears to the right of the scope name under the Update Status column. The Add Scope Rule window appears, as shown in Figure 14-23.

8. For scope rule type, select content source and then select the file share you specified in a previous example for a custom content source.

If you did not complete the exercise related to creating a custom content source earlier in this chapter, select web content instead and enter the address of a SharePoint site that might contain information on policies and procedures in the folder field.

9. For Behavior, select the Include–Any Item that Matches This Rule Will Be Included, Unless the Item is Excluded by Another Rule option.

11. Click the OK button.

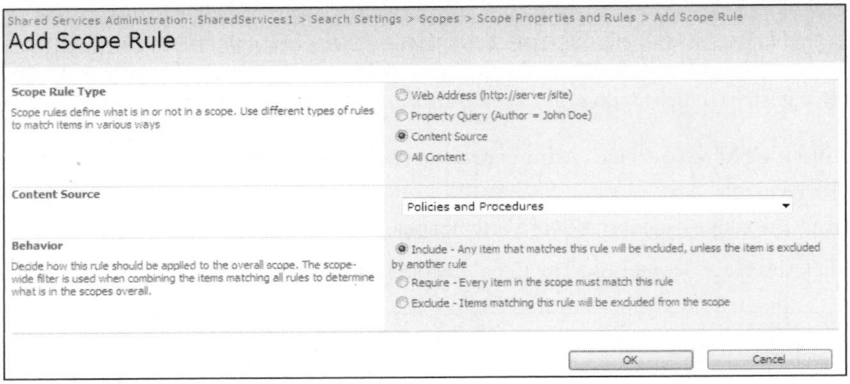

Figure 14-23

How It Works

Once your scope is created, it automatically updates during the next scheduled scope update process which is an automatic system process. However, you may also choose to force an update immediately. To do this you click the Start Update Now link, as shown in Figure 14-24 from the Scopes section of the Search Settings page. Once this happens, users can drill into the content stored only in that content source, thereby eliminating unrelated results from the other content sources or SharePoint sites. You can now add this scope as a tab to a Search Center site (using a process similar to one you will see the in the section "Using the Search Center" later in the chapter), as a selection item in the advanced search interface (see the section "Using the Advanced Search"), or as a value in the Scopes drop-down list of a site collection (discussed in the next Try It Out).

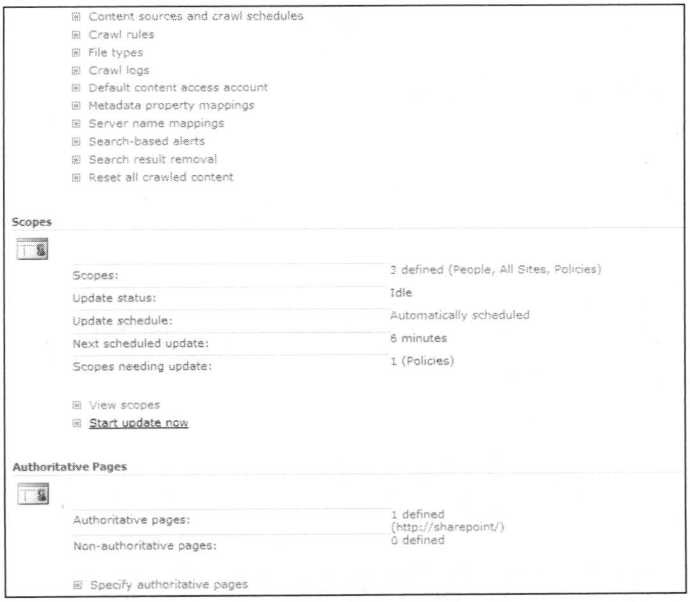

Figure 14-24

Try It Out   **Add a Search Scope to a Site Collection's Search Scope Drop-Down List**

When you create a scope from the Shared Services Administration site of your SharePoint environment, it automatically appears under the Unused Scopes group in each site collection. For users to access it, you must add it either to the Search drop-down list or Advanced Search Display groups using the following method. You must complete this process for all site collections in the farm where the scope will be used. In this example, you see how to add a scope to a site collection's Search Scope drop-down list.

1.   From the top-level site of your Corporate Intranet Portal site collection, select Site Settings ➪ Modify All Site Settings.

2.   Select Search Scopes from the Site Collection Administration links. The View Scopes window appears, as shown in Figure 14-25.

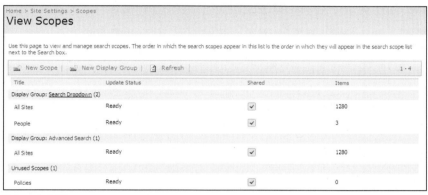

Figure 14-25

3.   Click the Search Dropdown link to the right of the Display Group text. You can also alternatively select the Advanced Search display group to have the scope appear there as well. The Edit Scope Display Group window appears, as shown in Figure 14-26.

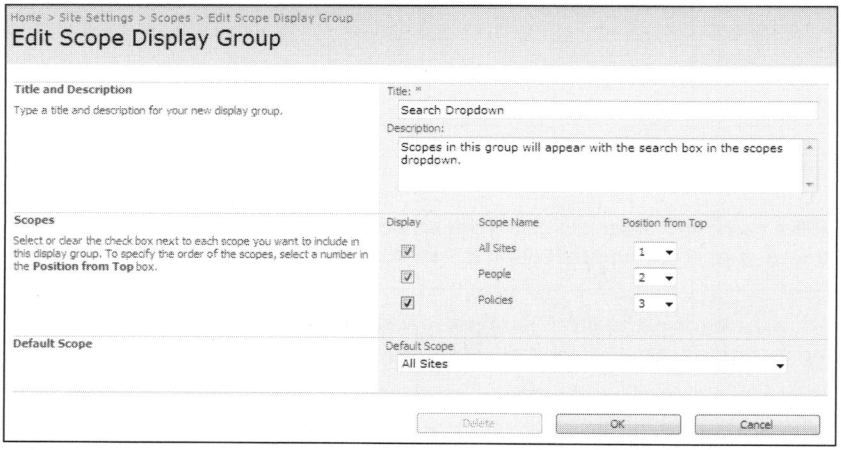

Figure 14-26

4. Select the check box associated with the Policies scope.

5. Click the OK button.

Site Level Search Scopes

In this example, you create a search scope that is limited to a single site collection. You're creating this for a graphics team, which only needs a subset of the content index that's on a single SharePoint site.

You can add this scope to either the scope's drop-down list or advanced search interface as you are creating it. This is different from the last Try It Out because you had to manually go in afterward and associate the scope with these locations on a per-site collection basis.

1. From the top-level site of your Corporate Intranet Portal site collection, select Site Actions ➪ Site Settings ➪ Modify All Site Settings.

2. Select Search Scopes from the Site Collection Administration links.

3. Click the New Scope link from the toolbar. The Create Scope window appears, as shown in Figure 14-27.

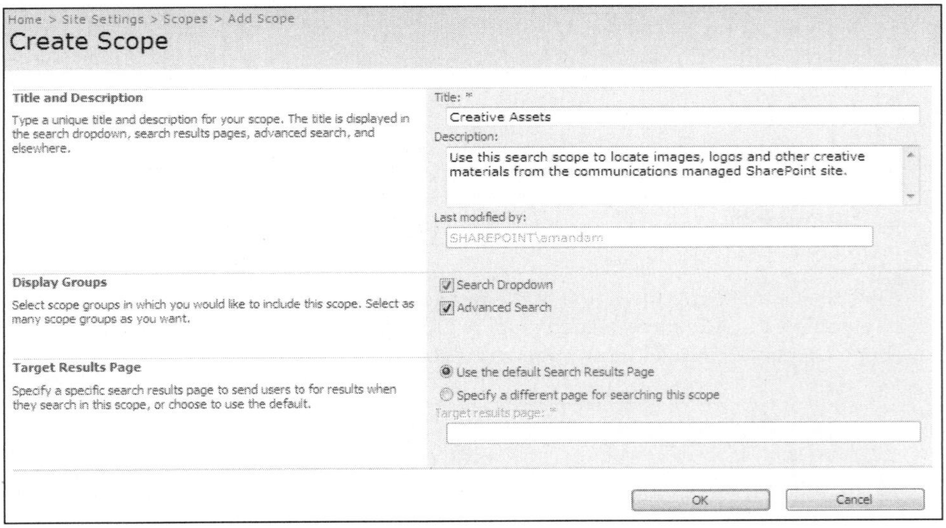

Home > Site Settings > Scopes > Add Scope
Create Scope

Title and Description	

Type a unique title and description for your scope. The title is displayed in the search dropdown, search results pages, advanced search, and elsewhere.	Title: *
	`Creative Assets`
	Description:
	`Use this search scope to locate images, logos and other creative materials from the communications managed SharePoint site.`
	
	Last modified by:
	`SHAREPOINT\amandam`

Display Groups	
Select scope groups in which you would like to include this scope. Select as many scope groups as you want.	☑ Search Dropdown ☑ Advanced Search

Target Results Page	
Specify a specific search results page to send users to for results when they search in this scope, or choose to use the default.	⦿ Use the default Search Results Page ○ Specify a different page for searching this scope Target results page: * `_____`

OK   Cancel

Figure 14-27

4. Enter a name and descriptive for your scope. In this example, enter **Creative Assets** for the name of your scope and the following for scope description:

> **Use this search scope to locate images, logos, and other creative materials from the communications managed SharePoint site.**

5. Select the check boxes to display the scope in the Search Dropdown and Advanced Search locations of the site.

6. Click the OK button.

7. Click the Add Rules link associated with the scope.

8. Select Web Address as the Scope Rule Type.

9. Enter the URL of the Advertising Materials site you created in Chapter 5 in the folder field. If you followed the example suggestion used in that exercise, it will be `http://yourservername/sitedirectory/advertising`. If you did not complete that exercise, enter the URL of a site containing creative documents and images.

10. For Behavior, select Require – Every Item in the Scope Must Match This Rule.

11. Click the OK button.

Using the Search Center

SharePoint 2007 has built-in page and site templates to aid you in creating an optimal search experience for your users. The Search Center, one of many built-in templates, gives you a rich and intuitive search interface, and includes the All Sites and People Search tabs, which search those two default scopes of a site collection. Using tabs, you can separate content sources and scopes so users can drill down to specific subsets of content depending on their needs. You can also create your own tabs so that a page only searches specific scopes. This gives users an interface where they can conduct searches based on predetermined criteria.

For more on the People Search scope, see the section "Finding People in your Organization" later in this chapter.

The Search Center is created automatically as part of the Collaboration Portal publishing template, shown in Figure 14-28. It can also be created as a subsite for other sites from the Enterprise tab of site templates. In the next example, you create a custom tab that will contain the Advanced Search Web Part.

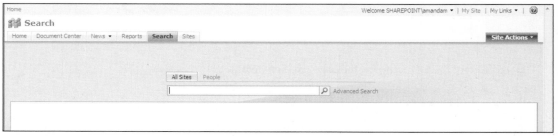

Figure 14-28

Try It Out   Add a Custom Tab to the Search Center

In the following example, you create a new page that becomes an Advanced Search page in your Search Center. From there you can customize the search interface to conduct searches based on properties relevant to that portion of the site. You can then add a new tab to the tabbed navigation; so rather than click an Advanced Search link to the right of the standard search box, users can select the tab. You commonly create tabs to narrow the results page to specific content. For example, you can create a scope that only shows content from a file share or Exchange public folder.

1. From the home page of your Corporate Intranet Portal, select the Search tab from the global navigation.

2. Select Site Actions ⇨ Create Page. The Create Page window appears, as shown in Figure 14-29.

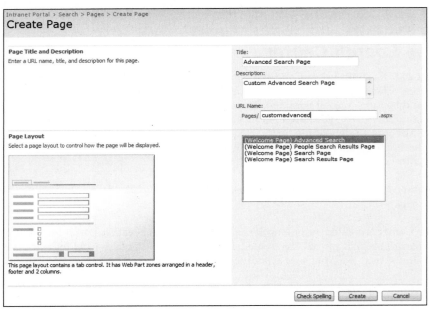

Figure 14-29

3. Specify the following for the page creation details:

Property	Value
Title	Advanced Search Page
Description	Custom Advanced Search Page
URL Name	Customadvanced
Page Layout	(Welcome Page) Advanced Search

4. Click the Create button. A new page is created containing Web Parts appropriate for an advanced search page.

5. From the Bottom Zone, select Add a Web Part.

6. Select Advanced Search Box from the suggested Web Parts listing.

7. Click the Add button.

8. Click the Add New Tab link as shown in Figure 14-30.

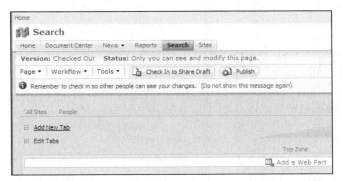

Figure 14-30

9. Enter a name for your tab. For this example, enter **Advanced Search**.

10. Specify customadvanced.aspx for the page.

11. Enter the following for the tooltip:

Search using advanced settings.

12. Click the OK button.

13. Publish your page by clicking the Publish button.

How It Works

Figure 14-31 shows what the new interface looks like to users visiting the search center.

Figure 14-31

Create Custom Keywords

When you perform an Internet or site search, you type a keyword in the search box and press Enter to receive your results (as in the "Perform a Basic Search for Content" Try It Out at the beginning of the chapter). A *keyword* is a word that summarizes the topic for which you are searching. Most search engines have ways of determining which words to treat as keywords, and you can do the same thing with SharePoint. You can define words that are strongly related to your business, business practices, or documentation and identify these as keywords within your environment so that when a user types a keyword to perform a search, she receives best bets for the returned results.

The next two Try It Outs show you how to use keywords to help your user get the information he needs. In the first Try It Out, you create a new keyword that your organization uses to describe collaboration and content sharing. You also identify synonyms for the keyword in case users type those instead of your keyword. Identifying synonyms increases the user's chances of pulling up the information you want them to receive. In the second Try It Out, you go one step further and use best bets to rank the results of a search. A best bet is the top returned values for a specific keyword and when you use them, users receive the most likely results at the top of their search. Best bet results are highlighted at the top of the returned results, and they display with a keyword and description to give users guidance and context. Figure 14-32 shows an example of best bet results.

Figure 14-32

Try It Out   **Create a Keyword**

In this example, you create a new keyword to represent the technology that your organization is using for the collaboration and sharing of content. When you create a keyword phrase, you can also identify synonyms that are words users may also use to refer to the same object or content. For example, if your keyword phrase is "SharePoint 2007," you define synonyms as WSS, MOSS, or OSS, because a user may type these words into the search box instead of SharePoint 2007.

You can assign expiration dates to your keyword to limit how long they are available in the system. This is helpful when you anticipate that a product, document, or program name may change. For example, you can define an expiration date if you think the name SharePoint 2007 will change to something else in a certain time frame. In addition, you can set a review date. For example, if SharePoint 2007 will change in three years, you can send an alert to a contact that will review the keyword's validity and determine whether it should be updated to a newer version.

1. From the top-level site of your Corporate Intranet Portal site collection, select Site Settings ⇨ Modify All Site Settings.

2. Select Search Keywords from the Site Collection Administration links.

3. Click the Add Keyword button from the toolbar. The Add Keyword window appears, as shown in Figure 14-33.

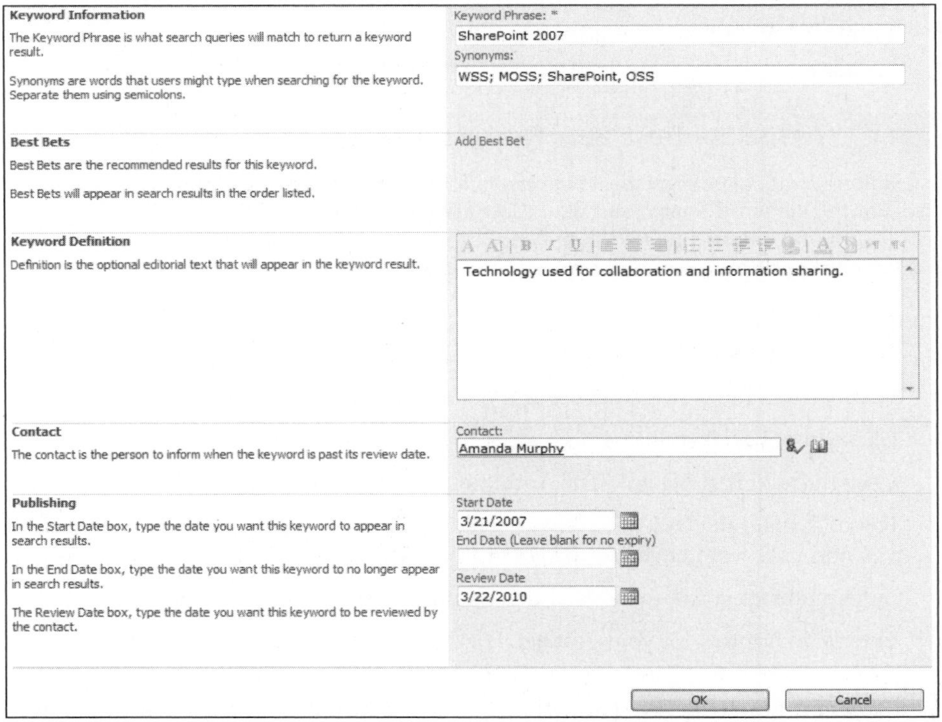

Figure 14-33

4. Enter the following values for the various properties that need to be defined for the keyword:

Property	Value
Keyword Phrase	SharePoint 2007.
Synonyms	WSS; MOSS; SharePoint; OSS.
Keyword Definition	Technology used for collaboration and information sharing.
Contact	Enter your own name.
Start Date	Enter the current date.
End Date	Leave blank.
Review Date	Enter a date three years from the current date.

5. Click the OK button.

Try It Out   Associate Best Bets Results with Specific Keywords

In this example, you create some best bet results for the custom keyword phrase created in the previous exercise. For the keyword SharePoint, you enter sites that you consider most likely to give the user relevant and useful information related to the application. Other best bets for this type of keyword might include links to specific user manuals or how-to videos.

1. From the top-level site of your Corporate Intranet Portal site collection, select Site Settings ⇨ Modify All Site Settings.

2. Select Search Keywords from the Site Collection Administration links.

3. Click your SharePoint keyword.

4. Click the Add Best Bet link. The Add Best Bet window appears, as shown in Figure 14-34.

5. For URL, enter the URL of a weblog you created in Chapter 8 to help share knowledge on what you and your team have learned about using SharePoint effectively for your organization.

6. Enter a title for your best bet. For this example, type **SharePoint Weblog**.

7. Enter a description for your best bet. For this example, enter the following:

> **SharePoint focused weblog designed to share information on how it can be used to improve how content is shared within our organization.**

8. Click the OK button.

9. Select Add Best Bet.

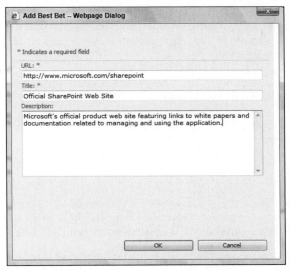

Figure 14-34

10. Enter the following information for the best bet:

URL	`http://www.microsoft.com/sharepoint`
Title	Official SharePoint Website
Description	Microsoft's official product website featuring links to white papers and documentation related to managing and using the application

11. Click the OK button. The Add Best Bet window closes.

12. Click OK to save changes to your keyword.

Finding People in Your Organization

Searches aren't all about locating documents and content; they're also important for locating information about the key people in the organization. Chapter 9 discussed how user profiles are an important element in SharePoint for sharing information related to members of an organization. Therefore it is important that the search support this type of information in addition to more standard content, such as documents and lists. To help users easily conduct a search on this type of information, a scope exists that points to the user profile database in SharePoint. In addition, specific tools and interface elements exist such as Web Parts, tabs and pages to facilitate the use of this scope. As mentioned in the section "Using the Search Center," you can use the People Search tab or scope to find details about a colleague's skills, business contact information, and other details in their user profile. For example, if you have Event Management as a skills property in your personal profile, when a co-worker performs a search for those keywords, in the People Search your name will appear in the results. The People Search scope helps you find the experts in your organization that will help resolve daily problems or whom you can use as resources for projects.

You can include a People Search Web Part to any standard team site or a portal sub site, in one of two ways. These two methods are covered in the next two Try It Outs.

❑ Add the People Search Box Web Part to your site so that users can directly enter a name into the Web Part to return results that are limited to the People scope.

❑ Have users use the standard search interface and select the People Search scope when performing their search.

In the third Try It Out of this section, you learn how you can use the People Search scope to perform a search for people in your organization. This can be done by either using the Search drop-down box on the primary search box or by selecting the People tab in the Search Center.

Try It Out · · · Add the People Search Box Web Part to a Site

In this example, you find out how to add the People Search box to a page and create a custom people search results page on the site to display the results of a search query. By default, SharePoint includes a People Search Box Web Part on the main page of a site created from the Collaboration Portal template. The title of the Web Part has been set to "Employee Finder," but it is the same Web Part you will use in this Try it Out. In most cases, an employee can go to the main page of the portal or People tab of the Search Center to conduct a people-specific search, but some circumstances warrant adding the Web Part to your own collaborative site or portal page. Following this exercise will help you understand how you can create your own people search interface.

1. From the main page of your Research and Development website, select Site Actions ➪ Create. You are redirected to the Content Creation page.

2. Select Web Part Page from the Web Pages section of the page. You are redirected to a Web Part Page Creation page.

3. Enter **peopleresults.aspx** for the page name and select Full Page, Vertical from the layout templates.

4. Select the Shared Documents library for the storage location of the page.

5. Click the Create button. Your new Web Part page is created.

6. Once the page is created, click the Add a Web Part button. The Add Web Parts selection window appears, as shown in Figure 14-35.

7. Select the People Search Core Results from the Search group and click the Add button.

8. Click Exit Edit Mode.

9. Return to the home page of the site.

10. Select Site Actions ➪ Edit Page.

11. From the Web Part zone on the left-hand side of the page, select Add a Web Part. The Add Web Parts selection window appears, as shown in Figure 14-36.

Figure 14-35

Figure 14-36

12. From the search group of Web Parts, select People Search Box and click the Add button.

13. Select Edit ⇨ Modify Shared Web Part on the People Search Web Part.

14. Expand the Miscellaneous group of properties.

15. Specify "Shared%20Documents/peopleresults.aspx" for the Target search results page URL.

16. Click the Apply, and then OK buttons on the Web Part.

17. Click Exit Edit Mode.

Try It Out   **Use the People Search Box Web Part**

For the next example, you see how to use the People Search Box Web Part to find users in an organization. You conduct a very basic search using the search box and then use the more advanced search options to find users based on details outlined in their user profiles. To prepare for this example, you should visit your own personal site and update your user profile to include "SharePoint Management" as a skill. You will need to run an incremental update of the SharePoint Sites content source before completing the next example. The process for doing this was covered in this chapter in a Try it Out called "Initiate a Manual Update of a Content Source."

1. From the home page of your Research and Development site, enter your own first name into the Search Box Web Part, as shown in Figure 14-37.

Figure 14-37

2. Click the Search icon to the right of the search box. Notice that your name appears in the search results on the custom page you created with a name of "me."

3. Click the Back button in your browser to return to the home page of the site.

4. Remove your name from the search box and click the Search Options link to the right of the search box.

5. Enter **SharePoint Management** in the Skills box.

6. Click the Search icon to the right of the search box. You receive results for any user who has SharePoint Management listed in their user profile property for skills. In Chapter 9, you added that value as a property in your skills so if you completed that exercise, you should see your own name listed.

How It Works

When you add the People Search Box Web Part to the main page of your site, users can search for people on your site with just a couple of quick clicks. When you ran the first query in this exercise, a link to your own personal profile appeared in the results. The system recognized that you were the user being displayed, which is why the results were shown as "me."

In your second query, you used the search options on the Web Part to perform a more advanced search to find people who had certain skills. This query helps when a user is looking for a specific field of expertise but doesn't know the exact name of the user they are looking for.

Try It Out   Use the People Search Scope

In this example, you perform a search using the term "SharePoint" limited to only the People scope. This eliminates links to documentation or training materials stored in the system and displays any users who have "SharePoint" featured in a property within their user profile.

1.   From the main page of your portal site, select the People Search scope from the Scope drop-down list, as shown in Figure 14-38. You can also select the People Search tab from the Search Center.

Figure 14-38

2.   Enter **SharePoint** into the search box.

3.   Click the Search icon to the right of the search box. You are redirected to a page listing all users that have SharePoint associated with their user profile.

Summary

This book has shown useful methods for adding content to your SharePoint site so you can share information with others. These efforts are wasted if you don't create a system that makes it easy for users to locate and find this content. After reading this chapter, you should know the different methods for searching for content, including the following:

❑   You enter keywords and search terms in the basic search box to receive results based on relevance or modified date.

❑   The Advanced Search interface, the Search Center, and the Scopes drop-down box refine your searches.

❑ You can create content sources to access data from multiple systems via a single index accessible throughout SharePoint. These systems may include files shares, Exchange folders, and line-of-business applications.

❑ You can create scopes to add drill-down capabilities in the index so users receive more direct and exact searches based on items such as location, content source, or properties.

❑ The crawl process recognizes a number of file types and adds them to the content index. You can include additional file types to this list, but these file types require you to install special iFilters to the SharePoint server.

❑ You can define keywords or terms to help users search for a common resource or sites. These words may relate to specific products you may sell or business activities in which you are involved. You can also give users best bets whenever they search for a specific phrase or synonyms.

Possibly the most important lesson you can take away from this chapter is that to properly configure the SharePoint environment to meet the needs of your users and business, you need their input. Where possible, the system should support existing business processes so that users can focus on their work and not the technology they use to complete their work.

Exercises

1. What types of storage locations can be crawled and indexed from SharePoint Server?

2. What is the difference between a Full Crawl and an Incremental Crawl?

3. While meeting with a group of users from the European region, you are requested to make it easier for the users to find content related to their region, by default. What are your alternatives for making this possible?

4. What is a best bet?

5. True or False. By default, SharePoint supports the indexing of Adobe Acrobat files.

Answers to Exercises

Chapter 1

Exercise 1 Solution

1. What is the difference between a team site and a document workspace?

The difference is that a team site typically manages the mass of information stored in lists and libraries, while a document workspace is a special site for collaborating on a single document or event.

Exercise 2 Solution

2. Your manager informs you that the organization is currently reviewing the need for a corporate portal. List two reasons to justify why organizations invest in portal technologies.

There are many reasons that organizations invest in portal technologies. Two major reasons are:

❏ People need to connect with information that will help them make informed business decisions regardless of their physical location. Because portals are web-based and are available via the Internet, large numbers of users can access information from a centralized location.

❏ Portal technologies scale with an organization as it grows and can accommodate business processes and information management.

Exercise 3 Solution

3. True or False. SharePoint Server 2007 is the next release of SharePoint Portal Server 2003.

True. While significant changes have been made to the system, SharePoint 2007 is still considered the next release of SPS 2003. Some major changes include improved support for web content publishing and management, content aggregation, workflow processes, and enterprise reporting.

Chapter 2

Exercise 1 Solution

1. If you wanted to receive an email notification every time a new item is added to a list, how would you do that?

To receive an email notification every time a new item is added to a list, you would create an alert. You create an alert by selecting Alert Me from the list's Action menu.

Exercise 2 Solution

2. Describe the difference between a lookup column and a choice column.

A choice column features a value list from which you can select that a site manager has manually entered into the column. A lookup column displays a value list based on the contents of an existing column from another list on the site.

Exercise 3 Solution

3. Describe how you would send a report of information stored in a list to a partner outside your organization that did not have access to your SharePoint list.

You can export SharePoint list views to an Excel spreadsheet from the Actions menu. This means you can take information from the SharePoint site, customize it, and send it to team members or partners that do not have direct access to the SharePoint list.

Exercise 4 Solution

4. What are the differences between a tasks list and a projects task list?

A projects tasks list is created with a Gantt chart view by default. Also, you can associate a tasks list with a workflow activity template whereas you can't do this with a projects task.

Exercise 5 Solution

5. True or False. You can allow users to skip specific questions based on their responses to specific survey questions.

True. SharePoint 2007 introduces a concept known as *branching logic* in surveys that define what the next question is that a user should answer based on his response to a specific question.

Chapter 3

Exercise 1 Solution

1.   Your project manager informs you that the version of the document you submitted for approval was not correct and that the version that was sent earlier in the week is more appropriate. How do you remedy the situation?

In this situation, you would browse the available versions of your document to find the version submitted earlier in the week. Once you have found the correct version, you would restore the previous version and finally resubmit the newly restored version to the project manager.

Exercise 2 Solution

2.   Your manager assigns your team a series of presentations for an upcoming conference. How can your team most efficiently collaborate on various slides?

In this case, you would browse to the View All site content page, select Create, and then select the Slide Library option to create a slide library where your team can collaborate and share slides.

Exercise 3 Solution

3.   You've been given the task of archiving an old document. Currently, these documents are stored in a common file share. What is the best method of mass-copying these documents to a document library?

Browse to the library that you want to use to archive your documents. Select Explorer View from the View's menu on the toolbar. Copy and paste your documents into the Explorer view.

Exercise 4 Solution

4.   You need to change the metadata information for multiple documents. What is the fastest way to change the metadata of a particular column for multiple documents?

In this situation, you could open your library in Datasheet mode (available from the Actions button). While in Datasheet mode, you can update a particular column for multiple documents, and change them all at the same time.

Chapter 4

You've just been assigned to customize the SharePoint site for your company's sales team. The team has struggled with having a central location that stores all information related to its various opportunities, contacts, meetings, and tasks. It has had a SharePoint site for a few months; however, the team has expressed some concerns that information is too difficult to find. The following exercises focus on ways in which you need to develop the site to become a more useful tool for the sales team.

Exercise 1 Solution

1. After conducting a planning workshop with some members of the sales team, you determine that while the sales manager wants to see all information stored in a single location, the actual sales team members struggle with seeing too much information. As a result, it takes sales team members longer than necessary to look up contact phone numbers. The sales team prefers to only see contacts from their own region. What can you do to make both groups happy?

By creating a site column for Region, lists, such as the contact list, can feature custom views that filter items to only show items for a specific region. The sales manager can use a list view that shows items across all regions and each regional office can have its own view that filters out information from regions other than its own. A list-centric column for Region would work specifically for this scenario as well. However, because you can assume this type of behavior is desired for other content lists on the site, a site column may be a better implementation choice.

Exercise 2 Solution

2. Whenever a sales person views the central list of contacts, he wants to see specific contacts that he himself has added. How would you accomplish that?

You can accomplish this by creating a custom view that has a filter to only show items where Created By is equal to [me]. It may also be beneficial to make the custom personalized view the default view so that users can see that view first when they enter a list.

Exercise 3 Solution

3. The sales manager wants to see a list of all opportunities that are in the pipeline for his staff. Because he has some concerns about the length of time certain sales staff members are taking to close their leads, he wants to visually identify leads that have the longest duration from the initial point of contact to the expected date of sale. What can you suggest to help address this situation?

By creating a Gantt view on the list, you can display visual indicators of items based on the date of initial contact and expected date of sale. The sales manager can easily identify the ones that are taking the longest to close.

Chapter 5

Exercise 1 Solution

1. What is the difference between an Approval Workflow template and the Collect Signatures workflow template?

Both the Approval Workflow template and Collect Signatures template generate decision-making processes that can potentially end in the approval of a specific document. However, the approval workflow tracks the acceptance or publishing of a document within the SharePoint site, whereas you can only launch the Collect Signatures workflow within a Microsoft Office application and you can only initiate it from a document containing a Signature Line element.

Exercise 2 Solution

2.   True or False. You can create a custom workflow in SharePoint Designer for use across all sites in a site collection.

False. When you use SharePoint Designer to create a custom workflow, you can only associate it with a single list or library, and you cannot add it to any central gallery or directory. To add a workflow to the central gallery, you must develop it using custom code and the .NET framework.

Exercise 3 Solution

3.   Explain the difference between a serial and parallel workflow process.

A serial workflow is one that requires users to complete activities in a predefined order so that they can only give feedback one at a time. A parallel workflow allows feedback or participation from a number of users and has a more informal structure related to when each user can join in or participate.

Exercise 4 Solution

4.   What two lists are required on a site that has workflow enabled on a document library?

When you define a workflow process for a document library, you must associate a task list and a history list with the workflow. When configuring a workflow, you may select an existing task or history list or create completely new instances of each. The task list tracks the assignments related to the workflow process. The history list is a solid reporting tool for tracking progress related to a specific activity or document.

Exercise 5 Solution

5.   Explain what happens when a change is requested during an approval workflow activity.

When an approver requests a change in a document during the workflow process, the current task for approval is marked as complete. The change request then generates a new task, and the approver designates a new member to handle the request. This member can either be the workflow owner or a specific user. When the new member marks the change request as complete, SharePoint creates a new task so an approver can review and approve the latest version of the document.

Chapter 6

Exercise 1 Solution

1. True or False. You can only associate one document template with a document library.

This is somewhat of a trick question so the answer is both true and false. Prior to enabling content type management via the Advanced settings of a document library, you may only associate a single document template with a document library. However, if you enable content type management on your library, you can then manage multiple content types from that single location and have more than one document template associated with the library.

Exercise 2 Solution

2. Imagine you are responsible for ensuring that all documents created and printed in your organization have the words Private and Confidential on them. What are your options for making this happen, and which would provide the best results?

You have two primary methods for accomplishing this.

Your first method is to add the words **Private** and **Confidential** to all the standard document templates within the organization. This method is tedious and requires you to constantly add these words to all new document templates. Also it's difficult to prevent users for removing the text directly from their document themselves.

The second method involves creating an information management policy on the base document content type so that all child document content types inherit the policy. This method also supports the creation of new content types that maintain the same information management policy setting. A setting exists on the label configuration to enter custom text such as Private and Confidential, and you can select a check box option to prevent users from removing the label or changing it after it's been added.

Exercise 3 Solution

3. People in your company have complained that recent job postings are being published on the corporate intranet website with typos and grammatical errors. Your management team demands a certain level of professionalism in any content that division posts. What are some steps you can take to ensure that future job postings are reviewed prior to publishing?

To manage approval processes around specific types of information such as job postings, you associate an Approval workflow template with the Job Postings content type. You can define the workflow activity to launch whenever an item is either created or modified. You can also select who needs to provide the approval for new content. Because the workflow is configured on the content type level, no matter how many location job postings exist throughout the portal, you can apply the same business process.

Chapter 7

Exercise 1 Solution

1. You get an email from marketing informing you that the executive team would like to add a list of key contacts to the main page of the corporate intranet. What do you do?

Each time you create a list or library such as a contact list, SharePoint creates a corresponding Web Part that you can add to a Web Part page, subsequently exposing its contents. To add a list of contacts to the main page of the corporate intranet, you browse to the site and create a contacts list. After entering the key contacts into the list, you expose the contacts on the home page by adding the Contacts List Web Part to a zone on the page.

Exercise 2 Solution

2. It's requested that you move the main news Web Part from the small right column to a more prominent section of the home page of the human resources team's collaboration site. How can you make this happen?

You can only add Web Parts to a special type of page called a *Web Part page*. These pages have zones where you add Web Parts. You cannot add a Web Part unless it is contained in a Web Part zone. Moving a Web Part from one zone to another is a simple drag-and-drop process. To move the News Web Part from the right zone to the main left zone, you enter the page editing mode via the Site Actions tab and then drag and drop the Web Part to a more prominent location, such as the center zone on the page.

Exercise 3 Solution

3. Sales makes a change in its division so that all current tasks displayed on the home page of the team site via a Web Part must also display which of the two team leads is responsible for the task. How can you modify the Web Part to display who the team lead is?

Many areas of this book talk about the importance of metadata columns on lists and libraries. Metadata is information about a list item or document, such as the document owner, date of creation, or team leader. In this chapter, you learned that by using views, you can expose metadata columns. You can create a metadata column to store team leader choices and then add this column to the selected view that the List Web Part displays. You can display any view that is available on the list from within the List Web Part.

Exercise 4 Solution

4. During a meeting, an executive asks if you can display a listing of all upcoming events for the organization. What is your answer?

You answer "Yes." Using the Content Query Web Part, you can display a listing of all upcoming events for the organization on the main page of the portal. You do this by running a query based on all Calendar list items. You can further refine your query by specifying certain content types or filtering based on metadata properties.

Exercise 5 Solution

5. The creative department recently analyzed their team site and think that the site would be more appealing if they added some background colors to the List Web Parts. How do you achieve this?

While you can place list data on a Web Part page using a List Web Part, this data is relatively flat and unreceptive to customization such as background color changes. However, you can use SharePoint Designer 2007 to convert your List view into a Data View Web Part. The Data View Web Part takes the code behind a list view (CAML) and transforms it into a more customizable template-based format (XSL). After converting to a Data View Web Part, you can then use Design view to modify things such as the background colors.

Chapter 8

Exercise 1 Solution

1. Describe the difference between a site and a site collection.

A *site* is the primary container for content in SharePoint. There are top-level sites and subsites. Each site has its own access configuration as well as content elements such as lists, libraries, or content types. *Site collections* represent a set of sites that exist in a hierarchy. Each site collection shares a set of templates and has a common top-level site.

Exercise 2 Solution

2. You have been asked to create a corporate portal for your company. What would be the appropriate site template to use to create the site?

Under the Publishing tab, you would select the Collaboration Portal because it contains many of the common elements contained in most corporate portals. You could then add more subsites and content elements as required.

Exercise 3 Solution

3. There is a growing need within your division to share more information between employees so that they can get to know each other better and stay on track with developments in their various projects and activities. What tool can you use to empower them to share more information with their peers and receive feedback on posted topics?

By encouraging employees to create their own blogs, you can enhance communication and sharing between employees on current activities and interests. Blogs provide a framework for employees to give feedback on activities and initiate additional collaboration activities. Other tools that they may choose to use include wikis and discussion boards.

Exercise 4 Solution

4. You have a site requirement that contains a document library, announcements list, tasks list, shared calendar, issues list, and discussion board. How would you go about creating that site?

You could start with a blank site template and create each of the required lists or libraries. However, because the Team Site template contains most of these elements, it may be more efficient to start with that template and add in the issues list after the fact. You could then save that site as a template to provide a starting point for other employees containing all the required elements.

Chapter 9

Exercise 1 Solution

1. Explain the difference between a SharePoint site group and an audience.

A SharePoint site group is a role in SharePoint to which users can be assigned. It can be associated with a specific set of permissions to perform tasks and duties. An audience is a membership group that helps target relevant content to users based on personal profile properties or memberships within Windows or SharePoint groups.

Exercise 2 Solution

2. True or False. By targeting content to users, you can ensure that only the right people have access to view items.

False. Targeting content to users via audiences has no impact on the user's access to an item. Instead, audiences filter through large amounts of data and target specific items as those to which a member will most likely have an interest.

Exercise 3 Solution

3. What are the three different types of audiences that you can create in SharePoint 2007?

You can create audiences in SharePoint 2007 based on Windows Group Memberships (distribution list or security groups), Profile Properties, or SharePoint Site Group Membership.

Exercise 4 Solution

4. What are the different levels of access that you can control in SharePoint?

There are several levels of access to information including:

❑ Site Level Access

❑ List or Library Level Access

❑ Item Level Access

Exercise 5 Solution

5. Explain from what sources you can import user profile information.

Users can update their profile information. They can also import it from external systems such as Active Directory, LDAP servers, or Business Data Catalog applications.

Chapter 10

Exercise 1 Solution

1. Explain the reasons why you would decide to create a form that supports editing in the browser.

Because not all users have access to the InfoPath application, creating a form template that is supported by the browser can expose the form to a wider audience. In addition, because the browser removes some of the interface elements that the InfoPath form itself offers, such as a view switcher or formatting controls, it may be a more controlled environment to have users complete and review form data. Finally, by using Forms Services to present the form to users, they see the form as a standard web-based form and can spend less time focusing on the technology and more time thinking about the information they are supplying and the decisions they are required to make as part of a business process.

Exercise 2 Solution

2. Explain the different scenarios by which you can publish a form template.

A form template can be published to SharePoint directly to a document library. This is suitable for scenarios where the form is only required to be hosted in a single location. Another alternative is to publish the form as a content type to a SharePoint Server. This method is most appropriate when there is a requirement to publish the form to multiple locations within a single site collection. Finally, there is an option to upload the form template via the Central Administration site as a server administrator. This method is most appropriate for complex forms featuring advanced customizations or custom code. It is also suitable for situations where a form template may be required to be accessible across multiple site collections within a single server farm.

Exercise 3 Solution

3. Describe a template part.

A template is reusable component that is comprised of form fields, controls, and customizations that can be saved as a single control and added to other form templates. An example of a template part might be a group of fields for entering contact information within a form. Because these fields are often exactly the same across all forms, it would be advantageous to save them once as a template part for reuse in other form templates.

Exercise 4 Solution

4. Explain the difference between a control and a data source element.

A data source element represents information and data that can be collected within a form. However, a control is the mechanism by which the data will be entered or viewed within the form. One single data source element may use multiple controls across different views depending on the requirements for data entry or viewing. However, each instance of a control that is added to a form can only be mapped to a single data source.

Exercise 5 Solution

5. True or False. InfoPath cannot submit to a data connection. It can only retrieve information.

False. InfoPath can submit data to an external data source as well as receive data.

Chapter 11

Exercise 1 Solution

1. Explain three benefits of using Excel Services for your organization's data reporting needs.

Three key benefits of using Excel Services for your organization's reporting needs include:

❑ Providing a centralized repository for reports rather than having them confined to individual hard drives or dispersed across many file-share folders or network locations.

❑ Rendering reports through the browser to display the data in a controlled setting and hiding any information related to formulas, calculations, or connections.

❑ Because Excel Services is built upon SharePoint technologies, all the standard benefits of working with SharePoint still exist such as versioning, item-level security, and content type management.

Exercise 2 Solution

2. True or False. When a workbook is published to a Reports Library, no one can change it.

False. You can assign users rights to edit or contribute to files. However, a key benefit of the Reports Library is that you can limit access to View or Read-Only for those who do not need edit access.

Exercise 3 Solution

3. Your manager informs you that whenever team members access the newly created Dashboard, they receive an "access denied" error message and cannot see the individual reports. What's the likely cause for this?

First, you need to make sure that users have access to the site and its data. You then want to check that the site's Reports Library and data connection libraries are configured as trusted locations within the SharePoint farm environment. You can do this by visiting the Excel Services Settings section of the Shared Services Administration site.

Chapter 12

Exercise 1 Solution

1. True or False. The Business Data Catalog contains important data from external applications.

False. The Business Data Catalog contains application definitions that describe the business data in the external applications, but does not actually contain the data. Instead, it defines how users will connect to the application to retrieve the data.

Exercise 2 Solution

2. Describe the difference between the roles of the application definition author and a developer.

The *application definition author* is the user who must understand both XML and the API of the business application well enough to describe access details of the application and the various data components. Once this person has completed the application definition file for an application, his role is generally complete. After a system administrator imports the application definition file, a *developer* accesses the business data to extend SharePoint's functionality or to create custom applications that interact with the business data. While the application definition author is not required to be a developer, a single individual may perform both roles.

Exercise 3 Solution

3. When an application is added to the BDC, can any user with list creation rights add a column to a list that points to the application?

Once the application is added to the BDC, only users with Select in Clients right can associate an entity with a list or library column. The system administrator controls this right via the Shared Services administration area for the application.

Exercise 4 Solution

4. Explain the difference between the Business Data List Web Part and Business Related Data List Web Part.

The Business Data List Web Part connects to an entity to show a grid view of items in that entity. The Business Related Data List Web Part is a connectable Web Part that depends on another Web Part, such as the Business Data List Web Part, to display details related to the selected item. For example, a listing of customers may be displayed in a Business Data List Web Part, and a Business Related Data List Web Part may contain information about orders. When a user selects a customer in the Business Data List Web Part, a related listing of orders would display in the other Web Part.

Chapter 13

Exercise 1 Solution

1. Your manager informs you that you have been selected to create a website for the communications department on the new SharePoint Server. The main requirement is to have the site allow non-technical employees in the communications division to publish monthly newsletters. What do you do?

In this situation, you begin by creating a Collaboration Portal. You would first create a Newsletter content type to have columns that represent such things as a title, body text, and a picture. Next, you create a page layout based on this content type. You would call the page layout "Newsletter," and the types of content you can create on this page would be the columns title, body text, and picture.

You can email communications to notify them that users with appropriate permissions can create newsletters by selecting Site Actions ⇨ Create Page, and selecting the Newsletter Page Layout before finally inputting the title, body text, and picture.

Exercise 2 Solution

2. Your organization has recently gone through a rebranding change, and your team must make the corporate intranet reflect these changes. What are your options?

Corporate branding ensures that your website will have a unique and consistent look and feel. If you find that your sites are not in tune with your corporate brand, you have the following options:

❑ You can use master pages to unify common elements of your sites. These elements, known as chrome, include headers or navigation menus.

❑ You can use themes to control the color scheme of your sites while maintaining the "SharePoint" layout. Themes let you change background colors, images, and fonts throughout your sites.

❑ A similar but slightly more advanced form of CSS customization is that an Alternate CSS URL can be specified in the Master Page property, enabling you to override default styles. While this customization type is similar to themes, it is slightly more flexible because it can ripple across numerous sites in the farm, provided they inherit from the parent site. While not covered in this chapter, it's important to realize this customization method exists.

Exercise 3 Solution

3. True or False. You can enable the Publishing feature after you create a team site.

True. Although initially you can create a website using a template, such as the Team Site, you can at a later date make it publishing-capable using the power of Features. You enable Features from the Site Collection Features and Site Features pages which you access by selecting Site Actions ➪ Site Settings. After enabling the Publishing feature on a team site, all publishing lists, libraries, and functionality are made available on your team site.

Exercise 4 Solution

4. The sales manager says a recent sale requires the implementation of an externally facing customer support portal in two languages, English and French. How do you proceed?

In this situation, you first create a Publishing Portal, the standard template for Internet-facing sites. To make your site accessible in two languages, you enable and set up Variations on your site. You then create labels for your languages, one named English and one named French. You must specify one of the sites as the source site. The source site is where users initially create content. As content is created, it's automatically replicated on the other sites where it remains in the source sites language until someone translates it.

Chapter 14

Exercise 1 Solution

1. What types of storage locations can be crawled and indexed from SharePoint Server?

Using SharePoint 2007, you can create content sources based on the following storage locations:

- ❑ SharePoint sites
- ❑ Websites (Non-SharePoint)
- ❑ File shares
- ❑ Exchange public folders
- ❑ Lotus Notes
- ❑ Applications via the Business Data Catalog

Exercise 2 Solution

2. What is the difference between a Full Crawl and an Incremental Crawl?

A Full Crawl is a complete inventory of content available in a content source. An Incremental Crawl is a review of all items that have been added or changed since the last update.

Exercise 3 Solution

3. While meeting with a group of users from the European region, you are requested to make it easier for the users to find content related to their region, by default. What are your alternatives for making this possible?

The first requirement is to identify how to distinguish content related to the European region from all other content. This may be best accomplished via a site column. However, you may identify that each region has a variety of content storage locations they take advantage of. Some of these may be within SharePoint; others may not.

Once you identify how to distinguish the content, you can create a custom scope that limits the index to items related only to the European region. This may be via a managed property based on a Regions site column, or it may be via a specific web address or content source. Once you create the scope, you can make it available via the Scope drop-down list, a custom search entry and results page, or via the Advanced Search interface.

Exercise 4 Solution

4. What is a best bet?

A best bet is a web address associated with a custom keyword that appears prominently when a user makes a search request using that keyword. Best bet results are returned in the right-hand column of the search results in an order that the administrator specifies.

Exercise 5 Solution

5. True or False. By default, SharePoint supports the indexing of Adobe Acrobat files.

False. In order for the system to index PDFs, you must add this file type to the list of extensions indexed by the system. Additionally, you must install an iFilter on the server. This iFilter is available for download from the Adobe website.

Index

A

Access (Microsoft)
creating Access view for list, 110–112
synchronizing SharePoint contact list with, 21–22
uploading Access database to SharePoint document library, 395–397
access levels. *see also* **user access**
enabling access requests, 302–304
item level, 308–310
list or library level, 306–308
overview of, 304
site level, 304–306
actions
launching from business items, 421–422
overview of, 415
Active Directory, 325
administrators
administrator-approved form templates, 373–376
BDC administrator role, 412
advanced search
adding managed property to Advanced Search Web Part, 488–490
creating managed property for, 484–488
interface, 479
overview of, 482–483
performing, 483
Advanced Search Web Part, 488–490
alerts, subscribing to list alerts, 39–40
announcement list, 26–27
columns, 26
views, 27
application definition author, 411

application definition files
adding actions to, 415
defined, 411
importing, 413
applications, BDC
adding users to, 415–416
configuring, 412–413
importing application definition file, 413
permissions, 415
Approval workflow, 144–148
associating with document libraries, 144–146
overview of, 126
removing from libraries, 147–148
requesting change in active workflow, 146–147
approvers, site groups, 295
ASP.NET
creating Web Parts with, 191
forms-based authentication and, 292
master pages and, 285, 457
audiences
distribution list as basis of, 318–320
membership-based, 318
overview of, 316–318
personalization and, 15
profiles as basis of, 325–326
targeting list item to specific, 320–322
targeting Web Part to specific, 322–325
view options, 103
Audiences column, 20
auditing, regulatory requirements and, 160
authentication
methods, 292
site log in process and, 291–292
Auto complete, text box control options, 341

B

back-end systems, 207, 409
basic search
  interface, 479
  performing, 480–482
  scope options, 479–480
BDC (Business Data Catalog), 409–435
  actions, 415
  adding users to applications, 415–416
  administrator role, 412
  application definition author role, 411
  application permissions, 415
  associating business data with SharePoint list
    items, 433–435
  business analyst or site manager role,
    411–412
  Business Data Actions Web Part, 431
  changing view of Business Data List Web Part,
    422–424
  configuring BDC applications, 412–413
  configuring Business Data List Web Part,
    418–420
  configuring Business Item Web Part, 428–431
  configuring Related Business Data List Web
    Part, 424–427
  creating columns for business data in
    SharePoint list, 432–433
  developer role, 412
  displaying items in Business Data List Web
    Part, 420–421
  enterprise features, 15
  extracting data from back-end systems, 207
  importing application definition file, 413
  launching actions from business items,
    421–422
  managing permissions on an entity, 416–417
  overview of, 409–410
  roles, 411
  SharePoint list integration with, 431–432
  summary and exercises, 435
  viewing entities, 414
  viewing Related Business Data, 427–428
  Web Parts and, 418
  what it is, 410
best practices, content management, 87–88
blank site template, 249–250
blog template
  commenting blog post, 260–262
  creating blog site, 256–257
  creating new entry, 259–260
  customizing, 257–259
  defined, 249
  elements of, 254–255
  overview of, 254
breadcrumb trail, site navigation, 240
business analyst, BDC roles, 411–412
Business Data Actions Web Part, 431
Business Data Catalog. *see* **BDC (Business
    Data Catalog)**
Business Data column, 19
Business Data List Web Part
  changing view of, 422–424
  configuring, 418–420
  displaying items in, 420–421
  overview of, 418
business environment, 85–87
business intelligence content types, 164
Business Item Web Part
  configuring, 428–431
  defined, 418
  overview of, 428
business scorecards, 397–398. *see also* **KPIs
    (key performance indicators)**
buttons, InfoPath controls, 344–345

C

Calculated column, 19
calendar, regional settings, 243–245
calendar list, 22–26
  columns, 22–23
  creating meeting workspace from item in,
    267–269

creating new event, 24–26
special features available, 23–24
Calendar view, 107–108
Cascading Style Sheets (CSS)
customizing sites, 283
site themes and, 474–475
check boxes, InfoPath controls, 344
Check In/Check Out, 55–58
checking in a document, 56–57
checking in a document from Office applications, 57–58
checking out a document, 55–56
document editing and, 119
document libraries and, 46
locking checked out documents, 54
managing and publishing content and, 439
choice, fill-in, 18
Choice column, 18, 92–93
chrome setting, Web Parts, 198
Closed Web Parts gallery, 195
**CMS (Content Management Server), 437–438.
see also WCM (Web Content
Management)**
collaboration
Approval workflow and, 144
forms for collecting information for, 329
SharePoint features, 8
WSS benefits, 5–6
Collaboration Portal
Document Center, 270–271
News template, 272–273
publishing templates, 279
Report Center, 271
Search Center, 278, 505
Site Directory, 273–278
collaboration templates, 249–265
blank site template, 249–250
blogs, 254–262
document workspace, 250–254
team site template, 249
wikis, 262–265
Collect Feedback workflow, 129–137
adding reviewers to workflow activity, 134–135

assigning workflow tasks, 136–137
associating with document libraries, 129–132
defined, 126
launching instance of, 132–134
overview of, 129
Collect Signatures workflow, 137–143
adding signature line to document template,
139–141
associating with document libraries, 138–139
defined, 126
launching from document, 141–143
overview of, 137–138
columns. see also site columns
adding to parent content type, 167–168
announcement list, 26
calendar list, 22–23
changing order on lists, 97–98
Choice, 92–93
contacts list, 20–21
content type, 12
creating, 88–90
creating columns for business data, 432–433
Currency, 94
Date and Time, 94–95
discussion board, 27
document libraries, 62
Hyperlink or Picture, 96
issue list, 31–32
link list, 28
list-centric compared with site, 102
Lookup, 95–96
Multiple Lines of Text, 90–92
Number, 93–94
overview of, 88
Person or Group, 96
related item columns, 432
Single Line of Text, 90
survey list, 32
tasks list, 29
types of information stored in list columns,
18–19
view options, 103
Yes/No, 96

combo boxes, 343

comments, blogs, 254, 260–262

conditional formatting, text box control options, 341

contact information page, 449–450

contacts list, 20–22
  adding items to, 21
  columns, 20–21

content
  adding items to lists, 33–35
  best practices for managing, 87–88
  editing items on lists, 35–37
  indexes, 478
  SharePoint features for managing and publishing, 438–439
  tracking updates, 39
  working offline with list content, 38–39

Content Editor Web Part, 201

Content Management Server (CMS), 437–438. *see also* **WCM (Web Content Management)**

content pages, 454

Content Query Web Part, 224–227, 317

content reports, 443

content rollup Web Parts, 208

content sources
  creating based on file shares, 492–494
  creating based on non-SharePoint web sites, 491–492
  overview of, 490–491
  scheduling updates, 494–496
  search scope and, 500
  updating manually, 496–497

content types, 159–190
  adding columns to parent types, 167–168
  anatomy of, 169–170
  business intelligence, 164
  creating, 161–162
  document, 164–165
  document information panel settings, 176–180
  editing existing, 162–163

  enabling content type management on a library, 184–185
  enabling document conversion on a content type, 467–470
  folder, 165
  grouping, 170–171
  issues, 166–167
  list, 165–166
  managing multiple, 185–187
  metadata associated with, 459–460
  naming/describing, 170
  overview of, 11–12, 159–161
  page layouts and, 168–169, 459–461
  parent content type, 170
  policy management and, 180–183
  publishing, 169
  publishing form template as content type, 372–373
  site columns and, 176
  specialized, 169
  storing custom, 160
  summary and exercises, 189–190
  templates, 171–172
  views based on, 187–189
  workflow for, 173–175

content versioning, 438

contextual menus
  document view options, 47
  editing documents via, 54

controls, InfoPath, 340
  buttons, 344–345
  check boxes, 344
  date pickers, 343
  option buttons, 344
  other options, 346
  rich-text boxes, 342
  sections, 345–346
  selection list boxes, 342–343
  text boxes, 340–342

crawled content
  creating managed property for advanced searches, 484

defined, 478
resetting, 497–498
CSS (Cascading Style Sheets)
customizing sites, 283
site themes and, 474–475
Currency column, 18, 94
currency data, 18
Current User Filter Web Part, 214–217

D

Dashboard
creating Dashboard page, 403–407
KPI Web Part, 210–213
overview of, 210
in Report Center, 378
data connection libraries
adding data connections to trusted data connection library, 394–395
data connection files stored in, 379
function of, 62
overview of, 78
data connections, Excel
adding data connections to trusted data connection library, 394–395
adding to form template, 367–371
overview of, 393–394
uploading data connection files to SharePoint,
395–397
using data connections from SharePoint
libraries, 397
data connections, InfoPath, 330
data management, WSS benefits, 6
data sources, InfoPath, 346–348
Data View Web Part, 228–230
databases
Data View Web Part, 228–230
user profiles, 310
Datasheet view, 108–109
creating, 108–109
editing/updating document metadata, 52–53
overview of, 107

date, regional settings, 243–245
Date and Time column, 19, 94–95
Date Picker, InfoPath controls, 343
deployment, WSS benefits, 5–6
Design Checker, 349
Design Tasks pane, InfoPath
controls. see controls, InfoPath
Layout task pane, 339–340
overview of, 338–339
designers, site groups, 294
designing forms, 350–355
developer, BDC roles, 412
discussion board, 27–28
display names, labels, 446
Disposition Approval workflow, 126
**distribution list, audience created from,
318–320**
**Document Center, enterprise templates,
270–271**
document content types, 164–165
document conversion
configuring, 466–467
converting document to a Web page, 470–472
defined, 454
enabling on a content type, 467–470
overview of, 465–466
**document information panel settings, content
types, 176–180**
document libraries
Approval workflow associated with, 144–146
Check In/Check Out, 55–58
Collect Feedback workflow associated with,
129–132
Collect Signatures workflow associated with,
138–139
creating documents, 49
document versions, 59–60
editing documents, 54
editing/updating metadata, 52–53
elements of, 62–63
emailing document links, 58–59
function of, 61

document libraries *(continued)*
opening in Windows Explorer, 63–64
publishing, 441
publishing form template to, 359–360
restoring documents to previous version, 60–61
templates, 48–49, 121–122
uploading Access database to, 395–397
uploading Excel workbooks to, 388–390
uploading multiple documents to, 51
uploading new documents to, 50
URLs for associating custom templates with, 122–123
view page, 47
working with documents offline, 58
document permissions, 308–310
document workspace template, 250–254
creating document workspace, 250–252
defined, 249
overview of, 250
publishing document back to source location from a document workspace, 252–254
downloads, files from picture libraries, 75–77
drop-down lists
adding search scope to, 503–504
InfoPath controls, 342

E

Edit mode, Web Parts, 194–195
editing content types, 162–163
editing document metadata, 52–53
editing documents
Check In/Check Out and, 119
version control and, 119
via contextual menus, 54
editing Excel workbooks, 384–387
editing list items, 35–37
editing wiki page, 264–265
elements
document library, 62–63
list, 18

emailing document links, 58–59
employee feedback, InfoPath, 330
enhanced text, column formatting options, 91
enterprise features, 14–15
enterprise templates
Document Center, 270–271
News, 272–273
overview of, 269–270
Records Center, 271–272
Report Center, 271
Search Center, 278
Site Directory, 273–278
entities, BDC
managing permissions on, 416–417
viewing details of, 414
Excel
document templates associated with content types, 171
exporting list data to, 42–43
Excel Services, 377–408
adding data connections to trusted data connection library, 394–395
adding Report Center to trusted file location, 381–382
business scorecards, 397–398
creating Dashboard page, 403–407
creating KPI list from manually entered data, 398–400
creating KPI list from SharePoint data, 400–403
creating Report Center site, 379–381
data connections, 393–394
displaying workbooks in a Web Part, 392–393
editing workbooks, 384–387
enterprise features, 15
Excel Web Access Web Part, 392
interacting with workbooks, 382–384
KPI Web Parts, 403–407
overview of, 377–378
publishing workbooks from Excel, 390–392
publishing workbooks to SharePoint, 388
Report Center default elements, 378–379

summary and exercises, 407–408

uploading data connection files to SharePoint, 395–397

uploading workbook to document library, 388–390

using data connections from SharePoint libraries, 397

viewing report snapshot, 387–388

Excel Web Access Web Part, 392

exports

list data to Excel, 42–43

list events, 24

Web Parts, 195

Web Parts from Web Parts page, 200–201

expression boxes, InfoPath controls, 346

F

FAQs (frequently asked questions), wikis and, 262

features

defined, 245

publishing features, enabling, 245–247

feedback, 330. *see also* **Collect Feedback workflow**

fields, list, 18

file attachments, InfoPath controls, 346

file items, document libraries, 62

file sharing

column structure compared with, 86

creating content source based on, 492–494

file types

adding to content index, 499

managing, 498

managing blocked types, 46

storage types, 46

files system, tree structure for organizing, 86

fill-in choices, list columns and, 18

Filter Web Parts

Current User Filter Web Part, 214–217

overview of, 213–214

filters

audience filtering, 317

Filter Web Parts, 213–217

folders

content types, 165

view options, 104

footer zones, Web Part pages, 192

form libraries, 65–68

creating from template, 66–68

function of, 61

overview of, 65–66

Form Services

activating, 358–359

adding data connections to form templates, 367–371

adding submit button to form template, 362–365

advanced publishing options, 371

creating forms, 333–336

creating template parts, 355–358

customizing templates, 336–338, 362

customizing toolbar, 365–367

designing forms, 350–355

enterprise features, 14

forcing form to open as Web page, 360–362

overview of, 331–333

publishing form template as administrator-approved template, 373–376

publishing form template as content type, 372–373

publishing form template to document library, 359–360

publishing form template to library, 358

publishing form templates, 349–350

Form Templates library, 441

formats

document conversion, 465

images, 71

text, 91

forms-based authentication, 292

frequently asked questions (FAQs), wikis and, 262

full crawl searches
defined, 478
scheduling content source updates, 494–495

G

galleries
browsing for Web Parts, 195
uploading template to, 118–119
Gantt view, 106–107
global navigation, sites, 236
global scope, searches, 500–502
Group By, view options, 103
groups
adding users to site groups, 298–299
content types, 170–171
creating site groups, 295–298
membership, 294–295
modifying permissions, 300–301
Person or Group column, 19, 96
groups/regions, InfoPath controls, 346
guidelines, best practices, 87–88

H

header zone, Web Part pages, 192
hierarchy managers, site groups, 294
history, workflow, 128
HTML, 439
Hyperlink or Picture column, 19, 96
hyperlinks
emailing document links, 58–59
InfoPath controls, 346

I

iFilter tool, 478
images
format options, 71
uploading multiple images to picture library, 73–74
images library, 441

implementation, WSS benefits, 5–6
imports, Web Parts to Web Parts page, 201–203
incremental crawl searches
defined, 478
overview of, 484
scheduling content source updates, 494–495
indexes. *see also* **searches**
adding file type to content index, 499
managing file types, 498
single content indexes, 497
InfoPath, 329–376
activating Form Services, 358–359
adding data connections to form templates, 367–371
adding submit button to form template, 362–365
advanced form publishing options, 371
buttons, 344–345
check boxes, 344
controls, 340, 346
creating forms, 333–336
creating template parts, 355–358
customizing document information panel, 176–180
customizing form templates, 336–338, 362
customizing toolbar, 365–367
data sources, 346–348
date pickers, 343
Design Checker, 349
Design Tasks pane, 338–339
designing forms, 350–355
forcing form to open as Web page, 360–362
functions of, 330
Layout Task pane, 339–340
new features, 331
option button, 344
overview of, 329–333
publishing form template as administrator-approved template, 373–376
publishing form template as content type, 372–373

publishing form template to document library, 359–360
publishing form template to library, 358
publishing form templates, 349–350
rich-text boxes, 342
sections, 345–346
selection list boxes, 342–343
summary and exercises, 376
text boxes, 340–342
views, 348
information management
goals for, 87
regulatory requirements, 160
information overload, 2
inheritance
navigation from parent site, 241–242
permissions, 304–306
ink pictures, InfoPath controls, 346
instructional information, Report Center, 378
issues content type, 166–167
issues list, 31–32
item level access, 308–310
assigning unique permissions to a document,
308–309
customizing on a list, 309–310
overview of, 308
items
adding to lists, 33–35
defined, 88
editing, 35–37
overview of list items, 18
targeting list items to specific audience,
320–322
view options for limiting, 104

K

keywords
associating best bets results with specific keywords, 510–511
creating, 508–509
defined, 508

knowledge base, 262
KPI list
creating from manually entered data, 398–400
creating from SharePoint data, 400–403
in Report Center, 378
templates, 398
KPI Web Part, 210–213, 403–407
KPIs (key performance indicators)
business intelligence content types and, 164
creating KPI list from manually entered data,
398–400
creating KPI list from SharePoint data,
400–403
KPI list in Report Center, 378
KPI Web Part, 210–213, 403–407

L

labels
creating for languages, 447–449
overview of, 446–447
languages
configuring lists of translators and languages,
151–152
creating labels for, 447–449
translation management and, 449–450
translation management libraries, 77
Layout task pane, InfoPath, 339–340
LDAP servers, 325
libraries, 45–83
adding data connections to trusted data connection library, 397
data connection library, 78
document library. see document libraries
enabling content type management on,
184–185
form libraries, 65–68
Library Web Part, 204
managing multiple content types in a library,
185–187
overview of, 10–11, 45–46
picture libraries. see picture libraries

libraries *(continued)*
 publishing form template to library, 358
 publishing portal lists and libraries, 441–443
 saving as a template, 116–118
 slide library, 79–82
 summary and exercises, 83, 124
 templates, 61–62
 translation management library, 77
 views. *see* views
 wiki page libraries, 68–71
library level access, 306–308
 assigning unique permissions to a list, 307
 overview of, 306
Library Web Part, 204
line of business. *see* **LOB (line of business)**
link list, 28–29
list boxes, 342–343
list content types, 165–166
list level access, 306–308
 assigning unique permissions to a list, 307
 overview of, 306
List Web Part
 changing toolbar of, 205–207
 changing view of, 204–205
 overview of, 204
list-centric columns. *see also* **columns**
 compared with site columns, 102
 defined, 88
lists, 17–44
 Access view for, 110–112
 adding items to, 33–35
 alert subscriptions for, 39–40
 announcement lists, 26–27
 associating business data with list items,
  433–435
 calendar lists, 22–26
 columns. *see* columns
 contacts lists, 20–22
 content types and, 187–189
 creating columns for business data in
  SharePoint list, 432–433
 creating custom, 112–116

 customizing item level access, 309–310
 discussion boards, 27–28
 editing items in, 35–37
 elements of, 18
 exporting data to Excel, 42–43
 InfoPath controls, 346
 integration with BDC, 431–432
 issues with, 31–32
 link lists, 28–29
 List Web Part, 204
 order of columns on, 97–98
 overview of, 10, 17, 112
 permissions, 307–308
 project tasks lists, 31
 publishing portal lists, 441–443
 RSS feed subscriptions for, 41–42
 saving as a template, 116–118
 site columns added to, 101–102
 summary and exercises, 43–44, 124
 survey lists, 32
 tasks lists, 29–30
 templates, 20
 tracking content updates, 39
 types of, 18–20
 uploading list template to gallery, 118–119
 views. *see* views
 working offline with list content, 38–39
LOB (line of business)
 BDC and, 409
 Business Data Web Parts and, 207
 Data View Web Part and, 228–230
 searches and, 477
locale, labels, 446
log in process, 290–293
 authentication and, 291–292
 overview of, 290–291
 signing in as different user, 293
Lookup column, 19, 95–96

M

Major versions, documents, 119

master pages
applying new, 455–457
ASP.NET and, 285
customizing, 457–459
overview of, 454–455
master/detail, InfoPath controls, 346
meeting templates, 266
membership-based audiences, 318
metadata
content types and, 459–460
defined, 88
document information panel settings,
176–180
document libraries, 46
editing/updating, 52–53
lists, 18
**Microsoft Content Management Server. see
CMS (Content Management Server)**
Microsoft Office
Access. see Access (Microsoft)
checking in a document from Office applications, 57–58
Excel. see Excel
Outlook. see Outlook
PowerPoint. see PowerPoint
SharePoint Server 2007. see SharePoint
Server 2007, getting started
UDC files in Office 2007, 78
Word. see Word
middle zones, Web Part pages, 192
Minor versions, documents, 119
Miscellaneous Web Parts
overview of, 217
Relevant Documents Web Part, 218–219
Mobile views, 104
monitoring business events, 8
**MOSS 2007. see SharePoint Server 2007, get-
ting started**
multi line, text box control options, 341
Multiple Lines of Text column, 18, 90–92

N
names, content type, 170
navigation, site
global navigation, 236
inherit navigation from parent site, 241–242
options, 240
tree view navigation, 242–243
**News template, enterprise templates,
272–273**
Number column, 18, 93–94
numeric data, 18

O
Office. see Microsoft Office
offline
working with documents, 58
working with list content, 38–39
option buttons, InfoPath controls, 344
Outlook
Outlook Web Access Web Parts, 219–220
synchronizing SharePoint contact list with, 22
tasks list integration with, 30
Outlook Web Access Web Parts, 219–220

P
page layouts
content types, 12, 168–169, 459–460
creating custom page, 464–465
creating page layout based on content type,
460–461
creating page layout with SharePoint Designer,
461–464
managing and publishing content, 438
overview of, 454
pages library, 442
parallel workflows, 126
parent content type
adding column to, 167–168
content type hierarchy and, 170

parent sites
inherit navigation from, 241–242
stopping inheritance of permissions from parent site, 305–306
PDFs, indexing, 478
people, searches
adding People Search Box Web Part to a site, 512–514
finding people within organization, 511–512
using People Search Box Web Part, 514–515
People scope, searches, 515
People Search Web Part
adding to a site, 512–514
using, 514–515
performance, 403–407. *see also* **KPIs (key performance indicators)**
permissions
adding users to site groups, 299–300
assigning unique permissions to a document, 308–310
assigning unique permissions to a list, 307–308
creating site groups, 295–298
item level access, 308
list or library level access, 306–308
modifying user or group permissions, 300–301
site level access, 304
stopping inheritance of permissions from parent site, 305–306
permissions, application
adding users to applications, 415–416
levels, 415
managing on BDC entity, 416–417
Person or Group column, 19, 96
personal information, updating in user profiles, 312–314
personalization, 15, 290. *see also* **audiences; user profiles**
picture libraries, 71–77
creating, 72–73
downloading files from, 75–77
function of, 62
image format options, 71
uploading multiple images to, 73–74
views, 72
pictures
Hyperlink or Picture column, 19, 96
InfoPath controls, 346
pivot table report, 378
placeholders, text box control options, 341
plain text format, 91
planning
reasons for choosing SharePoint Server, 9
reasons for choosing WSS, 6–7
policies
configuring expiration policy on a content type, 181–183
content types for policy management and, 180–181
portal technologies, 2–3
reasons for investing in, 2–3
what it is, 2
portals
creating publishing portal site, 439–441
defined, 2
publishing portal lists and libraries, 441–443
PowerPoint
creating presentations, 80–81
updating presentations, 81–82
uploading presentations to slide library, 79–80
practices, standardizing, 87
presentations. *see* **PowerPoint**
profiles. *see* **user profiles**
project tasks list, 31
Project Tasks view, 31
properties
items. *see* metadata
search scope and, 500
Web Parts, 194
Publishing column, 20
publishing content types
managing and publishing content, 438
WCM and, 169

publishing Excel workbooks
from Excel, 390–392
to SharePoint, 388
publishing features
creating publishing portal site, 439–441
enabling, 245–247
enabling on team site, 472–474
overview of, 439
publishing forms
as administrator-approved template, 373–376
advanced options, 371
as content type, 372–373
to document library, 359–360
to library, 358
templates for, 349–350
Publishing Portal, 279–280
publishing sites, 450–452
publishing templates
Collaboration Portal, 279
Publishing Portal, 279–280

Q

quick deploy users, site groups, 295

R

Really Simple Syndication. *see* RSS (Really Simple Syndication)
Records Center, enterprise templates, 271–272
recurring events, calendar lists, 23
regional settings, sites, 243–245
regions/groups, InfoPath controls, 346
regulatory requirements, Sarbanes-Oxley Act, 160
Related Business Data List Web Part
configuring, 424–427
overview of, 418, 424
viewing related business data on a page, 427–428
related item columns, 432

Relevant Documents Web Part, 218–219
Report Center
adding to trusted file location, 381–382
creating site for, 379–381
default elements, 378–379
enterprise templates, 271
report libraries, 62
Reporting Service, 439
reports
content and structure reports, 443
InfoPath for team reports, 330
sample reports in Report Center, 378
restricted readers, site groups, 295
reusable content, 443
reviewers, adding to workflow activity, 134–135
rich-text boxes, InfoPath controls, 342
rick text, column formats, 91
roles, BDC
administrator role, 412
application definition author role, 411
business analyst or site manager role, 411–412
developer role, 412
overview of, 411
RSS (Really Simple Syndication)
overview of, 39
RSS Viewer Web Part, 227–228
subscribing to RSS feed for list content, 41–42
RSS Viewer Web Part, 227–228

S

Sarbanes-Oxley Act, 160
scope, search
adding to drop-down list, 503–504
basic search, 480
global, 500–502
overview of, 499–500
People scope, 515
site-level, 504–505

Search Center
adding custom tab to, 506–507
enterprise templates, 278
overview of, 505
search scope. *see* scope, search
Search Web Parts, 220–221
searches, 477–516
adding People Search Web Part to a site, 512–514
adding properties to Advanced Search Web Part, 488–490
advanced, 482–483
basic, 479–480
content sources, 490–491
content sources based on file shares, 492–494
content sources based on non-SharePoint web sites, 491–492
creating managed property, 484–488
custom tab added to Search Center, 506–507
enterprise features, 14
facilities for, 477–479
file type management, 498
file types added to content index, 499
global scope, 500–502
keywords, custom, 508–509
keywords associated with best bets, 510–511
overview of, 477
People scope, 515
people within organization, 511–512
performing advanced search, 483
performing basic search, 480–482
resetting crawled content, 497–498
scheduling content source updates, 494–496
scope added to site collection drop-down list, 503–504
scope of, 499–500
Search Center, 505
Search Web Parts, 220–221
site-level scope for, 504–505
summary and exercises, 515–516
updating content sources manually, 496–497

using People Search Box Web Part, 514–515
sections, InfoPath controls, 345–346
selection, fill-in choices, 18
selection list boxes, InfoPath controls, 342–343
serial workflows, 126
Server Gallery Web Parts, 195
Shared Service Provider (SSP), 497
SharePoint Designer
creating custom workflows, 127, 154–157
creating page layouts, 461–464
customizing master pages, 457
SharePoint Portal Server 2003, 4
SharePoint Products and Technologies, 3
SharePoint Server 2007 for Search, 478
SharePoint Server 2007, getting started, 1–16
content types, 11–12
enterprise features, 14–15
libraries, 10–11
lists, 10
as offering of SharePoint Products and Technologies, 3
overview, 1
portal technologies, 2–3
primary features, 8
reasons for choosing, 8–10
SharePoint Portal Server 2003 compared with, 4
SharePoint Products and Technologies, 3
sites, workspaces, and site collections, 12–14
summary and exercises, 15
Web Parts, 11
workflow, 11
WSS compared with, 4–7
signatures. *see* Collect Signatures workflow
Single Line of Text column, 18, 90
Site Aggregator Web Part, 209–210
site collections
adding search scope to site collection drop-down list, 503–504
compared with workspaces and sites, 12
creating, 13–14, 234–236

documents and images, 442
enabling Variations, 445–446
moving sites within site collections, 452–454
overview of, 234
removing user from, 301–302
Report Center site template, 379
site columns. *see also* **columns**
adding to lists, 101–102
content types and, 12, 176
creating, 99–101
list-centric columns compared with, 102
overview of, 98–99
working with, 176
site definition files, 285
Site Directory, enterprise templates, 273–278
Site Directory Web Parts, 221–223
Site Gallery Web Parts, 195
site groups
adding users to site groups, 298–299
creating, 295–298
modifying permissions, 300–301
types of, 294–295
site level access, 304–306
overview of, 304
stopping inheritance of permissions from parent site, 305–306
site manager, BDC roles, 411–412
site members, site groups, 294
site owners, site groups, 294
site visitors, site groups, 294
site-level scope, 504–505
sites
applying site themes, 474–475
blank site, 249–250
blogs. *see* blog template
collaboration templates, 249
compared with workspaces and site collections, 12
creating Report Center site, 379–381
creating site hierarchy of publishing sites, 450–452
creating with team site template, 236–238

customizing, 454
document workspace, 250–254
enabling access requests, 302–304
enabling publishing features, 245–247
features, 245
inheriting navigation from parent site, 241–242
log in process, 290–293
managing, 239–240
master pages, 285
moving sites within site collections, 452–454
navigation options, 240
overview of, 234
publishing Excel workbooks to, 388
regional settings, 243–245
restoring site templates, 285–286
saving site as template, 280–282
Site Aggregator Web Part, 209–210
summary and exercises, 286–287
team site, 249
templates, 247–248
themes, 283–284, 474–475
tree view navigation, 242–243
wikis. *see* wiki sites
slide libraries, 79–82
creating new presentation, 80–81
function of, 62
overview of, 79
updating presentations, 81–82
uploading presentation to, 79–80
snapshots, viewing report snapshot in Excel, 387–388
Sort Order, view options, 103
spell check, text box control options, 341
spreadsheets. *see* **workbooks, Excel Services**
SSP (Shared Service Provider), 497
Standard view, 103–106
creating, 104–105
displaying, 106
elements of, 103–104
structure reports, 443
style library, 442

styles, view options, 104
submit button, adding to form template,
  362–365
subscriptions
  alert services, 39–40
  RSS feed services, 41–42
subsites, 234
survey list, 32
survey list template, 32

T

tables, InfoPath controls, 346
tasks, assigning workflow tasks, 136–137
tasks list, 29–30
  columns, 29
  new features, 30
  views, 30
  workflow associated with, 128
team site template
  creating new site with, 236–238
  overview of, 249
team sites
  collaboration, 12
  enabling publishing feature on team site,
    472–474
teams, InfoPath for team reports, 330
template parts
  creating, 355–358
  defined, 350
templates
  content types, 171–172
  document libraries, 48–49, 121–122
  enterprise. see enterprise templates
  libraries, 61–62
  lists, 20
  meeting workspace, 266–269
  restoring site templates, 285–286
  saving list or library as, 116–118
  saving site as, 280–282
  uploading list template to gallery, 118–119
  URLs for associating custom templates with
    document library, 122–123

templates, form
  adding data connections to, 367–371
  adding submit buttons to, 362–365
  creating template parts, 355–358
  customizing, 336–338, 362
  designing new form template, 351–355
  form libraries, 66–68
  publishing as administrator-approved tem-
    plate, 373–376
  publishing as content type, 372–373
  publishing options, 349–350
  publishing to document library, 359–360
  publishing to library, 358
templates, publishing
  Collaboration Portal, 279
  Publishing Portal, 279
templates, site
  blank site template, 249–250
  blog template, 255, 257–259
  collaboration templates, 249
  custom, 248
  Document Center, 270–271
  document workspace template, 250–254
  enterprise templates, 269–270
  News, 272–273
  overview of, 247
  Records Center, 271–272
  Report Center, 271
  saving site as, 280–282
  Search Center, 278
  SharePoint categories, 248
  Site Directory, 273–278
  team site template, 236–238, 249
  wikis, 262–265
templates, workflow
  Approval workflow. see Approval workflow
  Collect Feedback workflow. see Collect
    Feedback workflow
  Collect Signatures workflow. see Collect
    Signatures workflow
  overview of, 126–127
text, list columns and, 18, 90

text boxes, InfoPath controls, 340–342

themes, sites, 283–284, 474–475

threaded discussions, discussion boards for, 27

time

Date and Time column, 19

regional settings, 243–245

toolbars

changing toolbar of List Web Part, 205–207

customizing Forms Services toolbar, 365–367

totals, numeric columns, 104

tracking workflows, 128

translation management libraries

configuring lists of translators and languages, 151–152

creating, 149–151

function of, 62

overview of, 77

Translation Management workflow, 148–153

configuring lists of translators and languages, 151–152

creating translation management library, 149–151

languages and, 449–450

launching workflow, 152–153

overview of, 148–149

translators, 151–152

tree structure

business organization, 86

site collection organization, 234

tree view navigation

enabling, 242–243

overview of, 240

U

UDC (Universal Data Connection), 78

updates tracking list content, 39

updating content sources, 494–497

updating metadata, 52–53

updating presentations, 81–82

updating user profile, 312–314

user profiles, 316

uploads

images to picture libraries, 73–74

multiple documents, 51

new documents, 50

presentation to slide libraries, 79–80

URLs, for associating custom templates with document library, 122–123

user access

access levels, 304

access management vs. personalization, 290

adding users to site groups, 298–299

creating site groups, 295–298

group membership, 294–295

item level access, 308–310

list or library level access, 306–308

modifying user or group permissions, 300–301

vs. personalization, 290

removing user from site collection, 301–302

site access requests, enabling, 302–304

site level access, 304–306

site log in process, 290–293

user management

audiences. see audiences

overview of, 289

profiles. see user profiles

summary and exercises, 326–327

user access. see user access

user profiles

adding new user profile property, 314–315

audiences based on, 325–326

database, 310

overview of, 310–311

personalization and, 15

update configuration, 316

updating personal information, 312–314

V

Variations

enabling on site collection, 445–446

how they work, 444

Variations *(continued)*
labels and, 446–449
overview of, 443–444
reasons for choosing SharePoint Server, 9
versions
content versioning, 438
document versioning, 119–121
history feature, 46
major/minor, 46
options for storing, 119
restoring to previous, 60–61
viewing, 59–60
vertical labels, InfoPath controls, 346
viewers, site groups, 294
views, 102
Access view for list, 110–112
announcement list, 27
based on content types, 187–189
Calendar, 107–108
calendar lists, 24
changing list view, 37
creating view based on existing view, 109
Datasheet, 108–109
document libraries, 47, 63
Gantt, 107
InfoPath, 348
list, 18
picture libraries, 72
project tasks, 31
specialized, 106–107
Standard, 103–106
tasks list, 30
types and uses of, 102–103

W

WCM (Web Content Management), 437–476
applying new master page, 455–457
applying site themes, 474–475
CMS compared with, 437–438
configuring document conversion, 466–467
converting document to a Web page, 470–472
creating contact information page, 449–450

creating custom page, 464–465
creating page layout based on content type, 460–461
creating page layout with SharePoint Designer, 461–464
creating publishing portal site, 439–441
creating site hierarchy of publishing sites, 450–452
customizing master pages, 457–459
document conversion, 465–466
enabling document conversion on a content type, 467–470
enabling publishing features, 245–247, 472–474
enterprise features, 14
integration of Content Management Server with SharePoint Server, 168
labels, 446–449
moving sites within site collections, 452–454
options for customizing sites, 454
page layouts and content types, 459–460
publishing content types and, 169
publishing portal lists and libraries, 441–443
reasons for choosing SharePoint Server, 9
SharePoint features for managing and publishing content, 438–439
summary and exercises, 475–476
translation workflow management, 449
working with variations, 443–446
Web content
features for managing, 8
search scope and, 500
Web Content Management. *see* WCM (Web Content Management)
web forms, uses of InfoPath, 330
web pages
converting document to, 470–472
creating from browser, 438
forcing form to open as, 360–362
Web Part gallery, 11
Web Part pages
anatomy of, 191–193

creating, 194
Web Parts added to, 196–198
Web Parts exported from, 200–201
Web Parts imported to, 201–203
zones, 11, 191–193
Web Parts, 191–232
adding to Web Part pages, 196–198
Advanced Search Web Part, 488–490
anatomy of Web Part page, 191–193
BDC and, 207, 410
Business Data Actions Web Part, 431
Business Data List Web Part. see Business
    Data List Web Part
Business Item Web Part, 418, 428–431
changing toolbar of List Web Part, 205–207
changing view of List Web Part, 204–205
Content Query Web Part, 224–227, 317
content rollup Web Parts, 207, 208
creating Web Part page, 194
Current User Filter Web Part, 214–217
Dashboard Web Parts, 210
Data View Web Part, 228–230
defaults, 223–224
defined, 11
displaying Excel workbooks in, 392–393
Edit mode options, 194–195
exporting from Web Parts page, 200–201
Filter Web Parts, 213–214
importing to Web Parts page, 201–203
KPI Web Part, 210–213, 403–407
list and library, 204
Miscellaneous Web Parts, 217
modifying appearance of, 198–199
moving to new Web Part zone, 199–200
Outlook Web Access Web Parts, 219–220
overview of, 191
People Search Box Web Part, 512–515
Related Business Data List Web Part. see
    Related Business Data List Web Part
Relevant Documents Web Part, 218–219
RSS Viewer Web Part, 227–228
Search Web Parts, 220–221
Site Aggregator Web Parts, 209–210

Site Directory Web Parts, 221–223
summary and exercises, 231–232
targeting to specific audience, 322–325
types of, 418
Web Services, Data View Web Part, 228–230
web sites, content sources based on, 491–492
weblog. see blog template
what-you-see-is-what-you-get (WYSIWYG), 229
wiki articles, 68
wiki page libraries, 68–71
creating new library, 69–70
creating new wiki page, 70–71
function of, 61
overview of, 68–69
wiki sites, 69
creating, 263–264
defined, 249
editing wiki page, 264–265
overview of, 262–263
Wikipedia project, 68, 262
Windows Explorer
document libraries opened with, 63–64
document view options, 47
**Windows SharePoint Services 3.0. see WSS
    (Windows SharePoint Services 3.0)**
Windows Vista, 396
Windows Workflow Foundation
automated workflow solutions built on, 125
tasks list and, 30
Windows XP, 396
Word
checking in a document from, 57–58
creating documents and saving to SharePoint
    sites, 49
document templates associated with content
    types, 171
workbooks, Excel Services
displaying workbooks in a Web Part, 392–393
editing, 384–387
interacting with, 382–384
publishing to SharePoint, 388
publishing workbooks from Excel, 390–392
uploading to document library, 388–390

workflow, 125–158
Approval workflow. *see* Approval workflow
associating with tasks list, 128
Collect Feedback workflow. *see* Collect
    Feedback workflow
Collect Signatures workflow. *see* Collect
    Signatures workflow
for content types, 173–175
custom solution, 154–157
history, 128
managing and publishing content, 438
naming/creating, 127–128
overview of, 11, 125
removing workflows from libraries, 147–148
requesting change in active workflow,
    146–147
summary and exercises, 158
tasks list and, 30
templates, 126–127
Translation Management workflow. *see*
    Translation Management workflow
types of workflow solutions, 125–126
workflow tasks, 443
workspaces
calendar lists Web meeting space, 24
compared with sites and site collections, 12
creating from item in Calendar list, 267–269
document workspace, 250–254
meeting templates, 266
methods for creating, 266
overview of, 238
wraps, text, 341
WSS (Windows SharePoint Services 3.0)
compared with SharePoint Server 2007, 4–5
as offering of SharePoint Products and
    Technologies, 3
primary benefits of, 5–6
reasons for choosing, 6–7
search features, 478
WYSIWYG (what-you-see-is-what-you-get), 229

X

XML (CAML) based list data, 229
XSL transformation, 229

Y

Yes/No column, 19, 96

Z

zones, Web Part, 191–193
adding Web Parts to, 194
defined, 191
dragging Web Parts between, 194
features of, 192–193
moving Web Parts to new zone, 199–200
overview of, 11
types of, 192